Brooks - Cork Library
Shelton State
Community College

D1161071

DISCARD.

Handbook of Closeness
and Intimacy

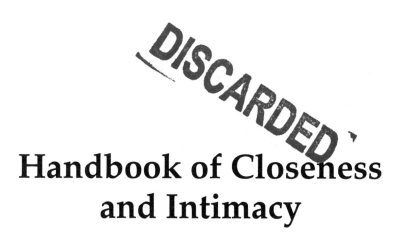

Handbook of Closeness and Intimacy

Debra J. Mashek

George Mason University

Arthur Aron

State University of New York at Stony Brook

Brooks - Cork Library
Shelton State
Community College

LEA
LAWRENCE ERLBAUM ASSOCIATES, PUBLISHERS
2004   Mahwah, New Jersey   London

Senior Editor: Debra Riegert
Cover Design: Sean Trane Sciarrone
Textbook Production Manager: Paul Smolenski
Full-Service Compositor: TechBooks
Text and Cover Printer: Hamilton Printing Company

This book was typeset in 10/11.25 pt. Palatino, Italic, Bold, and Bold Italic.
The heads were typeset in Palatino and Americana, Bold, Italics, and
Bold Italics.

Copyright © 2004 by Lawrence Erlbaum Associates, Inc.
All rights reserved. No part of this book may be reproduced in
any form, by photostat, microform, retrieval system, or any
other means, without prior written permission of the publisher.

Lawrence Erlbaum Associates, Inc., Publishers
10 Industrial Avenue
Mahwah, New Jersey 07430
www.erlbaum.com

Library of Congress Cataloging-in-Publication Data

Handbook of closeness and intimacy / [edited by] Debra J. Mashek, Arthur
    P. Aron.
        p. cm.
Includes bibliographical references and index.
    ISBN 0-8058-4284-5 (case : alk. paper)—ISBN 0-8058-4285-3
(paperbound : alk. paper)
1. Intimacy (Psychology)   I. Mashek, Debra J.   II. Aron, Arthur.

   BF575.I5H36   2004
   158.2—dc22   2003025838

Books published by Lawrence Erlbaum Associates are printed on
acid-free paper, and their bindings are chosen for strength and durability.

Printed in the United States of America
10 9 8 7 6 5 4 3 2

CONTENTS

CONCLUSION

PREFACE

The *Handbook of Closeness and Intimacy* brings together the latest thinking of some of the most active and influential researchers and clinicians in the area of closeness and intimacy—a core theme in relationship science that is currently extraordinarily lively in a variety of disciplines, including social psychology, family studies, clinical psychology, communication studies, and developmental psychology.

The *Handbook* is specifically about closeness and intimacy, though the ideas and findings presented here are embedded in a rich history of theorizing and research on close relationships more generally. As typically happens when a field of knowledge grows, the study of close relationships has developed nuance and complexity. Indeed, there is now a critical mass of work specifically on the topic of closeness and intimacy. Hence this *Handbook*.

As the various programs of research on closeness and intimacy are coming to the fore, it is important to bring these different voices together in one place, providing an opportunity for everyone interested in these topics to learn about the state of the scientific study of closeness and intimacy. The result is a volume likely to be indispensable to anyone interested in close relationships because of the distinction of its contributors, the breadth and inclusiveness of its coverage, the timeliness of the topic in light of the current surge of interest in it, and the array of creative new thinking it embodies.

CONTENTS

Chapters in this volume share four characteristics. First, they provide clear definitions of closeness or intimacy. Second, in addition to summarizing an existing program of research, many of the chapters also offer concise theoretical overviews that focus directly on the topics of closeness and intimacy (rather than on close relationships more generally). Third, the chapters introduce an array of new ideas, new applications, and previously unstated theoretical connections. Finally, most of the chapters benefited from peer reviews prepared by other chapter contributors.

The chapters are organized around six general, interrelated questions:

1. What are closeness and intimacy? Chapters 2–5 provide a foundation for understanding the issues and arguments addressed in subsequent sections.

2. How can closeness and intimacy be measured? Chapters 6–8 build on the first question by addressing the issue of measurement: How can one assess these complex constructs?

3. What are the general processes of closeness and intimacy? Chapters 9–12 overview nicely some of the general processes believed to drive closeness and intimacy.

4. What individual differences play a role in closeness and intimacy? Personal experience tells us that people differ both in their comfort with intimacy and in the nature

of the closeness experience. The contributors to Chapters 13–15 argue convincingly that some of these differences are a function of what the individual brings to the relationship.

5. What situational factors play a role in closeness and intimacy? Chapters 16–18 explore a few of the ways in which the situational context directs the experience of closeness and intimacy.

6. Is there a dark side to closeness and intimacy? Closeness and intimacy offer generally positive outcomes to most people. Chapters 19–22 challenge the boundaries of this assumed positivity by illuminating the dark side of closeness and intimacy.

In addition, a concluding chapter addresses systematically the state of knowledge surrounding each of the six organizing questions, including an articulation of what is not known (chapter 23).

ACKNOWLEDGMENTS

It is with great enthusiasm that we present the *Handbook of Closeness and Intimacy*. And, it is with even deeper appreciation that we thank the following people for playing pivotal roles in the completion of this project. First and foremost, we thank the authors of these chapters, who not only met our rigid deadlines, but also volunteered to review other authors' chapters and to revise their own chapters—often substantially—in light of our suggestions and those of their fellow authors. All of this was in addition to attending an early morning breakfast meeting at a research conference and being consistently responsive to our requests for advice and suggestions on what may have seemed like a million different issues.

We are also grateful to Debra Reigert of Lawrence Erlbaum Associates who was always ready to help at each juncture, to share our excitement as new ideas came along, and to serve as a wonderful facilitator of this *Handbook* coming to fruition, as well as to Larry Erlbaum himself for his great enthusiasm for the project from the start. In addition, we want to thank Julie Adeshchenko, who helpfully pulled together resource materials. We also thank those who reviewed the original proposal: Mark Fine, John Harvey, Dan Perlman, and Sandra Petronio.

Finally we thank our partners, Stewart Wattson and Elaine N. Aron, for supporting us consistently throughout this long project and for reminding us of the power of closeness and intimacy.

—DM

—AA

1

Introduction

Debra J. Mashek
George Mason University

Arthur P. Aron
State University of New York at Stony Brook

This *Handbook* is about closeness and intimacy, bringing together the latest thinking on these topics from a group of the most active and widely recognized relationship scholars in social psychology, clinical psychology, communication studies, and related disciplines. Precisely what we mean by closeness and intimacy is a topic in its own right (and a central theme of some of the chapters in this volume). There are indeed multiple definitions; in fact, some researchers see closeness and intimacy as very different things. However, the processes and experiences characterized as close or intimate generally include such features as a sense of connectedness, shared understandings, mutual responsiveness, self-disclosure, and intersubjectivity.

This *Handbook* is *specifically* about closeness and intimacy, not about processes occurring in the context of close relationships more generally. Nevertheless, one cannot study closeness and intimacy without considering its links with other relationship concepts and processes, such as love, satisfaction, sexuality, attachment, commitment, and passion, or with relationship development, maintenance, and loss. The chapters included in this volume maintain a tight focus on closeness and intimacy by considering these other relationship phenomena primarily in the context of their links with intimacy and closeness.

There are several other books that address relationship concepts and processes more generally, notably including the *Handbook of Personal Relationships* (Duck, 1997) and the *Blackwell Handbook of Social Psychology* Interpersonal Processes (Fletcher & Clark, 2000). What stands out about our *Handbook* is that for the first time the specific focus is on the pivotal phenomena of closeness and intimacy. Hence, this *Handbook* establishes closeness and intimacy as a substantial subarea of relationship science as well as reflects the latest thinking of a large group of top researchers in the rapidly advancing field of relationship science. Thus, at least for the moment, this volume serves as a compendium of the state of the art in relationship science. Most important, although more broadly focused books (or books on other subareas within relationship science) will inevitably supplant this one as a window on the science of relationships in general, we expect that this *Handbook* will for some time remain the key sourcebook for the specific area of closeness and intimacy.

SOME BACKGROUND

Relationships are central to human experience and thus have been discussed since the very earliest literary and scholarly work, dating from (in the West at least) ancient Greek civilization. Indeed, it is surprising that during the last two centuries, major disciplines such as psychology, sociology, and related fields, have generally relegated relationships to the margins. Only in the last twenty years or so has there been any major effort to apply the methods and theories of these fields to understanding relationships. The beginning of these major efforts is marked by the first International Conference on Personal Relationships held in Madison, Wisconsin in 1982 and the publication of Kelley et al.'s (1983) *Close Relationships*. These ground-breaking developments were quickly followed by the establishment of professional organizations, regular regional and international scientific meetings, and scholarly journals devoted specifically to relationships. Relationship researchers were appointed to editorships of major journals in the larger disciplines, substantial research grants were awarded by the chief funding agencies for research in this area, and many young scientists and scholars were devoting their careers to studying relationships. As a result, productive lines of research have been established, several fruitful theoretical models have been developed and tested, and there is now a solid and rapidly growing body of relationship knowledge.

As a field of study advances, it naturally penetrates deeper into the specifics. Thus, relationship science has moved to greater specialization, including considerable research and thinking focused on closeness and intimacy. The work in this area is still, necessarily, embedded in the larger field of relationship science, and there are few established relationship researchers who see themselves studying only closeness and intimacy. Indeed, many who contribute to understanding closeness and intimacy do not even see themselves as primarily relationship scientists. Yet, there is already a substantial body of work that is specifically focused on closeness and intimacy and a number of young scientists are building their laboratories and focusing their careers on these topics. Today, within the close relationship domain, and perhaps in the various relevant larger disciplines, the study of closeness and intimacy garners considerable respect comparable to the study of commitment, satisfaction, and interaction processes. Closeness and intimacy themes are also studied across relationship types, being central to the study of both friendships and romantic relationships, and are often given considerable attention in cross-generational and other family relationships. Thus, a critical mass of work has emerged. But the study of closeness and intimacy has not yet gelled into a fully coherent field with researchers regularly citing (or in some cases even being aware of) each other and building on each other's work: Hence this *Handbook*.

WHY THE NEED FOR A HANDBOOK?

Given the explosion of "handbooks" over the last decade, one might wonder whether there really is a need for yet another, especially one that focuses on what might at first appear to be a relatively narrow topic (after all, we already have *The Handbook of Personal Relationships*). Our opinion is admittedly biased, but we feel that a handbook is vital—in fact, and is,—if the accumulation of knowledge about these processes is to progress in an integrated fashion. As described above, many people, from many disciplines and many subdisciplines, explore phenomena that are either directly related to or richly informed by the ideas and traditions that lead to this volume. As a result, there is a wealth of knowledge and thinking on closeness and intimacy. Yet, and perhaps surprisingly, much of this knowledge is disjointed, lacking coherence and continuity. Rarely do we find an article (much less an entire book) that synthesizes meaningfully the tenets, findings, and applications of different perspectives on the central relationship processes of closeness and intimacy—stated metaphorically, many parallel roads traverse the closeness and intimacy map.

As the various programs of empirical research and theoretical thinking on closeness and intimacy swell, it is time to connect these parallel lines of inquiry in a way that both maintains their individual integrity and builds on their collective insights. This *Handbook* attempts to achieve this goal by bringing together active researchers, theorists, and clinicians—all of whom have made a substantial contribution to the study of closeness and intimacy. The result, we hope, is a book that will be of value to everyone interested in relationships because of the breadth and depth of its coverage, the timeliness of the topic in light of the current surge of interest in it, and the array of creative new thinking embodied in the chapters.

WHAT KIND OF HANDBOOK IS THIS?

The chapters that make up this handbook generally share four characteristics. First, most state clearly at the outset what the authors mean by closeness or intimacy. As the reader will notice, these oft-used terms are a challenge to pin down precisely. Nevertheless, the parallels among articulations are striking (these parallels are discussed directly chapter 23, "Conclusion"). Second, many of the contributors summarize an existing program of research, offering a clear overview of a theoretical framework focused directly on the topics of closeness and intimacy (rather than on close relationships more generally). Third, to complement rich ideological histories, the chapters contain a plethora of new ideas, new applications, and previously unstated theoretical connections. Instead of reviewing only already-published ideas and findings, contributors approached their chapters in a forward-thinking manner. Finally, most of the chapters benefited from peer reviews prepared by other chapter contributors (in addition to reviews from the two editors), which is an element of the book's production that we believe enhanced cross-chapter coherence and contributed to the quality of the finished product.

The resulting *Handbook* is more than a simple anthology of ideas. By weaving together arrayed tenets, findings, and applications, contributors have created a tapestry—a compendium of integrated knowledge. Most important, embedded in these chapters are findings that challenge commonly held assumptions about closeness and intimacy. In our concluding chapter, we complete the tapestry by attempting to articulate the places where many lines converge and by identifying the areas that will clearly benefit from additional attention.

HOW IS THIS HANDBOOK ORGANIZED?

The chapters are organized around the following six general, interrelated questions:

1. What are closeness and intimacy? (chapters 2–5)
2. How can closeness and intimacy be measured? (chapters 6–8)
3. What are the general processes of closeness and intimacy? (chapters 9–12)

4. What individual differences play a role in closeness and intimacy? (chapters 13–15)
5. What situational factors play a role in closeness and intimacy? (chapters 16–18)
6. Is there a dark side to closeness and intimacy? (chapters 19–22)

Section I, entitled *What are closeness and intimacy?* helps to define the domain addressed in this *Handbook* and provides a foundation for understanding the issues and arguments addressed in subsequent sections. This section, and indeed the book, begins logically with a chapter by Fehr (chapter 2) that focuses on the conventional understanding of intimacy and how that perception is constructed. Most important, Fehr addresses the question of whether men and women differ in how they interpret and develop intimacy. By beginning the book with an articulation of how most people understand the constructs of interest, Fehr helps the reader to more clearly make sense of psychological theory and findings. The other chapters in this section present theoretical views of closeness and intimacy, along with supporting research. A. Aron, Mashek, and E. Aron (chapter 3) argue that closeness, as defined by researchers, corresponds to including in one's self another person's resources, perspectives, and identities. Next, Prager and Roberts (chapter 4) argue that "deep intimate connection" is possible only when the organismic self is congruent with the self-concept, a state that allows for authentic self-disclosure and understanding. Finally, Laurenceau, Rivera, Schaffer, and Pietromonaco (chapter 5) examine empirical support for the notion that intimacy can be understood as an interpersonal process involving responses to emotional self-disclosures involving understanding, validation, and caring. Their chapter also highlights aspects of the interpersonal process model of intimacy that would benefit from additional theoretical investigation and empirical testing. Section I, then, presents a wide-lens picture of the closeness and intimacy map; subsequent sections aim to make the topography of the landscape even richer.

Section II addresses our second overarching question, *How can closeness and intimacy be measured?* This section builds on the first by addressing the issue of measurement. How can one assess these seemingly very complex constructs? First, Bersheid, Snyder, and Omoto (chapter 6) focus on their relationship closeness inventory (RCI), a measure based on interdependence theory that assesses closeness as the amount and diversity of interaction with the other and the amount of influence the other has over the self. They review research that has used this influential measure since its introduction 15 years ago, focusing on research demonstrating its successful application to diverse types of relationships across cultures. Agnew, Loving, Le, and Goodfriend (chapter 7) then describe a second influential and simple measurement tool, the inclusion of other in self (IOS) scale, a method based directly on the notion of closeness described in chapter 3 by A. Aron and colleagues. These authors offer new ideas concerning both the implementation and interpretation of the IOS scale, including the generality versus the specificity of inclusion and how it functions at different relationship stages. Section II concludes with a chapter by Kouneski and Olson (chapter 8) that overviews Enriching Relationship Issues, Communication and Happiness (ENRICH), a measurement tool that affords clinicians detailed information about the dynamics of intimacy across an array of domains. Further, these authors emphasize the value of typologies in assessing complex constructs such as intimacy.

Section III addresses the question, *What are the general processes of closeness and intimacy?* Actually, all of the chapters in the volume, to some extent, take on this question. Thus, it was with some reluctance that we placed only four chapters in this section. Nevertheless, we feel that these four chapters overview nicely some of the general processes believed to drive closeness and intimacy. First, Rusbult, Kumashiro, Coolsen, and Kirchner (chapter 9) summarize major aspects of Thibaut and Kelley's (1959) interdependence theory as it has been applied to close relationships, focusing on the implications of treating closeness as existing when the well-being of at least one partner is dependent on the other. In the process, this chapter emphasizes the importance of understanding closeness at a fundamentally interpersonal level of analysis. Collins and Feeney (chapter 10) work from an attachment-theory perspective to highlight how intimacy is expressed and received in the context of adult close relationships, again illuminating how insights about a particular phenomenon can be gleaned from a grand and widely influential perspective. The next chapter, by Vohs and Baumeister (chapter 11), elaborates a model of the link between passion and intimacy, arguing that passion is a function of the rate of increase in intimacy. Most important, this is the sole chapter in this volume that focuses specifically on a key aspect of intimacy–physical intimacy. Finally, Reis, Clark, and Holmes (chapter 12) offer a comprehensive integration of diverse views of intimacy pointing to an overarching core theme of perceived partner responsiveness.

Section IV focuses on the question, *What individual differences play a role in closeness and intimacy?* Personal experience tells us that people differ both in their comfort with intimacy and in the nature of the closeness experience. The contributors to this section argue convincingly that some of these differences are a function of what the individual brings to the relationship. Cross and Gore (chapter 13) start this section with a discussion of how relationship-interdependent self-construals might facilitate the development and maintenance of intimacy. Catherine Sanderson (chapter 14) explores variations of the extent to which people pursue intimacy goals in their relationships by considering why people with intense intimacy goals seem to report enhanced levels of relationship satisfaction. Finally, E. Aron (chapter 15) blends empirical findings from social, personality, and developmental psychology with clinical insight and comparative biology to argue that innate temperament, in interaction with early environmental influences, plays an important role in shaping closeness and intimacy throughout the lifespan.

Section V addresses the question, *What situational factors play a role in closeness and intimacy?* These chapters explore a few of the ways in which situational context directs the experience of closeness and intimacy. First, Arriaga, Goodfriend, and Lohmann (chapter 16) show that environments—both social and physical—can actually facilitate closeness. At the same time, this chapter shows how closeness can influence our social and physical environments. In the next chapter, Wortman, Wolff, and Bonanno (chapter 17) consider how the death of an intimate partner both alters closeness behaviors in other ongoing relationships and influences the desire to establish new intimacies. Finally, Adams, Anderson, and Adonu (chapter 18) consider the role of culture, a very broad and extremely influential sort of context. In this chapter, the authors challenge some of the assumptions of both relationship researchers and Westerners more generally about intimacy and relationships.

Section VI addresses the question, *Is there a dark side to the process of closeness and intimacy?* Clearly, closeness and intimacy offer generally positive outcomes to most people. Nevertheless, the chapters in this section challenge the boundaries of this assumed positivity by illuminating the dark side of closeness and intimacy. Mashek and Sherman (chapter 19) first make salient what it means to feel "too close" to a relationship partner; they then explore threat to control as a probable catalyst of the experience. Next, Ickes, Hutchinson, and Mashek (chapter 20) discuss a peculiar mode of social interaction characterized by a palpable aversion to closeness that is typified by a haunting psychological constellation. Next, drawing on experience and insights from their work with patients, R. Firestone and L. Firestone (chapter 21) consider how clinicians might reach out to people who are plagued by a genuine fear of intimacy with others, focusing foremost on individual defenses rather than on processes that occur at the dyadic level. Finally, Edelstein and Shaver (chapter 22) penetrate the apparent paradox of "avoidant attachment" (that is, how avoidance can be a style of attachment), arguing that avoidant individuals are indeed attached, but that they are also particularly skilled in shutting off thinking about painful topics.

Readers who study this volume cover to cover, as well as those who carefully select particular chapters, assist in our pursuit of an integrated synthesis of knowledge about closeness and intimacy. By being cognizant of the links between the chapters presented here, readers will likely be in a better position to forge the state of our future understanding of these relationship processes.

REFERENCES

Duck, S. (Ed.). (1997). *Handbook of personal relationships: Theory, research and interventions* (2nd ed.). New York: Wiley.

Fletcher, G. J. O., & Clark, M. S. (Eds.). (2000). *Blackwell handbook of social psychology: Interpersonal processes.* Oxford, England: Blackwell.

Kelley, H. H., Berscheid, E., Christensen, A., Harvey, J. H., Huston, T. L., Levinger, G., et al. (Eds.) (1983). *Close relationships.* New York: Freeman.

I

What Are Closeness and Intimacy?

2

A Prototype Model of Intimacy Interactions in Same-Sex Friendships

Beverley Fehr
University of Winnipeg

"I was so thankful that I could find such a good friend to share part of my life with. I told her she was the best friend I have ever had and I was happy that we're able to get so close" (Helgeson, Shaver, & Dyer, 1987, p. 226). These remarks, given by a respondent in Helgeson, Shaver, and Dyer's (1987) study of same-sex intimacy experiences, capture what psychologists are beginning to realize; namely, that friendships are an important source of intimacy in people's lives. Indeed, when Berscheid, Snyder, and Omoto (1989) asked 250 undergraduates about their deepest, closest, most intimate relationships, 36% named a friend (14% named a family member; 47% named a romantic partner, 3% were "other" (mostly work relationships)). Such effects are not limited to college students. Sapadin (1988) asked adults working in various professional capacities to complete the following sentence: "A friend is someone . . . ." The most frequent response from both women and men was " . . . with whom you are intimate." Other lines of research offer additional evidence that people find intimacy in friendships. For example, intimacy consistently emerges in research on conceptions of friendship (e.g., Candy, Troll, & Levy, 1981; Goldman, Cooper, Ahern, & Corsini, 1981; Parks & Floyd, 1996; see Fehr, 1996). Intimacy is also central in research on friendship expectations (e.g., Bigelow & La Gaipa, 1975; Clark & Ayers, 1993; La Gaipa, 1979). Finally, as the opening quotation suggests, people are able to meaningfully report on experiences of intimacy in a friendship when asked to do so (e.g., Helgeson et al., 1987; Oliker, 1989). These findings, taken from somewhat diverse areas of research, point to a clear conclusion, namely that people expect and value intimacy in their friendships.

A PROTOTYPE INTERACTION-PATTERN MODEL OF RELATIONSHIP EXPECTATIONS

It has been established that friendships are an important source of intimacy in people's lives. Less is known, however, about the process by which people come to regard a friendship as intimate. Return, for a moment, to the quotation with which this chapter opened. How did this woman come to the conclusion that her friendship was an intimate one? What knowledge did she draw on? In seeking answers to such questions, I first turned to interaction-pattern models of relationship expectations.

Interaction-Pattern Models of Expectations

The importance of interaction patterns in determining an individual's personality and quality of close relationships has long been recognized in psychology. For example, Sullivan (1953) posited that from childhood on, people learn the kinds of "me–you" patterns that promote feelings of security. Bowlby's (1969, 1973, 1980) seminal writings focused on the mental models of relationships children develop as a function of the caregiver's availability and responsiveness. Interdependence theory has explicated the contingent relations between the outcomes of self and other in relationships (Kelley & Thibaut, 1978; Rusbult, Arriaga, & Agnew, 2001; see also Rusbult, Kumashiro, Coolsen, & Kirchner, chap. 9, this volume). In addition, clinical psychologists have identified dysfunctional interaction patterns in marital relationships (e.g., the demand-withdraw pattern; Christensen, 1988; see also Gottman, 1979; Horowitz, 1989; Peterson, 1979). The basic theme that can be extracted from these writings is that positive and negative interaction patterns develop as self relates to other.

As McClintock (1983) has pointed out, the emphasis in this literature has been on the identification of interaction patterns, frequently through observations of interactions. In contrast, the cognitive representation of these patterns as a form of relational knowledge has received less attention. More recently, however, several theorists have formulated social cognitive models in which interaction patterns, as knowledge structures, are explicitly linked to relationship expectations. In developmental psychology, Bretherton (1990) created a model in which interactional schemas that are experience-near form the basis of higher level expectations. For example, a child might learn that "if I fall, my mommy will pick me up." A pattern of relating such as this is postulated to contribute to the more general expectation of comfort and care, which, in turn, contributes to the even more global expectation of being loved. Similar ideas have been articulated in clinical psychology, particularly in the marital literature. For instance, Baucom, Epstein, Sayers, and Sher (1989, p. 33) posited that,

> Individuals' expectations about interactions between spouses tend to take an "if–then" form and can involve predictions about reactions of the partner to one's own behavior, reactions of the self to the partner's behavior, and outcomes of a joint event (e.g., "If we argue in front of the children, they will be harmed psychologically.").

Baldwin (1992) drew on these ideas when formulating his social cognitive model of relational schemas. One component of a relational schema is an *interpersonal script*, defined as "an expected pattern of interaction, derived through generalization from repeated similar interpersonal experiences" (Baldwin, 1992, p. 462). Baldwin, too, posits that this kind of relational knowledge is represented in the form of if–then contingencies and forms the basis of interpersonal expectations. These models, developed in different areas of psychology, converge on a fundamental idea: On the basis of repeated experiences with a relationship partner, people develop cognitive representations of interaction patterns. Higher-order expectations are derived from this kind of relational knowledge.

A Prototype Analysis of Relationship Expectations

The proposition that interaction patterns underlie interpersonal expectations is based on a solid theoretical foundation. Moreover, as already discussed, theorists such as

Bretherton (1990) have proposed that this knowledge is hierarchically organized. However, the horizontal organization of this kind of relational knowledge has not been specified. In Bretherton's model, for example, a child's expectation of being loved by a parent might be based on knowledge of interaction patterns such as "if I am sick, mommy will take care of me," "if I am bored, mommy will play with me," and "if I am having a birthday, mommy will make a cake." Does each of these patterns equally contribute to an expectation of love, or are they weighted differentially in cognitive representation? An answer may be found in prototype theory, a well-established model of the organization of knowledge in cognitive representation. Rosch (1973; see Mervis & Rosch, 1981, for a review) argued that many natural language concepts are organized around prototypes (clearest cases, best examples). Prototypes shade into nonprototypes which shade into noninstances of a category. Boundaries between categories therefore are blurry and ill-defined. Consistent with the theory, Rosch found that people regard some instances of everyday concepts as better examples than others (e.g., apples are more representative of the concept of fruit than are figs). Moreover, this internal structure influenced information processing in predictable ways. For example, prototypical instances were more salient in memory, more easily substituted for the category name in a sentence, verified more quickly in reaction time studies (i.e., participants responded "yes" more quickly to statements such as "apple is a fruit" than to "fig is a fruit"), and so on (see Mervis & Rosch, 1981).

Rosch's theory was originally developed to explain the categorization of natural objects (e.g., vegetables, furniture), but has since been applied to a variety of social and relationship-relevant domains, including emotion (e.g., Fehr & Russell, 1984; Fitness & Fletcher, 1993; Shaver, Schwartz, Kirson, & O'Connor, 1987; Shaver, Murdaya, & Fraley, 2001), types and features of love (e.g., Aron & Westbay, 1996; Fehr, 1988, 1994; Fehr & Broughton, 2001; Fehr & Russell, 1991; Lamm & Weismann, 1997; Regan, Kocan, & Whitlock, 1998; see Fehr, 1993 for a review), anger (Russell & Fehr, 1994), jealousy (Sharpsteen, 1993), commitment (Fehr, 1988, 1999), relationship quality (Hassebrauck, 1997; Hassebrauck & Fehr, 2002) and most recently, respect (Frei & Shaver, 2002). Thus, by now there is considerable evidence that knowledge of many relationship-relevant concepts is organized as prototypes.

In the same way that some types and features of love, commitment, or anger are more prototypical than others, it is proposed that interaction patterns may vary in terms of prototypicality. For example, the interaction patterns, "if I reveal personal information to my friend, she will listen attentively" and "if I tell a joke, my friend will laugh" may both be indicative of an expectation of intimacy in a friendship. However, the former may be more likely to contribute to that expectation than the latter.

To summarize, based on theorizing in which interpersonal expectations are conceptualized in terms of underlying interaction patterns, it was proposed that there are specific patterns of relating that form the basis of intimacy expectations in friendships. Further, based on prototype theory, it was predicted that patterns of relating would have an internal structure such that some would be considered more prototypical (i.e., more likely to produce a sense of intimacy in a friendship) than others. As discussed next, a prototype analysis of intimacy interactions also had the potential to provide insight into the controversy over whether women's same-sex friendships are more intimate than men's.

Gender Differences in the Intimacy of Same-Sex Friendships

Women's same-sex friendships are frequently portrayed as more intimate than men's same-sex friendships. For example, a caption in an article on friendship in a women's magazine reads, "One woman savors the special intimacy that grows between women." In the article, the writer recalls a childhood summer spent with her extended family:

> I would find the men in the livingroom watching boxing—"the fights," they called them—on the black and white television, talking very little, coloring the air around them blue with their cigarette smoke . . . The women sat at the kitchen table drinking coffee, chatting excitedly, laughing, lightly caressing the children who passed by. I liked their grown-up hairdos and their earrings, their graceful hand movements, the humanistic bent of their conversation, and the intimacy of it. (Berg, 1991, p. 64)

The writer goes on to describe how as an adult, her same-sex friendships take a similar, intimate form. This portrait of women's friendships as highly intimate—more intimate than men's—is not just the stuff of magazine articles. Scientific research on women's and men's friendships has established that women's time with friends is spent in conversation, and that such conversations focus on relationship issues, feelings and emotions, and other personal matters. In contrast, men's friendships are activity-based, often revolving around sports. Further, their conversations tend to reflect these activities, focusing on topics such as sports, work, vehicles, and the like (e.g., Caldwell & Peplau, 1982; Johnson & Aries, 1983; Wellman, 1992; Wright, 1982; see Fehr, 1996, for a review). Women's friendships also are more likely to involve emotional support and physical affection, whereas men's friendships are more likely to entail the provision of practical forms of help or support. Accordingly, women's friendships have been characterized as face to face and men's friendships as side by side (Wright, 1982). This gender difference is generally not disputed. It has, however, fueled considerable controversy over whether women's friendships are necessarily more intimate than men's. As discussed next, there are three different camps in this debate:

Women and Men Agree on the Path to Intimacy, but Only Women Follow It.   The most widely-accepted interpretation of the documented gender differences in friendship experiences is that women's same-sex friendships are, in fact, more intimate than men's (see e.g., Bank & Hansford, 2000; Fehr, 1996; Reis, 1988, 1998; Sharabany, Gershon, & Hofman, 1981). This view is based on the assumption that intimacy is developed through responsive, personal self-disclosure (see e.g., Altman & Taylor, 1973; Reis & Patrick, 1996; Perlman & Fehr, 1987; Reis & Shaver, 1988). Importantly, there is evidence that both women and men agree with this assumption. Reis, Senchak, and Solomon (1985; see also Reis, 1998) found that when rating the intimacy of recorded conversations, women and men agreed that conversations involving personal self-disclosure (e.g., discussing a relationship breakup) were intimate. However, when interacting with a same-sex friend, men chose not to enact such behaviors. Thus, it appears that women are more likely to engage in the kinds of behaviors that both sexes regard as intimacy-producing.

"Different but Equal" Paths to Intimacy.   Another view is that women's and men's friendships are equally intimate, but that the sexes follow different paths to intimacy. Specifically, it is argued that for men, doing activities together is as meaningful and intimate as personal self-disclosure is for women (e.g., Swain, 1989, 1992; Wood & Inman, 1993). Swain (1989) coined the term "closeness in the doing" to describe men's route to intimacy. On the basis of interviews with male university students, he concluded that participation in activities such as backpacking, drinking, and sports create feelings of intimacy between male same-sex friends.

Two Paths to Intimacy for Men.   Theorists in yet another camp maintain that for women, intimacy in friendships is created via self-disclosure, whereas for men, intimacy is created through either self-disclosure or activities. For example, Helgeson et al. (1987) analyzed descriptions of a same-sex intimate experiences and found that women emphasized talking more than shared activities, whereas men focused on both talking and activities. Similarly, Camarena, Sarigiani, and Peterson (1990) found that in their sample of early adolescents, self-disclosure was the best predictor of intimacy in a close same-sex friendship for both boys and girls. However, for boys, intimacy was also predicted by shared experiences and adventures.

In summary, there are three competing views on the issue of whether women's friendships are more intimate than men's. A prototype analysis can inform this debate—not by ruling on which is the correct view, but rather by elucidating which perspective is most consistent with lay conceptions. To illustrate this point using another domain, theorists have offered various competing views of the relation between the concepts of love and commitment (ranging from the view that these concepts are synonymous to the view that they are completely independent; see Fehr, 1988). A prototype analysis revealed that laypeople's conceptions were most consistent with Kelley's (1983) model which conceptualized love and commitment as largely overlapping, but partially independent. For example, people generated many of the same features for both concepts, but also features that were unique to each (Fehr, 1988). In the same way, it was anticipated that a prototype analysis of intimacy interaction patterns would reveal which of the competing perspectives on the issue of sex differences in the intimacy of friendships most closely corresponded to lay people's conceptions. It is, after all, the social interactions of ordinary people that these theories are seeking to explain.

A PROTOTYPE INTERACTION-PATTERN MODEL OF INTIMACY EXPECTATIONS IN FRIENDSHIPS: PRELIMINARY EVIDENCE

A series of studies was conducted to validate the proposed interaction pattern model of intimacy expectations in same-sex friendships (see Fehr, in press, for details). It is important to note that because the focus was on laypeople's conceptions of intimacy, the term *intimacy* was not defined for the participants. Instead, they responded on the basis of what intimacy meant to them. Study 1 investigated whether people are able to describe ways of relating that contribute to an expectation of intimacy in a same-sex friendship. Study 2 examined whether the Study 1 findings, which were based on a university sample, would generalize to a community sample. Study 3 tested whether the interaction patterns identified in the first two studies were structured as prototypes, such that some patterns would be considered more indicative of intimacy in a friendship than others. Study 4 used reaction time methodology to verify the prototype structure of the intimacy interaction patterns. In Study 5, it was predicted that prototypical interaction patterns would be seen as characterizing close, established friendships to a greater extent than developing or deteriorating friendships. The applicability of nonprototypical patterns was expected to be less closely linked to friendship stage. In Study 6, it was hypothesized that violations of prototypical interaction patterns would be regarded as more damaging to a close friendship than violations of nonprototypical patterns. Finally, in Study 7, participants rated the applicability of intimacy interaction patterns to an actual friendship. It was expected that friendships characterized by prototypical patterns of relating would be more satisfying than those characterized by nonprototypical patterns. In each study, gender differences were examined in light of the competing perspectives on whose friendships are more intimate.

Study 1: Generating Intimacy Interaction Patterns

The purpose Study 1 was to identify the interaction patterns, or ways of relating, that people regard as contributing to an expectation of intimacy in a same-sex friendship.

Given that friendships figure prominently in the lives of young adults (e.g., Berscheid et al., 1989; Fehr, 1996) responses were gathered from a university sample. It was expected that the interaction patterns generated would reflect the ways in which women and men spend their time with friends. As already discussed, women self-disclose with friends, particularly about personal and relationship issues, whereas men are more likely to engage in activities (see Fehr, 1996, for a review). However, it was anticipated that the interaction patterns would extend beyond self-disclosure and activities. For example, research on conceptions of intimacy has identified emotional expressiveness (e.g., affection, compassion, caring), unconditional support, mutual appreciation, and mutual understanding, as among the important features of intimacy in friendships (e.g., Helgeson et al., 1987; Monsour, 1992). It seemed likely that such themes also would be reflected in the interaction patterns generated by participants in this study.[1]

Participants ($N = 121$) were 86 female and 35 male university students. They were asked to describe "interaction patterns or ways of relating that create a sense of intimacy in a friendship." Their responses were transcribed and coded by three judges, following a procedure in which and highly synonymous responses are combined (see Fehr, 1988). This coding process resulted in the identification of 48 interaction patterns listed by two or more participants (see Table 2.1 for a subset). First, and perhaps most noteworthy, participants appeared to have little difficulty reporting on this kind of relational knowledge. Second, consistent with a prototype perspective, there was considerable variability in the frequency with which patterns of relating came to mind. The pattern "If I need to talk, my friend will listen" was most frequently listed, indicating that self-disclosure is seen as an important in creating intimacy expectations. Patterns portraying emotional support also were listed frequently (e.g., "If I'm sad or depressed, my friend will cheer me up" ranked second), whereas patterns such as "If I need to borrow something, my friend will lend it" were rather infrequent. Overall, the patterns of relating captured a variety of themes that have been identified in the literature, such as the provision of emotional and practical support, loyalty, trust, having fun together, empathy, advice and guidance, and so on.

The contribution of this study is the specification of the kinds of interactions between self and other that give rise to these more global perceptions. Importantly, this study also uncovered patterns of relating that have received little, if any, attention in the intimacy literature. These included thoughtfulness (e.g., taking one another's wishes into account when making plans), respect (e.g., one's friend respecting one's need for time alone), forgiveness, shared emotion (e.g., one's friend sharing one's joys and sorrows), and so on. In short, the participants' responses reflected rich, complex knowledge of many ways of relating that could contribute to a sense of intimacy in a friendship.

Gender Differences. Most patterns of relating were listed by both women and men. Moreover, the frequencies with which they were generated were highly correlated, $r = .68$ ($r_s = .56$). Turning to the controversy over whether women's friendships are more intimate than men's, interaction patterns pertaining to self-disclosure (e.g., "If I talk, my friend will listen") were not listed more frequently by women than men—in fact, men were somewhat more likely to list such patterns (see Table 2.1). Moreover, men were not more likely than women to list patterns depicting shared activities (e.g., "If I want to have fun, my friend will go out with me"). In fact, women

---

[1] Note that the focus of the present research was on the patterns of relating that people believe produce a sense of intimacy in a friendship, rather than on their descriptions of a specific experience of intimacy (e.g., Helgeson et al., 1987; Register & Henley, 1992) or their definitions of the concept (e.g., Monsour, 1992; Waring, Tillman, Frelick, Russell, & Weisz, 1980).

TABLE 2.1
Patterns of Relating

Pattern of Relating	University Sample			Prototypicality Ratings			
	% Men	% Woman	% Total	Men	Women	Total	p
If I need to talk, my friend will listen.	48.57	36.05	39.67	7.31	8.17	7.77	.004
If I am upset or worried, my friend will comfort me.	11.43	20.93	18.18	6.53	7.70	7.19	.001
If I have a secret, I can trust my friend not to tell anyone else.	14.29	18.60	17.36	6.53	7.70	7.19	.006
If I have a problem, my friend will listen.	20.00	15.12	15.70	6.61	8.00	7.39	.001
If I have a problem, my friend will help me.	17.14	15.12	15.70	6.56	7.76	7.20	.003
No matter who I am or what I do, my friend will accept me.	11.43	15.12	14.05	6.97	7.53	7.24	ns
If I need to cry, my friend will be there for me.	2.86	15.12	11.57	5.97	7.96	7.11	.001
If I need support, my friend will provide it.	8.57	12.79	11.57	6.61	7.77	7.26	.001
If I need my friend, s/he will be there for me.	5.71	9.30	8.26	7.17	7.79	7.47	.057
If someone was insulting me or saying negative things behind my back, my friend would stick up for me.	5.71	6.98	6.61	7.08	7.59	7.35	ns
If I need love, my friend will give it.	14.29	1.16	4.96	5.89	7.53	6.83	.001
If I need a hug, my friend will hug me.	2.86	5.81	4.13	5.19	7.85	6.71	.001
If we have a fight or an argument, we will work it out.	0	3.49	2.48	6.56	7.74	7.24	.001
Even if it feels as though no one cares, I know my friend does.	2.86	2.33	2.48	6.56	7.74	7.24	.001
If my friend has upset me, I am able to let him/her know.	2.86	1.16	1.65	6.75	7.57	7.21	.031
If I want to have fun, my friend will go out with me.	17.14	19.77	19.00	6.36	6.66	6.46	ns
If I am sick, my friend will take care of me.	17.14	13.95	14.88	5.69	6.34	6.03	ns
If I need practical help (e.g., moving, a ride, studying), my friend will provide it.	5.71	12.79	10.74	5.86	6.64	6.26	.07
If I need money, my friend will lend it to me.	17.14	6.98	9.92	5.92	5.93	5.73	ns
If I need time alone, my friend will understand and give it to me.	11.43	9.30	9.92	5.81	6.94	6.45	.014
If I am happy, my friend will be happy with me.	11.43	9.30	9.92	5.47	6.43	6.02	.021
If I need an opinion, my friend will provide it.	8.57	9.30	9.09	5.58	6.85	6.29	.008
If I need to borrow something, my friend will lend it.	17.14	4.65	8.26	5.92	6.02	5.91	ns
If I need a favor, my friend will do it.	17.14	2.33	6.61	6.03	6.51	6.21	ns
If I'm joking or laughing, my friend will laugh with me.	5.71	6.98	6.61	5.81	6.64	6.23	.072
If I am bored, my friend will spend time with me.	8.57	3.49	4.96	5.75	6.13	5.94	ns
If I just want to do nothing, my friend will be fine with that.	5.71	3.49	4.96	5.44	6.09	5.77	ns
If I am thinking something, s/he is often on the same wavelength.	0	4.65	3.31	5.92	6.72	6.29	.074
If I am sad, my friend is sad too.	0	2.32	1.65	4.81	5.34	5.04	ns
If I am away, my friend will keep in touch.	0	2.33	1.65	6.31	7.02	6.69	ns

Note. For the university sample, $N = 121$ (86 women; 35 men). Prototypicality ratings were provided by 94 participants (53 women; 36 men; 5 participants did not indicate their gender). From Fehr, B. (in press). Intimacy expectations in same-sex friendships: A prototype interaction-pattern model. *Journal of Personality and Social Psychology.* Copyright © 2004 by the American Psychological Association. Reprinted with permission.

were somewhat more likely to generate such patterns (see Table 2.1). In sum, there was little evidence that men perceive shared activities as the route to intimacy—either in their own right or, as some camps would have it, in combination with personal self-disclosure. This is not to say that women and men agree on the kinds of interaction patterns that are most likely to produce intimacy in a friendship. Women and men could generate many of the same interaction patterns, but differ in terms of which patterns are perceived as most and least likely to produce an expectation of intimacy. (This issue was addressed in Study 3.)

Study 2: A Community Sample Replication

The purpose of Study 2 was to replicate the previous study with an older, community sample. Respondents ($N = 50$) were 30 married women and 20 married men with an average age of 39 years ($sd = 11.14$). They generated interaction patterns as in Study 1. Their responses were coded following the Study 1 procedure. First, it is noteworthy that all of the interaction patterns generated by the community sample also were listed by university students in the previous study. Moreover, the frequencies with which these responses were generated were highly correlated, $r = .76$. The relative ranking of the patterns also was highly similar ($r_s = .79$). As in the first study, the responses of women and men were highly correlated, $r = .60$ ($r_s = .73$). Thus, the patterns of relating identified in Study 1 were robust, extending to a community sample of middle-aged adults.

Study 3: Prototypicality Ratings

This study tested the key prediction, on the basis of prototype theory, that some patterns of relating would be seen as more likely to produce a sense of intimacy in a same-sex friendship than others. Participants ($N = 94$) were 53 women and 36 men (5 participants did not indicate their gender). They were asked to rate the 48 patterns of relating identified in Study 1 in terms of the likelihood that each would "produce a sense of intimacy in a same-sex friendship." Patterns pertaining to self-disclosure (e.g., "If I need to talk, my friend will listen") received the highest ratings, consistent with theories postulating that self-disclosure is the primary route through which people develop intimacy in their relationships (e.g., Altman & Taylor, 1973; Reis & Shaver, 1988). Reis and Patrick (1996) have commented that, "we suspect in actual practice, intimacy is predominantly created and maintained through verbal discourse" (p. 541). Interactions involving various kinds of social support, especially emotional support (e.g., "If I am worried or upset, my friend will comfort me"), loyalty (e.g., "If someone was insulting me or saying negative things behind my back, my friend would stick up for me"), and trust (e.g., "If I have a secret, I can trust my friend not to tell anyone else") also were seen as highly likely to produce a sense of intimacy in a same-sex friendship. The kinds of patterns that received the lowest ratings referred to practical help, being able to borrow things, including money, from one's friend, and turning to one's friend for advice or opinions. Thus, consistent with prototype theory predictions, some interaction patterns were seen as more likely to contribute to intimacy in a same-sex friendship than others.

Gender Differences.   Women rated the interaction patterns, overall, as more likely to create an expectation of intimacy than did men. Follow-up analyses in which women's and men's ratings of each interaction pattern were compared revealed that gender differences were most likely to occur for patterns that received the highest typicality ratings (see sample items in Table 2.1). A somewhat different picture emerged when within-gender comparisons were made. As expected, women assigned higher prototypicality ratings to interaction patterns depicting self-disclosure, emotional support, and so on than to patterns depicting shared activities and practical support. Interestingly, men did the same. Thus, two of the perspectives in the gender debate, namely that men would assign higher ratings to shared activities patterns than to patterns depicting self-disclosure and that men would assign equally high ratings to self-disclosure and activity patterns were not supported in this study. Instead, women and men agreed that interactions involving self-disclosure are more likely to produce intimacy in a same-sex friendship than those involving shared activities. The fact that women rated such patterns higher than did men may reflect women's greater propensity to engage in self-disclosure with friends.

Study 4: Reaction Time

The previous study found evidence that patterns of relating are structured as prototypes, such that some patterns are seen as more likely to produce a sense of intimacy in a same-sex friendship than others. The next step was to confirm this prototype structure. Study 4 examined prototype effects in the speed with which category relevant information is processed. On the basis of reaction time results in other domains (e.g., emotion, anger; see Fehr, Russell, & Ward, 1982; Russell & Fehr, 1994), it was predicted that prototypical patterns of relating (e.g., "If I want to talk, my friend will listen") would be verified more quickly as contributing to an expectation of intimacy than nonprototypical patterns (e.g., "If I need money, my friend will lend it"). Participants ($N = 30$) were 15 female and 15 male university students. The instructions and practice trials were presented on a computer screen. Twenty interaction patterns that were similar in length (10 patterns that received ratings above the median in Study 3 designated as prototypical; 10 patterns that received ratings below the median designated nonprototypical) were displayed one at a time, along with filler items. Participants were asked to make a yes–no decision in response to the question, "Would this way of relating create a sense of intimacy in a same-sex friendship?" Consistent with predictions, prototypical patterns of relating were verified more quickly than nonprototypical patterns of relating.

   Gender Differences.   There was a tendency for women to respond faster to the statements overall compared to men ($p = .051$). Although the Gender × Prototypicality interaction was not significant, follow-up tests indicated that women did, in fact, verify the prototypical patterns of relating more quickly than did men ($p < .05$), whereas the gender difference for nonprototypical was not significant ($p > .10$). Thus, women's tendency to respond more quickly was most evident for the prototypical patterns.

Study 5: Judgments of the Dynamics of Friendships

In this study, the implications of the prototype structure of interaction patterns for the dynamics of friendships were explored. It was hypothesized that the status of a friendship would be reflected in the applicability of prototypical intimacy interaction patterns—more so than that of nontypical patterns. For example, a newly formed friendship in which a prototypical pattern such as personal self-disclosure is increasing (e.g., "If I need to talk, my friend will listen" is becoming solidified as a pattern of relating) might be judged as more intimate than a friendship characterized by an increase in nonprototypical patterns (e.g., "If I need an opinion, my friend will provide it"). Conversely, the decline of a prototypical pattern (e.g., feeling one can no longer count on a friend to listen responsively) should be regarded as diagnostic of decreasing intimacy, more so than a decline in a nonprototypical pattern of relating. The key prediction, then, was an interaction between stage of friendship and prototypicality such that prototypical patterns would be seen as more applicable to close, established friendships than to developing or deteriorating friendships, whereas the applicability of nonprototypical patterns was not expected to vary systematically with friendship stage. Participants ($N = 253$) were 138 female 115 male university students (3 did not report their gender); each received a description of a same sex-friendship, depicted as in the development, maintenance, or deterioration stage.[2] They then rated 30 interaction patterns (15 prototypical and 15 nonprototypical based on the Study 3 ratings; see Table 2.1) in terms of how likely it was that the friendship pair in the scenario would interact in that way. As expected, prototypical interaction patterns received higher ratings than did nonprototypical patterns. Moreover, friendships at the development and deterioration stages were rated as lower in terms of intimacy interaction patterns, overall, than friendships at the maintenance stage. Thus, established, close friendships instantiated the prototype of intimacy interaction patterns to a greater extent than friendships that were either forming or declining. Most important, the predicted Prototypicality × Relationship Stage interaction was significant. Friendships at the development and deterioration stages were rated significantly lower in terms of prototypical intimacy interaction patterns than friendships at the maintenance stage (ratings of the development and deterioration stages did not differ significantly from one another). Nonprototypical patterns showed the same effects, but the differences were less pronounced.

Thus, as friendships progress, they are more likely to be characterized in terms of the overall prototype of intimacy interaction patterns. Conversely, as friendships begin to wane, they are less likely to approximate the prototype of intimacy. However, it is the prototypical interaction patterns that are the most accurate barometers of the state of the relationship, given that they showed greater differentiation between levels of friendship than did the nontypical patterns.

Gender Differences.   As in the previous studies, women assigned higher ratings overall to the interaction patterns than did men, and again, this difference was more pronounced for the prototypical patterns than for the nonprototypical patterns. Within-gender analyses revealed that both women and men assigned significantly higher ratings to the prototypical, than the nonprototypical, patterns of relating.

Study 6: Violations of Intimacy Interaction Patterns

In this study, it was predicted that violations of prototypical patterns of relating (e.g., discovering that a friend cannot be trusted with a secret) would be regarded as more damaging to a friendship than violations of nonprotoypical patterns (e.g., discovering that a friend could not be counted on for practical help). Participants ($N = 183$) were 96 female and 81 male university students (6 did not report their gender) received a description of an intimate friendship.[3] They were then presented with prototypical and nonprototypical interaction patterns, worded in the negative (e.g., "If

---

[2] The scenarios varied in terms of whether the friendship pair was presented as male or female. The patterns of relating received higher ratings, overall, when a female same-sex friendship was rated than when a male same-sex friendship was rated, and this difference was most pronounced for the prototypical patterns. Interestingly, gender of participant did not interact with gender of friendship pair, indicating that women and men agreed on the applicability of the interaction patterns to male and female friendships.

[3] As in the previous study, the friendship scenario depicted either a male or female same-sex friendship. Parallel to the previous study, violations of prototypical patterns were seen as more devastating if they occurred in a female, rather than a male, friendship. And, again, there were no gender of participant differences in these ratings.

someone was insulting Michelle or saying negative things behind her back, Jennifer would not stick up for her"), and were asked to rate the impact of that event on the friendship. Consistent with predictions, violations of prototypical intimacy patterns were regarded as more damaging to a friendship than violations of nonprototypical patterns. Thus, friendships are damaged when responsive self-disclosure, caring, comfort, and other prototypical intimacy interactions are no longer characteristic of the relationship. Friendships are more likely to weather failures of practical support, advice-giving, and other nonprototypical patterns of relating.

Gender Differences. Once again, women rated violations of the intimacy interaction patterns, overall, as more damaging than did men. This gender difference was greatest for the violation of prototypical patterns. Within-gender analyses revealed that both women and men regarded violations of prototypical intimacy patterns as having a more negative effect on a friendship than violations of nonprototypical patterns.

Study 7: Friendship Satisfaction

The studies discussed so far focused on laypeople's knowledge of intimacy interaction patterns. An important question is whether this knowledge has any bearing on people's evaluations of their own friendships. In other research, it has been shown that people's satisfaction in romantic relationships is correlated with the perception that prototypical features of love (Aron & Westbay, 1996) and relationship quality (Hassebrauck & Aron, 2001) apply to their relationship. On the basis of this research, it was predicted that friendships would be regarded as more satisfying if prototypical, rather than nonprototypical, patterns of relating were characteristic of the relationship. Further, it was anticipated that women's friendship satisfaction would be more closely linked to the prototypical patterns of relating than would men's. Participants ($N = 230$) were 128 female and 102 male university students; each rated the extent to which 30 patterns of relating (15 prototypical, 15 nonprototypical; see Table 2.1) characterized a same-sex friendship. They also reported how satisfied they were with the friendship. Results indicated that for both women and men, the more that prototypical patterns characterized their friendship, the greater the satisfaction ($r_s = .73$ and .41 for women and men respectively). This relation was stronger for women, however, than for men (i.e., the difference between these correlations was statistically significant, $Z = 3.80$, $p < .001$). It was also predicted that endorsement of nonprototypical patterns would not be as strongly correlated with satisfaction. This was true for women, although the correlation was still quite strong ($r = .60$, $p < .001$). For men, the correlation between nonprototypical patterns and satisfaction ($r = .47$, $p < .001$) was nearly identical to obtained between prototypical patterns and satisfaction. Thus, women were happiest in their friendships when they were characterized by prototypical patterns of relating. Men's satisfaction was not as highly dependent on having prototypical patterns of relating characterize a friendship—they were just as happy if a friendship was characterized by prototypical and nonprototypical patterns of relating. Thus, it appears that people's knowledge of patterns of relating is brought to bear on judgments of friendship satisfaction in ways that would be predicted by prototype theory.

IMPLICATIONS AND CONCLUSION

The model of intimacy expectations developed here and the research generated by it have wide-ranging implications. The findings are relevant to theories and research on intimacy, social cognitive models of relationship expectations, and to prototype theory. Moreover, the prototype approach adopted here provided a means of evaluating (using lay people's conceptions as the criterion) the various perspectives in the debate over whether women's same-sex friendships are more intimate than men's.

Intimacy Expectations in Friendships: The Value of an Interaction-Pattern Approach

Perhaps the single most important finding of this research is that people possess sophisticated, intricate knowledge of the many ways of relating that produce a sense of intimacy in a same-sex friendship. The complexity of human relationships is captured in the diversity of interaction patterns that were generated. According to university students and a community sample of married people, an expectation of intimacy is created when people experience responsive self-disclosure, when they can count on their friend for comfort and cheering up, when they can count on their friend for practical help, when they feel assured that problems will be resolved, when their friend helps them achieve important personal goals, and so on. Other researchers have found that people are able to report on a particular experience of intimacy (e.g., Helgeson et al., 1987) or provide definitions of the concept (e.g., Monsour, 1992). The present findings suggest that people are also able to articulate more complex forms of relational knowledge, specifically the patterns of relating, or contingencies between self and other, that give rise to a sense of intimacy in a same-sex friendship. This is important for a number of reasons. First, these results are consistent with theoretical claims that intimacy is inherently interactional (e.g., Prager, 1995, 2000; Reis, 1990; Reis & Shaver, 1988). As Reis (1998) recently pointed out, "[b]ecause intimacy is an interactional process, it depends not only on one partner's self expression, but also on the other's response" (p. 206). Indeed, the research reported here suggests that a sense of intimacy is not based on the knowledge that this is a friendship in which I talk, for example, but rather, the knowledge that my talking is likely to elicit listening, my sadness is likely to elicit a comforting response, and so on. Importantly, these are precisely the kinds of interactions that would be expected to result in feeling validated and understood in a relationship—feelings, which, according to Reis and Shaver's (1988) model, are fundamental to the experience of intimacy.

On a related note, in research on laypeople's definitions and experiences of intimacy, typical responses include social support, trust, mutual understanding, affection, and emotional expressiveness (see Fehr, 1996). The studies conducted here provide insight into the interaction patterns of relating that may underlie these more global evaluations. When people list *support* as an important feature of intimacy, for example, they are likely to be drawing on knowledge of patterns of relating such as "If I need my friend, s/he will be there" or "If I set a goal, my friend will support and encourage me." When people list *understanding* as a characteristic of intimacy, this response may well be based on interaction patterns such as "If I need time alone, my friend will understand and give it to me" or "If I am thinking something, she or he is often on the same wavelength." In short, the present findings provide a window into the kinds of interactions or ways of relating that are likely to contribute to these more abstract, global, indicators of intimacy. Of course, it is possible that causality actually runs in the opposite direction. People may arrive at general assessments of intimacy in a friendship, and consequently, might be especially attentive to, or more likely to recall (or perhaps even construct), intimate patterns of relating. Although it is unlikely that this chicken-and-egg problem can be conclusively solved, in research currently in progress, participants are being asked to enact prototypical or nonprototypical interaction patterns with a same-sex friend to see whether the instantiation of prototypical patterns leads to an increase in perceived intimacy in a friendship.

Finally, the findings have implications for social cognitive models of relationship expectations. The idea that relationship expectations are derived from patterns of relating (e.g., Baldwin, 1992; Bretherton, 1990) is a profound one, cutting to the very core of human relationships. The responses of participants in these studies suggest that this is a kind of relational knowledge that people are able to access and describe. As mentioned in the Introduction, Bretherton (1990) proposed that interaction patterns that are experience-near (e.g., "if I am hurt, my mommy will comfort me") contribute to higher order expectations such as an expectation of comfort, which in turn, may contribute to the more global expectation of being loved. If people are able to report on specific ways of relating, as the present findings suggest, then it becomes possible to test for evidence of such a hierarchy in the domain of intimacy.

Intimacy Expectations in Friendships: The Value of a Prototype Approach

One of the main hypotheses in this research was that intimacy interaction patterns would be structured as prototypes, such that some patterns would be regarded as more likely to produce a sense of intimacy in a friendship than others. Not only was it meaningful for participants to calibrate interaction patterns in terms of their centrality to intimacy expectations, but this prototype structure was found to influence information processing and judgments about friendships in predictable ways. Morever, the final study showed that the extent to which various patterns of relating are characteristic of people's actual friendships was related to friendship satisfaction. Women, in particular, were happiest in friendships that instantiated the prototypical patterns of relating such as "If I talk, my friend will listen."

A prototype approach to intimacy expectations also provides a framework for interpreting the results of research on lay conceptions of intimacy and intimate experiences. For example, on the basis of his analysis of lay people's conceptions of same-sex intimacy, Monsour (1992) identified four main intimacy dimensions: self-disclosure, emotional expressiveness (which included compassion and caring), unconditional support (e.g., being there for one another) and physical (nonsexual) contact. The results of the present studies suggest that these dimensions are not weighted equally in cognitive representation. More specifically, people seem to place the greatest importance on the first three dimensions, whereas the physical contact dimension appears to be less crucial, particularly for men. Men's greater discomfort with same-sex physical contact may account for why such interactions are not perceived as particularly intimacy producing (Bank & Hansford, 2000). Thus, a prototype analysis can be informative in highlighting the features, dimensions, or components of intimacy that are likely to be paramount in people's minds. The prototype findings also have implications for the kinds of intimacy-related issues that people are most likely to be struggling with or present as problematic in therapy. A friend's failure to provide comfort when needed, for example, should engender greater distress than a friend's failure to help with studying.

Finally, the methodology developed here would be well-suited for exploring whether people in non-Western cultures would generate similar patterns of relating as indicative of intimacy in a same-sex friendship. The patterns of relating identified in the present studies are clearly "me" oriented—intimacy is achieved when my friend listens to me, helps me, is loyal to me. People in collectivist cultures might be more likely to focus on "what I can do for my friend" when defining intimacy than on "what my friend can do for me." Moreover, as Adams, Anderson, and Adonu (chap. 18, this volume) have suggested, in cultures that emphasize independence, such as North America, self-disclosure may be more necessary to achieve intimacy because intimacy and connectedness are not the status quo. In contrast, in cultures that value interdependence, intimacy and connectedness to others already exist as part of the social fabric. An exploration of cultural differences in intimacy interaction patterns is an intriguing area for future research.

WHOSE FRIENDSHIPS ARE MORE INTIMATE? WOMEN'S OR MEN'S?

The most controversial issue in the friendship literature is whether women's same-sex friendship are more intimate than men's (Fehr, 1996). As already mentioned, a proto-type analysis does not provide a basis for pronouncements on which view is correct, but it does reveal which of the experts' views is most congruent with that of laypeople. The findings of the present studies, taken together, suggest that people's conceptions are not consistent with the view that women achieve intimacy through interactions involving self-disclosure whereas men achieve intimacy through shared activities. Nor was support found for the position that women achieve intimacy through self-disclosure interactions whereas men achieve intimacy through self-disclosure and ac-tivity interactions. The final perspective was that women and men would agree that self-disclosure interactions are more likely to contribute to intimacy than activity in-teractions; however, women would rate self-disclosure patterns higher than men, and men would rate activity patterns higher than women. The data were most consistent with this view.[4] Both women and men assigned the highest ratings to interactions in-volving responsive self-disclosure, emotional support, and the like, but women rated these patterns higher than did men. In addition, women and men assigned the lowest ratings to interactions involving activities (e.g., having fun) and various interactions involving practical support. The only departure from this view was that men did not rate these patterns of relating as more likely to produce a sense of intimacy in a same-sex friendship than did women. In other words, the findings did not take the form of a cross-over interaction because a gender difference was obtained only for the self-disclosure patterns.

To return to the key question, are women's friendships more intimate than men's? Those who answer yes to this question (e.g., Reis, 1998; Reis et al., 1985) point to the fact that women are more likely to engage in personal self-disclosure with friends than are men. The present findings reinforce this answer by showing that women are more likely than men to regard self-disclosure as contributing to a sense of intimacy. How-ever, any proclamations over whose friendships are more intimate must be tempered by a consideration of within-gender effects, namely, that men, like women, believe that self-disclosure interactions are more likely to create a sense of intimacy than are activity-based interactions. As Reis et al. (1985; see also Reis, 1998) have demonstrated, men simply prefer not to engage in such behaviors.

Do Men (and Their Friends) Live on Mars and Women (and Their Friends) Live on Venus?

The pattern of gender differences and similarities obtained here also speaks to the de-bate surrounding the different cultures explanation of gender differences. Proponents

---

[4] Note that in Studies 1 to 6, the experimenters were women. Thus, it is possible that the male partici-pants were responding to what they believed women researchers mean when they use the word "intimacy." However, in Study 7, a male experimenter was used. The fact that the results of this study also supported predictions would argue against this possibility. However, future studies will be conducted with male experimenters to explore this possibility more fully.

of the different cultures hypothesis (see e.g., Wood, 1997) argue that the socialization and experiences of women and men differ so vastly that the sexes can be characterized as inhabiting different cultures, with all of the attendant misunderstandings and failures of communication. (This view has been widely promoted in the popular press in which it takes the more extreme form of portraying women and men as inhabiting different planets, not merely different cultures.) The different cultures hypothesis also implies that the friendship worlds of women and men would be very different. Opponents of this view (e.g., Burleson, 1997; Burleson, Kunkel, Samter, & Werking, 1996; Duck & Wright, 1993; Vangelisti & Daly, 1997; Wright, 1988) have argued that a valid assessment of the magnitude of gender differences in any domain must be based on an examination of both between-sex and within-sex variability, not only the former. In the present studies, women rated self-disclosure and emotional support interaction patterns higher than did men, thereby inviting a different cultures explanation. However, the within-gender findings, namely that both women and men rated self-disclosure patterns higher than activity patterns, lend support to the similar cultures view. The similar cultures hypothesis is further bolstered by the finding that when gender of friendship pair was included as a variable (see Footnotes 2 and 3), prototypical patterns were seen as characterizing women's friendships to a greater extent than men's friendships—by both women and men. Thus, women and men agreed on the patterns of relating that are most likely to produce a sense of intimacy in a same-sex friendship and agreed that such patterns are more likely to typify women's friendships. The findings can perhaps best be summarized by Hyde's (1999) wry observation that, "men are from earth, women are from earth." That is not to say that women and men are immune from miscommunication and misunderstandings. Even though women and men inhabit the same planet, there are differences in their conceptions of intimacy, as indicated by the significant between-gender effects that were obtained in this research.

In conclusion, the prototype interaction pattern model of expectations proposed here and the research generated by it provide at least a preliminary answer to the question: How do people develop a sense of intimacy in their friendships? The findings suggest that intimacy expectations are based on knowledge of specific patterns of relating between self and other. If someone learns, on the basis of a history of repeated, similar interactions, that a friend is likely to respond to his or her expression of sadness with comfort and compassion, this sets the stage for the development of an expectation of intimacy in the friendship. Moreover, the present findings suggest that this person will place greater weight on this kind of interaction than on interactions pertaining to practical support, shared activities, and the like. Thus, people able to report not only on the kinds of interactions that they perceive as intimacy producing, but also on the structure of this kind of relational knowledge.

REFERENCES

Altman, I., & Taylor, D. A. (1973). *Social penetration: The development of interpersonal relationships*. New York: Holt, Rinehart & Winston.

Aron, A., & Westbay, L. (1996). Dimensions of the prototype of love. *Journal of Personality and Social Psychology, 70*, 535–551.

Baldwin, M. W. (1992). Relational schemas and the processing of social information. *Psychological Bulletin, 112*, 461–484.

Bank, B. J., & Hansford, S. L. (2000). Gender and friendship: Why are men's best same-sex friendships less intimate and supportive? *Personal Relationships, 7*, 1–23.

Baucom, D. H., Epstein, N., Sayers, S., & Sher, T. G. (1989). The role of cognition in marital relationships: Definitional, methodological, and conceptual issues. *Journal of Consulting and Clinical Psychology, 57*, 31–38.

Berg, E. (1991, August). The best of friends. *New woman*, pp. 62–64.

Berscheid, E., Snyder, M., & Omoto, A. M. (1989). Issues in studying close relationships: Conceptualizing and measuring closeness. In C. Hendrick (Ed.), *Review of Personality and Social Psychology*, Vol. 10, 63–91. Newbury Park, CA: Sage

Bigelow, B., & La Gaipa, J. (1975). Children's written descriptions of friendship: A multidimensional analysis. *Developmental Psychology, 11*, 857–858.

Bowlby, J. (1969). *Attachment and loss: Vol. 1. Attachment*. New York: Basic Books.

Bowlby, J. (1973). *Attachment and loss: Vol. 2. Separation, anxiety, and anger*. New York: Basic Books.

Bowlby, J. (1980). *Attachment and loss: Vol. 3. Loss, sadness, and depression*. New York: Basic Books.

Bretherton, I. (1990). Communication patterns, internal working models, and the intergenerational transmission of attachment relationships. *Infant Mental Health Journal, 11*, 237–252.

Burleson, B. R. (1997). A difference voice on different cultures: Illusion and reality in the study of sex differences in personal relationships. *Personal Relationships, 4*, 229–241.

Burleson, B. R., Kunkel, A. W., Samter W., & Werking, K. J. (1996). Men's and women's evaluations of communication skills in personal relationships: When sex differences make a difference and when they don't. *Journal of Social and Personal Relationships, 13*, 201–224.

Caldwell, M., & Peplau, L. (1982). Sex differences in same-sex friendship. *Sex Roles, 8*, 721–732.

Camarena, P., Sarigiani, P., & Peterson, A. (1990). Gender-specific pathways to intimacy in early adolescence. *Journal of Youth and Adolescence, 19*, 19–32.

Candy, S. G., Troll, L. E., & Levy, S. G. (1981). A developmental exploration of friendship functions in women. *Psychology of Women Quarterly, 5*, 456–472.

Christensen, A. (1988). Dysfunctional interaction patterns in couples. In P. Noller & M. A. Fitzpatrick (Eds.), *Perspectives on marital interaction* (pp. 31–52). Clevedon, Avon, England: Multilingual Matters.

Clark, M. L., & Ayers, M. (1993). Friendship expectations and friendship evaluations: Reciprocity and gender effects. *Youth and Society, 24*, 299–313.

Duck, S., & Wright, P. H. (1993). Reexamining gender differences in same-gender friendships: A close look at two kinds of data. *Sex Roles, 28*, 709–727.

Fehr, B. (1988). Prototype analysis of the concepts of love and commitment. *Journal of Personality and Social Psychology, 55*, 557–579

Fehr, B. (1993). How do I love thee . . . ? Let me consult my prototype. In S. Duck (Ed.). *Understanding personal relationships, Vol. 1: Individuals in relationships*. (pp. 87–120).

Fehr, B. (1994). Prototype-based assessment of laypeople's views of love. *Personal Relationships, 1*, 309–331.

Fehr, B. (1996). *Friendship processes*.

Fehr, B. (1999). Lay people's conceptions of commitment. *Journal of Personality and Social Psychology, 76*, 90–106.

Fehr, B. (in press). Intimacy expectations in same-sex friendships: A prototype interaction-pattern model. *Journal of Personality and Social Psychology*.

Fehr, B., & Broughton, R. (2001). Gender and personality differences in conceptions of love: An interpersonal theory analysis. *Personal Relationships, 8*, 115–136.

Fehr, B., & Russell, J. A. (1984). Concept of emotion viewed from a prototype perspective. *Journal of Experimental Psychology: General, 113*, 464–486.

Fehr, B., & Russell, J. A. (1991). The concept of love viewed from a prototype perspective. *Journal of Personality and Social Psychology, 60*, 425–438.

Fehr, B., Russell, J. A., & Ward, L. M. (1982). Prototypicality of emotions: A reaction time stydy. *Bulletin of the Psychonomic Society, 20*, 253–254.

Fitness, J., & Fletcher, G. J. O. (1993). Love, hate, anger, and jealousy in close relationships: A prototype and cognitive appraisal analysis. *Journal of Personality and Social Psychology, 65*, 942–958.

Frei, J. R., & Shaver, P. R. (2002). Respect in close relationships: Prototype definition, self-report assessment, and initial correlations. *Personal Relationships, 9*, 121–139.

Goldman, J. A., Cooper, P. E., Ahern, K., & Corsini, D. (1981). Continuities and discontinuities in the friendship descriptions of women at six stages in the life cycle. *Genetic Psychology Monographs, 103*, 153–167.

Gottman, J. M. (1979). *Marital interaction: Experimental investigations*. New York: Academic Press.

Hassebrauck, M. (1997). Cognitions of relationship quality: A prototype analysis of their structure and consequences. *Personal Relationships, 4*, 163–185.

Hassebrauck, M., & Aron A. (2001). Prototype matching in close relationships. *Personality and Social Psychology Bulletin, 27*, 1111–1122.

Hassebrauck, M., & Fehr, B. (2002). Dimensions of relationship quality. *Personal Relationships*.

Helgeson, V. S., Shaver, P., & Dyer, M. (1987). Prototypes of intimacy and distance in same-sex and opposite-sex relationships. *Journal of Social and Personal Relationships, 4*, 195–233.

Horowitz, M. J. (1989). Relationship schema formulation: Role-relationship models and intrapsychic conflict. *Psychiatry, 52*, 260–274.

Hyde, J. S. (1999, August). *Men are from earth, women are from earth: The media versus science on gender differences*. Paper presented at the Meeting of the American Psychological Association, Boston, MA.

Johnson, F. L., & Aries, E. J. (1983). The talk of women friends. *Women's Studies International Forum, 6*, 353–361.

Kelley, H. H. (1983). Love and commitment. In H. H. Kelley, E. Berscheid, A. Christensen, J. H. Harvey, T. L. Huston, G. Levinger, E. McClintock, L. A. Peplau, & D. R. Peterson (Eds.), *Close relationships* (pp. 265–314). New York: Freeman.

Kelley, H. H., & Thibaut, J. W. (1978). *Interpersonal relations: A theory of interdependence.* New York: Wiley.

La Gaipa, J. J. (1979). A developmental study of the meaning of friendship in adolescence. *Journal of Adolescence, 2,* 201–213.

Lamm, H., & Wiesmann, U. (1997). Subjective attributes of attraction: How people characterize their liking, their love, and their being in love. *Personal Relationships, 4,* 271–284.

Mervis, C. B., & Rosch, E. (1981). Categorization of natural objects. *Annual Review of Psychology, 32,* 89–115.

McClintock, E. (1983). Interaction. In H. H. Kelley, E. Berscheid, A. Christensen, J. H. Harvey, T. L. Huston, G. Levinger, E. McClintock, L. A. Peplau, & D. R. Peterson (Eds.), *Close relationships* (pp. 68–109). New York: Freeman.

Monsour, M. (1992). Meanings of intimacy in cross- and same-sex friendships. *Journal of Social and Personal Relationships, 9,* 277–295.

Oliker, S. J. (1989). *Best friends and marriage: Exchange among women.* Berkeley, CA: University of California Press.

Parks, M. R., & Floyd, K. (1996). Meanings for closeness and intimacy in friendship. *Journal of Social and Personal Relationships, 13,* 85–107.

Perlman, D., & Fehr, B. (1987). The development of intimate relationships. In D. Perlman & S. Duck (Eds.), *Intimate relationships: Development, dynamics and deterioration* (pp. 13–42). Beverly Hills, CA: Sage.

Peterson, D. R. (1979). Assessing interpersonal relationships by means of interaction records. *Behavioral Assessment, 1,* 221–236.

Prager, K. J. (1995). *The psychology of intimacy.* New York: Guilford.

Prager, K. J. (2000). Intimacy in personal relationships. In S. Hendrick & C. Hendrick (Eds.), *Close relationships: A sourcebook* (pp. 229–242). Thousand Oaks, CA: Sage.

Regan, P. C., Kocan, E. R., & Whitlock, T. (1998). Ain't love grand! A prototype analysis of the concept of romantic love. *Journal of Social and Personal Relationships, 15,* 411–420.

Register, L. M., & Henley, T. B. (1992). The phenomenology of intimacy. *Journal of Social and Personal Relationships, 9,* 467–481.

Reis, H. T. (1988). Gender effects in social participation: Intimacy, loneliness, and the conduct of social interaction. In R. Gilmour & S. Duck (Eds.), *The emerging field of personal relationships* (pp. 91–105). Hillsdale, NJ: Lawrence Erlbaum Associates.

Reis, H. T. (1990). The role of intimacy in interpersonal relations. *Journal of Social and Clinical Psychology, 9,* 15–30.

Reis, H. T. (1998). Gender differences in intimacy and related behaviors: Context and process. In D. L. Canary & K. Dindia (Eds.), *Sex differences and similarities in communication* (pp. 203–231). Mahwah, NJ: Lawrence Erlbaum Associates.

Reis, H. T., & Patrick, B. C. (1996). Attachment and intimacy: Component processes. In E. T. Higgins & A. W. Kruglanski (Eds.), *Social psychology: Handbook of basic principles* (pp. 523–563). New York: Guilford.

Reis, H. T., Senchak, M., & Solomon, B. (1985). Sex differences in the intimacy of social interaction: Further examination of potential explanations. *Journal of Personality and Social Psychology, 48,* 1204–1217.

Reis, H. T., & Shaver, P. (1988). Intimacy as an interpersonal process. In S. W. Duck (Ed.), *Handbook of personal relationships* (pp. 367–389). Chichester, England: Wiley.

Rosch, E. H. (1973). Natural categories. *Cognitive Psychology, 4,* 328–350.

Rusbult, C. E., Arriaga, X. B., & Agnew, C. R. (2001). Interdependence in close relationships. In G. J. O. Fletcher & M. S. Clark (Eds.), *Interpersonal Processes* (pp. 359–387). Oxford, England: Blackwell.

Russell, J. A., & Fehr, B. (1994). The varieties of anger: Fuzzy concepts in a fuzzy hierarchy. *Journal of Personality and Social Psychology, 67,* 186–205.

Sapadin, L. A. (1988). Friendship and gender: Perspectives of professional men and women. *Journal of Social and Personal Relationships, 5,* 387–403.

Sharabany R., Gershon, R., & Hofman, J. E. (1981). Girlfriend, boyfriend: Age and sex differences in intimate friendship. *Developmental Psychology, 17,* 800–808.

Sharpsteen, D. J. (1993). Romantic jealousy as an emotion concept: A prototype analysis. *Journal of Social and Personal Relationships, 10,* 69–82.

Shaver, P., Schwartz, J., Kirson, D., & O'Connor, C. (1987). Emotion knowledge: Further explorations of a prototype approach. *Journal of Personality and Social Psychology, 52,* 1061–1086.

Shaver, P. R., Murdaya, U., & Fraley, R. C. (2001). Structure of the Indonesian emotion lexicon. *Asian Journal of Psychology, 4,* 201–224.

Sullivan, H. S. (1953). *The interpersonal theory of psychiatry.* New York: Norton.

Swain, S. (1989). Covert intimacy: Closeness in men's friendships. In B. J. Risman & P. Schwartz (Eds.), *Gender in intimate relationships* (pp. 71–86). Belmont, CA: Wadsworth.

Swain, S. O. (1992). Men's friendships with women: Intimacy, sexual boundaries, and the informant role. In P. M. Nardi (Ed.), *Men's friendships* (pp. 153–171). Newbury Park, CA: Sage.

Vangelisti, A. L., & Daly, J. A. (1997). Gender difference in standards for romantic relationships. *Personal Relationships, 4,* 203–219.

Waring, E. M., Tillman, M. P., Frelick, M. D., Russell, L., & Weisz, G. (1980). Concepts of intimacy in the general population. *Journal of Nervous and Mental Disease, 168,* 471–474.

Wellman, B. (1992). Men in networks: Private communities, domestic friendships. In P. Nardi (Ed.), *Men's friendships* (pp. 74–114). Newbury Park, CA: Sage.

Wood, J. T., & Inman, C. C. (1993). In a different mode: Masculine styles of communicating closeness. *Journal of Applied Communication Research, 21,* 279–295.

Wood, J. T. (1997). Clarifying the issues. *Personal Relationships, 4,* 221–228.

Wright, P. H. (1982). Men's friendships, women's friendships, and the alleged inferiority of the latter. *Sex Roles, 8,* 1–20.

Wright, P. H. (1988). Interpreting research on gender differences in friendship: A case for moderation and a plea for caution. *Journal of Social and Personal Relationships, 5,* 367–373.

3

Closeness as Including Other in the Self

Arthur P. Aron
State University of New York at Stony Brook

Debra J. Mashek
George Mason University

Elaine N. Aron
State University of New York at Stony Brook

This chapter summarizes our conceptual framework and supporting research regarding the view that in a close relationship the other is, to some extent, part of the self—that closeness *is* including other in the self. Specifically, we consider five questions: (a) What is meant by including another person in the self? (b) What is the evidence that people do include close others in the self? (c) How is including another person in the self different from being familiar with or similar to the other person? (d) Why is it appropriate to consider including another person in the self to *be* closeness? And (e) what are some implications of this view?

WHAT IS MEANT BY INCLUDING ANOTHER PERSON IN THE SELF?

Our self-expansion model (Aron & Aron, 1986; Aron, Aron, & Norman, 2001) postulates that in a close relationship each person includes in the self, to some extent, the other's resources, perspectives, and identities.

The "resources" of the other that we argue are potentially included in the self include material goods, knowledge (conceptual, informational, procedural), and social assets that can facilitate the achievement of goals. Perceiving oneself as including a relationship partner's resources in the self refers to perceiving oneself as having access to those resources. It is as if, to some extent, the other's resources are one's own. In some cases, the other's resources are quite literally also one's own, as when one shares a house or bank account with the other. In other cases, one reasonably expects the other to make his or her resources available to self, such as with most knowledge resources (e.g., "I can do this because my partner will show me how."). In still other cases, one may feel as if what the other has is one's own even when it is not in actuality. This might occur, for example, when one feels that some particular possession of the partner is also one's own even when the partner might not see it that way. From the point of view of the self, these various cases are largely equivalent. (These may of course have quite different implications for future interactions, as for example when a grown child leaves home and wants to take his or her "own" possessions. But such issues are beyond the scope of the present chapter.)

The resource aspect of inclusion of other in the self is particularly central from a motivational point of view. This is because perceiving another's resources as ones own means that the outcomes (rewards and costs) the other incurs are to some extent also experienced as one's own. Thus, for example, helping other is helping self; interfering with other is interfering with self. This analysis also implies that the evaluative and affective responses to a close other's acquisition and loss of resources are to some extent the same as if the acquisition or loss was with regard to one's own resources.

The perspective aspect of inclusion refers to experiencing (consciously or unconsciously) the world to some extent from the other's point of view. Thus, for example, when another person is included in the self, various self-related attributional and cognitive biases should also apply to our attributions and cognitions with regard to that other person. The identity aspect, as we are using the term, refers to the features that distinguish the person from other people and objects, primarily the characteristics, memories, and other features that locate the person in social and physical space. Thus, for example, our model implies that people may easily confuse their own traits or memories with those of a close other.

In relation to these two general cognitive aspects of inclusion (that is, with regard to both perspectives and identities), we have described our model as implying shared cognitive elements of self and close others (e.g., Aron & Fraley, 1999). We should also note that our usage of the triad of resources, perspectives, and identities allows considerable room for overlap. However, our distinguishing among them has proven valuable heuristically for emphasizing different aspects of what we propose is included of a close other in the self, as we hope will be even clearer from the discussion to follow.

The inclusion of another's perspectives and identities in the self follows from the inclusion of that other's resources. A particular perspective or identity (as distinguished from other possible perspectives and identities) refers to the position (in time and space and in the social context) from which particular rewards and punishments are experienced; a person who has a particular perspective is the person who is affected by a specific set of outcomes. Thus, the way we distinguish a specific perspective or identity as belonging to a particular person is according to the person whose outcomes the perspective or identity is with reference to. If I am concerned about your outcomes, I am evaluating the world as would you, I am holding your perspectives. Similarly, if the material, knowledge, and social impact of events that happen to you are happening to me, then your place in the material and social world is my place in the material and social world, I am holding your identities.

Thus, from a motivational point of view, the main benefit of including other in the self would be the resources aspect; the perspectives and identities aspects may follow as a generally unconscious side effect, a restructuring of the cognitive system. Thus, we speculate that the process may operate as follows:

1. People are motivated (generally not consciously) to include another in the self in order to include that other's resources. (This motivation aspect is a central part of the larger self-expansion model in which the inclusion-of-other-in-the-self idea is embedded. For elaborations of the larger model, see Aron & Aron, 1986; Aron et al., 2001. For a specific focus on motivational issues, see Aron, Norman, & Aron, 1998).

2. As the relationship is forming, the partners make one another's resources readily available to the other.

3. This leads to the cognitive reorganization that makes the other's resources seem included in the self.

4. This leads to taking on to some extent the other's perspectives and identities.

5. This leads to a reciprocal ongoing process strengthening the conscious and unconscious experience of including other's resources in the self, which in turn leads back to Step 2. (As a caveat, different steps are likely involved when the self experiences relationship dissolution and relationship dissatisfaction more generally. We present here only the "typical" mechanism as a means of highlighting one possible process.).

In addition to the five-step process described above, there is another possible way that people may come to take on the perspectives and identities of the other as one's own. It may be that taking on the other's perspectives and identities as one's own may be direct goals in themselves (that is, not merely results of first including their resources). It does seem that there is a motivation (again, not usually conscious) to include more than the other's possessions, information, social networks, and other resources. It may be as if we also desire to *be* the other, not to lose one's self, but to add "substance" to it, to make it richer and more complex.

WHAT IS THE EVIDENCE THAT PEOPLE DO INCLUDE CLOSE OTHERS IN THE SELF?

Including Close Others' Resources in the Self

As we have noted, a central implication of including another's resources in the self is that one treats the other's outcomes as if they were one's own. That is, to the extent another person is part of myself, my responses to the others rewards and costs, opportunities and obstacles, successes and failures, should be as if they were my own rewards and so forth. Aron, Aron, Tudor, and Nelson (1991, Study 1 and follow-ups) examined this implication of this model in three studies in which participants made a series of allocation decisions involving themselves and another person. As predicted, in each study, participants distributed money about equally to themselves and the other when the other was their best friend, but they distributed more to themselves than the other when the other was a mere acquaintance. Importantly, these results held up even when participants believed that the other could not know about their allocations (thus ruling out interpretations involving expected effects of how the other would feel about their allocations.) Medvene, Teal, and Slavich (2000) adopted quite a different approach to this issue. In their study of couples in romantic relationships they found a standard equity effect. That is, there was greatest satisfaction for those who are neither under nor over benefitted. However, this pattern was significantly weaker for those who perceived their relationship as having high levels of interconnectednesss. Medvene et al. predicted this pattern based on the idea that if the partner is part of the self, the partner's benefits are one's own, and if partners do not distinguish between own and other's outcomes the meaning of over- or under-benefited in relation to the partner is undermined. (We will consider potential alternative explanations for this and related studies at the end of this section. However, in the context of this particular study it is notable that a measure of communal orientation—that is, tendency to attend to the other's needs—did not show a similar effect; Medvene, personal communication, June 12, 2003.)

Another relevant line of research has focused on social comparison processes. That is, several studies have found that social comparison processes are dramatically altered to be more like self-comparisons when the other is either already close to self or closeness is created by a priming manipulation (Beach et al., 1998; MacKay, McFarland, & Buehler, 1998; McFarland, Buehler, & MacKay, 2001; O'Mahen, Beach, & Tesser, 2000). For example, Beach et al. (1998) showed that participants' affective reaction to their task partner successfully outperforming (or failing to outperform) the self was less negative (or less positive) if the performance was in a domain believed to be important to the partner. Similarly, MacKay et al. (1998) showed that false feedback about a task partner's performance affected one's own mood only when the task partner was also a close relationship partner. Employing an experimental paradigm, Gardner, Gabriel, and Hochschild (2002) showed that priming inclusion of other in the self completely undermined the negative effect of partner outperforming the self and the degree of celebration in the close partner's success was correlated with the degree of including other in the self.

It is important to acknowledge that other models have been proposed to explain why people sometimes treat a close other's outcomes like their own For example, interdependence theory (Kelley & Thibaut, 1978; Rusbult, Kumsahiro, Coolsen, & Kirchner, chap. 4, this volume) emphasizes that individuals transform gut-level self-interest into joint- or other-interest as they evaluate long-term benefits to self. We think this is a likely mechanism that operates in close relationships. But we also think that there are important cases of acting for the benefit of close others that cannot be fully explained in this way, but that can be explained by including other in the self. Thus, for example, we believe that an interdependence analysis would have predicted a bigger difference between "other will know" and "other will not know" of ones allocation decisions in the Aron et al. (1991) allocation decision studies reviewed above.

Another theoretical model that seems to explain cases of acting for the benefit of close others is Clark and Mills' (1993) communal norm theory. In this model, people spontaneously attend to the needs of close others because it is normatively appropriate to do so. Again, we think that it is quite likely this mechanism operates in close relationships. But, also as before, we think that there are important cases of treating close others' outcomes like one's own that can not be fully explained in this way, but that can be explained by including close others in the self. Thus, for example, the communal norm view would seem to suggest that what determines degree of caring for others' outcomes is primarily the relationship category. However, several of the studies noted above found that even within relationship categories, the impact on the other's outcomes were moderated by degree of including other in the self.

Thus, we tentatively conclude that while multiple mechanisms may drive treating a close other's outcomes as one's own, there are various lines of data that seem specifically consistent with a mechanism of including close other's resources in the self.

Including Close Others' Perspectives in the Self

As noted, we propose that to some extent individuals take on a close other's perspective of appreciating the world. For example, when a long-term married individual attends a ballet, the individual may experience the ballet not only through the individual's own eyes, but also, as it were, through the spouse's eyes. This process also seems to apply to concern about the social impressions the other makes. That is, anecdotally, it seems that in social situations, people often seem to feel embarrassed or esteemed as a result of a close other's behaviors, as if those behaviors were one's own. In this light, Schlenker and Britt (2001) demonstrated that people will systematically manage information they convey about close friends to make a better impression on others. Similarly, Konrath and Ross (2003) examined whether people would extend to close others the usual effect found for self in which past successes are recalled as more recent and past failures as more distant than they actually were. Consistent with the notion of including a close other's perspectives in the self, Konrath and Ross found the same effect as is usually found for self when participants recalled past events for romantic partners, but only when those partners were close and not when they were distant. In addition, the social comparison studies we reviewed briefly in the previous section also can be interpreted as due to shared perspectives.

However, as we also noted earlier, the key implications of the perspectives aspect of the model is with regard to extending to close others self-related attributional and cognitive biases. With regard to attributional biases, several studies have found that the usual actor–observer difference in the tendency to make situational versus dispositional attributions (Jones & Nisbett, 1971) is smaller when the other is someone close to self, such as a best friend or romantic partner (Aron et al., 1991, introduction to Study 2; Aron & Fraley, 1999; Sande, Goethals, & Radloff, 1988). The idea here is that the self is experiencing the other's perspective as the self's own ("I know why he did it—like me, he did what was appropriate for the situation.").

To further study what it means to hold the perspective of the other, we extended a paradigm developed by Lord (1980, 1987) that focuses on another kind of self-relevant bias, in this case a cognitive bias in recall of imaged information. In the Lord paradigm, participants are presented with a series of nouns, for each of which they are to form a vivid, elaborated image of a particular person interacting with the object the noun represents. Later, participants are given a free recall test for the nouns. As predicted from his model of self as background to experience, Lord found consistently fewer nouns recalled that were imaged with self as compared to nouns imaged with others, such as media personalities. In our studies (Aron et al., 1991, Studies 2 and follow-up), in addition to self and a nonclose other, participants also imaged nouns with a close other, their mother. Our results replicated Lord's for self and nonclose other. But also, as predicted, we found that nouns imaged with the close other (i.e., the participant's mother) were recalled about the same as for those imaged with self. This result was found both when the nonclose other was an entertainment personality and in a replication in which the nonclose other was mother's best friend. Thus, just as our perspective as self is as a background to experience, our perspective with regard to close others—but not with regard to nonclose others—also seems to serve as a background to experience.

Including Close Others' Identities in the Self

A consistent finding in a long-standing line of work on what has come to be known as the *self-reference effect* is an advantage in terms of memory and response time for self-relevant versus other-relevant processing. For example, in a meta-analysis of 126 articles and book chapters on just the memory aspect of the self-reference effect, Symons and Johnson (1997) reported a consistent overall better memory for words studied in relation to self than for words studied in relation to other persons. However, they also found that the degree to which self-referent and other-referent processing differs seems to depend on the relationship to the other. Across the 65 relevant studies, Symons and Johnson found significantly smaller differences in the memory effect between self-reference and other-reference when the other was someone who was close to the self. Thus, being in a close relationship does indeed seem to subvert the seemingly fundamental distinction of self from other.

Our model posits that this apparent subversion by close relationships of the self-other distinction is due to specifically the other becoming part of the self—to the very structure of the self changing such that the self includes the other in its very make up. That is, we hypothesize that the knowledge structures of close others actually share elements (or activation potentials) with the knowledge structures of the self (Aron et al., 1991; Aron & Fraley, 1999; Smith, Coates, & Walling, 1999). For example, one's own and a close-other's traits may actually be confused or interfere with each other.

To test this idea, we evaluated the patterns of response latencies in making me–not me decisions (i.e., does the trait describe me?) about traits previously rated for their descriptiveness of self and of spouse (Aron et al., 1991, Study 3 and follow-up). We found that for traits on which the self matched the partner (the trait was true of both or false of both), me–not me responses were faster than when a trait was mismatched for self and partner (was true for one but false for the other). Further, in another study (Aron & Fraley, 1999), we found that this match–mismatch response-time index (serving as a measure of overlap of self and other) goes beyond simply distinguishing between a close and nonclose relationship partner. The magnitude of the effect correlates substantially with self-report measures of relationship quality, including predicting increases in self-reported closeness over a three month period. Using this same match–mismatch response-time paradigm, Smith et al. (1999) replicated both the overall difference between close and nonclose others and the correlation with the magnitude of self-reported closeness to the close other. Smith and colleagues eloquently articulated why such patterns may result: "If mental representations of two persons . . . overlap so that they are effectively a single representation, reports on attributes of one will be facilitated or inhibited by matches and mismatches with the second " (p. 873).

In another series of studies (Mashek, Aron, & Boncimino, 2003), participants rated one set of traits for self, a different set of traits for a close other, and still other traits for one or more nonclose others, such as media personalities. Participants were then given a surprise recognition task in which they were presented each trait and asked to indicate for which person they had rated it. The analysis focused on confusions; that is, it focused on traits on which the participant remembered having rated the trait for one person when the participant had actually rated the trait for a different person. Results were consistent with predictions. For example, if participants did not correctly recognize a trait as having been originally rated for the self, they were more likely to remember it as having been rated for the partner than as having been rated for the media personality. Similarly, if participants did not correctly recognize a trait as having been originally rated for the partner, they were more likely to remember it as having been rated for the self than as having been rated for the media personality. These results were replicated in two follow-up studies and held up after controlling for a variety of potential confounds, such as for any tendency to recall traits in general as having been rated for self or partner and for valence and extremity of ratings. (We will consider shortly the possible role of familiarity with and similarity to the target.)

Finally, we have done some work on people's perceptions that their selves overlap with those of close others. In these studies, we asked participants to describe their closest relationship using the Inclusion of Other in the Self (IOS) Scale (Aron, Aron, & Smollan, 1992). The IOS Scale consists of seven pairs of circles overlapping to different degrees from which the respondent selects the pair (the degree of overlap) that best describes his or her relationship with a particular person. The scale appears to have levels of reliability, as well as of discriminant, convergent, and predictive validity, that match or exceed other measures of closeness—measures which are typically more complex and lengthy. For example, Agnew, Van Lange, Rusbult, and Langston (1998) found that the IOS scale completed for a particular relationship correlated strongly with the number of plural pronouns (we, us, our) in the participant's free description of the relationship. It also correlates with scores on various other indirect measures of including other in the self, such as the match–mismatch response-time paradigm (e.g., Aron & Fraley, 1999). Since its development, the scale has been used effectively in a number of studies of relationships (for a review, see Agnew, Loving, Le, & Goodfriend, chap. 7, this volume). It seems plausible that this measure has been so successful because the metaphor of overlapping circles representing self and other corresponds to how people actually process information about self and others in relationships.

HOW IS INCLUDING OTHER IN THE SELF DIFFERENT FROM FAMILIARITY AND SIMILARITY?

A possible interpretation of these various results showing smaller (or absent) self-other differences for close others is that close others are more familiar or more similar to the self. We would be surprised if familiarity and similarity did not play an important role in this process. After all, one way in which people probably recognize anything as part of themselves is by its familiarity and by its similarity to other aspects of themselves. Further, familiarity and similarity are inevitably confounded with closeness. We are likely to be most familiar with those to whom we are close because we spend more time with them and do a wider variety of activities with them, seeing them in more situations (Berscheid, Synder, & Omoto, 1989). We are more likely to be similar with those to whom we are close because we are likely to select them as relationship partners (e.g., Byrne, 1971) and because close relationship partners become more similar over time (e.g., Zajonc, Adelmann, Murphy, & Niedenthal, 1987).

However, in this section we suggest that inclusion of other in the self is conceptually and empirically distinguishable from both familiarity and similarity.

Familiarity

Is it possible that what we are calling including other in the self is the same thing as being more familiar with the other? Conceptually, inclusion of other in the self and familiarity seem quite different. The former has to do with aspects of the other person treated as if they were one's own, the latter has to do with how much exposure to and attention one has given to those aspects or that person. For example, in terms of the resources aspect, perceiving the other's resources as one's own is quite distinct from being familiar with those resources. Consider the extent to which I treat some knowledge of my partner's as also my own. This depends on the degree of connection to my partner, not the amount of exposure or attention to either the knowledge or my partner. Similarly, in terms of the cognitive aspects, taking my partner's perspectives and identities is quite distinct from being familiar with those perspectives and identities. I can be very familiar with a person with whom I have little or no relationship, such as media personalities, enemies, some neighbors, or those in different positions in a hierarchy (e.g., supervisors or supervisees with whom we interact regularly). Familiarity with such a person may make it easier to see things from that person's perspective if I choose to do so, and familiarity may even make it easier to imagine what it is like to have that other person's role identities. But this is not the same thing as, for example, even when not with the person, spontaneously acting and experiencing the world as if I were this person. Contrast this situation with the case in which one feels very close to someone who is minimally familiar, such as a new baby son or daughter, someone with whom one has just fallen in love, or someone with whom one has shared a significant experience. In this case of the "close but not very familiar person," even when not with the person, one might well spontaneously experience the world from what he or she presumes is this person's perspective and as if he or she had this person's identities—at least one would be more likely to do so than for the "highly familiar but not close" other. In terms of our tentative model of including other in the self as shared cognitive elements in the representation of self and others, this is again quite different from the cognitive representations of self and other being highly familiar.

Still, even if familiarity and including other in the self are conceptually distinguishable, it remains possible that what is driving the various empirical findings we have reported for including close others in the self is the generally greater familiarity of close others. Indeed, such an interpretation seems plausible because presumably familiar others share with the self a high level of elaboration and organization (Klein & Kihlstrom, 1986). However, several findings suggest that familiarity does not account for the various findings we have reported regarding including close other in the self. Rather, these results seem to be driven by something different from familiarity that corresponds to what people generally call closeness. First, as part of their meta-analysis, Symons and Johnson (1997) coded all 65 of the relevant self-reference memory studies for degree of familiarity and degree of intimacy of the comparison other-referent. The mean difference between effect sizes in studies where the other referent was familiar versus studies where the other referent was not familiar, was not significant, and near zero; the mean difference between studies in which the other referent was intimate versus studies in which the other-referent was not intimate was significant and substantial. Second, in two of the source-memory confusion studies (Mashek et al., 2003, Studies 2 and 3), we attempted to pit the familiarity versus closeness explanations against each other. We did this by using a sample of those who were closer to their closest friend than to their closest parent, but more familiar with the closest parent by virtue of having known the parent substantially longer and in substantially more contexts. Both studies found significantly more confusions between self and one's closest friend than between self and one's closest parent. Finally, several studies have found that the match–mismatch response-time effect for partners to have consistent large correlations with subjectively reported closeness (Aron et al., 1991; Aron & Fraley, 1999; Smith et al., 1999), but to have near-zero correlations with reported familiarity and with variables that would seem to be relatively objective indicators of familiarity, such as number of different activities shared with other, amount of time spent with other, and relationship length (Aron et al., 1991; Aron & Fraley, 1999).

Similarity

If it is not familiarity, could it be that what we are calling *including other in the self* is actually just a stand in for perceived similarity? For example, the notion of confusing self and other may simply be a matter of confusing cognitive representations that share similar features. On the other hand, it is possible to differentiate inclusion of other from similarity conceptually. Consider that including another person in the self also means including the aspects of the other that are different from myself. For example, I may include a partner's shoes and eyeglasses in myself (being affected for example when the shoes are scuffed or the glasses lost), but I do not necessarily think that my own shoes are similar and I may not even wear eyeglasses. In the same way, one's own traits, and the traits of a close other, though very different, can still both be part of the self.

Put a little more precisely, including other in the self refers to the elements of other being available to and part of the structure and content of self; similarity refers to the elements of other sharing descriptive features with those of the self. Thus, with regard to including another's resources in the self, perceiving that the other's resources are my own is quite different from seeing them as similar to my own. Indeed, in the context of the motivational implications of our model, one would presumably prefer a potential partner whose resources are different from ones own because having access to such resources would maximally expand the self beyond that to which one already has access. In a like fashion, taking the perspective or identity of the other is quite different from elements of the other's perspective or identity sharing descriptive features with one's own. For example, as we have seen, taking the other's perspective implies a cognitive bias to making situational attributions for events happening to the other person. Realizing that the other person is similar to me and has similar experiences or circumstances could also make me appreciate the world from the other's point of view, but this would be a more indirect inference rather than a spontaneous mode of appreciating the world. In terms of identity, including other in the self leads to confusions of elements of self and other; similarity of elements of self and other may well lead to the opposite effect in that it is more important to distinguish such traits to avoid confusions. Indeed, the self-esteem maintenance literature generally shows greater distinctiveness between self and other in making social comparisons when the other is more similar to self (e.g., Tesser, 1988.)

Empirically, in the study where we used the cognitive bias measure (which is based on the Lord paradigm) of including other in the self, we also asked participants to rate similarity to the close other; correlations of the effect with rated similarity were small and not significant (Aron et al., 1991). Also, recall in two of the Mashek et al. (2003) source-confusion memory experiments we assessed confusions between self and two other people: one person who was close and similar and one person who was less close and similar. There were greater confusions of self with best friend (the closer other) than with closest parent (the less close other). The best friend and closest parent were about equally similar on the basis of separate trait ratings. Further, in one experiment, participants explicitly indicated whether they were more similar to their best friend or their father (the targets in that study). Rated similarity was essentially unrelated to confusions with self when closeness was controlled, and for those who were closer to their best friend, the greater confusions of self with friend versus of self with father held up strongly after controlling for who was rated as more similar.

WHY IS IT APPROPRIATE TO CONSIDER INCLUDING ANOTHER PERSON IN THE SELF TO BE CLOSENESS?

We believe it is appropriate to consider including other in the self to be closeness because it corresponds to how closeness has been understood in the relationship literature, in terms of both (a) what distinguishes a close relationship from other relationships and (b) what makes one relationship closer than another.

Inclusion of Other in the Self as Distinguishing a Close Relationship From Other Relationships

The notion that including other in the self is central to what makes a relationship a close relationship is consistent with a wide variety of social psychological ideas about relationships. Perhaps the most prominent social psychological notion directly related to the present theme is the *unit relation*, a fundamental concept in Heider's (1958) cognitive account of interpersonal relations. This idea is also related to the concept of *intersubjectivity*, emphasized by Ickes, Hutchison, and Mashek (chap. 20, this volume)—a concept they make vivid by citing Merleau-Ponty's (1945) description of a close relationship as a "double being" and Schutz's (1970) reference to two people "living in each other's subjective contexts of meaning" (p. 167).

Another sense in which people seem to distinguish relationships as close is the sense in which relationship partners feel they "possess" each other (e.g., Reik, 1944). In this light, it is notable that in the field of marketing, Belk (1988) proposed a notion of ownership in which "we regard our possessions as part of ourselves" (p. 139), an idea that has been the subject of considerable theoretical discussion and several studies. For example, Sivadas and Machleit (1994) found that items measuring an object's "incorporation into self" (items such as "helps me achieve my identity" and "is part of who I am") form a separate factor from items assessing the object's importance or relevance to the self.

In the relationship domain, Agnew et al. (1998) have explicitly linked the inclusion-of-other-in-the-self model with interdependence, describing it as "cognitive interdependence—a mental state characterized by a pluralistic, collective representation of self-in-relationship" (p. 939). Cialdini, Brown, Lewis, Luce, and Neuberg (1997) have linked the model to evolutionary theories of relationships, suggesting that interpersonal closeness as experienced as including other in the self may be how we recognize those with whom we share genes (a kind of literal, physical self-other inclusion) in the interest of knowing with whom one should share resources to enhance collective fitness. Finally, although there has been no explicit work on the possible link, we think that there may be a direct connection between self–other inclusion and communal relationships (e.g., Clark & Mills, 1979, 1993). That is, we see including other in the self as the foundation for spontaneously being concerned with the others' needs ("because others' needs are my needs") and thus both directly facilitating communal motivation (attention to and acting on others' needs) and having possibly functioned historically to help create a social norm of communal orientation in close relationships.

The notion of a close relationship as an overlap of selves has been popular more generally among psychologists and sociologists. For example, Bakan (1966) wrote about "communion" in the context of his expansion on Buber's (1937) "I–Thou" relationship. Jung (1925/1959) emphasized the role of relationship partners as providing or developing otherwise unavailable aspects of the psyche, so leading to greater wholeness. Maslow (1967) took it for granted that "beloved people can be incorporated into the self" (p. 103). And from a symbolic interactionist perspective, McCall (1974) described "attachment" as "incorporation of . . . [the other's] actions and reactions . . . into the content of one's various conceptions of the self" (p. 219).

Including Other in the Self as What Makes One Relationship Closer Than Another

The idea of including other in the self is certainly linked to notions of closeness and intimacy, so often used as descriptors of the degree of closeness found in a specific relationship. For example, Reis and Shaver (1988; see also Laurenceau, Rivera, Schaffer, & Pietromonaco, chap. 5, this volume) identified intimacy as mainly a process of an escalating reciprocity of self-disclosure in which each individual feels his or her innermost self validated, understood, and cared for by the other. That is, intimacy increases as each learns about and so presumably is able to include the other's perspective. The very word closeness as applied to interpersonal relationships suggests a metaphor for physical proximity. As we noted earlier, there is also an associated metaphor of union or overlap of self and other as a kind of end point of lack of distance. Our definition of degree of closeness as degree of including other in the self is a direct application of this metaphor to cognition—that greater closeness means that the cognitive representations of self and other are "nearer to" (more likely to mutually activate one another) or overlap more with (share more elements with) one another. Yet another sense of interconnection or even union is mutual influence and shared behavior. In this regard, Aron et al. (1992) and Aron and Fraley (1999) found significant moderate correlations between the overlapping circles IOS Scale and Berscheid et al.'s (1989) measure of perceived strength of influence of the partner on the self (median r across three samples = .32).

Further, in several studies (Aron et al., 1992; Aron & Fraley, 1999; Aron, Melinat, Aron, Vallone, & Bator, 1997) there are strong correlations between direct questions about how close the participant feels to his or her partner (subjective closeness index;

Berscheid et al., 1989) and the IOS scale (median r across six samples = .59). In a content analysis of an open-ended item about what the IOS Scale means, administered directly after participants rated their closest other on the Scale, 86% used some term that was reliably coded ($\kappa = .94$) by blind judges as *connectedness*. The IOS Scale, in turn, as a metaphor for closeness, was moderately to strongly correlated across a variety of samples with the more direct cognitive measures of including other in the self, such as the Sande et al. (1988) attribution task (Aron & Fraley, 1999), the match-mismatch response-time measure (Aron et al., 1991; Aron & Fraley, 1999; Smith et al., 1999), and the self–other confusion paradigm task (Mashek et al., 2002).

WHAT ARE SOME IMPLICATIONS OF TREATING CLOSENESS AS INCLUDING OTHER IN THE SELF?

Some Implications for Understanding Relationships

First, let us consider some implications of this model of closeness as including other in the self for the role of closeness in some major relationship theories. In an inter-dependence analysis (Rusbult et al., chap. 4, this volume) focusing on the perceived benefits and costs of relationship interactions, including other in the self means that one's outcomes in a relationship are to some extent directly a function of the other's outcomes, even over and above transformation of motivation which is due to consid-ering factors such as long-term benefits of caring about the partner's outcomes. More generally, as noted earlier, Agnew et al. (1998) describe inclusion of other in the self as a kind of "cognitive interdependence" (p. 939). If one applies an attachment perspective (e.g., Collins & Feeney, chap. 10, this volume), our model implies that, for example, part of what avoidants are avoiding (and preoccupieds are seeking) is incorporating into themselves aspects of others and having others incorporate aspects of them (es-sentially the same event from two different perspectives). Thus, one would look not only at the fears and opportunities for emotional states and actual interactions, but the fears and opportunities for changing the structure of the self. A quite different implication for attachment theory is Ruvolo and Fabin's (1999) finding that close rela-tionship partners confuse their own attachment style with that of their partners. That is, when we include a partner in the self, we also include their attachment style. Thus, part of what structures one's attachment style is one's partner's attachment style.

More generally, any question one asks about closeness, even outside of a particular theoretical context, is significantly reshaped by this view of closeness. For example, the issue of too much closeness (Mashek & Sherman, chap. 19, this volume) partly becomes one of the effect of including too much of the other in the self or feeling lost within the other's self; the impact of closeness during a relationship on how one ex-periences the loss of a relationship becomes one of how much of self was based on including the other (e.g., Lewandowski, 2002); or the question of how closeness devel-ops in a relationship over time (e.g., Aron et al., 1997) becomes one of the conditions that facilitates including other in the self.

Most of our own work regarding this model, however, has focused on the role of inclusion of other in the self as part of the larger self-expansion model (Aron & Aron, 1986; Aron et al., 2001). This model posits that people seek to expand their potential self-efficacy and that one way they seek to do so is through close relationships, because closeness in a relationship expands the self by including in the self the resources, perspectives, and identities of the relationship partner. This view has a number of important implications for understanding relationships. For example, Aron, Paris, and Aron (1995), in two prospective longitudinal studies, showed that entering a new relationship (operationalized as falling in love) expands the self in the sense that one's spontaneous self-description increases in diversity and in the sense of an increase in perceived self-efficacy.

Some Implications for Groups

Another major line of our work on the implications of this model has been outside of the relationship domain and in the area of groups. Thus, we have applied our model to the area of ingroup identification (Aron & McLaughlin-Volpe, 2001; Wright, Aron, & Tropp, 2003). The idea here is that identification with the ingroup, conceptualized as a kind of closeness to the ingroup, can be understood as including the ingroup in the self. Following this lead, Smith and his colleagues (Smith, 2002; Smith, et al., 1999; Smith & Henry, 1996), adapting our match–mismatch response-time paradigm, showed that we confuse ingroups but not outgroups with the self. (This result was also recently replicated by Cadinu & De Amicis, 1999.) Tropp and Wright (2001) extended this finding by showing that the degree of ingroup identification as indicated by standard measures correlates with both the degree of effect on the match-mismatch response-time paradigm and with the Including Ingroup in the Self (IIS) Scale. (The IIS is a self-report measure based on the IOS Scale in which the respondent selects among pairs of circles with different degrees of overlap that are labeled as *Self* and the name of the focal ingroup. The IIS has also been used successfully in a cross-cultural study by Uleman, Rhee, Bardoliwalla, Semin, & Toyama, 2000.)

A quite different application to groups of our model of closeness as including the other in the self focuses on the intergroup contact effect (Allport, 1954), which is the idea that contact with a member of an outgroup can lead to reduced prejudice toward that outgroup. Specifically, we have suggested, on the basis of our model, that intergroup contact is most likely to reduce prejudice when it involves a close, intimate friendship with an outgroup member (Aron & McLaughlin-Volpe, 2001; Wright, Aron, McLaughlin-Volpe, & Ropp, 1997). Specifically, we reasoned as follows: Ordinarily, in the self's conception of the world, the ingroup is part of the self and outgroups are not part of the self. Thus, one spontaneously treats ingroup members, to some extent, as the self, including feeling empathy with their troubles, taking pride in their successes, and generously sharing resources with them. Outgroup members, because they are not part of self, receive none of these advantages. However, what happens when one forms a friendship with an outgroup partner? Under these circumstances, we argue, the outgroup member—and hence to some extent the outgroup member's group identity, of which one inevitably becomes aware—becomes part of the self. That is, the representation of the outgroup comes to share elements with the representation of the self. The effect, we argue, is to undermine negative outgroup attitudes. Others have pointed to the specific role of friendship (e.g., Cook, 1984; Pettigrew & Tropp, 2000) but have not focused on the role of closeness or articulated particular mediating psychological mechanisms for why friendship should have a special effect.

Several studies, by ourselves and others, using a variety of nonexperimental and experimental methods, support the proposition that contact with a member of an outgroup is much more effective in reducing prejudice when one has a close versus a less close relationship with that outgroup member (e.g., McLaughlin-Volpe, 1998; Pettigrew, 1997; Wright & Van Der Zande, 1999). Other models, such as generalization of positive affect, dissonance, or balance theories might be applied to understand these effects. But such models do not articulate a mechanism to explain the generalization from the outgroup partner to the outgroup partner's group—an articulation that is explicitly provided by our closeness as inclusion of other in the self model. Further, McLaughlin-Volpe (2002) has recently shown that the closeness effects are directly mediated by including other in the self. In her study, including an outgroup member in the self, as measured by the match-mismatch response-time paradigm, predicted less outgroup stereotyping. Most important, this effect was significantly mediated by including the outgroup in the self, as also measured by the match-mismatch response-time paradigm.

Finally, the closeness as including other in the self model has led to the prediction of a new phenomenon, the extended (or vicarious) contact effect (Wright et al., 1997). The idea here is that a reduction in prejudice can occur as a result of mere knowledge that an ingroup member has a close relationship with an outgroup member. The logic is that when someone who is in the ingroup, and thus part of the self, is known to have an outgroup person as part of that person's self, the effect is that, to some extent, one begins to see members of that group as part of the self. Thus, the ingroup-outgroup distinction, vital to producing negative intergroup attitudes, is directly diminished by the connection of the outgroup member to an ingroup member. Also, negative attitudes towards the outgroup are reduced by this indirect connection of the outgroup with the self. This hypothesis has so far received support in a series of surveys and experiments (Wright et al., 1997) and in a recent field experiment involving Protestants and Catholics in Northern Ireland (Paolini, Hewstone, Cairns, & Voci, 2002). The latter study also demonstrated including other in the self as the mediating mechanism.

CONCLUSION

In this chapter we have articulated what we mean by including other in the self, presented data supporting the notion that close others are included in the self, and argued that this inclusion is not the same as familiarity or similarity. On this basis, we then preceeded to show inclusion of other in the self corresponds well conceptually and empirically to what social psychologists and ordinary people mean by closeness. Finally, we illustrated some significant implications of this view for understanding the role of closeness in a variety of contexts, including relationships and groups.

REFERENCES

Agnew, C. R., Van Lange, P. A. M., Rusbult, C. E., & Langston, C. A. (1998). Cognitive interdependence: Commitment and the mental representation of close relationships. *Journal of Personality and Social Psychology, 74,* 939–954.

Allport, G. (1954). *The nature of prejudice.* Reading, MA: Addison-Wesley.

Aron, A., & Aron, E. N. (1986). *Love as the expansion of self: Understanding attraction and satisfaction.* New York: Hemisphere.

Aron, A., Aron, E. N., & Norman, C. (2001). The self expansion model of motivation and cognition in close relationships and beyond. In M. Clark & G. Fletcher (Eds.), *Blackwell Handbook in Social Psychology, Vol. 2: Interpersonal Processes* (pp. 478–501). Oxford, England: Blackwell.

Aron, A., Aron, E. N., & Smollan, D. (1992). Inclusion of other in the self scale and the structure of interpersonal closeness. *Journal of Personality and Social Psychology, 63,* 596–612.

Aron, A., Aron, E. N., Tudor, M., & Nelson, G. (1991). Close relationships as including other in the self. *Journal of Personality and Social Psychology, 60,* 241–253.

Aron, A., & Fraley, B. (1999). Relationship closeness as including other in the self: Cognitive underpinnings and measures. *Social Cognition, 17,* 140–160.

Aron, A., & McLaughlin-Volpe, T. (2001). Including others in the self: Extensions to own and partner's group memberships. In C. Sedikides & M. B. Brewer (Eds.), *Individual self, relational self, and collective self: Partners, opponents, or strangers?* (pp. 89–109). Philadelphia: Psychology Press.

Aron, A., Melinat, E., Aron, E. N., Vallone, R., & Bator, R. (1997). The experimental generation of interpersonal closeness: A procedure and some preliminary findings. *Personality and Social Psychology Bulletin, 23,* 363–377.

Aron, A., Norman, C. C., & Aron, E. N. (1998). The self-expansion model and motivation. *Representative Research in Social Psychology, 22,* 1–13.

Aron, A., Paris, M., & Aron, E. N. (1995). Falling in love: Prospective studies of self-concept change. *Journal of Personality and Social Psychology, 69,* 1102–1112.

Bakan, D. (1966). *The duality of human existence: Isolation and commitment in western man.* Boston: Beacon Press.

Beach, S. R., Tesser, A., Fincham, F. D., Jones, D. J., Johnson, D., & Whitaker, D. J. (1998). Pleasure and pain in doing well, together: An investigation of performance-related affect in close relationships. *Journal of Personality and Social Psychology, 74,* 923–938.

Berscheid, E., Snyder, M., & Omoto, A. M. (1989). The relationship closeness inventory: Assessing the closeness of interpersonal relationships. *Journal of Personality and Social Psychology, 57,* 792–807.

Buber, M. (1937). *I and thou.* New York: Scribner.

Byrne, D. (1971). *The attraction paradigm.* New York: Academic Press.

Cadinu, M. R., & De Amicis, L. (1999). The relationship between the self and the in group: When having a common conception helps. *Swiss Journal of Psychology, 58,* 226–232.

Cialdini, R. B., Brown, S. L., Lewis, B. P., Luce, C., & Neuberg, S. L. (1997). Reinterpreting the empathy–altruism relationships: When one into one equals oneness. *Journal of Personality and Social Psychology, 73,* 481–494.

Clark, M. S., & Mills, J. (1979). Interpersonal attraction in exchange and communal relationships. *Journal of Personality and Social Psychology, 37,* 12–24.

Clark, M. S., & Mills, J. (1993). The difference between communal and exchange relationships: What it is and is not. *Personality and Social Psychology Bulletin, 19,* 684–691.

Cook, S. W. (1984). Cooperative interaction in multiethnic contexts. In N. Miller & M. B. Brewer (Eds.), *Groups in contact: The psychology of desegregation* (pp. 155–185). New York: Academic Press.

Gardner, W. L., Gabriel, S., & Hochschild, L. (2002). When you and I are "we", you are not threatening: The role of self-expansion in social comparison. *Journal of Personality and Social Psychology, 82,* 239–251.

Heider, F. (1958). *The psychology of interpersonal relations.* New York: Wiley.

Jones, E. E., & Nisbett, R. (1971). The actor and observer: Divergent perceptions of the causes of behavior. In E. E. Jones, D. Kanhouse, H. Kelley, R. Nisbett, S. Valins, & B. Weiner (Eds.), Attribution: Perceiving the causes of behavior (pp. 79–94). Morristown, NJ: General Learning Press.

Jung, C. G. (1959). Marriage as a psychological relationship (F. C. Hull, Trans.). In V. S. DeLaszlo (Ed.), *The basic writings of C. G. Jung* (pp. 531–544). New York: Modern Library. (Original work published 1925)

Kelley, H. H., & Thibaut, J. W. (1978). *Interpersonal relationships: A theory of interdependence.* New York: Wiley.

Klein, S. B., & Kihlstrom, J. F. (1986). Elaboration, organization, and the self-reference effect in memory. *Journal of Experimenatl Psychology: General, 115,* 26–38.

Konrath, S. H., & Ross, M. (2003, May). Our glories, our shames: Expanding the self in temporal self appraisal theory. Poster presented at the 111th Annual Meeting of the American Psychological Society, Atlanta, GA.

Lewandowski, G. (2002). *Relationship dissolution and the self-concept: The effects of interpersonal closeness and self-expansion.* Unpublished doctoral dissertation, State University of New York at Stony Brook.

Lord, C. G. (1980). Schemas and images as memory aids: Two modes of processing social information. *Journal of Personality and Social Psychology, 38,* 257–269.

Lord, C. G. (1987). Imagining self and others: Reply to Brown, Keenan, and Potts. *Journal of Personality and Social Psychology, 53,* 445–450.

MacKay, L., McFarland, C., & Buehler, R. (1998, August). *Affective reactions to performances in close relationships.* Paper presented at the 106th Annual Meeting of the American Psychological Association, San Francisco, CA.

Mashek, D. J., Aron, A., & Boncimino, M. (2003). Confusions of self with close others. *Personality and Social Psychology Bulletin, 29,* 382–392.

Maslow, A. H. (1967). A theory of metamotivation: The biological rooting of the value-life. *Journal of Humanistic Psychology, 7,* 93–127.

McCall, G. J. (1974). A symbolic interactionist approach to attraction. In T. L. Huston (Ed.), *Foundations of interpersonal attraction* (pp. 217–231). New York: Academic Press.

McLaughlin-Volpe, T. (1998). *Social interactions with members of ethnic outgroups and ethnic prejudice: A diary study.* Master's Thesis, State University of New York at Stony Brook.

McLaughlin-Volpe, T. (2002). *The intergroup contact effect as including an outgroup other in the self.* Unpublished doctoral dissertation, State University of New York at Stony Brook.

Medvene, L. J., Teal, C. R., & Slavich, S. (2000). Including the other in self: Implications for judgments of equity and satisfaction in close relationships. *Journal of Social and Clinical Psychology, 19,* 396–419.

Merleau-Ponty, M. (1945). *Phenomenologie de la perception.* Paris: Gallimard.

O'Mahen, H. A., Beach, S. R. H., & Tesser, A. (2000). Relationship ecology and negative communication in romantic relationships: A self-evaluation maintenance perspective. *Personality and Social Psychology Bulletin, 26,* 1343–1352.

Paolini, S., Hewstone, M., Cairns, E., & Voci, A. (2002). *Effects of direct and indirect cross-group friendships on judgments of Catholics and Protestants in Northern Ireland: The mediating role of an anxiety-reduction mechanism.* Unpublished manuscript, University of Newcastle, Callaghan, Australia.

Pettigrew, T. F. (1997). Generalized intergroup effects on prejudice. *Personality and Social Psychology Bulletin, 23,* 173–185.

Pettigrew, T. F., & Tropp, L. (2000). Does intergroup contact reduce prejudice? Recent meta-analytic findings. In S. Oskamp (Ed.), *Reducing prejudice and discrimination: Social psychological perspectives* (pp. 93–114). Mahwah, NJ: Lawrence Erlbaum Associates.

Reik, T. (1944). *A psychologist looks at love.* New York: Farrar & Reinhart.

Reis, H. T., & Shaver, P. (1988). Intimacy as interpersonal process. In S. Duck (Ed.), *Handbook of personal relationships: Theory, research and interventions* (pp. 367–389). Chichester, England: Wiley.

Ruvolo, A. P., & Fabin, L. A. (1999). Two of a kind: Perceptions of own and partners' attachment characteristics. *Personal Relationships, 6*, 57–79.

Sande, G. N., Goethals, G. R., & Radloff, C. E. (1988). Perceiving one's own traits and others': The multifaceted self. *Journal of Personality and Social Psychology, 54*, 13–20.

Schutz, A. (1970). *On phenomenology and social relations.* Chicago: Chicago University Press.

Schlenker, B. R., & Britt, T. W. (2001). Strategically controlling information to help friends: Effects of empathy and friendship strength on beneficial impression management. *Journal of Experimental Social Psychology, 37*, 357–372.

Sivadas, E., & Machleit, K. A. (1994). A scale to determine the extent of object incorporation in the extended self. *American Marketing Association, 5*, 143–149.

Smith, E. (2002). Overlapping mental representations of self and group: Evidence and implications. In J. P. Forgas & K. Williams (Eds.), *The social self: Cognitive, interpersonal and intergroup perspectives* (pp. 21–35). Philadelphia: Psychology Press.

Smith, E., Coats, S., & Walling, D. (1999). Overlapping mental representations of self, in-group, and partner: Further response time evidence and a connectionist model. *Personality and Social Psychology Bulletin, 25*, 873–882.

Smith, E., & Henry, S. (1996). An in-group becomes part of the self: Response time evaluation. *Personality and Social Psychology Bulletin, 22*, 635–642.

Symons, C. S., & Johnson, B. T. (1997). The self-reference effect in memory: A meta-analysis. *Psychological Bulletin, 121*, 371–394.

Tesser, A. (1988). Toward a self-evaluation maintenance model of social behavior. In L. Berkowitz (Ed.), *Advances in experimental social psychology, Vol. 21: Social psychological studies of the self: Perspectives and programs* (pp. 181–227). San Diego, CA: Academic Press.

Tropp, L. R., & Wright, S. C. (2001). Ingroup identification as the inclusion of ingroup in the self. *Personality & Social Psychology Bulletin, 27*, 585–600.

Uleman, J. S., Rhee, E., Bardoliwalla, N., Semin, G., & Toyama, M. (2000). The relational self: Closeness to ingroups depends on who they are, culture, and the type of closeness. *Asian Journal of Social Psychology, 3*, 1–17.

Wright, S. C., Aron, A., McLaughlin-Volpe, T., & Ropp, S. A. (1997). The extended contact effect: Knowledge of cross-group friendships and prejudice. *Journal of Personality and Social Psychology, 73*, 73–90.

Wright, S. C., Aron, A., & Tropp, L. R. (2002). Including others (and groups) in the self: Self-expansion and intergroup relations. In J. P. Forgas & K. Williams (Eds.), *The social self: Cognitive, interpersonal and intergroup perspectives.* Philadelphia: Psychology Press.

Wright, S. C., & Van Der Zande, C. C. (1999, October). *Bicultural friends: When cross-group friendships cause improved intergroup attitudes.* Paper presented at the Society for Experimental Social Psychology, St. Louis, MO.

Zajonc, R. B., Adelmann, R. K., Murphy, S. B., & Niedenthal, R. N. (1987). Convergence in the physical appearances of spouses. *Motivation and Emotion, 11*, 335–346.

4

Deep Intimate Connection: Self and Intimacy in Couple Relationships

Karen J. Prager
The University of Texas at Dallas

Linda J. Roberts
The University of Wisconsin-Madison

The famous epigraph to E. M. Forster's (1910/1998) novel *Howard's End* elegantly proclaims the penultimate importance of intimacy in human relationships: "Only connect . . . " These two words echo what psychological theorists and researchers alike have systematically articulated: True intimacy with others is one of the highest values of human existence; there may be nothing more important for the well-being and optimal functioning of human beings than intimate relationships (e.g., Bowlby, 1969; Kelly, 1955; Rogers, 1951; Sullivan, 1953; for recent reviews of supporting research, see Reis, Collins, & Bersheid, 2000). However, these two simple words convey two messages simultaneously: "Only connect—relationships give meaning to life; all else is background!"; and "only connect—it's as easy as that, simply connect!" For literary genius Forster, the dual surface of the message is intentional and carries a world of irony underneath. The characters and plot of his novel clearly support the notion that intimacy and connection are the bedrock of human happiness and meaning, but the story also convinces the reader that the exhortation to "only connect" is far from simple.

The novel establishes the inherent complexity and difficulty of intimate connection by examining the marriage of a man and a woman who stand as polar opposites of one another. The stage is set for Forster's (1910/1998) exploration of relational intimacy when Margaret Schlegel agrees to marry the widower Henry Wilcox despite her awareness of their profound differences—including his apparent lack of interest in real intimacy. With naive confidence, Margaret embraces the challenge of connecting with Henry Wilcox despite the gulf of their differences; she is determined to "build the rainbow bridge" between them:

It did not seem so difficult.... She would only point out the salvation that was latent in his own soul, and in the soul of every man. Only connect! That was the whole of her sermon. Only connect the prose and the passion and both will be exalted, and human love will be seen at its height.... By quiet indications the bridge would be built and span their lives with beauty. (pp. 134–135)

Forster deftly underscores the self-deception in the simplicity of her intention to "only connect!" when, in the very next sentence, the narrator abruptly informs the reader, "but she failed."

Like many other couples, Margaret and Henry were not able to achieve the "apex" of relational intimacy, deep intimate connection. Forster (1910/1998) helps us see that for Margaret and Henry an essential condition for intimate connection was lacking, one that was not easily surmounted. Henry was a man with little or no self-knowledge; he rejected his own inner life. As Forster put it: "Outwardly he was cheerful, reliable and brave; but within all had reverted to chaos" (p. 134). In Forster's view, the experience of intimate connection with another is not only dependent on relationship qualities such as love and commitment, but on the self that is shared with the other. Forster's insight is echoed by many psychological theorists, who argue that access to a true and authentic self is a necessary condition for intimate relating (e.g., Bowen, 1966; Erikson, 1959, 1963; Klein 1935; Rogers, 1951, 1959).

In this chapter, we will elaborate upon E. M. Forster's (1910/1998) insight regarding self, other, and the potential "bridge" of intimate relating in the context of committed couple relationships. We will argue that the process of achieving deep and abiding relational intimacy is not simple, nor does a marriage guarantee it, and most importantly, that relational intimacy both requires and touches the self as much as it does the relationship. We begin by presenting our definition and model of intimacy as manifest in both interpersonal interactions and ongoing relationships. We follow with an elaboration of relational intimacy in the special case of committed couple relationships. We then go on to examine some of the ways that the structures and strengths of the self enter, transform, and are transformed by an intimate couple relationship, using both Carl Rogers' (1951) and social cognitive frameworks for conceptualizing the "self." Finally, we examine the regulation of intimacy within couple relationships. Throughout, we draw on existing research on intimacy and on Karen J. Prager's clinical experience working with couples.

THE ESSENCE OF INTIMATE RELATING: NECESSARY AND SUFFICIENT CONDITIONS

Our goal is to articulate a conceptualization of intimacy that is clearly distinguished from other positive relationship processes such as love, caregiving, attachment, support, and relationship satisfaction. Further, whereas many previous conceptualizations of intimate relating are primarily based on the assumption of a verbal exchange (e.g., Jourard, 1971), we sought to define the conditions for intimate relating in such a way that nonverbal and sexual encounters are easily incorporated. Following Prager (1995), we organize our conceptualization by considering two basic phenomena and their interplay: intimate interactions and intimate relationships. Extending Prager's earlier work (Lippert & Prager, 2001; Prager, 1995), we define these two phenomena by specifying necessary and sufficient conditions for differentiating an intimate from a nonintimate interaction and an intimate from a nonintimate relationship. Further, we use the terms interactional intimacy and relational intimacy to capture the degree and quality of the intimate relating in intimate interactions and relationships, respectively, thus allowing for an analysis of the inherent variability within these basic categories.

Intimate Interactions and Interactional Intimacy

There is considerable variability among researchers and theorists in the specification of the essential features of an intimate interaction (see Perlman & Fehr, 1987; Prager, 1995 for reviews). Building on previous work (Lippert & Prager, 2001; Prager & Buhrmester, 1998; Reis & Shaver, 1988), we suggest that an intimate interaction is distinguished from other kinds of interactions by three necessary and sufficient conditions: self-revealing behavior, positive involvement with the other, and shared understandings. Self-revealing behaviors are those that reveal personal, private aspects of the self to another, or invite another into a zone of privacy. Both verbal behavior and nonverbal behavior (physical touch, sexual contact) can be self-revealing. Being self-revealing implies a willingness to drop defenses and invite the other to witness and to know private, personal aspects of the self. As a condition for an intimate interaction, then, some aspect of the self is willingly revealed or "exposed" to the other.[1] Deeply self-revealing behavior usually involves the expression of emotions, and often, "vulnerable emotions" such as guilt, hurt, or sadness, that expose the "innermost self" (see Johnson & Greenberg, 1994; Roberts & Greenberg, 2002).

For an interaction to be intimate, the individuals also need to be in a state of positive involvement with one another. Involvement refers to the partner's attentional focus on the unfolding interaction; an involved partner devotes full attention to the encounter as opposed to offering only a divided or intermittent attentional focus (Goffman, 1967; Roberts & Krokoff, 1990). Positive here refers to a basic positive regard for the other that is communicated through nonverbal cues, verbal cues, or both. Intimate relating thus precludes attacking, defensive, distancing, or alienating behavior. However, positive affect (such as happiness or love), is not an essential element of intimate relating—intimate interactions may involve soaring feelings of love, but they may also involve negative affect, such as feelings of remorse or sadness.

Positive involvement in the interaction is observable through both nonverbal and verbal behaviors. Behaviors that signify positive involvement evidence immediacy, a concept first identified, in the work of Mehrabian (1967). Immediacy is defined as the "directness and intensity of interaction between two entities (p. 325)." Mehrabian (1967, 1971) and others following him (e.g., Patterson, 1982) identified a host of behavioral cues that signal immediacy. Nonverbal cues include: decreased distance, increased gaze, touch, more direct body orientation, more forward lean, greater facial expressiveness, longer speech duration, more frequent or more intense interruptions, increased postural openness, more relational gestures, more frequent head nods, and more intense paralinguistic cues. Verbal cues include appropriate "tracking" of the partner's communication and thematic continuity (Thomas, 1977), and linguistic cues, such as pronouns and adverbs that place content of conversation in the present moment (e.g., this, here) versus those that place it in another place and time (e.g., then, there). Verb tense (present vs. past) also serves as a cue to immediacy (Mehrabian, 1971).

Finally, intimate interactions are characterized by shared understandings of one another's selves. In an intimate interaction, both partners experience a sense of knowing or understanding some aspect of the other's inner experience—from private thoughts, feelings, or beliefs, to characteristic rhythms, habits, or routines, to private sexual

---

[1] The models of the self put forth by Rogers (1951) and by contemporary social cognitive theorists may reflect the Western cultural context within which it was formulated. As social cognitive theorists (e.g., Markus & Kitayama, 1991; Oyserman & Markus, 1993) have argued, the surrounding culture actually defines what it means to be a self and would therefore also define what it means for two selves to be in an intimate relationship with one another. Our discussion may therefore be most applicable to a Western cultural context.

fantasies and preferences. Intimate relating is, at core, two selves knowing each other. This knowledge endures beyond the interaction and informs and deepens subsequent interactions between the partners. Knowledge of the other need not involve direct verbal disclosure. For example, an intimate mutually gratifying sexual encounter will involve the exchange of information about personal needs, desires and preferences, but usually without any explicit verbal communication. The (often implicit) understanding of the other's "sexual self" gained in an intimate sexual encounter can serve to shape and deepen future sexual relations.

When these three essential features (self-exposure, positive involvement, shared understanding) are present, at least some degree of interactional intimacy is present in the interaction. However, the degree and quality of intimacy in any given interaction varies widely as a function of the depth of self-exposure, the intensity of positive involvement and the extent of the shared personal understandings. Two partners sharing "knowing" looks during a boring lecture might represent one end of the continuum—the partners reveal their respective feelings, demonstrate momentary positive involvement with each other and share a private understanding of their joint position on the negative aspects of their current lecture hall experience; but the interaction lacks much depth, intensity, or generalizable shared understanding. In the most intimate interactions, on the other hand, partners invite one another into personal, private, and vulnerable aspects of their unguarded, undefended selves, visually, verbally, and nonverbally and thus experience intense feelings of connection and deep understanding. A deeply intimate encounter is exemplified by two partners maintaining eye contact and forward body orientation while disclosing feelings of uncertainty about themselves as relationship partners who nevertheless love one another deeply.

Intimate Relationships and Relational Intimacy

Intimate interactions are the essential building blocks, but not the entire structure, of an intimate relationship. The defining characteristics of intimate interactions provide the basic elements for defining an intimate relationship. Individuals who share an intimate relationship have necessarily conjointly experienced multiple interactions in which both partners have engaged in self-revealing behaviors, experienced positive involvement with the other, and achieved shared understandings. Through the process of intimate interaction, an intimate relationship comes to be distinguished from a casual or nonintimate relationship by virtue of accumulated knowledge or understanding of the other. In an intimate relationship, both partners must accumulate shared understandings of the other. An intimate relationship is thus characterized by mutual, accumulated, shared personal knowledge.

Beyond these minimal criteria for defining an intimate relationship is a continuum of relational intimacy that specifies the degree and quality of intimacy in the relationship. Relational intimacy varies as a function of two factors: extensiveness of intimate relating, and the accuracy of the accumulated shared personal understandings. By extensiveness of intimate relating we refer to the frequency of intimate interactions and the degree and quality of interactional intimacy in those interactions, as defined by the three necessary and sufficient conditions we discussed previously. Thus, higher levels of relational intimacy are characterized by frequent interactions involving high levels of personal disclosure, intense positive involvement and extensive domains of shared personal understanding. Understanding of the other takes on special significance in the context of an ongoing close relationship because the knowledge and understanding of the other and of the self-in-relation-to-other that is gained through intimate interactions endures and accumulates. Knowledge is stored in cognitive structures (or partner-and relationship-schemas) as internal representations that guide future interactive behavior (Baldwin, 1992; Bretherton, 1987, 1993; Kihlstrom & Cantor, 1984; Kihlstrom et al., 1988; Markus, 1977; Markus & Kunda, 1986). Thus, as we will discuss in more depth later in the chapter, not only the extensiveness but the accuracy of these enduring understandings of the partner are indicative and predictive of the degree and quality of the relational intimacy a couple achieves.

Relational Intimacy in Committed Couple Relationships

Our distinction between an intimate relationship and the degree of relational intimacy present in the relationship allows us to follow the common language convention of referring to any committed couple relationship as an intimate relationship, by definition, while at the same time acknowledging tremendous variability in the degree to which a particular couple's relationship is characterized by relational intimacy. All partners in couple relationships have extensive accumulated knowledge of each other, built up through years of common experiences and the process of each allowing the other to be a witness to his or her inner life. However, like Margaret and Henry, not all couples have high relational intimacy.

Clinical studies of distressed couples suggest the importance of relational intimacy for marital functioning. Conflicts regarding intimacy are common in clinic couples (e.g., Christensen & Shenk, 1991) and successful interventions for marital distress (e.g., Greenberg & Johnson, 1988) target changes in the pattern and style of partners' expressions of vulnerability and emotional responsiveness.

Further, it is well documented that high levels of self-reported intimacy are associated with marital satisfaction and stability (e.g., Talmadge & Dabbs, 1990). Self-revealing behavior (e.g., Haas & Stafford, 1998; Lippert & Prager, 2001; Prager, 1989, 1991; Sprecher,1987; Waring & Patton, 1984), the frequency and gratification of sexual contact (Prager & Buhrmester, 1998), emotional responsiveness as opposed to withdrawal (Gottman & Krokoff, 1989; Roberts & Krokoff, 1990; Smith, Vivian, & O'Leary, 1990), and the extent to which each partner perceives the other accurately (i.e., as self perceives self; Swann, De La Ronde, & Hixon, 1994) and positively (Murray, Holmes, & Griffin, 1996) are each closely associated with relationship satisfaction and stability. Although many marital researchers have pointed to the corrosive qualities of conflict and negative affect for marital health, Roberts (2000) has demonstrated that reports of partner withdrawal in response to confiding behavior (i.e., intimacy avoidance) contribute to marital dissatisfaction over and above the couples' level of conflict.

It is clear, nevertheless, that relational intimacy and relationship satisfaction are not isomorphic. Specifically, when the assessment of satisfaction is confined to the partners' global relationship evaluations, levels of relationship intimacy still correlate positively with satisfaction and neither totally accounts for the other (Lippert & Prager, 2001). Further supporting this contention, researchers (e.g., Fitzpatrick, 1988; Raush, Hertel, Barry, & Swain, 1974; Gottman, 1993) have identified a type of marital relationship that is high in satisfaction but low in relational intimacy. There are individual and couple differences in expectations and motivations for intimate relating in the context of a committed relationship (e.g., Prager, 1999). Indeed, it is important that relational intimacy is conceptualized as a possible component of relationship satisfaction but not as a process so general that it encompasses any and all positive relational processes. There are multiple pathways to the achievement of a satisfactory relationship. E. M. Forster (1910/1998) depicted Margaret and Henry's relationship in this complex light: Although they failed to achieve mutual understanding and a deep sense of intimate connection, their experiences of mutual affection and attachment were strong, and their commitment was enduring.

INTIMATE RELATING AND THE SELF-SYSTEM

To specify the conditions that account for the difference between a low degree of relational intimacy and the highest degree of relational intimacy—or deep, intimate connection as we will label it—requires an understanding of the self-system. Intimate relating, whether in an intimate interaction, or sustained over years in a couple relationship, involves the self-system and, in turn, shapes the self-system. The nature of the self-system an individual brings to a relationship can either contribute to or hinder the development and maintenance of high levels of relational intimacy. We will argue that deep intimate connection—or open, authentic sharing, positive absorption in the interaction, and high levels of shared understanding—requires a self-system that is accurately attuned to both self and partner experience. We have structured our exploration of the connections between intimate relating and the self-system around three essential features of the self-system: the self-concept, the experiencing organismic self, and their interplay (i.e., the congruence between the self-concept and organismic experience).

For our exploration of the self in intimate couple relationships, we draw on two approaches to understanding the self: the social-cognitive model of self (e.g., Markus, 1977; Neisser, 1976; Oyserman & Markus, 1993) and Carl Rogers' (1951, 1959) organismic model of self. The social-cognitive model of self arises out of a renewed surge of interest in the linkage between the self and social relationships, stimulated largely by research on "social cognition" using an information-processing paradigm. According to this model, schemas and related constructs (internal representations, working models, scripts) mediate the relationship between the individual organism and its social and interpersonal environment. From the perspective of social cognition theorists, the "self" is a multifaceted, hierarchically organized, dynamic memory structure composed of images, schemas, and prototypes (Markus & Wurf, 1987).

In our view, a full explication of the nature of intimate connection between two interacting selves requires a theory of self that additionally incorporates phenomenological experiencing and the notion of a "true" or "authentic" self. Initially seen as the exclusive purview of humanistic personality theorists (e.g., Allport, 1961; Bakan, 1966; Maslow, 1968; Rogers, 1951, 1959), the primacy of subjective experience and the relevance of the authenticity of self-representations are themes that are receiving increasing theoretical attention and research support (e.g., Arndt, Shimel, Greenberg, & Pyszczynski, 2002; Deci & Ryan, 1985; Harter, 1998, 2002; Ryan & Deci, 2000; Swann, De La Rond, & Hixon, 1995; Waterman, 1993).

Rogers' early (1951, 1959) theoretical work on the nature and development of the self remains a compelling and comprehensive articulation of self-functioning. Rogers' model of the self-system includes both the conceptual self (comparable to the self-concept in social cognitive theory) and the experiencing or organismic self, as well as specific postulates about their interplay and the resulting implications for psychological functioning. In contrast to the self-concept, which is the self-as-conceptualized by the person, the organismic self encompasses the moment to moment experiences of the organism (e.g., hunger, thirst, pain, love, joy) regardless of whether or not these experiences are consciously perceived and conceptualized. According to Rogers (1951), the organismic self "exists in a continually changing world of experience of which he is the center . . . [t]his perceptual (or experiential) field, for the person, is reality" (pp. 483–484). Thus, the organismic self may be thought of as the true self—the authentically experiencing, perceiving, and feeling self. Ideally, the experiences of the organismic self and the content of the self-concept are in harmony, or congruent. Perceptions and experiences are neither denied nor distorted in the congruent state, leaving the individual open to accurately understand his or her spontaneous reactions to the people and events encountered day to day. Because of the accessibility of the true self, congruence, as we will elaborate below, opens the door to optimum experiences of intimate connection between two selves.

Self-Concept and Intimate Relating

The self-concept has a dual function: It summarizes and categorizes previous self-defining experiences and, on the basis of prior experience, provides maps (or sets of expectations) for future experiences (Markus, 1977; Neisser, 1976). These self-representations or self-schemas offer cognitive short-cuts for the rapid interpretation of new experiences as well as the rapid determination of appropriate or effective interpersonal behavior. Some social cognition theorists (e.g., Epstein, 1994) argue that existing self-schemas provide such comfortable and efficient short-cuts that most individuals resist the emotional arousal and the concentrated effort that is required to operate outside of them. Therefore, the self-concept effectively limits each individual's repertoire of possible experiences and responses in an intimate context to those that are familiar and consistent with existing self-representations.

In couple relationships, the self-concept will determine the frequency and depth of intimate relating that a partner will seek or tolerate. Self-representations consistent with achieving relational intimacy may or may not be integral to a partner's self-concept (see also Collins & Read, 1994; Cross, Bacon, & Morris, 2000; Cross & Madsen, 1997). According to a recent review of this research (Aron, 2003), those who score high on "relationship interdependent self-construal" have closer and more committed relationships, and are more likely to consider their partners' needs. Similarly, Forster (1910/1998) suggests that Henry Wilcox's self-concept contributes to the lack of intimate connection he experiences with Margaret. He is proud to see himself as a practical and outwardly focused person. Because Henry's self-concept is inconsistent with intimate relating, he finds Margaret's requests for intimate contact mystifying. Forster aptly describes Henry's reaction when Margaret "scolds" him for not attending to the interpersonal world around him: "He was puzzled, but replied with a laugh: 'My motto is [c]oncentrate. I've no intention of frittering away my strength on that sort of thing.'" (p. 135). Whatever yearnings for intimacy Henry Wilcox may have experienced were outside of his self-definition. He was therefore unlikely to fully understand or act on Margaret's desire for—and expectation of—intimate connection.

Specific self-schemas about intimacy-relevant behaviors such as openness and self-disclosure will also have an impact on a couple's relational intimacy. For example, strong identification with the masculine role may predispose a husband to think of himself as a "sturdy oak" who is fully self-reliant. Open sharing of experienced interpersonal needs and desires may be associated with excess dependency or "sissy stuff" for him, with the result that these tendencies will not be readily incorporated into his self-representations and will not guide his actions (see Doyle, 1989, for more on these masculine stereotypes).[2]

In general, positive self-regard, or a positive evaluation of the self-concept, encourages more extensive intimate relating whereas negative self-regard discourages it.

---

[2] Whether a person favors verbal or sexual intimate relating also reflects self-schemas. Continuing our example of masculine role identification, it is common for married men, especially young men, to report that sexual relating is their favored type of intimate interaction (Peplau, Hill, & Rubin, 1993). Given the strong role that culture plays in shaping self-concept schemas (Markus & Kitayama, 1991; Oyserman & Markus, 1993), the close alignment between sexuality and "adequate masculinity" in U.S. society may well predispose many men to have self-schemas that foster sexual intimacy in their relationships while neglecting verbal intimacy. An opposite tendency may be seen in women.

Adult attachment research supports this link between positive representational models of self and relational intimacy. Individuals with secure attachment schemas (i.e., schemas that simultaneously evaluate the self as loveable and worthy and others as trustworthy and reliable) are more open and expressive of their emotions than individuals with avoidant attachment schemas (e.g., Bartholomew & Horowitz, 1991; Simpson, 1990). Moreover, individuals with secure attachment schemas offer more hugs and other affectionate touches, are more responsive to their partners' needs for care (Kunce & Shaver, 1994), engage in more self-disclosure (Mikulincer & Nachson, 1991), have higher reported needs for closeness and less need for distance (Feeney, 1999), and more readily offer and accept emotional support (Simpson, Rholes, & Nelligan, 1992).

Especially relevant to sexually intimate interactions is positive self-regard associated with body and sexual self-concepts. People who perceive their bodies as meeting cultural ideals derive a variety of psychological benefits, whereas those who believe they are not meeting these ideal standards may suffer from psychological and sexual problems (Goldenberg, McCoy, Pyszczynski, Greenberg, & Solomon, 2000). Evidence associating a positive body self-concept with protection from anxiety in stressful situations (Goldenberg et al., 2000) suggests that positive body and sexual self-concepts may protect individuals from feelings of anxiety and shame about sexual interactions. Because sexual interactions simultaneously expose many private aspects of the self, negative regard for one's body and sexual self likely interferes with deeply intimate sexual interactions.

Self-regard brought into the adult relationship is derived in part from self-schemas that reflect earlier relationship experiences (e.g., Bowlby, 1969; Collins & Read, 1994; Greenberg & Mitchell, 1983; Rogers, 1959; Sullivan, 1953). Self-regard develops in childhood in response to parents' positive regard for the child or, alternatively, in response to conditions of worth imposed on the child (Rogers, 1959). As a result, an intimate disclosure may elicit feelings of esteem or shame, not because of the partner's actual response, but because of expectations and self-evaluations which are based on internalized self-representations from childhood relationships (see, Benjamin, 1994, for an in-depth theoretical analysis of this issue). Fear of intimacy (i.e., in this case, fear of shame or rejection) may motivate people to avoid intimacy entirely (Firestone & Catlett, 1999).

Organismic Experiencing and Intimate Relating

The positive involvement of the organismic self in intimate interactions is so fully integral to experiences of deep intimate connection that we begin this section by discussing its impact on relational intimacy. Full involvement of the organismic self means that the person's moment-to-moment attention is not distracted but is instead fully focused upon self, partner, and interaction. The more access each individual has to his or her own organismic self experiences, the more both are able to tune into their own feelings, thoughts, and reactions to their interaction as they occur. Further, full attention to experience maximizes the individual's attunement to nuances of the partner's communication. The fully involved and highly accessible organismic self, then, permits spontaneity and a lack of defensiveness at the same time that it promotes an unfiltered, accurate understanding of the partner. The deep intimate connection partners experience when they are both so involved may well be similar to what Csikszentmihalyi (1990) has referred to as flow in his descriptions of intensely absorbing solo activities, such as rock climbing.

The association between full involvement of organismic self, and interactional intimacy is especially apparent in an intimate sexual encounter. Clinicians note that couples who have gratifying sexual interactions speak of a focused sexual playfulness

(Kaplan, 1974; Metz & Lutz, 1990). Sexual playfulness, as these authors describe it, is a form of sustained positive involvement in the interaction. This playful involvement is intrinsically motivated, and has been described as "regression in the presence of another . . . a spontaneous, creative, flowing out of the self within a dyadic relationship" (Betcher, 1981, p. 14). The full involvement of the organismic self in playful sexual intimacy brings depth and significance to the experience of sexual contact. When partners are able to sustain spontaneous organismic involvement with one another, they welcome one another into a process of profound mutual understanding and deep, intimate connection.

Finally, the verbal disclosure of organismic self experiences enhances immediacy and depth in intimate interactions because it invites partners to share a process of self-transformation. According to Rogers' theory (1951), organismic self experiences are represented and integrated into the self-concept when they are vividly experienced and accurately verbalized. Accurate verbalization of these experiences to another person enhances the self-transformative impact of this process, in part because disclosers are obliged to elaborate their experiences more fully than they would if thinking about them silently to themselves. Further, partners can offer their own impressions of the discloser's verbalized experiences, thereby becoming actively involved in the discloser's effort to incorporate the organismic experiences into his/her self-concept. Finally, the partner can validate the partner's organismic self experiences (i.e., encourage the other to evaluate those experiences as normal, understandable, reasonable, wise, perceptive, and realistic), and affirm the transformed self-concept (i.e., encourage the discloser to evaluate it more positively on dimensions such as valuable, worthwhile, lovable, and interesting). Because organismic self-disclosure welcomes the partner into the process as well as the content of self-transformation, intimate partners need never find their intimate interactions to be "stale" from over-familiarity, unless one or both are themselves rigidly entrenched or closed to new experience. Rather, they are more likely to achieve deep intimate connection as a result of their organismic self-disclosure.

Congruence, True and False Selves, and Intimate Relating

An incongruent self-system is one in which organismic experiences are denied or distorted (Rogers, 1959). An incongruent self-system directs the individual's focus disproportionately to defensive processes, thereby compromising positive involvement and erecting barriers to mutual understanding. Influential personality theorists (Freud, 1938; Horney, 1939; Dollard & Miller, 1950; Rogers, 1951, 1959) agree that keeping disturbing thoughts and emotions from awareness requires attention and emotional energy that might otherwise be directed more adaptively. Defensiveness is rarely effectively selective and must, of necessity, screen out (or distort) information in the immediate environment that might elicit experiences that disturb or threaten the self-concept. It follows, then, that when the partner is that immediate environment, defensiveness may prevent the partner's communication from being fully and accurately perceived.

Michael and Martha exemplify the effect of incongruence on intimacy.[3] Michael wants to convince himself, and convince Martha, that he is living up to his ambitious ideal-self–ideal-man image by making plans to advance his career. However, "ambitious Michael" is a false self—a self-concept that is incongruent with Michael's true, experiencing self. Michael's incongruence compromises mutual understanding in the

---

[3] Michael and Martha (and Warren and Wendy, introduced later) are fictitious amalgams of several couples treated by Karen J. Prager.

marriage due to the potential it creates for inaccurate and confusing communication. When an individual shares information about his or her self-concept that does not match his or her actual experience, the partner receives mixed messages: The organismic self signals one truth whereas the defended self-concept signals another. To the extent that Michael's presentation of this false self to himself and to Martha conflicts with his day-to-day behavior, Michael's false self circumscribes the couple's mutual understanding and thereby limits relational intimacy.

Further, because Michael believes he is being intimate with Martha when he describes his false self to her, both partners must accept the veracity of Michael's false self in order for either to believe that they have achieved an accurate, mutual understanding. On the one hand, Michael might well find Martha's acceptance of his false self to be a reassuring affirmation that he is the person he wishes he was. On the other hand, her acceptance of the false self may create more pressure on Michael to hide his true self. Regardless, Michael has made a "devil's pact" with himself. However temporarily effective Michael's defenses are, his true self will continue to be expressed (inadvertently) in his behavior (e.g., in Michael's case, procrastination, lethargy, and so forth). Martha will likely observe the contradictions between Michael's self-presentation and his behavior and, as a result, she will not believe that she understands Michael and Michael will not feel understood. Michael's negative evaluation of his true self, and his defensive projection of a false self, stand in the way of deep intimate connection with Martha.

In contrast, congruence contributes to deep intimate connection. Congruence deepens self-revealing behavior by providing the individual with an accurate, easily accessible picture of the true self. When a partner's self-system is congruent, moment-to-moment perceptions, feelings, motives, and interpretations of events are highly accessible and the true self can be revealed to the partner. Congruence also enhances mutual understanding. When the self-system is congruent, behaviors of the organismic self are consistent with what the person reveals about him or herself (i.e., the self-concept). Congruence therefore maximizes the perceived truth and authenticity of the self that is shared with the partner, not only from self's point of view, but also from the partner's perspective. Congruent individuals are able to communicate clearly and straightforwardly about their true selves, and that clarity helps the partner to receive the communication accurately.

The preceding sections on self-system and intimacy describe ways that each component of the self-system, and congruence among the self-system components, contributes to the level of interactional and relational intimacy partners can achieve in their relationship. As we will discuss next, however, even partners with highly functional self-systems must be able to reconcile their individual differences and collaborate with one another effectively enough to create opportunities for intimate connection and to sustain relational intimacy over time.

THE DYNAMICS OF INTIMACY REGULATION
IN COUPLE RELATIONSHIPS

Because many partners live together and occupy the same physical space for numerous hours each day, the potential for intimate contact is theoretically continuous. It is therefore necessary that couples develop coordinated strategies for moving in and out of intimate relating. We define intimacy regulation sequences as behavioral sequences that move partners back and forth from intimacy to separateness and back again to embrace intimate contact. For some couples, these sequences will quickly become automatic, well-coordinated, and mutually acceptable. For others, transitions in and out of intimate relating may be accompanied by anguish and conflict. Despite the importance of intimacy regulation sequences, little is known about how intimacy regulation operates within well-functioning relationships or how it contributes to (or reflects) relationship distress.

Intimacy regulation sequences are important not only because they define a core relationship process, but because they become patterned in a couple's relationship and begin to define the couple's intimate relating. Like any behavioral sequence that is repeated time and again, intimacy regulation sequences shape and confine the couple's relationship; characteristic intimacy regulation sequences create self-fulfilling behavioral outcome expectations associated with intimate relating.

Intimacy regulation sequences are inexorably linked to the self-systems of the two partners. This linkage is revealed in two important challenges couples face when they attempt to regulate intimacy in their relationship. First, intimacy regulation sequences must accommodate each partner's characteristic way of balancing autonomy with intimacy. Autonomy refers to self-determination, or people's freedom to control how they will spend their time and with whom they will spend it. We are interested here in autonomy as it serves the self-system; autonomy facilitates the development of a unique, richly complex, and clearly defined self-concept. Autonomy allows people to select the domains within which they will operate, with those domains, in turn, creating the categories with which people will organize (and expand) their self-concepts. Second, intimacy regulation sequences protect partners from being hurt by each other's insensitive or cruel behavior. On the one hand, partners are motivated to seek out intimate interactions in which they can disclose their true selves to a positively involved and accurately understanding partner. Such interactions potentially affirm and validate the true self. However, the same self-exposure also allows partners to attack, criticize, or denigrate those same true selves. Intimacy regulation sequences balance partners' needs to avoid being hurt with their desire to share their true selves with one another. Put another way, these sequences help partners balance their yearning for intimacy with their fear of intimacy (see Descutner & Thelen, 1991).

Our purpose here is to more closely examine intimacy regulation sequences and their linkages with partners' self-systems. We begin by describing three core types of intimacy regulation sequences. From there we examine processes by which these three types of intimacy regulation sequences address disparate partner needs for autonomy as well as intimacy. Finally, we consider the vulnerabilities that intimate relating introduces (or exacerbates) in the self-system, and the processes by which the three intimacy regulation sequences work together to keep the intimacy doors open while simultaneously protecting partner vulnerabilities.

Core Intimacy Regulation Sequences

We propose that there are three basic types of intimacy regulation sequences. It is our contention that these sequences affect the overall level of relational intimacy for a particular couple by (a) determining how often and under what circumstances partners will engage in intimate interactions, and (b) associating predictable consequences with intimacy relevant behaviors. Positive consequences will function to encourage partners to engage in more intimate interactions while negative consequences will function to discourage intimate relating.

The first type is the intimacy engage sequence. The two steps in this sequence are intimacy approach and intimacy reciprocation. In intimacy approach, one partner (the "intimacy initiator") signals his or her availability for an intimate interaction with the other (e.g., sitting next to the partner with a pleasant facial expression) or explicitly invites the other to participate (e.g., "do you want to make love?"). The "reciprocating partner's" behavior signals the initiator that he or she is available for intimacy using behaviors that are either parallel (e.g., one winks and the other winks back) or complementary to the initiator's behaviors (e.g., one starts talking and the other begins listening). Intimacy engage sequences should be experienced positively by both partners.

The second core intimacy regulation sequence is the intimacy withdrawal sequence. The two steps in this sequence are *intimacy withdrawal* and either withdrawal compliance or resistance. Once engaged in intimate interaction, partners must at some time withdraw, and either cease interacting altogether or shift their interaction mode to something else. As an intimate interaction winds down, one partner will initiate withdrawal with either a verbal statement or a behavioral shift (e.g., gets up out of bed, turns on the television) that moves the couple out of intimate relating and into either mutual alone time or another type of interaction (e.g., planning their day). The partner responding has two behavioral choices: to comply with or resist the withdrawal initiator's behavioral communication. For the most part, compliant behavior is unremarkable. In the absence of significant intimacy problems in the relationship, the behavior of the responder to withdrawal completes the intimacy withdrawal sequence and thereby completes the transition from intimate relating to another state. Intimacy withdrawal may create problems for the couple if the responding partner feels that the interaction should continue. In this case, the partner is likely to resist withdrawal and attempt to keep the other engaged. Sometimes the behaviors of the withdrawal resister are positive and playful; however, they can also be coercive, guilt-inducing, or accusatory (e.g., "so you'd rather watch TV than talk to me").

Withdrawal resistance opens the door to a third step in the sequence: response to resistance. Problems with withdrawal may be minimized if the withdrawal initiator responds warmly and sensitively to the resistance (without necessarily capitulating). However, problems escalate if an angry withdrawing partner ups the ante by turning withdrawal into rejection. Insistent, negatively toned resistance increases the likelihood of outright rejection by the withdrawal initiator; similarly, an escalated response to resistance could increase the likelihood of demanding, negative behavior from the resistor.

The third core intimacy regulation sequence is the decline intimacy sequence. The three steps in this sequence are intimacy approach, as described above, decline intimacy and response to decline. Declining intimacy includes any communication to the intimacy initiator that conveys the decliner's unavailability or lack of desire for intimate relating at that moment. The communication can be simply factual ("I have a headache"; "I have a deadline") with no negative emotional consequences. Any implied rejection in declining intimacy can be softened either by verbal reassurances or by postponement (although postponement is only positive if there is a history of follow through). However, declining an intimate overture can also be done in a way that is rejecting of the partner (e.g., "Oh come on, leave me in peace!" "Why do you always need to talk, talk, talk?").

The initiating partner's response to being declined is also an important aspect of this sequence. Graceful acceptance of a decline (presuming the decline is not conveyed in an overtly rejecting manner) can end this sequence without any negative emotional consequences. Conversely, the initiating partner can respond to hurt feelings by attacking, blaming, or criticizing the partner for declining. In the latter case, the response to being declined creates additional problems for the couple. Because initiating intimate contact makes the initiator vulnerable, an unremitting pattern of initiate and decline—whether overtly rejecting or simply not reciprocating—can create serious problems for the couple.

Together, these three intimacy regulation sequences control the way intimate partners enter into, withdraw from, and avoid intimate interactions. How these sequences are enacted determines the couple's level of relational intimacy—the more often initiations are offered and reciprocated, the more relational intimacy; the more quickly partners withdraw from intimate interactions, the less relational intimacy. We next examine the challenges addressed by intimacy regulation sequences, and the role of the partners' respective self-systems in determining how partners will confront those challenges.

CHALLENGE #1: MEETING DISPARATE PARTNER NEEDS FOR INTIMACY AND AUTONOMY

Rhythmic variations in relational intimacy are inevitable because needs for intimacy exist in "dialectical tension" with other needs (Baxter & Simon, 1993, p. 240). Intimacy needs and autonomy needs are often fulfilled through different behaviors and activities (e.g., Larson, 1990): The intimate interactions that meet needs for intimacy do not meet needs for autonomy whereas the pursuit of separate interests, activities, and goals that fulfill autonomy needs do not meet intimacy needs. Nonetheless, healthy adult functioning requires both intimacy and autonomy and neither is optimized without the other (e.g., Bakan, 1966; Blatt & Blass, 1996; Erikson, 1959; Gilligan, 1982; Guisinger & Blatt, 1994; Ryan & Deci, 2000). Intimacy and autonomy are therefore each essential, but dialectically opposed needs of the self-system.

Intimacy regulation sequences, then, can balance the intimacy and autonomy needs of the two partners. Partners who initiate and engage in intimate interactions frequently and who are able to be open with one another, remain positively involved, and maintain a dynamic and accurate perception of each other's true selves should enjoy high levels of relational intimacy. At the same time, intimacy withdrawal and decline sequences provide the space and time for partners to pursue the fulfillment of their individual autonomy needs. Well-functioning couples make continuous dynamic adjustments in their behavior to avoid emphasizing one pole—intimacy or autonomy—at the expense of the other.

Partners with excessively strong autonomy needs may be challenged if they also wish to sustain deep, intimate connections. Individuals whose self-concepts are defined primarily by autonomous pursuits may be so consumed by their autonomy needs that they fail to initiate intimate interactions, are quick to withdraw from them, and frequently decline their partner's initiations. Their relationships may lack intimacy because their autonomous pursuits are all-consuming. However, their less autonomy-motivated partners are likely to be lonely and unfulfilled. This pattern reflects the central dialectical tension Forster presents in *Howard's End*. The drama of the novel lies in the tension created by the opposing ideals of the two families united by Margaret and Henry's marriage. The Schlegels' romantic reverence for personal relations stands in opposition to the Wilcoxes' hard-working, action-oriented determination. Margaret's need "to connect" reflects a need to find regulation and balance between the two extremes.

Although the Schlegels and the Wilcoxes may represent polar extremes, no two partners will find their intimacy and autonomy needs to be perfectly synchronized and all couples will need well-coordinated intimacy regulation sequences to ensure that the intimacy and autonomy needs of both partners are met. Intimacy regulation sequences must accommodate at least two types of individual differences. First, differences in the strength of each partner's needs for intimacy and autonomy, respectively, are addressed by balancing engaging, withdrawing, and declining sequences in order to achieve an optimal balance between intimate interactions and autonomous activity. Second, differences in partner's favored ways of meeting intimacy needs (e.g., he wants more sex, she wants more conversation) are addressed when partners are willing to initiate and reciprocate one another's favored kinds of intimate interactions.

When partners have highly divergent needs for intimacy or autonomy, it is more difficult to develop intimacy regulation sequences that address both partners' needs. For example, Warren brought his wife Wendy to therapy because he frequently felt lonely in their relationship. Warren's loneliness signaled the failure of their intimacy regulation processes to fulfill both of their respective needs for intimacy and autonomy. Further into the interview, Wendy revealed that she rarely initiated intimacy and frequently declined Warren's initiatives, presumably because of her strong needs for autonomy. Wendy was not aware of overtly avoiding intimate relations with Warren; she was simply drawn into finding something "better" to do. However, the failure of the couple's intimacy regulation processes to address Warren's loneliness created additional problems. When Wendy initiated intimacy withdrawal, Warren, aware of his unmet intimacy needs, would angrily resist her withdrawal and blame her for not meeting his needs. Wendy, who felt inadequate because of her inability to meet Warren's needs, responded in a defensively rejecting manner to Warren. Wendy also reported that, as a result of the repetitive nature of these intimacy withdrawal sequences, she now anticipated Warren's negative behavior when he initiated intimate interactions, and found herself declining in the hopes of postponing indefinitely what had become a negative sequence. Warren's and Wendy's dilemma illustrates the crucial importance of effective intimacy regulation sequences in couple relationships, and the vicious cycle than can develop when the sequences are not mutually satisfying.

CHALLENGE #2: MAINTAINING OPENNESS VERSUS PROTECTING THE SELF

Because intimate partners have provided one another with extensive personal, private information about themselves, they are vulnerable to being hurt by the other. A partner who is uninvolved, misunderstands, or misuses personal, private information has the potential to inflict pain on the other. The need to protect the self-system from hurt therefore competes with needs for intimacy when partners have had (or fear) negative, hurtful experiences with one another as a result of their extensive, accumulated knowledge about each other.

Intimate relationship partners risk being hurt in two ways. In the short term, they risk that the partner may show indifference or disapproval in response to their self revealing behaviors, thereby turning a potentially intimate interaction into something else entirely. In the long term, partners may misuse personal, private information they have learned about one another as weapons of criticism, attack, or coercion during conflict. Part of what is destructive about these conflict behaviors is that they attack the self-concept of the partner rather than address the specific problem behaviors (see e.g., Baucom & Epstein, 1990). Partner misuse of personal information may therefore tip the balance in intimacy regulation sequences toward self-protection for one or both partners. If either partner experiences too much hurt as a result of insensitivity or misuse of personal vulnerabilities on the other's part, the couple's intimacy regulation sequences may function to reduce their level of relational intimacy (i.e., partners will engage in few, if any, intimate interactions, withdraw quickly, or decline initiations). This reduction in overall levels of relational intimacy causes further deterioration in the partners' satisfaction with the relationship, and may ultimately lead to its demise.

Summary and Conclusions

E. M. Forster's (1910/1998) ironic challenge to "only connect" reminds us that the highest level of intimacy—deep intimate connection—impels the vital participation of both partners' distinct, individual selves. An integrated model of the self, derived from

Carl Rogers' (1951, 1959) theory and social-cognitive self theory, afforded us insight into the variability in relational intimacy across couples. Specifically, the self-concept offers short-cut interpretations of relationship events, which in turn may either help or hinder partners from developing and maintaining high levels of relational intimacy. Aspects of the self-concept that stem from partners' earlier relationship experiences can also affect intimate relating in unpredictable and seemingly mysterious ways, further complicating the relationship between intimacy and self-concept. In contrast, positive self-regard should, in the main, encourage more extensive sharing of the self; in particular, we note the potentially facilitating effect of a positive body self-concept on gratifying sexual intimacy.

When the organismic self is accessible to awareness and congruent with the self-concept, a unique interactional intimacy becomes possible in which partners can simultaneously offer one another authentic self-revelation, full and uninterrupted positive involvement, and fully accurate mutual understanding. Self-disclosure of organismic experiences brings immediacy to intimate interactions and opens the door to deep, intimate connection.

Our integrated model of self also helps us to articulate the dynamics of intimacy regulation in couple relationships. Day-to-day, intimacy regulation processes determine how often partners engage in intimate interactions, how quickly they withdraw from them, and ultimately, whether each partner's needs for both intimacy and autonomy are met. Because deep intimate connection requires the full participation of two distinct selves, intimate relating must continually be negotiated; partners need to coordinate their different approaches to intimate relating and find balance in their respective yearnings for intimacy and its inherent risks.

To achieve and maintain relational intimacy is not an easy task in the context of a committed couple relationship. In the U.S. today, half of all couples experience marital dissolution and many more experience extended periods of marital distress and conflict. Misunderstandings, unmet needs, and alienation are commonplace. Although the process of achieving relational intimacy is often depicted as a simple algorithm in which layers of an onion are gradually shed to reveal an innermost core that is then known and understood by a partner, this analogy misses the complex interplay of selves that is involved in intimate couple relating. Further understanding of this interplay will allow us to more fully specify the nature of the differences between a low degree of relational intimacy and the highest, or what we have called deep intimate connection. As E. M. Forster (1910/1998) so aptly implied, to "only connect" is as challenging as it is meaningful.

REFERENCES

Allport, G. (1961). *Pattern and growth in personality*. New York: Holt, Rinehart & Winston.

Arndt, J., Schimel, J., Greenberg, J., & Pyszczynski, T. (2002). The intrinsic self and defensiveness: Evidence that activating the intrinsic self reduces self-handicapping and conformity. *Personality and Social Psychology Bulletin, 28*, 671–683.

Aron, A. (2003). Self and close relationships. In M. R. Leary & J. Tangney (Eds.), *Handbook of self and identity* (pp. 442–461). New York: Guilford.

Bakan, D. (1966). *The duality of human existence*. Chicago: Rand McNally.

Baldwin, M. W. (1992). Relational schemas and the processing of social information. *Psychological Bulletin, 112*, 461–484.

Bartholomew, K., & Horowitz, L. (1991). Attachment styles among young adults: A test of a four category model. *Journal of Personality and Social Psychology, 61*, 226–241.

Baucom, D. H., & Epstein, N. (1990). *Cognitive behavioral marital therapy*. New York: Brunner/Mazel.

Baxter, L. A., & Simon, E. P. (1993). Relationship maintenance strategies and dialectical contradictions in personal relationships. *Journal of Social and Personal Relationships, 10*, 225–242.

Benjamin, L. S. (1994). *Interpersonal diagnosis and treatment of personality disorders*. New York: Guilford.

Betcher, R. W. (1981). Intimate play and marital adaptation. *Psychiatry, 44,* 13–33.

Blatt, S. J., & Blass, R. B. (1996). Relatedness and self-definition: A dialectic model of personality develop-ment. In G. G. Noam & K. W. Fischer, (Eds.), *Development and vulnerability in close relationships: The Jean Piaget symposium series.* (pp. 309–338).

Bowen, M. (1966). The use of family therapy in clinical practice. *Comprehensive Psychiatry, 7,* 345–374.

Bowlby, J. (1969). *Attachment and loss, Vol. 1: Attachment.* New York: Basic Books.

Bretherton, I. (1987). New perspectives on attachment relations: Security, communication, and internal working models. In J. D. Osofsky (Ed.), *Handbook of infant development* (pp. 1061–1100). New York: Wiley.

Bretherton, I. (1993). From dialogue to internal working models: The co-construction of self in relationships. *Minnesota Symposia on Child Psychology* (Vol. 26, pp. 237–263).

Christensen, A., & Shenk, J. L. (1991). Communication, conflict, and psychological distance in nondistressed, clinic, and divorcing couples. *Journal of Consulting and Clinical Psychology, 59,* 458–463.

Collins, N. L., & Read, S. J. (1994). Cognitive representations of attachment: The content and function of working models. In K. Bartholomew & D. Perlman (Eds.), *Advances in personal relationships* (Vol. 5, pp. 53–90). London: Jessica Kingsley.

Cross, S. E., Bacon, P. L., & Morris, M. L. (2000). The relational-interdependent self-construal and relation-ships. *Journal of Personality and Social Psychology, 78,* 791–808.

Cross, S. E., & Madson, L. (1997). Models of the self: Self-construals and gender. *Psychological Bulletin, 122,* 5–37.

Csikszentmihalyi, M. (1990). *Flow: The psychology of optimal experience.* New York: Harper & Row.

Deci, E. L., & Ryan, R. M. (1985). *Intrinsic motivation and self-determination in human behavior.* New York: Plenum.

Descutner, C. J., & Thelen, M. H. (1991). Development and validation of a fear-of-intimacy scale. *Psychological Assessment, 3,* 218–225.

Dollard, J., & Miller, N. E. (1950). *Personality and psychotherapy: An analysis in terms of learning, thinking, and culture.* New York: McGraw–Hill.

Doyle, J. A. (1989). *The male experience* (2nd ed.). Dubuque, IA: Brown.

Epstein, S. (1994). Integration of the cognitive and the psychodynamic unconscious. *American Psychologist, 49,* 709–724.

Erikson, E. H. (1959). Identity and the life cycle: Selected papers. *Psychological Issues, 1,* 1–71.

Erikson, E. H. (1963). *Chilhood and Society.* New York: Norton.

Feeney, J. A. (1999). Issues of closeness and distance in dating relationships: Effects of sex and attachment style. *Journal of Social and Personal Relationships, 16,* 571–590.

Firestone, R. W., & Catlett, J. (1999). *Fear of intimacy.* Washington, DC: American Psychological Association.

Fitzpatrick, M. A. (1988). *Between husbands and wives: Communication in marriage.* Newbury Park, CA: Sage.

Forster, E. M. (1910/1998). *Howards end.* New York: Norton (Original work published 1910).

Freud, S. (1938). *The psychopathology of everyday life.* New York: Random House.

Gilligan, C. (1982). *In a different voice.* Cambridge, MA: Harvard University Press.

Goffman, E. (1967). Interaction ritual: Essays on face-to-face behavior. Garden City, NY: Doubleday.

Goldenberg, J. L., McCoy, S. K., Pyszczynski, T., Greenberg, J., & Solomon, S. (2000). The body as a source of self-esteem: The effect of mortality salience on identification with one's body, interest in sex, and appearance monitoring. *Journal of Personality and Social Psychology 79,* 118–130.

Gottman, J. (1993). The roles of conflict engagement, escalation, and avoidance in marital interaction: A longitudinal view of five types of couples. *Journal of Consulting and Clinical Psychology, 61,* 6–15.

Gottman, J. M., & Krokoff, L. J. (1989). Marital interaction and satisfaction: A longitudinal view. *Journal of Consulting and Clinical Psychology, 57,* 47–52.

Greenberg, J. R., & Mitchell, S. A. (1983). *Object relations in psychoanalytic theory.* Cambridge, MA: Harvard University Press.

Greenberg, L. S., & Johnson, S. M. (1988).*Emotionally-focused therapy for couples.* New York: Guilford Press.

Guisinger, S., & Blatt, S. (1994). Individuality and relatedness: Evolution of a fundamental dialectic. *American Psychologist, 49,* 104–111.

Haas, S. M., & Stafford, L. (1998). An initial examination of maintenance behaviors in gay and lesbian relationships. *Journal of Social and Personal Relationships, 15,* 846–855.

Harter, S. (2002). Authenticity. In *The Handbook of Positive Psychology.* C. R. Snyder & S. J. Lopez (Eds.) (pp. 382–394). London: Oxford University Press.

Harter, S. (2003). The development of self-representations during childhood and adolescence. In Leary, M. R. & Tangney, J. P. (Eds.). *Handbook of self and identity,* (pp. 610–642). New York: Guilford Press.

Horney, K. (1939). *New ways in psychoanalysis.* New York: Norton.

Johnson, S. M., & Greenberg, L. S. (1994). Emotion in intimate relationships. In S. M. Johnson & L. S. Greenberg (Eds.), *The heart of the matter: Perspectives on emotion in marital therapy.* (pp. 3–22). New York: Brunner/Mazel.

Jourard, S. (1971). *The transparent self.* New York: Van Nostrand.

Kaplan, H. S. (1974). *The new sex therapy: Active treatment of sexual dysfunctions.* New York: Brunner/Mazel.

Kelly, G. A. (1955). *The psychology of personal constructs.* Norton: New York.

Kihlstrom, J. F., Albright, J. S., Klein, S. B., Cantor, N., Chew, B. R., & Niedenthal, P. M. (1988). Information processing and the study of the self. *Advances in Experimental Social Psychology, 21,* 145–180.

Kihlstrom, J. F., & Cantor, N. (1984). Mental representations of the self. *Advances in Experimental Social Psychology, 17,* 1–47.

Klein, M. (1935). A contribution to the psychogenesis of manic-depressive states. *International Journal of Psycho-Analysis,* 16, 145–174.

Kunce, L. J., & Shaver, P. R. (1994). An attachment-theoretical approach to caregiving in romantic relationships. In K. Bartholomew & D. Perlman (Eds.), *Advances in personal relationships* (Vol. 5, pp. 205–237). London: Kingsley.

Larson, R. W. (1990). The solitary side of life: An examination of the time people spend alone from childhood to old age. *Developmental Review, 10,* 155–183.

Lippert, T., & Prager, K. J. (2001). Daily experiences of intimacy: A study of couples. *Personal Relationships, 8,* 283–298.

Markus, H. (1977). Self-schemata and processing information about the self. *Journal of Personality and Social Psychology, 35,* 63–67.

Markus, H., & Kitayama, S. (1991). Culture and the self: Implications for cognition, emotion, and motivation. *Psychological Review, 98,* 224–253.

Markus, H., & Kunda, Z. (1986). Stability and malleability in the self-concept in the perception of others. *Journal of Personality and Social Psychology, 51,* 858–866.

Markus, H., & Wurf, E. (1987). The dynamic self-concept: A social psychological perspective. *Annual Review of Psychology, 38,* 299–337.

Maslow, A. H. (1968). *Toward a psychology of being* (2nd ed.). New York: D. Van Nostrand.

Mehrabian, A. (1967). Orientation behaviors and nonverbal attitude communication. *Journal of Communication, 17,* 324–332.

Mehrabian, A. (1971). *Silent messages.* Belmont, CA: Wadsworth.

Metz, M. E., & Lutz, G. (1990). Dyadic playfulness differences between sexual and marital therapy couples. *Journal of Psychology and Human Sexuality, 3,* 169–182.

Mikulincer, M., & Nachshon, O. (1991). Attachment styles and patterns of self-disclosure. *Journal of Personality and Social Psychology, 61,* 321–331.

Murray, S., Holmes, J., & Griffin, D. (1996). The benefits of positive illusions: Idealization and the construction of satisfaction in close relationships. *Journal of Personality and Social Psychology, 70,* 79–98.

Neisser, U. (1976). *Cognition and reality: Principles and implications of cognitive psychology.* New York: Freeman.

Oyserman, D., & Markus, H. R. (1993). The sociocultural self. In J. Suls (Ed.), *Psychological perspectives on the self* (pp. 187–220). Hillsdale, NJ: Lawrence Erlbaum Associates.

Patterson, M. L. (1982). A sequential functional model of nonverbal exchange. *Psychological Review, 89,* 231–249.

Peplau, L. A., Hill, C. T., & Rubin, Z. (1993). Sex-role attitudes in dating and marriage: A 15-year followup of the Boston couples study. *Journal of Social Issues, 40,* 31–52.

Perlman, D., & Fehr, B. (1987). The development of intimate relationships. In D. Perlman & S. Duck (Eds.), *Intimate relationships: Development, dynamics, and deterioration* (pp. 13–42). Newbury Park, CA: Sage.

Prager, K. J. (1989). Intimacy status and couple communication. *Journal of Social and Personal Relationships, 6,* 435–449.

Prager, K. J. (1991). Intimacy status and couple conflict resolution. *Journal of Social and Personal Relationships, 8,* 505–526.

Prager, K. J. (1995). *The psychology of intimacy.* New York: Guilford Press.

Prager, K. J. (1999). The intimacy dilemma: A guide for couples therapists. In J. Carlson & L. Sperry (Eds.), *The intimate couple* (pp. 109–157). New York: Brunner/Mazel.

Prager, K. J., & Buhrmester, D. (1998). Intimacy and need fulfillment in couple relationships. *Journal of Social and Personal Relationships, 15,* 435–469.

Raush, H. L., Barry, W. A., Hertel, R. K. & Swain, M. A. (1974). *Communication, conflict and marriage.* San Francisco: Jossey-Bass.

Reis, H. T., Collins, W. A., & Berscheid, E. (2000). The relationship context of human behavior and development. *Psychological Bulletin, 126,* 844–872.

Reis, H. T., & Shaver, P. T. (1988). Intimacy as interpersonal process. In S. Duck (Ed.), *Handbook of personal relationships: Theory, relationships, and interventions* (pp. 367–389). Chichester, England: Wiley.

Roberts, L. J. (2000). Fire and ice in marital communication: Hostile and distancing behaviors as predictors of marital distress. *Journal of Marriage and the Family, 62,* pp. 693–707.

Roberts, L. J., & Greenberg, D. R. (2002). Observational windows to intimacy processes in marriage. In P. Noller & J. Feeny (Eds.), *Understanding marriage: Developments in the study of couple interaction. Advances in Personal Relationships Series* (pp. 118–149). Cambridge, MA: Cambridge University Press.

Roberts, L. J., & Krokoff, L. J. (1990). A time-series analysis of withdrawal, hostility, and displeasure in satisfied and dissatisfied marriages. *Journal of Marriage and the Family, 52,* 95–105.

Rogers, C. (1951). *Client-centered therapy: Its current practice, implications, and theory.* Boston: Houghton Mifflin.

Rogers, C. R. (1959). A theory of therapy, personality and interpersonal relationships, as developed in the client-centered framework. In S. Koch (Ed.), *Psychology: A study of a science* (Vol. 3, pp. 184–526). New York: McGraw Hill.

Ryan, R. M., & Deci, E. L. (2000). Self-determination theory and the facilitation of intrinsic motivation, social development, and well-being. *American Psychologist, 55,* 68–78.

Simpson, J. A. (1990). Influence of attachment styles on romantic relationships. *Journal of Personality and Social Psychology, 62,* 434–446.

Simpson, J. A., Rholes, W. S., & Nelligan, J. S. (1992). Support seeking and support giving within couples in an anxiety-provoking situation: The role of attachment styles. *Journal of Personality and Social Psychology, 62,* 434–446.

Smith, D. A., Vivian, D., & O'Leary, K. D. (1990). Longitudinal prediction of marital discord from premarital expressions of affect. *Journal of Consulting and Clinical Psychology, 58,* 790–798.

Sprecher, S. (1987). The effects of self-disclosure given and received on affection for an intimate partner and stability of the relationship. *Journal of Social and Personal Relationships, 4,* 115–127.

Sullivan, H. S. (1953). *The interpersonal theory of psychiatry.* New York: Norton.

Swann, W. B., Jr., De La Ronde, C., & Hixon, G. (1994). Authenticity and positivity strivings in marriage and courtship. *Journal of Personality and Social Psychology, 66,* 857–869.

Talmadge, L. D., & Dabbs, J. M. (1990). Intimacy, conversational patterns, and concomitant cognitive/emotional processes in couples. *Journal of Social and Clinical Psychology, 9,* 473–488.

Thomas, E. J. (1977). *Marital communication and decision-making: Analysis, assessment, and change.* New York: Free Press.

Waring, E. M., & Patton, D. (1984). Marital intimacy and depression. *British Journal of Psychiatry, 145,* 641–644.

Waterman, A. S. (1993). Two conceptions of happiness: Contrasts of personal expressiveness (eudaimonia) and hedonic enjoyment. *Journal of Personality and Social Psychology, 64,* 678–691.

5

Intimacy as an Interpersonal Process: Current Status and Future Directions

Jean-Philippe Laurenceau
University of Miami

Luis M. Rivera
University of Massachusetts, Amherst

Amy R. Schaffer
University of Miami

Paula R. Pietromonaco
University of Massachusetts, Amherst

INTIMACY AS AN INTERPERSONAL PROCESS: CURRENT STATUS AND FUTURE DIRECTIONS

The need for humans to establish and maintain intimate attachments and connections with others is a central and fundamental human motivation that appears to cut across cultures (Baumeister & Leary, 1995; Ryan & Deci, 2000; Sheldon, Elliot, Kim, & Kasser, 2001). A great deal of research has investigated the role of intimacy in the development and maintenance of interpersonal relationships, and researchers have advanced a variety of definitions and operationalizations of intimacy (e.g., Argyle & Dean, 1965; Chelune, Robinson, & Kommor, 1984; Fisher & Stricker, 1982; Fruzzetti & Jacobson, 1990; Hatfield, 1988; McAdams, 1988; Patterson, 1976, 1982; Schaefer & Olson, 1981; Waring, 1984). These definitions vary greatly and reflect the particular perspective on relationships taken by the particular theorist (Perlman & Fehr, 1987). Although each perspective has demonstrated explanatory power in its own right, theory and research on intimacy has needed a guiding conceptual model (Acitelli & Duck, 1987).

The overarching purpose of this chapter is to evaluate how an emergent interpersonal process model of intimacy (Reis & Patrick, 1996; Reis & Shaver, 1988) might assemble and organize various conceptualizations of intimacy in the field of personal relationships and to consider the utility of this process model for empirical inquiry into mechanisms linked to intimacy. Our specific goals are (a) to review the main components of Reis and Shaver's (1988) model of intimacy as an interpersonal process, (b) to examine existing evidence for the model, and (c) to elaborate on aspects of the interpersonal process model that warrant further theoretical and empirical attention. In particular, we focus on specific individual-difference factors that influence each partner's role in this process, and consider how social-cognitive processes help to clarify the concept of interpretive filters. To accomplish these goals, we draw on work from the many subdisciplines that make up relationship science (e.g., social and personality psychology, communications, sociology) as well as from basic and clinical research on relationship processes. A central assumption of our analysis is that intimacy is a personal, subjective (and often momentary) sense of connectedness that is the outcome of an interpersonal, transactional process consisting of self-disclosure and partner responsiveness.

AN EMERGENT PROCESS MODEL OF INTIMACY

Intimacy is a construct that has been conceptualized in a multitude of ways (Perlman & Fehr, 1987). These various conceptualizations differ on a variety of dimensions related to intimacy, including levels of analysis (e.g., at the level of individuals, at the level of interactions), central components (e.g., disclosure, responsiveness), and temporal aspects (e.g., static vs. process; Acitelli & Duck, 1987). With these varied views, it is understandable that the words intimacy and intimate have been used to refer to persons, interactions, relationships, environments, communications, thoughts, and feelings. Although several conceptualizations in the field of personal relationships have attempted to define and operationalize intimacy, many of these theories have lacked conceptual clarity or completeness. In contrast, the interpersonal-process model of intimacy (Reis & Patrick, 1996; Reis & Shaver, 1988), provides a comprehensive conceptualization of intimacy that encompasses individual, interactional, and relationship qualities, includes multiple components, addresses temporal features, and provides explicit guidelines for operationalizing and measuring intimacy.

Interpersonal Process Model of Intimacy

According to Reis and Shaver (1988), intimacy is an interpersonal, transactional process with two principal components: self-disclosure and partner responsiveness (see Figure 5.1). This process specifically refers to "the sequential unfolding of relevant thoughts, feelings, and behaviors, each of which is influenced by antecedent conditions and anticipated consequences" (Reis & Patrick, 1996, p. 524). Intimacy is initiated when one person communicates personally relevant and revealing information, thoughts, and feelings to another person. Expressions may also be nonverbal in nature, standing as communications in their own right or amplifying verbal disclosures and behaviors (Keeley & Hart, 1994). For the intimacy process to continue, the listener must emit emotions, expressions, and behaviors that are both responsive to the specific content of the disclosure and convey acceptance, validation, and caring for the individual disclosing. For the interaction to be experienced as intimate by the discloser, he or she must subjectively feel understood, validated, and cared for. The interpersonal process model of intimacy consists of various components and aspects that warrant further explanation.

Self-Disclosure. Operationalizations and definitions of intimacy all appear to have at least one aspect in common—a feeling of closeness developing from communication (Perlman & Fehr, 1987). Thus, it is not surprising that self-disclosure has traditionally been considered an important component and index of intimacy.

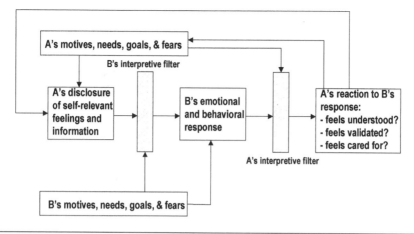

FIG. 5.1. The interpersonal process model of intimacy. *Note.* From *Intimacy as an Interpersonal Process* (p. 375), by H. T. Reis and P. Shaver, 1988, in S. Duck (Ed.), *Handbook of Personal Relationships*, Chichester: Wiley. © John Wiley & Sons Limited. Reproduced with permission.

Self-disclosure refers to the verbal communication of personally relevant information, thoughts, and feelings to another and has been implicated as an important factor in the development of intimacy between individuals (Jourard, 1971; Derlega, Metts, Petronio, & Margulis, 1993). In addition, nonverbal behaviors (e.g., gaze, touch, body orientation) are expressions that can augment and interact with verbal self-disclosures to affect the development of intimacy in a relationship (Patterson, 1984).

Intimacy and self-disclosure are not synonymous constructs, however. Self-disclosure is an important part of the process of engaging in intimate interactions and developing intimate relationships, but does not completely capture the phenomenon of intimacy (Chelune, Robison, & Kommor, 1984; Reis & Patrick, 1996). For example, self-disclosure has been found to account for just below half of the variance in ratings of couples' level of intimacy (Waring & Chelune, 1983). Moreover, disclosure reciprocity plays an important role in the acquaintance process where there is a strong demand for more immediate replies from a partner (Archer, 1987). Nevertheless, immediate reciprocity becomes less important as a relationship progresses, suggesting that other parts of partner responses become more important as relationships grow.

Although self-disclosure is a central component of the model, certain types of self-disclosure may be more related to the experience of intimacy than others. Disclosures have been categorized into one of two types: a) factual or descriptive (i.e., the communication of personal facts and information) and b) emotional or evaluative (i.e., the communication of personal feelings and opinions; Morton, 1978; Reis & Patrick, 1996). Although factual and emotional self-disclosures reveal personal information about oneself, emotional self-disclosures are considered to be more closely related to the experience of intimacy because they allow for the most core aspects of the self to be known, understood, and validated by another (Reis & Patrick, 1996). Furthermore, some researchers (Clark, Fitness, & Brissette, 2001; Johnson, 2000) have asserted that emotional disclosure in close relationships may play a more specific motivational function. As relationships become more communal in orientation (i.e., when each partner feels a sense of mutual responsibility for the other's needs), the expression of emotion serves to communicate needs to significant others as a step in the process of having these needs met (Clark et al., 2001). Therefore, emotional self-disclosures, in comparison to factual disclosures, may more often lead to having one's interpersonal needs met and thereby promote intimacy.

Partner Responsiveness.   Although verbal and nonverbal disclosures are central to the development of intimate relationships, relationship researchers have pointed to another variable, responsiveness, to help explain the development of intimacy in relationships. Miller and Berg (1984) explain that "responsiveness can be viewed as the extent to which and the way in which one participant's actions address the previous actions, communications, needs, or wishes of another participant in that interaction" (p. 191). To contribute to the development of intimacy in a relationship, an individual's responses have to demonstrate concern for the discloser, be sincere and immediate, capture the content of the original communication, and meet the need of the discloser (Berg, 1987). Responsiveness plays an important role in disclosure reciprocity, liking, and closeness in relationships (Berg & Archer, 1982). Researchers have conceptualized responsiveness as a component of the intimacy process whereby a person communicates understanding, validation, and caring in response to a partner's self-disclosure (Reis & Shaver, 1988; Reis & Patrick, 1996).

According to the interpersonal process model, partner responsiveness plays an important mediating role in the development of intimacy between interaction partners. Although responsiveness generally occurs when the listener's communications address the needs, wishes, or actions of the discloser (Berg, 1987; Davis, 1982; Miller & Berg, 1984), the model posits that responsive behaviors and expressions must also convey understanding, validation, and caring towards the disclosing partner (Reis & Patrick, 1996).

Perceptual Filters.   The speaker's perception and judgment of the listener's response as understanding, validating, and caring is an important factor in the experience of intimacy above and beyond the interactants' actual communications. Self-disclosures are thought to contribute to feelings of intimacy because the self is revealed in a way that triggers a partner's reaction that is perceived to be sufficiently responsive. Although a listener's reciprocal disclosure may be a genuine attempt to be understanding, validating, and caring, the speaker may not perceive the response as such. Ultimately, the extent to which a partner's disclosures contribute to feelings of intimacy is largely dependent on the speaker's perceptions of the quality of the partner's response (See Reis, Clark, and Holmes, chap. 12, this volume). In this way, perceptions of partner responsiveness should act as a mediator of the effects of self-disclosure and partner disclosure on intimacy. Moreover, the perceptions that partners have of each others' disclosures can be influenced by a multitude of individual difference factors.

Partner Motives, Needs, Goals, and Fears.   The way in which the process of intimacy unfolds between two partners is greatly influenced by individual differences (Reis & Patrick, 1996). Various classes of dispositional charateristics reflect variation in each partner's motivation, desire, intention, and ability towards engaging in intimate interactions across and within partner, time, and situation. These dispositional characteristics will moderate the degree to and the way in which individuals will self-disclose and respond to partners. For example, expressions on the part of the self-discloser may differ in quality, frequency, and depth, depending on the self-discloser's intentions (e.g., "I have a need to feel connected with my wife right now"). Individuals high in a need for connectedness would be more likely to disclose central aspects of the self and to behave in understanding, validating, and caring ways with partners (McAdams, 1988).

Davis (1982) has identified several dispositional factors that influence responsiveness in dyadic interactions. To begin, attending to a partner when interacting is probably essential for responsiveness to take place. Individual differences in this capacity to attend are reflected in the trait of self-monitoring, such that high self-monitors are likely to be more attentive and to respond more appropriately than are low self-monitors (Shaffer, Smith, & Tomarelli, 1982). A second determinant is communication accuracy, referring to the ability of a partner to decode (i.e., understand) the content expressed by a discloser. The capacity to decode disclosures has been associated with extraversion, self-consciousness, and self-monitoring (Davis, 1982). However, attending to one's partner and accurately decoding disclosures does not guarantee that one possesses the skills to appropriately elaborate a response. For this reason, differences in intelligence, memory, and interpersonal skill may affect response repertoires. Third, individuals will differ in their motivation to maintain responsiveness. Because responsiveness is believed to increase intimacy and social interaction, it is likely that those high in the intimacy motive and extraversion will maintain a higher motivation to be responsive.

Individual difference factors will influence not only self-disclosures and responses to disclosures, but also the interpretation of disclosures and responses from partners. For example, an interaction partner may interpret a self-disclosure (e.g., "It seems like you are spending more time at work lately") as an invitation to experience intimacy, a command to act, or an odd statement, depending on whether the partner seeks connectedness. Differences in the way individuals interpret disclosing and responsive behaviors are captured in the Reis and Shaver (1988) model as the influence of partner motives and needs on interpretive filters. Thus, Partner A may choose to disclose personally relevant information, thoughts, and feelings to Partner B, yet B may interpret this disclosure in a variety of different ways (e.g., as a threat, sexual advance, gesture of friendliness, invitation for intimacy) and the interpretation of the disclosure will influence the degree to which and the way in which B responds. Correspondingly, B may choose to communicate genuine understanding, validation, and caring, yet A may interpret this veridical attempt at responsiveness in a variety of different ways. A's interpretation will influence the degree to which A deems B's behavior as responsive, thus affecting A's feelings of intimacy.

Utility of a Process Model of Intimacy

The interpersonal process model of intimacy is useful for several reasons. First, the model acknowledges that aspects of intimacy reflect a quality of persons and relationships, but it also emphasizes what takes place at the level of specific interactions (Acitelli & Duck, 1987; Berscheid, 1999). Some relationships can be rated as more intimate than others; some individuals have a greater need for intimacy than others. The central characteristic that ties together these levels of analysis is the interaction that reflects engagement in the interpersonal process model. Second, the model conceptualizes intimacy as a dynamic process unfolding over time. This focus mirrors the claim "that relationships themselves are processes, not states, and are made up of several continually interacting components" (Duck & Sants, 1983, p. 28). Although, while stable charateristics may make a relationship intimate, variability exists in the degree of intimacy that is experienced in the moment-to-moment interactions of an intimate relationship. Third, the interpersonal process model posits a theoretical mechanism by which intimacy develops and is influenced by individual difference factors. As a result, the model produces a set of specific, tenable, and testable hypotheses that reflect mediators and moderators of the intimacy process. Fourth, the model acknowledges that intimate relationships consist of repeated intimate interactions over time that contribute to more global evaluations of the quality of the relationship. For example, an individual's interpretation, assimilation, and expectations of repeated intimate interactions give rise to a general judgment about relationships as satisfying, meaningful, and trustworthy (Prager, 1995; Reis, 1994). A methodological implication of the model is that an understanding of the process of intimacy may be informed by assessing self-disclosure and partner responsiveness repeatedly over time within a relationship.

Evidence for the Interpersonal Process Model

Basic Research.   Several empirical studies support central tenets of the interpersonal process model of intimacy. First, the evidence suggests that both self-disclosure and partner responsiveness are implicated in the intimacy process. In an unpublished experience sampling study (Lin, 1992, cited in Reis, 1994; Reis & Patrick, 1996), college students' average ratings of self-disclosure and partner responsiveness predicted the degree to which they reported greater overall relationship intimacy. Interestingly, their ratings of partner responsiveness predicted intimacy ratings to a greater extent than did self-disclosure. Moreover, emotional self-disclosure predicted relationship intimacy, but factual self-disclosure did not.

Two additional experience sampling studies (Laurenceau, Feldman Barrett, & Pietromonaco, 1998) have replicated and extended these findings. Participants reported on a range of interpersonal interactions and social relationships, including those with best friends, romantic partners, parents, siblings, and acquaintances over either a one week (Study 1) or two week (Study 2) period. Both self-disclosure and partner disclosure significantly predicted intimacy on an interaction-by-interaction basis. Furthermore, perceived partner responsiveness emerged as a partial mediator of these effects, suggesting that the effects of disclosures on the experience of intimacy occurred, in part, through perceptions of the partner's responsiveness. In addition, emotional self-disclosures again emerged as a more important predictor of intimacy than disclosures of facts and information.

More recent work has replicated and extended predictions from the Reis and Shaver (1988) interpersonal process model of intimacy using reports of daily interactions from romantic and marital relationships. In a study of 113 romantic, cohabiting couples (Lippert & Prager, 2001), interaction diaries were used to assess intimacy, disclosure of private information, expression of emotion, and perceptions of being understood by one's partner. Ratings of intimacy on an interaction-by-interaction basis were significantly predicted by both disclosures and perceptions of partner understanding. In addition, couples higher in global relationship satisfaction rated their interactions as more intimate. In another study (Laurenceau, Feldman Barrett, & Rovine, 2002), 96 married couples reported levels of self-disclosure, partner disclosure, perceived partner responsiveness, and intimacy across the day's interactions with their partner on each of 42 consecutive days. As predicted from the interpersonal process model, self-disclosure and partner disclosure both significantly and uniquely contributed to the prediction of intimacy, whereas perceived partner responsiveness was a partial mediator of the effects of self-disclosure and partner disclosure on intimacy. Once again, findings suggested that emotional disclosure is a stronger predictor of intimacy than is factual disclosure.

Clinical Research.   Increasing or enhancing intimacy is often one of the central goals of marital or couples-based therapies across several different therapeutic orientations (Dandeneau & Johnson, 1994; Jacobson & Christensen, 1996; Waring, 1988). Not surprisingly, within the field of applied marital research, several findings and observations provide evidence relevant to the interpersonal process model of intimacy.

The importance of both self-disclosure and partner responsiveness to developing a close, satisfying, and intimate relationship has been supported by marital research. Marital researchers have found that dissatisfied couples often invalidate expressed feelings about relationship problems, eroding the impact of positive exchanges (Gottman, 1994). Furthermore, as marriages develop over time, couple communication and relationship satisfaction are influenced more by the disclosure of feelings than by the disclosure of information (Fitzpatrick, 1987). The *speaker–listener technique,* used as a central couples communication exercise in the Prevention and Relationship

Enhancement Program (PREP; Markman, Renick, Floyd, Stanley, & Clements, 1993; Markman, Stanley, & Blumberg, 2001), focuses on the role of self-disclosure and responsiveness in couples communication. The PREP program specifically teaches couples how to express emotions about problems and how to respond to such expressions in a way that promotes understanding and validation, ultimately leading to problem solving and resolution. The "speaker" is given specific directions on how to disclose thoughts and feelings effectively, whereas the "listener" is explicitly told to respond by reflecting the content of the disclosure back to the speaker in order to demonstrate understanding. Moreover, expression of emotions and receiving validation from one's partner have been identified as two significant change processes in couples therapy (Greenberg, James, & Conry, 1988). Behavioral marital therapy, an empirically well-supported form of couples therapy (see Baucom, Shoham, Mueser, Daiuto, & Stickle, 1998), specifically trains couples in the skills of appropriate self-disclosure of thoughts and feelings, as well as listening and validation (Gottman, Notarius, Gonso, & Markman, 1976).

Some clinical researchers have operationalized intimacy on the basis of the observations of behavioral interaction patterns in couples. Although couples who seek marital therapy often describe their relationship problems as an increase in negative sentiment and a loss of closeness or connection, an astute observer will note that indicators of complaints lie in their pattern of behavioral exchanges (Fruzzetti, 1996; Fruzzetti & Jacobson, 1990). From an observational perspective, intimacy may be understood as consisting of arousal-interaction-feedback cycles that result in either conflict escalation/couple disengagement or conflict de-escalation/couple engagement (Fruzzetti & Jacobson, 1990). This conceptualization of intimacy posits the interaction of physiological arousal levels and behavioral interactions that lead to increased positive emotional experience, closeness, and understanding which may become reciprocally reinforcing. If spouses learn that collaborative engagement in couple interactions often leads to conflict resolution and closeness, they may begin to predict that future interactions will likely result in the same outcome which reinforces continued collaborative engagement.

Evaluation.   Taken together, our review of findings from both the basic and applied relationship literatures lends support to aspects of the interpersonal process model. Both self-disclosure and partner responsiveness appear to make important, and independent, contributions to intimacy at an interaction-by-interaction or day-to-day basis. Moreover, disclosures that are evaluative in nature (i.e., emotional disclosures) seem to contribute more to intimacy than disclosures of that are descriptive in nature (i.e., disclosure of facts and information). Finally, perceptions of a partner's responsiveness (particularly in the form of perceived understanding and validation) should mediate the effects of disclosures on intimacy.

Despite the evidence presented, some limitations and gaps warrant further attention. First, research has yet to examine transactional and dynamic aspects of the intimacy process. Partners often play the roles of both discloser and responder over the course of an interaction. In addition, the model posits a feedback loop that suggests the continued experience of intimacy for an undetermined period of time. However, existing work has not yet examined the dynamic way in which interaction partners engage and disengage in the intimacy process. Second, the vast majority of the evidence is based on self-report methods, and as a consequence, the associations are potentially inflated because of shared method variance. Thus, it will be important for further work to incorporate other methods such as behavioral observations. Third, although the model acknowledges that interactions are digested into more general relationship evaluations, we are unaware of findings that speak to the process by which interactions experienced as intimate are aggregated, intepreted, and therefore give rise to broader-level perceptions. Fourth, empirical evidence for the interpersonal process model of intimacy thus far has focused primarily on the components of disclosures, responsiveness, and perceived partner responsiveness. Little work has been directed toward investigating individual differences and social-cognitive factors that influence these components. For example, the role of the perceptual filters have received little attention. An important next step is to examine some of the specific factors that are presumed to influence the disclosure and responsiveness components central to the interpersonal process model of intimacy.

FACTORS INFLUENCING THE INTERPERSONAL PROCESS MODEL OF INTIMACY

In this section, we attempt to expand on the interpersonal process model by (a) examining a select set of individual difference variables including attachment, empathic ability, and gender that might specifically influence components in the intimacy process; and (b) considering how social cognitive processes help to clarify the role of each partner's interpretive filter. We also identify factors, such as expression of emotion, culture, and shared activities, that we believe influence the intimacy process in important ways.

Romantic Attachment

Adult attachment and intimacy are related interpersonal processes (Reis & Patrick, 1996). In adults, attachment style is related to how people experience and regulate their emotions in their interactions with significant others (Pietromonaco & Feldman Barrett, 2000), and may influence how people go about engaging in the process of intimacy.

Attachment style has been associated with patterns of self-disclosure in adults. In a study assessing self-disclosure at a dispositional level (Mikulincer & Nachshon, 1991), secure and anxious-ambivalent participants reported greater self-disclosure than did avoidant participants. In an experience sampling study examining perceptions immediately following social interactions (Tidwell, Reis, & Shaver 1996), individuals with avoidant attachment styles reported less disclosure and intimacy in their interactions with opposite-sex partners than both securely and ambivalently attached individuals. Other work (Pietromonaco & Feldman Barrett, 1997) suggests that anxious-ambivalent (preoccupied) individuals may be more likely to self-disclose and feel intimacy in interactions that are high in conflict than those who are either secure or dismissing-avoidant. Thus, the way that intimacy evolves in a relationship may depend, in part, on the attachment styles of the partners involved.

Using the interpersonal process model of intimacy as a theoretical framework, Schaffer and Laurenceau (2002) examined specific pathways by which attachment anxiety and avoidance might influence responsiveness in everyday interactions between romantic partners. Both partners in 109 committed romantic relationships completed measures of attachment dimensions and reported on the degree to which partner responsiveness was provided and perceived by means of an experience sampling methodology. As predicted, males and females with lower levels of avoidance reported responding more to their partners as well as perceiving more responsiveness from partners in everyday interactions.

In addition, several teams of researchers (Collins & Feeney, 2000; Feeney & Collins, 2001; Fraley & Shaver, 1998; Rholes, Simpson, Orina, & Grich, 2002; Simpson, Rholes, & Nelligan, 1992; see also Collins & Feeney, chap. 10, this volume) have investigated the relationship between adult attachment style/dimensions and a specific form of responsiveness, caregiving, during attachment-related threats. A consistent finding is that more insecurely attached individuals were poorer caregivers than more securely attached individuals according to both objective third party ratings and subjective reports from both participants and their partners. Interestingly, one set of findings (Rholes et al., 2002) indicated that securely attached women were more likely to offer support to their partner if their partner was seeking support and avoidantly attached women were less likely to offer support to their partner regardless of whether the partner was seeking support. However, are responsive behaviors such as caregiving and support relevant only in the presence of a stressor?

We believe that a distinction should be made between responsive behaviors that occur within the context of an attachment-related stressor and responsive behaviors that occur in non-reactive contexts. One of the central goals of the attachment system is to organize resources towards the goal of attaining security. As suggested by Pietromonaco and Feldman Barrett (2000), one of the likely subgoals towards this higher-order goal of security is the experience of intimacy. Nevertheless, social relationships are pursued, developed, and maintained not only because of the support and security that is afforded during times of stress, but also because of the companionship and connection that is experienced during times of relative calm (Rook, 1987). Although several studies have pointed to the influence of attachment style/dimensions on intimacy-related behaviors and emotions when security is threatened, the literature has focused little on whether attachment shows the same influences in more neutral (or positive), relationship contexts. This issue is theoretically important because much of what occurs in the daily ebb and flow of relationships may not occur in the context of acute stressors and threats.

Empathic Ability and Intimacy

Empathic ability may moderate how individuals interpret and respond to a partner's disclosure. Ickes and colleagues (Ickes, 1997; Ickes & Simpson, 1997; Ickes, Stinson, Bissonnette, & Garcia, 1990) have expanded the definition of empathy to include *empathic accuracy*, which is "the degree to which one interactant is able to accurately infer the specific content of another interactant's thoughts and feelings" (p. 731, Ickes et al., 1990). Within the context of the Reis and Shaver (1988) model, empathic ability or accuracy may influence the degree to which individuals correctly interpret another's self-disclosure and, in turn, whether they respond in a way that shows that they understand, care for, and accept their partner.

Although little work has examined the link between empathy and intimacy as a process, we would expect that, in general, partners with high empathic ability may be more likely to engage in intimate transactions that promote understanding, validation, and caring. This prediction is indirectly supported by work showing that greater empathic accuracy is associated with greater satisfaction in marital relationships (Ickes, 1997; Geoff, Fletcher, & Lange, 1997). However, too much empathic accuracy may lead to increased conflict during intimate interactions which, as a result, may lead to relationship dissatisfaction. These detrimental effects may occur when: (a) the partners' emotional and cognitive capacities include irreconcilable differences that must remain unresolved; (b) their empathic accuracy modifies, and even eradicates, illusions that have helped to sustain the relationship (Ickes & Simpson, 1997); and (c) empathic accuracy by one partner is interpreted by the other partner as intrusive, blunt, or crude (Ickes & Simpson, 1997; Sillars, 1985). These findings suggest that accuracy may be avoided under some conditions.

What factors may help to explain how empathic accuracy plays a role in the intimacy process? Research suggests that empathic accuracy may be greater under some conditions. For example, some researchers (Ickes & Simpson, 1997) have outlined how empathic accuracy is managed across threatening versus nonthreatening relationship contexts, such as in laboratory tasks in which partners engage in self-esteem or relationship threatening experiences (e.g., listening to a romantic partner's thoughts and feelings about past romantic relationships or evaluating photos of attractive members of the opposite sex). When people experience threatening situations, they appear to be motivated to engage in empathic inaccuracy as a way of maintaining relationship satisfaction and stability (Simpson, Ickes, & Blackstone, 1995).

The link between empathic ability and intimacy as a transactional process has received little attention. Instead, research has focused primarily on the relation between empathy and relationship quality in general (Ickes, 1997), leaving open many questions about intimacy as a dynamic process. For example, how is empathic accuracy related to partners' interpretations of each other's disclosures and their responsiveness to each other? How might individual differences in empathic accuracy be associated with variability in the development and experience of intimacy? Future investigations addressing questions such as these will help to clarify whether and how empathic ability contributes to the intimacy process.

Perception and the Intimacy Process

Each partner's perceptual processes during interactions can influence their interpretations of disclosures and partner responsiveness (Berscheid, 1994; Fletcher & Fitness, 1996). Reis and colleagues (Reis & Patrick, 1996; Reis & Shaver, 1988) conceptualize the role of social perception in the intimacy process as the "interpretive filters" that individuals use to register and interpret partner interaction behaviors, including the motives and goals that affect the kinds of interpretations and appraisals that are made.

Following from Figure 1, when Partner A initiates an interaction with an emotional and self-revealing disclosure, the way in which Partner B perceives and reacts to A's disclosure is influenced by B's interpretive filter and by the dispositional and contextual factors that affect the filter. Partner B may interpret this disclosure in a variety of different ways (e.g., as a threat, a romantic advance, a gesture of friendliness, or an invitation for intimacy) and the interpretation of the disclosure will influence the degree and manner in which B responds. A, in turn, interprets B's reaction to the disclosure in light of his or her filter. In a situation that promotes intimacy, the intent of A's emotional disclosure is to allow a central aspect of the self to be revealed to B, who interprets the intention and reacts by engaging in behaviors intended to communicate understanding of the disclosure's content, acceptance, and valuing of A's perspective, and caring and affection. For the interaction to be experienced as intimate, A must then come to perceive B's intent to be understanding, validating, and caring.

As with any social interaction process (e.g., Patterson, 1984), the interpersonal process model of intimacy contains several points at which differences in interpersonal perception can influence evaluative appraisals during or immediately following an interaction. Although the literature on interpersonal perception has focused largely on judging global personality traits and dispositions (e.g., Funder, 1995), the focus here is on how perceptions of relationship behaviors correspond to the actual behaviors they are supposed to reflect. An important social-cognitive factor that influences the way in which individuals interpret interpersonal behavior and respond in social situations is one's representations of past relationships. Past experiences will influence the processing of social information and shape expectations about future interactions (Andersen & Berk, 1998; Zajonc & Markus, 1985). These past influences may be captured in the conceptualization of relational schemas that contain scripts for interpersonal interaction and schemas for self and others (Baldwin, 1992; Safran, 1990), internal working models that reflect expectations for partner availablility and accessibility (Bartholomew & Horowitz, 1991; Bowlby, 1973; Hazan & Shaver, 1987), or lay relationship theories that reflect beliefs about how relationships should develop (Fletcher & Thomas, 1996; Knee, 1998).

To what degree do social perceptual processes influence intimacy? A growing body of research is beginning to suggest that some relationship experiences, such as intimacy, may be largely in the eye of the beholder. For example, it is now well known that happily married couples tend to attribute undesired, negative spouse behavior to situational characteristics rather than to specific, dispositional character-istics of the spouse (Bradbury & Fincham, 1990). Work by Murray and colleagues (Murray, Holmes, & Griffin, 1996a; Murray & Holmes, 1997; Murray, Holmes, & Griffin, 1996b) points to the biases that romantic couples use in the service of main-taining a positive spin in the face of partner/relationship shortcomings (positive illu-sions). Members of committed, romantic relationships are biased toward maintaining positive relationship perceptions and are likely to focus and attend to positive infor-mation, and even reinterpret undesirable information in a more positive or benign way (Murray & Holmes, 1993). Nevertheless, findings such as these have raised the following question: To what degree are perceptions of behaviors, actual behaviors, or both, related to relationship experiences such as intimacy (Reis & Downey, 1999)? The likely answer is both: Perceptions between relationship partners simultaneously reflect accuracy and bias (Kenny & Acitelli, 2001; Murray, Rose, Bellavia, Holmes, & Kusche, 2002). Relationship perceptions are neither correct nor incorrect, but re-flect a constructed social reality between partners. Findings from Laurenceau et al. (2002) revealed that although actual and perceived partner disclosures were only moderately related to each other, both actual and perceived behaviors contributed to the experience of intimacy, suggesting that perceptions alone do not solely drive the intimacy process.

Little work has explored the interpretive filter component of the intimacy process. How is it that one partner's behaviors and expressions intended to reflect engagement in the intimacy process do not match the impact that is made on the other partner? How do partner responses and relationship expectations and beliefs interact to contribute to perceived partner responsiveness? Future investigations will need to address this gap in the literature by examining the connection between social cognitive processes and the development of intimacy.

The Role of Gender in Intimacy

Within the Reis and Shaver (1988) model, gender socialization might influence the intimacy process at the level of motives, needs, goals, and fears about intimacy as well as at the interpretive phase. For example, women tend to focus on interpersonal connections to a greater extent than do men (Cross & Madson, 1997), and therefore they may be more likely to perceive that partner disclosures are relevant to the development and maintenance of intimacy.

The empirical literature suggests a more complex picture. Women experience greater intimacy related behaviors and feelings than do men, but only under some conditions (for reviews see Dindia & Allen, 1992; Reis, 1998). For example, women are more likely than men to disclose personal information to a stranger (Dindia & Allen, 1992). Furthermore, a meta-analysis of eight studies (Reis, 1998) showed that, when interacting with same-sex partners, women evidenced greater intimacy than did men. Nevertheless, the same meta-analysis (Reis, 1998) found that, when interacting with opposite-sex partners, men and women appeared to show little or no difference in disclosing their personal information. Thus, when intimacy is assessed by means of disclosures, men and women may be most likely to differ when they interact with same-sex others.

Only two studies have investigated gender differences in intimacy within the specific framework of the Reis and Shaver (1988) model, but they provide initial evidence that men and women may focus on different components when judging relationship intimacy. In a diary study in which married couples reported on their experiences with their partner for 42 days (Laurenceau, et al., 2002), wives reported greater average levels of self-disclosure (on the basis of both husband and wife reports) but ratings of perceived partner responsiveness and intimacy showed little or no difference between husbands and wives. Nevertheless, when the authors examined the predictors of intimacy, perceptions of the partner's responsiveness more strongly predicted intimacy for wives than for husbands. In contrast, self-disclosure more strongly predicted intimacy for husbands than for wives. These findings suggest that, for women, the development of intimacy may depend more heavily on their interpretation of the partner's responses (i.e., what is happening within the interpretive filter), whereas, for men, intimacy may be more tied to whether they express their own thoughts and feelings. Interestingly, for both men and women, perceptions of intimacy are connected to the male partner's behavior or to the perception of his behavior. This pattern invites further work investigating the relative weight of men's versus women's behaviors in the intimacy process.

Another study of gender differences within the Reis and Shaver framework focused on same-sex friendships (Grabill & Kerns, 2000). Friends engaged in a conversation, which judges later coded for self-disclosure and responsiveness. Female friends were more likely than male friends to disclose, to be responsive, and to feel validated and understood. These findings extend work (Reis, 1998) showing that women evidence greater intimacy in their same-sex friendships than do men by documenting actual behavioral differences in the intimacy process.

The intimacy patterns for men and women reported so far are based on North American populations, but because gender socialization practices vary from culture to culture, gender differences in intimate interaction processes may vary as well. For example, some work (Reis, 1998) suggests that men and women differ (in ways noted previously) in their same-sex intimacy interactions in countries like the United States and Germany, but not in non-Western countries such as Jordan and Hong Kong. However, intimacy in opposite-sex interactions, as reported by both men and women, do not differ significantly across these countries. The next step should be to investigate potential mediating factors that might vary across cultures, such as people's perceptions of masculinity and femininity and attitudes toward traditional gender roles, to gain a more comprehensive understanding of the link between gender and intimacy processes.

Taken together, the research suggests that the effects of gender vary with situational context (e.g., interaction partner, relationship type) and cultural context (e.g., Western versus non-Western countries). However, it is likely that men and women have equal capacities to experience intimacy (Reis, Senchak, & Solomon, 1985; Shaffer & Ogden, 1986) if their socialization processes are the same. Thus, differences between men and women may be more likely to arise in the way in which they establish and experience intimacy than in the degree to which they report intimacy (Laurenceau et al., 2002).

Role of Shared Activities

Models of intimacy typically have focused almost exclusively on verbal and nonverbal expressions (i.e., self-disclosure, gaze, touch) that initiate intimacy processes. Other forms of nonverbal communication, however, may also serve to launch and maintain intimacy processes. For example, one group of researchers (Berscheid, Snyder, & Omoto, 1989) has emphasized the number of different shared activities (i.e., specific behaviors that partners engage in together) that promote closeness between partners. In order to assess shared activities, Berscheid and colleagues developed the relationship closeness inventory (RCI) which surveyed specific activities such as doing laundry together, going to a restaurant, and going dancing. Overall, the amount of time spent engaging in activities together demonstrates a significant positive association with perceived relationship quality and intimacy (Hill, 1988).

All shared activities, however, may not have equivalent effects on feelings of intimacy or closeness. Aron and colleagues (Aron, Norman, & Aron, 2001) have developed converging evidence that novel and arousing shared couple activities, in particular, lead to self-expansion (increases in self-efficacy by including the other in the self) above and beyond the positivity or amount of shared activities (Aron, Norman, & Aron, 2001). A series of studies (Aron, Norman, Aron, McKenna, Heyman, 2000) has shown that couple members who engage together in self-expanding activities experience increased relationship satisfaction. These findings also have been replicated in a field study (Reissman, Aron, & Bergen, 1993) in which married couples who engaged in self-expanding activities reported more relationship satisfaction than did couples who engaged in merely pleasurable activities.

Aron and colleagues hypothesize that self-expanding (i.e., novel and arousing) activities lead to increased relationship quality because they provide opportunities for the members of the couple to increase self-efficacy and self-knowledge by accessing the partner's resources, perspectives, and identities. In addition to being arousing, novel activities also have the potential to generate a greater degree of vulnerability than more commonplace ones. For example, a novel activity, such as engaging in a wheel-barrel contest with your partner or going out salsa dancing for the first time, puts partners in a situation where each are revealing aspects of the self (verbally and nonverbally) that may not be expected or controllable. For example, a couple (Anna and Bob) may enroll in dancing lessons. At their first session, Bob may not know what to expect, and he may feel tentative and awkward, and his body language may indicate his insecurities (e.g., he may constantly look at his feet). In a sense, Bob is providing a nonverbal disclosure to his partner. Anna may try to reassure Bob in nonverbal rather than verbal terms, for example, by providing a physical response to Bob (e.g., she might smile or squeeze his hand reassuringly). If Bob perceives her behavior in the mutually shared activity as caring, validating and understanding, he will likely experience increased intimacy, just as a verbal interaction would in the interpersonal process model. Although this process is likely to be more strongly linked to intimacy in initially developing relationships, people in longer-term relationships also may capitalize on this effect by continuing to engage regularly in shared novel, arousing, and self-revealing activities.

FUTURE DIRECTIONS FOR THEORY AND RESEARCH

Emotional Expression and Intimacy

Although research on the interpersonal process model has generally supported the contribution of emotional disclosures to the experience of intimacy, it is doubtful whether all emotion revealed to partners is associated with increases in intimacy. Not surprisingly, most conceptions of intimacy focus on the presence of frequent and intense positive emotion with a relative absence of negative emotion (Berscheid, 1983). However, the detrimental effects of particular negative emotions on adaptive relationship functioning have been identified. For example, research has indicated that the expression of "noxious" negative emotions such as belligerence and contempt, particularly when directed against a relationship partner, is associated with partner withdrawal and defensiveness and is often the beginning of a cascade toward dissatisfaction (Gottman, 1994). Nevertheless, the expression of other types of negative emotion, such as sadness, hurt, and vulnerability, have been observed to promote increases in closeness and intimacy (Sloan & L'Abate, 1985). When emotion is experienced and expressed to a responsive partner, it often evokes predictable responses and can be used as a means of having relationship needs met. For example, a spouse's expression of anger, fear, and sadness may indicate that intimacy needs are not being met by the partner (Clark et al., 2001; Kobak, Ruckdeschel, & Hazan, 1994). If the partner can respond to this expression of negative affect in a way that addresses the other person's underlying needs, feelings of intimacy may ultimately be increased. The role of specific emotions, and the conditions under which they facilitate versus hinder intimacy, is an aspect of the intimacy process that warrants further attention.

Culture and Conceptions of Intimacy

The lion's share of the intimacy literature is based on Western partners in relationships. It is likely that the interpersonal process model of intimacy will need to be extended when applied to relationship partners from diverse cultures. Current conceptions of intimacy that emphasize mutual self-expression and feeling responded to by one's partner may not necessarily be culturally universal because of differences in collectivism–individualism. Approximately two-thirds of the world's population live in collectivist countries where focusing on the other's needs and playing expected social roles are major central norms (Triandis, 1995). In collectivist cultures, intimacy, connectedness, and belongingness may be better predicted by partners' perceptions that they are correctly anticipating their partner's needs and that they are fulfilling their role in the relationship (Markus & Kitayama, 1991). In contrast to whether one feels responded to by one's partner, an alternative view consistent with both collectivist and individualist views may place greater importance on the role of relationship goals.

Relationship researchers (e.g., Gable & Reis, 2001; Fincham & Beach, 1999) are beginning to invoke goal-related concepts to understand relationship processes, and a goal theoretic framework may guide a culturally diverse conceptualization of intimacy. As foreshadowed by Aristotle in *Nichomachean Ethics*, when partners identify shared values, transform these shared values into shared goals, and work together towards those goals, they likely experience a sense of connectedness and intimacy. The specific values that partners come to share and develop into goals are influenced by their individual and shared cultural contexts. Thus, a pancultural conception of intimacy may be thought of as a by-product of partners' joint pursuit of mutually shared relationship goals (Fowers, 2001). Important work for the future will be examining the generalizability of the interpersonal process model of intimacy in relationship partners who come from diverse cultural backgrounds and determining which components may need to be broadened or reconceptualized. For example, partners from individualist cultures may focus on asking, "do I feel that my partner understands, validates, and cares for me?", whereas partner's from collectivist cultures may focus on asking, "do I feel that I am understanding, validating, and caring for my partner?"

CONCLUSION

We believe that the conceptualization of intimacy as an interpersonal process provides a rich framework from which to understand and investigate the development of intimacy in relationships. The empirical work we have reviewed largely supports central components of the model as well as targets some factors that influence these components. Nevertheless, several gaps exist in knowledge about intimacy related processes and we have suggested some directions and questions that may serve to guide continued work in this area. Continuing to identify the mediators, moderators, and contexts that influence how intimacy develops will contribute to a deepening understanding of this most fundamental of human experiences.

ACKNOWLEDGMENTS

We are thankful to Art Aron, Bill Ickes, Deb Mashek, and Harry Reis for their valuable comments and suggestions on earlier versions of this chapter. Preparation of this chapter was facilitiated by National Institute of Mental Health Scientist Development Award (1K01MH064779-01A1) to Jean-Philippe Laurenceau.

REFERENCES

Acitelli, L. K., & Duck, S. (1987). Intimacy as the proverbial elephant. In D. Perlman & S. Duck (Eds.), *Intimate relationships: Development, dynamics, and deterioration* (pp. 297–308). Newbury Park, CA: Sage.

Andersen, S. M., & Berk, M. S. (1998). The social-cognitive model of transference: Experiencing past relationships in the present. *Current Directions in Psychological Science, 7*, 109–115.

Archer, R. L. (1987). Self-disclosure: A very useful behavior. In V. J. Derlega & J. H. Berg (Eds.), *Self-disclosure: Theory, research, and therapy* (pp. 329–342). New York: Plenum.

Argyle, M., & Dean, J. (1965). Eye contact, distance, and affiliation. *Sociometry, 28*, 289–304.

Aron, A., Norman, C. C., & Aron, E. N. (2001). Shared self-expanding activities as a means of maintaining and enhancing close romantic relationships. In J. H. Harvey & A. E. Wenzel (Eds.), *Close romantic relationships: Maintenance and enhancement* (pp. 47–66). Mahwah, NJ: Lawrence Erlbaum Associates.

Aron, A., Norman, C. C., Aron, E. N., McKenna, C., & Heyman, R. E. (2000). Couples' shared participation in novel and arousing activities and experienced relationship quality. *Journal of Personality and Social Psychology, 78*, 273–284.

Baucom, D. H., Shoham, V., Mueser, K. T., Daiuto, A. D., & Stickle, T. R. (1998). Empirically supported couple and family interventions for marital distress and adult mental health problems. *Journal of Consulting and Clinical Psychology, 66*, 53–58.

Baumeister, R. F., & Leary, M. R. (1995). The need to belong: Desire for interpersonal attachments as a fundamental human motivation. *Psychological Bulletin, 117*, 497–529.

Bartholomew, K., & Horowitz, L. M. (1991). Attachment styles among young adults: A test of a four-category model. *Journal of Personality and Social Psychology, 61*, 226–244.

Berg, J. H. (1987). Responsiveness and self-disclosure. In V. J. Derlega & J. H. Berg (Eds.), *Self-disclosure: Theory, research, and therapy* (pp. 101–130). New York: Plenum.

Berg, J. H., & Archer, R. L. (1982). Responses to self-disclosure and interaction goals. *Journal of Experimental Social Psychology, 18*, 501–512.

Berscheid, E. (1983). Emotion. In H. H. Kelley, E. Berscheid, A. Christensen, J. H. Harvey, T. L. Huston, G. Levinger, E. McClintock, L. A. Peplau, & D. R. Peterson, *Close relationships* (pp. 110–168). New York: Freeman.

Berscheid, E. (1994). Interpersonal relationships. *Annual Review of Psychology, 45*, 79–129.

Berscheid, E. (1999). The greening of relationship science. *American Psychologist, 54*, 260–266.

Berscheid, E., Snyder, M., & Omoto, A. M. (1989). The Relationship closeness inventory: Assessing the closeness of intepersonal relationships. *Journal of Personality and Social Psychology, 57*, 792–807.

Bowlby, J. (1973). *Attachment and loss: Vol. 2. Separation: Anxiety and anger.* New York: Basic Books.

Bradbury, T., & Fincham, F. (1990). Attribution in marriage: Review and critique. *Psychological Bulletin, 107*, 3–33.

Chelune, G. J., Robinson, J. T., & Kommor, M. J. (1984). A cognitive interactional model of intimate relationships. In V. J. Derlega (Ed.), *Communication, intimacy, and close relationships.* New York: Academic Press.

Clark, M. S., Fitness, J., & Brissette, I. (2001). Understanding people's perceptions of relationships is crucial to understanding their emotional lives. In G. J. Fletcher & M. S. Clark (Eds.), *Blackwell handbook of social psychology: Interpersonal processes* (pp. 253–278). Oxford, England: Blackwell.

Collins, N. L., & Feeney, B. C. (2000). A safe haven: An attachment theory perspective on support seeking and caregiving in intimate relationships. *Journal of Personality and Social Psychology, 78*, 1053–1073.

Cross, S. E., & Madson, L. (1997). Models of the self: Self-construals and gender. *Psychological Bulletin, 122*, 5–37.

Dandeneau, M. L., & Johnson, S. M. (1994). Facilitating intimacy: Interventions and effects. *Journal of Marital and Family Therapy, 20*, 17–33.

Davis, D. (1982). Determinants of responsiveness in dyadic interaction. In W. I. Ickes & E. S. Knowles (Eds.), *Personality, roles, and social behaviors* (pp. 85–139). New York: Springer-Verlag.

Derlega, V. J., Metts, S., Petronio, S., & Margulis, S. (1993). *Self-Disclosure*. Newbury Park, CA: Sage.

Dindia, K., & Allen, M. (1992). Sex differences in self-disclosure: A meta-analysis. *Psychological Bulletin, 112*, 106–124.

Duck, S., & Sants, H. K. (1983). On the origins of the specious: Are personal relationships really interpersonal states? *Journal of Clinical and Social Psychology, 1*, 27–41.

Feeney, B. C., & Collins, N. L. (2001). Predictors of caregiving in adult intimate relationships: An attachment theoretical perspective. *Journal of Personality and Social Psychology, 80*, 972–994.

Fincham, F. D., & Beach, S. R. H. (1999). Conflict in marriage: Implications for working with couples. *Annual Review of Psychology, 50*, 47–77.

Fisher, M., & Stricker, G. (1982). *Intimacy*. New York: Plenum.

Fitzpatrick, M. A. (1987). Marriage and verbal intimacy. In V. J. Derlega & J. Berg (Eds.), *Self-disclosure: Theory, Research, and Therapy* (pp. 131–154). New York: Plenum.

Fletcher, G. J., & Fitness, J. (1996). *Knowledge structures in close relationships: A social psychological approach*. Hillsdale, NJ: Lawrence Erlbaum Associates.

Fletcher, G. J., & Thomas, G. (1996). Close relationship lay theories: Their structure and function. In G. J. Fletcher & J. Fitness (Eds.), *Knowledge structures in close relationships: A social psychological approach* (pp. 3–24). Hillsdale, NJ: Lawrence Erlbaum Associates.

Fowers, B. J. (2001). The limits of a technical concept of a good marriage: Exploring the role of virtue in communication skills. *Journal of Marital and Family Therapy, 27*, 327–340.

Fraley, C., & Shaver, P. (1998). Airport separations: A naturalistic study of adult attachment dynamics in separating couples. *Journal of Personality and Social Psychology, 75*, 1198–1212.

Fruzzetti, A. E. (1996). Causes and consequences: Individual distress in the context of couple interactions. *Journal of Consulting and Clinical Psychology, 64*, 1192–1201.

Fruzzetti, A. E., & Jacobson, N. S. (1990). Toward a behavioral conceptualization of adult intimacy: Implications for marital therapy. In E. A. Blechman (Ed.), *Emotions and the family: For better or for worse* (pp. 117–135). Hillsdale, NJ: Lawrence Erlbaum Associates.

Gable, S. L., & Reis, H. T. (2001). Appetitive and aversive social interaction. In J. Harvey & A. Wenzel (Eds.), *Close romantic relationships: Maintenance and enhancement* (pp. 169–194). Mahwah, NJ: Lawrence Erlbaum Associates.

Geoff, T., Fletcher, G. J. O., & Lange, C. (1997). On-line empathic accuracy in marital interaction. *Journal of Personality and Social Psychology, 72*, 839–850.

Gottman, J. M. (1994). *What predicts divorce: The relationship between marital processes and marital outcomes*. Hillsdale, NJ: Lawrence Erlbaum Associates.

Gottman, J. M., Notarius, C., Gonso, J., & Markman, H. J. (1976). *A couple's guide to communication*. Champaign, IL: Research Press.

Grabill, C. M., & Kerns, K. A. (2000). Attachment style and intimacy in friendship. *Personal Relationships, 7*, 363–378.

Greenberg, L. S., James, P., & Conry, R. (1988). Perceived change processes in emotionally focused couples therapy. *Family Psychology. 2*, 4–23.

Hatfield, E. (1988). Passionate and companionate love. In R. J. Sternberg & M. L. Barnes (Eds.), *The psychology of love* (pp. 191–217). New Haven, CT: Yale University Press.

Hazan, C., & Shaver, P. (1987). Romantic love conceptualized as an attachment process. *Journal of Personality and Social Psychology. 52*, 511–524.

Hill, M. S. (1988). Marital stability and spouses' shared time: A multidisciplinary hypothesis. *Journal of Family Issues, 9*, 427–451.

Ickes, W. (1997). *Empathic accuracy*. New York: Guilford.

Ickes, W., Gesn, P. R., & Graham, T. (2000). Gender differences in empathic accuracy: Differential ability or differential motivation? *Personal Relationships, 7*, 95–109.

Ickes, W., & Simpson, J. A. (1997). Managing empathic accuracy in close relationships. In W. Ickes (Ed.), *Empathic accuracy* (pp. 218–250). New York: Guildford.

Ickes, W., Stinson, L., Bissonmette, V., & Garcia, S. (1990). Naturalistic social cognition: Empathic accuracy in mixed-sex dyads. *Journal of Personality and Social Psychology, 39*, 730–742.

Jacobson, N. S., & Christensen, A. (1996). *Integrative couple therapy: Promoting acceptance and change*. New York: Norton.

Johnson, S. M. (2000). Emotionally focused couples therapy. In F. M. Dattilio & L. J. Bevilacqua (Eds.), *Comparative treatments for relationship dysfunction* (pp. 163–185). New York: Springer.

Jourard, S. M. (1971). *Self-disclosure: An experimental analysis of the transparent self*. New York: Wiley.

Keeley, M. P., & Hart, A. J. (1994). Nonverbal behavior in dyadic interactions. In S. Duck (Ed.), *Dynamics of relationships* (pp. 135–179). Thousand Oaks, CA: Sage.

Kenny, D. A., & Acitelli, L. K. (2001). Accuracy and bias in the perception of the partner in a close relationship. *Journal of Personality & Social Psychology, 80*, 439–448.

Knee, C. R. (1998). Implicit theories of relationships: Assessment and prediction of romantic relationship initiation, coping, and longevity. *Journal of Personality and Social Psychology, 74*, 360–370.

Kobak, R., Ruckdeschel, K., & Hazan, C. (1994). From symptom to signal: An attachment view of emotion in marital therapy. In S. M. Johnson & L. S. Greenberg (Eds.), *The heart of the matter: Perspectives on emotion in marital therapy* (pp. 46–71). New York: Bruner/Mazel.

Laurenceau, J.-P., Feldman Barrett, L., & Pietromonaco, P. R. (1998). Intimacy as an interpersonal process: The importance of self-disclosure, and perceived partner responsiveness in interpersonal exchanges. *Journal of Personality and Social Psychology, 74,* 1238–1251.

Laurenceau, J.-P., Feldman Barrett, L., Rovine, M. J. (2002). *Intimacy in marriage: A daily-diary and multilevel modeling approach.* Manuscript submitted for review.

Lin, Y.-C. (1992). *The construction of the sense of intimacy from everyday social interaction.* Unpublished doctoral dissertation, University of Rochester, Rochester, New York.

Lippert, T., & Prager, K. J. (2001). Daily experiences of intimacy: A study of couples. *Personal Relationships, 8,* 283–298.

Markman, H. J., Renick, M. J., Floyd, F. J., Stanley, S. M., & Clements, M. L.(1993). Preventing marital distress through communication and conflict management training: A 4–5-year follow-up. *Journal of Consulting & Clinical Psychology, 61,* 70–77.

Markman, H. J., Stanley, S. M., & Blumberg, S. (2001). *Fighting for your marriage: Positive steps for preventing divorce and preserving a lasting love, new and revised.* San Francisco: Jossey-Bass.

Markus, H., & Kitayama, S. (1991). Culture and the self: Implications for cognition, emotion, and motivation. *Psychological Review, 98,* 224–253.

McAdams, D. P. (1988). Personal needs and personal relationships. In S. Duck (Ed.), *Handbook of personal relationships* (pp. 7–22). Chichester, England: Wiley.

Mikulincer, M., & Nachshon, O. (1991). Attachment styles and patterns of self-disclosure. *Journal of Personality and Social Psychology, 61,* 321–331.

Miller, L. C., & Berg, J. H. (1984). Selectivity and urgency in interpersonal exchange. In V. J. Derlega (Ed.), *Communication, intimacy, and close relationships* (pp. 262–206). New York: Academic Press.

Morton, T. L. (1978). Intimacy and reciprocity of exchange: A comparison of spouses and strangers. *Journal of Personality and Social Psychology, 36,* 72–81.

Murray, S. L., & Holmes, J. G. (1993). Seeing virtues in faults: Negativity and the transformation of interpersonal narratives in close relationships. *Journal of Personality and Social Psychology, 65,* 707–722.

Murray, S. L., & Holmes, J. G. (1997). A leap of faith? Positive illusions in romantic relationships. *Personality and Social Psychology Bulletin, 23,* 586–604.

Murray, S. L., Holmes, J. G., & Griffin, D. (1996a). The benefits of positive illusions: Idealization and the construction of satisfaction in close relationships. *Journal of Personality and Social Psychology, 70,* 79–98.

Murray, S. L., Holmes, J. G., & Griffin, D. (1996b). The self-fulfilling nature of positive illusions in romantic relationships: Love is not blind, but prescient. *Journal of Personality and Social Psychology, 71,* 1155–1180.

Murray, S. L., Rose, P., Bellavia, G., Holmes, J., & Kusche, A. (2002). When rejection stings: How self-esteem constrains relationship-enhancement processes. *Journal of Personality and Social Psychology, 83,* 556–573.

Patterson, M. L. (1976). An arousal model of interpersonal intimacy. *Psychological Review, 83,* 235–245.

Patterson, M. L. (1982). A sequential model of nonverbal exchange. *Psychological Review, 89,* 231–249.

Patterson, M. L. (1984). Intimacy, social control, and nonverbal involvement: A functional approach. In V. J. Derlega (Ed.), *Communication, intimacy, and close relationships* (pp. 105–132). New York: Academic Press.

Perlman, D., & Fehr, B. (1987). The development of intimate relationships. In D. Perlman and S. Duck. *Intimate Relationships: Development, dynamics and deterioration* (pp. 13–42). Thousand Oaks, CA: Sage.

Pietromonaco, P. R., & Feldman Barrett, L. (1997). Working models of attachment and daily social interactions. *Journal of Personality and Social Psychology, 73,* 1409–1423.

Pietromonaco, P. R., & Feldman Barrett, L. (2000). The internal working models concept: What do we really know about the self in relation to others? *Review of General Psychology, 4,* 155–175.

Prager, K. J. (1995). *The psychology of intimacy.* New York, Guilford.

Reis, H. T. (1994). Domains of experience: Investigating relationship processes from three perspectives. In R. Erber & R. Gilmour (Eds.), *Theoretical frameworks for personal relationships* (pp. 87–110). Hillsdale, NJ: Lawrence Erlbaum Associates.

Reis, H. T. (1998). Gender differences in intimacy and related behaviors: Context and process. In D. J. Canary & K. Dindia (Eds.), *Sex differences and similarities in communication: Critical essays and empirical investigations of sex and gender in interaction* (pp. 203–231). Mahwah, NJ: Lawrence Erlbaum Associates.

Reis, H. T., & Downey, G. (1999). Social Cognition in relationships: Building essential bridges between two literatures. *Social Cognition, 17,* 97–117.

Reis, H. T., & Patrick, B. C. (1996). Attachment and Intimacy: Component Processes. In E. T. Higgins & A. W. Kruglanski (Eds.), *Social psychology: Handbook of basic principles* (pp. 523–563). New York: Guilford.

Reis, H. T., Senchank, M., & Solomon, B. (1985). Sex differences in the intimacy of social interaction: Further examination of potential explanations. *Journal of Personality and Social Psychology, 48,* 1204–1217.

Reis, H. T., & Shaver, P. (1988). Intimacy as an interpersonal process. In S. Duck (Ed.), *Handbook of personal relationships* (pp. 367–389). Chichester, England: Wiley.

Reissman, C., Aron, A., & Bergen, M. R. (1993). Shared activities and marital satisfaction: Causal direction and self-expansion versus boredom. *Journal of Social and Personal Relationships, 10,* 243–254.

Rholes, S. W., Simpson, J. A., Orina, M. M., & Grich, J. (2002). Working models of attachment, support giving, and support seeking in a stressful situation. *Journal of Personality and Social Psychology, 28,* 598–608.

Rook, K. S. (1987). Social support versus companionship: Effects on life stress, loneliness, and evaluations by others. *Journal of Personality and Social Psychology, 52,* 1132–1147.

Ryan, R. M., & Deci, E. L. (2000). Self-determination theory and the facilitation of intrinsic motivation, social development, and well-being. *American Psychologist, 55,* 68–78.

Schaefer, M. T., & Olson, D. H. (1981). Assessing intimacy: The PAIR inventory. *Journal of Marital and Family Therapy, 7,* 47–60.

Schaffer, A., & Laurenceau, J.-P. (2002). *Responding to a romantic partner and perceptions of partner responsiveness in everyday interactions: The influence of adult attachment.* Manuscript submitted for review.

Shaffer, D. R., & Ogden, J. K. (1986). On sex differences in self-disclosure during the acquaintance process; The role of anticipated future interaction. *Journal of Personality and Social Psychology, 51,* 92–101.

Shaffer, D. R., Smith, J., & Tomarelli, M. M. (1982). Self-monitoring as a determinant of self-disclosure reciprocity during the acquaintance process. *Journal of Personality and Social Psychology, 43,* 163–175.

Sheldon, K. M., Elliot, A. J., Kim, Y., & Kasser, T. (2001). What is satisfying about satisfying events? Testing 10 candidate psychological needs. *Journal of Personality & Social Psychology, 80,* 325–339.

Sillars, A. L. (1985). Interpersonal perception in relationships. In W. Ickes (Ed.), *Compatible and incompatible relationships* (pp. 277–305). New York: Springer-Verlag.

Simpson, J. A., Ickes, W., & Blackstone, T. (1995). When the head protects the heart: Empathic accuracy in dating relationships. *Journal of Personality and Social Psychology, 69,* pp. 629–641.

Simpson, J. A., Rholes, W. S., & Nelligan, J. S. (1992). Support seeking and support giving within couples in an anxiety-provoking situation. *Journal of Personality and Social Psychology, 62,* 434–446.

Sloan, S. Z., & L'Abate, L. (1985). Intimacy. In L. L'Abate (Ed.), *The handbook of family psychology and therapy* (pp. 405–427). Homewood, IL: Dorsey Press.

Tidwell, M., Reis, H. T., & Shaver, P. R. (1996). Attachment, attractiveness, and daily social interactions: A diary study. *Journal of Personality and Social Psychology, 71,* 729–745.

Triandis, H. C. (1995). *Individualism and collectivism.* Boulder, CO: Westview Press.

Waring, E. M. (1984). The measurement of marital intimacy. *Journal of Marital and Family Therapy, 10,* 185–192.

Waring, E. M. (1988). *Enhancing marital intimacy through cognitive self-disclosure.* New York: Brunner/Mazel.

Waring, E. M., & Chelune, G. J. (1983). Marital intimacy and self-disclosure. *Journal of Clinical Psychology, 39,* 183–190.

Zajonc, R., & Markus, H. (1985). Affect and cognition: The hard interface. In C. E. Izard & J. Kagan (Eds.), *Emotions, cognition, and behavior* (pp. 73–102). New York: Cambridge University Press.

II

How Can Closeness and Intimacy Be Measured?

6

Measuring Closeness: The Relationship Closeness Inventory (RCI) Revisited

Ellen Berscheid and Mark Snyder
University of Minnesota

Allen M. Omoto
Claremont Graduate University

THE CONCEPTUAL FRAMEWORK OF THE RCI

The conceptual analysis of relationships presented by Kelley et al. (1983/2002) in *Close Relationships* was the heuristic for the development of the RCI (Berscheid, Snyder, & Omoto, 1989a; 1989b). As Berscheid and Peplau (1983/2002) note, at the time Kelley and his colleagues were attempting to construct a conceptual blueprint to facilitate the study of close relationships, little attention had been given to the construct *relationship*. Thus, Kelley et al. found it necessary to provide a conceptual analysis of the relationship construct before proceeding to consider its frequently used descriptor *close*.

Kelley et al. (1983/2002) argued that the essence of a relationship lies in the interaction that takes place between two people. Evidence that two people are interacting is provided by observation that they are influencing each other's behavior. Such influence can be observed, described, and its causal antecedents and consequences ultimately discovered. Thus, Kelley et al. maintained that two people can be viewed as being in a relationship with one another if their interaction pattern reveals that they are interdependent—each person's behavior is influenced by the other's behavior.

Other relationship theorists have independently concluded that the essence of an interpersonal relationship lies in the interaction that occurs between two people. They have differed, however, with respect to the number of interactions, and the type of interaction, that is necessary to occur before concluding that two people are in a relationship (see Berscheid & Kelley, 2002).

Close Relationships

The adjective *close,* and its many antonyms (e.g., *superficial*), are perhaps the most fre-quently used descriptors of relationships, both by laypersons and relationship schol-ars. The latter have long assumed that the property and processes of closeness underlie many, if not most, of the relationship phenomena they hope to understand (e.g., Clark & Reis, 1988). As a consequence, the descriptor *close* historically has embodied a wide variety of meanings. Berscheid and Peplau (1983/2002) stated, in the late 1970s and early 1980s, the following: "Such words as *love, trust, commitment, caring, stability, at-tachment, one-ness, meaningful,* and *significant,* along with a host of others, flicker in and out of the numerous conceptions of what a 'close relationship' is" (p.12).

Kelley et al. (1983/2002) concluded that the development of a systematic body of knowledge about close human relationships would continue to be problematic if in-vestigators could neither agree on an issue so fundamental as when two people are or are not in relationship with one another, nor reach agreement on the criteria that should be used to classify a relationship as *close* or *not close.* Having located the essence of a relationship in the interaction between two people, Kelley et al. reasoned that all descriptors of a relationship—including the descriptor *close*—must necessarily refer to properties of the partners' interaction pattern. Having defined the existence of a *relationship* with respect to the partners' interdependence, it was a logical next step to conceptualize a *close* relationship as one in which the partners' interaction pattern displays a high degree of interdependence.

How investigators would (or should) ascertain the partners' degree of interdepen-dence was not explicitly prescribed by Kelley et al. (1983/2002). They merely prophe-sized that most investigators probably would want to examine at least four properties of the interaction pattern characteristic of two people: the frequency with which the two persons interact, the diversity of activities each individual influences, the strength with which the interactants respond to each other's behavior, and the duration of time the foregoing properties have been represented in the interaction pattern. Kelley et al. argued that these properties of the interaction pattern are especially likely to reflect the degree to which the partners are interdependent.

Although Kelley et al. (1983/2002) highlighted the properties of frequency, diver-sity, and strength of influence (and the length of time these properties have been characteristic of the partners' interaction) as especially diagnostic of closeness (i.e., high interdependence), they also anticipated that many other properties of the inter-action pattern would and should be of interest to relationship investigators. Other properties that they believed to be of high interest for understanding relationship phenomena were the symmetricality of the partners' influence and the nature of the activities influenced.

Closeness and Sentiment

Perhaps the most controversial feature of the Kelley et al. (1983/2002) conceptual-ization of closeness proved to be their exclusion of the partners' sentiment for each other and for their relationship. Indeed, this issue was difficult for the authors of *Close Relationships* to resolve among themselves (see Berscheid & Kelley, 2002). At the time they undertook their conceptualization effort, it was commonly believed by most laypersons, and by some relationship scholars as well, that because most close relationship partners experience positive emotions and feelings in their inter-actions, a *close* relationship should be identified by assessing the positivity of the partners' sentiment toward each other and toward the relationship itself. Relatedly, it also was widely believed that the association between interdependence and positivity of sentiment was so strong and inevitable that positive sentiment for the partner and the relationship should be included in the very conceptualization of the descriptor *close*.

Berscheid and Kelley (2002) note that, in retrospect, several factors were probably responsible for the belief that a relationship characterized by high interdependence also is invariably characterized by positive sentiment and that the emotions and feelings the partners typically experience in response to the others' behavior are almost uniformly positive. First, that widely shared belief rarely had been examined. The first highly publicized attack on the belief that many relationships considered to be *close* on other grounds (e.g., marital and other family relationships) were invariably positive in emotional tone and consequence occurred when sociologists Straus, Gelles, and Steinmetz published *Behind Closed Doors: Violence in the American Family* in 1980. Their data startled both relationship researchers and the general public, who had not suspected that physical mayhem was so prevalent "behind closed doors." Rook's (1984) seminal research on the negative effects of relationships further weakened the assumption and, today, the "dark side" of many highly interdependent relationships is being examined by relationship scholars (see, for example, Spitzberg & Cupach, 1998).

Berscheid and Kelley (2002) also note that there was at least one other reason for the strong association that prevailed between the concept of closeness and the partners' positive sentiment for each other and the relationship. In Western, individualistic societies, people believe that whether they establish and maintain a relationship with another person is a matter of their own personal choice and volition (see Johnson, 1991). As a consequence, it is not readily apparent to most people why an individual would choose to establish and to continue a relationship with a person for whom positive sentiment is not felt and in which negative emotions and feelings are frequently experienced. However, the fact that many close relationships—close in terms of their high interdependence—are often formed and maintained in "closed" fields (see Berscheid & Reis, 1998), in which the partners are likely to pay a high penalty for not continuing to interact with each other, generally has been overlooked by laypersons. Some relationship scholars, too, have neglected to consider the partners' extrinsic motivations for continuing an unhappy relationship, despite the facts that at least one early model of relationship stability, Levinger's (1965) cohesiveness model, emphasized the importance of considering the barriers to dissolving a relationship with a person for whom negative sentiment is felt and that Thibaut and Kelley (1959) had discussed "involuntary relationships" in their original presentation of interdependence theory.

Kelley et al. (1983/2002) concluded that the partners' sentiment for each other and for the relationship should not be folded into the concept of a close relationship but, rather, should be examined independently of examinations of interdependence. Although most highly interdependent relationships are also positive relationships (e.g., in terms of the partners' sentiments for each other, their sentiments toward the relationship itself, and the relationship's effects on the partners' well-being), they need not be. Relationships that are incongruent in interdependence and sentiment are often of special interest to relationship scholars (e.g., stable but unhappy relationships that threaten one or both partner's psychological and physical health).

It might be noted that, as Berscheid and Kelley (2002) discuss, there is no "correct" or "incorrect" conceptualization of the relationship descriptor *close*. Nor can there be. Basic scientific principles only require that a construct be clearly defined and stated, that its elements be tied to an observational base accessible to other scientists, and, finally, that the construct, however it is defined, prove useful in advancing the understanding of phenomena of interest.

It is to the RCI as a measure of relationship closeness that we now turn our attention. First, we will briefly recapitulate the considerations that guided the development of the RCI and the results of our initial tests of its reliability and validity. Then, we will consider its usefulness as a measure of relationship closeness. Berscheid et al. (1989b) concluded their presentation of the RCI and their description of its development with the comment that "[O]nly additional use of the inventory will determine if it is useful within other relationship populations and for predicting a variety of relationship phenomena" (p. 805).

The RCI now has been used in empirical investigations of a wide variety of relationship phenomena. Much as we would like to be exhaustive in our coverage of these investigations, we can highlight here only a handful, selecting and focusing on those that provide some particular insights into the construct validity of the RCI, its psychometric performance in populations other than the one in which the instrument was developed, and, finally, its usefulness in a number of different relationship research arenas, including both basic research as well as applied investigations of practical and important societal problems.

THE DEVELOPMENT OF THE RCI

The RCI and Its Scales

With the Kelley et al. (1983/2002) framework as our guide, we set out to create a multidimensional measure of relationship closeness. We sought to keep this measure closely grounded in observable events, and especially to patterns of interaction (and hence potential influence) between relationship partners. Rather than assume that certain types of relationships (e.g., romantic relationships, family relationships) are close, we endeavored to create a measure that could be used with virtually any type of relationship, and not incidentally, allow for comparisons of closeness and its dimensions across relationship types. For such a measure to be practically useful and efficient, we reasoned, it would need to be based on self-report. To minimize some of the deficiencies of self-report data that derive from reporting biases, faulty memory, and halo effects, we decided to make the reports highly structured and time-bound. As such, we intended our measure to provide a current snapshot of the interaction patterns and interdependence in a relationship.

To assess frequency of impact, we considered the conditions under which relationship partners are most likely to affect one another. Our analysis suggested that assessing instances of face-to-face interaction, although neither necessary nor sufficient for interpersonal influence, might well capture the situations or conditions most facilitative of impact. In addition, the potential for impact seemed greatest and clearest when partners were alone with each other. Whereas it might prove unwieldy for individuals to report on interaction sequences (unless, perhaps, diary methods are used; Duck, Rutt, Hurst, & Strejc, 1991; Wheeler & Nezlek, 1977; Wheeler, Reis, & Nezlek, 1983), we thought people might be able easily to report on the amount of time they spent together. Our indicator of frequency, therefore, represented the opportunity for influence, and was simply the estimated amount of time that participants spent together without others present during a typical day (we also suggested that these assessments be made by breaking the day into parts and with reference to the past week).

Having committed to one means of assessing frequency, we next considered the issue of diversity of impact. Given our criteria for the measure we were developing, we believed that one indicator of diversity of impact would be the number of different activities and activity domains relationship partners engaged in with one another during a fixed period of time. Assessment of a range of heterogeneous behavioral domains should suggest the extensiveness or breadth of interpersonal influence. It was important that the activities surveyed run the gamut from the mundane tasks of everyday life (e.g., doing laundry, eating a meal) to those more unusual (e.g., going on an outing). Consequently, we developed a checklist of activities specifically targeted to the population we planned to use to develop the RCI—the college student population—and asked respondents to indicate which of these activities they had participated in alone with their relationship partner. As with the frequency measure, we assumed that diversity of impact would be clearest when participants were alone with each other rather than in group contexts. Our intent, then, was to develop an exhaustive list of typical weekly activities for the population under study. We made no claims that this particular list would be representative or appropriate for populations other than the college student population.

Finally, in considering strength of influence, we grappled with issues of how best to scale the magnitude of instances of impact, especially as they occur across a wide variety of domains. Complicating our operational task further, we sought to develop a measure of strength of influence that would be independent of frequency and diversity. Developing separate indicators of these dimensions was important for conceptual and operational reasons, but also to facilitate examination of patterns of impact as distinguished from overall closeness scores. For example, we hoped that investigators would be able to discover if certain relationship outcomes were more reliably linked to variation in strength (or frequency or diversity) of impact despite comparable levels of overall closeness.

We ultimately decided to ask participants to scale for us the degree to which their relationship partner influenced their everyday behaviors, decisions, plans, and goals. Like diversity, we inquired about influence both on mundane and important activities and plans. Respondents were presented with a set of specific and itemized activities, decisions, and plans and asked to rate the extent to which their relationship partner influenced each one of them. We concluded that summing over this wide range of behaviors and plans was likely to provide a reasonable, if imperfect, assessment of strength of impact.

Having devised measures of frequency, diversity, and strength of influence that were concrete, timebound, composed of multiple items, easy to complete, and reasonably reliable (see Berscheid et al., 1989b), we devised scoring procedures for these scales that permitted them to be summed to create an overall measure of relationship closeness (for a complete listing of the items of the RCI, and the scoring criteria for the RCI scales, see Appendix A and Table 6.1). Because Kelley et al.'s (1983/2002) definition of closeness hinges on relationships that are characterized by relatively frequent, diverse, and strong impact (that lasts over some duration of time, as discussed further

TABLE 6.1

Scoring Criteria for Relationship Closeness Inventory Scales

Scale Score	Frequency (Number of Min)	Diversity (Number of Activity Domains)	Strength (Total)
1	0–12	0	34–53
2	13–48	1	54–73
3	49–108	2–3	74–93
4	109–192	4–6	94–113
5	193–300	7–9	114–133
6	301–432	10–13	134–153
7	433–588	14–18	154–173
8	589–768	19–24	174–193
9	769–972	25–30	194–213
10	973–1200	31–38	214–238

subsequently), we expected covariation among these scales for close relationships but no necessary pattern of covariation between the scales for less close relationships. In our original sample of respondents, who evaluated their "closest" relationship, we found that the three scales were moderately and positively correlated (r range $= .31$ to .41). In fact, the overall internal consistency of our three-scale closeness index was .62. Although for statistical and psychometric reasons we might have hoped for better, we considered this indication of reliability to be adequate for the multidimensional construct we were attempting to measure with no previous empirical guides to build on. (See also Aron, Aron, & Smollan, 1992; Omoto, 1989; Simpson, 1987, for reports of overall RCI reliability that are similar if not slightly higher.) In addition, the test–retest reliability of the RCI was a substantial .82 over a 3-to-5 week time interval.

Next, we will discuss several important considerations in the development and use of the RCI, each of which addresses questions that are frequently asked of us. First, we consider the diversity scale, and the need to be attentive to possible modifications in its content when using the RCI with different populations of respondents and their relationships. Second, we revisit our decision to omit Kelley et al.'s (1983/2002) duration criterion from the total RCI score. Third, we discuss the success of our attempt to construct the RCI scale in such a way as to measure interdependence independent of the individual's sentiment for the partner and the positivity of emotions experienced in the relationship.

Use of the Diversity Scale With Different Populations

As we have discussed, the diversity scale was intended to list, as comprehensively as possible, the kinds of activities frequently performed by persons in the population from which the sample is drawn (although an "open end" opportunity to name other activities is always provided respondents). The diversity scale reported by Berscheid et al. (1989b) was developed from the authors' previous investigations of the activities typical of the college student population. In many private communications, we have found it necessary to remind potential users of the RCI that, unless a college student sample is used, the activities listed in the diversity scale may need to be modified to reflect those of the population from which the sample will be drawn and to which generalizations will be made. If the sample is to be drawn from an elderly population, for example, it probably would be wise to include the item *went to see physician* and other such activities that are infrequently performed by college students but are typical of older persons.

It should be noted that even the activities listed for college students may need to be modified to better reflect those of a specific student sample. For example, in their preliminary inquiries, Gudykunst and Nishida (1993) found that Japanese college student respondents said that "attending festivals" and "moon viewing" were important omissions from the activities list in the diversity scale. Accordingly, these investigators modified the diversity scale to explicitly include these activities before administering the RCI to their Japanese respondents (a study we shall discuss further subsequently).

The Omission of Longevity From the RCI

Kelley et al. (1983/2002) emphasize that the duration of time two persons' interaction pattern has exhibited the properties of high frequency, diversity, and strength is an important consideration in classifying a relationship as a close one. After much consideration of the possible role of duration in the RCI, however, we concluded that this factor could not be adequately assessed by self-report. We also believed that the length of time the relationship partners had influenced each other's activities could not be assessed by determining the length of the relationship itself (a factor that could be readily assessed by self-report), that is, "it is not the duration of the relationship alone that is of significance; rather, it is the duration of the properties of high frequency, high diversity, and high strength (Berscheid et al., 1989b, p. 796). We termed our length of relationship measure "longevity" to distinguish it from duration of influence and were curious to learn whether longevity and RCI score were associated (given the common belief that long-term relationships are more likely to be close than short-term relationships) and whether longevity might be associated with different phenomena than closeness as measured by the RCI. Thus, a longevity item (i.e., *how long have you known this person*) is included in the RCI, although responses to this item never contribute to the total RCI score.

In our presentation of the RCI, we also recommended that the association between relationship longevity and RCI score as well as the association between longevity and the relationship phenomenon of interest be reported (Berscheid et al., 1989b, p. 796). Part of the impetus for this recommendation was that our initial examinations of the performance of the RCI within our U.S. college student sample revealed that, although longevity did not predict the later dissolution of the romantic relationships we examined (only the RCI did), it was longevity alone that significantly predicted the individual's emotional distress if the relationship later dissolved (the RCI and other putative measures of closeness did not predict distress). In addition, our initial investigations found small negative (not positive) correlations between longevity and total RCI score. Analyses subsequently revealed that friend relationships were mostly responsible for the negative correlation; there was no significant association between longevity and total RCI score within either romantic or family relationships (see 1989b, p. 798). These findings were encouraging, for they supported our decision to keep our measurement of length of relationship separate from our measurement of closeness, and they also supported our hunch that both measurements might prove useful in furthering understanding of different types of relationships and relational phenomena.

That relationship closeness as measured by the RCI and relationship longevity are measuring two different things (and that close relationships are not necessarily long-term relationships) has been confirmed by other investigators. For example, Gudykunst and Nishida (1993) found significant negative correlations between longevity and RCI score in both their United States and their Japanese samples, but when type of relationship (romantic, friend, family) and sex of respondent were taken into consideration, total RCI score was negatively correlated with longevity only for the male respondents in their combined sample.

The Omission of Sentiment From the RCI

In accord with Kelley et al.'s (1983/2002) conceptual framework of closeness, and the view that behavioral interdependence and sentiment for the partner and the relationship are conceptually (if not often empirically) independent of each other, we attempted to keep our focus on measuring the degree of influence the partners had on each other, as revealed in their pattern of activity. To determine how successful we had been in achieving that aim, and also to investigate the extent to which positive sentiment is associated with behavioral interdependence and with other putative measures of closeness, we included in our initial studies of the RCI two measures of sentiment. In our first sentiment measure, we asked respondents to rate the frequency with which they experienced several positive and negative emotions in their relationship. From this information, we created an emotional tone index (ETI). This measure demonstrated adequate psychometric properties and has been used in subsequent research. In our second measure of sentiment, we asked respondents to complete a measure of "Affect for Partner," which incorporated traditional dimensions of loving and liking.

We expected our sentiment measures to reveal positive sentiment for the person evaluated (who was nominated as the one with whom respondents believed they had their closest relationship). However, we hoped that scores on these sentiment measures would not be correlated with RCI scores. We expected however, that sentiment would be positively correlated with the respondent's subjective feelings of closeness. To examine this hypothesis, we constructed a subjective closeness index (SCI), a simple and face-valid two-item measure assessing the individual's feelings about the closeness of their relationship relative to their other relationships and to the relationships of other people. As we had hoped, the RCI was not related to the ETI (see Berscheid, 1983/2002, for possible explanations for the absence of association). However, both the RCI and the ETI were modestly correlated with the SCI, although in no case did the shared variance between any two of these measures exceed 4%. Moreover, the affect for partner measure was significantly more strongly related to the SCI than it was to the RCI. On the basis of this pattern, our simple conclusion was that none of these relationship closeness indexes could be substituted for any other. Although they might converge on some construct of relationship closeness, in our view it was more accurate to say that they offered different perspectives on relationship closeness. In fact, we held out the possibility that these measures—the RCI, the SCI, and the sentiment measures—might prove differentially useful in characterizing people's relationships and in predicting different relationship outcomes. At the least, however, the pattern of (low) associations obtained constituted evidence for the discriminant validity of the RCI, as well as evidence that it tapped something meaningfully different than sentiment for the partner.

Other Putative Indicants of Closeness

Others have added to the set of closeness measures that we created. Prominent among them was Aron, Aron, and Smollan's (1992) development of the single-item inclusion-of-other-in-self scale (IOS), a pictorial measure. In one study, Aron et al. compared the IOS to the RCI, the SCI, and Sternberg's (1988) intimacy scale. The pattern of correlations among these scales and the results of factor analyses revealed two important, and to our minds, conceptually distinct dimensions of relationship closeness: feelings of closeness and behaviorally based closeness. As we would anticipate from our psychometric work and findings, the SCI and the intimacy scale fell squarely on the feeling close dimension. The three scales of the RCI, meanwhile, loaded on the dimension named *behaving close*, as expected given their conceptual roots. The IOS in this study loaded on both the feeling and behaving dimensions. These results were replicated in a second study that employed confirmatory factor analytic techniques.

Aron et al.'s (1992) findings offer further evidence of the discriminant validity of the RCI as a measure of behaviorally based closeness and, in addition, of the SCI as a measure of sentiment for the partner. What it says about the meaning of the IOS is less clear, especially in light of the fact that this measure was found to substantially overlap with measures of marital satisfaction, commitment, emotional closeness, and attraction in several subsequent secondary studies. However, none of the relationship measures were consistently and significantly related to measures of social desirability across these studies (save for a consistent positive relationship between intimacy scale scores and tendencies toward self-deception). Thus, these measures of relationship closeness seem to assess at least two separate dimensions of the closeness construct.

We suspect that the IOS, with its roots in cognitive representations of self and other and felt interconnectedness, may be strongly related to a dimension that might be termed *thinking close*. Indeed, in research conducted by Aron and colleagues (Aron et al., 1992; Aron, Aron, Tudor, & Nelson, 1991), the IOS has proved useful in predicting cognitive outcomes related to relationship involvement and development. (See also Omoto, 1989; Omoto & Gunn, 1994, for the potential utility of the RCI to predict cognitively based outcome measures.) It remains for future research to explore this possibility in greater depth.

In sum, we see potential value in the availability of multiple measures of relationship closeness to characterize relationships and to investigate relational phenomena. The issue that we would like to bring clearly into focus, however, is that ideally the choice of measure should be guided by the perspective on relationship closeness the researcher deems most appropriate for the task at hand. In short, when making choices among alternative measures of relationship closeness, we suggest that careful attention be given to theoretical guides—not simply to pragmatic considerations. The results of the studies we have described above suggest that attempting to characterize the closeness of relationships in terms of subjective feelings of closeness, behavioral influence patterns, sentiment and emotional tone would lead to the choice of different measures. Moreover, not all measures are likely to predict all outcomes equally well. Arguing for the superiority of one measure over another, it seems to us, depends critically on theoretical approach and the measure's reliability and its validity—discriminant, construct, and predictive.

THE PREDICTIVE VALIDITY OF THE RCI

In this vein, in our initial presentation of the RCI, we sought to determine if the RCI, SCI, and ETI, as well as relationship longevity, could prospectively predict relationship stability among those of our research participants who had nominated a romantic relationship as their closest current relationship. Because our participants had given us the initials of their closest relationship partner at the time of our initial assessment, it was relatively easy to recontact participants 3 months later and again 9 months after our initial assessment to ask them if they were still romantically involved with the relationship partner they had identified. We then set about trying to predict relationship dissolution from the relationship measures we had collected with the straightforward prediction that longer and closer relationships would be more likely to have endured.

Our analyses revealed that, in combination, the three closeness measures and relationship longevity (at the time of assessment) were associated with relationship stability. Among this set of predictors, however, only the RCI emerged as a significant predictor. In subsequent analyses we found that the RCI alone could predict relationship stability and that the contributions of the other measures above and beyond the RCI were negligible and nonsignificant. Furthermore, the RCI's predictive power seemed to derive from each of its components. Each of the RCI scales was related to relationship stability in the expected fashion, although only the associations of the diversity and strength scales were significant. In other analyses, we also found that the participants themselves could not reliably predict the outcomes of their relationships. Their responses to a question of how long they anticipated the relationship to last were not significantly related to the relationship outcomes we tracked (Berscheid et al., 1989a).

In predicting relationship stability, therefore, we found that behaviorally based closeness, as instantiated by the RCI, was a significant predictor (for other research using the RCI and its scales to predict relationship dissolution, see Attridge, Berscheid, & Simpson, 1995; Simpson, 1987). This finding speaks to the predictive validity of the RCI and its value in forecasting a relationship event that is of considerable interest to laypersons as well as relationship researchers. Other research has established the predictive power of the RCI in influencing distress at relationship dissolution (e.g., Attridge, Berscheid, & Sprecher, 1995; Simpson, 1987) as well as partners' responses to potential relationship-threatening situations (e.g., Omoto, 1989; Simpson, Ickes, & Blackstone, 1995).

FURTHER EVIDENCE FOR THE CONSTRUCT
VALIDITY OF THE RCI

As we have discussed, our initial tests of the RCI indicated that it was a reliable instrument which possessed both discriminant and predictive validity. Subsequent empirical studies have demonstrated that the RCI also possesses construct validity. When the RCI has been used in research, it appears to function well and effectively as a measure of closeness. Moreover, when used in tests of hypotheses derived from theories about relationship phenomena, the RCI appears to perform well to the extent that the theories involved invoke or engage the construct of closeness. Here, we can only briefly highlight a few of the many studies that have used the RCI to measure closeness. Our selection of studies was guided by a desire to show the ways in which research with the RCI has helped to document its construct validity and to demonstrate its utility for investigating diverse issues of theoretical and practical importance in the study of close relationships. To do so, we will focus on studies that have expanded the kinds of relationships studied, the populations for which they are studied, and the settings in which they are studied.

We begin with a study that examined the RCI's performance in a collectivistic culture (i.e., Japan) as opposed to the individualistic culture (i.e., United States) in which the inventory was developed. As a result of the growing concern of psychology and related social sciences with cultural influences on behavior, it has become increasingly important to document how the phenomena and processes of individual and social functioning are embedded in their cultural contexts.

Cross-Cultural Investigations

Gudykunst and Nishida (1993) have observed that in order for a measure of relationship closeness to be useful in studying relationships across cultures, it must satisfy at least three requirements: (a) the theoretical framework on which the instrument is based must be applicable across cultures (i.e., it must not be culturally biased); (b) the instrument must be translatable without loss of meaning; and (c) the closeness scores on the instrument must show similar associations with similar relationship processes across cultures. To investigate the extent to which the RCI met these requirements, Gudykunst and Nishida administered the RCI to college students in the United States and Japan.

Because members of collectivistic cultures tend to engage in activities in larger groups rather than in dyads, Gudykunst and Nishida (1993) predicted that RCI Frequency and Diversity scale scores would be lower in their Japanese respondents than in their American respondents. They were: Scores on these two scales, but not on the RCI strength scale, for the relationship selected by the respondent as his or her closest relationship, were significantly higher for American respondents than they were for Japanese respondents. However, these investigators also found that the general pattern of mean scores on the frequency, diversity, and strength dimensions, as well as that of total RCI scores, across the two cultures were the same as those evident in Berscheid et al.'s (1989b) data. Moreover, even though the Japanese respondents were more likely than American respondents to select a friend relationship than a romantic relationship as their closest, RCI data revealed that in both cultures romantic relationships were closer than family or friend relationships. Gudykunst and Nishida also found that the reliability coefficients for the strength scale and for total RCI score in their two samples were virtually the same as those reported by Berscheid et al. for their U.S. sample. Also like Berscheid et al., these investigators found that RCI scores were not associated with the longevity of the respondent's relationship in either their Japanese or American samples.

To determine whether closeness as measured by the RCI was associated with relationship processes in similar ways across American and Japanese cultures, Gudykunst and Nishida (1993) examined the degree to which the RCI measure of closeness was associated with *attributional confidence* (i.e., the extent to which individuals are confident they can predict their partner's behavior, including the partner's attitudes, feelings, and values, and there is mutual understanding when they communicate). These investigators found, as predicted, small but significant positive correlations between attributional confidence and RCI score in both their American and Japanese respondents and, moreover, the pattern of correlations was consistent across relationship type and gender of respondent within the two cultures.

On the basis of their investigations, Gudykunst and Nishida (1993) concluded that the RCI is a valid cross-cultural measure of relationship closeness; that is, in terms of the criteria that they set forth for studying relationships across cultures, the theoretical framework on which the RCI is based provides a culturally unbiased description of close relationships, the RCI is translatable (at least into Japanese) without loss of meaning, and the RCI shows similar associations with relationship processes across cultures. Gudykunst and Nishida also observed that the cultural differences they found in the frequency and diversity scales are not problematic if the RCI is used as an independent variable in cross-cultural research (e.g., if median RCI scores within culture are used to classify relationships as *close* or *not close*). They suggested, however, that it would be interesting to examine a slight alteration in respondents' instructions for the frequency and diversity scales. At present, these scales ask respondents to indicate the amount of time spent *alone with X (the partner), with no one else around* and indicate the activities engaged in *alone with X*. As previously discussed, the rationale for this instruction was that individuals are more likely to influence each other when they are alone than when they are in the presence of others because those others also are likely to be exerting influence on the individual's behavior. Although this assumption may be warranted in an individualistic culture, Gudykunst and Nishida (1993) have questioned whether it is a sound assumption in a collectivistic culture where people tend not to spend much time alone with their relationship partners. As a consequence, these investigators suggest that the instructions might be modified to eliminate the *alone* specification for both time spent together and activities engaged in.

The RCI also has been translated into German and used to investigate differences between adolescents' relationships with their mothers, fathers, and friends (Laursen, Wilder, Noack, & Williams, 2000). Again, the results suggest that the RCI possesses construct validity. Similar processes associated with relationship closeness were found in the United States and Germany. Friend relationships, not parental relationships, were at the center of the cross-cultural differences found (i.e., distinctions between peer and family systems are more prominent in the United States than in Germany). Accordingly, it would appear that, to the extent that the RCI has been used in cross-cultural research, it does transfer well across the range of cultures thus far investigated.

Parent-Adolescent Relationships

A continuing objective of relationship researchers is to track and account for the transformations that occur within relationships over time. This is an acute problem for developmental psychologists, particularly those who focus on parent-child relationships. Toward this end, Collins and Repinski (2001) set out to test predictions from Collins' (1995) expectancy violation-realignment model, which hypothesizes that expectancy violations are especially likely to occur in early adolescence as a consequence of the extensive physical, cognitive, and social changes adolescents undergo during this period. Collins and Repinski administered the RCI, as well as Berscheid et al.'s

(1989b) SCI and ETI, to a sample of male and female adolescents and to their mothers and fathers. Each adolescent completed each measure with reference to their relationship with each of their parents and each parent with reference to their relationship with the adolescent, providing four different views of the same relationship.

Collins and Repinski (2001) found that the RCI, SCI, and ETI were not redundant measures of the properties of these parent-adolescent relationships. Whereas adolescents' perceptions of behavioral interdependence (i.e., RCI score) showed moderate positive correlations with their SCI and ETI scores, mothers' and fathers' reports of behavioral interdependence (i.e., RCI scores) were not significantly correlated with either their SCI or ETI scores. In contrast, and reflecting Berscheid et al.'s (1989b) findings, SCI and ETI scores were consistently correlated in all four types of dyads (i.e., mother-daughter, mother-son, father-daughter, and father-son) according to both parents' and adolescents' reports. The investigators note that expectancy violations may arise not only from the lack of concordance in views of the relationship, but also from divergence in the degree to which one aspect of the relationship is believed to be related to other aspects of the relationship.

In addition, Collins and Repinski (2001) found that adolescents' reports of their relationships with their parents varied by the age but not the sex of the adolescent. As expected, younger adolescents (ages 12–13) reported greater behavioral interdependence, as measured by the RCI, with both their mothers and their fathers than did older adolescents (ages 16–17). Younger adolescents also reported that their relationships with their fathers were more positive in emotional tone and higher in subjective closeness than did older adolescents, but no age differences were found in adolescents' reports of subjective closeness or emotional tone of their relationships with their mothers. Over all ages, Collins and Repinski (2001) found, adolescents' reports of their relationships with their fathers and their mothers were positively and significantly correlated; but mothers' and fathers' reports of their relationships with their adolescent child were significantly related only in subjective closeness.

Historically, frequent experiences of intense, positive emotion and reports of subjective opinion have been used as indicators of closeness in parent-child relationships. However, on the basis of their findings, Collins and Repinski (2001) conclude that:

> The relative independence of measures of relationships once considered interchangeable points to the need to examine multiple dimensions of relationship simultaneously. . . . Recognizing multiple dimensions of relationships permits researchers to study how changes in some aspects of relationships can occur amid continuity in others. (p. 439)

Laursen and Williams (1997), too, found the RCI useful in their examination of the changing dynamics of close relationships across adolescence. Alterations in interdependence captured developmental distinctions between horizontal (e.g., peer) relationships and vertical (e.g., child–parent) relationships. They also found that changes in subjective closeness appeared to precede changes in different aspects of interdependence.

Finally, in a study of parent–adolescent relationships, Repinski (1993) modified the frequency scale of the RCI in a potentially useful way: On the basis of the investigator's belief that weekdays and weekend days provide different opportunities for interaction between children and their parents, distinct time estimates were obtained for a typical weekday (morning, afternoon, and evening) and for a typical weekend day, for each of the three time periods, these two estimates were added, and then divided by 2. It should be noted that the reliability of the frequency scale in this study ranged from .69 (*adolescent–friend*) to .79 (*mother–adolescent*).

Closeness, Relationship Threat, and Cognitive Processes

The closeness of a relationship is presumed by relationship theorists to be associated with many cognitive processes. For example, the closeness of a relationship has been hypothesized to interact with threats to the relationship to generate certain cognitive and perceptual outcomes, including modifying the individual's degree of empathic accuracy for the partner's thoughts and feelings. Sillars (1985) proposed that among the factors that may undermine accurate empathic understanding of the partner is a high level of behavioral interdependence between the partners. As Ickes and Simpson (1997) discuss:

> One manifestation of *behavioral interdependence* is the degree to which the partners have developed unique rules of interaction or special ways of communicating with each other. . . . As interdependence increases, the actions of each partner must be interpreted within an increasingly complicated interpersonal context. . . . For this reason, greater behavioral interdependence should, at times, actually reduce empathic understanding. (p. 232)

In an experimental investigation of the hypothesis that empathic inaccuracy sometimes furthers relationship maintenance, Simpson, Ickes, and Blackstone (1995) assessed the closeness of individuals' relationships with their romantic partners and then, with both partners present, asked each partner to evaluate and discuss the attractiveness of opposite-sex persons who were purported to be members of a local "dating pool." Half the participants evaluated highly attractive opposite-sex persons, whereas the other half evaluated persons of lesser attractiveness. Following this task, the participants viewed a videotape of their evaluation session and inferred their partner's thoughts and feelings when the tape was stopped (at points at which the partner had indicated they had experienced a thought or feeling). Empathic accuracy scores were calculated by having independent coders rate how closely each inferred thought or feeling corresponded to the actual thought or feeling the partner had reported. Four months later, the investigators determined whether the relationship was intact or whether it had ended.

Simpson et al. (1995) predicted that motivated inaccuracy about their partners' thoughts and feelings would be evident when the partners enjoyed a close, interdependent relationship (as measured by the RCI), when they were insecure about the future of the relationship (as measured by Fei & Berscheid's insecurity scale; see Attridge, Berscheid, & Sprecher, 1998), and when they experienced a situational threat to the relationship (i.e., in the form of the experimental manipulation of having half the participants evaluate highly attractive potential partners). The results confirmed these predictions. Couples possessing this constellation of features were significantly less accurate at reading their partner's thoughts and feelings than those whose relationships had not been threatened, and they were even less accurate than opposite-sex strangers had been in a previous study. The prediction that such motivated inaccuracy might operate in the service of maintaining a valued relationship was also confirmed.

Path analyses conducted by Simpson et al. (1995) indicated that the effects they observed were mediated by the degree to which the partners believed their relationship was threatened during the evaluation task. Specifically, along with the experimental threat manipulation, and the individual's insecurity score, the closeness of the relationship, as measured by the RCI, significantly contributed to the individual's perceived threat. Perceived threat, in turn, was significantly, and negatively, associated with that individual's degree of empathic accuracy. Thus, this experiment provides additional evidence of the construct validity of the RCI; that is, relationship closeness was predicted to contribute to perceived threat, and closeness as measured by the RCI did show the associations it was predicted to show.

Research by Omoto (1989) also speaks to the potential role of relationship closeness as assessed with the RCI, relationship threat, and cognitive processes. In an experimental paradigm, members of heterosexual dating partners were assigned to "overhear" their partner in conversation with an opposite-sex stranger. Unbeknownst to participants, these conversations were actually scripted interactions. Half of the participants heard their partner engaged in an animated and positive conversation, whereas the remaining participants overheard a relatively dry and uninteresting conversation. Unlike the Simpson et al. (1995) work, then, participants in this study did not themselves directly observe their partner's evaluations nor were they asked to report on the likely thoughts and feelings of their partners.

Omoto (1989) found that partners in less close relationships, who did not have the same extensive behavioral history and routines as members of closer relationships, appeared to be more threatened when they overheard the positive conversation and subsequently devoted substantial cognitive effort to tracking and remembering it. Members of closer relationships, however, were generally attentive to their partners regardless of the nature of the conversation (i.e., potential threat). The attributions that participants produced in response to the conversations also differed. Threatened members of less close relationships tended to denigrate the potential relationship interloper whereas members of closer relationships produced attributions that focused on their own relationship partners and the positive qualities of their relationships.

In sum, relationship closeness, as assessed by the RCI, has implications for cognitive processes in relationships. It appears that cognitive processing may vary not only as a function of closeness, but also as a function of closeness and other relationship or situational characteristics such as insecurity or threat (see also Omoto & Gunn, 1994).

Women's Sexual Satisfaction

Hurlbert, Apt, and Rabehl (1993) observed that sexuality in nondistressed marital relationships has been seldom studied, despite the fact that a couple's sex life is an important component of their marital relationship. Moreover, researchers of sexual satisfaction have tended to focus on the role that such objective sexual variables as frequency of activity, number of orgasms, sexual desire, and sexual excitability play in marital sexual satisfaction. Hurlbert et al. investigated sexual satisfaction among women whose scores on the dyadic adjustment scale (Spanier, 1976) indicated they were satisfied with their marriages, comparing the roles of ostensibly objective sexual variables with personality variables (e.g., sexual assertiveness) and with relationship variables (e.g., communication quality, closeness as measured by the RCI). The women's scores on a sexual satisfaction scale (Hudson, 1982) were significantly correlated with virtually all of the measures included in the study (e.g., number of orgasms, sexual excitability), including the closeness of the wife's relationship with her husband as measured by the RCI.

Although Hurlbert et al. (1993) found that all of their measures were highly intercorrelated, a step-wise multiple-regression analysis found that only three variables added to the prediction of sexual satisfaction over and above the other variables assessed; two of these were the personality variables of "assertiveness" and "erotophilia" and the third was closeness as assessed by the RCI. These three variables alone accounted for well over half the variance in women's sexual satisfaction. As well as providing additional construct validity for the RCI, this study illustrates in yet another context that relationship closeness does indeed underlie many different kinds of relationship phenomena, just as relationship scholars initially suspected.

Volunteer Relationships

As a behaviorally based measure of closeness, the RCI should be relevant to nearly all relationship types, and not merely those in which partners merge identities, express positive affect, or experience feelings of love and liking. It should be relevant, for example, to volunteer caregiving relationships in which people agree to offer practical and emotional support to one or more individuals who are suffering from terminal illnesses or temporarily debilitating conditions (e.g., Omoto & Snyder, 1995). These relationships present provocative opportunities for extending relationship theories and measures because, although individuals voluntarily initiate the relationship, they are often paired to work with persons they do not know and with whom they may have little in common. In addition, terminating these relationships can be relatively easy, at least as compared to marital or family relationships for which there are clear structural and legal (if not moral) barriers to dissolution. Volunteer–caregiver relationships also tend to be asymmetrical in that partners possess different resources and abilities. Moreover, there are unambiguous expectations about the purposes of these relationships and the roles that relationship partners are designed to fill. Despite the fact that volunteer caregiving is quite common, these relationships have yet to receive much attention from relationship researchers.

Omoto and Snyder (1999) asked people who were active as volunteers in an AIDS service organization to complete measures of relationship closeness, including one patterned after the RCI (but with some of the item content, such as the diversity scale, modified to reflect this participant population), stress, satisfaction, and perceptions of their relationship partner (a person living with HIV or AIDS). Each volunteer completed measures at several points in time, so it was possible to track relationship development and change. Relationship closeness was found to moderate the effects of partner illness on volunteers' perceptions of stress and satisfaction with their volunteer service (Omoto, Gunn, & Crain, 1998). Specifically, to the extent that volunteers worked with relatively sick patients and reported greater closeness to them, they tended to experience stress in their work. Work with relatively more healthy patients or less close relationships did not produce the same levels of stress for volunteers. In addition to these stressful consequences for volunteers, some benefits of relationship closeness for people living with HIV or AIDS also have been investigated. Crain, Snyder, and Omoto (2000) found that those HIV or AIDS clients who reported closer relationships with a volunteer tended to use more effective coping strategies in dealing with their illness, which in turn were related to their better overall psychological health. These studies speak to the generalizability of the closeness construct to relationship domains not extensively included in the literature to date and to the utility of the RCI to predict important relationship and health outcomes.

In other longitudinal work on volunteers in AIDS service organizations (Omoto, Snyder, & Smith, 2002; Smith, Omoto, & Snyder, 2000), one component of the RCI, the diversity dimension, was examined as an outcome of the volunteer process (Omoto & Snyder, 1995, 2002; Omoto, Snyder, & Berghuis, 1993). When the range of activities in which volunteers and their HIV or AIDS clients engaged in together was examined, it was found that greater diversity of activities could be predicted from emotional investment in and commitment to the relationship. Volunteers who reported greater feelings of closeness and emotional investment in their relationship with their client were likely to report greater commitment to volunteering and, subsequently, to actually engage in more activities with their client; that is, they behaved so as to expand the number of domains in which their client was likely to have influence on them. Not incidentally, greater diversity also was related to an index of relationship longevity.

Other studies have explored closeness in the context of other types of volunteer relationships. For example, in a study of hospice volunteers of varying ages who volunteered their time to visit and provide companionship to persons with terminal illnesses, Omoto, Snyder, and Martino (2000) examined the role of closeness in predicting various outcomes of volunteer service, such as increases in self-esteem. In addition, within an intergenerational mentoring program for at-risk Latinas, relationship closeness, as assessed with a composite measure that included the RCI (with the diversity and strength scales modified to make the item content more relevant to this particular sample), predicted both relationship persistence and relationship satisfaction for program mentors and their mentees (see Aldrich, 2002). This finding, which is reminiscent of the original findings of Berscheid et al. (1989b) in which lesser relationship closeness reliably predicted relationship dissolution, has considerable practical import for organizations that depend on volunteer efforts. Structuring volunteer–client (or mentor–mentee) relationships so as to increase actual or likely relationship closeness may produce volunteers who report greater commitment to and actual behavioral investment in their volunteer tasks. Taken together, these studies of voluntary-helping relationships deliver a consistent message about the potential importance of conceptualizing closeness according to the framework of Kelley et al. (1983/2002) and measuring it along the lines of the RCI (Berscheid et al., 1989a, 1989b).

CONCLUDING COMMENTS

In this chapter, we have reviewed the conceptual foundations of the RCI, its development, and its validation. The accumulating body of evidence suggests that as a measure of closeness in relationships the RCI possesses both reliability and validity and that it has proven its applicability to a wide range of relationship contexts. Its demonstrated utility in investigating closeness in diverse forms of relationships and across cultures also attests to the broad and integrative scope of the conceptualization of closeness that guided the development of the RCI. We trust that this conceptualization, and particularly this measure, will continue to be useful as researchers expand the scope of relationships and relationship phenomena that they seek to understand.

REFERENCES

Aldrich, C. D. (2002). *Predicting relationship closeness, satisfaction, and persistence within a mentoring program.* Unpublished Masters thesis, Claremont Graduate University, Claremont, CA.

Aron, A., Aron, E., & Smollan, D. (1992). Inclusion of other in the self scale and the structure of interpersonal closeness. *Journal of Personality and Social Psychology, 63,* 596–612.

Aron, A., Aron, E., Tudor, M., & Nelson, G. (1991). Close relationships as including other in self. *Journal of Personality and Social Psychology, 60,* 241–253.

Attridge, M., Berscheid, E., & Simpson, J. A. (1995). Predicting relationship stability from both partners versus one. *Journal of Personality and Social Psychology, 69,* 254–268.

Attridge, M., Berscheid, E., & Sprecher, S. (1998). Dependency and insecurity in romantic relationships: Development and validation of two companion scales. *Personal Relationships, 5,* 31–58.

Berscheid, E., & Kelley, H. H. (2002). Introduction to the Percheron Press edition. In H. H. Kelley, E. Berscheid, A. Christensen, J. H. Harvey, T. L. Huston, G. Levinger, E. McClintock, L. A. Peplau, & D. R. Peterson, *Close relationships* (pp. vii–xxvi). Clinton Corners, NY: Percheron. (Original work published 1983)

Berscheid, E., & Peplau, L. A. (2002). The emerging science of relationships. In H. H. Kelley, E. Berscheid, A. Christensen, J. H. Harvey, T. L. Huston, G. Levinger, E. McClintock, L. A. Peplau, & D. R. Peterson, *Close relationships* (pp. 1–19). Clinton Corners, NY: Percheron. (Original work published 1983)

Berscheid, E., & Reis, H. T. (1998). Attraction and close relationships. In D. T. Gilbert, S. T. Fiske, & G. Lindzey (Eds.), *The handbook of social psychology* (4th ed., pp. 193–281). New York: McGraw-Hill.

Berscheid, E., Snyder, M., & Omoto, A. M. (1989a). Issues in studying relationships: Conceptualizing and measuring closeness. In C. Hendrick (Ed.), *Close Relationships, Vol. 10: Review of Personality and Social Psychology* (pp. 63–91). Newbury Park, CA: Sage.

Berscheid, E., Snyder, M., & Omoto, A. M. (1989b). The relationship closeness inventory: Assessing the closeness of interpersonal relationships. *Journal of Personality and Social Psychology, 57,* 792–807.

Clark, M. S., & Reis, H. (1988). Interpersonal processes in close relationships. *Annual Review of Psychology, 39*, 609–672.

Collins, W. A. (1995). Relationships and development: Family adaptation to individual change. In S. Shulman (Ed.), *Close relationships and socioemotional development* (pp. 128–154). New York: Ablex.

Collins, W. A., & Repinski, D. J. (2001). Parents and adolescents as transformers of relationships: Dyadic adaptations to developmental change. In J. R. M. Gerris (Ed.), *Dynamics of parenting: International perspectives on nature and sources of parenting* (pp. 429–443). Leuven, The Netherlands: Garant Publishers.

Crain, A. L., Snyder, M., & Omoto, A. M. (2000, May). *Volunteers make a difference: Relationship quality, active coping, and functioning among PWAs with volunteer buddies.* Paper presented at the Annual meeting of the Midwestern Psychological Association, Chicago, IL.

Duck, S., Rutt, D. J., Hurst, M., & Strejc, H. (1991). Some evident truths about everyday communication: All conversations are not created equal. *Human Communication Research, 18*, 228–267.

Gudykunst, W. B., & Nishida, T. (1993). Closeness in interpersonal relationships in Japan and the United States. *Research in Social Psychology, 8*, 85–97.

Hudson, W. W. (1982). *The clinical measurement package.* Homewood, IL: Dorsey.

Hurlbert, D. F., Apt, C., & Rabehl, S. M. (1993). Key variables to understanding female sexual satisfaction: An examination of women in nondistressed marriages. *Journal of Sex & Marital Therapy, 19*, 154–165.

Ickes, W., & Simpson, J. A. (1997). Managing empathic accuracy in close relationships. In W. Ickes (Ed.), *Empathic accuracy* (pp. 218–250). New York: Guilford.

Johnson, M. P. (1991). Commitment to personal relationships. In W. H. Jones & D. Perlman (Eds.), *Advances in personal relationships, Vol. 3: A Research annual* (pp. 117–143). London: Jessica Kingsley.

Kelley, H. H., Berscheid, E., Christensen, A., Harvey, J. H., Huston, T. L., McClintock, E., Peplau, L. A., & Peterson, D. R. (2002). *Close relationships.* Clinton Corners, NY: Percheron. (Original work published 1983)

Laursen, B., Wilder, D., Noack, P., & Williams, V. (2000). Adolescent perceptions of reciprocity, authority and closeness in relationships with mother, father, and friends. *International Journal of Behavioral Development, 24*, 461–471.

Laursen, B., & Williams, V. A. (1997). Perceptions of interdependence and closeness in family and peer relationships among adolescents with and without romantic partners. *New Directions for Child Development, 78*, 3–20.

Levinger, G. (1965). A social psychological perspective on marital dissolution: An integrative review. *Journal of Marriage and the Family, 27*, 19–29.

Omoto, A. M. (1989). *Relationship involvement and closeness: Implications for the processing of relationship relevant events.* Unpublished doctoral dissertation, University of Minnesota, Minneapolis, MN.

Omoto, A. M., & Gunn, D. O. (1994, May). *The effect of relationship closeness on encoding and recall for relationship-irrelevant information.* Paper presented at the International Network for Personal Relationships, Iowa City, IA.

Omoto, A. M., Gunn, D. O., & Crain, A. L. (1998). Helping in hard times: Relationship closeness and the AIDS volunteer experience. In V. J. Derlega & A. P. Barbee (Eds.), *HIV infection and social interaction* (pp. 106–128). Thousand Oaks, CA: Sage Publications.

Omoto, A. M., & Snyder, M. (1995). Sustained helping without obligation: Motivation, longevity of service, and perceived attitude change among AIDS volunteers. *Journal of Personality and Social Psychology, 68*, 671–686.

Omoto, A. M., & Snyder, M. (1999). [Unpublished data from a longitudinal study of AIDS volunteers]. Kansas: University of Kansas, Lawrence, and University of Minnesota, Minneapolis, MN.

Omoto, A. M., & Snyder, M. (2002). Considerations of community: The context and process of volunteerism. *American Behavioral Scientist, 45*, 846–867.

Omoto, A. M., Snyder, M., & Berghuis, J. P. (1993). The psychology of volunteerism: A conceptual analysis and a program of action research. In J. B. Pryor & G. D. Reeder (Eds.), *The social psychology of HIV infection* (pp. 333–356). Hillsdale, NJ: Lawrence Erlbaum Associates.

Omoto, A. M., Snyder, M., & Martino, S. C. (2000). Volunteerism and the life course: Investigating age related agendas for action. *Basic and Applied Social Psychology, 22*, 181–198.

Omoto, A. M., Snyder, M., & Smith, D. M. (2002). *Relationship closeness and duration of service of volunteers.* Unpublished manuscript, Claremont Graduate University, Claremont, CA; University of Minnesota, Minneapolis, MN; and University of Michigan, Ann Arbor, MI.

Repinski, D. J. (1993). *Adolescents' close relationships with parents and friends.* Unpublished doctoral dissertation, University of Minnesota, Minneapolis, MN.

Rook, K. S, (1984). The negative side of social interaction: Impact on psychological well-being. *Journal of Personality and Social Psychology, 46*, 1097–1108.

Sillars, A. L. (1985). Interpersonal perception in relationships. In W. Ickes (Ed.), *Compatible and incompatible relationships* (pp. 277–305). New York: Springer-Verlag.

Simpson, J. A. (1987). The dissolution of romantic relationships: Factors involved in relationship stability and emotional distress. *Journal of Personality and Social Psychology, 59*, 971–980.

Simpson, J. A., Ickes, W., & Blackstone, T. (1995). When the head protects the heart: Empathic accuracy in dating relationships. *Journal of Personality and Social Psychology, 69*, 629–641.

Smith, D. M., Omoto, A. M., & Snyder, M. (2000, May). *Helping others: Effects of similarity and relationship closeness and duration of service.* Paper presented at the Annual meeting of the Midwestern Psychological Association, Chicago, IL.

Spanier, G. (1976). Measuring dyadic adjustment: New scales for assessing the quality of marriage and similar dyads. *Journal of Marriage and the Family, 38*, 15–30.

Spitzberg, B. H., & Cupach, W. R. (Eds.). (1998). *The dark side of close relationships*. Mahwah, NJ: Lawrence Erlbaum Associates.

Sternberg, R. J. (1988). *Construct validation of a triangular theory of love*. Unpublished manuscript, Yale University, New Haven, CT.

Straus, M. A., Gelles, R. J., & Steinmetz, S. (1980). *Behind closed doors: Violence in the American family*. New York: Doubleday.

Thibaut, J. W., & Kelley, H. H. (1959). *The social psychology of groups*. New York: Wiley.

Wheeler, L., & Nezlek, J. (1977). Sex differences in social participation. *Journal of Personality and Social Psychology, 45*, 742–754.

Wheeler, L., Reis, H. T., & Nezlek, J. (1983). Loneliness, social interaction, and sex roles. *Journal of Personality and Social Psychology, 45*, 943–953.

APPENDIX A

The Relationship Closeness Inventory

We are currently investigating the nature of interpersonal relationships. As part of this study, we would like you to answer the following questions about your relationship with another person. Specifically, we would like you to choose the *one* person with whom you have the *closest, deepest, most involved, and most intimate relationship,* and answer the following questions with regard to this particular person. For some of you, this person may be a dating partner or someone with whom you have a romantic relationship. For others of you, this person may be a close, personal friend, family member, or companion. It makes no difference exactly who this person is as long as she or he is the one person with whom you have the closest, deepest, most involved, and most intimate relationship. *Please select this person carefully since this decision will affect the rest of this questionnaire.*

   With this person in mind, please respond to the following questions:

1. Who is this person? (initial of first name only)_____
   a. What is this person's age? _____   What is your age?_____
   b. What is this person's sex? _____   What is your sex?_____
2. Which one of the following best describes your relationship with this person? (Check *only one*)

WORK:
_____co-worker _____your boss/supervisor _____your subordinate

FAMILY:
_____aunt/uncle _____sister/brother _____parent _____cousin

ROMANTIC:
_____married _____engaged _____living together
_____dating: date only this person
_____dating: date this person and others

FRIEND:
_____close friend (non-romantic) _____casual friend

OTHER:
_____(please specify _____)

3. How long have you *known* this person? Please indicate the *number* of years and/or months (for example,____3____years, ____8____months)
____years ____months

We would like you to estimate the amount of time you typically spend alone with this person (referred to below as "X") during the day. We would like you to make these time estimates by breaking the day into morning, afternoon, and evening, although you should interpret each of these time periods in terms of your own typical daily schedule. (For example, if you work a night shift, "morning" may actually reflect time in the afternoon, but is nevertheless time immediately after waking.) Think back over the past week and write in the average amount of time, per day, that you spent *alone with X, with no one else around*, during each time period. If you did not spend any time with X in some time periods, write ____0____ hour(s) ____0____ minutes.

4. DURING THE PAST WEEK, what is the average amount of time, per day, that you spent *alone with X* in the MORNING (e.g., between the time you wake and 12 noon)?

____hour(s)   ____minutes

5. DURING THE PAST WEEK, what is the average amount of time, per day, that you spent *alone with X* in the AFTERNOON (e.g., between 12 noon and 6 pm)?

____hour(s)   ____minutes

6. DURING THE PAST WEEK, what is the average amount of time, per day, that you spent *alone with X* in the EVENING (e.g., between 6 pm and bedtime)?

____hour(s)   ____minutes

Compared with the "normal" amount of time you usually spend alone with X, how typical was *the past week*? (Check one)

____ typical   ____ not typical . . . if so, why? (please explain)

The following is a list of different activities that people may engage in over the course of one week. For each of the activities listed, please check all of those that you have engaged in *alone with X in the past week*. Check only those activities that were done *alone with X* and *not* done with X in the presence of others.

In the past week, I did the following activities *alone with X*: (Check all that apply)

____did laundry
____prepared a meal
____watched TV
____went to an auction/antique show
____attended a non-class lecture or presentation
____went to a restaurant
____went to a grocery store
____went for a walk/drive
____discussed things of a personal nature
____went to a museum/art show
____planned a party/social event
____attended class

_____went on a trip (e.g., vacation or weekend)
_____cleaned house/apartment
_____went to church/religious function
_____worked on homework
_____engaged in sexual relations
_____discussed things of a non-personal nature
_____went to a clothing store
_____talked on the phone
_____went to a movie
_____ate a meal
_____participated in a sporting activity
_____outdoor recreation (e.g., sailing)
_____went to a play
_____went to a bar
_____visited family
_____visited friends
_____went to a department, book, hardware store, etc.
_____played cards/board game
_____attended a sporting event
_____exercised (e.g., jogging, aerobics)
_____went on an outing (e.g., picnic, beach, zoo, winter carnival)
_____wilderness activity (e.g., hunting, hiking, fishing)
_____went to a concert
_____went dancing
_____went to a party
_____played music/sang

The following questions concern the amount of influence X has on your thoughts, feelings, and behavior. Using the 7-point scale below, please indicate the extent to which you agree or disagree by writing the appropriate number in the space corresponding to each item.

1	2	3	4	5	6	7
I strongly disagree						I strongly agree

1. _____X will influence my future financial security.
2. _____X does *not* influence everyday things in my life.*
3. _____X influences important things in my life.
4. _____X influences which parties and other social events I attend.
5. _____X influences the extent to which I accept responsibilities in our relationship.
6. _____X does *not* influence how much time I spend doing household work.*
7. _____X does *not* influence how I choose to spend my money.*
8. _____X influences the way I feel about myself.
9. _____X does *not* influence my moods.*
10. _____X influences the basic values that I hold.
11. _____X does *not* influence the opinions that I have of other important people in my life.*
12. _____X does *not* influence when I see, and the amount of time I spend with, my family.*
13. _____X influences when I see, and the amount of time I spend with, my friends.
14. _____X does *not* influence which of my friends I see.*

15. _____X does *not* influence the type of career I have.*
16. _____X influences or will influence how much time I devote to my career.
17. _____X does *not* influence my chances of getting a good job in the future.*
18. _____X influences the way I feel about the future.
19. _____X does *not* have the capacity to influence how I act in various situations.*
20. _____X influences and contributes to my overall happiness.
21. _____X does *not* influence my present financial security.*
22. _____X influences how I spend my free time.
23. _____X influences when I see X and the amount of time the two of us spend together.
24. _____X does *not* influence how I dress.*
25. _____X influences how I decorate my home (e.g., dorm room, apartment, house).
26. _____X does *not* influence where I live.*
27. _____X influences what I watch on TV.

Now we would like you to tell us how much X affects your future plans and goals. Using the 7-point scale below, please indicate the degree to which your future plans and goals are affected by X by writing the appropriate number in the space corresponding to each item. If an area does not apply to you (e.g., you have no plans or goals in that area), write a 1.

1	2	3	4	5	6	7
not at all						a great extent

1. _____my vacation plans
2. _____my marriage plans
3. _____my plans to have children
4. _____my plans to make *major* investments (house, car, etc.)
5. _____my plans to join a club, social organization, church, etc.
6. _____my school-related plans
7. _____my plans for achieving a particular financial standard of living

* reverse-scored item

7

Thinking Close: Measuring Relational Closeness as Perceived Self-Other Inclusion

Christopher R. Agnew
Purdue University

Timothy J. Loving
University of Texas at Austin

Benjamin Le
Haverford College

Wind Goodfriend
Purdue University

As with other psychological constructs, *closeness* represents a significant challenge to the measurement-minded social scientist. Although the closeness that people can feel for others is undeniably palpable, it is not easily captured by the standard methods and approaches used to assess other important relationship constructs. This chapter focuses on a social psychological attempt to meet this measurement challenge, the inclusion of other in the self scale (IOS scale; Aron, Aron, & Smollan, 1992). The IOS scale has been used in research to measure closeness as conceptualized in the frame works of self-expansion (Aron & Aron, 1997) and cognitive interdependence (Agnew, 2000; Agnew, Van Lange, Rusbult, & Langston, 1998).

As Aron and colleagues have noted (Aron, Aron, & Norman, 2001), the measurement of closeness has been approached from multiple angles, including affective ("feeling close") and behavioral ("acting close") perspectives. In our research, we have taken a decidedly cognitive approach to the measurement of relationship constructs (e.g., Agnew, Loving, & Drigotas, 2001; Agnew, 2000; Agnew et al., 1998; Le & Agnew, 2001; Loving & Agnew, 2001) and, not surprisingly, we approach closeness from a cognitive perspective ("thinking close"). For example, we have offered the term *cognitive interdependence* to refer to the mental state characterized by pluralistic, collective representations of the self-in-relationship (Agnew, 2000; Agnew et al., 1998) and have found that this state covaries with levels of relationship commitment in

Please circle the picture below which best describes your relationship with your romantic partner.

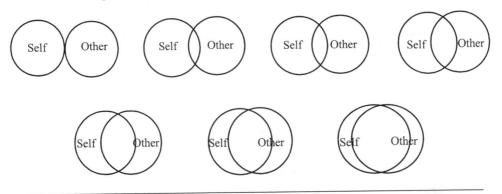

FIG. 7.1. Inclusion-of-Other-in-the-Self (IOS) Scale, Including Original Instructions (Aron et al., 1992).

romantic relationships. To assess cognitive interdependence, we have employed a diverse assortment of measures, including standard pencil-and-paper self-reports, a covert linguistic analysis of spontaneous plural pronoun use in relationship-relevant cognitions, and the IOS scale.

We see this last measure as a particularly useful one, clearly aligned with our view of a "close" relationship as one that involves the cognitive incorporation of one's relationship partner into one's self. Aron et al.'s IOS scale offers a significant departure from extant measures of relational closeness (Aron et al., 1992; see Figure 7.1). This single-item, graphic-based measure has demonstrated desirable psychometric properties and, since its development, has been used in studies of various relationship topics (e.g., Agnew et al.'s, 2001, work on social network perceptions; Knee's, 1998, work on implicit relationship theories; Medvene, Teal, and Slavich's, 2000, work on relationship equity and satisfaction) and nonrelationship topics (e.g., Blanchard, Perreault, and Vallerand's, 1998, work on sport participation; Li's, 2002, work on cultural differences in self construals; Smith, Coats, and Walling's, 1999, work on mental representations of in groups).

Despite the measure's popularity across a range of topics, a number of important questions about the IOS scale remain unexamined. We focus here on two such issues, each informed by data that we have collected in our lab from people involved in romantic relationships: the generality versus specificity of self–other inclusion (focusing on domains of the self), and the extent to which the IOS scale assesses perceived similarity at different relationship stages. The first issue, arising from the general nature of the measure's instructions (see Figure 7.1), raises an intriguing question: What aspect of another is included in one's self? It is possible that the global nature of the scale obscures insightful information regarding the precise nature of self–other inclusion. In our work, we sought to shed light on what aspects of the self-concept are (and are not) perceived as included in general IOS scale judgments.

The second issue revolves around another provocative question: To what extent are increasing levels of closeness (or inclusion) associated with perceived self–other similarity? In other words, is the IOS scale's assessment of closeness driven by perceptions of similarity (vs. differences) with one's partner, and does relationship longevity influence this association? We begin with a description of the development of the IOS scale, including information concerning past validity and reliability assessments and then provide tentative responses to these questions on the basis of our research.

INCLUSION OF OTHER IN THE SELF (IOS) SCALE

As can be seen in Figure 7.1, the IOS scale consists of a series of seven Venn-like diagrams depicting different degrees of overlap between two circles (Venn, 1880). Respondents are instructed to *Please circle the picture below which best describes your relationship with your romantic partner.* A respondent's choice is thought to represent the degree of closeness he or she perceives in his or her relationship with his or her partner. A novel aspect of the measure is that each of the seven response diagrams is constructed such that it contains the same amount of total area. Thus, as the degree of overlap between the two circles increases, the diameter of each one also increases.

In the article in which the IOS scale was first introduced (Aron et al., 1992), the authors presented a thorough examination of the scale's empirical merits. Although it is impossible to conduct tests of interitem consistency for a one-item measure, the authors demonstrated that the IOS had alternate form ($\alpha = .95$ for romantic relationships) and test–retest validity ($r = .85$ for romantic relationships). In addition, the IOS was found to be significantly correlated with other popular closeness measures, including the relationship closeness inventory (RCI; Berscheid, Snyder, & Omoto, 1989; $r = .22$), the subjective closeness index (SCI; Berscheid et al., 1989; $r = .34$), and the Sternberg intimacy scale (SIS; Sternberg, 1988; $r = .45$). These significant correlations support both the concurrent and convergent validity of the IOS scale. Finally, discriminant validity was established by demonstrating a negligible .09 correlation with an anger–sadness measure that used similar overlapping circle diagrams (all correlations reported here are from Study 1, Aron et al., 1992).

Of course, a useful closeness measure should also predict important relationship outcomes. In Aron et al.'s original 1992 article, predictive validity was established by showing that the IOS scale was significantly correlated with likelihood a relationship remained intact three months later ($r = .46$) and, for those couples still together at that time, with expected distress if the relationship were to end ($r = .34$). In more recent work on cognitive interdependence, the IOS scale was found to be highly correlated with a variety of other relationship variables including satisfaction, commitment, investment in the relationship, and centrality of the relationship to the individual's life (Agnew et al., 1998).

Five supplemental studies were also included in the original presentation of the IOS scale as evidence of its convergent and construct validity. Three of these studies used married couple samples and established that the IOS predicts a variety of important relationship constructs and outcomes, including marital quality and dyadic adjustment. The other two supplemental studies made use of experimental manipulations of closeness with strangers in laboratory settings. In these studies, dyad members indicated high degrees of self–other overlap on the IOS scale following a closeness manipulation (Aron, Melinat, Aron, Vallone, & Bator, 1997). In sum, the psychometric properties of the IOS scale have been found to match or exceed other extant multi-item measures of closeness that typically require much longer to complete (Aron & Aron, 1997).

In addition to the validation work reviewed above, other research has examined the social cognitive underpinnings of the IOS scale. Aron and colleagues (Aron & Fraley, 1999) have suggested that, with respect to the IOS scale, "this symbolic description of overlapping selves may tap a readily accessible cognitive structure of self–other overlap" (Aron & Fraley, 1999, p. 142). Making use of reaction-time methodology and past research on actor–observer attributional processes, Aron and Fraley (1999) examined the cognitive makeup of closeness in two ways. First, romantically involved participants rated trait adjectives by indicating how much each word described both themselves and their partners. After completing filler tasks, participants then underwent a reaction time procedure in which the traits were presented again, this time on a computer screen, and participants had to press either a *me* or *not me* key to indicate whether the word described them. Consistent with the cognitive underpinnings of the IOS scale, it took longer to make this *me–not-me* decision when the trait was true for the participant, but not true for his or her partner, as compared with when the trait was true for both couple members. In addition, this latency increased as closeness increased, as measured by the IOS scale. The authors argued that this slower processing speed occurred because, when making this type of decision for oneself, if one's partner is cognitively close, one will also automatically make the decision for a partner as well; however, confusion ensues if the trait is not in fact true for both couple members (Aron & Fraley, 1999; see also Mashek, Aron, & Boncimino, 2003).

Second, the authors argued that if one's partner is cognitively overlapped with one's self, one should be more likely to make situational attributions for that partner as well. This notion is based on the well-known *actor–observer bias* in the social cognition literature (Goldberg, 1981; Jones & Nisbett, 1971). This term describes the tendency for people to attribute their own behavior to a situational cause, but to assign a dispositional cause to the behavior of others. Participants in this study were again asked to describe their partner, only this time using opposite-trait adjective pairs, such as *serious* versus *carefree*. If a participant indicated that both ends of this spectrum were true of his or her partner, the authors inferred that this represented situational attributions (i.e., my partner is serious in some situations, but carefree in others). Again, consistent with the inclusion of other aspect of the IOS scale, participants who were closer to their partners exhibited this effect more so than did those not as close (as measured by the IOS scale), which was interpreted by the authors as evidence of "taking the [partner's] perspective" (Aron & Fraley, 1999, p. 155).

GENERALITY VERSUS SPECIFICITY OF SELF–OTHER INCLUSION

According to Aron and Aron's (1997) self-expansion model, people seek to expand themselves in a variety of ways. The desire for self-expansion is held to exist as a fundamental human motive. Specifically, they suggest four areas in which an individual may strive toward self-expansion: (a) *physical and social influence* (e.g., having physical possessions), (b) *cognitive complexity* (e.g., possessing general knowledge or insight), (c) *social and bodily identity* (e.g., identifying with others), and (d) *awareness of position in universe* (e.g., knowledge of one's place in the "grand scheme" of life).

Close, romantic relationships are one aspect of life wherein these four areas may become intertwined and, accordingly, may be seen as key venues for self-expansion. Aron and Aron (1997) state that "a central human motivation is *self-expansion* and that one way people seek such expansion is through close relationships in which each includes the other in the self" (p. 251). For example, individuals involved in a close relationship may gain the use of their partners' memories (e.g., Wegner, Erber, & Raymond, 1991), such that each participant in a relationship has access to the memory of the other as an available knowledge source when necessary. Furthermore, individuals gain access to the material possessions of their partners. This acquisition or expansion of one's personal belongings to include a partner's is an ongoing process, potentially corresponding to the move from selfish to unselfish motivations within a relationship (Aron & Aron, 1997). In other words, as individuals become more interdependent with their partners, they are less likely to think in terms of "my stuff," and more likely to think in terms of "our stuff" (Agnew et al., 1998).

The concept of self–other inclusion has intuitive appeal and corresponds to the way individuals may already view relationships. For example, the term *break up* implicitly refers to the process of dividing something that was one "unit" (Aron &

Aron, 1997). Furthermore, it is not uncommon for people to stop thinking of dating friends as, for example, "Hillary" and "Bill," and start thinking of them as "Hillaryand-Bill" (the emphasis put on the contiguity with which the names are spoken; they have become linguistically and cognitively linked). In addition, the self-expansion concept has been used to explain such relationship dynamics as increases and decreases in reported relationship satisfaction, the importance of shared activities, the role of arousal and novelty in attraction to a potential partner, and unrequited love (Aron & Aron, 1997). Finally, a number of studies have tested and confirmed that individuals demonstrating higher levels of self–other overlap with their partner also demonstrate more communal allocation of resources, fewer differences in actor–observer perspectives, and a higher likelihood of adopting the partner's characteristics as one's own (Aron, Aron, Tudor, & Nelson, 1991).

The research reviewed above clearly demonstrates the cognitive effects of self–other inclusion as assessed by the IOS scale. But, while there is a relatively large amount of evidence supporting the notion of the self–other inclusion metaphor within the domain of close relationships, specific aspects of the self that are included have not received research attention. To begin filling the gap, we conducted two studies to determine which components of one's identity are most associated with judgments of global inclusion of other in the self. Specifically, using Aron and colleagues' IOS scale (Aron et al., 1992), we investigated the extent to which individuals' reports of global self–other inclusion were related to four specific areas of self-identity, as delineated in past research on the self (cf. Hoyle, 1991): (a) personal self, (b) physical self, (c) work self, and (d) social self.

Our first study included 175 heterosexual introductory psychology students from the United States (46% women; 54% men) who were each involved in an exclusive, romantic relationship of at least two weeks duration. The mean age of the sample was 19.68 ($SD = 1.69$), with over half of the participants (53%) being freshmen. The majority of participants (83%) were White (9% Asian; 2% Black; 3% Hispanic) and average length of relationship involvement was 18.55 months ($SD = 19.17$; $Mdn = 11.5$). The students participated in the questionnaire study in partial fulfillment of a course requirement. In addition to demographic items, participants completed a questionnaire consisting of several measures of self–other inclusion, including the original IOS scale (Aron et al., 1992), which was used to measure global self–other inclusion. We then modified the original IOS scale instructions to assess the degree of overlap between respondents' and their partners' personal, physical, work, and social selves. To measure the degree of self–other inclusion concerning these dimensions of the self, we asked respondents four variations of the following question (in random order).

Please circle the picture below which best describes your personal (physical/work/social) relationship with your romantic partner (i.e., how you and your partner relate with one another)/(i.e., how you and your partner are physically intimate with one another)/(i.e., how you and your partner's work lives include one another)/(i.e., how you and your partner's individual social lives include one another).

Table 7.1 displays the correlations between the global IOS measure and the specific personal, physical, work, and social indexes of one's identity. As can be seen, all four specific measures were significantly correlated with global IOS. More importantly, we wanted to assess the degree to which the correlations were significantly different from one another. We used techniques described by Cohen and Cohen (1983) to investigate whether the relative magnitudes of the obtained correlations differed significantly. These analyses revealed that personal relationship inclusion with one's partner was a significantly stronger predictor of global IOS than the other measures. Furthermore, the social relationship measure displayed stronger correlations with the

TABLE 7.1

Correlations Between Specific Components of the
Self-Concept and Global IOS

	Global IOS	
Component	Study 1	Study 2
Personal	.67*	.73*
Physical	.38*,a	.48*,a
Work	.35*,a	.40*,a
Social	.55*	.67*

Note. $N = 175$ for Study 1; $N = 128$ for Study 2; IOS = inclusion-of-other-in-the-self scale.

[a] Indicates correlations that share superscripts in a given column are not significantly different from one another; all other correlations in a given column are different from one another at $p < .05$.

*$p < .01$.

global measure than either the physical or work relationship measures. Finally, the correlations between the physical and work relationship measures and global IOS were not significantly different from one another. These findings suggest that individuals may be more likely to consider their personal and social relationship with their partner when considering the general level of closeness or self–other inclusion they perceive within their relationship.

To build upon these findings, we assessed the association between perceived self–other inclusion (both global and specific) and relationship quality. Specifically, we sought to determine whether the inclusion of some aspects of the self-concept is more highly associated with relationship satisfaction than is the inclusion of other self aspects. In light of the results reported above, we see such findings as adding to the existing body of literature on self–other inclusion that exclusively uses the global IOS measure.

Our second study included 128 undergraduate participants from the United States (64 couples) who were involved in an exclusive, romantic relationship of at least 5 months duration. The mean age of the sample was 19.65 ($SD = 1.17$), with 47% of the participants being freshmen. The majority of participants were White (88%), 3% were Asian, 2% were Black, and 2% were Hispanic. Average length of relationship involvement was 16.55 months ($SD = 13.27$; $Mdn = 9.5$). Participants completed a questionnaire consisting of demographic items as well as the general and modified IOS measures described above for the previous study. To measure relationship quality, the investment model scale's (Rusbult, Martz & Agnew, 1998) index of satisfaction level was used: five items, with a 9-point response scale ranging from 0 (do not agree at all) to 8 (agree completely) and an alpha level of .90.

To confirm the findings from our first study, correlations were computed between the global IOS measure and the specific personal, physical, work, and social indexes of one's identity. As Table 1 illustrates, all four specific measures were again significantly correlated with global IOS. Furthermore, the relative strengths and patterns of these associations were very similar to those obtained in the first study.

Next, correlations were computed between each IOS measure and the measure of satisfaction to investigate whether the measures of global and specific IOS were differentially related to relationship satisfaction (see Table 7.2). As can be seen (see "Total" panel), all IOS measures were significantly associated with satisfaction (all $ps < .01$). Furthermore, measures of global, personal, and social IOS demonstrated

TABLE 7.2

Correlations Between IOS Measures and Relationship
Satisfaction

IOS	Satisfaction
Total	
Global	.57[*,a]
Personal	.60[*,a]
Physical	.37[*,b]
Work	.27[*,b]
Social	.54[*,a]
Women	
Global	.63[*,a,b]
Personal	.72[*,a]
Physical	.49[*,b]
Work	.34[*,b]
Social	.51[*,b]
Men	
Global	.53[*,a]
Personal	.47[*,a]
Physical	.22[b]
Work	.20[b]
Social	.58[*,a]

Note. $N = 128$ (64 women; 64 men); IOS = inclusion-of-other-in-the-self, scale.

[a,b] Within each grouping, correlations that share superscripts are not significantly different from one another; all other correlations are different from one another at $p < .05$.

[*] $p < .01$.

significantly stronger associations with reported relationship satisfaction than did measures of physical and work IOS.

We also computed the above correlations by sex to investigate possible sex differences in the relative importance applied to the different IOS measures concerning judgments of relationship satisfaction (and because of problems inherent with combining data from couple members in analyses). For females, all IOS measures were significantly correlated with relationship satisfaction (see Table 7.2). Furthermore, the global and personal IOS measures demonstrated significantly stronger associations than did the other IOS measures. In contrast, although the males' patterns of results mirrored those of the total sample, physical and work IOS measures were not significantly associated with reported relationship satisfaction (see Table 7.2). This finding suggests that females tend to derive more relationship satisfaction from the inclusion of their work and physical selves with their partner's than do males.

Taken together, these two studies revealed that inclusion of the personal and social selves were significantly more strongly related to global IOS than were inclusion of the physical and work selves. These findings suggest that, at least with our undergraduate samples, personal and social overlaps are strong indicators of general closeness within romantic relationships. Additionally, the second study demonstrated that reports of relationship quality (assessed by reported relationship satisfaction) might be influenced differentially by these specific components of the self, and males and females may not hold the same concerns or needs within their relationships.

In light of the differential associations between satisfaction and global and specific measures of IOS, we suggest that valuable information can be gained by continuing to investigate the underpinnings, or specific aspects, of self-identity comprising the global IOS scale. Future research efforts could continue to explore why or how individuals might seek differing amounts of self–other overlap in specific domains of their identities. Furthermore, it would be interesting to investigate how these relationships between the global measure and specific IOS measures change with age. For example, in the current study, overlapping personal and social selves were most related to the global IOS measure. Although this makes some intuitive sense, one might investigate the potential moderating role of career salience on this effect. It is reasonable to posit that those at different life stages may have different goals and needs within their relationships. Finally, whereas the second study demonstrated associations between the specific measures and relationship satisfaction, ultimately it would be beneficial to determine if these specific measures are predictive of break up. In other research we have found that discrepancies between one's own IOS assessment and perceived partner IOS assessment predict break up five months later, with the larger the discrepancy, the greater the likelihood of termination (Le & Agnew, 1997). However, we have not investigated specific facets of the self that might be more or less predictive of relationship termination.

SIMILARITY, RELATIONSHIP DURATION, AND SELF–OTHER INCLUSION

The idea of cognitively connected or overlapping selves is the basis for the IOS scale (Aron et al., 1992). With this in mind, our next study focused more closely on this cognitive aspect of the original IOS scale. Specifically, we investigated whether individuals view similarity (as assessed by activity preferences) between themselves and their partners as associated with perceived self–other inclusion. Above, we briefly review a number of studies that have demonstrated that increasing levels of self–other inclusion are associated with cognitive changes such that individuals appear to view themselves as increasingly connected to their partners. These cognitions are associated with, among other things, greater equality in allocation of resources to another, pluralistic representations of self and other (*us* rather than *you and I*), and increased perspective taking. To add to this literature, we investigated whether increasing levels of self–other inclusion are associated with perceived similarity for self and other activity preferences. To the extent that individuals perceive more cognitive inclusion with their partners, they should also view themselves as having the same preferences as their partners.

Our study included 204 introductory psychology students from the United States (100 women; 104 men) who were each involved in a dating relationship for at least one week. The mean age of the sample was 19.70 (*SD* = 2.08). The majority of participants were White 86%, 6% were Asian, 4% were Black, 3% were Hispanic, and 1% other. Average length of relationship involvement was 15.60 months (*SD* = 17.36; *Mdn* = 10 months). The students participated in the questionnaire study in partial fulfillment of a course requirement.

In addition to standard demographic items, participants completed the IOS scale to measure global self–other inclusion. To measure degree of perceived similarity in activity preferences, a list of possible activities that close relationship partners might enact was constructed. Activities were considered in three broad categories: (a) leisure activities, (b) task activities, and (c) relationship activities. Initial activities were drawn from past research (e.g., Surra & Longstreth, 1990). In addition, pilot participants were asked to generate examples of types of activities and several additional examples were generated by the authors. The final version of the measure included a total of 62 leisure activities (e.g., go out to eat at a restaurant, play cards or board games), 22 task activities (e.g., do laundry, shop for groceries), and 22 relationship activities (e.g., talk about relationship problems, kiss). For each activity, respondents indicated the degree to which their partner and themselves felt similarly about preference for this activity using a 7-point scale ranging from $1 = $ (*my partner and I feel the same about this activity*) to $7 = $ (*my partner and I greatly differ on our preference for this activity*).

Factor analyses were conducted on each of the three broad activity types in order to isolate possible distinct activity subtypes. For leisure activities, three factors were found, labeled "Sports and games" (e.g., play cards or board games, play tennis; Eigenvalue = 11.02; 22.7% of the variance), "Water-Related leisure" (e.g., go water skiing, go boating; Eigenvalue = 18.07; 37.3% of the variance), and "Cultural events" (e.g., go to a live theatre performance, go to the symphony or orchestra; Eigenvalue = 4.52; 9.3% of the variance). Collectively, these three factors accounted for 69.3% of the variance underlying the set of items. Three factors were also found to underlie the set of task activities. These factors were labeled "Domestic chores" (e.g., grocery shop, do dishes; Eigenvalue = 9.68; 57.7% of the variance), "Professional pursuits" (e.g., go to classes, prepare applications or resumes; Eigenvalue = 2.47; 14.7% of the variance), and "Correspondence" (e.g., write letters, read letters; Eigenvalue = 1.83; 10.9% of the variance). Collectively, these three factors accounted for 83.2% of the variance. Finally, two factors were found to underlie the relationship activities. These factors were labeled "Conversation" (e.g., talk about events in the news, talk about work; Eigenvalue = 5.77; 21.1% of the variance) and "Affection" (e.g., cuddle, hug, kiss; Eigenvalue = 13.05; 47.6% of the variance) and accounted for 68.7% of the variance. On the basis of these results, total scores were calculated for each factor and used in the analyses described below.

Table 7.3 displays the correlations between the IOS scale and perceived similarity for general and specific activity preferences across all participants. Self–partner similarities for all three general types of activity (leisure, task, and relationship) were positively correlated with the IOS scale. Further note that similarity on 6 of the 8 subtypes of activity was also positively correlated with the IOS scale.

TABLE 7.3

Correlations of IOS Scale With Perceived
Similarity for General and Specific Activity
Preferences, Overall

Activity	IOS
General leisure	.28**
Water-Related leisure	.19**
Sports and games	.19**
Cultural events	.26**
General task	.20**
Domestic chores	.10
Professional pursuits	.17*
Correspondence	.09
General relationship	.33**
Conversation	.17*
Affection	.30**

Note. $N = 204$. IOS = inclusion-of-other-in-the-self scale.
$*p < .05$. $**p < .01$.

TABLE 7.4

Correlations of IOS Scale With Perceived Similarity for General and Specific
Activity Preferences, by Relationship Duration and Gender

	IOS Scale			
	New Relationships		Established Relationships	
Activity	Female (n = 52)	Male (n = 55)	Female (n = 48)	Male (n = 49)
General leisure	.38**	.36**	.25†	.11
Water-related leisure	.38**	.24†	.10	−.16
Sports and games	.29*	.30*	.16	.01
Cultural events	.44**	.23†	.27†	.12
General task	.32*	.22†	.26†	.05
Domestic chores	.27†	.05	.04	−.03
Professional pursuits	.26†	.13	.37**	.02
Correspondence	.23†	.15	.11	.01
General relationship	.38**	.45**	.24†	.35*
Conversation	.32*	.07	.30*	.27†
Affection	.18	.57**	.08	.31*

Note. IOS = inclusion-of-other-in-the-self scale.
†$p < .10$, *$p < .05$, **$p < .01$.

Table 7.4 displays correlations between perceived similarity in activity preferences and IOS responses broken down by gender and by relationship duration. To examine the role of relationship duration, a median split was computed to divide participants into two groups. Those relationships below the median (with a duration of 10 months or less) are labeled "New relationships," whereas those above the median (10 months or longer) are labeled "Established relationships." Note that similarity in activity preference seems to be most important in new relationships regardless of gender. It is also interesting to note that regardless of relationship duration, women have higher correlations between the IOS scale and similar activity preferences for the conversation aspect of relationship activities, whereas males have higher correlations between the IOS and similar activity preferences for the affection aspect of relationship activities. This seems consistent with stereotypes of women relating closeness to talking to their partners about the relationship and related aspects of life, whereas males relate closeness to the physical aspects of the relationship.

Overall, self–other inclusion was found to be significantly and positively associated with perceived similarity in activity preferences; the more similarity dating individuals' perceived in their activity preferences, the closer they reported being. This finding is especially robust in new relationships, in which 11 of the 22 activity types (across women and men) were significantly correlated with IOS (in comparison with only 4 of 22 in established relationships). These results pose an interesting question: Why was this pattern of associations primarily found for new relationships and not for established relationships? Although speculative, we suggest that this result is a reflection of the motivational component of self-expansion theory.

Self-expansion theory (Aron & Aron, 1997) suggests that individuals are motivated to expand themselves and that close relationships provide a forum for this expansion to occur. According to our results, dating participants report more similarities in activity preferences when the relationship is relatively "fresh," versus when it is more established. Perhaps individuals in less established relationships perceive more similarity because it is at this junction of a relationship that perceptions of similarity with

one's partner are particularly important. The developmental phases of dating relationships include a great deal of time spent getting to know one another. New partners
spend a great deal of time talking and learning about each other's likes and dislikes.
As they get closer through this self-disclosure process, according to the self-expansion
model, they should be motivated to "take on" their partners' activity preferences.

On the other hand, in established relationships, expansion has already occurred. As
a result, the motivation to include the other has passed (i.e., it has already happened),
and we subsequently see far fewer associations between the IOS scale and perceived
similarity for activity preferences. In other words, individuals no longer feel the need
to assume they like the same things as their partners, and in fact, their perceptions
of similarity for activity preferences may be less "clouded" and more realistic. For
example, consider the significant association between professional pursuits and IOS
for women in established relationships. We find it interesting that this association
occurs in established relationships but not in new relationships. Could it be that
in established relationships, individuals are now thinking more "long term," which
would make professional issues more salient and relevant?

Newer couples may also be thought of as in the initial phases of expansion with
their partners, becoming increasingly close to a partner and potentially becoming
similar to them as they expand. However, at some point later in a relationship, the
initial expansion phase runs its course (i.e., one partner has "included" all the new
knowledge–resources from the other partner) and boredom may ensue (Aron & Aron,
1997). Aron has proposed that the couple members may engage in novel activities
and hobbies together, thus "jump starting" the expansion process (i.e., to keep from
getting bored in the relationship). It may also be the case that these couples bias their
perceptions of similarity as a way of maintaining the relationship. Theoretically, if
couples perceive differences, they would be motivated to stay together because of the
possibilities for future expansion.

It also may be possible that the perception of similarities between partners becomes
more fine-tuned over time. For example, suppose two people, David and Susan, have
just met. They discover that they are both from California and like Mexican food—
thus there is an immediate overlap that begins to form on the basis of similarity
(reflected in the results reported above for early stage couples). David and Susan
both share a California connection. However, as their relationship grows, they realize
that although they are both Californians, he is from Los Angeles and she is from
San Francisco (which, among Californians at least, are considered very distinct cities).
Likewise, David may like Baja cuisine whereas Susan may be a fan of Tex–Mex dishes.
So, over time, David and Susan begin to discover differences in their similarities.

CONCLUDING THOUGHTS

Because of the IOS scale's simplicity, it is an extremely provocative base from which
to branch into exciting new research directions. Some of the work presented here is an
example. But there is ample room for additional work along these lines. For instance,
it would be interesting to consider further what is salient in each respondent's mind
as he or she responds to the scale. Differences in interpretation could indicate problems in a relationship (e.g., "if I think about yesterday's fight regarding who did the
laundry, that may influence how I answer the question") or, alternatively, particularly
good things about a relationship. Asking for respondents' spontaneous interpretations of the IOS diagrams may serve as a practical and useful supplement to obtaining only the response itself. It may also be possible to experimentally manipulate
how an individual interprets the measure by making different aspects of the self, the
partner, or the relationship salient. This is an important area for future work.

We think it is also important to fully consider whether the IOS scale is an appropriate measure of self-expansion theory. There are two distinct yet interrelated areas of inquiry that are operating (and thus, ripe for measurement) as delineated by self-expansion theory. The first is the process of self-expansion, which is held to be driven by a fundamental motivation to seek new experiences and relationships, obtain novel information and possessions, and gain personal enlightenment. This motivation guides individuals toward others as a means for gaining these experiences and resources (in a sense, acting as an attracting force). From this perspective, attraction is then a balance between the possibility of the great amount of self-expansion that would occur with a dissimilar partner and the potential to maintain a relationship (thus, to have continual access to a partner and his or her resources over time) with a similar partner. Attraction is maximized when these two dimensions are in balance—a partner who is similar enough to "get along" with you, yet different enough to "be exciting" (and *expanding*).

This process of self-expansion can lead to, but is not the same as, the end state of self–other inclusion itself (as demonstrated by the low correlation between the IOS scale and the new self-expansion questionnaire recently reported by Lewandowski & Aron, 2002). Self–other inclusion represents the degree to which partners are cognitively and emotionally intertwined with one another, sharing preferences, memories, and a joint motivation for maintaining their relationship. It is this self–other inclusion which is subjectively experienced as closeness and is similar to what we have described and investigated as cognitive interdependence in our own research. From this perspective, the positions of self-expansion and interdependence theories converge, and the IOS scale represents but one measure tapping into the cognitive overlap that can occur in close relationships (other measurement strategies, such as Agnew et al.'s [1998] pronoun coding technique are also useful).

The implications for measurement are, therefore, twofold. First, a researcher must have a sense of which of these areas are of interest. Is it the self-expansion process itself, or the relational state of self–other overlap that is of interest? The hypotheses that stem from the answer to this question will differ, as will the measurement strategy chosen. Second, are the self-expansion process and content of the resulting self–other inclusion general in nature, or are they specific in their domains of expansion and overlap? The first two studies described in this chapter begin to examine this question, with results indicating that personal and social self-other inclusion are most central to the overall general experience of inclusion and closeness. We encourage continued work in this area.

REFERENCES

Agnew, C. R. (2000). Cognitive interdependence and the experience of relationship loss. In J. H. Harvey & E. D. Miller (Eds.), *Loss and trauma: General and close relationship perspectives* (pp. 385–398). Philadelphia: Brunner-Routledge.

Agnew, C. R., Loving, T. J., & Drigotas, S. M. (2001). Substituting the forest for the trees: Social networks and the prediction of romantic relationship state and fate. *Journal of Personality and Social Psychology, 81*, 1042–1057.

Agnew, C. R., Van Lange, P. A. M., Rusbult, C. E., & Langston, C. A. (1998). Cognitive interdependence: Commitment and the mental representation of close relationships. *Journal of Personality and Social Psychology, 74*, 939–954.

Aron, A., & Aron, E. (1997). Self-expansion motivation and including other in the self. In S. Duck (Ed.), *Handbook of personal relationships* (2nd ed., pp. 251–270). New York: Wiley.

Aron, A., Aron, E., & Norman, C. (2001). Self-expansion model of motivation and cognition in close relationships and beyond. In G. J. O. Fletcher & M. S. Clark (Eds.), *Blackwell handbook of social psychology: Interpersonal processes* (pp. 478–501). Malden, MA: Blackwell.

Aron, A., Aron E. N., & Smollan, D. (1992). Inclusion of other in the self scale and the structure of interpersonal closeness. *Journal of Personality and Social Psychology, 63*, 596–612.

Aron, A., Aron, E. N., Tudor, M., & Nelson, G. (1991). Close relationships as including other in the self. *Journal of Personality and Social Psychology, 60,* 241–253.

Aron, A., & Fraley, B. (1999). Relationship closeness as including other in the self: Cognitive underpinnings and measures. *Social Cognition, 17,* 140–160.

Aron, A., Melinat, E., Aron, E. N., Vallone, R. D., & Bator, R. J. (1997). The experimental generation of interpersonal closeness: A procedure and some preliminary findings. *Personality and Social Psychology Bulletin, 23,* 363–377.

Berscheid, E., Snyder, M., & Omoto, A. M. (1989). The relationship closeness inventory: Assessing the closeness of interpersonal relationships. *Journal of Personality and Social Psychology, 57,* 792–807.

Blanchard, C., Perreault, S., & Vallerand, R. J. (1998). Participation in team sport: A self-expansion perspective. *International Journal of Sport Psychology, 29,* 289–302.

Cohen, J., & Cohen, P. (1983). *Applied multiple regression/correlational analysis for the behavioral sciences.* Hillsdale, NJ: Lawrence Erlbaum Associates.

Goldberg, L. R. (1981). Unconfounding situational attributions from uncertain, neutral, and ambiguous ones: A psychometric analysis of descriptions of oneself and various types of others. *Journal of Personality and Social Psychology, 41,* 517–552.

Hoyle, R. H. (1991). Evaluating measurement models in clinical research: Covariance structure analysis of latent variable models of self-conception. *Journal of Consulting and Clinical Psychology, 39,* 67–76.

Jones, E. E., & Nisbett, R. (1971). The actor and the observer: Divergent perceptions of the causes of behavior. In E. E. Jones, D. Kanouse, H. Kelley, R. Nisbett, S. Valins, & B. Weiner (Eds.), *Attribution: Perceiving the causes of behavior* (pp. 79–94). Morristown, NJ: General Learning Press.

Knee, C. R. (1998). Implicit theories of relationships: Assessment and prediction of romantic relationship initiation, coping, and longevity. *Journal of Personality and Social Psychology, 74,* 360–370.

Le, B., & Agnew, C. R. (1997, June). *Discrepancy between own and perceived partner inclusion-of-other-in-the-self predicts relationship dissolution.* Paper presented at the Annual Meeting of the International Network on Personal Relationships (INPR) Young Scholars Pre-Conference, Oxford, Ohio.

Le, B., & Agnew, C. R. (2001). Need fulfillment and emotional experience in interdependent romantic relationships. *Journal of Social and Personal Relationships, 18,* 423–440.

Lewandowski, G., & Aron, A. (2002, February). *The self-expansion scale: Construction and validation.* Paper presented at the Annual Meeting of the Society for Personality and Social Psychology, Savannah, GA.

Li, H. Z. (2002). Culture, gender and self—close-other(s) connectedness in Canadian and Chinese samples. *European Journal of Social Psychology, 32,* 93–104.

Loving, T. J., & Agnew, C. R. (2001). Socially desirable responding in close relationships: A dual-component approach and measure. *Journal of Social and Personal Relationships, 18,* 551–573.

Mashek, D., Aron, A., & Boncimino, M. (2003). Confusions of self with close others. *Personality and Social Psychology Bulletin, 29,* 1–11.

Medvene, L. J., Teal, C. R., & Slavich, S. (2000). Including the other in self: Implications for judgments of equity and satisfaction in close relationships. *Journal of Social and Clinical Psychology, 19,* 396–419.

Rusbult, C. E., Martz, J. M., & Agnew, C. R. (1998). The investment model scale: Measuring commitment level, satisfaction level, quality of alternatives, and investment size. *Personal Relationships, 5,* 357–391.

Smith, E. R., Coats, S., & Walling, D. (1999). Overlapping mental representations of self, in-group, and partner: Further response time evidence and a connectionist model. *Personality and Social Psychology Bulletin, 25,* 873–882.

Sternberg, R. J. (1988). *Construct validation of a triangular theory of love.* Unpublished manuscript.

Surra, C. A., & Longstreth, M. (1990). Similarity of outcomes, interdependence, and conflict in dating relationships. *Journal of Personality and Social Psychology, 59,* 501–516.

Venn, J. (1880). On the diagrammatic and mechanical representation of propositions and reasonings. *The London, Edinburgh, and Dublin Philosophical Magazine and Journal of Science, 9,* 1–18.

Wegner, D. M., Erber, R., & Raymond, P. (1991). Transactive memory in close relationships. *Journal of Personality and Social Psychology, 61,* 923–929.

8

A Practical Look at Intimacy: ENRICH Couple Typology

Edward F. Kouneski and David H. Olson
University of Minnesota

Imagine an evening out with your intimate partner at a favorite restaurant. The atmosphere engages your senses as you share your thoughts.

Mmmm, taste the rosemary in this bread; it's warm. I'm really glad we're making time together away from the kids.

You overhear the conversations of couples seated nearby.

At the table to the left, a man speaks, "You can take our order now. I'll have the breaded veal cutlets. She'll have the chicken cacciatore. And for an appetizer, bring the stuffed mushrooms with crab."

When the waiter leaves, the woman says, "You know, I'm allergic to shellfish." He gestures for the waiter to return. "No, never mind," she says, "I'll just eat around the crabmeat. Oh, I have something important to tell you. Jonie's teacher called today, and the parent conference is this Friday at four o'clock."

Why didn't he know that she was allergic? Why won't she order something else?

"I'll have to reschedule a meeting that afternoon, but that's okay," the man says. "I'll be there. Count on it."

No misunderstanding there. They value co-parenting.

Beyond them is a younger couple laughing, talking of ballroom dancing. One reaches for the other's hand. They lean forward, gazing at each other, not yet noticing the waiter standing above.

Ahh, to be young again with few cares.

"Look, time to order," one says. "Let's have wine. Red or white?"

"You decide. Let's have what you want," the other replies.

"No, let's have what you want." The banter continues.

"But I'd really like to have what you want."

At the table to the right, two persons eat quietly, attending only to their own plates. After several minutes, the woman breaks the silence. "I bought wallpaper today, for the den."

"That's nice," the man replies without looking up. "Pass the salt."

A salty old fellow, eh?

Behind you, a woman says "You aren't ready yet?"

The man points to his menu, showing the waiter. "I'm trying to decide between . . . "

She interrupts, "You can never make a decision, not even what to eat."

He announces, "She can talk. That's her third hair color in a week."

Now your partner turns to you with a smile and says, "I wonder if I should color mine to cover the gray," and before you can respond, adds, "On second thought, I like me just the way I am."

Exactly my thought, I like you just the way you are!

This vignette portrayed five couples. Look again at the interactions to see how you would characterize each one. Which couple is the most conflicted? Whose relationship seems devitalized? Is one couple interacting in a traditional manner? Which relationship could be described as harmonious? Is your own relationship one that you would call vitalized?

These portraits may seem like caricatures, but they are not greatly exaggerated. Rather, each of these couples resembles a distinct type identified by research. The *traditional* couple responds well to their child's needs, not their own. The *harmonious* pair attends mostly to themselves. The *conflicted* couple speaks harsh words, while the *devitalized* hardly speaks a word. Observing these interactions, the *vitalized* pair seems able to complete each other's sentences, yet they speak their own.

In this chapter, the reader will see that intimacy and closeness is experienced differently among these types of couples. We present detailed profiles of the couple types that go behind this restaurant scene to reveal some of the complexity in these relationships. Our findings are based on a national survey of married couples who completed enriching relationship issues, communication and happiness (ENRICH) a comprehensive 165-item self-report couples assessment.

The ENRICH inventory contains 10 highly reliable scales (Cronbach alphas ranged from .75 to .90; test–retest reliabilities ranged from .77 to .92) that were used in cluster analysis to derive the ENRICH couple typology (Olson & Fowers, 1993). To assess couple intimacy, we organized these scales into three areas representing the following:

1. Skills that facilitate intimacy, specifically how well couples communicate with each other ("my partner is a very good listener") and resolve conflicts ("at times, I feel some of our differences never get resolved").

2. Different kinds of intimacy, such as social ("I really enjoy being with most of my partner's friends"), recreational ("I am concerned that my partner has too many activities or hobbies"), sexual ("we try to find ways to keep our sexual relationship interesting and enjoyable"), and spiritual ("we rely on our spiritual beliefs during difficult times").

3. Some common stressors or potential barriers to intimacy in marriage include raising children ("we agree on how to discipline our children"), managing finances ("we have trouble saving money"), dealing with personality issues ("I wish my partner were more reliable and followed through on more things"), and negotiating roles ("I am concerned that I do more than my share of the household tasks").

ENRICH also contains scales that were not used to create the typology, and we used these to explore other characteristics associated with intimacy, such as couple and family system dynamics, relationship behaviors, and individual functioning (psychological well-being). In developing profiles of the couple types, we relied on the original 10 scales and all of the new scales to present a complete portrait of each couple type.

The ENRICH couple types have been characterized as follows (Olson & Olson, 1999): Vitalized are the happiest, satisfied couples, with the most relationship strengths and the lowest risk of divorce. Harmonious are happy and satisfied, with many strengths. Traditional are generally happy and have more external strengths (family, friends, and spiritual community) than internal strengths (e.g., communication skills). Conflicted are unhappy and dissatisfied; they have few strengths and a high divorce risk. Devitalized are the unhappiest, least satisfied couples, with the fewest strengths and the highest divorce risk.

Looking at relationships through the lens of an empirically derived typology such as ENRICH is one way to respond to the call by Prager (2000) for innovative strategies to help couples increase satisfaction and intimacy. A stronger link between assessment and intervention is needed. This has been advocated before with proposals for systematic research to determine which types of couples would benefit from what kinds of interventions (Olson, 1981). By tailoring treatment goals to specific types of couples, therapy outcomes can be improved, but this requires a sound assessment tool (Beach & Bauserman, 1990).

In organizing the content of this chapter, we present background information on couple typologies and the ENRICH program before defining intimacy and closeness. After discussing several principles that shape our perspective on intimacy, we present detailed profiles of the ENRICH couple types and note practical implications. Next, we report statistical analyses that demonstrate the relevance and validity of the ENRICH typology. We conclude with an intervention strategy aimed at helping less intimate couples develop and sustain a happy, satisfying relationship.

TYPOLOGIES OF INTIMATE RELATIONSHIPS

Typologies of intimate relationships have been developed over decades of research. The ENRICH couple typology is one of many that attempts to capture the complexity of couple and family systems. An important and necessary property of classification—one that determines whether a typology is meaningful, and not arbitrary—is whether it predicts additional characteristics of the types (Filsinger, McAvoy, & Lewis, 1982). Early typologies were intuitively derived based on in-depth interviews (e.g., Cuber and Haroff, 1955) and are difficult to replicate. Later typologies were empirically derived, either based on self-report (e.g., Fitzpatrick, 1984) or observation (e.g., Gottman, 1993), but only a few have been extensively researched and proven useful.

Typologies examine many characteristics at once to identify clusters of cases that fit together naturally. Compared with traditional multivariate analysis, the typological method offers the advantage of greater statistical power, by combining multiple variables into a single analytical framework (Olson, 1981). This method has practical appeal because it focuses attention on couples, not just variables. Typologies, therefore, can bridge the gap between research and practice.

AN INTRODUCTION TO ENRICH

ENRICH is a component of the PREPARE/ENRICH program (Olson & Olson, 1999), developed to help couples learn skills for a happy marriage. The program gives couples the opportunity to talk openly and directly about important issues in their relationship. ENRICH is for couples who have been married at least two years. Preparing personal and relationship evaluation (PREPARE) is for couples planning to be married. Each has national norms developed with data from more than 250,000 culturally and ethnically diverse couples.

Counselors certified to use the PREPARE/ENRICH program include clergy and pastoral counselors, marriage and family therapists, and psychologists. In practice, partners complete an inventory without consulting each other. Results are summarized in a computer report used by the counselor to guide a couple through communication and goal setting exercises (see Olson & Olson, 1999) after discussing relationship strengths and issues. Counselors have the flexibility to determine how best to use the program materials, according to their own skills and on the basis of their judgment of the couple's readiness for change.

Development

ENRICH was developed after an extensive review of conceptual and empirical studies to identify the many factors that influence marital quality (Fournier, Olson, & Druckman, 1983). This process led to the development of the 10 scales that represent the core domains of the inventory: communication, conflict resolution, family and friends, leisure activities, sexual relationship, spiritual beliefs, children and parenting, financial management, personality issues, and egalitarian roles. Using dyadic scores on these scales, the cluster analysis for the couple typology was done in three stages involving exploratory, replication, and cross-validation procedures (Olson & Fowers, 1993).

Application

A unique feature of ENRICH is its use of dyadic scores to denote the level of agreement between husbands and wives on positive qualities in the relationship. Couples with high agreement scores have similarly positive perceptions and understand each other's experience in the relationship. This fits our conceptualization of intimacy, and it has practical applications.

Positive agreement items help couples see strengths to build on in their relationship, unlike a total agreement score, which would mix agreement on positive aspects with agreement on negative aspects of the relationship. This distinction is useful because each set of information serves a different purpose. Negative agreement items signal issues that require special focus. When couples see "eye to eye" on an issue, there is a starting point for problem solving. To resolve it, however, success is more likely if there is a base of positive agreement on which to build. No matter how few, an identifiable strength becomes a resource the couple can call upon to address a problem.

INTIMACY AND CLOSENESS

There are many ways to define intimacy (see Heller & Wood, 1998; Prager, 2000; Schaefer & Olson, 1981; Waring, 1988), which suggests that it is an elusive concept to measure. Our goal is to make a practical contribution, first by bringing attention to the literature that views intimacy as *similar perceptions* and *mutual understanding* of the experience. Heller and Wood (1998) advanced these concepts in research with the personal assessment of intimacy in relationships (PAIR) inventory (Schaefer & Olson, 1981). They found highly intimate couples had congruent scores (similar perceptions) on the intimacy scales, and these couples accurately predicted each other's scores (mutual understanding). Other researchers, too, have found that a couple's level of intimacy corresponds to the degree to which each person shares perceptions of the relationship (Talmadge & Dabbs, 1990, cited in Prager, 2000); and similarity in perceptions contributes significantly to satisfaction with the relationship (Deal, Wampler, & Halverson, 1992).

To begin constructing a framework for a theory of intimacy that is supported by the ENRICH program, we present five principles, each of which contain assumptions that we would like to make explicit.

1. Intimacy is a process and an experience that optimally occurs in a caring, committed relationship. Intimacy is a dynamic process. It evolves over time as both partners create positive ways of being in the relationship. Intentional focus and active efforts are required to build and sustain intimacy. Process implies movement, in either direction, toward higher or lower levels, and this suggests there are relationship characteristics that either facilitate or impede the experience of intimacy. How couples communicate, resolve conflicts, and manage stressors in the relationship, matters. When there is a sense of inclusion, or commitment to the relationship, couples may make communication a priority and find it easier to collaborate as equal partners in facing any challenges or issues that arise. These characteristics, in a long term relationship, foster a quality of intimacy that endures.

2. Intimacy implies that many positive qualities are present in the relationship. As a process, intimacy involves constructing a shared reality about what is working well in the relationship. By identifying strengths, couples become more connected and build a foundation for new strengths to emerge. Therefore, intimacy reflects an accumulation of strengths in the relationship. So defined, it can be measured as the degree to which couples share positive perceptions of the relationship. Highly intimate partners are in close agreement about their strengths as a couple. They see many positives, in multiple areas of the relationship, while less intimate couples see few.

3. Couples experience various kinds of intimacy. There are variations in the levels and the kinds of intimacy that couples experience. Intimacy as a multidimensional construct was advanced by the developers of the PAIR Inventory (Schaefer & Olson, 1981). PAIR measures five kinds of intimacy: intellectual, emotional, sexual, social, and recreational. ENRICH, a precursor to PAIR, measures sexual, social, and recreational in addition to spiritual intimacy; it does not measure intellectual, and it taps emotional intimacy differently. PAIR combines two concepts, openness in communication and a sense of togetherness, for its emotional intimacy scale, but ENRICH separates these into two scales (i.e., communication and couple closeness).

4. Couples can learn skills that facilitate intimacy. Communication and conflict resolution skills can be learned. These skills are taught in most marriage and couples education programs, which emphasize building competencies for a healthy relationship. They are also conceptualized as necessary facets of intimacy by Waring (1981). ENRICH defines *communication* as the couple's ability and freedom to communicate openly in an atmosphere of supportiveness and genuine understanding; and *conflict resolution* as acknowledging issues and using effective strategies to resolve them (Olson, 1996).

A couples communication style that promotes intimacy is both *assertive* and *respectful*. To be assertive means knowing what you want and need in the relationship, and taking the risk to disclose this information. To be respectful involves actively listening to your partner's needs and concerns, to understand and validate them. Respect is also marked by the absence of controlling behaviors such as avoidance or partner dominance. ENRICH incorporates exercises for couples to practice assertiveness and active listening skills and to learn concrete steps for conflict resolution. The exercises are designed to encourage disclosure, responsiveness, and collaboration.

5. Intimacy is linked to patterns of flexibility and closeness in the relationship. We hypothesize that highly intimate couples function at optimal levels of flexibility and closeness, and they use communication skills to maintain these levels. Optimal *flexibility* is a balance of stability and change in the relationship (Olson, 2000). In response to stress, flexible couples can shift roles and responsibilities as needed. Optimal *closeness* is a balance of togetherness and separateness (Olson, 2000). Close couples are emotionally connected, and they rely on each other for support. They enjoy being together and share many interests, yet they also accept each other's individuality. In effect, close couples experience a secure sense of belonging in the relationship. This creates an atmosphere for intimacy to flourish.

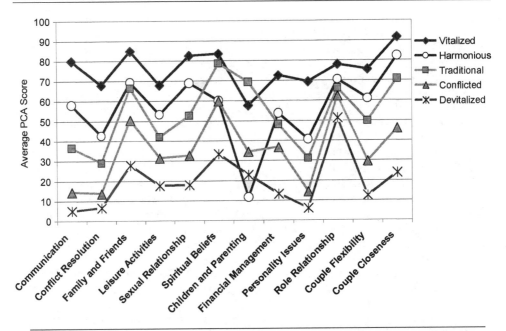

FIG. 8.1. Five couple types were derived using cluster analysis and positive couple agreement (PCA) scores on 10 scales from the ENRICH inventory. On a continuum from most to least intimate, the types range from *vitalized* to *devitalized*. PCA scores on two additional scales, flexibility and closeness, demonstrate that the typology predicts other meaningful characteristics. The PCA score is the percentage of items that both partners rated as a positive quality in their relationship.

PROFILES AND IMPLICATIONS

Figure 8.1 provides a glimpse at how the ENRICH typology works. It displays positive couple agreement (PCA) scores on the 10 original scales used to create the typology and on two additional scales that measure flexibility and closeness. The scores are linearly distributed across the types, a pattern which suggests that from most to least intimate, the couple types are vitalized, harmonious, traditional, conflicted, and devitalized. The major characteristics of each couple type are summarized below.

ENRICH classifies couples as *stable* (vitalized, harmonious, traditional) or *unstable* (conflicted, devitalized), a distinction supported by longitudinal research over the first three years of marriage that demonstrated the latter group is the most likely to divorce (Fowers, Montel, & Olson, 1996). Our data replicate other validating evidence reported by Olson and Fowers (1993) using two items, relationship satisfaction and divorce potential, which is a proven indicator of marital distress (Fowers & Olson, 1989). Relationship satisfaction was indicated by nine of every 10 highly intimate couples (vitalized; 93%; harmonious, 86%) and three of every four moderately intimate couples (traditional, 75%); in contrast, satisfaction was indicated by only one in three conflicted, (32%) and one in 10 devitalized (9%) couples. The ratings of divorce potential show an increase in marital distress across the types. Many vitalized (70%) couples had never considered divorce; this is also true for a majority of harmonious (59%), and traditional (57%) couples but only a minority of conflicted (34%) and devitalized (21%) couples.

More Intimate Couples

Vitalized Type. Vitalized couples are the most intimate and skilled of the types, and the most successful in preventing stressors from interfering with their relationship. In addition, Vitalized couples are the most emotionally connected of the types, and the most flexible in adapting to stress and transitions in their relationships. They are highly assertive and rarely engage in avoidant or controlling behaviors. They have mutually high levels of self confidence, and they share a sense of happiness and enjoyment in life. These findings suggest that vitalized couples are the most likely to understand and respond to each other's needs in the relationship.

Harmonious Type. Harmonious couples are somewhat skilled in communication and conflict resolution, and they have moderate to high levels of intimacy. They tend to experience more sexual and social, than spiritual or recreational, intimacies. Harmonious couples handle some stressors more effectively than others. They are not in agreement on children and parenting, yet many do not yet have children. For some harmonious couples, knowing how to deal with personality issues is a source of stress; and to some extent so is coming to agreement on how to manage finances. Personality issues refer to behaviors such as moodiness, stubbornness, and jealousy.

Harmonious couples are nearly as close but not as flexible as vitalized, who are more skilled in communication. This suggests that harmonious couples may eventually have difficulty resolving issues, or adapting to stressors including normative transitions such as the birth of children. Harmonious couples can be assertive, but not as consistently as vitalized. Avoidant and controlling behaviors, if not kept in check, could lead a decline in relationship satisfaction.

Harmonious couples have a strong sense of togetherness, but they need to increase flexibility in the relationship. A high level of closeness, without a high level of flexibility, suggests more dependence than interdependence in the relationship. Communication exercises must focus not only on what each person wants or needs, but also on how to listen well, accepting each other's perspective as valid. Long term, these couples need to embrace their relationship as an equal partnership.

Resolving personality issues may require changes in behavior as well as accepting each other's imperfections and flaws. Harmonious couples are likely to be motivated to improve their communication and conflict resolution skills. Their strong emotional bond is an asset that can help bolster these efforts.

Moderately Intimate Couples

Traditional couples are the most stable (i.e., least likely to divorce) type (Fowers et al., 1996) after vitalized, and they are nearly as satisfied as harmonious. On most measures, their scores are average, falling between the more intimate (vitalized, harmonious) and the less intimate (conflicted, devitalized) couples' scores.

Traditional Type. Traditional couples are moderately skilled in communication and conflict resolution. Intimacy generally declines across the types, however, Traditional couples break this pattern by experiencing high levels of spiritual and social intimacies. In addition, traditional couples are highly compatible on values related to children and parenting, much like vitalized. They experience moderate levels of sexual and recreational intimacies. Personality issues and financial management are two stressors in these relationships.

Although traditional couples have social support from external sources (such as family, friends, and religious institutions), support within the relationship is less clear. Traditional couples experience closeness, but they do not perceive much flexibility.

Traditional couples can be assertive, but they are not highly responsive to each other's needs. They may avoid communicating on some issues, or at certain times, yet harshly confront each other on other issues, or at other times. There are signs of psychological distress in these marriages. Self-confidence is not as mutually high as it is for vitalized. Traditional couples report happiness and enjoyment in life, but this could be attributed to factors outside the relationship.

More flexibility is needed, before focusing on intimacy to increase sexual satisfaction, physical affection, and shared leisure time. For collaborative problem solving, responsiveness to each other's concerns needs to be emphasized. Personality issues, a major source of stress, are linked to perceptions of control and dominance in these relationships. In statistical analyses not yet reported, partner dominance was the most important variable discriminating traditional from vitalized couples. Unless traditional couples can interrupt this negative pattern of rigidity and control, their experience of intimacy likely will remain mixed.

To ensure success, therapeutic and educational interventions can build on traditional couples' strong values related to children, family, and spiritual community. This can be done, for example, by placing emphasis on developing character and practicing virtues in marriage, such as loyalty, friendship, and kindness. This approach goes beyond skill building as a means to promote greater flexibility and respect in the relationship.

Less Intimate Couples

To learn how to develop intimacy and closeness is a particularly challenging task for couples in distress. They often seek therapy when the relationship seems beyond repair, and even then, one of the partners may be reluctant to participate. Sometimes these couples may seek other ways to find help. For instance, conflicted and devitalized types have begun to represent the majority of attendees at some marriage and couples education programs (Olson & Olson, 1999). Therefore, strategies in working with conflicted and devitalized types of couples are critical to develop. If distressed couples are willing to work on the relationship, they need to be given a clear picture of the challenges ahead. Solidifying commitment to the relationship may be a necessary first step.

Conflicted Type.   Conflicted couples are much less skilled in communication and conflict resolution than the previous types. They experience low levels of intimacy, in every form. They are much less emotionally connected and less flexible than the more intimate types. Of the different kinds of intimacy, spiritual intimacy ranks above the others. Of the various stressors, personality issues seem the most problematic. Lack of agreement on childrearing is another source of stress.

In general, conflicted and devitalized couples' scores on the various measures differ by degree, but some of the differences are more pronounced than others. Conflicted couples experience more spiritual and social intimacies. They have less stress related to financial management. Their controlling, avoidant behaviors are problematic, but not as extreme as devitalized. Although conflicted couples are less happy than the more intimate types, they are not as unhappy as devitalized. Their self-confidence, however, which reflects self-esteem and mastery, is similarly low.

Devitalized Type.   Devitalized couples are discouraged, either unmotivated or unwilling to develop communication and conflict resolution skills for the relationship. They experience the lowest levels of intimacy and have less capacity to deal with stressors than any other couple type. Personality issues, financial management, and children and parenting are all major sources of stress in the relationship. Devitalized couples can be characterized as *disengaged*, the least close, and as *rigid*, the least flexible, of the types. Devitalized couples are much less assertive than other types. They are the most likely to avoid communication and to perceive disrespect, or hostility, from their partner. (In twice as many devitalized as conflicted marriages, both partners reported high levels of avoidance and partner dominance.) Their states of psychological well-being are the worst, with both partners prone to feeling unworthy, incompetent, and unhappy in their lives.

Overall, conflicted and devitalized couples both are in distress. As portrayed in the opening vignette, the conflicted partners spoke harshly, and the devitalized hardly spoke, yet both pairs displayed criticism and contempt. These are two forms of hostility, overt and covert, that were observed by Gottman (1993). The unstable types in his typology are labeled hostile-engaged and hostile-disengaged. These styles of interaction affect the psychological states of both partners, with covert hostility appearing to do even more damage than overt hostility.

Less intimate couples are embroiled in a negative cycle of avoiding issues at times, and desperately trying to control each other at other times. Whereas this pattern reflects ineffective communication and conflict resolution skills, it also signals a lack of trust or a loss of hope in the relationship. In the struggle for power and control, less intimate couples may be as reluctant as they are unable to resolve issues.

Discrepant perceptions characterize less intimate couples. As reported later in this chapter, wives view these relationships as more rigid and less egalitarian, and they report more problems with communication, personality issues, and children and parenting, than do their husbands. Unless conflicted and devitalized couples can construct a common view of the relationship and elicit caring responses from each other, progress toward intimacy seems unlikely.

Couples With Children

Research shows couple intimacy declines with the birth of children, and relationship satisfaction dips to its lowest level when children reach adolescence (Olson et al., 1989). More avenues of research are needed to determine how intimacy changes after couples have children, what can be done to normalize this experience, and which strategies work to maintain or increase intimacy during the childrearing years.

In our findings, among all of the background characteristics examined as predictors, only the presence of children was important, and it was negatively associated with intimacy. Making the relationship a priority is often advised, and there are practical ways to help couples "take back" their marriage (Doherty, 2001). Another approach worth exploring is to add a parenting-skills component to marriage and couples education programs. This has several potential benefits. For the less intimate couples, conflicted and devitalized, it could help reduce stress in the relationship by increasing their confidence in coparenting, and this could strengthen their emotional connectedness. In addition, skills practiced in the context of parenting may be transferable to the relationship; this applies particularly well to Traditional couples, who place a strong value on children and parenting yet do not communicate well in the marriage.

Prevalence

The typological findings are based on a secondary data set of 21,501 couples who completed the ENRICH inventory between 1997 and 1999.[1] The sample is one of

---

[1] A detailed profile of the characteristics of this sample is provided in the book *Empowering Couples: Building on Your Strengths* by Olson and Olson (2000).

convenience, because couples entered it either by referral or self-selection. For the analyses reported below, we randomly selected 2,000 couples of each type, in order to have equal group sizes for the statistical procedures that compare and contrast the types. When surveyed, the couples had been married an average of eight years. Nearly three-fourths (72%) had children, and a majority (55%) had two or more children. The couples resided in both urban (56%) and rural (44%) areas across every region of the United States.

In an earlier typological study ($N = 6{,}267$; data collected between 1983 and 1985) couple types were found in the following proportions: vitalized, 12%; harmonious, 11%; traditional, 16%; conflicted, 25%; and devitalized, 36% (Olson & Fowers, 1993). In the current data set, the types are represented in nearly the same proportions: vitalized, 21%; harmonious, 11%; traditional, 14%; conflicted, 25%; and devitalized, 29% (Kouneski, 2002). The exception is there are more vitalized (21% vs. 12%) and fewer devitalized (29% vs. 36%) couples now—perhaps due to greater prevention and couples education efforts in the span of 12–16 years between the two data collection periods.

Summary

The results of statistical analyses show that couple type is linked to many meaningful characteristics. The observed patterns of differences across the types are useful in generating new insights for couples intervention. Overall, couples who function at optimal levels of closeness and flexibility are highly assertive, respectful, and self confident. They are satisfied with their relationship, and their marriages are stable. They have the capacity to experience intimacy in all of its forms. Their communication skills promote mutual understanding, enabling the full development of intimacy.

Couples who function as *disengaged* (not close) or *rigid* (not flexible) tend to be avoidant and controlling, and one or both partners experience psychological distress. They have divergent perceptions of the relationship, with both partners dissatisfied. They may be passive or aggressive in expressing resentment and hostility toward each other. These couples are likely to be ambivalent about their commitment to the relationship, and therefore, not risk self disclosure, which requires the willingness to be vulnerable and to trust one's partners. Their experience of intimacy, therefore, is restricted.

These findings have implications for researchers and clinicians who rely on relational assessments. To determine whether a marriage is healthy or in distress, it is clear that couple dynamics, relationship behaviors, and individual functioning (psychological well-being) are intricately linked. Close and flexible patterns of functioning distinguish highly intimate couples. So does the mutual experience of psychological well-being. Furthermore, highly intimate couples engage in communication behaviors that convey respect and positive regard for each other and lead to their mutual understanding that the relationship has value.

DETAILED FINDINGS

This research was exploratory and primarily serves a descriptive purpose. In examining patterns to produce detailed profiles of the types, statistical analyses were undertaken to (a) identify meaningful characteristics that distinguish the couple types, (b) determine the most important predictors of success in intimate relationship, and (c) examine gender differences within each type. Given the large sample, even trivial differences can be statistically significant; therefore, to gauge the practical significance of the findings, effect size measures were used. (For a complete description of the statistical procedures and results, see Kouneski, 2002).

Meaningful Characteristics of the Types

The core characteristics of the types were graphically depicted in Figure 8.1. For each domain, there were significant differences between the types and large effects. This finding is based on multivariate analyses of variance (MANOVA), follow-up analyses of variance (ANOVAs), and the univariate effect-size measure, partial η squared (η^2). Of the 10 scales used to create the typology, in descending order, the best discriminators were communication, conflict resolution, and personality issues (η^2 range, .65 to .75); followed by family and friends, sexual relationship, leisure activities, and children and parenting (η^2 range, .46 to .51); then by financial management, spiritual beliefs, and role relationship (η^2 range, .23 to .37).

Additional characteristics of the types are displayed in Table 8.1. Categorical variables (both couples rating the domain highly, both couples rating the domain lowly, and couples responding in a moderate or mixed fashion) were constructed for couple closeness, couple flexibility, assertiveness, avoidance, partner dominance, self-confidence, and happiness in life. Each variable was significantly associated with couple type and showed medium-to-large effects based on chi-square tests and the effect-size measure Cramer's V. The variables for family closeness and family flexibility, and most others examined, were also significant but had trivial-to-small effects.

If we view intimacy as a continuum across the five couple types, from high (vitalized; harmonious) to moderate (traditional) to low (conflicted; devitalized), the data on additional characteristics of the types can be used to deepen our understanding of the links between intimacy levels, couple dynamics, relationship behaviors, and psychological well-being.

Couple Dynamics. Among the more intimate types, harmonious (93%) couples are very close, much like vitalized (98%); yet fewer harmonious (67%) are highly flexible, compared with vitalized (88%). Closeness is mutually high in many more traditional (76%) than conflicted (35%) or devitalized (8%) couples, while flexibility is high in less than half of Traditional (44%) and in very few conflicted (15%) and devitalized (2%) couples.

Relationship Behaviors. Among the more intimate types, many harmonious (74%) couples are mutually high in assertiveness; and this is true for even more vitalized (95%). A slight majority of traditional (52%) couples are highly assertive, compared with very few conflicted and devitalized (14% and 4%, respectively). On the measures of avoidance and partner dominance, it useful to note the proportion that is not mutually low, because it signals one or both partners are engaging in controlling behaviors, or disrespectful communication. Harmonious couples are not as mutually low in avoidance as vitalized (58% and 86%, respectively). The proportions are much lower for traditional (28%), conflicted (9%), and devitalized (2%). In addition, harmonious couples are not as mutually low in partner dominance as vitalized (32% and. 77%, respectively), and the proportions decline from traditional (13%), to conflicted (2%), to devitalized (nearly 0%). Among the less intimate types, one fifth of conflicted (18%) and one third of devitalized (36%) couples are mutually high in avoidance; in addition, one third of conflicted (35%) and two thirds of devitalized (65%) are mutually high in partner dominance.

Psychological Well-Being. Vitalized and harmonious couples enjoy mutually high levels of psychological well-being. Harmonious couples are not quite as high in self-confidence as vitalized (58% and 79%, respectively), but happiness in life (76% and. 89%, respectively) is somewhat comparable. Less than half of traditional (41%) couples share a high level of self-confidence, whereas two thirds (66%) report happiness.

TABLE 8.1

Additional Characteristics of the ENRICH Couple Types

Characteristics	Proportions by Couple Type				
	Vitalized	Harmonious	Traditional	Conflicted	Devitalized
Couple closeness					
Both high	98.4	92.7	75.6	34.8	8.2
Both low	.1	.4	1.3	13.4	38.8
Moderate/mixed	1.5	6.9	23.1	51.8	53.0
Couple flexibility					
Both high	87.8	66.7	43.9	14.9	2.1
Both low	—	—	.9	11.7	34.5
Moderate/mixed	12.2	33.3	55.2	73.4	63.4
Assertiveness					
Both high	95.4	74.1	51.8	13.7	4.0
Both low	.2	.3	1.9	15.0	33.1
Moderate/mixed	4.6	25.6	46.2	71.3	62.9
Avoidance					
Both high	.2	1.1	4.3	17.5	36.2
Both low	85.9	58.2	28.9	9.3	2.1
Moderate/mixed	13.9	40.7	66.8	73.2	61.7
Partner dominance					
Both high	.2	2.8	7.3	35.3	64.1
Both low	77.1	31.6	13.0	1.6	.1
Moderate/mixed	22.7	65.6	79.7	63.1	35.8
Self-Confidence					
Both high	78.5	57.5	41.1	22.6	11.2
Both low	.7	2.2	5.0	17.2	29.5
Moderate/mixed	20.8	40.3	53.9	60.2	59.3
Happiness in life					
Both	88.7	76.1	65.9	34.2	15.8
Neither	2.1	4.3	8.0	23.7	40.7
One only	9.3	19.6	26.1	42.1	43.5
Family closeness					
Both high	37.8	26.0	21.8	18.2	17.7
Both low	7.2	11.0	11.4	15.9	16.5
Moderate/mixed	55.1	63.0	66.9	66.1	66.0
Family flexibility					
Both high	49.0	37.6	29.7	27.2	23.1
Both low	2.4	3.0	3.0	5.2	6.6
Moderate/mixed	48.7	59.4	67.4	67.7	70.4

Note. Individual percentile rank scores were categorized as "high" (60% and above); "moderate" (40 to 59%); or "low" (39% and below), to assign categorical values of "both high," "both low," and "moderate/mixed" (based on national norms). Dashes indicate proportions less than .05.

Among the less intimate types, only one fifth of conflicted (22%) couples are mutually high in self-confidence. In devitalized couples, self-confidence was more likely to be mutually low (30%) than high (11%). In addition, one or both partners did not report happiness in many conflicted (66%) and devitalized (84%) couples, and neither partner did in 24% and 41%, respectively.

Most Important Predictors of Intimacy

Hierarchical logistic regression was used to determine the relative importance of variables that predict intimacy. For the dichotomous, categorical dependent variable, the highly intimate (vitalized, harmonious) and the less intimate (conflicted, devitalized) couple types were contrasted. Independent variables, called *predictors* in logistic regression, were entered stepwise in blocks representing demographics, family system, couple dynamics, and individual functioning. Relationship behaviors were omitted from this analysis because of item overlap with the scales that determined couple type, the dependent variable. Demographics included the presence of children, length of marriage, and other characteristics such as age, education, and income. Family system and couple dynamics, besides the measures of closeness and flexibility, included abuse (emotional, physical, or sexual) and problem drug or alcohol use, by one's partners or parents. Individual functioning comprised the two measures of psychological well-being.

Couple dynamics were the best predictors of intimacy. Closeness was the most important predictor. When both partners in the relationship perceived a high level of closeness (odds ratio [OR] = 11.6), they were 12 times more likely to be classified as vitalized or harmonious than those with moderate or mixed levels. Flexibility was the second most important predictor. Similarly, couples who perceived high levels of flexibility (OR = 5.2) were five times more likely to be vitalized or harmonious.

Psychological well-being was a good predictor of intimacy. When both partners had high scores in self-confidence (OR = 2.0) and each reported feeling happiness in life (OR = 1.9), they were twice as likely as others, with moderate or mixed levels, to be classified as vitalized or harmonious.

On demographics, the presence of children (OR = .60) was the only important background characteristic discriminating between the most intimate and least intimate couple types. Conflicted and devitalized couples were more likely to have children. No other background or couple and family system characteristics had predictive value except for abuse by partner (OR = 3.4). The link between spouse abuse and couple type was examined in a separate study (Asai & Olson, 2000).

Gender Differences by Couple Type

Paired-samples *t* tests were conducted to determine whether husbands and wives had different perceptions of their relationship and, if so, to what degree. The analyses used every ENRICH scale available, including two not yet mentioned. Marriage satisfaction, a composite scale, has one item for each of the 10 core domains. The idealistic distortion scale measures marital conventionalization and is used to correct social desirability bias; this scale has been newly interpreted as a measure of "positive illusions" about the marriage because it is strongly associated with satisfaction (Fowers, Applegate, Olson, & Pomerantz, 1994).

Couple satisfaction and idealism scores were distributed linearly across the types, as expected, with vitalized couples the most satisfied and the most idealistic (Kouneski, 2002). Overall, highly intimate couples had similar perceptions on nearly every measure. However, in the less intimate couple types divergent perceptions were common. Wives were less satisfied and more realistic than their husbands in conflicted (C) and devitalized (D) marriages. On skills, stressors, and couple dynamics, small-to-medium effects were found using Cohen's (1988) standardized-mean difference, *d*, as an effect-size measure. Husbands reported more satisfaction (C: $d = .34$; D: $d = .43$) and a more idealistic view of the marriage (C: $d = .28$; D: $d = .42$) than their wives, who reported more problems with communication (C: $d = .30$; D: $d = .38$) as well as egalitarian roles (C: $d = .41$; D: $d = .47$), personality issues (C: $d = .19$; D: $d = .25$), and children and parenting (C: $d = .18$; D: $d = .25$). In addition, wives perceived less flexibility in the relationship than did their husbands (C: $d = .21$; D: $d = .28$).

Curiously, in the highly intimate couple types, vitalized (V) and harmonious (H), wives perceived more closeness than did their husbands (V: $d = -.39$; H: $d = -.40$), yet both spouses reported a high level of closeness. For these couples, there were no differences in perceptions of flexibility or self-confidence. In conflicted marriages, however, there was an indication that husbands experienced more self-confidence than did their wives ($d = .15$); in devitalized marriages, both partners were equally low in self-confidence.

INTERVENTION STRATEGY

To help couples achieve greater satisfaction, stability, and happiness in marriage, the most effective interventions may be those that have a dual focus on skill building and pattern change (Buetler, 2000). Whether skill building alone can have lasting effects is a point of some controversy. Short-term gains have been demonstrated, but long-term outcomes are less certain (Gottman, Coan, Carrere, & Swanson, 1998). Efforts to build skills therefore, must lead to a change in functional patterns (e.g., rigidity, hostility, avoidance, defensiveness). If attempts to improve skills are not successful, there may be absent in the relationship an ethic of caring, or a genuine concern for each other's well-being. In these cases, little value is placed on developing strengths in the relationship. This may be due in part to a sense of personal inadequacy and a fear of rejection by one's partner.

For couples in great distress, an indirect intervention may be more successful than a direct one. For example, stating that the goal is to become closer or more intimate may be too anxiety provoking. These couples may balk at acquiring skills because communication facilitates closeness. They may be more receptive to interventions focused on shared problem solving aimed at increasing flexibility not closeness. In therapy, such problem solving initially can be channeled toward resolving the presenting symptoms (Walsh & Olson, 1989) or uniting to cope with an external stressor.

When couples have few positive perceptions of their relationship and no clearly identified strengths to reinforce, some caution should be exercised in communicating their type. The act of labeling conflicted and devitalized types could disempower rather than empower them. One or both partners may view this label as pathologizing, or fixed and permanent.

No typology fits everyone perfectly. Despite the statistical patterns that can be discerned, there will be exceptions and unique cases including those that fall near the boundary of two types. Couples of the same type may differ in their agreement on individual items, even though they agree on the same *percentage* of items. Therefore, it is important to view each couple as unique, except perhaps vitalized couples who are all overwhelmingly positive in their perceptions.

Following is an outline of an intervention strategy, based on ENRICH, that targets the less intimate, more distressed couples.

1. Focus on problem solving at the start to increase levels of flexibility in the relationship. Give couples hope. Help them create small successes in problem solving by finding ways to better manage an identified stressor. Instill a sense of mutual care and support in this process. Find common ground by highlighting "special focus" items, or negative couple agreement, to identify issues that both partners perceive as problems and are willing to address.

2. Assess patterns and behaviors in the relationship that affect individual health and well-being. Examine self-confidence, assertiveness, avoidance, and partner

dominance. If one or both partners are unassertive, explore signs of psychological distress or negative communication behaviors that may be contributing factors. If couples do not engage well in this process, each partner's commitment to the relationship will need to be clarified.

3. Explore how positive regard is communicated despite personality issues and differences. Find ways to help partners communicate what they like and appreciate about each other. With conflicted and devitalized couples, it is often useful to revisit the early years of their marriage, and even the courtship period, to rediscover what attracted them to each other. In this context, given the hope of renewing a relationship once valued, intimacy and closeness may be viewed as less threatening.

4. Help couples create a common understanding of their experience of intimacy in the relationship. Have both partners discuss their satisfaction with current levels of intimacy. This is necessary before discussing goals or plans for increasing intimacy. Cover all forms of intimacy (family and friends, leisure activities, sexual relationship, spiritual beliefs) including closeness and communication (emotional intimacy). This may be difficult for couples who feel hostility or are not invested in the relationship. Perceptions of abuse in the relationship may need to be addressed, given the damage to trust in the relationship. The use of positive communication skills (assertiveness and active listening) is extremely important for this discussion.

5. Encourage couples to discuss what each person needs and can do to enhance the value of their relationship. It may be difficult for couples to have this discussion when one or both partners lacks self-confidence (i.e., self-esteem and mastery). If persons do not value their own needs in the relationship, they will surely find it difficult to attend to a partner's. Emphasize that active listening conveys respect for other, whereas assertiveness stems from respect for self. These skills go hand in hand with self-confidence.

Persons with low self-esteem need a sense of belonging in order to risk getting closer and more deeply attached. According to Murray and Holmes (2000), "enhancing the value of the relationship is likely to be seen as a viable or safe strategy of self-enhancement only by individuals who trust in the continued stability of their relationships" (p. 179). This could explain some of the variability in the effectiveness of interventions aimed solely at skill building. To understand the value placed on developing intimacy and closeness, it is important to examine both individual and couple characteristics. Psychological well-being, relationship behaviors, and couple dynamics (i.e., closeness and flexibility) all are interrelated.

CONCLUSION

Intimacy is complex to measure because it is a relational phenomenon. It is also a reciprocal experience. Either both partners are intimate or neither is. We have emphasized the role of shared, positive perceptions in creating and sustaining intimacy. As couples build consensus on positive qualities in their relationship, they are affirming its value. Happy couples share the beliefs that "we belong together" and "we are good for each other."

There is wisdom in proverbs. Leo Tolstoy's novel Anna Karenina opens with the saying that happy families are all alike, but each unhappy family is miserable in its own way. Perhaps the true power of a typology rests not so much in predicting multiple characteristics of the types as in capturing the essence of a happy relationship toward which couples can aspire. Couples with high levels of intimacy are close, flexible, assertive, respectful, self-confident, and happy. These are the vitalized couples, who openly communicate their needs and feel genuinely supported in the relationship, caring for each other's well being.

Next time you are in your favorite restaurant, you might notice how other couples are interacting. Look around, but also look within. Consider the qualities of your own relationship that you appreciate and value. Share your reflections with your partner. Together, you might decide the kind of intimate relationship that you can have and keep.

REFERENCES

Asai, S. G., & Olson, D. H. (2000). *Spouse abuse and marital system: Based on ENRICH.* Retrieved from http://www.lifeinnovations.com/pdf/abuse.pdf, May 11, 2003.

Beach, S. R. H., & Bauserman, S. A. K. (1990). Enhancing the effectiveness of marital therapy. In F. D. Fincham & T. N. Bradbury (Eds.), *The psychology of marriage* (pp. 402–419). New York: Guilford.

Buetler, L. E. (2000). Empirically based decision making in clinical practice. *Prevention and Treatment, 3.* Available from http://journals.apa.org/prevention/volume3/pre0030027a.html

Cohen, J. (1988). *Statistical power analysis for the behavioral sciences* (2nd ed.). Hillsdale, NJ: Lawrence Erlbaum.

Cuber, J. F., & Haroff, P. B. (1955). *The significant Americans: A study of sexual behavior among the affluent.* Englewood Cliffs, NJ: Prentice-Hall.

Deal, J. E., Wampler, K. S., & Halverson, Jr., C. F. (1992). The importance of similarity in the marital relationship. *Family Process, 31,* 369–382.

Doherty, W. J. (2001). *Take back your marriage: Sticking together in a world that pulls us apart.* New York: Guilford.

Filsinger, E. E., McAvoy, P., & Lewis, R. A. (1982). An empirical typology of dyadic formation. *Family Process, 21,* 321–335.

Fitzpatrick, M. A. (1984). A typological approach to marital interaction: Recent theory and research. *Advances in Experimental Social Psychology, 18,* 1–47.

Fournier, D. G., Olson, D. H., & Druckman, J. M. (1983). Assessing marital and premarital relationships: The PREPARE/ENRICH inventories. In E. E. Felsinger (Ed.), *Marriage and family assessment* (pp. 229–250). Beverly Hills, CA: Sage.

Fowers, B. J., Applegate, B., Olson, D. H., & Pomerantz, B. (1994). Marital conventionalization as a measure of marital satisfaction: A confirmatory factor analysis. *Journal of Family Psychology, 8,* 98–103.

Fowers, B. J., Montel, K. H., & Olson, D. H. (1996). Predicting marital success for premarital types based on PREPARE. *Journal of Marital and Family Therapy, 22,* 103–119.

Fowers, B. J., & Olson D. H. (1989). ENRICH marital inventory: A discriminant validity and cross-validation assessment. *Journal of Marital and Family Therapy, 15,* 65–79.

Gottman, J. M. (1993). The roles of conflict engagement, escalation, and avoidance in marital interaction: A longitudinal view of five types of couples. *Journal of Consulting and Clinical Psychology, 61,* 6–15.

Gottman, J. M., Coan, J., Carrere, S., & Swanson, C. (1998). Predicting marital happiness and stability from newlywed interactions. *Journal of Marriage and the Family, 60,* 5–22.

Heller, P. E., & Wood, B. (1998). The process of intimacy: Similarity, understanding, and gender. *Journal of Marital and Family Therapy, 24,* 273–288.

Kouneski, E. F. (2002). *Five types of marriage based on ENRICH: Linking intrapersonal and interpersonal characteristics.* Unpublished doctoral dissertation, University of Minnesota, Twin Cities.

Murray, S. L., & Holmes, J. G. (2000). Seeing the self through a partner's eyes: Why self-doubts turn into relationship securities. In A. Tesser, R. B. Felson, & J. M. Suls (Eds.), *Psychological perspectives on self and identity.* Washington, D.C.: American Psychological Association.

Olson, D. H. (1981). Family typologies: Bridging family research and family therapy. In E. E. Filsinger & R. A. Lewis (Eds.), *Assessing marriage: New behavioral approaches.* Newbury Park, CA: Sage.

Olson, D. H. (1996). *PREPARE/ENRICH counselor's manual: Version 2000.* Minneapolis, MN: Life Innovations, Inc.

Olson, D. H. (2000). Circumplex model of marital and family systems. *Journal of Family Therapy, 22,* 144–167.

Olson, D. H., & Fowers, B. J. (1993). Five types of marriage: An empirical typology based on ENRICH. *The Family Journal: Counseling and Therapy for Couples and Families, 1,* 196–207.

Olson, D. H., & Olson, A. K. (1999). PREPARE/ENRICH program: Version 2000. In R. Berger & M. T. Hannah (Eds.), *Preventive approaches in couples therapy.* Philadelphia: Brunner/Mazell.

Olson, D. H., & Olson, A. K. (2000). *Empowering couples: Building on your strengths.* Minneapolis, MN: Life Innovations, Inc.

Olson, D. H., McCubbin, H. I., Barnes, H. L., Larsen, A. S., Muxen, M. J., & Wilson, M. A. (1989). *Families: What makes them work.* Beverly Hills, CA: Sage.

Prager, K. J. (2000). Intimacy in personal relationships. In S. Hendrick and C. Hendrick (Eds.), *Close relationships* (pp. 229–244). Thousand Oaks, CA: Sage.

Schaefer, M. T., & Olson, D. H. (1981). Assessing intimacy: The PAIR Inventory. *Journal of Marital and Family Therapy, 7,* 47–60.

Walsh, F., & Olson, D. H. (1989). Utility of the circumplex model with severely dysfunctional family systems. In D. H. Olson, C. S. Russell, & D. H. Sprenkle (Eds.), *Circumplex model: Systemic assessment and treatment of families* (pp. 51–78). New York: Haworth.

Waring, E. M. (1988). *Enhancing marital intimacy through facilitating cognitive self-disclosure.* New York: Brunner/Mazel.

III

What Are the General Processes of Closeness and Intimacy?

9

Interdependence, Closeness, and Relationships

Caryl E. Rusbult, Madoka Kumashiro,
Michael K. Coolsen, and Jeffrey L. Kirchner
University of North Carolina at Chapel Hill

What is closeness? And what is a close relationship? Should closeness and close relationships be defined in terms of legal or material properties, such as marital status or economic resources (cf. Sweeney, 2002)? Should these constructs be defined in terms of observable behaviors, such as the frequency with which partners engage in shared activities or exhibit positive reciprocity during everyday conversation (cf. Berscheid, Snyder, & Omoto, 1989; Gottman, 1998)? Should these constructs be construed in terms of mental experiences such as love or satisfaction (cf. Sternberg, 1986) or in terms of personal dispositions such as childhood attachment history (cf. Hazan & Shaver, 1994)? Should we emphasize the process by which partners become increasingly intimate (cf. Reis & Shaver, 1988), examine the progressive merger of partners' identities (cf. Aron & Aron, 2000), or identify the norms that govern partners' dealings with one another (cf. Clark & Mills, 1993)?

Each of these orientations has illuminated the field's understanding of closeness and relationships; to be sure, each theory has enriched our own work. At the same time, we suggest that the concepts of *closeness* and *relationship* should first and foremost be understood by adopting an inherently interpersonal analysis. Indeed, it is instructive that dictionary definitions of these concepts include terms such as *association, connection, join,* and *existing only in relation to something else.* Toward understanding "that which exists only in relation to something else," we propose to analyze closeness not primarily in terms of material properties or mental experiences or personal dispositions, but in terms of the nature of the interdependence between persons. Specifically, this chapter describes the relevance of interdependence theory principles to understanding closeness and relationships (Holmes, 2002; Kelley et al., 2003; Kelley & Thibaut, 1978; Rusbult & Van Lange, 1996). In this review, we hope to illustrate that an interdependence theoretic analysis complements alternative theoretical orientations, providing an overarching framework in which to understand the interrelations among those orientations.

We begin by introducing the key dimensions of interdependence structure, proposing that closeness should be conceptualized in terms of outcome interdependence, or the character of the relations between persons. Next, we discuss the relevance of interdependence structure to understanding motivation, cognition, and communication. Then we describe the emergence of habitual transformational tendencies, suggesting that relationships should be conceptualized in terms of the relatively stable motives that guide partners' interactions with one another. Finally, we illustrate important features of our analysis via a review of interaction processes in two common classes of interdependence situation—those involving conflicting interests and those involving nonmutual dependence. The goal of this review is to link interdependence principles with the orientations to which we alluded above, demonstrating the relevance of interpersonal structure to explaining intrapersonal processes, and thereby illuminating our understanding of phenomena such as conflict, attachment, and intimacy.

INTERDEPENDENCE STRUCTURE

In contemporary physics, the relations between particles are as real and meaningful as the particles themselves. In interdependence theory, the relations between individuals are as real and meaningful as the individuals themselves. Interdependence theory characterizes the relations between individuals in terms of outcome interdependence, or the ways in which partners cause one another to experience good versus poor outcomes, pleasure versus displeasure. The theory describes the impact that individuals exert on one another in terms of interdependence structure, advancing a taxonomic description of this structure and outlining its implications for motivation, cognition, and interaction. In short, interdependence structure is the "foundation" that affords other social psychological processes—it is the "interpersonal reality" within which specific motives are activated, toward which cognition is oriented, and around which interaction unfolds.

Formal Representations of Structure

The options and outcomes of interaction are formally represented using outcome matrices and transition lists. An *outcome matrix* describes interdependence patterns involving two persons, each of whom can enact either of two behaviors yielding four possible combinations, the consequences of which are represented in terms of outcomes for each person (see Figure 9.1; Kelley & Thibaut, 1978; Von Neumann & Morgenstern, 1944).[1] Matrices are useful descriptions of the intricate ways in which (and degrees to which) people affect their own and one another's outcomes. However, a matrix is a "snapshot" of interdependence as it exists at a single point in time. Given that the behaviors individuals enact on earlier occasions may modify the options or outcomes that are available on future occasions, the theory also uses a second tool for representing interdependence. A *transition list* not only describes the behavioral

---

[1] For example, Figure 9.1 displays the well-known prisoner's dilemma situation (Kelley et al., 2003). In this situation, if both John and Mary enact Behavior 1, both enjoy moderately good outcomes (8 and 8); if both enact Behavior 2, both experience moderately poor outcomes (4 and 4); if one enacts Behavior 1 whereas the other enacts Behavior 2, the former suffers very poor outcomes (0) whereas the latter enjoys very good outcomes (12). Behavior 2 yields better outcomes for each person on average, so from this point of view, it seems "rational" for both persons to enact Behavior 2. Unfortunately, if both engage in Behavior 2, both experience poorer outcomes (4 and 4) than they would if both were to engage in Behavior 1 (8 and 8). If John and Mary trusted one another and were committed to helping one another, both would enact Behavior 1, the "cooperative" choice. Thus, this situation pits individual rationality against collective rationality, and can be construed in terms of the conflict between "me versus we."

"Me Versus We":
The Prisoner's Dilemma Situation

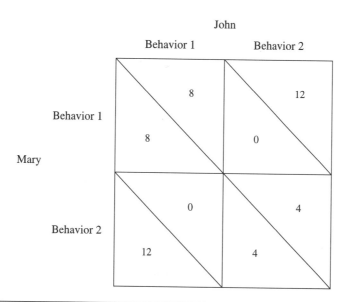

FIG. 9.1. Matrix Representation of Situation Structure (modified from Kelley & Thibaut, 1978).

options and outcomes that are available at a particular point in time, but also specifies the means by which interacting individuals proceed from one pattern of interdependence to another (see Figure 9.2; Kelley, 1984b).[2] (For the purposes of the present chapter, it is not critical that readers fully master the intricacies of matrix and transition list representations. We present relevant information in footnotes for those who wish to address these intricacies.)

Interaction describes the choices of two persons, the outcomes each experiences, and the future options or outcomes that become available as a result of interaction. That is, *interaction* describes two persons' needs, thoughts, and motives in relation to one another (A and B) in the context of the specific interdependence situation (S) in which their interaction transpires (Kelley et al., 2003). Expressed formally, $I = f(S, A, B)$. Interaction processes are essential to understanding closeness and relationships, in that through interaction, people provide themselves and their partners with good versus poor outcomes. Whether a given interaction yields pleasure versus displeasure depends on whether it gratifies (vs. frustrates) important needs, such as security, companionship, sexuality, and exploration (cf. Baumeister & Leary, 1995; Hazan & Shaver, 1994; Kenrick & Trost, 2000). Interaction not only yields *concrete outcomes*,

---

[2] For example, Figure 9.2 displays a transition list describing rescue from the consequences of an unwise action (Kelley, 1984b). At Time 1 (List X), each person's outcomes are influenced by his or her own actions—John enjoys moderately good outcomes by enacting J1 (8) irrespective of what Mary does, and Mary enjoys very good outcomes by enacting M1 (12) irrespective of what John does. Unfortunately, Mary's choice of M1 takes the two to a new situation (List Y) in which her outcomes are extremely poor, and in which control over both persons' outcomes is entirely in John's hands. At this point, if John follows his direct impulse and continues with J1, Mary suffers extremely poor outcomes. It is only by enacting a new, somewhat costly behavior (J3) that John can rescue Mary and return the two to the safer, initial situation (List X).

Rescue From the Consequences of an Unwise Action

Junctures	Possible Behaviors	Joint Selections	John	Mary	Movement To Next Juncture
X	(J1, J2)	J1 and M1	8	12	Y
	(M1, M2)	J1 and M2	8	4	X
		J2 and M1	0	12	Y
		J2 and M2	0	4	X
Y	(J1, J2, J3)	J1 and M3	8	-12	Y
	(M3, M4)	J1 and M4	8	-12	Y
		J2 and M3	0	-12	Y
		J2 and M4	0	-12	Y
		J3 and M3	-4	0	X
		J3 and M4	-4	0	X

FIG. 9.2. Transition List Representation of Situation Structure (modified from Kelley, 1984b).

or immediate experiences of pleasure versus displeasure, but also yields *symbolic outcomes,* or experiences that rest on the broader implications of interaction (Holmes, 1981; Kelley, 1979). For example, if John and Mary disagree about where to dine and John suggests Mary's preferred restaurant, Mary not only enjoys the concrete benefits of good food and wine, but also enjoys the symbolic pleasure of perceiving that John loves her and is responsive to her needs.

Properties of Interdependence Structure

Components of Structure. How do matrices and transition lists illuminate interdependence structure? By examining the main effects and interaction of each person's possible behaviors, we can discern the impact on each person's outcomes of the person's own actions (*actor control*: a main effect of Mary's actions on Mary's outcomes), the partner's actions (*partner control*: a main effect of John's actions on Mary's outcomes), and the partners' joint actions (*joint control*: an interaction of John's and Mary's actions on Mary's outcomes; Kelley et al., 2003). Moreover, by examining the within-cell association between partners' outcomes, we can discern *covariation of interests,* or the extent to which outcomes for actor and partner are positively correlated (corresponding interests) versus negatively correlated (conflicting interests). These components define four properties of structure, each of which is described below (Kelley & Thibaut, 1978).

Level of Dependence. *Level of dependence* describes the degree to which an individual "relies on" an interaction partner, in that his or her outcomes are influenced by the partner's actions. To the extent that Mary can obtain good outcomes for herself irrespective of John's actions (high actor control), she is independent. Mary is dependent to the extent that John can unilaterally cause her pleasure or displeasure (partner control) or can behave in such a manner as to govern her own behavioral choice (joint control). Increasing dependence tends to activate increased situation- and person-relevant attention and cognition, in that when Mary's outcomes are governed by John's actions, she will dedicate considerable thought to what the situation is "about" and to developing expectancies regarding John's behavior (Arriaga & Rusbult, 1998; Fiske, 1993; Holmes, 2002). Given that dependence constitutes reliance on a partner for fulfilling important needs, increasing dependence tends to promote perseverance in interactions and commitment to relationships (Bui, Peplau, & Hill, 1996; Drigotas & Rusbult, 1992; Rusbult, 1983). Moreover, because dependence sometimes entails vulnerability, it may inspire motivated forms of cognition such as positive illusion and downward social comparison. For example, Mary may quell feelings of insecurity by translating John's faults into virtues, or by identifying flaws in other relationships that are not evident in her own (Murray, Holmes, & Griffin, 1996; Rusbult, Van Lange, Wildschut, Yovetich, & Verette, 2000). Dependence can also constitute a "trap": For example, Mary may remain involved in an abusive relationship due to high dependence, in that although she suffers poor outcomes, she cannot obtain better outcomes elsewhere (she has poor alternatives due to limited education or poor job prospects) or because important resources bind her to the relationship (she has high investments, in the form of effort or shared material possessions; Johnson, 1995; Rusbult & Martz, 1995). Dependence situations afford cognition, motivation, communication, and interaction centering on issues of comfort (vs. discomfort) with interdependence and independence (see Figure 9.3).

Mutuality of Dependence.   *Mutuality of dependence* describes the degree to which two people are equally dependent on one another. Interactions with nonmutual dependence involve a power differential, in that to the extent that Mary is relatively more dependent, John holds relatively greater power. The less dependent, more powerful partner tends to exert greater control over decision making and the allocation of resources, whereas the more dependent partner tends to carry the greater burden of interaction costs (accommodation, sacrifice) and is more vulnerable to possible abandonment (Attridge, Berscheid, & Simpson, 1995; Rusbult, 1983; Witcher, 1999). Therefore, nonmutual dependence tends to magnify the dependent partner's situation- and person-relevant attention and cognition, along with other adaptations geared toward reducing vulnerability. For example, when Mary is unilaterally dependent, she is likely to be very attentive to the ways in which her outcomes might be affected by John's actions, to predicting John's probable behavior, and to engaging in motivated cognition that may reduce her feelings of anxiety. In contrast, interactions with mutual dependence tend to be more stable and congenial, yielding benefits that accrue from balance of power—more tranquil and positive emotional experience (less anxiety, guilt), reduced use of threat or coercion, and more "easy" and harmonious interaction (Baumeister, Wotman, & Stillwell, 1993; Drigotas, Rusbult, & Verette, 1999; Fiske, 1993). In short, situations with nonmutual dependence afford the expression of comfort (vs. discomfort) with vulnerability on the part of the dependent partner, along with comfort (vs. discomfort) with responsibility on the part of the powerful partner (see Figure 9.3).

Basis of Dependence.   *Basis of dependence* describes the way in which partners influence one another's outcomes, or whether dependence derives from partner control (Mary's outcomes are controlled by John's unilateral actions) versus joint control (Mary's actions are controlled by the partners' joint actions). Partner control is experienced as relatively absolute and externally controlled, in that the individual's outcomes rest in the hands of the partner. Interactions with partner control frequently involve adaptation in the form of exchange (tit-for-tat: "I'll scratch your back if you'll scratch mine"), exhibit communication involving promises and threats, and are governed by morality norms (Axelrod, 1984; Clark & Mills, 1993; Fiske, 1992). In contrast,

Situation Structure and Affordances

Situation Dimension	Relevant Motives
Level of dependence	Comfort versus discomfort with dependence; and Comfort versus dis comfort with independence
Mutuality of dependence	Comfort versus discomfort with vulnerability (as dependent) Comfort versus discomfort with responsibility (as powerholder)
Basis of dependence	Dominance versus submissiveness; and Assertiveness versus passivity
Covariation of interests	Prosocial versus self-interested motives (rules for self) Trust versus distrust of partner motives (expectations about others)
Temporal structure	Dependability versus unreliability; and Loyalty versus disloyalty
Uncertainty of information	Openness versus need for certainty; and Optimism versus pessimism

FIG. 9.3. Situation Structure and Affordances (modified from Holmes, 2002).

joint control is experienced as relatively contingent, in that the individual's outcomes rest on coordination with the partner's actions; in such situations, individuals can achieve more desirable versus less desirable outcomes by synchronizing with the partner ("I need to wait and see what he does"). Interactions with joint control frequently involve adaptation in the form of coordination ("follow my lead"; "you decide"), activate ability-relevant traits (problem solving, taking the initiative), and are governed by rules of conventional behavior rather than morality norms (Buss & Craik, 1980; Fiske, 1992; Turiel, 1983). In short, basis of dependence affords the expression of dominance (vs. submissiveness) and assertiveness (vs. passivity; see Figure 9.3).

Covariation of Interests. A fourth structural dimension, *covariation of interests*, describes the degree to which partners' outcomes correspond versus conflict, or whether the course of action that benefits John similarly benefits Mary. Covarying interests may entail either common behaviors or complementary behaviors. For example, both John and Mary may find it congenial to cook together (shared activities), or both may prefer that he cook while she cleans (division of labor). Covariation ranges from perfectly corresponding patterns through "mixed motive" patterns to perfectly conflicting patterns ("zero-sum" patterns). Covariation so thoroughly defines the possibilities for congenial versus uncongenial interaction that humans readily develop mental representations to determine whether "what's going on" is good or bad for them. Given corresponding outcomes, interaction is relatively "easy"—each person can simply pursue his or her own interests, simultaneously yielding good outcomes for the partner. Situations with conflicting interests tend to generate potentially destructive cognition and emotion (greed, fear), yield more active and differentiated information-seeking and self-presentation ("can Mary be trusted?"), and afford the expression of cooperation versus competition and trust versus distrust (Holmes & Murray, 1996; Surra & Longstreth, 1990; Van Lange et al., 1997; Wieselquist, Rusbult, Foster, & Agnew, 1999). Thus, although situations with conflicting interests are potentially uncongenial, such situations also serve as a "foundation" on which people may demonstrate their own prosocial versus self-interested motives, and on which they may display trust versus mistrust of their partners' motives (see Figure 9.3).

Temporal Structure.   Actor control, partner control, joint control, and covariation of interests define the preceding four structural properties. However, *temporal structure* is a fifth important property, in that interaction situations change over time, and may entail dynamic or sequential processes. Partners may be passively moved from one situation to another as a result of their earlier actions, or they may be active agents in seeking such movement. Thus, interdependence should be understood not only in terms of static structure, but also in terms of the future behaviors and outcomes that are made available (vs. eliminated) as a consequence of interaction (Kelley, 1984b; Kelley et al., 2003). *Extended situations* involve a series of steps prior to reaching a goal. For example, John and Mary may engage in a temporally extended investment process, whereby each person must enact specific behaviors at specific junctures (disclosing to one another, meeting kin) if the two are to proceed toward a remote but desirable goal (a close and committed relationship). *Situation selection* describes movement from one situation to another, bringing the actor, partner, or dyad to a situation differing from the previous one in terms of options or outcomes. For example, on the basis of her attachment history, Mary may seek situations with greater (vs. lesser) interdependence or with more (vs. less) partner control (Collins & Feeney, 2000; Simpson, Rholes, & Nelligan, 1992). Situation selection also describes the juncture between a present relationship and alternative relationships. For example, people ensure the continuation of committed relationships by cognitively derogating tempting alternatives; movement from one relationship to another is facilitated by cognitive enhancement of alternatives (Johnson & Rusbult, 1989; Miller, 1997). In short, temporally extended situations afford the expression of goals and motives involving self-control and the inclination to "stick with it"—dependability versus unreliability, as well as loyalty versus disloyalty (see Figure 9.3).

Uncertainty of Information.   The *uncertainty of information* is a sixth structural property. The nature of adaptation to specific situations rests on whether individuals possess certain (vs. uncertain) information about (a) the impact of each person's actions on each person's outcomes ("if we go to Rome, will he like the food?"); (b) each person's goals and motives ("will he be responsive to my needs?"); and (c) future interaction opportunities that will be made available (vs. eliminated) as a consequence of each person's actions ("if we do this your way, where will it 'take' us?"; Holmes, 2002; Kelley et al., 2003). Uncertain information gives rise to ambiguity and misunderstanding, challenging the flow of interaction. Accurate information is most critical in novel or risky situations and in interactions with unfamiliar partners. Accordingly, partners engage in a good deal of information exchange during the early stages of relationships, and such exchange frequently is governed by agreed-on rules. For example, reciprocal displays of intimacy are normative; such exchanges foster mutual attraction (Collins & Miller, 1994; Reis & Patrick, 1996). People also rely on probabilistic assumptions about one another's preferences and motives. For example, when an unfamiliar partner exhibits traits possessed by a significant other, individuals often respond to the person in a manner that mirrors prior experiences with the significant other (Andersen & Baum, 1994; Andersen, Reznik, & Manzella, 1996). That is, people use mental representations of significant others to "fill in the informational gaps" in interaction with new partners. Moreover, individuals may develop "frozen expecta-tions" that powerfully shape their perceptions of situations and partners (Holmes, 2002, p. 22). For example, people with avoidant attachment style perceive a wide range of dependence situations as "risky," anticipate that partners are likely to be self-interested or unresponsive, and readily forecast problematic future interaction situations (Mikulincer, 1998; Tidwell, Reis, & Shaver, 1996). Thus, although the true nature of partners' interdependence tends to "make itself known" over the course of extended interaction, uncertain information affords the expression of openness versus the need for certainty, as well as optimism versus pessimism (see Figure 9.3).

Combinations of Structural Properties.   Most interdependence situations are de-fined by their properties with respect to two or more structural dimensions. For exam-ple, a situation termed *twists of fate* involves temporal structure, dependence, and un-certain information; the situations termed *prisoner's dilemma, hero,* and *chicken* involve moderately high mutual dependence and moderately conflicting interests, but differ in magnitude of actor control, partner control, and joint control (Kelley et al., 2003). All possible combinations of the six properties define a very large number of patterns. However, a smaller number of prototypical patterns can be identified (perhaps 20 to 25; Kelley et al., 2003). Everyday situations resemble these abstract patterns, sharing common interpersonal problems and opportunities. For example, the so-called *twists of fate* situation is one wherein each partner, at some point, might unexpectedly find himself or herself in a position of extreme unilateral dependence; this sort of situation is characteristic of health crises and other reversals of fortune. The *prisoner's dilemma* situation (described earlier) is characteristic of interactions involving mutual sacri-fice, trading favors, and free riding. Everyday situations that share the same abstract pattern have parallel implications for motivation, cognition, and interaction.

We propose that closeness exists to the extent that at least one person in an in-teraction is dependent—to the extent that one or both interacting persons affect one another's well-being. Of course, closeness (or dependence) is a continuum; some interactions involve very low closeness (interactions with one's butcher), whereas others involve very high closeness (interactions with lovers and kin). By combin-ing dependence with other properties, we may define many types of closeness and predict their important features. For example, combinations involving nonmutual dependence have properties of caretaker interactions, wherein one person (the pow-erholder) is responsible for the other's well-being (the dependent's). Combinations of dependence with uncertain information are somewhat unpredictable, wherein part-ners fortuitously provide one another with good versus poor outcomes ("let's see where this takes us") or apply mental representations in ways that are not entirely explicable to the two parties ("he doesn't seem to be interpreting this as I do"; "is he 'in the same situation' as I am?"). And combinations involving conflicting interests force partners to confront the conflict between pursuit of personal interests versus prosocial goals. Thus, whereas lay construals of closeness frequently emphasize the more congenial forms of interdependence—the combination of high mutual depen-dence with corresponding interests representing the closest thing to paradise—our analysis suggests that closeness takes many forms. Indeed, "enemy" interactions may be very close, entailing extended mutual dependence with a partner whose interests chronically conflict with one's own.

Importance of Interdependence Structure

Structure Directly Affects Behavior.   Why should we concern ourselves with the structure of outcome interdependence? To begin with, structure sometimes governs behavior somewhat independent of individuals' goals and motives. For example, the communication literature has identified a *demand–withdraw* pattern of interaction characterized by repeated demands for change on the part of wives, met by chronic withdrawal on the part of husbands (Christensen & Heavey, 1993; Berns, Jacobson, & Gottman, 1999). Despite the fact that reversals of this pattern sometimes are evident (men may "demand," women may "withdraw"), in light of the prevalence of gender-based demand–withdraw patterns, this type of interaction typically has been explained in terms of social norms or sex differences in confrontation versus avoidance. In contrast to prevailing gender-based explanations, an interdependence theoretic analysis suggests that this type of interaction transpires in situations resembling the so-called *threat* situation, wherein one partner controls resource allocations to both persons, and the only course of action available to the other is to deliver a threat that harms both persons (Holmes & Murray, 1996).[3]

In what sense does demand–withdraw interaction reflect interdependence structure paralleling the threat situation? Typically, men hold greater power than women in deciding who receives what resources and who is responsible for what tasks ("you change the diapers"; "let's take turns cooking dinner"), with women being dependent upon their partners' fairness. Ideally, John might allocate resources and tasks in a 50–50 manner, thereby satisfying both partners' needs and promoting harmony in the relationship. However, if John is exploitative, Mary may push to discuss matters, perhaps threatening to quit cooking in the meantime (the "demand" component). It is in John's interests to avoid discussion (the "withdraw" component), in that inaction will maintain the status quo. Hoping to bring about change, Mary may voice increasingly strong complaints. Thus, the demand–withdraw interaction. Although it might be tempting to explain this type of communication in terms of social norms or sex differences, the pattern plausibly results from a specific type of interdependence situation in which men act in such a manner as to maintain a beneficial status quo, and women seek to bring about change. Granted, cultural norms play a role in producing and sustaining this sort of power differential. However, contemporary behavior in the situation may simply reflect each person's pursuit of self-interest. Thus, outcome interdependence "matters" because interaction sometimes is driven more by interdependence structure than by social norms or personal dispositions.

Structure and Affordances.   As implied in the preceding review, there is a second important reason to attend to structure. Specific interdependence patterns present specific sorts of interpersonal problems and opportunities, and therefore (a) logically imply the relevance of specific goals and motives, and (b) permit the expression of those goals and motives (see Figure 9.3). *Affordance* describes what a situation "makes possible" or "may activate" in interaction partners (Kelley et al., 2003). For example, interactions with uncertain information afford misunderstanding and invite the application of fixed expectations regarding situations and partners ("I'm in a risky situation with a potentially unresponsive partner"; Fiske, 1993; Hazan & Shaver, 1994; Ickes & Simpson, 1997); these processes become less relevant as information

---

[3] From a technical point of view, the threat situation is an interdependence pattern that combines high mutual partner control (both John and Mary have the wherewithal to benefit one another) with high bilateral actor control (each has the wherewithal to benefit the self) in a moderately noncorrespondent manner, such that Mary's actor control favors behaving in a manner that benefits John, but John's actor control favors behaving in a manner that does not benefit Mary. If John uses his control in a consistently self-interested manner, Mary may react to his unfair behavior by threatening him using the only means available—by enacting a behavior that yields poor outcomes for both persons. Alternatively, John might utilize his control in a benevolent manner, alternating between self-benefiting and other-benefiting behavior so as to produce moderately good outcomes for both persons. The latter form of adaptation represents "trading justice for loyalty," in that John's evenhanded actions are likely to yield loyalty on the part of Mary.

about interdependence becomes increasingly certain. And for example, interactions with conflicting interests afford the expression of self-centeredness versus concern with collective interests, and therefore inspire predictable sorts of cognition and affect (greed, fear) and invite predictable forms of attributional activity and self-presentation ("is John essentially benevolent?"; "trust me"; Frank, Gilovich, & Regan, 1993; Van Lange & Kuhlman, 1994); these processes become less relevant as interactions involve increasingly correspondent interests. In short, interdependence structure "matters" because it is the interpersonal reality within which motives are activated, toward which cognition is oriented, and around which interaction unfolds. As highlighted in a truism noted by Holmes (2002), "the mind has the structure it has because the world has the structure it has" (Anderson, 1991, p. 428).

Summary. In this section, we introduced matrices and transition lists as tools for representing interdependence structure, noting that outcome patterns in these representations vary in actor control, partner control, joint control, and covariation. These components define four structural properties: level of dependence, mutuality of dependence, basis of dependence, and covariation of interests. Two additional properties are also important: temporal structure and uncertainty of information. We proposed that closeness exists to the extent that one or both interacting persons are dependent, suggesting that combinations of dependence with other properties define the myriad forms of closeness (mutual vs. nonmutual, discrete vs. extended, with corresponding vs. conflicting interests). We argued that knowledge of interdependence structure is critical because (a) interaction sometimes is driven primarily by situation structure, and (b) interdependence structure affords the expression of important social psychological goals and motives.

INTERDEPENDENCE PROCESSES

Recall that interaction is shaped not only by interdependence structure, but also by partners' needs, thoughts, and motives in relation to one another in the context of the specific situation in which their interaction unfolds ($I = f[S, A, B]$). Thus, to fully understand the concept of closeness, we must add to our structural analysis a complementary analysis that describes how John and Mary react to the interdependence situations they encounter. In this section we explain how close partners psychologically transform specific interdependence situations, responding not only on the basis of the sorts of structural properties described above, but also on the basis of broader considerations (e.g., long-term goals, concern for the partner). We discuss the role of mental events and habits in shaping this process, and outline the role of attribution and self-presentation in close partners' attempts to understand one another. We also describe the process of adaptation, or the means by which people develop relatively stable tendencies to react to specific situations in specific ways.

Transformation Process

In discussing interdependence structure, the phrase *given situation* is used to describe the direct consequences of both partners' actions on each person's outcomes (Kelley & Thibaut, 1978). These outcomes are "given" in that they describe gut level, autistic effects on each person, ignoring the partner's interests and ignoring long-term relationship-relevant concerns. In a sense, given outcomes represent the "virtual structure" of a situation. People sometimes behave in such a manner as to maximize direct, given outcomes. This is especially probable in simple situations for which no broader considerations are relevant, among people who lack the inclination or wherewithal to

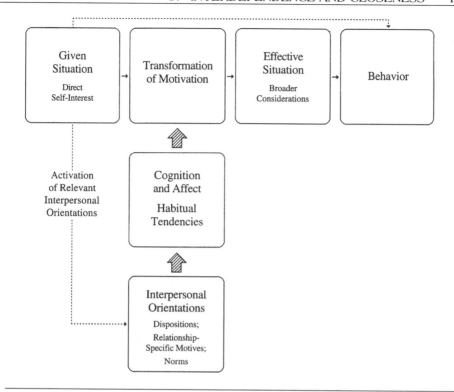

FIG. 9.4. The Transformation Process (modified from Rusbult & Van Lange, 1996).

take broader considerations into account, and in situations involving time pressure or other factors that constrain cognitive capacity (Baumeister, Bratslavsky, Muraven, & Tice, 1998; Mischel, Cantor, & Feldman, 1996).

However, close partners frequently depart from their direct, gut level interests, instead basing their behavioral choices on broader considerations. Acting on the basis of broader considerations results from psychological *transformation* of the given situation. Transformation entails "making something" of the given situation, and essentially frees individuals from control by direct self-interest, allowing them to be responsive to strategic concerns, long-term goals, or desire to influence a partner's outcomes (see Figure 9.4). For example, Mary may behave in ways that yield poor direct outcomes because in doing so she can promote John's welfare, encourage future reciprocity, or enhance the quality of their relationship. The preferences resulting from this process constitute the *effective situation* in which effective preferences directly guide behavior.

Transformation constitutes an implicit "rule" that the individual adopts in the course of interaction (Kelley & Thibaut, 1978). Some rules are prosocial (oriented toward benefiting others), some are antisocial (oriented toward harming others), and some are asocial (indifferent to others' outcomes). Some rules involve sequential or temporal considerations, such as waiting to see how the partner behaves, or adopting strategies such as tit-for-tat or turn-taking ("I'll cooperate as long as you do"; "let's do it your way this time, my way next time"; Axelrod, 1984). Other rules center on the weighting of one's own and a partner's outcomes, such as (a) altruism, or maximizing the partner's outcomes; (b) cooperation, or maximizing the partners' combined outcomes; (c) competition, or maximizing the relative difference between one's own and the partner's outcomes; and (d) individualism, or maximizing one's own outcomes irrespective of the partner's outcomes (Kelley & Thibaut, 1978; Messick & McClintock, 1968).

The empirical literature includes many demonstrations of the transformation process, not only in close relationships, but also in stranger interactions (Dehue, McClintock, & Liebrand, 1993; Rusbult, Verette, Whitney, Slovik, & Lipkus, 1991; Yovetich & Rusbult, 1994). Transformation is particularly "visible" when a given situation structure dictates one type of behavior (e.g., self-interest dictates other-harming behavior), yet personal values dictate another type of behavior (e.g., prosocial motives dictate other-benefiting behavior). For example, when Mary helps John with yard work rather than going out with her friends, she communicates her concern for his welfare. Thus, when people act on the basis of transformed preferences, we are able to "see them for who they are," discerning their personal goals and motives. As such, the transformation process represents the point at which the "rubber meets the road," or the point at which intrapersonal processes—individual cognition, affect, and motivation—operate on specific interdependence situations in such a manner as to reveal the individual's unique self.

Cognition, Affect, and Habit

Humans are social animals, and human intelligence is highly interpersonal. Both cognitively and affectively, we are well-prepared to construe the world in terms of interdependence—to recognize interest-relevant features of situations, identify regularities in properties across diverse settings, and recognize that classes of situations possess common features and implications (Cosmides & Tooby, 1992; Kelley, 1997). Cognition and affect are geared toward (a) discerning what a given situation is "about" (recognizing patterns, identifying key properties) and evaluating that structure in terms of one's own needs and motives; (b) understanding the partner's needs and predicting his or her motives; and (c) forecasting the implications of present actions for future interactions (Kelley, 1979, 1984a). Interdependence structure plays a role in shaping the content of cognition and affect. For example, situations with the basic structure of the prisoner's dilemma situation involve conflict between (a) benefiting the partner at low cost to the self versus (b) benefiting the self at substantial cost to the partner (e.g., making a small sacrifice for the partner, pitching in on a project vs. loafing and letting the partner do the work).[4] Issues of fear and greed readily come to mind in such situations ("will John treat me kindly?"; "shall I try to take a free ride?"). In a sense, the characteristic blend of fear and greed inspired by such situations serves as a "flag" for this interdependence pattern—a rather automatic indicator of the essential opportunities and constraints implicit in this type of situation.

The transformation process frequently is driven by the cognition and affect that accompany a given situation. For example, Mary is likely to exhibit self-centered or antisocial transformation to the extent that she experiences greedy thoughts and desires ("it would be nice to take a free ride and let John suffer the costs"), and to the extent that she is fearful about John's motives ("is he likely to exploit me?"). Cognition

---

[4] From a technical point of view, the prisoner's dilemma situation is a pattern that combines moderate bilateral actor control (both John and Mary have the wherewithal to produce moderate benefits for themselves) with high mutual partner control (each person has the wherewithal to greatly benefit the other) in a moderately noncorrespondent manner, such that each person's actor control favors behaving in a manner that yields poor outcomes for the other (see Figure 1). Thus, each person may be tempted to behave in a competitive manner (to "defect"), either in an attempt to exploit the other (inspired by greed) or to protect the self from the other's exploitation (inspired by fear). Alternatively, both John and Mary may cooperate, yielding moderately good outcomes for both persons. Over the course of extended interaction, it is adaptive for close partners to develop patterns of mutual cooperation (Axelrod, 1984; Kelley et al., 2003).

and emotion are also colored by distal causes, including the values, goals, and dispositions that are afforded by the situation (Mikulincer, 1998; Wieselquist et al., 1999). For example, Mary's reaction to situations with conflicting interests may be colored by the value she places on fairness, loyalty, or communal norms (affecting her experience of greed), as well as by the degree to which she trusts John (affecting her experience of fear). Thus, the mental events that underlie transformation are functionally adapted to situation structure, and take forms that are relevant to that structure.

Of course, the transformation process does not necessarily rest on extensive mental activity. As a consequence of adaptation to repeatedly encountered patterns, people develop habitual tendencies to react to specific situations in specific ways, such that transformation comes about with little or no conscious thought (Kelley, 1983; Rusbult & Van Lange, 1996). For example, following repeated interactions with one another in situations with the structure of the prisoner's dilemma, John and Mary may quite automatically exhibit mutual cooperation, with little or no cognition or affect. Mediation by mental events is more probable in novel situations with unknown implications, in risky situations with the potential for harm, and in interactions with unfamiliar partners who possess unpredictable goals and motives (Baumeister, Bratslavsky, Finkenauer, & Vohs, 2001; Fincham, 2001; Holmes, 2002).

Communication, Attribution, and Self-Presentation

During the course of interaction, close partners seek to convey their goals, values, and dispositions using both direct and indirect means (e.g., verbally, nonverbally, via intimation). Communication entails self-presentation on the part of one person and attribution on the part of the other. As implied earlier, the material for self-presentation and attribution resides in the disparity between the given and effective situations, in that deviations from self-centered choice reveal the actor's goals and motives (Holmes, 1981; Kelley, 1979). Thus, possibilities for communicating self-relevant information are limited by interdependence structure—that is, specific situations afford the display of specific motives. For example, it is difficult for close partners to convey kindness (or to discern it) in situations with highly correspondent interests, in that in such situations, "kind" behavior aligns with "self-interested" behavior.

People engage in *attributional activity* in their attempts to understand the implications of a partner's actions, seeking to predict future behavior, and explaining prior behavior in terms of underlying dispositions (Fincham, 2001; Gilbert, 1998). Expectations are not particularly accurate in new relationships, in that they must be based on probabilistic assumptions about how the average person would react in a given situation; in long-term relationships, expectations can also be based on knowledge of how a partner has behaved across a variety of situations (Kelley, 1979). Of course, the attribution process is not always geared toward forming accurate inferences. For example, highly dependent partners may develop quite positive interpretations of one another, exhibiting positive illusion and engaging in downward comparison so as to place one another in a favorable light (Murray et al., 1996; Rusbult et al., 2000; Simpson, Fletcher, & Campbell, 2001). So long as attributions are not wildly out of touch with reality, positively biased interpretations appear to have considerable functional value, in that positive illusion is associated with greater couple adjustment and more congenial patterns of interaction.

Self-presentation describes individuals' attempts to communicate their abilities, motives, and dispositions to one another. Conveying that one loves another is most directly (and perhaps most convincingly) communicated by departing from one's interests in order to enhance that person's outcomes (Van Lange et al., 1997; Wieselquist et al., 1999). Given that people do not always hold complete information about their partners' given outcomes, they may sometimes mistakenly assume that a partner's behavior reflects his or her simple preferences, when in fact the behavior resulted from prorelationship transformation. For example, Mary's acts of loyalty, kindness, or sacrifice may not be visible if John fails to recognize the costs she incurred—John may assume that Mary's acts reflect simple pursuit of self-interest rather than prosocial departures from the dictates of given structure (Drigotas, Whitney, & Rusbult, 1995). In addition, self-presentation may sometimes be geared toward concealing one's true preferences and motives. For example, Mary may misrepresent her given preferences, overstating her desire to dine at an Italian restaurant so as to highlight the benevolence of her agreement to dine at John's preferred Thai restaurant. Socially desirable self-presentation is particularly evident during the early stages of developing relationships (Leary, 2001; Tice, Butler, Muraven, & Stillwell, 1995).

Adaptation

When people initially encounter specific interdependence situations, the problems and opportunities inherent in the situation are likely to be unclear. In such novel situations, Mary may systematically analyze the situation and reach an active decision about how to behave, or she may simply react in an impulsive manner. Either way, experience is acquired. If her choice yields good outcomes, Mary is likely to react similarly to future situations with parallel structure; if her choice yields poor outcomes, she is likely to modify her behavior in future situations with parallel structure. *Adaptation* describes the process by which repeated experience in situations with similar structure gives rise to habitual response tendencies that on average yield good outcomes (Kelley, 1983; Rusbult & Van Lange, 1996). Stable adaptations may be embodied in interpersonal dispositions, relationship-specific motives, or social norms.

Interpersonal Dispositions. *Interpersonal dispositions* are actor-specific inclinations to respond to particular situations in a specific manner across numerous partners (Kelley, 1983). Dispositions emerge because over the course of development, different people experience different histories with different close partners, undergoing different sorts of interaction with parents and siblings, and confronting different problems and opportunities in peer interactions. As a result of adaptation, people acquire dispositions, reflected in the way in which they approach specific situations; they develop tendencies to perceive situations and partners in specific ways, and to apply transformations with greater or lesser probability. Thus, beyond inherited temperament, the "interpersonal self" can be construed as the sum of one's adaptations to previous interdependence situations and partners. For example, children's experiences with their parents form the basis for attachment style (Bowlby, 1969). To the extent that caregivers benevolently use their power, responding to the child's needs and serving as a secure base from which the child can explore, the child will develop trusting and secure expectations regarding dependence; to the extent that caregiving is unresponsive or exploitative, children develop anxious expectations regarding dependence, or come to avoid situations in which they need and rely on others (Ainsworth, Blehar, Waters, & Wall, 1978). To the extent that Mary develops an avoidant adaptation, she will tend to perceive that many types of situation involve dangerous dependencies, she will anticipate antisocial partner motives, and accordingly she will tend to avoid dependence situations or exhibit defensive or hostile motives when she finds herself in such situations (Collins & Feeney, 2000; Hazan & Shaver, 1994; Simpson, Rholes, & Phillips, 1996). To the extent that Mary develops a secure adaptation, she will later perceive dependence situations as safe, readily trusting others and finding it easy to commit to close partners.

Relationship-Specific Motives. *Relationship-specific motives* are inclinations to respond to particular situations in a specific manner with a specific partner (Holmes,

1981). For example, commitment emerges as a consequence of dependence on a partner, and is strengthened as a result of high satisfaction (John gratifies Mary's most important needs), poor alternatives (Mary's needs could not be gratified independent of her relationship), and high investments (important resources are bound to her relationship; Rusbult, Olsen, Davis, & Hannon, 2001). Commitment colors emotional reactions to interaction situations (feeling affection rather than anger when a partner is neglectful) and gives rise to habits of thought that support sustained involvement (use of plural pronouns, positive illusion, derogation of alternatives; Agnew, Van Lange, Rusbult, & Langston, 1998; Johnson & Rusbult, 1989; Rusbult et al., 2000). In turn, benevolent thoughts encourage prosocial transformation and behavior. For example, strong commitment is associated with prosocial acts such as sacrifice, accommodation, and forgiveness (Finkel, Rusbult, Kumashiro, & Hannon, 2002; Rusbult et al., 1991; Van Lange et al., 1997). Moreover, whereas commitment reflects the individual's own transformational tendencies, trust reflects beliefs about a close partner's transformational tendencies. Mary develops trust in John—or becomes increasingly confident of his prosocial values, goals, and motives—as a result of observing him behave in such a manner as to promote her welfare in situations wherein doing so is antithetical to his direct self-interest ("he was tempted to be unfaithful, but remained loyal"; Holmes & Rempel, 1989). Trust shapes affective reactions to interdependence situations (feeling less fearful in situations involving conflicting interests), and encourages patterns of perception and cognition that support prosocial transformation (relaxed record keeping, benevolent memory; Clark & Mills, 1993; Wieselquist, Rusbult, Kumashiro, & Finkel, 2003).

Social Norms.   *Social norms* are rule-based, socially transmitted inclinations to respond to particular interdependence situations in a specific manner (Thibaut & Kelley, 1959). For example, most societies develop rules regarding the expression of anger; such rules help groups avoid the chaos that would ensue if people were to freely express hostility. Likewise, rules of civility and etiquette represent efficient solutions to interdependence dilemmas, regulating behavior in such a manner as to yield harmonious interaction. For example, close partners frequently follow agreed-on rules regarding resource allocation, adhering to distribution rules such as equity, equality, or need, and experiencing discomfort when these standards are violated (Walster, Walster, & Berscheid, 1978). Such rules may govern a wide range of interactions or may be relationship-specific. For example, in parent–child relationships or other communal involvements, the norms guiding behavior typically are need-based rather than contributions-based (Clark & Mills, 1993; Fiske, 1992). Frequently, norms not only govern behavior, but also shape cognitive experiences. For example, in interactions guided by communal norms, partners neither monitor nor encode the extent of each person's contributions to the other's welfare.

Summary.   As noted earlier, interdependence structure is the "interpersonal reality" within which specific motives are activated, toward which cognition is oriented, and around which interaction unfolds. In this section, we briefly outlined the relevance of interdependence structure to understanding such processes. We explained how close partners may transform specific interdependence patterns, responding to a given pattern not on the basis of direct self-interest, but also on the basis of broader considerations, such as long-term goals or concern with the partner's well-being. We described the role of cognition and affect in this process, noting that mental events are functionally adapted to situation structure and take forms that are relevant to that structure. We also discussed communication, explaining how individuals seek to reveal their own goals and motives via self-presentation, and seek to understand their partners' goals and motives by means of attributional activity. We outlined the relevance of interdependence structure for understanding each process, explaining how situation structure affords the expression of motives, shapes the character of cognition, and serves as the foundation for communication. Finally, we noted that people develop habitual tendencies to react to specific sorts of interdependence situations in specific ways, explaining that such habitual adaptations are embodied in interpersonal dispositions, relationship-specific motives, and social norms.

INTERACTION AND RELATIONSHIPS

Of what relevance are interdependence structure and process to understanding relationships? Recall that specific structural properties afford specific intrapersonal processes in Persons A and B, which in turn shape the course of their interaction ($I = f[S, A, B]$). From this point of view, a close relationship can be described as "a state of interaction process among two or more persons" (Kelley, 1994, p. 2). That is, a relationship exists to the extent that partners exhibit somewhat characteristic patterns of cognition, affect, communication, and motivation in interaction with one another. Thus, a relationship is not defined solely in terms of its structural properties, nor is it something that resides solely in Person A or in Person B or even in the sum of the two persons' cognition or motivation. And of course, to describe a close relationship as "a state of interaction process" is not to imply that a relationship is static or invariant: John and Mary may change over time (as a result of fatigue, maturation), and the nature of their interactions will vary as a function of the range of situations the two confront. In this section, we illustrate how structure and process combine to shape interaction in two important classes of situation—in situations with conflicting interests and in those with nonmutual dependence. For each class of situation, we begin by outlining the central structural issues with which close partners must contend, identifying key features of common interaction patterns. We also illustrate important interaction- and relationship-relevant phenomena via a review of empirical work relevant to each class of situation, thereby illustrating the ways in which phenomena such as conflict, attachment, and intimacy may be illuminated by an interdependence-based analysis of close relationships.

Conflicting Interests, Interaction, and Relationships

Conceptual Analysis. Interactions with conflicting interests involve challenging problems of adaptation ("I want my way!"; "do you care about my needs?"). At the same time, such situations provide opportunities for people to "display their true colors," and for partners to clearly discern one another's goals and motives. In short, this type of situation affords the expression of prosocial (vs. asocial or antisocial) motives, and yields self-presentation and attributional activity centering on issues of trustworthiness and benevolence. As such, situations with conflicting interests are termed *diagnostic situations*, in that they are revealing of each person's transformational tendencies as well as each person's expectancies regarding others' tendencies (Holmes & Rempel, 1989). For example, Mary can display her own trustworthiness by being sexually faithful even when tempted to behave otherwise; she can discern John's trustworthiness when she recognizes that he was tempted to be unfaithful but declined to do so.

In reacting to situations with conflicting interests, close partners may exhibit three basic patterns of interaction. A first pattern involves bilateral negativity, wherein both partners engage in antisocial or self-interested behavior. This type of interaction comes about when partners hold fixed expectations that cause them to perceive many interdependence situations as zero-sum ("this is a competitive situation"), experience greedy or hostile cognition regarding the partners' respective outcomes ("I need to 'beat' him"), or hold fearful expectations regarding the partner's goals and motives ("she can't be trusted"). Because each person seeks to gain good outcomes at the other's expense—or because each is fearful that the other may wish to do so—both partners exhibit self-interested or antisocial behavior. In an otherwise happy and congenial relationship—and irrespective of their concrete outcomes—poor symbolic outcomes are likely to ensue, including shame, disappointment in oneself and the partner, and bilateral distrust. In future interactions, the partners may experience escalation of conflict (increasing hostility, reciprocal destructiveness), or they may disengage from the relationship, seeking reduced interdependence.

A second pattern involves unilateral positivity, wherein (a) John perceives that the situation affords cooperation, experiences benevolent and trusting cognition, and exhibits prosocial behavior, whereas (b) Mary exhibits antisocial or distrustful motives and behavior. John will suffer poor concrete outcomes along with a mix of symbolic outcomes—he may be pleased that he demonstrated his benevolence, but is unlikely to find solace in Mary's failure to "come through" on his behalf and may feel betrayed. John's unilateral prosocial act will yield positive concrete outcomes for Mary, but her symbolic outcomes, too, are likely to be mixed—she may enjoy receiving unambiguous evidence of John's love, but may suffer remorse or shame regarding her own behavior. In future interactions, Mary may decide to reciprocate John's prosocial act (perhaps initiating prosocial turn-taking), the two might enter into a pattern of chronic exploitation on the part of Mary, or John might choose to reduce interdependence by withdrawing from the involvement.

A third pattern involves bilateral positivity, wherein both partners perceive the potential for cooperation, and both experience prosocial and trusting thoughts and motives, such that both exhibit prosocial behavior. Above and beyond the concrete outcomes of their interaction, both partners will enjoy positive symbolic outcomes—each will enjoy the pleasure of displaying personal benevolence, along with the pleasure of discerning the other's benevolence. Bilateral prosocial acts not only enhance mutual trust, but also yield other benefits to close partners, including strengthened commitment and enhanced prosocial motivation. We return to this point later, in a discussion of mutual cyclical growth. For the moment, this simple conceptual analysis should suffice to illustrate the importance of examining all three elements in the $I = f(S, A, B)$ equation: Through their reactions to conflict situations, both partners' motives and expectancies not only govern each person's concrete and symbolic outcomes, but also serve to select the future situations that become available to the pair.

Sacrifice, Accommodation, and Forgiveness.   Many interaction patterns identified in the empirical literature transpire in situations with conflicting interests. For example, through no fault of either person, partners' interests and preferences may conflict. Such situations call for sacrifice—willingness to depart from one's direct interests in order to promote the partner's interests (Van Lange et al., 1997; Wieselquist et al., 1999). For example, for Mary's sake, John may spend the weekend with his in-laws rather than watching World Cup Soccer.[5] Another common pattern emerges when one partner "behaves badly," engaging in inconsiderate or irritating acts. Such situations call for accommodation, that is, inhibiting the impulse to retaliate and instead behaving in a conciliatory manner (Gottman, 1998; Rusbult et al., 1991). For example,

---

[5] Situations involving sacrifice benefit from communication. If partners engage in simultaneous, uncoordinated acts of sacrifice, their interaction will resemble the "gift of the Magi," whereby each person sacrifices for the other and neither enjoys his or her most preferred outcome. For example, John might find himself spending the weekend with his in-laws while Mary remains at home watching soccer.

when John says something rude, Mary may bite her tongue, "let the remark roll off her back," and nicely ask John how his day went. A third common pattern centers on acts of betrayal, wherein a partner departs from relationship-relevant norms in such a manner as to yield very poor outcomes for the actor. Such situations call for forgiveness, that is, forgoing grudge and seeking to restore congenial relations (Finkel et al., 2002; McCullough, Worthington, & Rachal, 1997). For example, when John reveals private information to a third party and thereby humiliates Mary, she may control her impulse toward retribution, search for extenuating circumstances that help explain his actions, and find it in her heart to accept his sincere apology.

What are the common elements of these patterns of interaction? First, situations with conflicting interests inspire powerful tendencies toward reciprocity, even under circumstances of close interdependence. Indeed, the impulse toward negative reciprocity ("fighting fire with fire") appears to be stronger than the tendency toward positive reciprocity ("I'll scratch your back if you'll scratch mine"; Epstein, Baucom, & Rankin, 1993; Gottman, 1998). Second, given that reciprocal negativity is a strong impulse, prosocial reactions come about as a consequence of transformation. For example, when close partners confront accommodative dilemmas or betrayal incidents and are allowed limited versus plentiful reaction time, those given limited time exhibit more antisocial behavior; those given plentiful time for the transformation process are more likely to exhibit accommodation and forgiveness (Rusbult, Davis, Finkel, Hannon, & Olsen, 2003; Yovetich & Rusbult, 1994). Third, parallel sorts of dispositions and relationship-specific motives inspire prosocial transformation across the three patterns. For example, tendencies toward sacrifice, accommodation, and forgiveness are promoted by strong commitment, a variable that embodies concern for the interests of the partner and relationship (Finkel et al., 2002; Rusbult et al., 1991; Van Lange et al., 1997). Prosocial motives and acts are also more probable among people with greater self-control, more secure attachment, greater psychological femininity, and stronger perspective-taking tendencies (Arriaga & Rusbult, 1998; Finkel & Campbell, 2001; McCullough et al., 1997; Rusbult et al., 1991, 2001).

Mutual Cyclical Growth.   In situations with conflicting interests, mutual prosocial behavior appears to represent good adaptation, in that it yields greater couple adjustment and longevity (Carstensen, Gottman, & Levenson, 1995; Van Lange et al., 1997). Longitudinal studies of both dating relationships and marital relationships have revealed a pattern of *mutual cyclical growth* involving reciprocal, temporally extended associations among commitment, prosocial behavior, and trust (Wieselquist et al., 1999): Specifically, high dependence on a partner promotes strong commitment to the relationship, and strong commitment promotes prosocial acts such as sacrifice and accommodation, which in turn tend to be perceived by partners with some degree of accuracy. Perceiving an actor's prosocial acts yields enhanced partner trust; because the partner trusts the actor, the partner becomes more willing to become dependent on the actor, and high dependence promotes strong commitment on the part of the partner, which in turn promotes prosocial acts that are perceived by the actor, which in turn enhance the actor's trust . . . and so on, in a pattern of mutual cyclical growth (or mutual cyclical deterioration, when things "begin to go south"). As such, trust serves as an implicit gauge of the strength of a partner's commitment. Which comes first, commitment or trust? Adopting an interdependence theoretic analysis makes it clear that in understanding real interaction in ongoing close relationships, causes and effects are not so clearly distinguishable: In the context of temporally extended interactions with across-partner associations, the effect on Mary of John's prosocial acts can serve as the cause of her own enhanced trust; the effect of her enhanced trust can serve as the cause of her own strengthened commitment.

Dependence, Interaction, and Relationships

Conceptual Analysis. In understanding the implications of dependence on a close partner, it is important to recognize that dependence entails needing or relying on another; dependence implies potential vulnerability. As such, dependence situations afford the expression of comfort with (vs. avoidance of) independence and interdependence. High dependence is unlikely to be problematic (a) when partners' interests correspond, in that behaviors benefiting the actor simultaneously benefit the partner, or (b) when dependence is mutual, in that mutuality yields the sorts of payoffs that accrue from balance of power. The risks of dependence become particularly evident when dependence is nonmutual, involves conflicting interests, or both.[6] Under such circumstances, the less dependent person will be particularly concerned with issues concerning responsibility, and must decide whether to use power in a benevolent or malevolent manner; the more dependent person will be particularly oriented toward issues concerning vulnerability, and will seek to detect signs of partner responsiveness versus unresponsiveness.

Situations involving nonmutual dependence are quite common in everyday life, including requests for assistance, seeking support for one's goal pursuits, and simple self-revelation (Collins & Feeney, 2000; Drigotas, Rusbult, Wieselquist, & Whitton, 1999; Reis & Shaver, 1988; Simpson et al., 1992). Nonmutual dependence can be construed in terms of a 2×2 matrix wherein (a) an actor may request aid (rendering the self vulnerable) or may forego requesting aid (remaining invulnerable), and (b) the partner may react in a responsive or unresponsive manner. For example, John may wish to tell Mary of his dream to become an accomplished novelist. Although such a revelation might seem innocuous, John cannot be sure how Mary will react. If he is inclined to perceive even simple dependencies as dangerous, dislikes placing himself in a vulnerable position, or fears that Mary may respond with indifference or ridicule, he may decide not to reveal his goal. By remaining invulnerable, John simultaneously maximizes the odds that his needs remain unfulfilled—it is difficult for a partner to provide assistance if she is unaware of the need for it. If, because of a serendipitous turn of events or insightful empathy, Mary perceives John's dream despite his reticence, she may nevertheless behave in an affirming manner. John is likely to experience extreme gratitude for such an unanticipated gift of responsiveness and may become more comfortable placing himself in positions of dependence on future occasions.

If John perceives that dependence is not terribly "dangerous," summons his courage, and renders himself vulnerable by revealing his dream, he hopes that Mary will respond with warmth, encouraging him to pursue his goal. If Mary is a skilled and committed caregiver and responds to his needs, he is likely to feel understood and supported, and will develop increased trust. At the same time, Mary might react to John's disclosure with indifference or boredom; she might even belittle his dreams or turn the information against him. If Mary wishes to avoid the responsibility or costs of caregiving and is accordingly unresponsive, John may feel disappointed or demeaned, and will become increasingly distrustful of Mary and the experience of dependence. Although this is a rather elementary 2×2 analysis, we hope that it suffices to once again illustrate the importance of examining all three elements in the $I = f(S, A, B)$ equation: Through John's initiating act and Mary's response to his act, both

---

[6] Social psychologists are at least implicitly aware of this situationally defined "hot zone": A variety of interesting interaction phenomena have been examined in situations involving nonmutual dependence (infant behavior in the "strange situation," adult behavior in support-seeking or self-disclosure situations) and conflicting interests (behavior during arguments or following transgressions).

partners' tendencies not only govern each person's concrete and symbolic outcomes, but also serve to select the future situations that become available to the pair. [7]

Security of Attachment. Work regarding attachment processes illuminates our understanding of dependence situations, in that issues of dependence are at the heart of attachment concerns. The adult attachment literature suggests that the intrapersonal and interpersonal adaptations acquired in childhood are carried into adult interactions. For example, securely attached individuals perceive a wide range of dependence situations as "safe," experience more positive cognition and affect in such situations, exhibit more trusting expectations about their partners' motives, enact fewer exploitative behaviors, and adopt more constructive strategies in response to violations of trust (Baldwin, Keelan, Fehr, Enns, & Koh-Rangarajoo, 1996; Mikulincer, 1998; Simpson et al., 1996; Tidwell et al., 1996). Insecurely attached individuals exhibit distrustful and destructive cognitive, motivational, and behavioral tendencies not only when they are the more dependent persons in interaction, but also when their partners are dependent upon them. What comes first, attachment style or patterns of interaction? These variables appear to exhibit reciprocal patterns of cause and effect, in that (a) attachment style is shaped by adaptation to repeatedly encountered dependence situations with important partners; and (b) attachment style shapes cognition, motivation, communication, and the selection of partners and future interaction situations. Moreover, and consistent with the claim that dependence situations afford attachment-relevant issues, the liabilities of unreliable, rejecting, and unresponsive partner behavior are most pronounced when interdependence structure is most problematic—in situations involving nonmutual dependence and conflicting interests (Pietromonaco & Feldman-Barrett, 1997; Simpson et al., 1996). In short, the more problematic the dependence situation, the more attachment concerns come to the fore.

Rejection Sensitivity. Research on rejection sensitivity further enriches our understanding of dependence, illuminating the process by which expectancies operate in extended dependence situations (Downey & Feldman, 1996; Downey, Freitas, Michaelis, & Khouri, 1998). The empirical literature suggests that predispositions toward comfort with (vs. avoidance of) interdependence may operate in a self-reinforcing manner: Women with greater sensitivity to possible rejection develop fearful expectancies regarding partner behavior—they anxiously expect and readily perceive negativity from their partners. As a consequence, they overreact to signs of possible exploitation in dependence situations with conflicting interests, frequently behaving in a provocative and hostile manner. Their partners respond with elevated anger and reciprocal negativity, thereby confirming the woman's worst fears. As a consequence of such maladaptive interaction, the relationships of rejection sensitive women exhibit poor adjustment and are more likely to terminate. In contrast, more adaptive patterns of interaction are evident among people who are less fearful of dependence and less sensitive to possible rejection, and who therefore exhibit prosocial expectations and transformations, exhibiting positive and responsive behavior, and trusting that the partner will reciprocate.

Intimacy Processes. Work regarding intimacy processes is also relevant to discussions of dependence, in that when people disclose self-relevant information, they

---

[7] Dependence situations become more complex when partners possess incomplete or inaccurate information. For example, although Mary may intend to respond in an encouraging manner, John may perceive her behavior as nagging or critical. Noting his irritation, Mary may feel confused or angry with John for so thoroughly misinterpreting her intentions, and may behave in such a manner as to lead the two to future situations with more problematic situation structure.

make themselves vulnerable to possible rejection. In such situations, individuals confront a tradeoff between the benefits of disclosure in comparison with the risks of exploitation. Individuals display trust when they disclose important self-relevant information, thereby placing themselves in a dependent position (Omarzu, 2000; Reis & Patrick, 1996). When partners exhibit prosocial motives and do not exploit this vulnerability (i.e., they exhibit understanding, caring, and acceptance) interactions become more trusting, reciprocal disclosure is elicited, and mutual attraction is enhanced (Collins & Miller, 1994; Laurenceau, Barrett, & Pietromonaco, 1998; Reis & Shaver, 1988). In light of the vulnerabilities inherent in intimacy situations, it is not surprising that dependencies of this sort are regulated by norms. For example, partners tend to disclose at roughly equal levels of intimacy (it is rude to respond to a tearful confession of childhood sexual abuse with "nice weather we've been having"), and regard it as unacceptable to transmit a close partner's secret to a nonclose third party (Mary can tell John about a colleague's childhood abuse, but should not transmit such information to her masseuse; Reis & Patrick, 1996; Yovetich & Drigotas, 1999).

Summary.   In this section of the paper, we proposed that a close relationship exists to the extent that partners develop a "state of interaction process," exhibiting relatively characteristic forms of cognition, affect, communication, and motivation across the range of interdependence situations they routinely confront. To demonstrate the utility of this analysis, we reviewed interaction processes in two common classes of interdependence situation: those involving conflicting interests and those involving nonmutual dependence. We explained how partners' fixed expectations regarding interdependence may color their perceptions of a given situation, as well as how well-established goals and motives shape their cognition, affect, and communication. Thus, it becomes clear that situations afford the expression of close partners' personal values and dispositions, and that both persons' thoughts and motives shape their joint adaptations to interdependence situations ($I = f[S, A, B]$). This review links interdependence principles with the theoretical orientations to which we alluded at the beginning of the chapter, demonstrating the relevance of interdependence structure to explaining important intrapersonal and interpersonal processes involving conflict, attachment, and intimacy.

SUMMARY AND CONCLUSIONS

We have proposed that closeness and close relationships can fruitfully be understood using an interdependence theoretic analysis. Interdependence theory presents a logical analysis of the structure of interpersonal situations, offering a conceptual framework in which interdependence situations can be analyzed in terms of six properties: level of dependence, mutuality of dependence, basis of dependence, covariation of interests, temporal structure, and availability of information. We propose that closeness exists to the extent that at least one person in an interaction is dependent, that is, to the extent that one or both interacting persons affect the other's well-being. Combinations of dependence with other structural properties define the character of close interdependence, presenting partners with specific sorts of problems and opportunities, logically implying the relevance of specific motives, and permitting the expression of those motives. Via the concept of transformation, the theory explains how interaction is shaped by broader considerations, such as individuals' long-term goals and concern for others' welfare. The theory also illuminates our understanding of social-cognitive processes such as cognition and affect, attribution, and self-presentation, and explains how adaptations to repeatedly encountered patterns become embodied in dispositions, relationship-specific motives, and norms.

Close partners can be said to be in a relationship to the extent that they exhibit characteristic patterns of cognition, affect, communication, and motivation across the range of interdependence situations they routinely confront, such that their interactions with one another to some degree are predictable (albeit not static or invariant). As such, close relationships take many forms, and are more than the material properties of which they are comprised, more than the sum of the partners' dispositions, and more than the observable behaviors that characterize partners' conversation or the rules that govern their dealings with one another. It should be clear that many of the theoretical and empirical traditions reviewed in this chapter are compatible with the interdependence orientation, and that interdependence theory provides an overarching framework in which to understand the interrelations among these orientations. We hope that this chapter helps to convey the comprehensiveness of interdependence theory, and to illustrate the utility of interdependence principles toward developing a fundamentally interpersonal analysis of closeness and relationships.

ACKNOWLEDGMENTS

The authors contributed equally to preparation of this chapter; order of authorship is based on seniority. Correspondence regarding this chapter should be addressed to Caryl Rusbult, Department of Psychology, University of North Carolina at Chapel Hill, Chapel Hill, North Carolina 27599-3270 (rusbult@unc.edu).

REFERENCES

Agnew, C. R., Van Lange, P. A. M., Rusbult, C. E., & Langston, C. A. (1998). Cognitive interdependence: Commitment and the mental representation of close relationships. *Journal of Personality and Social Psychology, 74*, 939–954.

Ainsworth, M., Blehar, M. C., Waters, E., & Wall, S. (1978). *Patterns of attachment: A psychological study of the strange situation.* Hillsdale, NJ: Lawrence Erlbaum Associates.

Andersen, S. M., & Baum, A. B. (1994). Transference in interpersonal relations: Inferences and affect based on significant–other representations. *Journal of Personality, 62*, 460–497.

Andersen, S. M., Reznik, I, & Manzella, L. M. (1996). Eliciting facial affect, motivation, and expectancies in transference: Significant other representations in social relations. *Journal of Personality and Social Psychology, 71*, 1108–1129.

Anderson, J. R. (1991). The adaptive nature of human categorization. *Psychological Review, 98*, 409–429.

Aron, A., & Aron, E. (2000). Self-expansion motivation and including other in the self. In W. Ickes & S. Duck (Eds.), *The social psychology of personal relationships* (pp. 109–128). New York: Wiley.

Arriaga, X. B., & Rusbult, C. E. (1998). Standing in my partner's shoes: Partner perspective-taking and reactions to accommodative dilemmas. *Personality and Social Psychology Bulletin, 9*, 927–948.

Attridge, M., Berscheid, E., & Simpson, J. A. (1995). Predicting relationship stability from both partners versus one. *Journal of Personality and Social Psychology, 69*, 254–268.

Axelrod, R. (1984). *The evolution of cooperation.* New York: Basic Books.

Baldwin, M. W., Keelan, J. P. R., Fehr, B., Enns, V., & Koh-Rangarajoo, E. (1996). Social-cognitive conceptualization of attachment working models: Availability and accessibility effects. *Journal of Personality and Social Psychology, 71*, 94–109.

Baumeister, R. F., Bratslavsky, E., Finkenauer, C., & Vohs, K. D. (2001). Bad is stronger than good. *Review of General Psychology, 5*, 323–370.

Baumeister, R. F., Bratslavsky, E., Muraven, M., & Tice, D. M. (1998). Ego depletion: Is the active self a limited resource? *Journal of Personality and Social Psychology, 74*, 1252–1265.

Baumeister, R. F., & Leary, M. R. (1995). The need to belong: Desire for interpersonal attachments as a fundamental human motivation. *Psychological Bulletin, 117*, 497–529.

Baumeister, R. F., Wotman, S. R., & Stillwell, A. M. (1993). Unrequited love: On heartbreak, anger, guilt, scriptlessness, and humiliation. *Journal of Personality and Social Psychology, 64*, 377–394.

Berns, S. B., Jacobson, N. S., & Gottman, J. M. (1999). Demand-withdraw interaction in couples with a violent husband. *Journal of Consulting and Clinical Psychology, 67*, 666–674.

Berscheid, E., Snyder, M., & Omoto, A. M. (1989). The relationship closeness inventory: Assessing the closeness of interpersonal relationships. *Journal of Personality and Social Psychology, 57*, 792–807.

Bowlby, J. (1969). *Attachment and loss, Vol. 1: Attachment.* New York: Basic Books.

Buss, D. M., & Craik, K. H. (1980). The frequency concept of disposition: Dominance and prototypically dominant acts. *Journal of Personality, 48,* 379–392.

Bui, K. T., Peplau, L. A., & Hill, C. T. (1996). Testing the Rusbult model of relationship commitment and stability in a 15-year study of heterosexual couples. *Personality and Social Psychology Bulletin, 22,* 1244–1257.

Carstensen, L. L., Gottman, J. M., & Levenson, R. W. (1995). Emotional behavior in long-term marriage. *Psychology and Aging, 10,* 140–149.

Christensen, A., & Heavey, C. L. (1993). Gender differences in marital conflict: The demand/withdraw interaction pattern. In S. Oskamp & M. Costanzo (Eds.), *Gender issues in contemporary society* (pp. 113–141). Newbury Park, CA: Sage.

Clark, M. S., & Mills, J. (1993). The difference between communal and exchange relationships: What it is and is not. *Personality and Social Psychology Bulletin, 19,* 684–691.

Collins, N. L., & Feeney, B. C. (2000). A safe haven: An attachment theory perspective on support seeking and caregiving in intimate relationships. *Journal of Personality and Social Psychology, 78,* 1053–1073.

Collins, N. L., & Miller, L. C. (1994). Self-disclosure and liking: A meta-analytic review. *Psychological Bulletin, 116,* 457–475.

Cosmides, L., & Tooby, J. (1992). Cognitive adaptations for social exchange. In J. H. Barkow, L. Cosmides, & J. Tooby (Eds.), *The adapted mind: Evolutionary psychology and the generation of culture* (pp. 163–228). New York: Oxford University Press.

Dehue, F. M. J., McClintock, C. G., & Liebrand, W. B. G. (1993). Social value related response latencies: Unobtrusive evidence for individual differences in information processes. *European Journal of Social Psychology, 23,* 273–294.

Downey, G., & Feldman, S. (1996). Implications of rejection sensitivity for intimate relationships. *Journal of Personality and Social Psychology, 70,* 1327–1343.

Downey, G., Freitas, A., Michaelis, B., & Khouri, H. (1998). The self-fulfilling prophecy in close relationships: Rejection sensitivity and rejection by romantic partners. *Journal of Personality and Social Psychology, 75,* 545–560.

Drigotas, S. M., & Rusbult, C. E. (1992). Should I stay or should I go?: A dependence model of break ups. *Journal of Personality and Social Psychology, 62,* 62–87.

Drigotas, S. M., Rusbult, C. E., & Verette, J. (1999). Level of commitment, mutuality of commitment, and couple well-being. *Personal Relationships, 6,* 389–409.

Drigotas, S. M., Rusbult, C. E., Wieselquist, J., & Whitton, S. (1999) Close partner as sculptor of the ideal self: Behavioral affirmation and the Michelangelo phenomenon. *Journal of Personality and Social Psychology, 77,* 293–323.

Drigotas, S. M., Whitney, G. A., & Rusbult, C. E. (1995). On the peculiarities of loyalty: A diary study of responses to dissatisfaction in everyday life. *Personality and Social Psychology Bulletin, 21,* 596–609.

Epstein, N., Baucom, D. H., & Rankin, L. A. (1993). Treatment of marital conflict: A cognitive-behavioral approach. *Clinical Psychology Review, 13,* 45–57.

Fincham, F. D. (2001). Attributions in close relationships: From Balkanization to integration. In G. J. O. Fletcher & M. S. Clark (Eds.), *Blackwell handbook of social psychology: Interpersonal processes* (pp. 3–31). Oxford: Blackwell.

Finkel, E. J., & Campbell, W. K. (2001). Self-control and accommodation in close relationships: An interdependence analysis. *Journal of Personality and Social Psychology, 81,* 263–277.

Finkel, E. J., Rusbult, C. E., Kumashiro, M., & Hannon, P. A. (2002). Dealing with betrayal in close relationships: Does commitment promote forgiveness? *Journal of Personality and Social Psychology, 82,* 956–974.

Fiske, A. P. (1992). The four elementary forms of sociality: Framework for a unified theory of social relations. *Psychological Review, 99,* 689–723.

Fiske, S. T. (1993). Controlling other people: The impact of power on stereotyping. *American Psychologist, 48,* 621–628.

Frank, R. H., Gilovich, T., & Regan, D. T. (1993). The evolution of one-shot cooperation: An experiment. *Ethology and Sociobiology, 14,* 247–256.

Gilbert, D. T. (1998). Ordinary personology. In D. T. Gilbert, S. T. Fiske, & G. Lindzey (Eds.), *Handbook of social psychology, Vol. 2* (4th ed., pp. 89–150). Boston: McGraw-Hill.

Gottman, J. M. (1998). Psychology and the study of marital processes, *Annual Review of Psychology, 49,* 169–197.

Hazan, C., & Shaver, P. R. (1994). Attachment as an organizational framework for research on close relationships. *Psychological Inquiry, 5,* 1–22.

Holmes, J. G. (1981). The exchange process in close relationships: Microbehavior and macromotives. In M. J. Lerner & S. C. Lerner (Eds.), *The justice motive in social behavior* (pp. 261–284). New York: Plenum.

Holmes, J. G. (2002). Interpersonal expectations as the building blocks of social cognition: An interdependence theory perspective. *Personal Relationships, 9,* 1–26.

Holmes, J. G., & Murray, S. L. (1996). Conflict in close relationships. In E. T. Higgins & A. Kruglanski (Eds.), *Social psychology: Handbook of basic principles* (pp. 622–654). New York: Guilford.

Holmes, J. G., & Rempel, J. K. (1989). Trust in close relationships. In C. Hendrick (Ed.), *Review of personality and social psychology* (Vol. 10, pp. 187–220). London: Sage.

Ickes, W., & Simpson, J. A. (1997). Managing empathic accuracy in close relationships. In W. Ickes (Ed.), *Empathic accuracy* (pp. 218–250). New York: Guilford.

Johnson, D. J., & Rusbult, C. E. (1989). Resisting temptation: Devaluation of alternative partners as a means of maintaining commitment in close relationships. *Journal of Personality and Social Psychology, 57,* 967–980.

Johnson, M. P. (1995). Patriarchal terrorism and common couple violence: Two forms of violence against women. *Journal of Marriage and the Family, 57,* 283–294.

Kelley, H. H. (1979). *Personal relationships: Their structures and processes.* Hillsdale, NJ: Lawrence Erlbaum Associates.

Kelley, H. H. (1983). The situational origins of human tendencies: A further reason for the formal analysis of structure. *Personality and Social Psychology Bulletin, 9,* 8–30.

Kelley, H. H. (1984a). Affect in interpersonal relations. In P. Shaver (Ed.), *Review of personality and social psychology* (Vol. 5, pp. 89–115). Newbury Park, CA: Sage.

Kelley, H. H. (1984b). The theoretical description of interdependence by means of transition lists. *Journal of Personality and Social Psychology, 47,* 956–982.

Kelley, H. H. (1994). Personal commentary. *Bulletin of the International Society for the Study of Personal Relationships, 11,* 1–3.

Kelley, H. H. (1997). The "stimulus field" for interpersonal phenomena: The source of language and thought about interpersonal events. *Personality and Social Psychology Review, 1,* 140–169.

Kelley, H. H., Holmes, J. G., Kerr, N. L., Reis, H. T., Rusbult, C. E., & Van Lange, P. A. M. (2003). *An atlas of interpersonal situations.* New York: Cambridge.

Kelley, H. H., & Thibaut, J. W. (1978). *Interpersonal relations: A theory of interdependence.* New York: Wiley.

Kenrick, D. T., & Trost, M. R. (2000). An evolutionary perspective on human relationships. In W. Ickes & S. Duck (Eds.), *The social psychology of personal relationships* (pp. 9–35). New York: Wiley.

Laurenceau, J. P., Barrett, L. F., & Pietromonaco, P. R. (1998). Intimacy as an interpersonal process: The importance of self-disclosure, partner disclosure, and perceived partner responsiveness in interpersonal exchanges. *Journal of Personality and Social Psychology, 74,* 1238–1251.

Leary, M. R. (2001). The self we know and the self we show: Self-esteem, self-presentation, and the maintenance of interpersonal relationships. In G. J. O Fletcher & M. S. Clark (Eds.), *Blackwell handbook of social psychology: Interpersonal processes* (pp. 457–477). Oxford: Blackwell.

McCullough, M. E., Worthington, E. L., Jr., & Rachal, K. C. (1997). Interpersonal forgiving in close relationships. *Journal of Personality and Social Psychology, 73,* 321–336.

Messick, D. M., & McClintock, C. G. (1968). Motivational basis of choice in experimental games. *Journal of Experimental Social Psychology, 4,* 1–25.

Mikulincer, M. (1998). Attachment working models and the sense of trust: An exploration of interaction goals and affect regulation. *Journal of Personality and Social Psychology, 74,* 1209–1224.

Miller, R. S. (1997). Inattentive and contented: Relationship commitment and attention to alternatives. *Journal of Personality and Social Psychology, 73,* 758–766.

Mischel, W., Cantor, N., & Feldman, S. (1996). Principles of self-regulation: The nature of willpower and self-control. In E. T. Higgins & A. Kruglanski (Eds.), *Social psychology: Handbook of basic principles* (pp. 329–360). New York: Guilford.

Murray, S. L., Holmes, J. G., & Griffin, D. W. (1996). The self-fulfilling nature of positive illusions in romantic relationships: Love is not blind, but prescient. *Journal of Personality and Social Psychology, 71,* 1155–1180.

Omarzu, J. (2000). A disclosure decision model: Determining how and when individuals will self-disclose. *Personality and Social Psychology Review, 4,* 174–185.

Pietromonaco, P., & Feldman-Barrett, L. (1997). Working models of attachment and daily social interactions. *Journal of Personality and Social Psychology, 73,* 1409–1423.

Reis, H. T., & Patrick, B. C. (1996). Attachment and intimacy: Component processes. In E. T. Higgins & A. W. Kruglanski (Eds.), *Social psychology: Handbook of basic principles* (pp. 523–563). New York: Guilford.

Reis, H. T., & Shaver, P. (1988). Intimacy as an interpersonal process. In S. Duck (Ed.), *Handbook of personal relationships: Theory, relationships, and interventions* (pp. 367–389). Chichester, England: Wiley.

Rusbult, C. E. (1983). A longitudinal test of the investment model: The development (and deterioration) of satisfaction and commitment in heterosexual involvements. *Journal of Personality and Social Psychology, 45,* 101–117.

Rusbult, C. E., Davis, J. L., Finkel, E. J., Hannon, P., & Olsen, N. (2003). *Forgiveness of betrayal in close relationships: A dual-process model of the transformation from self-interested impulses to relationship-oriented actions.* Unpublished manuscript, University of North Carolina at Chapel Hill, Chapel Hill, NC.

Rusbult, C. E., & Martz, J. M. (1995). Remaining in an abusive relationship: An investment model analysis of nonvoluntary commitment. *Personality and Social Psychology Bulletin, 21,* 558–571.

Rusbult, C. E., Olsen, N., Davis, J. L., & Hannon, P. (2001). Commitment and relationship maintenance mechanisms. In J. H. Harvey & A. Wenzel (Eds.), *Close romantic relationships: Maintenance and enhancement* (pp. 87–113). Mahwah, NJ: Lawrence Erlbaum Associates.

Rusbult, C. E., & Van Lange, P. A. M. (1996). Interdependence processes. In E. T. Higgins & A. Kruglanski (Eds.), *Social psychology: Handbook of basic principles* (pp. 564–596). New York: Guilford.

Rusbult, C. E., Van Lange, P. A. M., Wildschut, T., Yovetich, N. A., & Verette, J. (2000). Perceived superiority in close relationships: Why it exists and persists. *Journal of Personality and Social Psychology, 79,* 521–545.

Rusbult, C. E., Verette, J., Whitney, G. A., Slovik, L. F., & Lipkus, I. (1991). Accommodation processes in close relationships: Theory and preliminary empirical evidence. *Journal of Personality and Social Psychology, 60,* 53–78.

Simpson, J. A., Fletcher, G. J. O., & Campbell, L. (2001). The structure and function of ideal standards in close relationships. In G. J. O. Fletcher & M. S. Clark (Eds.), *Blackwell handbook of social psychology: Interpersonal processes* (pp. 86–106). Oxford: Blackwell.

Simpson, J. A., Rholes, W. S., & Nelligan, J. S. (1992). Support seeking and support giving within couples in an anxiety-provoking situation: The role of attachment styles. *Journal of Personality and Social Psychology, 62,* 434–446.

Simpson, J. A., Rholes, W. S., & Phillips, D. (1996). Conflict in close relationships: An attachment perspective. *Journal of Personality and Social Psychology, 71,* 899–914.

Sternberg, R. J. (1986). A triangular theory of love. *Psychological Review, 93,* 119–135.

Surra, C. A., & Longstreth, M. (1990). Similarity of outcomes, interdependence, and conflict in dating relationships. *Journal of Personality and Social Psychology, 59,* 501–516.

Sweeney, M. M. (2002). Two decades of family change: The shifting economic foundations of marriage. *American Sociological Review, 67,* 132–147.

Thibaut, J. W., & Kelley, H. H. (1959). *The social psychology of groups.* New York: Wiley.

Tice, D. M., Butler, J. L., Muraven, M. B., & Stillwell, A. M. (1995). When modesty prevails: Differential favorability of self-presentation to friends and strangers. *Journal of Personality and Social Psychology, 69,* 1120–1138.

Tidwell, M. C. O., Reis, H. T., & Shaver, P. R. (1996). Attachment, attractiveness, and social interaction: A diary study. *Journal of Personality and Social Psychology, 71,* 729–745.

Turiel, E. (1983). *The development of social knowledge: Morality and convention.* Cambridge, England: Cambridge University Press.

Van Lange, P. A. M., & Kuhlman, D. M. (1994). Social value orientations and impressions of a partner's honesty and intelligence: A test of the might versus morality effect. *Journal of Personality and Social Psychology, 67,* 126–141.

Van Lange, P. A. M., Rusbult, C. E., Drigotas, S. M., Arriaga, X. B., Witcher, B. S., & Cox, C. L. (1997). Willingness to sacrifice in close relationships. *Journal of Personality and Social Psychology, 72,* 1373–1395.

Von Neuman, J., & Morgenstern, O. (1944). *Theory of games and economic behavior.* Princeton, NJ: Princeton University Press.

Walster, E., Walster, G. W., & Berscheid, E. (1978). *Equity: Theory and research.* Boston: Allyn and Bacon.

Wieselquist, J., Rusbult, C. E., Foster, C. A., & Agnew, C. R. (1999). Commitment, prorelationship behavior, and trust in close relationships. *Journal of Personality and Social Psychology, 77,* 942–966.

Wieselquist, J., Rusbult, C. E., Kumashiro, M., & Finkel, E. J. (2003). *Benevolent memory in close relationships: The impact of trust on memory for positive and negative partner behaviors.* Unpublished manuscript, University of New England, Biddeford, ME.

Witcher, B. S. (1999). *The effects of power on relationships and on individuals.* Unpublished dissertation, University of North Carolina at Chapel Hill, Chapel Hill, NC.

Yovetich, N. A., & Drigotas, S. M. (1999). Secret transmission: A relative intimacy hypothesis. *Personality and Social Psychology Bulletin, 25,* 1135–1146.

Yovetich, N. A., & Rusbult, C. E. (1994). Accommodative behavior in close relationships: Exploring transformation of motivation. *Journal of Experimental Social Psychology, 30,* 138–164.

10

An Attachment Theory Perspective on Closeness and Intimacy

Nancy L. Collins
University of California, Santa Barbara

Brooke C. Feeney
Carnegie Mellon University

> *Attachment theory regards the propensity to make intimate emotional bonds to particular individuals as a basic component of human nature, already present in germinal form in the neonate and continuing through adult life into old age.*
>
> —Bowlby (1988, pp. 120–121)

Close relationships are essential to health and well-being (Cohen, 1988; Sarason, Sarason, & Gurung, 2001; Uchino, Cacioppo, & Kiecolt-Glaser, 1996), and most people regard their intimate relationships as their most important source of personal happiness (Myers & Diener, 1995; Ryff, 1989). Moreover, the capacity to form intimate bonds with others is considered to be a principal feature of effective personality development and a key marker of mental health (Bowlby, 1988; Epstein, 1994). But despite the importance of close relationships for health and well-being, many people find it difficult to develop and sustain intimate relationships with others, and many relationships fail to provide partners with the deep sense of emotional closeness that is necessary for optimal functioning. In this chapter, we use attachment theory as a framework for understanding closeness and intimacy processes within adult close relationships and for exploring individual differences in the capacity for intimate relating (see also Cassidy, 2001; Reis & Patrick, 1996). Attachment theory provides a useful perspective from which to understand intimacy processes for a number of reasons. First, attachment theory highlights the importance of closeness and intimacy processes for the development and maintenance of trust and felt security in close relationships. In doing so, attachment theory emphasizes the central role of care-seeking–caregiving exchanges as a special class of intimate interactions. Second, attachment theory identifies the ways in which individual differences in attachment style shape the quality of intimate interactions within a relationship, as well as partners' subjective perceptions of these interactions. Finally, attachment theory provides insight into the role of early family experiences in the development of intimacy-related goals and skills.

Before discussing attachment theory, it is important to clarify our use of the terms *closeness* and *intimacy*. We use the term *closeness* to refer to the degree to which relationship partners are cognitively, emotionally, and behaviorally interdependent with one another. By interdependent, we mean the degree to which partners' lives are deeply intertwined such that partners influence one another's outcomes and rely on one another for the fulfillment of important social, emotional, and physical needs (Berscheid, Snyder, & Omoto, 1989; Kelly et al., 1983). Whereas closeness refers to a general pattern of interdependence, intimacy refers to a specific type of social interaction. On the basis of models of intimacy advanced by Reis and Shaver (1988; Reis & Patrick, 1996) and by Prager (1995; Prager & Roberts, chap. 4, this volume), we use the term *intimacy* to refer to a special class of social interactions in which one partner expresses self-relevant feelings and information and, as a result of the other partner's responsiveness and positive regard, the individual comes to feel understood, validated, and cared for (see Laurenceau, Rivera, Schaffer, & Pietromonaco, chap. 5, this volume, for a review of Reis & Shaver's [1988] intimacy model). Although intimate interactions often involve verbal self-disclosure, physical forms of intimacy (e.g., touching, hugging, sexual contact) provide an equally important channel through which individuals can express their true selves, and through which partners can communicate acceptance and caring (Prager, 1995; Reis & Patrick, 1996). Furthermore, although this model of intimacy emphasizes the importance of studying specific interactions, it is also useful for understanding patterns of intimate relating within a relationship. Individuals will come to experience their relationship as emotionally intimate to the extent that they feel understood, validated, and cared-for by their partner on central self-relevant dimensions (Reis & Patrick, 1996); and these intimate feelings should result from accumulated experiences in intimate interactions, along with each partner's subjective interpretations of those experiences and relevant goals and needs (Prager & Roberts, chap. 4, this volume).

Because attachment bonds are characterized by profound psychological and physical interdependence not found in other social bonds (Hazan & Zeifman, 1999), attachment relationships are among people's closest and most intimate relationships. Attachment relationships are unique from other close relationships in their ability to satisfy needs for security, in their central importance to the self, and in their implications for health and well-being (Cassidy, 2001). Moreover, it is within attachment relationships that individuals are most likely to express the types of "vulnerable emotions" (e.g., sadness, hurt, fear) that are considered to be the most self-revealing and the most intimate (Prager & Roberts, chap. 4, this volume; Reis & Patrick, 1996), and to engage in physical forms of intimacy (e.g., cuddling, kissing, comforting) that do not typically occur in other close relationships (Hazan & Zeifman, 1999; Shaver, Hazan, & Bradshaw, 1988). As such, attachment relationships provide an important context within which to explore the dynamics of closeness and intimacy, and the implications of these dynamics for personal and interpersonal adaptation across the lifespan.

In the pages that follow, we examine closeness and intimacy processes from the perspective of attachment theory. We begin by providing an overview of the basic tenets of attachment theory, focusing on both normative processes and individual differences. In doing so, we explore how early experiences in the family may shape the capacity for intimate relating in childhood and adulthood. Next, we discuss how intimacy and attachment processes are regulated in adult close relationships, and how these processes are shaped by individual differences in attachment style.

THE ATTACHMENT BEHAVIORAL SYSTEM

In discussing the attachment behavioral system, it is useful to distinguish between normative processes and individual differences. Normative processes refer to the general operation of the attachment behavioral system in terms of its adaptive function and its social and psychological dynamics, which are presumed to be universal. Individual differences refer to the specific ways in which the attachment system is expressed in different people depending on their history of attachment experiences, current relationship circumstances, and cultural context.

Normative Processes

Attachment theory was first developed to explain why infants become attached to their primary caregivers and emotionally distressed when separated from them. Drawing from principles of evolutionary theory, Bowlby (1969/1982) argued that attachment behaviors in infants (e.g., crying, clinging, smiling) are regulated by an innate *attachment behavioral system* that functions to promote safety and survival by maintaining a child's proximity to a nurturing caretaker. According to this approach, the attachment system will be activated most strongly in adversity so that when a child is frightened, tired, ill, or in unfamiliar surroundings, the child will seek protection and comfort from an attachment figure (Bowlby, 1969/1982; Bretherton, 1985). As the child matures and his or her cognitive system becomes increasingly sophisticated, the goal of the attachment system is not simply to maintain physical proximity to a caregiver, but to maintain a psychological sense of *felt security* (Bretherton, 1985; Sroufe & Waters, 1977).

An attachment bond is therefore a specific type of emotional bond that has four defining features: (a) *proximity maintenance*, in which the attached individual wishes to be in close proximity (either physically or psychologically) to the attachment figure, (b) *separation distress*, in which the attached individual experiences an increase in anxiety during unwanted or prolonged separation from the attachment figure, (c) *safe haven*, in which the attachment figure serves as a source of comfort and security for the attached individual, and (d) *secure base*, in which the attachment figure serves as a base of security from which the attached individual engages in explorations of the social and physical world (Hazan & Zeifman, 1999). A child's ability to rely on his or her attachment figure as a safe haven when comfort is needed, and as a secure base from which to explore the world, is considered to be a principal feature of well-functioning attachment bonds and a key predictor of healthy emotional development.

In order for attachment bonds to function effectively, the attachment behavior of a child must be coordinated with the caregiving behavior of his or her attachment figure. Indeed, Bowlby (1969/1982) referred to attachment bonds as a "shared dyadic programme" (p. 377) in which care seekers and caregivers play complementary roles and in which the behavior of one partner commonly meshes with that of the other. The *caregiving behavioral system* is thus an integral component of attachment bonds (Bowlby, 1969/1982; George & Solomon, 1999; Kunce & Shaver, 1994). From a normative perspective, the caregiving system alerts individuals to the needs of others and motivates them to provide comfort and assistance to those who are dependent upon them (Collins & Feeney, B. C., 2000; Feeney, B. C., & Collins, 2001). Just as infants are motivated to remain in close proximity to their primary caregivers, caregivers feel a strong urge to remain close to their infants and young children; they routinely monitor their infant's whereabouts and remain ready to respond on short notice should any threat arise. Of course, effective caregiving involves more than simply monitoring a child's whereabouts and remaining alert to signs of distress. In its optimal form, caregiving includes sensitivity and responsiveness to the child's expressed needs and signals, and should include a broad array of behaviors (e.g., holding, soothing, reassuring, problem-solving) that complement the child's attachment behavior (George & Solomon, 1999; Kunce & Shaver, 1994).

Individual Differences

Although the need for felt security is believed to be universal, children differ systematically in the way they cope with distress and regulate feelings of security; these differences are thought to be contingent on the child's history of regulating distress with attachment figures (Ainsworth, Blehar, Waters, & Wall, 1978; Bowlby, 1973, 1969/1982). Attachment scholars have identified three primary patterns or styles of attachment in infant-caregiver dyads (secure, anxious-ambivalent, and avoidant), and these attachment styles are systematically linked to differences in caregiver warmth and responsiveness (Ainsworth et al., 1978; Egeland & Farber, 1984). *Secure* attachment is associated with a caregiver who is sensitive and responsive (thereby inducing feelings of support and security), *anxious-ambivalent* attachment is associated with a caregiver who responds in an inconsistent manner (inducing anxiety, vigilance, and anger), and *avoidant* attachment is associated with a caregiver who is cool, rejecting, and unsupportive (inducing premature self-reliance and suppression of neediness and vulnerability). These individual differences in *attachment style* are thought to reflect differences in the psychological organization of the attachment system, a central part of which is the child's perception of whether the caretaker can be trusted to be emotionally available and responsive when needed (Main, Kaplan, & Cassidy, 1985).

Thus, central to Bowlby's theory (1973, 1969/1982) is the notion that early child/caregiver interactions provide a critical context within which the child organizes emotional experience and learns to regulate attachment needs. On the basis of these early interactions, Bowlby (1973) argued that children develop *internal working models* of attachment, which contain beliefs and expectations about whether the caretaker is emotionally available and responsive when needed (a working model of other), and whether the self is worthy of care and attention (a working model of self). These working models tend to be mutually confirming such that positive (or negative) expectations about a caretaker's responsiveness tend to be linked to positive (or negative) images of the self. Working models are cognitive-affective-motivational schemas that enable individuals to forecast the responsiveness and availability of others and to plan their own behavior accordingly. They include conscious and unconscious elements that direct not only feelings and behavior, but also attention, memory, and cognition in attachment-relevant contexts (Bowlby, 1973; Bretherton & Munholland, 1999; Collins & Allard, 2001; Collins & Read, 1994; Main, Kaplan, & Cassidy, 1985). Once developed, working models tend to be relatively stable because they operate automatically and unconsciously, and because they influence how new information is processed and construed (Shaver, Collins, & Clark, 1996; Collins & Read, 1994). Therefore, enduring cognitive models will be carried forward into new relationships where they influence how one expresses and regulates attachment needs (Bowlby, 1988; Bretherton, 1985, 1987).

Attachment Processes in Adulthood

Although Bowlby focused primarily on infants and young children, he acknowledged the importance of studying attachment processes across the lifespan and he suggested that the basic functions of the attachment system continue to operate in adulthood and old age (Bowlby, 1988). At present, most of the empirical work on adult attachment processes has focused on adult romantic relationships, which Bowlby viewed as the prototypical attachment bond in adulthood. Just as children derive a sense of felt security from becoming emotionally connected to a primary caregiver who is invested in their welfare and responsive to their needs, adults will derive a sense of security from becoming emotionally and behaviorally interdependent with a romantic partner who is uniquely committed to them and deeply invested in their welfare (Hazan & Zeifman, 1999). Hence, from a normative perspective, emotional (and physical) well-being in adulthood, as in childhood, will depend in part on having an accessible attachment figure who can serve as a reliable safe haven in times of need and a secure base from which to explore autonomous activities outside of the relationship. In addition, feeling nurtured and cared for by a responsive partner should be a critical component of secure and well-functioning intimate relationships in adulthood. We discuss these issues in greater detail subsequently.

In addition to these normative processes, Bowlby suggested that individual differences in adult attachment behavior and emotion regulation will be guided by internal working models of attachment that have their developmental origins in early attachment relationships. Consistent with these claims, adult attachment researchers have shown that the patterns of attachment that characterize adult romantic relationships are similar to those observed in childhood, and these patterns are systematically linked to retrospective reports of early experiences with attachment figures (e.g., Collins & Read, 1990; J. A. Feeney & Noller, 1990; Hazan & Shaver, 1987; Levy, Blatt, & Shaver, 1998; Rothbard & Shaver, 1994). Moreover, the cognitive, emotional, and behavioral consequences of these attachment patterns in adult romantic relationships appear to be similar to those observed in parent-child relationships (see Feeney, J. A., 1999 for a review of these findings).

Adult attachment researchers typically define four prototypic attachment styles derived from two underlying dimensions: *anxiety* and *avoidance* (Bartholomew & Horowitz, 1991; Brennan, Clark, & Shaver, 1998; Crowell, Fraley, & Shaver, 1999; Fraley & Waller, 1998). The *anxiety* dimension refers to one's sense of self-worth and acceptance (versus rejection) by others, and this dimension appears to be closely linked to working models of the self. The *avoidance* dimension refers to the degree to which one approaches (versus avoids) intimacy and interdependence with others, and this dimension appears to be closely linked to working models of others. *Secure* adults are low in both attachment-related anxiety and avoidance; they are comfortable with intimacy, willing to rely on others for support, and confident that they are valued by others. *Preoccupied* (anxious/ambivalent) adults are high in anxiety and low in avoidance; they have an exaggerated desire for closeness and dependence, coupled with a heightened concern about being rejected. *Dismissing avoidant* individuals are low in attachment-related anxiety but high in avoidance; they view close relationships as relatively unimportant and they value independence and self-reliance. Finally, *fearful avoidant* adults are high in both attachment anxiety and avoidance; although they desire close relationships and the approval of others, they avoid intimacy because they fear being rejected.

These differences in attachment style represent theoretical prototypes that individuals can approximate to varying degrees (Bartholomew & Horowitz, 1991); they are most often assessed through self-report scales, although structured interview measures have also been developed (see Crowell, Fraley, & Shaver, 1999 for a review of adult attachment style measures). Individual differences in adult attachment style are thought to reflect underlying differences in working models of self and others that are presumed to develop, at least in part, from early experience with attachment figures during childhood and adolescence (Collins & Read, 1990). And, much like children's working models direct their attachment behavior in parent-child interactions, working models in adulthood should shape the way that adults express and regulate their attachment needs. For example, the different styles of attachment can be understood in terms of rules that guide responses to emotionally distressing situations (Fraley & Shaver, 2000; Mikulincer, Shaver, & Pereg, 2003). Kobak and Sceery (1988) suggest that secure attachment is organized by rules that allow acknowledgment of distress and turning to others for support. In contrast, avoidant attachment is organized by rules that restrict acknowledgment of distress, as well as any attempts to seek comfort and support from others, whereas preoccupied attachment is organized by rules that direct attention toward distress and attachment figures in a hypervigilant manner that inhibits autonomy and self-confidence. These different strategies for coping with distress will, of course, have important implications for closeness and intimacy processes, which we discuss in detail at a later point in this chapter.

It is important to note that the attachment styles observed in adulthood (between romantic partners) are not identical to those formed in infancy (between children and parents). Although longitudinal studies reveal moderate levels of continuity across childhood and adolescence (given a stable family environment; see Allen & Land, 1999), and across different time points in adulthood, we do not yet have clear evidence of a simple or direct link between parent-child attachment and adult romantic attachment (see Crowell, Fraley, & Shaver, 1999). Complexities in the conceptualization and measurement of attachment styles at different points in the lifespan make it difficult to establish strong links at this time, but attachment scholars are continuing to study the continuity, and lawful discontinuity, of attachment patterns across the lifespan. Nevertheless, regardless of whether the attachment patterns observed in adulthood are a continuation of those formed in childhood, adults as well as children will have developed characteristic strategies for regulating their attachment needs (i.e., strategies for seeking support, reducing feelings of distress, increasing feelings of security), and the specific strategies used to achieve this goal are believed to be at least partly contingent on an individual's history of regulating distress with attachment figures.

In summary, attachment theory proposes that individuals of all ages will have a propensity to form intimate bonds with a small number of significant others who provide a safe haven of support in times of need, and a secure base from which to explore the world. And, while the need for intimate bonds is presumed to be universal, people will differ systematically in their willingness and ability to develop such bonds, and in the way they regulate and express their attachment needs. These differences in attachment style are presumed to reflect underlying differences in working models of self and others, which guide cognition, emotion, and behavior in attachment-relevant contexts.

ATTACHMENT PROCESSES IN ADULTHOOD: CLOSENESS, INTIMACY, AND FELT SECURITY

As the above review suggests, attachment theory has obvious relevance to closeness and intimacy processes in adulthood. Not only is security maintained through the regulation of physical proximity and psychological closeness to attachment figures, intimate interactions provide the interpersonal foundation for the development of secure attachment bonds. In the sections that follow, we limit our discussion of attachment processes to those involving adult romantic relationships because romantic bonds are considered the prototypical attachment bond in adulthood (see Hazan & Zeifman, 1999) and because most of the empirical work in adulthood has been conducted on romantic relationships. However, we believe that the processes described below would apply equally well to other adult relationships that qualify as attachment bonds.[1]

In discussing attachment and intimacy, it is once again useful to distinguish between normative processes and individual differences. In the sections that follow, we begin by discussing the normative functioning of the attachment system in adulthood and its implications for intimacy processes. In doing so, we argue that intimate interactions are critical for the development of secure attachment bonds, and that support-seeking/caregiving interactions are especially important in this regard. Furthermore, we suggest that intimacy and security have reciprocal effects on one another, that is, effective intimacy processes enhance feelings of security, and feelings of security facilitate effective intimacy processes. Finally, we provide a detailed review of attachment style differences in the capacity for closeness and intimacy.

Attachment, Intimacy, and Closeness: Normative processes

Proximity Seeking. One of the primary assumptions of attachment theory is that individuals will regulate feelings of safety and security by regulating closeness and proximity to attachment figures. According to this approach, the attachment behavioral system will be activated whenever an individual experiences a threat to the self or a threat to their primary attachment relationship. And, although adults have the capacity for self-protection and self-reliance, they nevertheless benefit greatly from seeking contact with an attachment figure who is deeply invested in their welfare and reliably available to help if needed (Hazan & Zeifman, 1999). As Bowlby (1988) states, "To remain within easy access of a familiar individual known to be willing and able to come to our aid in an emergency is clearly a good insurance policy—whatever our age" (p. 27). There is, of course, ample evidence that romantic relationships serve important security-regulating functions in adulthood. Seeking social support is a common method of coping with stress, and romantic partners are often an individual's most important source of emotional and instrumental support (Cutrona, 1996). Moreover, a large body of research indicates that receiving social support from significant others helps individuals cope more effectively with stressful life events and has long-term benefits for physical health and emotional well-being (Cohen, 1988; Sarason, Sarason, & Gurung, 2001; Uchino, Cacioppo, & Kiecolt-Glaser, 1996).

In addition to evidence highlighting the importance of close relationships for coping with stress, a number of studies provide more direct evidence for attachment dynamics in couples by showing that stressful events motivate individuals to express their distress and to seek closeness to their romantic partner. For example, Collins and Feeney (2000) found that when individuals were asked to discuss a personal worry or concern with their partner, disclosers who rated their problem as more serious and stressful disclosed more openly to their partner and sought more social support. Moreover, disclosers felt better after the discussion (in terms of their overall mood)

---

[1] As discussed in detail by Hazan and Zeifman (1999), a relationship qualifies as an attachment bond to the extent that it is characterized by the four defining features of attachment, (a) proximity maintenance, (b) separation distress, (c) safe haven, and (d) secure base. Bonds of attachment are found in some but not all relationships of emotional significance – only those that are critical to an individual's continuing security and to the maintenance of emotional stability (Weiss, 1982). Bowlby suggested that adult pair bonds—in which sexual partners mutually derive and provide security to one another—are the prototypical attachment relationship in adulthood, and there is evidence that adults direct most of their attachment behavior toward their primary romantic partner (Hazan & Zeifman, 1999). It is important to note, however, that other long-term relationships may also function as attachment bonds in adulthood. For example, adults may continue to desire proximity to their parents and to depend on their parents as an important source of safety and security. Under some circumstances, sibling relationships and close friendships may also qualify as attachment bonds, but only if they serve an important safety-regulating function.

when their partner displayed more responsiveness and understanding during their discussion. Similarly, in a diary study in which couples were asked to report patterns of support-seeking and caregiving behavior over a 3-week period, respondents reported seeking more support from their partners on days when they experienced more stressful life events, and this behavior was corroborated by their partner's report (Collins & Feeney, B. C., 2003). Evidence for the normative activation of the attachment system was also obtained in a clever field study in which couples were unobtrusively observed at an airport (Fraley & Shaver, 1996). In this study, couple members who were separating from each other displayed higher levels of proximity-maintaining behavior (e.g., kissing, hugging, clinging, eye-to-eye contact) than did couples who were not separating from each other. Finally, in a series of studies, Mikulincer, Gillath, and Shaver (2002) found that when individuals were primed with threatening words, mental representations of attachment figures became more accessible in memory (and this was true regardless of the individual's chronic attachment style). These findings suggest not only that working models of attachment will be automatically activated in response to threat, but also that adults may derive a psychological sense of proximity (and perhaps felt security) by simply accessing mental representations of attachment figures in memory. Taken together, these studies provide evidence that adults respond to threats to the self, or threats to their attachment relationship, by regulating physical as well as psychological closeness to their romantic partner.

Intimacy and Closeness as Necessary for Felt-Security.   To say that romantic relationships qualify as attachment bonds means only that such relationships have the *potential* to provide partners with a sense of physical and emotional security. The existence of a relationship by no means guarantees that the relationship will provide couple members with the deep sense of emotional closeness and security that is essential for optimal functioning. Just as parent-child relationships differ in their attachment quality, adult romantic relationships will differ in the degree to which they provide partners with a safe haven of comfort and security and a secure base from which to explore the world. If the basic functions of the attachment system continue to operate in adulthood, and if romantic relationships qualify as attachment bonds, then felt security in adulthood will depend in large part on whether one's romantic partner is perceived to be both willing and able to be responsive to one's needs (Collins & Feeney, B. C., 2000).

It is important to clarify what we mean by *felt security* in adulthood. We distinguish between two different but compatible uses of the term. First, felt-security refers to a situational state that reflects the degree to which the individual feels free from physical and emotional threat. When felt-security is threatened (by either a threat to the self or a threat to the attachment relationship) the attachment system will be activated and the individual will tend to seek contact with attachment figures. Thus, acute threats to felt security trigger the attachment system and motivate attachment behavior (as previously discussed). We distinguish this situation-specific form of felt security from relationship-specific felt security, which refers to an individual's overall sense of confidence in the partner's love and commitment, and expectations concerning the partner's responsiveness to need. Relationship-specific felt security reflects the degree to which the self is perceived to be accepted and cared for by the partner, and the degree to which the partner is judged to be emotionally available and responsive. Individuals will feel more secure in their relationship to the extent that they feel nurtured and cared for by a responsive partner. It is useful to conceptualize relationship-specific felt security in terms of a relationship-specific working model (Collins & Read, 1994). Consistent with this approach, Murray et al. (2001) argue that felt-security in romantic relationships requires two conjunctive beliefs, (a) that the partner loves the self and is thus *willing* to be available and caring, and (b) that the partner is a good, responsive person who is *capable* of fulfilling one's needs. Thus, a secure relationship-specific working model simultaneously evaluates the self as loved and the partner as trustworthy and reliable.

If relationship-specific felt security requires the belief that a responsive partner is uniquely committed to the self, such inferences should be based on past experience in diagnostic situations that enable individuals to draw inferences about a partner's motives and feelings (Holmes & Rempel, 1989; Weiselquist, Rusbult, Foster, & Agnew, 1999). We suggest that intimate interactions, in which partners reveal private aspects of the self, provide a critical testing ground for drawing such inferences. Intimate interactions—in which individuals express self-relevant information and, as a result of their partner's responsiveness, come to feel validated, understood, and cared for— are central to felt security because they provide the interpersonal context in which individuals can gather diagnostic information about their partner's acceptance of the self. After all, in order for individuals to feel secure in their partner's love, they must perceive that their partner knows, understands, and values their true self.

Although intimate interactions of all kinds provide valuable information about a partner's attitude toward the self, a sense of felt security also requires evidence that the partner is willing and able to be responsive to one's needs. Therefore, we suggest that care-seeking–caregiving interactions, which are a special form of intimate inter- actions, will be especially critical for drawing inferences about a partner's respon- siveness. Through care-seeking–caregiving interactions, individuals learn whether they can count on their partner to understand their needs and to be emotionally (and physically) available when needed. They also learn about their partner's willingness to follow communal norms and to accept responsibility for their well-being (Clark, Fitness, & Brissette, 2001). Furthermore, it is precisely because care-seeking interac- tions involve vulnerability (e.g., expressions of fear, weakness, sadness, hurt) that they provide such a critical testing ground for felt security. Such interactions provide evidence of a partner's willingness to care for us when we are at our weakest (e.g., when we are emotionally vulnerable, socially isolated, physically ill, down on our luck) and perhaps least able to reciprocate. Under these circumstances, a partner's continued acceptance and care provide diagnostic evidence of their deep investment in our well-being (Tooby & Cosmides, 1996). It is precisely this type of information that is necessary for an individual to develop a sense of confidence and trust in a partner's love and commitment (Holmes & Rempel, 1989).

Consistent with this idea, a number of studies have shown an association between relationship security and the receipt of responsive support and care. For example, questionnaire studies indicate that relationship satisfaction in dating and married couples depends in large part on the degree to which one's partner is perceived as a responsive caregiver who provides a safe haven of comfort and support (Carnelley, Pietromonaco, & Jaffe, 1996; Feeney, B. C., & Collins, 2003; Feeney, J. A., 1996). Links between effective caregiving and relationship security have also been found in labo- ratory studies of dyadic interaction, and in diary studies of ongoing interactions in couples. For example, Collins and Feeney (2000) brought couples into the lab and asked one member of the couple to disclose a personal worry or concern to his or her partner. Couples who rated their relationship as happier and more secure engaged in interactions that were judged—by members of the couple and by independent raters— to be much more supportive and responsive. Similarly, Kobak and Hazan (1991) asked couples to engage in two laboratory activities, a problem-solving activity and a con- fiding activity. Husbands who reported greater attachment security (as indexed by the degree to which they rated their wife as psychologically available) had wives who dis- played less rejection and greater support validation during the problem-solving task. In addition, wives who reported greater attachment security (as indexed by the degree to which they felt they could rely on their husband and that he was psychologically available) had husbands who displayed more effective listening and greater accep- tance during the confiding task. Finally, in a daily diary study of romantic couples,

Collins and B. C. Feeney (2003) found that respondents reported feeling more secure in their relationship (more loved and valued by their partner) on days when their partner provided more responsive care and support. Moreover, responsive support (or lack thereof) predicted changes in security from one day to the next, and the effects of social support were independent of the effects of social conflict. Taken together, these studies provide support for the idea that care-seeking/caregiving interaction play a critical role in the development of relationship-specific security.

Felt Security as Necessary for Closeness and Intimacy. We have argued that intimacy processes (especially care-seeking and care giving interactions) are critical to the development of felt security in adult romantic relationships. However, it is also likely that felt-security will have reciprocal effects on relational intimacy and interdependence. After all, individuals take considerable risk in revealing the self, not only because partners might show signs of disapproval or rejection but also because partners might misuse the information for future criticism or exploitation (Prager and Roberts, chap. 4, this volume; Reis & Patrick, 1996). Individuals also place themselves at risk when becoming interdependent with a partner because their personal outcomes may be linked to a partner who is unwilling or unable to fulfill important social and emotional needs, or who fails to behave in pro-social ways. Thus, a sense of trust and felt security should increase the likelihood that partners will be willing to engage in the types of behaviors that are necessary for intimacy and for the development of closeness and interdependence (see also Murray et al., 2003). For example, individuals should be more willing to express vulnerable emotions and to seek comfort and support when they feel confident that their partner is willing and able to respond in a sensitive manner. Moreover, confidence in a partner's love should enhance one's willingness to self-disclose because individuals readily anticipate acceptance rather than rejection (Prager & Roberts, chap. 4, this volume).

Consistent with this proposition, a number of studies provide evidence for the link between relationship security and the willingness to seek closeness and intimacy. In the diary studied mentioned above (Collins & Feeney, B. C., 1993), individuals were more likely to seek social support from their partner on stressful days if they perceived, in general, that their partner loved them and was responsive to their needs. Likewise, in another diary study, Murray et al. (2003) found that respondents who felt chronically more valued by their partner (a secure relationship-specific working model) tended to draw closer to their partner on days when they felt most vulnerable (and in need of support and affirmation), whereas those who felt less valued by their partner tended to distance themselves from their partner on days when they felt more vulnerable. Likewise, Kobak and Hazan (1991) found that when married couples were asked to engage in a confiding interaction in which partners discussed a personal disappointment or loss, both husbands and wives engaged in more self-disclosure when they felt more secure in their relationship. Finally, in an experimental study in which women were primed to feel more secure, respondents said that they would be more likely to seek social support in response to a hypothetical stressor relative to women who received neutral primes (Pierce & Lydon, 1998).

Attachment, Intimacy, and Closeness: Individual Differences

Thus far we have discussed normative attachment processes, and we have argued that felt security requires the belief that one's partner is committed to the self and can be trusted to be available and responsive when needed. Moreover, we have suggested that intimate interactions (especially support and caregiving interactions) provide critical diagnostic opportunities for drawing inferences about a partner's love and responsiveness. And finally, we have suggested that felt-security within a relationship will have reciprocal effects on one's willingness to engage in intimate interactions and to become close and interdependent with one's partner. But, in addition to these normative attachment dynamics, it is important to consider individual differences in the capacity for intimate relating. After all, not everyone is equally skilled at intimate relating or equally motivated to seek out intimacy and interdependence. Thus, closeness and intimacy processes within a relationship will be shaped by the needs, expectations, and behavioral tendencies of each member of a dyad. Individuals who enter their relationships with dispositional insecurities (who have negative working models of self, others or both) may have difficulty engaging in the types of behaviors necessary for intimacy, and may find it difficult to develop a sense of confidence in their partner's love and commitment. Thus, individual differences in attachment styles should play a critical role in shaping the nature and quality of intimate interactions, and partners' subjective perceptions of those interactions.

Before discussing attachment-style differences in closeness and intimacy, it is useful to consider the skills and abilities that are necessary for intimate relating and for the effective regulation of attachment processes (see also Cassidy, 2001). Based on our discussion of normative attachment processes, we suggest that intimacy requires (a) willingness and ability to disclose the true self (one's thoughts, feelings, wishes, fears) and to be a responsive and accepting of the partner's true self, (b) willingness and ability to rely on one's partner for comfort, support, and nurturance, and to provide nurturance and support to the partner, and (c) willingness and ability to share physical intimacy. In addition to these essential abilities, Cassidy (2001) argues that intimacy also requires the ability to feel comfortable with an autonomous self (an appropriate balance between autonomy and intimacy), and the ability to negotiate with one's partner. As we discuss in detail subsequently, individuals who enter their relationships with insecure working models may have difficulty with effective intimacy processes because they lack one or more of these essential abilities.

Below we provide a detailed description of each attachment style, and we review and discuss evidence regarding attachment style differences in the capacity for intimate relating. (See also Edelstein & Shaver, chap. 22, this volume, for a detailed discussion of avoidant attachment and its relation to intimacy and interdependence in close relationships.) For theoretical and conceptual clarity, we have organized our discussion of individual differences around the four attachment prototypes (secure, preoccupied, dismissing, fearful); however, we note that individual differences in attachment styles are best measured in terms of continuous dimensions rather than discrete categories (see Brennan, Clark, & Shaver, 1998; Crowell, Fraley, & Shaver, 1999; Fraley & Waller, 1998).

Secure Attachment and Intimacy.   Secure adults are comfortable with intimacy and closeness, view themselves as being valued and worthy of care and affection from others, and they perceive that others are generally responsive and dependable (Bartholomew, 1990; Bartholomew & Horowitz, 1991; Collins & Read, 1990; Feeney, J. A., & Noller, 1990; Hazan & Shaver, 1987; Simpson, 1990). Secure individuals perceive attachment figures to be generally well-intentioned, trustworthy, good-hearted, and accessible. Thus, these individuals are able to depend on others and they are not worried about being abandoned or unloved. They tend to be involved in relationships characterized by frequent positive emotion and high levels of interdependence, commitment, trust, and satisfaction. They value intimate relationships, they are able to maintain close relationships without losing personal autonomy, and they are coherent and thoughtful in discussing relationship issues. Moreover, secure individuals report positive, warm, and responsive relationship histories, have high self-esteem and perceptions of personal competency, are generally positive and self-assured in their interactions with others, and report an absence of serious interpersonal problems (Bartholomew, 1990; Bartholomew & Horowitz, 1991; Collins & Read, 1990; Feeney, J. A., & Noller, 1990; Hazan & Shaver, 1987; Rothbard & Shaver, 1994; Simpson, 1990).

They appear to maintain a healthy interdependence such that they effectively balance both intimacy and independence needs.

Secure individuals exhibit their comfortable approach to relationship intimacy in a number of ways. They are willing to seek both emotional and instrumental forms of support from others in stressful situations (Armsden & Greenberg, 1987; Collins & Feeney, B. C., 2000; Feeney, J. A., 1998; Florian, Mikulincer, & Bucholtz, 1995; Mikulincer & Florian, 1995; Mikulincer, Florian, & Weller, 1993; Ognibene & Collins, 1998; Simpson, Rholes, & Nelligan, 1992), they exhibit a willingness to disclose to others, and they both like and are responsive to interaction partners who disclose to them (Grabill & Kerns, 2000; Mikulincer & Nachshon, 1991). In contrast to individuals with insecure attachment styles, securely attached individuals discriminate among recipients of self-disclosure by showing more intimate levels of self-disclosure (and comfort with disclosure) when it is directed toward a close relationship partner rather than a stranger of the opposite sex (Keelan, Dion, & Dion, 1998). In addition, relative to avoidant individuals, secure individuals report higher levels of intimacy, enjoyment, promotive interaction, and positive emotion in their daily interactions with others (Tidwell, Reis, & Shaver, 1996). Secure individuals use touch to express affection and to seek care from relationship partners (Brennan, Wu, & Loev, 1998), and they are less likely than other individuals to respond to physical separation from relationship partners with feelings of insecurity (Feeney, J. A., 1998), perhaps because they are able to regulate security with a sense of psychological closeness as well as with physical closeness. Finally, secure individuals are comfortable with sexual intimacy and are less likely than insecure individuals to engage in risky sexual behavior. For example, relative to their insecure counterparts, secure adults are less likely to have sex outside their primary relationship, more likely to be involved in mutually initiated sex, and more likely to enjoy physical contact that is both intimate and sexual (Hazan, Zeifman, & Middleton, 1994, as cited in Feeney, J. A., 1999). In addition, secure women are less likely to agree to unwanted sex (Impett & Peplau, 2002).

When in the caregiving role, they exhibit responsiveness and sensitivity to their partner's needs, they freely display proximity-seeking behaviors, they take a cooperative (noncontrolling) approach when assisting their partner, and there is an absence of compulsive over-caregiving and negativity (Collins & Feeney, B. C., 2000; Feeney, J. A., 1996; Kunce & Shaver, 1994; Simpson et al., 1992). When conversing with their partners, they exhibit high levels of receptivity, gazing, facial pleasantness, vocal pleasantness, interest, and attentiveness (Guerrero, 1996). Compared to insecure individuals, they are more expressive (Tucker & Anders, 1998), and they are skilled at interpreting their partner's nonverbal behaviors and feelings (Noller & Feeney, J. A., 1994). Thus, individuals with a secure attachment style have the general characteristics and interpersonal skills necessary for the development and maintenance of intimate relationships with others.

It is also important to consider individual differences in cognitions about relationship behaviors, as these thoughts and interpretations should have important implications for the closeness/intimacy experienced within the relationship. Secure adults have been shown to provide positive explanations for ambiguous and potentially negative relationship events—construing these events in ways that minimize their negative impact on the relationship (Collins, 1996; Collins, Ford, Guichard, & Allard, 2003). They are also less likely than insecure individuals to interpret a lack of support from their partner in pessimistic ways (e.g., by attributing negative intent to their partner) and to let an intervening negative event bias their perceptions of earlier relationship events (Collins & Feeney, B. C., in press). In addition, when their partner behaves in ways that are kind and caring, secure individuals are more likely to infer that their partner was motivated by altruistic rather than selfish concerns (Collins, Ford, Guichard, & Allard, 2003). This type of thinking is likely to promote intimacy by engendering feelings of goodwill and understanding, and by reducing the likelihood of conflict and ill feelings toward one's partner. Interestingly, attachment security has been shown to enhance perceptions of intimacy in daily interactions with others (Grabill & Kerns, 2000; Kerns & Stevens, 1996). For example, in conversations with friends, secure dyads perceive their conversations as being more intimate than observers perceive them to be, and they perceive having received greater validation from their friends than is evident in observers' ratings. Thus, a secure attachment style appears to foster the types of perceptions that facilitate closeness and connectedness to others.

Preoccupied (Anxious–Ambivalent) Attachment and Intimacy. Preoccupied (or anxious-ambivalent) individuals are comfortable with intimacy and closeness, but they view themselves as being somewhat unworthy of care and affection from others. They possess mental models of themselves as being misunderstood, underappreciated, and lacking in confidence; they tend to report inconsistent, unpredictable, and relatively unsupportive attachment histories. Anxious–ambivalent individuals place a great deal of importance on, and are therefore strongly motivated to form, intimate relationships with others. They seek others' approval because they depend on other people's acceptance for a sense of personal well-being and to maintain positive self-regard; however, they experience a great deal of anxiety in their relationships with others because they are worried about being abandoned and unloved, and because they perceive significant others as being inconsistent, unreliable, and unwilling to commit to relationships (Bartholomew, 1990; Bartholomew & Horowitz, 1991; Collins & Read, 1990; Feeney, J. A., & Noller, 1990; Hazan & Shaver, 1987; Simpson, 1990). These perceptions and concerns appear to result in an over-dependence on close relationship partners, a tendency to desire extreme levels of intimacy, and a controlling (overdominating) interpersonal style. As a result, preoccupied/anxious individuals tend to be involved in relationships characterized by frequent negative affect and low levels of trust and satisfaction. They generally experience an approach-avoidance conflict in social situations as a result of their inconsistent experiences with attachment figures in the past—a conflict which typically results in extreme approach behaviors (Bartholomew, 1990; Bartholomew & Horowitz, 1991; Collins & Read, 1990; Feeney, J. A., & Noller, 1990; Hazan & Shaver, 1987; Rothbard & Shaver, 1994; Simpson, 1990). The dialectic between intimacy and independence for these individuals is heavily pulled toward concerns for intimacy over independence. Consistent with this idea, when Mashek and Sherman (chap. 19, this volume) asked adults to rate their actual level of closeness and their desired level of closeness in their current relationship, adults who were high in attachment-related anxiety reported a much larger gap between how much closeness they had and how much they desired.

Issues of closeness and distance (and struggles over this issue) are particularly salient for preoccupied–anxious individuals (Feeney, J. A., 1999; Pistole, 1994). Preoccupied individuals' comfort with and desire for intimacy is reflected in their desire to seek support from others when feeling distressed (Mikulincer & Florian, 1995; Ognibene & Collins, 1998), their willingness to disclose to others (Mikulincer & Nachshon, 1991), and their positive feelings toward individuals who disclose to them. Preoccupied individuals report a use of touch to express affection similar to that of secures; however, they report a desire for more touch from relationship partners, and they are the most likely (of all attachment groups) to use touch in a careseeking capacity (Brennan, Wu, & Loev, 1998). Although both secure and preoccupied individuals disclose to others, preoccupied–anxious individuals show less topical reciprocity (i.e., fewer of their statements refer to something that had been mentioned by the interaction partner), suggesting that the self-disclosure of preoccupied individuals may be self-focused and aimed more at meeting their own intimacy needs. Finally, like their secure counterparts, preoccupied–anxious individuals report enjoying sexual contact that is also intimate (holding, caressing) and they tend not to endorse accepting attitudes toward casual sex (Feeney, Noller, & Patty, 1993; Hazan, Zeifman, & Middleton, 1994, as cited in Feeney, J. A., 1996). However, preoccupied individuals appear to be less discriminating about their sexual partners and more willing to engage in risky sexual behavior, perhaps because they use sexual contact as a way to satisfy their need for closeness and acceptance. For example, relative to secure and avoidant individuals, preoccupied–anxious individuals (especially women) tend to engage in intercourse at a younger age and to report a larger number of lifetime sexual partners (Bogaert & Sadava, 2002); they are also more likely to experience unwanted pregnancy (Cooper, Shaver, & Collins, 1998). In addition, preoccupied/anxious women are more likely to agree to unwanted sex, and they report doing so because they fear that their partner will lose interest in them (Impett & Peplau, 2002).

It is also interesting to note that the support-seeking behavior of preoccupied individuals does not differ under conditions of high and low stress, which suggests that they may be less discriminating in their need and desire for support and intimacy (Ognibene & Collins, 1998) and reflecting their chronic desire for a high level of intimacy and responsiveness from relationship partners. Although their caregiving behavior can be responsive with regard to the provision of instrumental support (in that they provide support in response to the partner's need—more when it's needed and less when it's not), anxious individuals have been shown to provide emotional support to their partners irrespective of the partner's need for it, again highlighting their desire for intimacy and closeness (Feeney, B. C., & Collins, 2001). Preoccupied (or anxious) individuals report relatively high levels of compulsive over-caregiving, controlling caregiving, and provision of physical comfort, but low levels of sensitivity (Feeney, J. A., 1996; Feeney, B. C., & Collins, 2001; Kunce & Shaver, 1994). The caregiving pattern exhibited by these individuals suggests that although they are capable of providing affectionate caregiving, their caregiving may be somewhat intrusive and out of synch with their partner's needs—perhaps because they are focusing more on meeting their own intimacy needs. In fact, preoccupied–anxious individuals report that when they help their partners, they are motivated by a desire to achieve relationship goals (e.g., to develop a closer relationship with the partner, to keep the partner in the relationship) and to achieve some self-benefit (e.g., being rewarded for helping the partner), in addition to helping because of love and concern about the partner's well-being (Feeney, B. C., & Collins, 2003).

Similar to secure individuals, preoccupied/anxious individuals exhibit high levels of receptivity, gazing, facial pleasantness, vocal pleasantness, interest, attentiveness, and depth when conversing with their partners; however, they also exhibit high levels of vocal anxiety (Guerrero, 1996). Preoccupied/anxious individuals are less expressive when interacting with dating partners (Tucker & Anders, 1998), they use less adaptive negotiation and conflict resolution strategies (Levy & Davis, 1988; Pistole, 1989; Simpson, Rholes, & Phillips, 1996), they show deficits in the ability to decode a close relationship partner's nonverbal behavior and feelings (Noller & J. A. Feeney, 1994; Tucker & Anders, 1999), they have a tenuous sense of trust (Mikulincer, 1998; Shaver & Hazan, 1993), and they are more likely than secure individuals to respond to physical separation from relationship partners with feelings of insecurity (Feeney, J. A., 1998). A lack of interpersonal competence and skills is at least part of the reason why preoccupied–anxious individuals have difficulty developing satisfying social support networks. Despite their preoccupation with relationships and desire for closeness, preoccupied/anxious individuals appear to lack the skills necessary to be truly responsive to others and to develop the type of close, supportive relationships they desire.

With regard to cognitions about relationship events and behaviors that may have important implications for the closeness and intimacy experienced within the relationship, preoccupied/anxious individuals have been shown to provide relatively negative attributions for their partner's transgressions—construing these events as rejecting and motivated by hurtful intent—in ways that are likely to have a negative impact on the relationship (Collins, 1996; Collins et al., 2003). They are also more likely than secure individuals to interpret an ambiguous support message in pessimistic ways (e.g., by perceiving their partner as insensitive and by attributing harmful intent to their partner) and to let an intervening negative event bias their perceptions of an earlier interaction (Collins & Feeney, B. C., in press). In addition, when their partner behaves in ways that are kind and caring, they appreciate this behavior but have doubts about their partner's benevolent motivation (Collins et al., 2003). This type of thinking is likely to reflect a low sense of self-worth and a concern about rejection, and it is likely to impede intimacy by engendering suspicion, conflict, and ill feelings toward one's partner. Interestingly, preoccupied individuals also have been shown to differ from individuals with other attachment styles in the way in which they organize knowledge about conflictual romantic relationships. Probably because their relationship goals involve achieving a high level of intimacy and maximal responsiveness from their partners, they tend to view their conflict interactions in a more positive light than other individuals—noticing not only the negative side of conflict, but also its more positive, intimacy-promoting aspects (Fishtein, Pietromonaco, & Barrett, 1999; Pietromonaco & Barrett, 1997). With regard to perceptions of intimacy in their social interactions, preoccupied individuals are less likely than secure individuals to report intimacy in their relationships and to feel understood, validated, and cared for by others (Grabill & Kerns, 2000). Thus, although preoccupied individuals desire intimacy, they may have difficulty developing and maintaining the intimacy they desire because of their anxiety about having their needs met (which may lead them to be less responsive to the needs of others and use ineffective intimacy-seeking strategies), and because they may fail to appreciate the level of intimacy they have obtained at each stage in their relationships.

It is important to mention that patterns of findings for preoccupied individuals have been less clear (sometimes apparent and sometimes unrelated to the various constructs of interest) than those obtained for individuals characterized by the other attachment styles. The inconsistent findings for preoccupied–anxious individuals are supportive of the notion that they may have the desire to engage in situationally appropriate intimacy-related behaviors (e.g., willingness to self-disclose, comfort with physical intimacy, and desire for interdependence); however, their efforts may sometimes be counterbalanced or interfered with by their insecurities related to fear of rejection. It is also worth noting that because preoccupied attachment is the least common attachment style, inconsistent findings may also be due to low statistical power.

Dismissing Avoidance and Intimacy.[2] Dismissing avoidant individuals are low in attachment-related anxiety but high in attachment-related avoidance. They perceive

---

[2] Since Hazan and Shaver's (1987) original formulation of adult attachment styles, the conceptualization and measurement of adult attachment has shifted from the original three-category model (secure, anxious, avoidant), to a four-category model (secure, anxious, dismissing avoidance, fearful avoidance). The primary difference between these models is the identification of two forms of avoidant attachment in the four-category model. As a result of these changes in the field, some studies report results for a single "avoidant" style and others report results for "dismissing avoidants" and "fearful avoidants." In our review of this literature, we describe results for the single "avoidant" category under the heading of "dismissing avoidant" because the dismissing avoidant prototype most closely matches the original "avoidant" category. Furthermore, contemporary work on adult attachment no longer uses a categorical approach; most scholars now use a dimensional approach in which individual differences in attachment style are assessed along two continuous dimensions of "attachment-related anxiety" and "attachment-related avoidance." Once again, in our review of this literature, we discuss findings related to "attachment-related avoidance" under the heading of "dismissing avoidance," unless the authors conducted special analyses in which they identified differential effects for individuals who fit the fearful versus dismissing prototype.

attachment figures as being generally unreliable, unavailable, and uncaring; however, they view themselves as being worthy and adequate individuals, and as being invulnerable to negative feelings. They maintain a positive self-image in spite of previous rejection from attachment figures by denying attachment needs, downplaying the importance of close relationships, placing much value on independence and self-reliance, distancing themselves from others, and restricting expressions of emotionality (Bartholomew, 1990; Bartholomew & Horowitz, 1991; Rothbard & Shaver, 1994). Therefore, dismissing avoidants tend to be compulsively self-reliant, and their relationships tend to be characterized by low levels of commitment and interdependence. Although avoidant individuals report a high sense of self-worth, they lack clarity or credibility in discussing close relationships (Bartholomew, 1990; Bartholomew & Horowitz, 1991). The dialectic between intimacy and independence for both avoidant styles appears to be heavily pulled toward independence over intimacy, with the major difference being that dismissing avoidant individuals claim not to want or need intimacy, whereas fearful avoidant individuals admit that they want it but are concerned about rejection (see below). Consistent with this argument, Mashek and Sherman (chap. 19, this volume) found that the when adults were asked to rate their actual level of closeness and their desired level of closeness in their current relationship, individuals who were high in attachment-related avoidance but low in attachment-related anxiety (the pattern associated with dismissing avoidance) wanted much less closeness than they currently had. In contrast, those who were high in avoidance and high in anxiety (the pattern associated with fearful avoidance) reported wanting much more closeness.

Issues of closeness and distance (and struggles over this issue) are also salient for avoidant individuals who are characteristically uncomfortable with intimacy (Feeney, J. A., 1999; Pistole, 1994). Avoidant individuals' discomfort with intimacy and closeness is apparent in their use of distancing strategies (as opposed to support-seeking strategies) when coping with stressful situations (Mikulincer et al., 1993; Mikulincer & Florian, 1995; Fraley & Shaver, 1998; Ognibene & Collins, 1998; Simpson et al., 1992), their low levels of self-disclosure, their increases in negative emotion following the disclosure of others (Bradford, Feeney, J. A., & Campbell, 2002; Mikulincer & Nachshon, 1991), and, compared to secure and preoccupied individuals, their lower likelihood of using touch to express affection or seek care from relationship partners, and their greater aversion to touch (Brennan et al., 1998). Avoidant individuals also appear to be uncomfortable with intimate sexual contact as evidenced by their tendency to separate sex and love. For example, avoidant individuals are more likely than secure individuals to engage in "one-night stands" and to have sex outside of their primary relationship (Brennan & Shaver, 1995; Hazan, Zeifman, & Middleton, 1994, as cited in Feeney, J. A., 1999). They also tend to have more accepting attitudes toward casual sex (Feeney, J. A., Noller, & Patty, 1993) and are more likely to endorse the idea that sex without love is pleasurable (Brennan & Shaver, 1995).

Characteristic of avoidant individuals is their tendency to pull away from partners as their levels of distress increase (Collins & Feeney, B. C., 2000; Fraley & Shaver, 1998; Simpson et al., 1992). For example, Simpson et al. (1992) showed that as the anxiety level of avoidant individuals rises, they show more resistance to touch from their partners. When in the caregiving role, they are generally unresponsive, controlling, insensitive, and unlikely to provide physical comfort (Feeney, J. A., 1996; Feeney, B. C., & Collins, 2001; Kunce & Shaver, 1994; Simpson et al., 1992). Their caregiving pattern reflects underlying motives including a dislike of distress and perceptions that the partner is too dependent and difficult (Feeney, B. C., & Collins, 2003). Avoidant individuals appear to experience negative emotion when their partners display behaviors that threaten their ability to avoid intimacy.

When conversing with close relationship partners, they exhibit (in comparison to secure and preoccupied individuals) lower levels of receptivity, gazing, facial and vocal pleasantness, interest, and attentiveness (Guerrero, 1996). Similar to anxious individuals, avoidant individuals are less expressive when interacting with dating partners (Tucker & Anders, 1998), they use less adaptive conflict resolution strategies (Levy & Davis, 1988; Pistole, 1989; Simpson et al., 1996), and they show deficits in the ability to decode a close relationship partner's nonverbal behavior and feelings (Noller & Feeney, J. A., 1994; Tucker & Anders, 1999). In addition, compared to secure and anxious-ambivalent adults, avoidant adults report lower levels of intimacy, enjoyment, promotive interaction, and positive emotions, and higher levels of negative emotion in their daily interactions with others (Tidwell, Reis, & Shaver, 1996). In fact, Anders and Tucker (2000) have shown that a lack of interpersonal competence and skills may be an important reason why avoidant individuals have difficulty developing satisfying social support networks (see also Feeney, B. C., & Collins, 2003, for evidence indicating that avoidant individuals cite a lack of skills as a reason for not supporting their relationship partners). For example, by not opening up to others and communicating their needs, avoidant individuals reduce the likelihood that close, supportive relationships will develop and endure. Consistent with this idea, in a prospective study of young adults, Collins, Cooper, Albino, and Allard (2002) found that individuals who were high in avoidance during adolescence went on (six years later) to develop relationships that were less satisfying and less intimate, as reported by both members of the couple. For example, avoidant respondents described their relationship as low in intimacy, low in mutual disclosure, low in effective problem-solving communication, and high in conflict.

It is important to note, however, that these overt distancing strategies are characteristic of avoidant individuals primarily in situations in which the attachment system is activated (when the self or relationship partner is feeling alarmed or distressed). At lower levels of anxiety (when the attachment system is not activated), avoidant individuals do not distance themselves, and they do seek and provide support and establish intimacy with others. Thus, these individuals cannot be characterized as cold, distant, or aloof in general. It is distress or anxiety that appears to impede the establishment of proximity and intimacy in dyadic interactions involving avoidant individuals. It appears that distressed adult partners (similar to distressed infants in the developmental literature) present significant relationship problems for avoidant individuals. Because the proximity needs of avoidant individuals have been frequently frustrated and rarely satisfied, these individuals may overcompensate with proximity-seeking in nonthreatening circumstances.

Although it may appear (on the basis of self-reports and overt behaviors) that intimacy and closeness is not important to avoidant individuals, these individuals (similar to avoidant children in the strange situation) do exhibit physiological arousal when separated from their relationship partners in stressful situations (Feeney, B. C., & Kirkpatrick, 1996), they are more likely than secure individuals to respond to physical separation from relationship partners with feelings of insecurity (Feeney, J. A., 1998), and they appear to be somewhat more calmed than even secure individuals by supportive partner comments, which indicates that avoidant individuals do benefit from support and do have intimacy needs (Simpson et al., 1992). Fraley, Davis, and Shaver (1998) have shown that although dismissing adults attempt to avoid attachment-related emotions and are able to block emotional responses (or prevent them from surfacing) when asked to think about separation and loss, they show substantial arousal when made to focus on such thoughts. If dismissing-avoidant individuals are truly dismissing of attachment and intimacy, we would not expect them to react physiologically to the presence versus absence of a romantic partner or to be calmed by a partner's conversational behavior when feeling stressed. Thus, even avoidant individuals benefit from intimacy and closeness and appear to need it (albeit not overtly) even in threatening situations.

With regard to cognitions about relationship events and behaviors that may have important implications for the closeness and intimacy experienced within the relationship, dismissing individuals are more optimistic than fearful or preoccupied individuals (but less optimistic than secure individuals) in their explanations for their partner's transgressions—perhaps reflecting their positive views of themselves and their lack of dependence on relationship partners (Collins, 1996; Collins et al., 2003). However, relative to secure individuals, they are much more likely to draw negative inferences about their partner's caring behavior (e.g., to believe that their partner was motivated by selfish rather than altruistic concerns; Collins et al., 2003) and to view their partner's ambiguous support attempts as relatively unhelpful and unsupportive (Collins & Feeney, in press). Thus, dismissing individuals appear to draw inferences that protect them from the negative consequences of their partner's transgressions, but may also undermine their ability to benefit from their partner's kindness and goodwill.

Because avoidant individuals' behaviors do not always match their underlying feeling, it is interesting to speculate about the factors that may be driving their behaviors with regard to establishing closeness and intimacy in a relationship—particularly with regard to the degree to which cognition or emotion drives their behavior when the attachment system is activated. That is, there are likely to be individual differences in the degree to which emotional versus cognitive cues drive intimacy-related behaviors—particularly in stressful situations. It is possible that the behavior of secure individuals is the result of balanced attention to both cognitive and affective cues such that a focus on either will lead to the same overt behavior. That is, in stressful situations they will feel emotionally distressed and perceive the situation as one in which intimate contact with an attachment figure would be appropriate and helpful in coping with distress. However, it seems likely that the behavior of insecure individuals may be driven either by their cognitive response to the situation or their emotional response to it—which may or may not correspond—and that one set of cues will take precedence over the other in determining the behavioral outcome. For example, because dismissing individuals value self-reliance and seek to minimize interdependence, they may over rely on their cognitive cues and may tend to suppress or minimize the importance of attending to their emotional cues. Therefore, their cognitions about the importance of self-reliance may not match their desire for closeness to, and support from, their attachment figures—at least in stressful situations when their attachment systems have been activated. Therefore, cognitive cues would most likely drive the behavior of dismissing individuals because they are likely to suppress the opposing affective component. However, the opposite may be true for anxious individuals who may over rely on their emotional cues. As a result, they may indiscriminately desire and seek closeness and intimacy, even when their pessimistic cognitions concerning the responsiveness of others, if considered, would contradict those feelings. Additional research is greatly needed to uncover the mechanisms that underlie the intimacy-seeking and distancing behaviors of individuals with different attachment characteristics—particularly insecure individuals as their behavioral strategies for terminating the activation of the attachment system are not as direct or as easily understood as the behaviors of secure individuals.

Fearful Avoidance and Intimacy.   Finally, fearful avoidant individuals are high in both attachment-related anxiety and avoidance. Like dismissing individuals, they perceive attachment figures as being generally unreliable, unavailable, and uncaring; however, they differ from dismissing individuals in their lower sense of self-worth. Fearful individuals view themselves as being unlovable, emotionally distant, and mistrusting. They desire social contact and intimacy, but they avoid putting themselves in situations where they feel vulnerable to rejection (Bartholomew, 1990; Bartholomew & Horowitz, 1991). Thus, the approach-avoidance conflict they experience is typically resolved in favor of avoidance of close relationships. Fearful individuals tend to experience subjective distress and disturbed social relationships characterized by a hypersensitivity to social approval. Because they fear rejection and actively avoid social situations and close relationships in which they perceive themselves as vulnerable to rejection, they undermine the possibility of establishing satisfying, intimate social relations which could serve to modify their views of close relationships (Bartholomew, 1990; Bartholomew & Horowitz, 1991).

Because fearful individuals are high in both anxiety and avoidance, they have some characteristics in common with both preoccupied and dismissing individuals regarding their approach to intimacy. Their caregiving is characterized by low levels of physical contact, sensitivity, and responsiveness (similar to dismissing avoidants), but they also engage in relatively high levels of compulsive over-caregiving (Carnelley, Pietromonaco, & Jaffe, 1996; Feeney, J. A., 1996; Kunce & Shaver, 1994). The caregiving patterns of the two avoidant types (dismissing and fearful) support Bartholomew and Horowitz's (1991) hypothesis that the two styles are similar in their avoidance of intimacy, but differ in their need for others' acceptance and approval and in their desire for intimate social contact. Fearful individuals are likely to be similar to dismissing avoidants in their use of distancing strategies when coping with stressful situations (Mikulincer et al., 1993; Mikulincer & Florian, 1995; Ognibene & Collins, 1998; Simpson et al., 1992) and in their low levels of self-disclosure (Mikulincer & Nachshon, 1991; however, see Grabill & Kerns, 2000 for an exception). When having conversations with a close relationship partner, fearful avoidants are vocally anxious and, compared to individuals characterized by the other attachment styles, they sit farthest from the partner, they display the least conversational fluency, and they have the longest response latencies (Guerrero, 1996). Similar to dismissing avoidant individuals, they are less likely than secure or preoccupied individuals to use touch to express affection or seek care from relationship partners, and they are more likely to report touch aversion (Brennan, Wu, & Loev, 1998). Interestingly, however, they report a desire for more touch equivalent to that of preoccupied individuals. Perhaps fearful adults have historically received more insensitive and controlling than affectionate forms of touch from relationships partners. If so, their reports may reflect their aversion to insensitive forms of touch and a desire for more affectionate touch. Alternatively, because avoidant individuals report histories with relatively unaffectionate caregivers, they may desire touch yet, at the same time, they may feel uncomfortable with the unfamiliar experience.

With regard to cognitions about relationship events and behaviors that may have important implications for the closeness and intimacy experienced within the relationship, fearful individuals (similar to preoccupied individuals) tend to make relationship-threatening attributions for their partner's transgressions (Collins, 1996; Collins et al., 2003) and (similar to dismissing individuals) tend to draw negative inferences about their partner's caring behavior (Collins et al., 2003). In addition, when faced with a stressful laboratory task, fearful individuals are much more likely than secure individuals to view their partner's support attempts as hurtful and unsupportive, especially when those attempts are somewhat ambiguous (Collins & Feeney, in press). Thus, fearful individuals tend to perceive their relationship experiences in ways that are likely to impede the continuance or establishment of intimacy. We suspect that fearful individuals' cognitions about the hazards of relationships frequently override their emotional desires for intimate contact. However, in some situations in which they perceive rejection to be less likely (e.g., in situations in which the relationship partner is in need of support or care), their behavior is likely to be guided by their emotional desire for intimate contact. The compulsive caregiving they exhibit in some of these "safer" situations may reflect an overcompensation for their frequent lack of intimate contact with relationship partners.

Concluding Comments Regarding Individual Differences. It is important to remember that attachment patterns are presumed to develop as an adaptation to the particular caregiving environments that individuals are currently experiencing or have experienced in the past (George & Solomon, 1999; Main, 1990). That is, all individuals, at some point in their lives obtain knowledge about the most effective ways of terminating attachment system activation in times of distress, of meeting attachment needs, and of deriving security and protection from attachment figures. For example, avoidant children have learned that overt expressions of distress and contact-seeking are frequently rebuffed; therefore, they developed an attachment strategy of keeping the caregiver or attachment figure in check while inhibiting direct expressions of need for intimate contact. This is an effective strategy for an avoidant child's particular caregiving environment as he or she is able to maintain a sufficient amount of intimacy with, and proximity to, the attachment figure to feel safe while not alienating the attachment figure. This behavior probably does not reflect the child's ideal degree of intimate contact with the attachment figure, but it has proven to be the best strategy for the particular caregiving environment in which the child has been placed. Similarly, preoccupied/anxious children have learned that clinging is an effective strategy for maintaining proximity to attachment figures, given the inconsistent and independence-restricting caregiving environment in which they have been placed.

Attachment theorists (e.g., Main, 1990) have proposed that although security is the ideal attachment pattern, anxious and avoidant attachment are alternative patterns that allow the child to maintain a sufficient amount of proximity to (or intimacy with) the caregiver. These alternative attachment strategies are thought of as "good enough" strategies for deriving a sufficient amount of security from, and intimate contact with, the attachment figure. Although these strategies leave insecure children more vulnerable than secure children, they afford the insecure child some degree of proximity to the attachment figure on whom the child depends for protection (George & Solomon, 1999).

If we extend this thinking to adult attachment patterns, it is likely that adults have either (a) continued the strategies for deriving protection and security from attachment figures they learned earlier in life, which are strategies they employ without having reexamined their adequacy for new caregiving environments; (b) developed the most adaptive attachment patterns and strategies that fit their current adult experiences with attachment figures; or (c) selectively enter adult relationships or caregiving environments for which their learned attachment strategy is appropriate. Therefore, even in adulthood, each attachment strategy (whether secure or insecure) affords the individual some degree of acceptable proximity to (or intimate contact with) the attachment figure. For example, the research evidence reviewed above indicates that it is not the case that avoidant adults wish to have no intimacy in their lives. To the contrary, they do appear to derive security from their relationship partners, and they do seek intimacy when the attachment systems (of both the self and the partner) are deactivated. They appear to have learned that they can most effectively derive comfort and security from relationship partners if they do not express their attachment needs directly and risk alienating the partner or attachment figure. Thus, from an attachment perspective, some degree of intimacy is important for all individuals' sense of security and well-being, and most adults appear to obtain it and benefit from it to some degree. Adult attachment patterns may have evolved as "good enough" strategies for maintaining a safe degree of intimate contact with attachment figures and for maintaining adequate levels of security within the context of the particular caregiving environment in which the individual is placed. All individuals learn to regulate emotions (and thereby terminate attachment system activation) by maintaining a certain degree of closeness and proximity to the caregiver or attachment figure. Although the insecure strategies are not ideal for developing and maintaining the type of close, intimate relationships that secure individuals enjoy, they are likely "good enough" strategies for maintaining an acceptable degree of intimacy to attachment figures. In adulthood, these strategies are adaptive if they match the individual's current caregiving environment. If not, they may prevent the experience of a deeper intimate connection with relationship partners.

Although a secure attachment style is not the only one that allows individuals to derive security and closeness, it does appear that closeness and intimacy are more easily and ideally obtained for those who enter their relationships with secure working models of self and others. Secure individuals appear to have the closest, most ideally intimate relationships in that they are comfortable with expressing their thoughts and feelings, comfortable with physical forms of intimacy, and able to give and receive care as needed. Preoccupied/anxious individuals appear to have relationships that are not intimate in the ideal sense in that their insecurities and learned strategies for maintaining closeness to attachment figures are likely to frustrate and tax their relationship partner. Although the preoccupied–anxious attachment strategy allows them to obtain some degree of intimate contact with the attachment figure, the anxiety experienced by these individuals (and the resulting behavioral manifestation of this anxiety) is likely to impede the deeper intimate connection they crave. Avoidant individuals appear to have the least close and intimate relationships. They behaviorally appear not to let the partner in—perhaps because too much intimacy and closeness has been dangerous in the past; however, the research evidence indicates that even avoidant individuals derive some degree of security from their close relationship partners. They have simply learned not to overtly seek intimate contact—particularly in times of distress.

In conclusion, although we have learned a great deal about the ways in which intimacy is expressed and received in the context of adult close relationships as a function of the relationship partners' attachment characteristics, the intimacy dynamics surrounding each attachment pattern (particularly the insecure attachment patterns), as well as the interactive effects of various combinations of attachment patterns, require some unraveling in future research. It remains to be seen if attachment strategies in adulthood (as in childhood) can be viewed as "good enough" adaptations to particular caregiving environments, and it remains to be discovered exactly how good is "good enough" with regard to the development and maintenance of well functioning relationships in adulthood.

ACKNOWLEDGMENTS

Preparation of this chapter was supported by National Science Foundation Grant SBR-0096506 awarded to Nancy L. Collins.

Correspondence concerning this chapter should be addressed to Nancy L. Collins, Department of Psychology, University of California, Santa Barbara, California, 93106 or to Brooke C. Feeney, Department of Psychology, Carnegie Mellon University, Pittsburgh, Pennsylvania, 15213. E-mail: ncollins@psych.ucsb.edu or to bfeeney@andrew. cmu.edu

REFERENCES

Ainsworth, M. D. S., Blehar, M. C., Waters, E., & Wall, S. (1978). *Patterns of attachment: A psychological study of the strange situation.* Hillsdale, NJ: Lawrence Erlbaum Associates.
Allen, J. P., & Land, D. (1999). Attachment in adolescence. In J. Cassidy & P. R. Shaver (Eds.), *Handbook of attachment: Theory, research, and clinical applications* (pp. 319–335). New York: Guilford Press.

Anders, S. L., & Tucker, J. S. (2000). Adult attachment style, interpersonal communication competence, and social support. *Personal Relationships, 7*, 379–389.

Armsden, G. C., & Greenberg, M. T. (1987). The inventory of parent and peer attachment: Individual differences and their relationship to psychological well-being in adolescence. *Journal of Youth and Adolescence, 16*, 427–455.

Bartholomew, K. (1990). Avoidance of intimacy: An attachment perspective. *Journal of Social and Personal Relationships, 7*, 147–178.

Bartholomew, K., & Horowitz, L. M. (1991). Attachment styles among young adults: A test of a four-category model. *Journal of Personality and Social Psychology, 61*, 226–244.

Berscheid, E., Snyder, M., & Omoto, A. M. (1989). The relationship closeness inventory: Assessing the closeness of interpersonal relationships. *Journal of Personality and Social Psychology, 57*, 792–807.

Bogaert, A. F., & Sadava, S. (2002). Adult attachment and sexual behavior. *Personal Relationships, 9*, 191–204.

Bowlby, J. (1982). *Attachment and loss: Vol. 1. Attachment.* New York: Basic Books. Original work published 1969.

Bowlby, J. (1973). *Attachment and loss: Vol. 2. Separation.* New York: Basic Books.

Bowlby, J. (1988). *A secure base.* New York: Basic Books.

Bradford, S. A., Feeney, J. A., & Campbell, L. (2002). Links between attachment orientations and dispositional and diary-based measures of disclosure in dating couples: A study of actor and partner effects. *Personal Relationships, 9*, 491–506.

Brennan, K. A., Clark, C. L., & Shaver, P. R. (1998). Self-report measurement of adult attachment: An integrative overview. In J. A. Simpson & W. S. Rholes (Eds.), *Attachment theory and close relationships* (pp. 46–76). New York: Guilford Press.

Brennan, K. A., Wu, S., & Loev, J. (1998). Adult romantic attachment and individual differences in attitudes toward physical contact in the context of adult romantic relationships. In J. A. Simpson & W. S. Rholes (Eds.), *Attachment theory and close relationships* (pp. 394–428). New York: Guilford Press.

Bretherton, I. (1985). Attachment theory: Retrospect and prospect. *Monographs of the Society for Research in Child Development, 50*, 3–35.

Bretherton, I. (1987). New perspectives on attachment relations: Security, communication, and internal working models. In J. D. Osofsky (Ed.), *Handbook of infant development* (2nd ed., pp. 1061–1100). New York: Wiley.

Bretherton, I., & Munholland, K. A. (1999). Internal working models in attachment relationships: A construct revisited. In J. Cassidy & P. R. Shaver (Eds.), *Handbook of attachment: Theory, research, and clinical applications* (pp. 89–111). New York: Guilford Press.

Carnelley, K. B., Pietromonaco, P. R., & Jaffe, K. (1996). Attachment, caregiving, and relationship functioning in couples: Effects of self and partner. *Personal Relationships, 3*, 257–278.

Cassidy, J. (2001). Truth, lies, and intimacy: An attachment perspective. *Attachment and Human Development, 3*, 121–155.

Clark, M. S., Fitness, J., & Brissette, I. (2001). Understanding people's perceptions of relationships is crucial to understanding their emotional lives: In G. J. O. Fletcher & M. S. Clark (Eds.), *Blackwell Handbook of Social Psychology: Vol. 2. Interpersonal Processes.* United Kingdom: Blackwell.

Cohen, S. (1988). Psychosocial models of the role of social support in the etiology of physical disease. *Health Psychology, 7*, 269–297.

Collins, N. L. (1996). Working models of attachment: Implications for explanation, emotion, and behavior. *Journal of Personality and Social Psychology, 71*, 810–832.

Collins, N. L., & Allard, L. M. (2001). Cognitive representations of attachment: The content and function of working models. In G. J. O. Fletcher & M. S. Clark (Eds.), *Blackwell Handbook of Social Psychology: Vol. 2. Interpersonal Processes* (pp. 60–85). United Kingdom: Blackwell.

Collins, N. L., Cooper, M. L., Albino, A., & Allard, L. (2002). Psychosocial vulnerability from adolescence to adulthood: A prospective study of attachment style differences in relationship functioning and partner choice. *Journal of Personality, 70*, 965–1008.

Collins, N. L., & Feeney, B. C. (2000). A safe haven: An attachment theory perspective on support seeking and caregiving in intimate relationships. *Journal of Personality and Social Psychology, 78*, 1053–1073.

Collins, N. L., & Feeney, B. C. (in press). Working models of attachment shape perceptions of social support: Evidence from experimental and observational studies. *Journal of Personality and Social Psychology.*

Collins, N. L., & Feeney, B. C. (2003). *Social support and caregiving in daily interaction: Feeling supported and feeling secure.* Unpublished manuscript, University of California, Santa Barbara.

Collins, N. L., Ford, M., Guichard, A., & Allard, L. M. (2003). *Working models of attachment and social construal processes in romantic relationships.* Under review.

Collins, N. L., & Read, S. J. (1990). Adult attachment, working models, and relationship quality in dating couples. *Journal of Personality and Social Psychology, 58*, 644–663.

Collins, N. L., & Read, S. J. (1994). Cognitive representations of adult attachment: The structure and function of working models. In K. Bartholomew & D. Perlman (Eds.), *Advances in Personal Relationships, Vol. 5: Attachment processes in adulthood* (pp. 53–90). London: Jessica Kingsley.

Cooper, M. L., Shaver, P. R., & Collins, N. L. (1998). Attachment styles, emotion regulation, and adjustment in adolescence. *Journal of Personality and Social Psychology, 74*, 1380–1397.

Crowell, J. A., Fraley, R. C., & Shaver, P. R. (1999). Measurement of individual differences in adolescent and adult attachment. In J. Cassidy & P. R. Shaver (Eds.), *Handbook of attachment: Theory, research, and clinical applications* (pp. 434–465). New York: Guilford Press.

Cutrona, C. E. (1996). *Social support in couples: Marriage as a resource in time of stress.* Thousand Oaks, CA: Sage.

Egeland, B., & Farber, E. A. (1984). Infant-mother attachment: Factors related to its development and changes over time. *Child Development, 55,* 753–771.

Epstein, S. (1994). Integration of the cognitive and psychodynamic unconscious. *American Psychologist, 49,* 709–724

Feeney, B. C., & Collins, N. L. (2001). Predictors of caregiving in adult intimate relationships: An attachment theoretical perspective. *Journal of Personality and Social Psychology, 80,* 972–994.

Feeney, B. C., & Collins, N. L. (2003). Motivations for caregiving in adult intimate relationships: Influences on caregiving behavior and relationship functioning. *Personality and Social Psychology Bulletin, 29,* 950–968.

Feeney, B. C., & Kirkpatrick, L. A. (1996). The effects of adult attachment and presence of romantic partners on physiological responses to stress. *Journal of Personality and Social Psychology, 70,* 255–270.

Feeney, J. A. (1996). Attachment, caregiving, and marital satisfaction. *Personal Relationships, 3,* 401–416.

Feeney, J. A. (1998). Adult attachment and relationship-centered anxiety: Responses to physical and emotional distancing. In J. A. Simpson & W. S. Rholes (Eds.), *Attachment theory and close relationships* (pp. 189–218). New York, NY: Guilford Press.

Feeney, J. A. (1999). Adult romantic attachment and couple relationships. In J. Cassidy & P. R. Shaver (Eds.), *Handbook of attachment: Theory, research, and clinical applications* (pp. 355–377). New York: Guilford Press.

Feeney, J. A., & Noller, P. (1990). Attachment style as a predictor of adult romantic relationships. *Journal of Personality and Social Psychology, 58,* 281–291.

Feeney, J. A., Noller, P., & Patty, J. (1993). Adolescents' interactions with the opposite sex: Influence of attachment style and gender. *Journal of Adolescence, 16,* 169–186.

Fishtein, J., Pietromonaco, P. R., & Barrett, L. F. (1999). The contribution of attachment style and relationship conflict to the complexity of relationship knowledge. *Social Cognition, 7,* 228–244.

Florian, V., Mikulincer, M., & Bucholtz, I. (1995). Effects of adult attachment style on the perception and search for social support. *The Journal of Psychology, 129,* 665–676.

Fraley, R. C., Davis, K. E., & Shaver, P. R. (1998). Dismissing-avoidance and the defensive organization of emotion, cognition, and behavior. In J. A. Simpson & W. S. Rholes (Eds.), *Attachment theory and close relationships* (pp. 249–279). New York: Guilford Press.

Fraley, R. C., & Shaver, P. R. (1998). Airport separations: A naturalistic study of adult attachment dynamics in separating couples. *Journal of Personality and Social Psychology, 75,* 1198–1212.

Fraley, R. C., & Shaver, P. R. (2000). Adult romantic attachment: Theoretical developments, emerging controversies, and unanswered questions. *Review of General Psychology, 4,* 132–154.

Fraley, R. C., & Waller, N. G. (1998). Adult attachment patterns: A test of the typological model. In J. A. Simpson & S. W. Rholes (Eds.), *Attachment theory and close relationships* (pp. 77–114). New York: Guilford Press.

George, C., & Solomon, J. (1999). Attachment and caregiving: The caregiving behavioral system. In J. Cassidy & P. R. Shaver (Eds.), *Handbook of attachment: Theory, research, and clinical applications* (pp. 649–670). New York: Guilford Press.

Grabill, C. M., & Kerns, K. A. (2000). Attachment style and intimacy in friendship. *Personal Relationships, 7,* 363–378.

Guerrero, L. K. (1996). Attachment-style differences in intimacy and involvement: A test of the four-category model. *Communication Monographs, 63,* 269–292.

Hazan, C., & Shaver, P. R. (1987). Romantic love conceptualized as an attachment process. *Journal of Personality and Social Psychology, 52,* 511–524.

Hazan, C., & Zeifman, D. (1999). Pair bonds as attachments: Evaluating the evidence. In J. Cassidy & P. R. Shaver (Eds.), *Handbook of attachment: Theory, research, and clinical applications* (pp. 336–354). New York: Guilford Press.

Holmes, J. G., & Rempel, J. K. (1989). *Trust in close relationships.* In C. Hendrick (Ed.), *Close relationships* (pp. 187–220). Thousand Oaks, CA: Sage Publications.

Impett, E. A., & Peplau, L. A. (2002). Why some women consent to unwanted sex with a dating partner: Insights from attachment theory. *Psychology of Women Quarterly, 26,* 360–370.

Keelan, J. P. R., Dion, K. K., & Dion, K. L. (1998). Attachment style and relationship satisfaction: Test of a self-disclosure explanation. *Canadian Journal of Behavioural Science, 30,* 24–35.

Kerns, K. A., & Stevens, A. C. (1996). Parent-child attachment in late adolescence: Links to social relations and personality. *Journal of Youth & Adolescence, 25,* 323–342.

Kobak, R., & Hazan, C. (1991). Attachment in marriage: Effects of security and accuracy of working models. *Journal of Personality and Social Psychology, 60,* 861–869.

Kobak, R. R., & Sceery, A. (1988). Attachment in late adolescence: Working models, affect regulation, and perception of self and others. *Child Development, 59,* 135–146.

Kunce, L. J., & Shaver, P. R. (1994). An attachment-theoretical approach to caregiving in romantic relationships. In K. Bartholomew & D. Perlman (Eds.), *Advances in personal relationships* (Vol. 5, pp. 205–237). London: Jessica Kingsley.

Levy, K. N., Blatt, S. J., & Shaver, P. R. (1998). Attachment styles and parental representations. *Journal of Personality and Social Psychology, 74*, 407–419.

Levy, M. B., & Davis, K. E. (1988). Lovestyles and attachment styles compared: Their relations to each other and to various relationship characteristics. *Journal of Social and Personal Relationships, 5*, 439–471.

Main, M. (1990). Cross-cultural studies of attachment organization: Recent studies, changing methodologies, and the concept of conditional strategies. *Human Development, 33*, 48–61.

Main, M., Kaplan, N., & Cassidy, J. (1985). Security in infancy, childhood, and adulthood: A move to the level of representation. *Monographs of the Society for Research in Child Development, 50*, 66–104.

Mikulincer, M. (1998). Attachment working models and the sense of trust: An exploration of interaction goals and affect regulation. *Journal of Personality and Social Psychology, 74*, 1209–1224.

Mikulincer, M., & Florian, V. (1995). Appraisal of and coping with a real-life stressful situation: The contribution of attachment styles. *Personality and Social Psychology Bulletin, 21*, 406–414.

Mikulincer, M., Florian, V., & Weller, A. (1993). Attachment styles, coping strategies, and posttraumatic psychological distress: The impact of the gulf war in Israel. *Journal of Personality and Social Psychology, 64*, 817–826.

Mikulincer, M., Gillath, O., & Shaver, P. R. (2002). Activation of the attachment system in adulthood: Threat-related primes increase the accessibility of mental representations of attachment figures. *Journal of Personality and Social Psychology, 83*, 881–895.

Mikulincer, M., & Nachshon, O. (1991). Attachment styles and patterns of self-disclosure. *Journal of Personality and Social Psychology, 61*, 321–331.

Mikulincer, M., Shaver, P. R., & Pereg, D. (2003). Attachment theory and affect regulation: The dynamics, development, and cognitive consequences of attachment-related strategies. *Motivation and Emotion, 27*, 77–102.

Murray, S. L., Bellavia, G. M., Rose, P., & Griffin, D. W. (2003). Once hurt, twice hurtful: How perceived regard regulates daily marital interactions. *Journal of Personality and Social Psychology, 84*, 126–147.

Murray, S. L., Holmes, J. G., Griffin, D. W., Bellavia, G., & Rose, P. (2001). The mismeasure of love: How self-doubt contaminates relationship beliefs. *Personality and Social Psychology Bulletin, 27*, 423–436.

Myers, D. G., & Diener, E. (1995). Who is happy? *Psychological Science, 6*, 10–19.

Noller, P., & Feeney, J. A. (1994). Relationship satisfaction, attachment, and nonverbal accuracy in early marriage. *Journal of Nonverbal Behavior, 18*, 199–221.

Ognibene, T. C., & Collins, N. L. (1998). Adult attachment styles, perceived social support, and coping strategies. *Journal of Social and Personal Relationships, 15*, 323–345.

Pierce, T., & Lydon, J. (1998). Priming relational schemas: Effects of contextually activated and chronically accessible interpersonal expectations on responses to a stressful event. *Journal of Personality and Social Psychology, 75*, 1441–1448.

Pietromonaco, P. R., & Barrett, L. F. (1997). Working models of attachment and daily social interactions. *Journal of Personality and Social Psychology, 73*, 1409–1423.

Pistole, M. C. (1989). Attachment in adult romantic relationships: Style of conflict resolution and relationship satisfaction. *Journal of Social and Personal Relationships, 6*, 505–512.

Pistole, M. C. (1994). Adult attachment styles: Some thoughts on closeness-distance struggles. *Family Process, 33*, 147–159.

Prager, K. J. (1995). *The psychology of intimacy.* New York: Cambridge University Press.

Reis, H. T., & Patrick, B. C. (1996). Attachment and intimacy: Component processes. In E. T. Higgins & A. W. Kruglanski (Eds.), *Social psychology: Handbook of basic principles* (pp. 523–563). New York: Guilford Press.

Reis, H. T., & Shaver, P. (1988). Intimacy as an interpersonal process. In S. Duck, D. F. Hay, S. E. Hobfoll, W. Ickes, & B. M. Montgomery (Eds.), *Handbook of personal relationships: Theory, research and interventions* (pp. 367–389). Oxford, England: Wiley.

Rothbard, J. C., & Shaver, P. R. (1994). Continuity of attachment across the life span. In M. B. Sperling & W. H. Berman (Eds.), *Attachment in adults: Clinical and developmental perspectives* (pp. 31–71). New York: Guilford Press.

Ryff, C. D. (1989). Happiness is everything, or is it? Explorations on the meaning of psychological well–being. *Journal of Personality and Social Psychology, 57*, 1069–1081.

Sarason, B. R., Sarason, I. G., & Gurung, R. A. R. (2001). Close personal relationships and health outcomes: A key to the role of social support. In B. R. Sarason & S. Duck (Eds.), *Personal relationships: Implications for clinical and community psychology* (pp. 15–41). New York: Wiley.

Shaver, P. R., Collins, N., & Clark, C. L. (1996). Attachment styles and internal working models of self and relationship partners. In G. J. O. Fletcher & J. Fitness (Eds.), *Knowledge structures in close relationships: A social psychological approach* (pp. 25–61). Hillsdale, NJ: Lawrence Erlbaum Associates.

Shaver, P., & Hazan, C. (1993). Adult romantic attachment: Theory and evidence. In D. Perlman & W. H. Jones (Eds.), *Advances in personal relationships* (Vol. 4, pp. 29–70). London: Jessica Kingsley.

Shaver, P. R., Hazan, C., & Bradshaw, D. (1988). Love as attachment. In R. J. Sternberg & M. L. Barnes (Eds.), *The psychology of love.* New Haven, CT: Yale University Press.

Simpson, J. A. (1990). Influence of attachment styles on romantic relationships. *Journal of Personality and Social Psychology, 59*, 971–980.

Simpson, J. A., Rholes, W. S., & Nelligan, J. S. (1992). Support seeking and support giving within couples in an anxiety-provoking situation: The role of attachment styles. *Journal of Personality and Social Psychology, 62*, 434–446.

Simpson, J. A., Rholes, W. S., & Phillips, D. (1996). Conflict in close relationships: An attachment perspective. *Journal of Personality and Social Psychology, 71*, 899–914.

Sroufe, L. A., & Waters, E. (1977). Attachment as an organizational construct. *Child Development, 48*, 1184–1199.

Tidwell, M. C. O., Reis, H. T., & Shaver, P. R. (1996). Attachment, attractiveness, and social interaction: A diary study. *Journal of Personality & Social Psychology, 71*, 729–745.

Tooby, J., & Cosmides, L. (1996). Friendship and the banker's paradox: Other pathways to the evolution of adaptations for altruism. *Proceedings of the British Academy, 88*, 119–143.

Tucker, J. S., & Anders, S. L. (1998). Adult attachment style and nonverbal closeness in dating couples. *Journal of Nonverbal Behavior, 22*, 109–124.

Tucker, J. S., & Anders, S. L. (1999). Attachment style, interpersonal perception accuracy, and relationship satisfaction in dating couples. *Personality and Social Psychology Bulletin, 25*, 403–412.

Uchino, B. N., Cacioppo, J. T., & Kiecolt-Glaser, J. K. (1996). The relationship between social support and physiological processes: A review with emphasis on underlying mechanisms and implications for health. *Psychological Bulletin, 488*–531.

Wieselquist, J., Rusbult, C. E., Foster, C. A., & Agnew, C. R. (1999). Commitment, pro-relationship behavior, and trust in close relationships. *Journal of Personality and Social Psychology, 77*, 942–966.

Weiss, R. S. (1982). Attachment in adult life. In C. M. Parkes & J. Stevenson-Hinde (Eds.), *The place of attachment in human behavior* (pp. 171–184). New York: Basic Books.

11

Sexual Passion, Intimacy, and Gender

Kathleen D. Vohs
University of British Columbia

Roy F. Baumeister
Florida State University

Passion and intimacy are widely recognized as important components of successful close romantic relationships. Few people would wish that their marriage would lack passion or fail to achieve intimacy. Both emotional and sexual forms of passion and intimacy are desirable aspects of a good relationship.

Unfortunately, both passion and intimacy are often misunderstood, and the link between the two has proven elusive. Colloquial usage of the terms often seems to regard them as almost synonyms. Thus, the phrase "being intimate" is sometimes used to express sexual intercourse, even though "being passionate" would seemingly be a more precise and literal way to express it.

This chapter examines the relationship between passion and intimacy. We first suggest that passion is a subjective, inherently ephemeral feeling created by change in intimacy. Understanding the link in that way can resolve some of the apparent contradictions in how passion and intimacy co-occur and can perhaps shed light on how relationships develop and vary. Next, we propose that there is an important gender difference in the passion-intimacy link, such that the same increment in intimacy produces higher passion in males than in females. This difference will then be considered in the context of gender differences in sexual drive and passion generally. We will close with a brief consideration of the differential impact of cultural, social, and situational influences on male versus female sexuality.

Several notices before we review the evidence: Our analyses mainly apply to romantic pairings because, for the most part, our theories were informed by data from the sex and love literatures. There are, however, some ties from the theories presented here to other types of relationships. The passion–intimacy theory could be applicable to and family and friendship relationships, if the same conditions are present. For the most part, however, these theories are perhaps most useful when considering romantic or sexual relationships. Regarding culture, we note that a great deal of the literature that informed these theories was conducted in Western cultures (viz. the United States). We believe that the theories are equally applicable to people from a variety of cultures, with the most important differences found in the ways that cultures affect the antecedent variables; the processes involved in each of the theories are regarded as basic to the operations of the human psyche and not specifically tied to culture.

DEFINITIONS

Many writers have sought to define passion and intimacy. In our view, intimacy refers to a condition of a relationship, whereas passion is a property (a state) of an individual person. Thus, one person can experience passion regardless of what the relationship partner is feeling, but intimacy exists between two people rather than inside one of them.

On the basis of writings of Hatfield (1984), Lewis (1973), Reis and Patrick (1996), and Sternberg (1986), we define intimacy in terms of three main dimensions. First, intimacy involves mutual understanding of inner, personal material. It typically develops from self-disclosure and mutual observation, and it leads to an empathic, sympathetic, mutual understanding. The two people feel that they understand each other and that they are in turn understood. We also assume that there is some accuracy to this mutual understanding: A relationship could not be described as intimate if the partners misunderstood each other egregiously.

Second, intimacy involves positive feelings about each other. Intimate partners have a deep concern for each other's welfare. They also regard each other favorably.

Third, intimacy typically entails communication. Accurate mutual understanding is created and sustained by communication. Also, the partners communicate their positive feelings about each other (especially affection, warmth, and caring) to each other.

Passion, meanwhile, is a strong emotional state. Passionate love involves powerful feelings of attraction to the partner, including physiological arousal and a desire to be united with that person. In romantic relationships, passionate love normally includes a substantial element of sexual desire and attraction. To be sure, love is not the only kind of passion, but the arousal and emotional intensity are still defining features. For example, the difference between passionate hatred and other (cold) hatred would lie precisely in the emotional intensity.

THE PARADOX

In order to explain how passion and intimacy may be related, one must reconcile certain seeming contradictions. Obviously there must be some kind of positive correlation: A good relationship would consist of high degrees of both passion and intimacy. Conversely, weak or failed relationships have neither intimacy nor passionate love (although they may sometimes produce other passions!). In support of this idea, one-shot survey data show that when people rate their relationships, their ratings of passion and intimacy are positively correlated (e.g., Patton & Waring, 1985).

Then again, in other respects there must seemingly be a lack of positive correlation or even a negative correlation between passion and intimacy. The time courses of passion and intimacy are quite different, as Sternberg (1986) and others have argued. Specifically, passion rises rapidly early in a relationship and then declines. Intimacy, conversely, rises more slowly and then may tend to reach a plateau. Thus, after several good years together, a couple may have achieved a high degree of intimacy, but the passion that first drew them together is likely to have subsided. The standard view holds that long-term romantic relationships make a transition from passionate love to companionate love, and the transition is essentially a shift from passion to intimacy as the main foundation.

The divergent time courses of passion and intimacy have been confirmed in multiple studies. One of the most thorough was an ambitious study by Acker and Davis (1992) based on Sternberg's (1986) theory. They found that passion declined over time in long-term relationships, whereas intimacy continued to rise. Studies of sexual behavior confirm the waning of passion over time. Many studies have shown that the frequency of sexual intercourse declines progressively over the course of a marriage or relationship (see Baumeister & Bratslavsky, 1999, for review). Indeed, the decline is not uniform: It is sharpest in the early years of a marriage, whereas after many years it drops more slowly (e.g., Ard, 1977)—in a sense the mirror image of intimacy, which rises most sharply at first and then may increase more slowly as the couple gradually exhausts the stock of new things to find out about each other. In one study, the frequency of intercourse dropped by half from the first to the second year of marriage, whereas in subsequent years the decreases were smaller (James, 1981).

To be sure, there are multiple factors that contribute to the decrease in sexual frequency. Undoubtedly one is simply that people's sexual desires become less frequent and less urgent with aging. Yet when a middle-aged couple gets a divorce and starts over with new partners, the frequency of intercourse tends to be high again, and so age alone cannot explain the effect.

The discrepant time courses are probably rooted in the very nature of passion and intimacy. Intimacy is a kind of knowing, and building up a substantial stock of knowledge and understanding of another person takes time. In contrast, passion is essentially an emotion, and emotions are by nature temporary. Emotions also respond more to change rather than stable circumstances.

Thus, we have a problem: Passionate love and intimacy are seemingly positively related, yet their time course is so different that the one is going up when the other is going down. How can this paradox be resolved?

PASSION AND CHANGE IN INTIMACY

The solution to the paradox may be that passion derives not from intimacy per se but from change in intimacy (Baumeister & Bratslavsky, 1999). That is, increases in intimacy generate positive feelings of passion. In mathematical terms, passion is a function of the first derivative of intimacy over time.

The divergent time courses of passion and intimacy can be reconciled if passion is understood as arising from change in intimacy. Early in the relationship, intimacy is low but rising, and these increases produce the first feelings of passionate attraction. When intimacy is rising most rapidly, such as when the couple begins to express affection and caring and attraction, passion may reach its height, which will be felt as a blossoming of love. After a few years, the rises in intimacy will be more subtle and gradual, and passion will therefore decline (even though intimacy is still rising). And farther down the line, intimacy may have leveled off, causing passion to diminish toward zero.

Each new step toward greater intimacy has considerable power to elicit an emotional and passionate response. Repeating that step over and over gradually robs it of its power, however. The first time someone says "I love you" is likely to elicit waves of strong emotion and physical sensations. The four hundredth time that same person says those same words, the reaction is likely to be closer to a yawn and something along the lines of "that's nice, can you get me a beer?" (or even, "OK, what is it you want?")

Although it is undoubtedly more difficult to generate romantic or sexual passion after many years together, it is not impossible. Baumeister and Bratslavsky (1999) noted that when developing their ideas about passion and intimacy, many people told them that the most passionate sexual episodes in long-lasting relationships often accompanied making up after fights. They proposed that a fight or argument is experienced by the couple as a drop in intimacy, because the two feel that they are at cross-purposes and not feeling the sort of loving concern for each other that defines intimacy. Reconciliation after the fight therefore produces a rise in intimacy, even if the net effect is merely a resumption of the level of intimacy that existed before. This short-term increase may be enough to fuel passion.

An ambitious program of research by Aron and Aron (e.g., Aron & Aron, 2001; Aron, Norman, Aron, McKenna, & Heyman, 2000) found other ways for long-term couples to stimulate passion. These researchers found that when couples participate together in novel, exciting activities, the experience can kindle new feelings of passionate love for the partner. To be sure, Aron et al. (2000) discussed their ideas in the context of expansion and merger of selves. In our view, however, engaging in novel and exciting activities allows for a further increase in intimacy, insofar as the couple adds a new shared experience and sees each other in a new light and context, and so an increase in passion would follow naturally from this rise in intimacy.

Individual differences furnish another perspective on the link between passion and intimacy. Some people increase intimacy faster than others. Extraverts, who show the pattern of rapidly rising intimacy, are marked by multiple patterns indicating high passion, such as rapid sexual involvements (see Baumeister & Bratslavsky, 1999, for review). Tellingly, their relationships also tend to reach plateaus faster, therefore losing passion. Extraverts are therefore more prone than others to have multiple sexual partners, because the dwindling passion toward their current partner does not compete well with the rapid rise of intimacy (and hence passion) that they may feel toward a new partner. Introverts also eventually reach the asymptote at which intimacy levels off and passion dwindles, of course, but because intimacy with a new person develops more slowly, they are less prone than extraverts to fall into the whirlwind romance pattern and hence less likely to have a high turnover in their romantic relationship partners.

Gender differences represent another dimension of variation among individuals. The next section will consider likely gender differences in the link between passion and intimacy.

GENDER AND THE INTIMACY GRADIENT

Whereas extraverts and introverts differ on the speed with which they become intimate, men and women may differ in the power with which increments in intimacy are translated into passion. Specifically, it is likely that identical increments in intimacy will produce stronger doses of passion in males than in females. This is an assumption rather than a proven fact, but it is an extremely useful assumption in the sense that it enables one to predict and explain a series of differences between the genders in their relationship behavior.

First, men are likely to feel passionate love sooner than women. As we said, intimacy is a property of the relationship rather than of the person (although two people may perceive it differently). As the couple begins to disclose personal information to each other, express positive feelings about each other, and develop some mutual understanding, each increment in intimacy will produce a stronger emotional response in the man than in the woman. Hence the man is likely to reach the point of feeling that he is in love before the woman does. Evidence supports this. With a large and well-selected sample of students in dating relationships, Kanin, Davidson, and Scheck (1970) found that over a quarter of the men but only 15% of the women reported feeling in love by the fourth date. In a similar vein, almost half the women still did not feel love by the 20th date, whereas less than a third of the men still felt no love. Similar evidence that males fall in love faster than females was reported in other studies, including evidence about relationship development (Huston, Surra, Fitzgerald, & Cate, 1981) and studies of unrequited love (Baumeister, Wotman, & Stillwell, 1993).

It is also worth considering that there is an upper limit on how much passion one can feel on any one occasion. If the person is moved to feel strong affection and sexual desire on the basis of three intimate disclosures, there is no point in making an additional ten disclosures—in fact, it would seem better to save them so as to generate passion on another occasion. But the gender difference becomes relevant here. The woman may require a large dose of intimacy in order to generate maximum passion, whereas the man may reach the same level of passion with much less intimacy. Hence there may be a tendency for the man to hold back his intimate disclosures to some degree, whereas the woman may press for more intimate exchanges.

The different impact could be seen in homosexual relationships. Gay males may be able to generate considerable sexual passion without extensive self-disclosures, and so they would tend to become sexually active early in the relationship and remain so for a long period of time. Lesbians, in contrast, might use up much of the intimacy gradient in generating passion, and so they may tend to find that the intimacy approaches its asymptote fairly soon after they begin to generate enough passion to produce sex, leading to a decline in passion. There is indeed evidence supporting both points (especially Blumstein & Schwartz, 1983). First, gay males appear to generate sexual passion more rapidly than lesbians. Second, lesbians exhibit much more rapid and severe dropoffs in sexual activity than gay males, suggesting that they have reached the point at which intimacy levels off and hence fails to generate passion.

Within heterosexual relationships, the difference between men and women may produce a series of changes. Almost all studies have found that men are ready for sex sooner than women, consistent with the view that they require less intimacy to generate high passion (e.g., McCabe, 1987; Cohen & Shotland, 1996). Next there may then be a period when intimacy is blossoming rapidly, and so the man and woman may briefly feel that their levels of passion match each other. Gender differences in sexual responsiveness would likely diminish at this period. As the level of intimacy approaches the plateau, however, and the increments become smaller, the gender difference in sexual passion may resurface, with the man have sexual desires more frequently and more strongly than the woman. Consistent with this view, multiple studies have found that most marital conflicts concerning sexual behavior involve the husband wanting more frequent sex than the wife (e.g., Kinsey, Pomeroy, & Martin, 1948; Kinsey et al., 1953; Blumstein & Schwartz, 1983).

The differences may produce other possible misunderstandings and disagreements between the genders. Abbey (1982) proposed that when women express mildly positive, friendly sentiments, men tend to overinterpret them as indications of sexual and romantic attraction. Her data were admittedly weak and the conclusion—that the error is entirely on the men's part—seems biased and one-sided. We suggest that there may be an honest basis for reacting differently to the same conversation, even if both perceive it accurately and similarly. A friendly interaction that produces a mild increase in intimacy will often be enough to evoke some degree of romantic passion in the man, whereas the same interaction may fail to produce much of a comparable response in the woman.

Baumeister and Bratslavsky (1999) also suggested that the gender difference in desire for foreplay may be traced to the gender difference in how intimacy translates into passion. Foreplay can be regarded as communication of physical affection, and as such it may function as a sign of increments in intimacy. If men can reach high levels of sexual passion from smaller doses of intimacy, then men will need less foreplay to reach full sexual arousal than women. The female requirement of foreplay may therefore be taken, not as any lack of sensitivity in the female body, but rather as a further consequence of the slower and smaller conversion of intimacy into passion.

The idea that changes in intimacy produce more passion in men than women can also be tested by looking at changes in the opposite direction—decreases in intimacy, when a relationship deteriorates and breaks up. Some evidence has in fact found that men suffer more than women over the end of a relationship (Hill, Rubin, & Peplau, 1976). More recent evidence has also indicated that marital arguments are more distressing to husbands than to wives, and husbands take longer than wives to recover from them (Levenson, Carstensen, & Gottman, 1994).

SEX DRIVE

The findings covered in the previous section suggest that men may be more passionate than women, or at least more prone to experience strongly passionate responses than what women feel under identical circumstances. Whether that impression is generally true across the full emotional spectrum is open to debate and beyond the scope of this chapter. We will however address one particular, relevant issue: sexual desire.

The notion of gender differences in sex drive is important to consider because, as noted previously, levels and changes in passion affect intimacy in a complex and important manner. (Sex drive refers more to sexual motivation generally, whereas passion refers to feelings and motivations directed toward a specific person.) If men and women have different sexual motivations generally, this may help to explain some of the problems couples encounter, especially later in the relationship when the passion (i.e., specific sexual desire) dwindles and overall sex drive becomes a central determinant of sexual preferences.

The question of whether men have a stronger sex drive than women became a political football in the 1970s. Undoubtedly stereotypes suggested that women desired sex less than men, and indeed some Victorian authors were moved to wonder whether typical or decent women experienced sexual desire at all except perhaps on rare occasions (Acton, 1857). These extreme views were quickly recognized as absurd during the 1970s, which saw high points of both the sexual revolution and the modern feminist movement. Ideologically passionate theorists moved to the opposite extreme and insisted that women had just as much sexual desire as men and possibly more. Even today, Hyde and DeLamater's (1997) textbook on human sexuality deals with the question of gender differences in sex drive by proposing that the evidence fails to confirm any real difference, especially in view of how society has conspired to suppress female sexuality, and it concludes by proposing that eventually everyone will realize that women have a stronger sex drive than men.

However, there is no inherent value judgment to be made about almost any degree of sexual desire, with the possible exception of the two extremes (i.e., having no desire at all, or having an obsessive and insatiable craving). It is clear that the average man and the average woman are comfortably removed from either of those extremes, and so no value judgment is riding on whether one gender or the other has a somewhat milder appetite. In particular, it seems unsound and plain silly to treat desire for sex as a kind of competition in which more is better.

The alleged lack of evidence regarding gender differences in sex drive is wildly overstated. We recently published a review of empirical findings pertinent to the question (Baumeister, Catanese, & Vohs, 2001). Our approach was to begin by imagining two hypothetical women (or two men), one of whom had a much stronger sex drive than the other. What would be the likely behavioral manifestations of the difference in sex drive? We made a list of predicted differences and then searched the literature for evidence that compared men against women on each of these.

To anticipate the conclusion, our review found that men have a higher sex drive than women (Baumeister, Catanese, & Vohs, 2001). This conclusion was supported by every measure and every study. There were no findings indicating that women desire sex more than men. To be sure, women are capable of more sexual activity and more orgasms than men, but capability is not desire. Thus, although women may be able to have more orgasms than men, they do not necessarily want more orgasms than men. On the contrary, men seem to want more orgasms and devote more time and effort into obtaining them (including by masturbation; see Oliver & Hyde, 1993).

The findings can be summarized roughly as follows. Men think about sex more than women, have more frequent sexual fantasies, and have more variety in their fantasies. Men experience spontaneous sexual arousal more frequently than women. Men desire sexual intercourse more frequently than women, a pattern that is found among young single people, young married people, middle-aged couples, and elderly couples. Men desire more sexual partners and actually claim to have more. (To be sure, the latter finding is somewhat suspect insofar as the average number of sex partners must be the same, provided that the population contains equal numbers of men and women and that they use the same criteria for counting sex partners.) Men desire a greater variety of activities than women. Men expend more time, effort, money, and other resources trying to obtain sex. Men find it more difficult and aversive to live without sex—indeed, even among Catholic clergy. Men masturbate more than women. Men are less likely to complain (or be the target of partner complaints) of lack of sex drive. Men initiate sex more than women, whereas women refuse or avoid sex more than men. Men have more favorable attitudes about sex than women, and men also have more favorable attitudes toward both their own and their partner's genitals than women.

Thus, the difference in sex drive is undeniable. At most one can question whether the difference is innate or possibly the product of cultural suppression of female sexuality. Some degree of cultural suppression of female sexuality seems likely, but it seems inadequate to account for all the gender differences in sex drive. Thus, the difference in masturbation is one of the largest and most robust differences (e.g., Oliver & Hyde, 1993), yet masturbation is much less affected by social norms and pressures than interpersonal activities, and if anything society has directed more strenuous efforts toward curtailing male than female masturbation. (It was the boys who were supposed to go blind or insane from masturbation, after all.) Furthermore, research on people who do not masturbate has suggested that guilt and socialized concerns play a more prominent role in deterring male than female masturbation (Arafat & Cotton, 1974). Women who do not masturbate generally cite a lack of desire as the main reason (Arafat & Cotton, 1974).

Another difference that cannot easily be ascribed to social norms or pressures is found in the behavior of Catholic clergy. Both priests and nuns subscribe to the single standard of absolute sexual abstinence, and purity, and the pressures to live up to one's vows is backed by force, tradition, institutional pressures, and ostensibly God's divine commands. Yet the nuns succeed far better than the priests by any measure, including masturbation, incidence of intercourse, number of sex partners, and number of sexual experiences (e.g., Murphy, 1992). The pressures are similar, but the women are able to live without sex more easily than the men—most likely because their desire for sex is less insistent.

Again, this is not to deny that society has generally put particular pressures on women to curtail their sexual interest. In other works, we have cited evidence of this cultural suppression of female sexuality and sought to explain it (Baumeister &

Twenge, 2002). The explanation that best fits the evidence is partly based on there being an initial difference in sex drive. Because women desire sex less than men, gender interactions throughout history have conformed to the pattern in which men try to persuade women to engage in sex, and this persuasion typically takes the form of offering women other resources (such as respect, commitment, money, attention, love, status) in exchange for sex (see Baumeister & Vohs, in press). This creates a kind of sexual marketplace, and female sexuality is thus a resource subject to the laws of supply and demand. As with any resource, there is a market incentive for women to restrict each other's sexual behavior, so that the price will be higher. Hence the pressures on individual women to hold back on sex come not from society at large nor from men but rather, typically, from the female peers in the local community.

We also reiterate that the gender difference in sex drive is descriptive and not prescriptive. In particular, we reject any suggestion that women should not desire sex, or should not enjoy it, or are not entitled to sexual pleasure, or cannot have a rich and intensely satisfying sex life. Furthermore, there is substantial variation within gender, and certainly there are some women who have more sexual desires than many men. The data indicate only that men want sex more often and more intensely than women, on average.

The gender difference in sex drive has important implications for close relationships. During the formation of a new relationship, the man will typically desire sex earlier than the woman, and so the early stages of relationships will often include efforts by the man to persuade the woman to engage in sex (rather than the reverse). This puts the woman in the so-called gatekeeper role: Women decide whether and when sexual relations will commence (Baumeister & Vohs, in press).

We suggested previously that there may often be a phase during which the blossoming intimacy produces high degrees of sexual passion in both partners. During this phase, then, the gender difference in sexual desire may diminish or even seem to disappear. The man and woman are likely to conclude from this that they are well matched and well attuned to each other in terms of their sexual wants and needs. The odds are, however, that they will discover this to be an illusion and that their seeming mutual attunement was temporary. When the task of increasing intimacy is largely completed and the bloom of romantic passion begins to wear off, they will go back to their respective baselines of sexual desire, which usually means that the man wants more sex than the woman. Hence when couples argue or fight about sex, the dispute is generally that the man wants more sex or more particular sexual activities than the woman. Indeed, in one large sample of couples, around half of them had disputes about sex, and in every case the dispute involved the man wanting more sex than the woman (Byers & Lewis, 1988). There were no contrary cases in which the problem was that the woman wanted more sex than the man.

Other relationship problems may also reflect the gender difference in sex drive, albeit possibly combined with other factors. Males have been found to be somewhat more prone than females to use coercive means, even physical force, to obtain sex (Anderson & Struckman-Johnson, 1998). Men are also more prone than women to engage in extramarital affairs and other extradyadic sexual activity (e.g., Laumann et al., 1994). Although we are not addressing the moral issues and do not wish to make excuses for immoral behavior, the asymmetry in these patterns does seem to be consistent with and probably motivated by the difference in sex drive.

Homosexual relationships may diverge because of the gender difference in sex drive. Prior to AIDS, homosexual men often accumulated hundreds of sex partners, and in some venues gay men would routinely expect to have sex half a dozen times with as many different partners in a single night (e.g., Shilts, 1987). This kind of promiscuity was much rarer among lesbians. Meanwhile, even within established relationships, gay males have a higher frequency of sexual intercourse than lesbians

(Blumstein & Schwartz, 1983). A sizeable minority of lesbian couples appear to cease having sex altogether after some years together, whereas gay males are less likely to cease (Blumstein & Schwartz, 1983). Gay males are also more likely to have sex with other partners even when in a partnered relationship.

EROTIC PLASTICITY

Strength and frequency of sexual desires are not the only aspects of sexuality where men and women differ. Another important difference concerns erotic plasticity, which is defined as the degree to which the sex drive is shaped by cultural, social, and situational factors. A review by Baumeister (2000) concluded that women have higher erotic plasticity than men. Thus, whereas the male sex drive appears to conform to the pattern of an innate set of desires that are relatively immune to sociocultural influence, the female sex drive is much more malleable.

If women are more affected by social, cultural, and personal conditions than men, then a number of closeness and intimacy issues may arise. According to this model, men and women are differentially affected by the same factors and, likewise, different factors are central determinants of men's and women's sexual responses. For researchers of sex in relationships, it is beneficial to know, a priori, that the same conditions and treatments are likely to have different effects on men and women. At a personal level, too, men and women in sexual relationships may gain increased insight into oneself or one's partner through an understanding of erotic plasticity differences. Thus, the establishment and maintenance of closeness and intimacy may depend on an accurate understanding of the factors propelling men's and women's sexual responses, and erotic plasticity provides a basis for such understanding.

The difference in erotic plasticity takes multiple forms, according to the evidence reviewed by Baumeister (2000). First, individual women show more variation in their sexuality across the course of their adult lives as compared with men. Women show more peaks and valleys in sexual activity, adapt and change more over the course of a marriage, and are more willing to change back and forth in sexual orientation.

Second, specific social and cultural variables have larger effects on female than on male sexuality. Educational and religious institutions have stronger effects on women, in the sense that the most versus least educated (or most versus least religious) women are quite different in their sexual activities, whereas the corresponding differences for men are smaller. Peer groups and parents appear to have more impact on shaping a young woman's sexuality than a young man's. Cross-cultural differences in female sexuality are greater than the corresponding differences in male behavior. Behavioral–genetic studies of sexual behavior generally show stronger hereditary and genetic effects among men than among women, which supports the view that the social environment plays a more decisive role among women.

Third, attitude-behavior consistency in the sexual realm is lower for women than men. Female erotic plasticity means that general attitudes will be less effective at predicting actual behavior, because a woman's sexual response depends much more on the specific context and circumstances than a man's response. Women are more likely than men to engage in sexual activities that go against their broad, general attitudes, and they are also more likely to fail to follow through on sexual activities that they do find appealing in the abstract. (Men do often suffer from lack of opportunity to act out all their sexual inclinations.)

The reasons for the difference in plasticity are not entirely clear. One likely candidate, however, is that the gender difference in sex drive is a contributing factor. Because women have milder desires for sex, these desires are more subject to social and cultural influences. If one considers other desires, such as the desire to have and care for children, it appears that when women have stronger motivations than men, male behavior shows higher plasticity (as indicated in the cultural and historical variations in the father role).

Applied to relationships, the gender difference in plasticity entails that women can probably adjust their sexual behavior and perhaps their expectations more effectively than men. Relationships often require compromise and accommodation, and in the sexual sphere at least women will find these easier to accomplish. There is indeed some evidence that women adjust sexually to a relationship more than men (Ard, 1977).

CONCLUSION AND SUMMARY

In this chapter we focus on several points. First, we propose that passion typically results from change in intimacy, such that rapidly increasing intimacy produces high passion whereas stable intimacy (even stable high intimacy) tends to produce low passion. Second, we propose that there are gender differences in the formula by which intimacy leads to passion, so that identical increases in intimacy will cause more passion in the man than in the woman. Third, we contend that there is a gender difference in sex drive, such that men generally have more frequent and more intense sexual desires than women. Fourth, we propose that the female sex drive is more dependent than the male sex drive on social, cultural, and situational factors.

REFERENCES

Abbey, A. (1982). Sex differences in attributions for friendly behavior: Do males misperceive females' friendliness? *Journal of Personality and Social Psychology, 42*, 830–838.

Acker, M., & Davis, M. H. (1992). Intimacy, passion, and commitment in adult romantic relationships: A test of the triangular theory of love. *Journal of Social and Personal Relationships, 9*, 21–50.

Acton, W. (1857). *The functions and disorders of the reproductive organs.* Philadelphia:

Anderson, P. B., & Struckman-Johnson, C. (1998). *Sexually aggressive women: Current perspectives and controversies.* New York: Guilford.

Angier, N. (1999). *Woman: An intimate geography.* Boston: Houghton-Mifflin.

Arafat, I. S., & Cotton, W. L. (1974). Masturbation practices of males and females. *Journal of Sex Research, 10,* 293–307.

Ard, B. N. (1977). Sex in lasting marriages: A longitudinal study. *Journal of Sex Research, 13,* 274–285.

Aron, A., & Aron, E. N. (2001). The self expansion model of motivation and cognition in close relationships and beyond. In M. Clark & G. Fletcher (Eds.), *Blackwell Handbook of Social Psychology, Vol. 2: Interpersonal Processes.* Oxford, England: Blackwell.

Aron, A., Norman, C. C., Aron, E. N., McKenna, C., & Heyman, R. (2000). Couples shared participation in novel and arousing activities and experienced relationship quality. *Journal of Personality and Social Psychology, 78,* 273–283.

Baumeister, R. F. (2000). Gender differences in erotic plasticity: The female sex drive as socially flexible and responsive. *Psychological Bulletin, 126,* 347–374.

Baumeister, R. F., & Bratslavsky, E. (1999). Passion, intimacy, and time: Passionate love as a function of change in intimacy. *Personality and Social Psychology Review, 3,* 49–67.

Baumeister, R. F., Catanese, K., & Vohs, K. D. (2001). Is there a gender difference in strength of sex drive? Theoretical views, conceptual distinctions, and a review of relevant evidence. *Personality and Social Psychology Review, 5,* 242–273.

Baumeister, R. F., & Twenge, J. M. (2002). The cultural suppression of female sexuality: Who is the proximal cause? *Review of General Psychology, 6,* 166–203.

Baumeister, R. F., & Vohs, K. D. (in press). Sexual economics: Sex as female resource for social exchange in heterosexual interactions. *Personality and Social Psychology Review.*

Baumeister, R. F., Wotman, S. R., & Stillwell, A. M. (1993). Unrequited love: On heartbreak, anger, guilt, scriptlessness, and humiliation. *Journal of Personality and Social Psychology, 64,* 377–394.

Blumstein, P., & Schwartz, P. (1983). *American couples.* New York: Simon & Schuster.

Byers, E. S., & Lewis, K. (1988). Dating couples' disagreements over the desired level of sexual intimacy. *Journal of Sex Research, 24,* 15–29.

Cohen, L. L., & Shotland, R. L. (1996). Timing of first sexual intercourse in a relationship: Expectations, experiences, and perceptions of others. *Journal of Sex Research, 33*, 291–299.

Hatfield, E. (1984). The dangers of intimacy. In V. Derlega (Ed.), *Communication, intimacy, and close relationships* (pp. 207–220). New York: Academic Press.

Hill, C. T., Rubin, Z., & Peplau, L. A. (1976). Breakups before marriage: The end of 103 affairs. *Journal of Social Issues, 32*, 147–168.

Huston, T. L., Surra, C. A., Fitzgerald, N. M., & Cate, R. M. (1981). From courtship to marriage: Mate selection as an interpersonal process. In S. Duck & R. Gilmour (Eds.), *Personal Relationships. 2: Developing personal relationships*, (pp. 53–88). New York: Academic Press.

Hyde, J. S., & DeLamater, J. (1997). *Understanding human sexuality* (6th ed.). Boston, MA: McGraw-Hill.

James, W. H. (1981). The honeymoon effect on marital coitus. *Journal of Sex Research, 17*, 114–123.

Kanin, E. J., Davidson, K. D., & Scheck, S. R. (1970). A research note on male–female differentials in the experience of heterosexual love. *Journal of Sex Research, 6*, 64–72.

Kinsey, A. C., Pomeroy, W. B., & Martin, C. E. (1948). *Sexual behavior in the human male*. Philadelphia: Saunders.

Kinsey, A. C., Pomeroy, W. B., Martin, C. E., & Gebhard, P. H. (1953). *Sexual behavior in the human female*. Philadelphia: Saunders.

Laumann, E. O., Gagnon, J. H., Michael, R. T., & Michaels, S. (1994). *The social organization of sexuality: Sexual practices in the United States*. Chicago, IL: University of Chicago Press.

Levenson, R. W., Carstensen, L. L., & Gottman, J. M. (1994). The influence of age and gender on affect, physiology, and their interrelations: A study of long-term marriages. *Journal of Personality and Social Psychology, 45*, 587–597.

Lewis, R. A. (1973). Parents and peers: Socialization agents in the coital behavior of young adults. *Journal of Sex Research, 9*, 156–170.

McCabe, P. (1987). Desired and experienced levels of premarital affection and sexual intercourse during dating. *Journal of Sex Research, 23*, 23–33.

Murphy, S. (1992). *A delicate dance: Sexuality, celibacy, and relationships among Catholic clergy and religious*. New York: Crossroad.

Oliver, M. B., & Hyde, J. S. (1993). Gender differences in sexuality: A meta-analysis. *Psychological Bulletin, 114*, 29–51.

Patton, D., & Waring, E. M. (1985). Sex and marital intimacy. *Journal of Sex and Marital Therapy, 11*, 176–184.

Reis, H. T., & Patrick, B. C. (1996). Attachment and intimacy: Component processes. In E. Higgins & A. Kruglanski (Eds.), *Social psychology: Handbook of basic principles* (pp. 523–563). New York: Guilford.

Shilts, R. (1987). *And the band played on: Politics, people, and the AIDS epidemic*. New York: Viking Penguin.

Sternberg, R. J. (1986). A triangular theory of love. *Psychological Review, 93*, 119–135.

12

Perceived Partner Responsiveness as an Organizing Construct in the Study of Intimacy and Closeness

Harry T. Reis
University of Rochester

Margaret S. Clark
Carnegie Mellon University

John G. Holmes
University of Waterloo

Human kind cannot bear very much reality.

—T. S. Eliot

It may really be too hard and too late, not even desirable, after such long, familiar cold, to be known, and heard, and seen.

—Amy Bloom, "Love Invents Us"

There is no shortage of distinct and conceptually imaginative constructs in the relationship literature. With the rapid expansion of the field in the last two decades, relationship scholars have defined, operationalized, and investigated a plethora of constructs, each delineating a particular quality or process describing behavior in personal relationships, and each distinguishable to varying degrees from other constructs. With every new issue of leading journals, the list of relationship constructs grows, and no moratorium on the proliferation of new constructs appears on the horizon. Such a moratorium would not be desirable, of course; new constructs enter the field precisely because their advocates believe that they are capable of adding new knowledge and insights to our understanding of interpersonal behavior and relationships.

Understandably, then, as the field has grown, so has its armoire of theoretical constructs and assessment tools. Early research focused on relatively broad, inclusive concepts such as satisfaction, love, intimacy, and commitment. As knowledge about these and related processes has accumulated, the field has come to recognize that these constructs are multifaceted. For example, Fehr and Russell (1991) identified literally dozens of types of love associated with a wide variety of distinct features (Aron & Westbay, 1996; Fehr, 1988). Reflecting the desire to move away from global, unidimensional constructs, Gottman (1998) suggested that satisfaction is too broad and imprecise a construct (he called it "glop"; p. 172) to be useful. Furthermore, the field's theoretical development necessarily focuses attention on relatively more finely differentiated distinctions, such that concepts become more sharply and carefully defined, both conceptually and operationally. The consequence is an increasingly sophisticated and specialized literature, encompassing many seemingly diverse theories and constructs, each laying out a series of carefully articulated and precisely differentiated principles, supported in the best of circumstances by a program of empirical research that not only verifies those principles but also documents differences from their conceptual neighbors and variants. It is no wonder, then, that when competing theories are discussed, scholars typically conclude not that one or another account is better, but rather that they appear to address somewhat different aspects of the phenomenon and therefore are not directly comparable (Bradbury, 2002).

In broad principle, we have no quarrel with this state of affairs; scientific disciplines advance through the ever more detailed refining of their theories and concepts. Because relationships are highly complex phenomena whose influences span multiple levels of analysis—the persons, their interaction, the social, cultural, and historical context of their interaction, and the systematic interplay among these levels of analysis (Hinde, 1997; Reis, Collins, & Berscheid, 2000)—theoretical models inevitably will be complex. Nevertheless, the benefits of specialization notwithstanding, we suggest that single-minded attention to conceptual and operational nuance may obscure the central core principles that underlie these more complex variables. It is useful to identify core principles for several reasons. For one, highlighting commonalities helps organize differentiated constructs in a conceptually coherent and parsimonious manner. A good example of this is the hierarchical model of attachment processes proposed by Collins and Read (1994), which allows for the integration of trait dispositions, role-related categories, and partner-specific representations within a multidimensional organizational model. Another benefit is that a deep understanding of commonalities in a diverse and specialized literature makes possible the generalization of knowledge and insights from one body of research and theory to another. A third reason concerns the application of knowledge to real-world relationships. Because theories typically deal with abstract principles rather than concrete behaviors, there are times when seemingly disparate behaviors represent common underlying processes. For example, one husband's tendency to overlook his wife's attraction to their handsome new neighbor and another husband's deepened commitment to his marriage upon discovering that he has a potentially fatal illness may be understood in tandem as relationship maintenance mechanisms reflecting the importance of felt security (as we discuss later in this chapter). In short, we suggest that in the field's commendable zeal to differentiate the many species of trees in the relationship forest, we may have become distracted from the important fact that they are all trees.[1]

---

[1] Although our approach resembles, in certain respects, the goal of theory development, there is one important difference: We seek less to articulate a novel set of principles describing the causes, consequences, and underlying mechanisms of perceived partner responsiveness and more to identify its many manifestations in the relationship literature (as well as in everyday social relationships). To the extent that this approach serves the purposes of theory development, we are delighted.

In this chapter, we propose that a construct we call *perceived partner responsiveness to the self* provides one such core organizing principle for the study of personal relationships. We define this construct as a process by which individuals come to believe that relationship partners both attend to and react supportively to central, core defining features of the self. The processes involved in perceived partner responsiveness to the self, we further propose, are central to creating intimacy and closeness, which we define for present purposes as a state that results from the operation of these processes. That is, the belief that one participates in an intimate close relationship arises from processes of interaction during which, or as a result of which, partners feel mutually responsive to each other's important goals, needs, dispositions, and values. Perceived partner responsiveness, in other words, contributes to the development of intimacy in a close relationship. This definition does not equate perceived partner responsiveness with intimacy or closeness; rather we see this process as one path (albeit a key one) by which people become intimate or close.[2]

The chapter begins with a review of evidence from diverse phenomena, ideas, and theoretical principles, each of which speaks to the relevance and impact of perceived partner responsiveness. Subsequently, we outline a theoretical model for describing this process and its various components. We then discuss the relative contributions of social construction and social reality as mechanisms underlying the perception of a partner's responsiveness to the self. Finally, we consider how perceived responsiveness, a construct usually examined in the context of intimate relationships, applies broadly across social networks.

REVIEW OF EXISTING CONSTRUCTS AND PRINCIPLES

The definition offered above is deliberately broad, encompassing diverse phenomena. For example, perceived partner responsiveness encompasses such constructs as reflected appraisal (believing that a partner esteems one's personal qualities), emotional rapport (feeling an emotional bond with others), and responsiveness to needs (believing that a partner will respond supportively to expressions of need). These diverse examples fit together, we suggest, as indications of a person's belief that central features of the self (personal qualities, emotions, needs, etc.) are recognized, valued, and behaviorally supported by the partner. By spanning a wide conceptual swath in this review, we hope to provide a compelling picture of the diverse forms that perceived partner responsiveness takes, and to illustrate its sundry manifestations in social interaction. Our review begins with studies of interpersonal processes, then moves to studies of social cognition and self-regulation, and concludes by examining dispositional (i.e., individual difference) research. We include both studies that examine actual processes of responsive interaction as well as research that focuses on one partner's perception of the other's behavior. This broad review provides a platform for the more integrated discussion that follows in the subsequent two sections.

Evidence From Interpersonal Processes

Consider first research examining perceived partner responsiveness from the perspective of interpersonal transactions, that is, in terms of social interactions likely to give rise to the perception that a partner understands, values, and responds supportively

---

[2] We do not equate intimacy and closeness. Space does not allow us to address this issue in this chapter. However, we see intimacy as one type of closeness, emphasizing validation and caring (Reis & Patrick, 1996). Other types of closeness include more behaviorally based forms of independence, in which partners influence each other's behavior (e.g., Berscheid, Snyder, & Omoto, 1989). Feeling close and behaving close represent independent forms of closeness (Aron, Aron, & Smollan, 1993).

to the self. Here we emphasize studies that examine interaction process directly, in most cases by incorporating both partners' perspective.

Many studies document the importance of factors like understanding and empathic accuracy for close relationships (see Ickes & Simpson, 1997, 2001, for reviews). Prototypical is Noller and Ruzzene's (1991) observation that "it is taken for granted that marital harmony is strongly related to effective communication between spouses, and that effective communication, to some optimal degree, involves spouses' understanding of each others' thoughts and feelings" (p. 204). Nevertheless, one partner's insights into the other's thoughts, feelings, and needs, when used to exploit or damage the other, are unlikely to engender perceived responsiveness. From a communications perspective, responsiveness has been defined in terms of the patterning and relevance of one person's verbal or nonverbal response to a partner's verbal or nonverbal expression (e.g., Davis, 1982). Responsive listening has been shown to characterize effective communication in several types of dyads, such as spouses, friends, and the doctor–patient relationship, and is thought by some to be central to the development of intimacy. Because critical or hostile comments often meet the definition of responsiveness, however, it is apparent that something more than a content-relevant, well-timed response is needed to foster perceived partner responsiveness to the self. That something is likely to involve a sense of supportiveness, caring, and valuation.

Marital interaction research highlights the impact of perceiving that a partner is responsive and supportive. For example, in some of the earliest observational studies of marital interaction, Gottman (1979) found that nondistressed couples exhibited mutual validation in their problem-focused communications to a greater extent than distressed couples did. Since then, numerous replications and variations on this basic finding have been published, all pointing to a basic principle: When discussing conflicts, happy spouses tend to listen openly and nondefensively to their partner's complaints and generally communicate understanding and empathy for the partner's point of view, whereas distressed spouses tend to reject, criticize, or ignore their partner's point of view. For this reason, most of the major marital interaction coding systems include codes for behaviors that indicate responsiveness and unresponsiveness. For example, the popular marital interaction coding system (MICS; Heyman, Weiss, & Eddy, 1995) has specific codes to index validation (agree, approve, accept responsibility, comply) and invalidation (disagree, disapprove, deny responsibility, excuse, and noncomply); the rapid couples interaction scoring systems (RCISS; Gottman, 1994) codes one spouse's response to the other's problem description for indications of responsive listening, understanding, and acceptance as opposed to distance and denial (e.g., facial responses, defensiveness, humor). It bears noting that research appears to show that perceived invalidation is more pernicious than perceived validation is salutary (although to be sure methodological limitations make this conclusion somewhat tenuous; Reis & Gable, 2003).

Reflecting such findings, most marital therapies incorporate strategies designed not merely to increase each partner's ability to respond supportively and constructively to the other's problem descriptions, but also to heighten each one's awareness of the other's efforts in this regard; in other words, to foster the perception that partners are attempting to be responsive to one's needs. For example, the concept of emotional acceptance is central to integrative behavioral couple therapy (IBCT; Jacobson, Christensen, Prince, Cordova, & Eldridge, 2000): Therapists attempt to create a context in which partners learn to accept in each other what cannot be changed, change what they can, and compassionately recognize the difference (paraphrasing the well-known "serenity prayer"). In IBCT, clear communication about needs and emotional acceptance is central to distress reduction; we would argue that this is because clear communication promotes feeling that one's important needs will be understood, accepted, and supported by partners. Emotionally focused couple therapy (Johnson & Greenberg, 1995) incorporates a similar premise.

Responsiveness to the self plays a pivotal role in another kind of close relationship, between parents and children. For example, a key proposition of attachment theory is that caregiver responsiveness to the child's expressions of distress and wish for comfort is essential to the development of secure internal models of self and other. Other theoretical accounts of the relationship between parent and child also stress the value of responsiveness, defined in terms of the parent's awareness of, and willingness to actively and supportively address, the child's needs, wants, and concerns (see Dix, 1991, for a review). Key to our conceptualization is the idea that responsive parenting goes beyond simple emotional warmth to entail thoughtful appraisals of the child's needs, goals, and abilities; supportive encouragement to realistic levels of the child's autonomous strivings and self-regulation; and translation of both of these into specific action plans (e.g., Dix, 1992; Gottman, Katz, & Hooven, 1997). Understanding emotions and regulating them constructively is fundamental to this process (Bell & Richard, 2000; Dix, 2000).

Interpersonally oriented researchers have devoted special attention to responsiveness in the affective domain. Because affect is central to the self, and because affective communication is deeply ingrained in human evolutionary heritage, affective signals provide some of the most important clues about another person's response to the self (Hatfield, Cacioppo, & Rapson, 1994). For example, Stern (1985) proposed that infants develop strong feelings of security and connection when caregivers match the timing, intensity, and patterning of their emotional displays, a process he termed *affective attunement.* Existing research supports the importance of this process in building the infant–caregiver relationship and in nurturing the infant's emerging sense of self (Reddy, Hay, Murray, & Trevarthen, 1997; Trevarthen, 1994). A somewhat similar process, emotional synchrony, plays a significant role in regulating adult social interaction. Tickle-Degnen and Rosenthal (1990) have argued that feelings of rapport follow from a combination of mutual attentiveness, nonverbal coordination, and affective positivity. (Affective positivity is needed because, although nonverbal coordination tends to be associated with couple satisfaction [e.g., Noller, 1984], reciprocated hostility and negative affect is common in distressed couple's interaction [Gottman, 1994].) *Emotional contagion* (the process of "catching" an interaction partner's emotions) and emotional understanding, both of which typify intimate relationships, are also associated with the synchronicity of emotional and other nonverbal expressions (Bernieri & Rosenthal, 1991; Hatfield et al., 1994; Levenson & Ruef, 1997). Some scholars have suggested that nonverbal signals convey more information about acceptance and responsiveness than verbal communications do (e.g., Mehrabian, 1972).

A special kind of interpersonal responsiveness, pertaining to needs, provides the central theoretical distinction between communal and exchange relationships (Clark & Mills, 1979; Mills & Clark, 1982). In communal relationships, partners feel responsible for one another's welfare, give benefits in response to the other's needs, and expect the other to respond to one's own needs. In contrast, in exchange relationships benefits are provided, received, and expected according to equity norms—for example, to repay past benefits or to obligate future benefits. Existing research shows that the process of attending to and responding to a partner's need underlies several phenomena; for example, the perceived availability of social support (discussed below); emotional responses to the success and failure of the help provided to a partner; the willingness to express emotions and needs to partners; and various mechanisms for maintaining martial satisfaction (see Clark, Fitness, & Brissette, 2001, for a review). Perceiving that a partner is responsive to one's needs is a cardinal process in determining which relationships will be most central to the self, reflecting the high value most people in Western culture ascribe to communal norms as a relationship ideal.

Current conceptualizations of social support point to a similar conclusion. Across different theoretical models and research programs, there is consistent evidence for the idea that the perceived availability of support (as distinguished from the actual receipt of support) most reliably predicts health and emotional well-being; that is, people who perceive higher levels of support to be available if needed from their social networks tend to be healthier and happier across diverse outcomes (see Stroebe & Stroebe, 1996, for a review). Furthermore, Cutrona (1996) has suggested that support availability is most beneficial when it is perceived to contribute or enhance resources specifically matched to the demands of a stressor—in other words, when available support helps one address pressing needs. Although perceived support availability is typically assessed multidimensionally (Wills & Shinar, 2000), emotional support is most relevant to our theoretical analysis—feeling aware of a partner's regard and sympathetic caring. For example, Feeney and Collins (2001, 2002) demonstrated that interactions in which one partner responded to the other's need for support with behaviors that communicated support and caring fostered feelings of security in a relationship and heightened beliefs about the availability of support.

In sum, although interpersonal process research has clearly implicated responsiveness in several behavioral domains as a key component of social interaction, much more research and theorizing is needed. A phenomenon like responsiveness is intrinsically difficult to study: By definition, it requires examining one partner's behavior as contingent on the other's. Nevertheless, as Kelley (1983) persuasively theorizes, such patterns of interconnected behaviors and responses are the essence of interaction and relationship. Better understanding of the process of responsiveness will by necessity advance our understanding of interaction within relationships.

Evidence From Social Cognition and Self-Regulation

In this section we review research that addresses interpersonal processes primarily from the perspective of motivated social cognition. Many such processes potentially fit under the conceptual umbrella of perceived responsiveness to the self. Each of the processes we discuss addresses mechanisms by which interpersonal feedback directly influences either the self-concept (Markus & Cross, 1990) or self-regulation and which in turn influence the development and maintenance of close relationships. By considering these somewhat diverse constructs together, we highlight a premise common to all of them: The impact of partner feedback on self-regulatory activity depends on whether that feedback is seen as fitting and supporting core elements of the self.

One well-known example is Swann's (1990) self-verification theory. Swann proposes that people desire and proactively pursue evaluations from close relationship partners that confirm existing self-conceptions, reinforcing those self-views and bolstering the seeming coherence of the social world. For example, Swann and colleagues have shown that people prefer to interact with others who confirm their self-views, even when those views are unflattering, and that marriages are experienced as more intimate when one spouse's perceptions of the other are concordant with the other's self-perceptions (e.g., Swann, De La Ronde, & Hixon, 1994). Central to self-verification theory is the goal of having one's core sense of self understood by relationship partners.

Murray and Holmes maintain that close relationships are enhanced by "positive illusions;" that is, by perceiving partners somewhat more favorably than objective circumstances would seem to warrant (Murray & Holmes, 2000). Such positive illusions predict increased relationship satisfaction and stability over time, presumably because such beliefs, and the interactions they engender, foster feelings of security and acceptance that buffer against the inherent vulnerabilities, disappointments, and conflicts of interest that closeness and commitment entail. Their research shows, among various manifestations of this basic principle, that persons with low self-esteem often underestimate their partners' regard and acceptance, a process that may instigate cycles of relationship deterioration; in contrast, the belief by middling and high self-esteem persons that their partners value them helps to facilitate beneficent interactions (Murray, Holmes, MacDonald, & Ellsworth, 1998). Another recent study showed that intimates tend to assume a greater degree of similarity with each other than actually exists, an assumption that enhances the sense of feeling understood by the partner and, correspondingly, relationship satisfaction (Murray, Holmes, Bellavia, Griffin, & Dolderman, 2002). Their research highlights the important issue of accuracy and inaccuracy in perceived partner appraisals, an issue to which we turn later in this chapter.

The *Michelangelo phenomenon* described by Drigotas, Rusbult, and their colleagues indicates that personal growth and couple well-being is enhanced when people believe that their partners view and treat them in a manner consistent with their ideal self (Drigotas, Rusbult, Wieselquist, & Whitton, 1999). These two processes, called perceived perceptual affirmation and perceived behavioral affirmation, respectively, implicate mechanisms by which partners are felt to be active participants in the process of goal pursuit and personal development. Deci and Ryan (1987) discuss a related process, called autonomy support, which they define as the provision of support for self-ascribed needs, values, and goals (Ryan & Solky, 1996). Perceived autonomy support is associated with various positive outcomes in health care, learning, and helping organizations. For example, Williams, Rodin, Ryan, Grolnick, and Deci (1998) found that perceived autonomy support by physicians predicted patient adherence with medication regimes. Although the concepts of affirmation and autonomy support are both distally rooted in a partner's actual response to the self, both models give proximal priority to the recipient's perception of the partner's support.

This latter proposition is reminiscent in certain key respects of the concept of validation, popularized in psychodynamically oriented theories of intimacy and closeness, such as Sullivan's (1953) interpersonal theory of the self. Sullivan theorized that intimacy was a process of mutual self-revelation, in which partners sought and expressed support for each other's personal attributes and world view. This collaboration, when successful, fosters relationship security and a mutual sense of worth. The general idea of validation has been incorporated into numerous social psychological theories; for example, social comparison theory, which posits that the desire for validation underlies selective affiliation and the preference for similar others as comparison targets. This is because similar others are more likely to endorse one's own values and attitudes (Goethals & Darley, 1977) and also because performance assessments are more likely to be validating when the other's level of ability is comparable to one's own (Miller, Turnbull, & McFarland, 1988). That validation represents a process more complex than simple praise is demonstrated in a series of experiments reported by Schimel, Arndt, Pyszczynski, and Greenberg (2001), which reveals that being liked for who one is intrinsically reduced defensiveness whereas being praised for one's achievements did not.

Validation figures prominently in the intimacy model advanced by Reis and Shaver (1988). They proposed that intimacy results when a partner's response to one's own self-disclosure is perceived to be understanding, validating, and caring. Thus, their model highlights several factors intrinsic to the current analysis of perceived partner responsiveness such as awareness and recognition by a partner of core aspects of the self, actual responses by a partner that signal this recognition, and some awareness of these responses by the self. Existing research shows that perceived responsiveness is central to intimacy, somewhat more so, in fact, than self-disclosure is (e.g., Laurenceau, Barrett, & Pietromonaco, 1998; Lin, 1992). Also, Reis and Patrick (1996) reported a pair of experiments in which high praise by an evaluating other who was misinformed about the target's true self actually undermined liking and the desire for further interaction. Rudich and Vallacher (1999) obtained similar results, although in their research low self-esteem persons were less discriminating in their preferences. Validation can also be provided by identity support—feedback from friends that affirms and enhances a desired identity (Schlenker & Britt, 1999).

Yet one further example of the impact of validating feedback is suggested by Steele's research on self-affirmation (summarized by Steele, 1988). Although not directly concerned with relationships, his model is readily generalized to the interpersonal realm. Steele describes a network of processes designed to maintain:

> . . . a phenomenal experience of the self—self-conceptions and images—as adaptively and morally adequate, that is, as competent, good, coherent, unitary, stable, capable of free choice, capable of controlling important outcomes, and so on. I view these self-affirmation processes as being activated by information that threatens the perceived adequacy or integrity of the self and as running their course until this perception is restored, through explanation, rationalization, and/or action. (Steele, 1988, p. 262)

Of course, these threats and restorations often occur in interaction with relationship partners, and are likely to impair and foster, respectively, the security and stability of close relationships. In the next section of this chapter we discuss several examples of this process.

In sum, these and many other theories and research programs not discussed indicate that feedback from relationship partners is central to developing, maintaining, and enhancing a coherent, stable, and valued self-conception. The familiarity of this conclusion, which is axiomatic in longstanding models of the interpersonal self and of motivated social cognition (e.g., Fiske & Taylor, 1991; Markus & Cross, 1990), illustrates the pervasiveness of the general construct we describe—perceived partner responsiveness to the self—across many, if not most, models of interpersonal feedback in self-regulation.

Evidence From Personality Processes

This section reviews research on personality processes relating to stable individual differences in the tendency to perceive others as more or less responsive to the self, as well as research linking these individual differences to interpersonal functioning.

Among the many theories of personality development, none emphasizes feedback from others more than symbolic interactionism does: One learns about oneself, in this view, by reflecting on appraisals provided by other persons, especially significant others (e.g., Mead, 1934). Although the original theorizing emphasized the link between self-perception and actual interpersonal feedback, an influential review by Shrauger and Schoeneman (1979) concluded that self-perception was more clearly related to the individual's perceptions of how others viewed the self. Research in the symbolic interactionist tradition generally has not addressed the supportive aspects of responsiveness.

Internalized representations of others, and more particularly of their responsiveness to the core self, are a staple of psychoanalytic theories of personality development. For example, most object relations theories emphasize that mental models of others (called *object representations*) are central to the development of self-representations in childhood and profoundly influence later interpersonal functioning (Baldwin, 1992; Westen, 1991). Prominent in object relations theorizing is the ability of parents and other caregivers to accurately assess and respond to the child's needs (as distinguished from the caregiver's own needs), thereby facilitating the development of coherent mental models that neither overvalue nor undervalue the self or the other, and that allow the individual to feel secure enough to become invested in close relationships.

Presumably, this occurs because experience-based object representations allow the individual both to trust that others will respond empathically and appropriately to important personal needs, and to feel safe in providing such support to partners. Sullivan (1953), as discussed earlier, combined these constructs with insights from symbolic interactionism, theorizing that shared understanding and validation are central to the development of all types of close relationships across the lifespan.

Arguably no psychoanalytic theory emphasizes caregiver responsiveness more than attachment theory does. Central to Bowlby's (1969/1982) original theorizing was the idea that caregiver responses to the child's expressions of distress and wishes for closeness and comfort play a predominant role in shaping the child's *internal working model* of self-in-relation-to-others that guides affect, cognition, and behavior in close relationships "from the cradle to the grave" (Bowlby, 1979, p. 129). Extensive evidence supports Bowlby's proposition (see Belsky, 1999, for a review), although to be sure debate continues about the extent to which these effects should be attributed to caregiver behavior, temperament, or motivated cognition (Vaughn & Bost, 1999). The pioneering studies of Ainsworth and her colleagues (Ainsworth, Blehar, Waters, & Wall, 1978) categorized attachment relationships in large part according to responsiveness: An avoidant relationship is said to result when caregivers consistently rebuff or otherwise ignore the child's expressions of distress and need whereas an anxious-ambivalent relationship ensues when caregivers are inconsistently unavailable or intrusive (reflecting concern about their own rather than the child's needs). Secure relationships are typified by the caregiver's appropriately comforting responses to the child's expressions of distress, accompanied by support of exploration and autonomy when the child is not distressed.

These categories basic to infant–caregiver attachment map well onto adult romantic relationships, as a burgeoning literature demonstrates. Adults with an avoidant attachment style tend to see romantic partners as distant and cold, and feel uncomfortable relying on them; anxious–ambivalent individuals are preoccupied with worry about their partner's trustworthiness and the possibility of abandonment; and secure individuals tend to feel confident about their partner's dependability and regard. These interpersonal differences may be understood in dispositional terms as chronically accessible expectations about the availability and responsiveness of relationship partners to one's needs (Baldwin, 1992; Collins, 1996). Although these prototypes are thought to be rooted in early relationships, adult experiences commonly reinforce existing beliefs through several mechanisms, one of which involves behavior confirmation: Expectations and other self-regulatory processes channel interaction in a manner that evokes behaviors by self and partner that confirm existing expectations (Snyder & Stukas, 1999). Thus, although chronic expectations about the availability and responsiveness of close relationship partners may be grounded in early relationships, subsequent relationships also play an important role in maintaining those beliefs.

One construct that illustrates the self-fulfilling nature of expectancies about a partner's responsiveness is rejection sensitivity, which refers to the tendency to anxiously expect, readily perceive, and behaviorally and emotionally overreact to the possibility of rejection by relationship partners (Downey & Feldman, 1996; Levy, Ayduk, & Downey, 2001). Rejection sensitivity is assessed by asking participants to report their concerns and expectations about a series of interpersonal requests, ranging from instrumental assistance (e.g., "extra money to cover living expenses") to emotional needs (e.g., "ask your boyfriend or girlfriend if he or she really loves you"). Individuals high in rejection sensitivity tend to perceive their partners as unsupportive and rejecting, an expectation that may be confirmed by hostile behaviors elicited from the partner (in the manner of a self-fulfilling prophecy) as reactions to the rejection-sensitive person's provocations (Downey, Freitas, Michaelis, & Khouri,

1998). In other words, anticipating that a partner will be unresponsive may evoke self-protective behavior that begets a reaction likely to confirm the anticipated lack of support. This cycle contributes to the deterioration of relationships with family members, peers, and romantic partners (Levy et al., 2001).

In a related vein, low self-esteem has been characterized as a deficiency in perceived acceptance by others. For example, Leary and Baumeister (2000) define self-esteem as a feedback system designed to monitor, gauge, and regulate perceived inclusion and acceptance: Self-esteem denotes, " . . . the sense that other people regard their relationships with the individual as valuable, important, and close" (pp. 11–12). Consistent with this definition, and compared to persons high in self-esteem, persons with low self-esteem tend to believe that others value them less and to react with stronger emotions to interpersonal threats (e.g., Leary, Haupt, Strausser, & Chokel, 1998; Murray et al., 1998). Perceived inclusion reflects several important functions of relationships, one of which is to ensure that others will be available as a resource for meeting one's needs.

Finally, the tendency to seek from others reassurance of personal worth has been implicated in the maintenance of depressed affect and clinical depression (Joiner, Metalsky, Katz, & Beach, 1999). One such theory, Coyne's (1976) interpersonal model of depression, proposes that depressed individuals seek reassurance about personal worthiness and caring, feedback that partners often strive to provide, at least initially. Because depressed persons tend to discount such reassurance, however, and because the symptoms of depressed affect often do not abate following reassurance, partners may become frustrated and rejecting over time, thereby confirming the depressed person's impaired sense of interpersonal worth and anticipated support. In other words, perceptions of partners' unwillingness or inability to fulfill the pressing desire for reassurance are prototypical of depressed persons' interpersonal schemas. Although the depressed person's portrayal of his or her social environment may be valid, as Segrin and Abramson (1994) conclude in a comprehensive review, it fails to acknowledge the extent to which one's own behavior may elicit this response. Consistent with the self-esteem research discussed above, these tendencies are most pronounced among high validation seekers, who tend to "see their basic worth, competence, or likability as being 'on the line' when faced with challenging or difficult situations" (Dykman, 1998, p. 143).

In conclusion, many theories of personality emphasize the impact of early relationships on interaction in later life, drawing on the mediating mechanism of chronic expectations about others' responsiveness. This principle need not imply a static view of perceived partner responsiveness, in which perceptions are essentially "frozen" in place: There is clear evidence that later social interactions contribute to the ongoing reinforcement and potential revision of mental models of perceived partner responsiveness. In the next section, we discuss this latter perspective.

PERCEIVED PARTNER RESPONSIVENESS: SOCIAL CONSTRUCTION OR SOCIAL REALITY?

Over the past decade, research on responsiveness to the self has raised some intriguing and important questions about whether *actual*, "objective" responsiveness and support by others is central to well-being, or instead, whether it is largely *perceptions* of responsiveness and support that are most crucial to adjustment. This distinction has gained prominence in recent years, in the wake of research on motivated construal and the social construction of reality in close relationships (e.g., Ickes & Simpson, 1997; Murray, 1999). In this section, we provide a brief overview of this debate because the lessons learned seem important to our model of perceived partner responsiveness. Much of our discussion focuses on social support research because this area has dealt most directly with this issue. Further, as we argued earlier, behavior communicating positive regard and sympathetic caring quite closely resembles our definition of perceived responsiveness (e.g., Feeney & Collins, 2001; 2002). We believe that these processes apply generally across intimate relationships.

Evidence for Social Construction

As mentioned earlier, by the early 1990s it was well-established that perceptions of social support availability predicted better adjustment to stressful events (e.g., Cohen, 1992). Much of this research relied on subjective reports of support availability without direct evidence that support had been provided, or for that matter, that a partner was willing to provide it, if needed. Most theories implicitly assumed that such perceptions reflected the reality of social experiences. However, other studies suggested that provider and recipient reports may be only moderately correlated (e.g., Abbey, Andrews, & Halman, 1995; Bolger, Zuckerman, & Kessler, 2000; Coriell & Cohen, 1995). Indeed, one influential review concluded that subjective perceptions of support are more strongly tied to personality than to social experience (Dunkel-Schetter & Bennett, 1990). Other researchers have expanded on this social construction theme by demonstrating that, most generally, support perceptions are a function of existing beliefs, schemas, and expectations (e.g., Lakey & Cassady, 1990; Pierce, Sarason, & Sarason, 1992).

Perhaps not surprisingly, attachment style dimensions have been a major focus in discussions of the influence of personality factors, and starting with the pioneering work of Sarason, Pierce, and Sarason (1990), several studies now show that working models of attachment shape social construals of support (see Cutrona, 1996, for a review). The link between perceived support and attachment beliefs seems natural. The avoidance (or, in Bartholomew and Horowitz's, 1991, terms, model of other) dimension of attachment reflects a belief or expectation that others typically will be (or not be) available and responsive in times of need. The anxiety (or model of self) dimension of attachment reflects an expectation that others will (or will not) respond to one's own needs, in particular because they do (or do not) value and care for oneself.

Such generalized expectations about the world as benign and supportive and the self as worthy of acceptance and caring seem likely to color beliefs about the potential availability of support resources. That is, at times perceived support may largely reflect a sense of "felt security" that if help were needed, attachment figures "would be there" for the person. However, personality factors also influence judgments of responsiveness in actual interactions with specific people, consistent with the extensive evidence that social perception is guided by relational schemas (Laurenceau, Rivera, Schaffer, & Pietromonaco, chap. 5, this volume; see Baldwin, 1992, for a review).

In support of these propositions, Murray, Holmes, and Griffin's (2000) findings for self-esteem essentially paralleled their results for the anxiety or "self" dimension. That is, people with low self-esteem in close dating and married relationships seriously underestimated their partners' regard for them (and thus their potential support) and reacted to these (unwarranted) insecurities by self-protectively distancing themselves from their partners. One might have thought that expectations in specific, well-established close relationships such as these would be more accurately attuned to the realities of potential support, but that was not the case. Apparently, a general sense of unworthiness was projected onto their partners, the invalidity of these *naïve realism* assumptions notwithstanding. Murray et al. (2002), using daily diary methods with married couples, have shown that such general conclusions about a partner's lack of caring also contaminate perceptions of acceptance and negative evaluations in specific everyday interactions. Low self-esteem individuals were more likely to interpret a partner's negative but ambiguous behavior in personal ways, seeing it as an example of a lack of support and validation. This finding is similar to those of Downey

et al. (1998), discussed earlier, which showed that chronically rejection sensitive individuals were more likely to anxiously expect, readily perceive, and negatively react
to signs of a partner's less-than-positive reaction to the self.

What are we to make of such findings? Demonstrating that personality and chronic
expectations contribute an important component to perceived social support through
social construction processes does not mean that "reality" influences are inconsequen-
tial. There is also good evidence of these latter influences. For example, Lakey, McCabe,
Fisicaro, and Drew (1996) used round-robin generalizability methods to study the role
played by both members of a dyad on perceived support. They found that perceiver–
supporter *interaction effects* played the largest role in determining perceived support,
followed by supporter characteristics, and then by perceiver biases. An interaction
effect implies that the unique pairing of perceiver and supporter characteristics determines perceived support. Cook (2000) used Kenny's social relations model (Kenny &
La Voie, 1984) to identify similar influences on perceived attachment security in a family context. That is, some people may be insecure no matter with whom in the family
they interact, as attachment theory implies. Alternatively, family members may all feel
more secure around a particular support provider, such as the mother, which is evidence for an interpersonal "reality" effect on perceptions of responsiveness. Cook also
found that felt security depended on the particular qualities of specific within-family
relationships. Some caution is warranted in interpreting the latter relationship or interaction term findings in Cook's (see also Lakey et al., 1996) study because the error
term is included in the relationship-variance estimate and will thus inflate its value.

Nonetheless, the overall pattern of findings is reasonably persuasive in suggesting
that dyadic or relationship-specific effects, which reflect the particular "chemistry" of
two people, may be significant, as are the personal qualities of potential supporters.
In this regard, Trobst (2000) used circumplex methods to categorize different types of
support transactions and to link them to the supporter's personality (again, evidence
of a reality effect). She showed that certain supporters are more capable of providing
love and acceptance (the *communion* dimension); others are more inclined to grant
status and reinforcing competence (the *agency* dimension). Trobst's work underscores
the fact that social support, and responsiveness to needs more generally, may take
diverse forms. Each of the different "media" (Foa & Foa, 1974) through which support
may be communicated have interpersonal meanings that depend on the recipient's
attributions. For example, Trobst notes that in early work on support, Cobb (1976)
suggested that the key is "information leading the subject to believe that he is cared
for and esteemed" (p. 300), parallel to the circumplex's primary dimensions of granting
love and status in interpersonal exchanges. These distinctions remind us of Reis and
Shaver's (1988) intimacy model: Intimacy and closeness depend on the extent to which
the communication process is seen by the discloser (or support seeker) as indicating
understanding, validation, and caring by the partner.

The complexity of this process suggests that support recipients face the difficult and
often vexing task of identifying and distinguishing valid indications of support from
"noise" in the interaction process (Bernieri, Gillis, Davis, & Grahe, 1996). A further
complication is that a provider's well-intentioned efforts at support may not meet
the target's particular needs, resulting in "miscarried" support (Coyne, Wortman,
& Lehman, 1988). In other words, there is much room for subjective interpretation in
process of receiving social support, allowing personality and other relational schemas
to color construals of responsiveness to needs.

Does Actual Support Matter?

Given the potential for slippage, it is not surprising that some commentators have
questioned the value of actual support. For example, Bolger, Zuckerman, and Kessler

(2000) noted the weak connection between perceived and actual support and suggested that the realization of having received support may have deleterious self-esteem costs because it challenges a recipient's sense of competence in valued domains. (Bolger et al., 2000, note that this effect is independent of negative effects attributable to the substantial stress that people who receive support often experience.) In a study of support transactions among persons preparing for bar admission exams, they found that "invisible" support—support about which recipients were unaware—was successful in alleviating anxiety, whereas support visible to recipients was actually associated with increased anxiety.

If the support process is considered in signal detection terms (Gable, Reis, & Downey, 2003), *misses* involve invisible support where support is provided but not seen, *hits* involve actual support that is detected, and *false alarms* describe the perception of support (such as, perhaps, by optimistic or securely attached persons) when it was not actually provided. We surmise that misses may not always be beneficial, as in the Bolger et al. (2000) study. For instance, in a daily diary study, Clark (2002) found that acts viewed by donors as important and helpful were often not reported as support, perhaps because donors felt that they were unimportant or unhelpful. Moreover, research has not yet identified the conditions that dictate when support is best kept outside of the recipient's awareness (such as, perhaps, involving ongoing stressors or self-esteem threat). A further issue is the distinction between the effects of support on the recipient's affective state as opposed to the relationship. Gable et al. (2003) found that although support hits did not improve the recipient's mood, they did increase positive feelings about the relationship with the donor.

One way or another, the degree to which support perceptions contain a kernel of truth poses a key question that must be addressed. We see compelling evidence consistent with a significant role for the reality of received support, as reviewed above. Moreover, other studies that have explored the perspectives of both partners have reached similar conclusions. For example, Murray et al. (1996) found that partner's "positive illusions" were grounded in reality, in the sense that they exaggerated actual characteristics (as reported both by the partners themselves and by other friends). Ickes and Simpson's (1997) review of the literature on empathic accuracy and mutual understanding concluded that, although certain relationship-threatening conditions may promote defensive inaccuracy, in general people are motivated by accuracy concerns and valid perceptions of partners' intentions and goals are the norm in successful relationships. Direct evidence from further studies (e.g., Cutrona, Hessling, & Suhr, 1997) also indicates that support perceptions often contain an important kernel of truth.

Perhaps the clearest evidence documenting the reality of support comes from observational studies of actual support transactions. For example, Simpson, Rholes, and Nelligan (1992) found that perceptions by women exposed to an anxiety-provoking stressor of their dating partners' responses were associated with judges' ratings of the men's behavior (as well as with the women's attachment style). Similarly, Collins and Feeney (2000) coded videotaped laboratory discussions of a personal problem between support seekers and their dating partners. Their results showed clearly that support perceptions can be traced to specific behavioral exchanges and are not pure social constructions.[3] In general, these transactions reflected the communal concerns of caregivers seeking to be responsive to their partners' needs (Clark & Mills, 1993); for example, participants who found their problem most stressful received the most

---

[3] These results are correlational and one must be concerned with the possibility of third variable influences (such as personality styles). However, such alternatives would require that something about an actor's personality led to perceiving support, *and* in the short lab session, also induced supportive behavior by the partner in specific transactions that were detectable by the independent observer–judges.

support. Furthermore, support seekers felt more supported when their partners' behavior was rated by judges as offering more instrumental and emotional support, showing clearer signs of responsiveness (e.g., active listening and communicating understanding) and engaging in less negative support (e.g., blaming, dismissing, and escaping). Caregiver reports of the support provided also were correlated with perceived support. Triangulation among the perspectives of recipient, donor, and outside observer is useful because it obviates the issue of whether intimate partners have private, idiosyncratic ways of communicating support derived from a history of repeated interactions, as well as possible confounding by the partner's global perceptions (whether positive or negative) of the overall quality of their relationship.

In addition to providing evidence for the importance of actual support, Collins and Feeney (2000) also reported findings consistent with the perceptual bias perspective. Individuals who were more satisfied with their relationship and who had more trust in their partners' caring rated their partners' (real) support even more favorably than did observers or even the partners themselves. These results provide the first evidence of positive illusions in the context of actual dyadic interaction. They also demonstrate that relationship-specific working models or expectations must be considered as influences on social construction quite apart from generalized expectations such as attachment styles or chronic personality factors (Holmes, 2000).

In sum, if nothing else, it seems apparent that the field has begun to apply sophisticated theories and methods to this important question. Even at this early stage, it seems safe to conclude that both reality and social construction matter—that is, that reports of social support are likely to possess both a kernel of truth and a shell of motivated elaboration. Thus, we see the field ready to move forward to the next level of investigation, which is to determine how these elements combine in particular individuals, interactions, relationships, and situations. Understanding these combinations seems likely to implicate processes that are more complex than "one or the other," involving, for example, dynamic associations among dispositional factors, relationship-specific schemas, interaction qualities, and the situational context in which those interactions take place.

THE STRUCTURE OF SOCIAL NETWORKS AND PERCEIVED PARTNER RESPONSIVENESS

In the preceding sections of this chapter, we have repeatedly noted that propositions about the importance of responsiveness to the self for individual well-being and for relationship intimacy and closeness pervade the literature. We have also pointed out consensus about the importance of individual differences in expectations about other's responsiveness. At this point, it is reasonable to pose two questions: Exactly what do we expect our partners to be responsive to? And, whom do we expect to be responsive to us? The answers to these two seemingly distinct questions are closely tied to each other because the nature of expected responsiveness depends upon who the partner is and the niche in our social network that the partner fills.

Imagine trying to answer the first question without specifying who the partner is. It can be answered only in a general way. As stated earlier, people want their partners to be responsive to the self—that is, to whichever qualities, characteristics, and drives are most central to their core sense of self. Broadly speaking, such responsiveness should involve recognition and acceptance of just who (or what) the self (or the ideal self) is and it should also help maintain, enhance, or repair the self's well-being. Beyond this generalization, however, we cannot describe which actual behaviors would entail responsiveness because the appropriately responsive acts are predicated upon the existing relationship. What type of relationship do we have or desire with this person?

Do we feel that he or she should be responsible for our needs? If so, which needs and to what extent?

This point may be illustrated with a few examples. Will a partner saying, "I love you," be perceived as responsive? Probably yes if the partner is one's spouse, but probably not if the partner is a casual acquaintance or coworker. Will a partner providing advice about formatting one's résumé be perceived as responsive? Probably yes if he or she is a supervisor or colleague at school or work, but probably not if he or she is our child or housecleaner. Will the provision of money for taking one to the airport be perceived as responsive? Yes if the recipient is a taxi driver, but probably not if the recipient is one's best friend (cf. Clark & Mills, 1979). The point is that the actions constituting responsiveness depend crucially on the nature of the relationship with the other (and sometimes, as we will argue shortly, on the wider social network in which this relationship is embedded).

Each of us encounters many other people in day-to-day activity: parents, siblings, friends, acquaintances, neighbors, teachers, shopkeepers, business associates, and so on. No one perceives or expects all these social contacts to be equally responsive to their needs, and moreover, most people do not expect all others to be responsive in the same way. For example, most people expect their mothers to be more responsive to their needs than their neighbors.

Clearly, then, expected responsiveness to the self varies not only according to individual differences (for example, in rejection sensitivity, attachment style, and communal orientation), but also according to social roles and according to social networks. Thus, successful responsiveness depends critically on recognizing the type of relationship that exists. An added consideration is that the impact of individual differences will also vary depending on the nature of the social environment. For example, it seems unlikely that individual difference variables make much difference in judgments about the responsiveness of store clerks or flight attendants. Most people will see prompt courteous service as expected and the lack of such service as unresponsive. However, such individual differences are likely to be important in serious dating relationships. Ideally, romantic partners are expected to be consistently responsive in many complex ways across diverse situations and at considerable costs in terms of time, effort, money, and psychological resources. Thus, the adequacy of their responsiveness is often ambiguous and open to the influence of individual differences in tendencies to view partners as responsive or not.

One line of research that has emphasized consideration of the structure of social networks to better understand perceptions of responsiveness to the self is Clark and Mills' (1979, 1993) work on communal relationships. Communal relationships are those relationships in which partners mutually provide non-contingent benefits in response to each other's needs. Although responsiveness to the self involves more dimensions than simply personal needs, it is useful to discuss the more limited domain of responsiveness to needs in communal relationships to illustrate more general points about the importance of perceived partner responsiveness to the self in intimacy and closeness.

Needs, Expectations, and Actual Responsiveness: Distinct but Related Constructs

In exploring social structure and perceived responsiveness to needs, it is important to distinguish the belief that a partner ought to respond to one's needs from the perception that a partner is actually responsive to one's needs. Although related, these entities differ meaningfully. For example, although most children believe that their parents ought to respond to their needs, they also often feel that their parents have not been sufficiently responsive. Judgments about actual responsiveness depend critically on expectations of the degree of obligation ascribed to that partner: The greater the perceived obligation, the more responsiveness that is expected. Thus, given identical acts, different partners may be perceived as differentially responsive or unresponsive. For example, a child may pay his mother little heed for preparing his or her lunch every day but may perceive a friend who provides a lunch treat as exceptionally responsive. This important link between expected obligations and perceptions of responsiveness will be familiar to those acquainted with expectancy violation processes, but is nonetheless often overlooked. Perhaps this is because most research on perceived partner responsiveness (and individual differences therein) focuses on relationships typically characterized by high normative expectations—that is, dating and family relationships.

Another important distinction concerns personal needs and a partner's perceived responsive to those needs. Needs vary over time and situations, of course, besides varying chronically from one person to another. For example, attachment theorists have pointed out that individuals high in attachment anxiety tend to report chronically greater neediness than secure and avoidant individuals do (Hazan & Shaver, 1994). As several studies reviewed earlier suggest, feeling needy is likely to influence perceptions of a partner's behavior (and perhaps more importantly, perceptions that partners have not been responsive). When all is going well, people tend not to feel needy (or at least those needs may not be salient), making it unlikely that partners will be seen as unresponsive (unless, perhaps, he or she commits a harmful act). Thus, for example, when thriving and happy, a college student is unlikely to perceive parents who call once a month as unresponsive; but if struggling academically and socially, the same student is likely to feel that even weekly calls are unresponsive to her needs. This logic suggests that needs must be at least somewhat salient to engender perceptions of partner unresponsiveness. It also suggests that chronically needy persons are likely to be chronically high in perceiving partners as unresponsive.

Need is not a precondition for the perception of partner responsiveness, however. Even in the absence of salient specific needs, partners can display responsiveness, for example through actions that indicate caring and attentiveness (e.g., seemingly random acts of kindness, affectionate cards or emails, or surprise gifts). Such messages, which signify that a partner cares about one's welfare and is taking proactive steps to promote it, are likely to enhance perceived partner responsiveness and relationship well-being.

It follows from the above that expectations about a partner's responsibility for one's welfare will interact with levels of self-experienced needs to influence perceived partner responsiveness. An elderly parent may believe that her adult child is responsible for addressing her needs in daily living whereas a neighborhood acquaintance has little responsibility. When doing well—for example, being active in volunteer and social activities while both the child and acquaintance, busy with their own lives, pay little attention—the parent is unlikely to perceive either her child or neighbor as unresponsive to her needs. Indeed, she probably thinks little about responsiveness. But if she falls ill and requires assistance, she is likely to perceive the child's lack of aid but not the acquaintance's as unresponsive. Chronic accessibility of concerns about responsiveness (e.g., predispositions such as rejection sensitivity or attachment anxiety) may alter the threshold and sensitivity of this process.

Expected Levels of Responsibility and Their Implications for Perceived Partner Responsiveness

Of course we do not expect all others to be responsible for our personal welfare (beyond, perhaps, minimal politeness and emergency assistance); that would be impractical, impossible, and unnecessary. Rather, expected levels of responsiveness vary

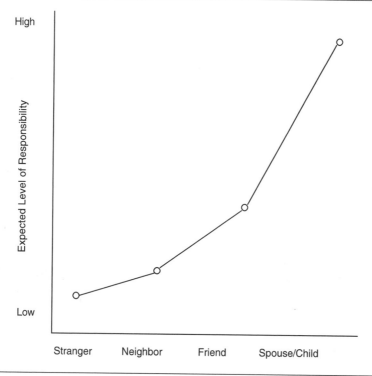

FIG. 12.1. Expected responsiveness varies as a function of role relationships.

from partner to partner within a social network. We expect little responsiveness from some partners, moderate levels from others, and an abundance from still others. Clark and Mills (1993; Mills & Clark, 1982; 1994) have referred to these differences as variations in the strength of communal relationships, or *communal strength*. In common language people often use the term *close* to refer to the same quality.

Clark and Mills (1993) suggest that relationships with strangers generally are weak in communal strength. Typically, we expect strangers and acquaintances to assume low levels of responsibility for our welfare, commensurate with acts of responsiveness that have negligible cost. Thus, when we ask a stranger for the time or directions, we expect an informative response, and if we experience a medical emergency, we expect strangers to summon assistance. Generally, most people expect higher levels of responsiveness from friends. Friends should listen to our problems, should remember our birthdays, and should offer a ride home when our car is in the shop. Most people expect even greater levels of responsiveness from others in certain very close relationships: parents, spouses, best friends, and children. For example, most children expect their parents to provide housing, food, clothing, transportation, entertainment, and comfort on a daily basis. The substantial costs of these provisions are so deeply ingrained in the definition of certain relationships that neither donor or recipient attends closely to the expectation (although they can become highly salient during conflictual interactions). Figure 12.1 depicts these variations within a social network.

We propose that relationships are experienced as satisfying when the other's responsiveness is perceived to meet or exceed one's expectations. That is, people are likely to deem partners as unresponsive when their willingness to exert effort and incur costs falls short of expected levels commensurate with the communal strength of the relationship.[4] On the other hand, partners who provide benefits beyond expectations are likely to be seen as extraordinarily responsive. Thus, the same behavior may be seen as unresponsive in the context of a very close relationship, appropriately responsive in the context of a moderately close relationship, and exceptionally responsive in a distant relationship. For example, imagine a woman celebrating her 75th birthday. Three small bouquets are delivered to her door, one from her only child, one from a casual friend, and one from her newly-moved-in neighbor. Her child is likely to be perceived as insufficiently responsive, the casual friend as appropriately attentive, and the neighbor as extraordinarily thoughtful.

That benefits and attention provided to a partner can exceed expectations raises another interesting issue. In certain cases, being seen as exceptionally responsive depends on the perceiver's desire to develop a stronger communal relationship than currently exists. In the above example we assumed that the birthday celebrant would be pleased to have a closer relationship with her new neighbor. However, sometimes the benefits and attention provided by another person may exceed both expectations and the desired level of communal relationship. For example, imagine a woman receiving a large bouquet of flowers from a suitor she wishes to be rid of. This behavior is unlikely to be perceived as responsive to the self; indeed, by our own definition of perceived partner responsiveness it cannot be so, because the suitor has not accurately assessed the woman's needs and wishes: His act is more likely responsive to his own needs and wishes.

Hierarchies of Communal Strength and Perceived Partner Responsiveness

As Reis et al. (2000) noted, dyadic relationships do not exist in a social vacuum. Our partners have relationships with others, for whose welfare they have varying degrees of responsibility. People are usually aware of these hierarchies and of their own approximate position in them. For example, we usually expect close friends to be responsive to our needs but not more responsive than to the needs of their spouses or children. Such tacit knowledge may influence perceived partner responsiveness to the self in several ways. For one, evidence of a partner's responsiveness in the face of conflicting responsibilities in other equally strong or stronger communal relationships (including responsibilities to the self) is diagnostic of a caring orientation, and, in attribution theory terms, is likely to augment the resulting attribution (Kelley, 1973). For example, foregoing long-awaited theater tickets to attend a friend's piano recital will make one seem especially responsive. Similarly, a child choosing to sit with one friend over another friend at lunch is likely to be seen as more responsive than the same act in the absence of a choice. Knowledge of communal strength hierarchies may also affect inferences of perceived unresponsiveness. Failing to attend to a partner's needs is typically excused (and will not result in low perceived responsiveness) in the face of conflicting responsibilities with another relationship consensually seen as higher in communal strength. For example, an aunt skipping her niece's wedding ordinarily would be interpreted as a serious lapse of responsiveness, but she is likely to be forgiven (and perhaps even admired) if she is at the hospital coping with her own child's critical illness.

Variations in the communal strength of an individual's many relationships may be represented within a polygon, organized according to the extent to which partners

---

[4] Throughout this chapter we have discussed individual differences and relationship context as determinants of expected levels of responsiveness. One additional determining factor, studied little to date, is cultural prescriptions, which may also lead individuals to expect higher or lower levels of responsiveness in particular relationships.

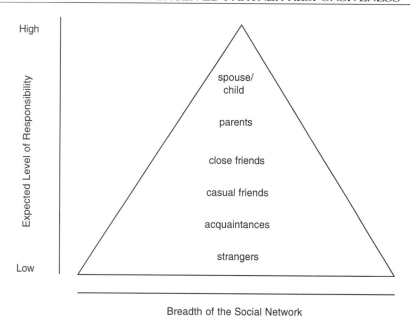

FIG. 12.2. Social network breadth and expected responsiveness.

are expected to respond to each other's needs. Relationships with very high levels of expected responsiveness are placed at the top, relationships with moderate levels of expected responsiveness are located in the middle, and those with low levels of expected responsiveness are situated at the bottom. Most people's social networks are likely to form a triangle, as depicted in Figure 12.2. Few partners (limited, perhaps, to children and spouses) appear at the top, several partners will appear a bit lower in the hierarchy (good friends and siblings, perhaps), more people below that (friends and good colleagues), many more near the bottom (casual acquaintances), and strangers, from whom minimal responsiveness is expected, at the very bottom. In other words, as relationships become more exclusive, greater levels of responsiveness to personal needs are expected.

Although a triangular model may characterize most people's social networks, we speculate that individuals likely differ in the height and width of their responsiveness triangles. Consider, for example, the implications of an avoidant attachment style, of rejection sensitivity, or of low self-esteem (all discussed earlier in this chapter). We would expect the height of such people's expected responsiveness triangles to be lower than those of secure, nonrejection sensitive, and high self-esteem individuals, respectively, indicating that the former tend to have fewer strong communal relationships in which high levels of responsiveness are expected. The width of their triangles also may be narrower, especially near the top of the triangle, because they may have relatively fewer friends from whom they expect moderate to high levels of responsiveness. Precisely how these and other individual differences in chronic tendencies to perceive others as more or less responsive to one's needs are reflected in relationships and interactions is an important empirical question.

An interesting complication may arise when interaction takes place in a group context. When all members of the group are relatively low in one another's hierarchies (e.g., strangers on a bus), no one person is likely to be singled out as particularly nonresponsive if the entire group fails to respond to one person's sudden need. But if the group includes individuals high in each other's responsiveness triangle (e.g., when close friends ride the bus together), because it is expected that a friend will respond to an emergency, even in the absence of relevant expertise, he or she is likely to be singled out as especially unresponsive (and more so than the others) should the entire group fail to intervene. In other words, although responsibility tends to diffuse among strangers or casual acquaintances in social groups, as has been shown in many studies of bystander intervention, it is less likely to diffuse when at least one member of a group is higher in the needy person's triangle.

A Caveat

The principles articulated above refer to perceived partner responsiveness within communal relationships, defined by Clark and Mills (1979, 1993) as those relationships in which people expect their partners to have a "special" (that is, over and above strangers) concern with their welfare. Indeed, people tend to be most concerned with partner responsiveness in close relationships, which is probably why researchers interested in these processes (and in their dispositional moderators) tend to focus their attention on close relationships. However, responsiveness may also be consequential in relationships governed by other norms. For example, in exchange relationships benefits are given with the expectation of comparable benefits being returned. Although thoughts about responsiveness seldom arise in exchange-governed interactions (e.g., when a shopper and storekeeper exchange money for merchandise), probably because the norms regulating these exchanges are well-practiced and rarely violated, perceptions of partner responsiveness may also vary within exchange relationships. A partner who violates an exchange norm is likely to be seen as unresponsive—for example, when one member of a car pool is consistently late when it is his turn to drive. Alternatively, partners who go to extraordinary lengths to adhere to exchange norms may be seen as especially responsive—for example, a homeowner who gives a bonus to a remodeler who exceeded her expectations may be perceived as unusually responsive (presumably because the bonus gives priority to the remodeler's need for money over her self-interest).

In short, although perceived partner responsiveness is ordinarily discussed and investigated in the context of communal relationships, the process is not limited to such relationships. We note, however, that our various points about expected responsiveness hierarchies apply to communal and not to exchange or other types of relationships, inasmuch as it is only in communal relationships that people expect partners to respond to their needs.

CONCLUSION

In this chapter we argue that perceived partner responsiveness to the self represents a cardinal process in closeness and intimacy. We began by discussing several variations in which this construct, or ideas closely related to it, appear in the literature. These variations spanned interpersonal, social cognitive, self-regulatory, and personality processes, suggesting a diverse range of relevance for this construct. We then examined the important question of whether perceived partner responsiveness is grounded in social construction or social reality, a question of considerable interest not only to researchers but also to therapists, counselors, and ordinary advice-givers seeking to make sense of certain social interactions. We concluded that both inputs matter. Finally, we presented a model of perceived partner responsiveness to needs, one important dimension of the self to which these ideas seem particularly pertinent. Of course, many other attributes are central to the self—motives, goals, ideals, traits, values, fears, and fantasies—and perceived partner responsiveness is important for them, too. This model will, we hope, prove useful for researchers seeking to study those other attributes.

Perceived partner responsiveness is a fitting topic for a handbook on closeness and intimacy for several reasons. For one, as discussed in the section on needs, responsiveness is not universally expected (or perhaps even desired) but rather is expected primarily in close relationships. For another, research on perceived partner responsiveness highlights the importance of conceptualizing closeness and intimacy as dyadic, and not individual, phenomena (Reis, Capobianco, & Tsai, 2002). As we have discussed in regard to perceived responsiveness, closeness and intimacy are not just about how each person feels about the other but also about how each perceives the other's feelings about the self. This simple yet far-reaching point has important implications for how we conceptualize and study closeness and intimacy. Minimally, it suggests that theoretical models and empirical methods solely adopting the perspective of a single individual are likely to be limited in the kinds of insights they are capable of generating. Something more complex is needed, and that something involves explicit recognition of the fundamental interdependence inherent in close relationships.

If indeed it is the case, as we argue, that perceived responsiveness to the self is a basic concept in the study of closeness and intimacy, then it might prove useful to begin to organize research, theory, and application around this concept. For example, the many specific exemplars illustrated in the review section of this chapter might be organized among themselves in a manner that reveals similarities, differences, and shared mediating mechanisms. Similarly, insights from one set of phenomena might be generalized to others—for example, our discussion about the relative role of social construction and social reality, or of the importance of expectations in providing a context for social judgment, might be extrapolated to design studies for other specific manifestations of perceived responsiveness. In many ways, the advantage of identifying core principles among related phenomena is similar to the advantage of a structural equation model over a table of bivariate correlations: The underlying coherence among multifaceted, multidimensional phenomena and processes is emphasized.

We began this chapter by noting that in their search for the particular, researchers often overlook the general (which is, to us, somewhat ironic; after all, by definition, generalities apply across a wider variety of settings and situations than particulars do). We do not recommend that researchers eschew ever-greater specialization and detail, but we do suggest that, from time to time, they might pointedly consider connections among seemingly diverse, but perhaps fundamentally linked, phenomena. Doing so seems essential to the critical task of identifying and understanding the conceptual infrastructure of close relationships.

ACKNOWLEDGMENTS

We thank both editors and Jean-Phillippe Laurenceau for their insightful and very helpful comments on an earlier version of this chapter.

REFERENCES

Abbey, A., Andrews, F., & Halman, L. (1995). Provision and receipt of social support and disregard: What is their impact on the marital life quality of infertile and fertile couples? *Journal of Personality and Social Psychology, 68,* 455–469.
Ainsworth, M. D. S., Blehar, M. C., Waters, E., & Wall, S. (1978). *Patterns of attachment: Assessed in the strange situation and at home.* Hillsdale, NJ: Lawrence Erlbaum Associates.

Aron, A., & Aron, E. N., & Smollan, D. (1992). Inclusion of other in the self scale and the structure of interpersonal closeness. *Journal of Personality and Social Psychology, 63*, 596–612.

Aron, A. & Westbay, L. (1996). Dimensions of the prototype of love. *Journal of Personality and Social Psychology, 70*, 535–551.

Baldwin, M. W. (1992). Relational schemas and the processing of social information. *Psychological Bulletin, 112*, 461–484.

Bartholomew, K., & Horowitz, L. M. (1991). Attachment styles among young adults: A test of a four-category model. *Journal of Personality and Social Psychology, 61*, 226–244.

Bell, D. C., & Richard, A. J. (2000). Caregiving: The forgotten element in attachment. *Psychological Inquiry, 11*, 69–83.

Belsky, J. (1999). Interactional and contextual determinants of attachment security. In J. Cassidy & P. R. Shaver, (Eds), *Handbook of attachment: Theory, research, and clinical applications* (pp. 249–264). New York: Guilford.

Bernieri, F., Gillis, J., Davis, J., & Grahe, J. (1996). Dyad rapport and the accuracy of its judgments across situations: A lens model analysis. *Journal of Personality and Social Psychology, 71*, 110–129.

Bernieri, F. J., & Rosenthal, R. (1991). Interpersonal coordination: Behavior matching and interactional synchrony. In R. S. Feldman & B. Rimé (Eds), *Fundamentals of nonverbal behavior: Studies in emotion and social interaction* (pp. 401–432). New York: Cambridge University Press.

Berscheid, E., Snyder, M., & Omoto, A. M. (1989b). The Relationship Closeness Inventory: Assessing the closeness of interpersonal relationships. *Journal of Personality and Social Psychology, 57*, 792–807.

Bloom, A. (1997). *Love Invents Us.* New York: Random House. Taken from p. 205.

Bolger, N., Zuckerman, A., & Kessler, R. (2000). Invisible support and adjustment to stress. *Journal of Personality and Social Psychology, 79*, 953–961.

Bowlby, J. (1979). *The making and breaking of affectional bonds.* London: Tavistock.

Bowlby, J. (1982). *Attachment and loss: Vol. 1. Attachment.* New York: Basic. (Original work published 1969).

Bradbury, T. N. (2002). Research on relationships as a prelude to action. *Journal of Social and Personal Relationships, 19*, 235–263.

Clark, M. S., Fitness, J., & Brissette, I. (2001). Understanding people's perceptions of relationships is crucial to understanding their emotional lives. In M. Hewstone & M. Brewer (Eds.), *Blackwell handbook of social psychology: Vol. 2. Interpersonal processes* (pp. 253–278). Oxford, England: Blackwell.

Clark, M. S., & Mills, J. (1979). Interpersonal attraction in exchange and communal relationships. *Journal of Personality and Social Psychology, 37*, 12–24.

Clark, M. S., & Mills, J. (1993). The difference between communal and exchange relationships: What it is and is not. *Personality and Social Psychology Bulletin, 19*, 684–691.

Cobb, S. (1976). Social support as a moderator of life stress. *Psychosomatic Medicine, 38*, 300–314.

Cohen, S. (1992). Stress, social support, and disorder. In H. O. Veiel & U. Baumann (Eds.), *The meaning and measurement of social support* (pp. 109–124). New York: Hemisphere.

Collins, N. L. (1996). Working models of attachment: Implications for explanation, emotion, and behavior. *Journal of Personality and Social Psychology, 71*, 810–832.

Coriell, M., & Cohen, S. (1995). Concordance in the face of a stressful event: When do members of a dyad agree that one person supported the other? *Journal of Personality and Social Psychology, 69*, 289–299.

Collins, N. L., & Feeney, B. C. (2000). A safe haven: An attachment theory perspective on support seeking and caregiving in intimate relationships. *Journal of Personality and Social Psychology, 78*, 1053–1073.

Collins, N. L., & Read, S. J. (1994). Cognitive representations of attachment: The content and function of working models. In K. Bartholomew & D. Perlman (Eds.), *Advances in personal relationships, Vol. 5* (pp. 53–90). London: Kingsley.

Cook, W. L. (2000). Understanding attachment security in family context. *Journal of Personality and Social Psychology, 78*, 285–294.

Coyne, J. C. (1976). Depression and the response of others. *Journal of Abnormal Psychology, 85*, 186–193.

Coyne, J., Wortman, C., & Lehman, D. (1988). The other side of support: Emotional overinvolvement and the miscarried helping. In B. H. Gottlieb (Ed.), *Marshaling social support* (pp. 305–330). Thousand Oaks, CA: Sage.

Cutrona, C. E. (1996). *Social support in couples: Marriage as a resource in times of stress.* Thousand Oaks, CA: Sage.

Cutrona, C., Hessling, R., & Suhr, J. (1997). The influence of husband and wife personality on marital social support interactions. *Personal Relationships, 4*, 379–393.

Davis, D. (1982). Determinants of responsiveness in dyadic interaction. In W. I. Ickes & E. S. Knowles (Eds.), *Personality, roles, and social behaviors* (pp. 85–139). New York: Springer-Verlag.

Deci, E. L., & Ryan, R. M. (1987). The support of autonomy and the control of behavior. *Journal of Personality and Social Psychology, 53*, 1024–1037.

Dix, T. (1991). The affective organization of parenting: Adaptive and maladaptative processes. *Psychological Bulletin, 110*, 3–25.

Dix, T. (1992). Parenting on behalf of the child: Empathic goals in the regulation of responsive parenting. In I. E. Sigel, A. V. McGillicuddy-DeLisi, et al. (Eds), *Parental belief systems: The psychological consequences for children* (2nd ed., pp. 319–346). Hillsdale, NJ: Lawrence Erlbaum Associates.

Dix, T. (2000). Understanding what motivates sensitive parenting. *Psychological Inquiry, 11*, 94–97.

Downey, G., & Feldman, S. I. (1996). Implications of rejection sensitivity for intimate relationships. *Journal of Personality and Social Psychology, 70*, 1327–1341.

Downey, G., Freitas, A. L., Michaelis, B., & Khouri, H. (1998). The self-fulfilling prophecy in close relationships: Rejection sensitivity and rejection by romantic partners. *Journal of Personality and Social Psychology, 75*, 545–560.

Drigotas, S. M., Rusbult, C. E., Wieselquist, J., & Whitton, S. W. (1999). Close partner as sculptor of the ideal self: Behavioral affirmation and the Michelangelo phenomenon. *Journal of Personality and Social Psychology, 77*, 293–323.

Dunkel-Schetter, C., & Bennett, T. (1990). Differentiating the cognitive and behavioral aspects of social support. In B.R. Sarason, I.G. Sarason, & G. Pierce (Eds.), *Social support: An interactional view* (pp. 267–296). New York: Wiley.

Dykman, B. M. (1998). Integrating cognitive and motivational factors in depression: Initial tests of a goal-orientation approach. *Journal of Personality and Social Psychology, 74*, 139–158.

Eliot, T. S. (1936). *Collected Poems*. New York: Harcourt Brace and World. Taken from p. 176.

Feeney, B. C., & Collins, N. L. (2001). Predictors of caregiving in adult intimate relationships: An attachment theoretical perspective. *Journal of Personality and Social Psychology, 80*, 972–994.

Feeney, B. C., & Collins, N. L. (2002, February). Caregiving from the perspective of self and partner. Paper presented at the 3rd Annual Social for Personality and Social Psychology Meeting, Savannah, Georgia.

Fehr, B. (1988). Prototype analysis of the concepts of love and commitment. *Journal of Personality and Social Psychology, 55*, 557–579.

Fehr, B., & Russell, J. A. (1991). The concept of love viewed from a prototype perspective. *Journal of Personality and Social Psychology, 60*, 425–438.

Fiske, S. T., & Taylor, S. E. (1991). *Social cognition*. New York: McGraw-Hill.

Foa, U. G., & Foa, E. B. (1974). *Social structures of the mind*. Springfield, IL: C. C. Thomas.

Gable, S. L., Reis, H. T., & Downey, G. (2003). He said, she said: A quasi-signal detection analysis of daily interactions between close relationship partners. *Psychological Science, 14*, 100–105.

Goethals, G. R., & Darley, J. (1977). Social comparison theory: An attributional perspective. In J. Suls & R. Miller (Eds.), *Social comparison processes: Theoretical and empirical perspectives* (pp. 259–278). Washington, D. C.: Hemisphere.

Gottman, J. M. (1979). *Marital interaction: Experimental investigations*. New York: Academic Press.

Gottman, J. M. (1994). *What predicts divorce? The realtionship between marital processes and marital outcomes*. Hillsdale, NJ: Lawrence Erlbaum Associates.

Gottman, J. M. (1998). Psychology and the study of marital processes. *Annual Review of Psychology, 49*, 169–197.

Gottman, J. M., Katz, L. F., & Hooven, C. (1997). *Meta-emotion: How families communicate emotionally*. Hillsdale, NJ: Lawrrence Erlbaum Associates.

Hatfield, E., Cacioppo, J. T., & Rapson, R. L. (1994). *Emotional contagion*. New York: Cambridge University Press.

Hazan, C., & Shaver, P. R. (1994). Attachment as an organizational framework for research on close relationships. *Psychological Inquiry, 5*, 68–79.

Heyman, R. E., Weiss, R. L., & Eddy, J. M. (1995). Marital interaction coding system: Revision and empirical evaluation. *Behavioral Research Therapy, 33*, 737–746.

Hinde, R. A. (1997). *Relationships: A dialectical perspective*. East Sussex, England: Psychology Press.

Holmes, J. G. (2000). Social relationships: The nature and function of relational schemas. *European Journal of Social Psychology, 30*, 447–496.

Holmes, J. G., & Rempel, J. K. (1989). Trust in close relationships. In C. Hendrick (Ed.), *Review of Personality and Social Psychology. Vol. 10* (pp. 187–219). Newbury Park, CA: Sage.

Ickes, W., & Simpson, J. A. (1997). Managing empathic accuracy in close relationships. In W. Ickes (Ed.), *Empathy accuracy* (pp. 218–260). New York: Guilford.

Ickes, W., & Simpson, J. A. (2001). Motivational aspects of empathic accuracy. In M. Hewstone & M. Brewer (Eds.), *Blackwell handbook of social psychology: Vol. 2. Interpersonal Processes* (pp. 229–249). Oxford, England: Blackwell.

Jacobson, N. S., Christensen, A., Prince, S. E., Cordova, J., & Eldridge, K. (2000). Integrative behavioral couple therapy: An acceptance-based, promising new treatment for couple discord. *Journal of Consulting and Clinical Psychology, 68*, 351–355.

Johnson, S. M., & Greenberg, L. S. (1995). The emotionally focused approach to problems in adult attachment. In N. S. Jacobson & A. E. Gurman (Eds.), *Clinical handbook of couple therapy* (pp. 121–141). New York: Guilford.

Joiner, T. E., Jr., Metalsky, G. I., Katz, J., & Beach, S. R. H. (1999). Depression and excessive reassurance-seeking. *Psychological Inquiry, 10*, 269–278.

Kelley, H. H. (1973). The process of causal attribution. *American Psychologist, 28*, 107–128.

Kelley, H. H. (1983). Analyzing close relationships. In H. H. Kelley, E. Berscheid, A. Christensen, J. H. Harvey, T. L. Huston, G. Levinger, et al. (Eds.), *Close Relationships* (pp. 20–67). New York: Freeman.

Kenny, D. A., & La Voie, L. (1984). The social relations model. In L. Berkowitz (Ed.), *Advances in Experimental Social Psychology, Vol. 18* (pp. 142–182). Orlando, FL: Academic Press.

Lakey, B., & Cassady, P. (1990). Cognitive processes in perceived social support. *Journal of Personality and Social Psychology, 59,* 337–343.

Lakey, B., McCabe, K., Fisicaro, S., & Drew, J. (1996). Environmental and personal determinants of support perceptions: Three generalizability studies. *Journal of Personality and Social Psychology, 70,* 1270–1280.

Laurenceau, J. P., Barrett, L. F., & Pietromonaco, P. (1998). Intimacy as an interpersonal process: The importance of self-disclosure, partner disclosure, and perceived partner responsiveness in interpersonal exchanges. *Journal of Personality and Social Psychology, 74,* 1238–1251.

Leary, M. R., & Baumeister, R. F. (2000). The nature and function of self-esteem: Sociometer theory. In M. P. Zanna (Ed.), *Advances in experimental social psychology, Vol. 32* (pp. 1–62). San Diego, CA: Academic Press.

Leary, M. R., Haupt, A. L., Strausser, K., & Chokel, J. T. (1998). Calibrating the sociometer: The relationship between interpersonal appraisals and the state self-esteem. *Journal of Personality and Social Psychology, 74,* 1290–1299.

Levenson, R. W., & Ruef, A. M. (1997). Physiological aspects of emotional knowledge and rapport. In W. J. Ickes (Ed.), *Empathic accuracy* (pp. 44–72). New York: Guilford.

Levy, S. R., Ayduk, O., & Downey, G. (2001). The role of rejection sensitivity in people's relationships with significant others and valued social groups. In M. R. Leary (Ed.), *Interpersonal rejection* (pp. 251–289). New York: Oxford University Press.

Lin, Y. C. (1992). *The construction of the sense of intimacy from everyday social interaction.* Unpublished doctoral dissertation, University of Rochester, Rochester, New York.

Markus, H. M., & Cross, S. (1990). The interpersonal self. In L. A. Pervin (Ed.), *Handbook of personality: Theory and research* (pp. 576–608). New York: Guilford.

Mead G. H. (1934). *Mind, self, and society.* Chicago: University of Chicago Press.

Mehrabian, A. (1972). *Nonverbal communication.* Chicago: Aldine-Atherton.

Mills, J., & Clark, M. S. (1982). Communal and exchange relationships. In L. Wheeler (Ed.), *Review of Personality and Social Psychology, Vol. 3* (pp. 121–144). Beverly Hills, CA: Sage.

Mills, J., & Clark, M. S. (1994). Communal and exchange relationships: Controversies and research. In R. Erber & R. Gilmour (Eds.), *Theoretical frameworks for personal relationships* (pp. 29–42). Hillsdale, NJ: Lawrence Erlbaum Associates.

Miller, D. T., Turnbull, W., & McFarland, C. (1988). Particularistic and universalistic evaluation in the social comparison process. *Journal of Personality and Social Psychology, 55,* 908–917.

Murray, S. L. (1999). The quest for conviction: Motivated cognition in romantic relationships. *Psychological Inquiry, 10,* 23–34.

Murray, S. L., & Holmes, J. G. (2000). Seeing the self through a partner's eyes: Why self-doubts turn into relationship insecurities. In A. Tesser, R. B. Felson, et al. (Eds.), *Psychological perspectives on self and identity* (pp. 173–197). Washington, D.C.: American Psychological Association.

Murray, S. L., Holmes, J. G., & Griffin, D. (1996). The benefits of positive illusions: Idealization and the construction of satisfaction in close relationships. *Journal of Personality and Social Psychology, 70,* 79–98.

Murray, S. L., Holmes, J. G., & Griffin, D. W. (2000). Self-esteem and the quest for felt security: How perceived regard regulates attachment processes. *Journal of Personality and Social Psychology, 78,* 478–498.

Murray, S. L., Holmes, J. G., Bellavia, G., Griffin, D. W., & Dolderman, D. (2002). Kindred spirits? The benefits of egocentrism in close relationships. *Journal of Personality and Social Psychology, 82,* 563–581.

Murray, S. L., Holmes, J. G., MacDonald, G., & Ellsworth, P. (1998). Through the looking glass darkly? When self-doubts turn into relationship insecurities. *Journal of Personality and Social Psychology, 75,* 1459–1480.

Noller, P. (1984). *Nonverbal communication and marital interaction.* Elmsford, NY: Pergamon.

Noller, P., & Ruzzene, M. (1991). Communication in marriage: The influence of affect and cognition. In G. J. O. Fletcher & F. D. Fincham (Eds.), *Cognition and close relationships* (pp. 203–234). Hillsdale, NJ: Lawrence Erlbaum Associates.

Pierce, G., Sarason, B. R., & Sarason, I. G. (1992). General and specific support expectations and stress as predictors of perceived supportiveness: An experimental study. *Journal of Personality and Social Psychology, 63,* 297–307.

Reddy, V., Hay, D., Murray, L., & Trevarthen, C. (1997). Communication in infancy: Mutual regulation of affect and attention. In G. Bremner, A. Slater, et al. (Eds.), *Infant development: Recent advances* (pp. 247–273). Hove, England: Psychology Press.

Reis, H. T., Capobianco, A., & Tsai, F. F. (2002). Finding the person in personal relationships. *Journal of Personality, 70,* 813–850.

Reis, H. T., Collins, W. A., & Berscheid, E. (2000). The relationship context of human behavior and development. *Psychological Bulletin, 126,* 844–872.

Reis, H. T., & Gable, S. L. (2003). Toward a positive psychology of relationships. In C. L. Keyes & J. Haidt (Eds.), *Flourishing: The positive person and the good life* (pp. 129–159). Washington, D.C.: American Psychological Association.

Reis, H. T., & Patrick, B. C. (1996). Attachment and intimacy: Component processes. In A. Kruglanski & E. T. Higgins (Eds.), *Social psychology: Handbook of basic principles* (pp. 523–563). New York: Guilford.

Reis, H. T., & Shaver, P. (1988). Intimacy as an interpersonal process. In S. Duck (Ed.), *Handbook of personal relationships* (pp. 367–389). Chichester, England: Wiley.

Rudich, E. A., & Vallacher, R. R. (1999). To belong or to self-enhance? Motivational bases for choosing interaction partners. *Personality and Social Psychology Bulletin, 25,* 1387–1404.

Ryan, R. M., & Solky, J. A. (1996). What is supportive about social support? On the psychological needs for autonomy and relatedness. In G. R. Pierce, B. R. Sarason, & I. G. Sarason (Eds.), *Handbook of social support and the family* (pp. 249–267). New York: Plenum Press.

Sarason,. B. R., Pierce, G., & Sarason, I. G. (1990). Social support: The sense of acceptance and the role of relationships. In B. R. Sarason, I. G. Sarason, & G. Pierce (Eds.), *Social support: An interactional view* (pp. 267–296). New York: Wiley.

Schimel, J., Arndt, J., Pyszczynski, T., & Greenberg, J. (2001). Being accepted for who we are: Evidence that social validation of the intrinsic self reduces general defensiveness. *Journal of Personality and Social Psychology, 80,* 35–52.

Schlenker, B. R., & Britt, T. W. (1999). Beneficial impression management: Strategically controlling information to help friends. *Journal of Personality and Social Psychology, 76,* 559–573.

Segrin, C., & Abramson, L. Y. (1994). Negative reactions to depressive behaviors: A communication theories analysis. *Journal of Abnormal Psychology, 103,* 655–668.

Shrauger, J. S., & Schoeneman, T. J. (1979). Symbolic interactionist view of self-concept: Through the looking glass darkly. *Psychological Bulletin, 86,* 549–573.

Simpson, J. A., Rholes, W. S., & Nelligan, J. (1992). Support-seeking and support-giving within couples within an anxiety provoking situation: The role of attachment styles. *Journal of Personality and Social Psychology, 62,* 434–446.

Snyder, M., & Stukas, A. A. (1999). Interpersonal processes: The interplay of cognitive, motivational, and behavioral activities in social interaction. *Annual Review of Psychology, 50,* 273–303.

Steele, C. M. (1988). The psychology of self-affirmation: Sustaining the integrity of the self. In L. Berkowitz (Ed.), *Advances in experimental social psychology, Vol. 21: Social psychological studies of the self: Perspectives and programs* (pp. 261–302). San Diego, CA: Academic Press.

Stern, D. N. (1985). *The interpersonal world of the infant.* New York: Basic Books.

Stroebe, W., & Stroebe, M. (1996). The social psychology of social support. In A. Kruglanski & E. T. Higgins (Eds.), *Social psychology: Handbook of basic principles* (pp. 597–621). New York: Guilford.

Sullivan, H. S. (1953). *The interpersonal theory of psychiatry.* New York: Norton.

Swann, W. B., Jr. (1990). To be adored or to be known: The interplay of self enhancement and self verification. In R. M. Sorrentino & E. T. Higgins (Eds.), *Motivation and cognition. Vol. 2.* (pp. 408–488). New York: Guilford Press.

Swann, W. B., Jr., De La Ronde, C., & Hixon, J. G. (1994). Authenticity and positivity strivings in marriage and courtship. *Journal of Personality and Social Psychology, 66,* 857–869.

Tickle-Degnen, L., & Rosenthal, R. (1990). The nature of rapport and its nonverbal correlates. *Psychological Inquiry, 1,* 285–293.

Trevarthen, C., & Aitken, K. J. (1994). Brain development, infant communication, and empathy disorders: Intrinsic factors in child mental health. *Development and Psychopathology, 6,* 597–633.

Trobst, K. K. (2000). An interpersonal conceptualization and quantification of social support transactions. *Personality and Social Psychology Bulletin, 26,* 971–986.

Vaughn, B. E., & Bost, K. K. (1999). Attachment and temperament: Redundant, independent, or interacting influences on interpersonal adaptation and personality development? In J. Cassidy & P. R. Shaver, (Eds.), *Handbook of attachment: Theory, research, and clinical applications* (pp. 198–225). New York: Guilford Press.

Westen, D. (1991). Social cognition and object relations. *Psychological Bulletin, 109,* 429–455.

Williams, G. C., Rodin, G. C., Ryan, R. M., Grolnick, W. S., & Deci, E. L. (1998). Autonomous regulation and long-term medication adherence in adult outpatients. *Health Psychology, 17,* 269–276.

Wills, T. A., & Shinar, O. (2000). Measuring perceived and received social support. In S. Cohen, L. Underwood, & B. Gottlieb (Eds.), *Social support measurement and intervention: A guide for health and social scientists* (pp. 86–135). New York: Oxford University Press.

IV

What Individual
Differences Play a Role in
Closeness and Intimacy?

13

The Relational Self-Construal and Closeness

Susan E. Cross and Jonathan S. Gore
Iowa State University

Close and intimate relationships are a much desired element of American society. Americans report that satisfying close relationships are necessary for happiness (Berscheid & Reis, 1998), and they spend considerable time, money, and energy seeking to increase their acceptance and love from others. Yet relationships seem to be increasingly problematic in American society. Divorce rates are high, more people than ever live alone, and levels of social connections and social support are declining (Myers, 1999, 2000).

What accounts for this problematic view of relationships? By extension, why is closeness and intimacy such a seemingly difficult and complex issue in American society? To answer these questions, we first must clarify our perspective on closeness and intimacy. Although definitions abound, and pinning down a concrete definition is difficult (and perhaps impossible), we adopt the viewpoint articulated by Reis and Patrick (1996; building on earlier work by Reis & Shaver, 1988) that intimacy is "an interactive process in which, as a result of a partner's response, individuals come to feel understood, validated, and cared for" (p. 536). According to the Reis and Patrick (1996) model of intimacy development, individuals share important self-relevant information, and their partners respond with understanding and caring. As Prager and Roberts (chap. 4, this volume) note, "Intimate relating is, at core, two selves knowing each other; this knowledge endures beyond the interaction and informs and deepens subsequent interactions between the partners" (p. 46). Thus, in close and intimate relationships, one is free to express the "real" self, one feels that the other knows and understands one's real self, and one seeks to know and understand the real self of the other. The construct of the self is integral to these definitions of closeness and intimacy, yet in many ways it is the self that makes relationships difficult and problematic for contemporary Americans. To understand the American view of relationships, one must first understand the American view of the self.

VIEWS OF THE SELF

The United States is one of the most individualistic societies in the world (Hofstede, 1991; Triandis, 1995), and individualism shapes many Americans' understanding of the self, particularly those from European-American backgrounds. The basis of individualism American style is the fundamental assumption that a person is a unique person, separate from others and social relationships, with inalienable rights and freedoms (Lukes, 1973). These beliefs are established in the religious and political foundations of the nation (e.g., the Bill of Rights and the American legal system), and are transmitted through cultural practices and norms. For example, childrearing practices emphasize the development and necessity of independence and autonomy (Rothbaum, Weisz, Pott, Miyake, & Morelli, 2000). Advertising and the media promote a cultural ideal of the person as unique, special, and required to choose his or her own path in life (Kim & Markus, 1999; see Cross & Gore, 2002, for a review). The cultural messages that one should do one's own thing, be one's own person, stand on one's own two feet, and follow one's own dream results in an understanding of the self as autonomous, freedom seeking, defined by own's unique assemblage of interests, pursuits, beliefs, and attitudes, and obligated to no one and nothing except by one's own choice.

Consequently, social-personality psychology theories assume a self that is autonomous, independent from others, unique, and fundamentally separate from others, which Markus and Kitayama (1991) termed the *independent self-construal*. This construction of the self includes beliefs that the person is defined by internal characteristics, abilities, preferences, choices, goals, and desires; these internal, stable attributes then direct behavior. Most research conducted by social-personality researchers has focused on the ways that motivation, emotion, cognition, behavior, and personal relationships support and maintain this independent view of the self. Behavior, goals, or relationships that threaten the self or do not express the "real" self (defined as independent and separate from other influences) are viewed as inauthentic and lacking in power to provide persistence or happiness (Sheldon & Elliott, 1999).

This view of the primacy of the individual and individual desires, needs, and interests may make close and intimate relationships problematic, however. As Bellah and his colleagues (1985) point out, "American cultural traditions define personality, achievement, and the purpose of human life in ways that leave the individual suspended in glorious, but terrifying, isolation" (p. 6). We would substitute "the self" for "personality" in Bellah et al.'s statement and suggest that it is the importance placed on independence, autonomy, and freedom from constraints that makes Americans wary of close relationships. Yet other research points out that belonging is a basic human need (Baumeister & Leary, 1995), and that relationships are central to Americans' perceptions of happiness and satisfaction (Myers, 1999). The culturally valued independent self-construal may lead people to frame commitment to close and intimate relationships as limiting one's freedom and threatening to the self. When the self is defined as autonomous, independent, bounded, and free of obligation or duty, the pursuit of and commitment to intimate relationships may be both desired and feared.

Other elements of American society, however, emphasize a different way of being a person and a different stance toward the self and relationships. African Americans, Hispanics, and Asian Americans have been described as less individualistic and more collective than European Americans (Allen, Dawson, & Brown, 1989; Marin & Triandis, 1985; McCombs, 1985). Similarly, women in American society tend to be less individualistic and more oriented toward the development and maintenance of close relationships than are men (Gilligan, 1982; Maccoby, 1990; see Cross & Madson, 1997, for a review). As a result of gendered socialization practices or other nondominant cultural influences, many people in the United States may define the self in terms of close relationships, resulting in what has been termed the *relational-interdependent self-construal* (Cross, Bacon, & Morris, 2000; we will use *relational self-construal* in the remainder of this chapter). For these persons, close relationships are self-defining; the self-space includes representations of close others as well as representations of one's own attributes, abilities, wishes, goals, and experiences. When representations of the self are activated, representations of close others will be engaged also. Given this self-construal, close relationships are essential for self-definition, self-expression, and self-enhancement. Individuals who have defined themselves in terms of close relationships will therefore tend to think and act in ways that develop, enhance, and maintain harmonious and close relationships with important others. In short, the relational self-construal is a higher order self-representation that directs and regulates lower order self-views and self-related processes (Cross, Morris, & Gore, 2002). Not only will this self-construal influence overt and intentional relationship-oriented processes (such as self-disclosure and responsiveness), but it will also shape the cognitive, emotional, and motivational processes that underlie relational behavior.

In this chapter we review the emerging research on the relational self-construal and its role in the development and maintenance of closeness and intimacy. The foundation of this work is the voluminous research that demonstrates the "executive function" of the self in cognition, emotion, motivation, and behavior (Baumeister, 1998). Although much of the existing research on the self assumed an independent self-construal, we expect the relational self-construal also to direct and guide cognition, emotion, motivation, and behavior. If the self is conceptualized as fundamentally motivated to develop and maintain close relationships, rather than fundamentally motivated to maintain autonomy and independence, then the self-related processes involved in close and intimate relationships may reflect this difference in orientation. We focus on individual differences in the relational self-construal in Western cultural contexts (primarily the United States). Members of collectivist cultures are also quite likely to articulate relational selves, but the exact nature and expression of these selves are likely shaped by culture-specific values and beliefs. We begin our review of this literature with an examination of the influence of the relational self-construal on processes that develop and nurture close and intimate relationships. First, however, we briefly describe the development of a measure of the relational self-construal.

MEASURING THE RELATIONAL SELF-CONSTRUAL

Although women in Western cultural contexts are more likely than men to develop a relational self-construal, there are also individual differences within the sexes on this dimension. To avoid using gender as a proxy for the relational self-construal, Cross and her colleagues developed a brief measure of this construct, the relational-interdependent self-construal scale (Cross, Bacon, & Morris, 2000). This measure taps explicit views of the self as defined by relationships with others, in contrast to other measures that assess collective, group-oriented aspects of the interdependent self-construal (e.g., Singelis, 1994), affective consequences of investment in close relationships (e.g., Kashima et al., 1995), or the desire for reciprocity and expectations of equity in close relationships (communal orientation scale; Clark, Ouellette, Powell, & Milberg, 1987). Sample items include the statements "when I think of myself, I often think of my close friends or family also" and "when I feel very close to someone, it often feels to me like that person is an important part of who I am."

The scale has good reliability ($\alpha = .85-.90$) and good stability over time (test–retest reliability over 2 months is .76). The scale correlates moderately positively with other measures of relatedness or communal orientation, and is uncorrelated with measures of independence or individualism. Women usually score higher on the scale than do men ($ds = -.17 - -.57$) (see Cross et al., 2000, for more psychometric data and evidence of the scale's validity). In summary, the relational-interdependent self-construal scale (RISC) taps a form of self-structure that is defined by relationships with close others. Now we turn to studies examining the association of the relational self-construal with the pursuit of closeness and intimacy with others.

THE SELF AND RELATIONSHIP DEVELOPMENT

If individuals have constructed a relational self-construal, then they should seek to develop and maintain close, intimate relationships. These relationships serve as the foundation for self-expression, self-verification, and self-enhancement. Thus, we expect that individuals with a highly relational self-construal will tend to be open to relationships and will engage in the self-disclosure and responsiveness that leads to closeness and intimacy. Although many researchers have tended to use the term *intimate relationships* to refer to romantic or sexual relationships, we have assumed instead that a friendship or family relationship can also by characterized as intimate, given the Reis and Patrick (1996) definition. Our studies focus on closeness in same-sex friendships.

Our initial investigations examined the early stages of relationship development. In one of our early studies (Study 3; Cross et al., 2000), unacquainted pairs of women engaged in a get-acquainted exercise that modeled the kinds of exchanges that people may experience in the beginning of a friendship (Aron, Melinat, Aron, Vallone, & Bator, 1997). Participants were asked to respond to a series of questions that elicited their thoughts, feelings, and experiences on a variety of topics. For example, one question asked, "given the choice of anyone in the world, whom would you want as a dinner guest?" Participants exchanged responses for fifteen minutes, and then separately evaluated their interaction and their partner's openness and responsiveness. As expected, participants with a highly relational self-construal were perceived by their partners as more self-disclosing and responsive than were others. Moreover, the partners of the highly relational participants were more satisfied with the interaction than were the partners of participants with a low relational self-construal. Thus, in this laboratory context, the highly relational participants were more likely to engage in the behaviors that promote close and satisfying relationships.

Is this also true in ongoing relationships? We sought to answer this question in two studies of new college roommates. We focused on new roommates for several reasons. First, we could select for roommate pairs who did not know each other before the semester started—they had been assigned to live together by the residence hall staff. Thus, they participated in this study during the early stages of their relationship, when they were still learning about each other and negotiating how to live together. Consequently, deliberate attempts to develop the relationship may have been more salient than among pairs of friends who had known each other for a very long time.

Second, the roommate relationship is generally unavoidable and somewhat difficult to leave. When other friendships become dissatisfying or fail to live up to one's expectations, they are usually fairly easy to end—the partners can simply quit seeing each other. In contrast, students are often forced by economic or other considerations (e.g. convenient location, a lease) to continue to live in a dissatisfying roommate situation at least until a semester break. Living with another person, especially in tight quarters, requires a high degree of coordination and cooperation. Roommates who share a bedroom, bathroom, or kitchen must communicate and agree on standards of cleanliness, schedules, how to share space, and many other issues. Although a student may come to realize that he or she will never be emotionally close to a new roommate, he or she may seek to have positive, harmonious interactions with the person so that the situation is as livable as possible. Thus, we expected that the highly relational participants in this study would desire a close and harmonious relationship with their new roommate, and would seek out opportunities to get to know the roommate better.

College students who were living with a same-sex roommate they had not known or lived with previously participated in this study. The participants completed the following measures at Time 1: The relational-interdependent self-construal scale, measures of emotional disclosure to the roommate and emotional disclosure from the roommate, perceived roommate responsiveness, and relationship quality (a composite of liking, perceived depth of the relationship, commitment, subjective closeness, and conflict). With permission from the participants, the same questionnaire was mailed to their roommates. Participants from the first phase then returned one month later to complete follow-up measures of emotional disclosure to and from the roommate, perceived roommate responsiveness, and relationship quality.

To assess emotional disclosure, participants and their roommates were asked to indicate the extent to which they talked with their roommate about, and the extent to which their roommate talked with them about, several topics (e.g., "what I like and dislike about myself"). To assess responsiveness, participants and their roommates rated the extent to which the other person was receptive and supportive (e.g., "my roommate seems sensitive to my feelings," "my roommate tries to see things from my point of view"). We operationalized relationship quality as the sum of the z scores of relationship strength (Murray, Holmes, & Griffin, 1996a), relationship commitment (Rusbult, 1983), relationship depth (Pierce, Sarason, & Sarason, 1991), liking for one's roommate (Stafford & Canary, 1991), and subjective closeness (Berscheid, Snyder, & Omoto, 1989), then subtracted the z score of conflict (Lepore, 1992). All measures of relationship quality were adapted to be specific to the roommate relationship. Roommate pairs ($N = 140$) provided complete data. We refer to the two persons as the *participant* and the *roommate*.

Using Reis and Shaver's (1988) intimacy process model as a framework, we examined a roommate intimacy model that illustrates the process through which highly relational people are able to create a social atmosphere that fosters closeness (Gore, Cross, & Morris, 2003). As shown in Figure 13.1, participants with a highly relational self-construal begin by disclosing information to their roommate that is emotional in nature (e.g. one's deepest feelings, one's worst fears). The association between self-construal and emotional disclosure remains even after controlling for initial perceptions of relationship quality. By disclosing this information, high relationals are establishing a sense of trust with their roommates. This disclosure is then recognized by the roommate (*R's perception of P's disclosure*, see Figure 13.1), and this perception leads to feelings of being understood, validated and cared for. Taken together, these feelings compose the construct termed *perceived responsiveness* (Reis & Patrick, 1996), which is a key element in the development of intimacy (Lin, 1992, reported by Reis & Patrick, 1996). Responsiveness has also been found to mediate the association between self-disclosure and closeness in a relationship (Laurenceau, Barrett, & Pietromonaco, 1998), as we found in this study of roommate intimacy (see Figure 13.1).

Further examination provided support that this process is ongoing. By including later assessments of participants' perceptions of their roommates' disclosure and responsiveness, and the participants' relationship quality and emotional disclosure (Time 2 was one month after the initial session), we were able to explore positive changes in these relationship variables as a result of ongoing communication. Starting near the left of Figure 13.1 (Time 1), when the roommate perceives the participant's disclosure as a sign of responsiveness, he or she should view the relationship as being of high quality. As a result, he or she emotionally discloses back to the participant.

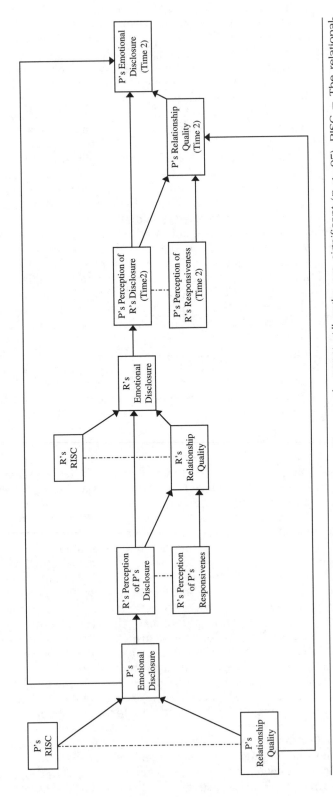

FIG. 13.1. The roommate model of intimacy maintenance (Gore et al., 2002). All paths are significant ($p < .05$). RISC = The relational-interdependent self-construal scale (Cross et al., 2000). Relationship quality = strength + commitment + depth + subjective closeness + liking – conflict. P = participant, R = roommate.

234

The roommate's self-construal also predicts his or her emotional disclosure after controlling for the level of perceived relationship quality. The participant will then perceive the roommate as "returning the favor" by disclosing and therefore showing trust. This leads the participant to perceive the roommate as responsive, contributing to increased levels of relationship quality. As with the roommate, positive changes in perceived relationship quality are then associated with positive changes in emotional disclosure. Thus, persons with highly relational self-construals are able to create a social atmosphere with their roommates that establishes trust by disclosing personal information. This not only influences the roommate's intimacy perceptions and behaviors, but also ultimately leads to increases in the participant's perception of relationship quality. It is unclear whether these increases in quality and disclosure continue or if they eventually plateau over time. What this model suggests, in accordance with Reis and Shaver (1988), is that the intimacy process is cyclical, particularly if an atmosphere of trust is developed, and that this intimate social atmosphere is pursued and nurtured by persons with a highly relational self-construal. For people with low relational self-construals, intimacy is still attainable but developing an intimate relationship with one's roommate may involve other behaviors, such as shared activities.

TAKING RESPONSIVENESS A STEP FURTHER: KNOWING AND UNDERSTANDING THE OTHER

Simply responding positively and supportively when a friend discloses important or sensitive information is not adequate for a long-term relationship. Consider the case of new roommates, Shirley and Laverne, placed together by residence hall staff. As they get to know each other, they begin with small talk about hometowns and majors, interests and hobbies, likes and dislikes. As the relationship deepens, they begin to reveal their values and beliefs, what's important to them, and their cares and concerns (Hays, 1985). Imagine that Shirley shares with her roommate Laverne that she is hundreds of miles away from a long-term boyfriend and misses him terribly. Laverne may nod encouragingly, respond empathically, and seek to support Shirley at the time. But if Laverne fails to act on this knowledge, her behavior may undermine the relationship. If she fails to relay messages that Shirley's boyfriend has called, or monopolizes the phone when Shirley has arranged to call him, she demonstrates insensitivity to Shirley's concerns, an incomplete understanding of Shirley's disclosures, and ultimately a lack of investment in the relationship.

Thus, if individuals seek to develop and build a new relationship, they will not only respond sensitively and warmly when the relationship partner discloses to them, but they will also remember and act on this information. In a study of new roommates who were strangers before living together, Cross and Morris (2003) hypothesized that persons with a highly relational self-construal would tend to listen carefully and remember their roommate's disclosures, and so would be better able than others to predict a new roommate's values and beliefs. In this study, one member of a roommate pair described herself or himself on a variety of values and beliefs items (for example, they indicated how important it was to stay close to their families). The other member of the pair (whom we'll call the *judge*) was asked to respond to the items as they thought their roommate would respond. A type of profile analysis was used to assess agreement between the two roommates (Bernieri et al., 1994). In this analysis, correlation coefficients are computed for each pair down the set of items. This raw accuracy correlation is corrected for implicit profile accuracy, which is the degree to which the target fits a typical prototype (e.g., most college students may report that it is important to them to do well in classes) and the degree to which the judge reflects awareness of this prototype in his or her judgements. The resulting measure reflects "[t]he degree to which peer judges accurately predicted how their roommates reported their own *constellation* of [values and beliefs] as they deviated from the most typical (aggregate) values of these [attributes]" (Berneiri, et al., 1994, p. 373), termed *ideographic accuracy*.[1]

We found that judges who defined themselves in terms of their close relationships (i.e., scored high on a measure of the relational self-construal) were more likely than others to accurately predict their roommate's values and beliefs. This association, however, depended on the depth of the relationship. In relationships described as very close by the judges, there was no association between the judges' relational self-construal scores and their ideographic accuracy scores. In relationships described as distant and lacking closeness, there was a much stronger association. Thus, in very close relationships, individuals seem to attend to and remember their roommate's disclosures because doing so supports and enhances an already rewarding relationship. In more distant relationships, however, individuals who chronically tend to think of themselves in terms of their close relationships appear to be more motivated than others to attend to and remember their roommate's disclosures.

This attention to and memory for information about a new relationship partner may have important consequences for the development of the relationship. The person who knows his roommate well can predict his behavior and perhaps avoid conflict in the relationship. A person may steer away from sensitive topics to avoid disagreements or change his behavior to maintain harmony in the relationship. Moreover, accurate knowledge of one's partner may make the partner feel known and understood, a critical component of intimacy (Reis & Shaver, 1988). The importance of feeling known and understood in the development and maintenance of closeness and intimacy has been frequently noted (Gottman, 1994; see Murray, Holmes, Bellavia, Griffin, & Dolderman, 2002, for a review). For example, de la Ronde and Swann (1998), in a study of 93 married couples, found that the couples reported higher levels of intimacy when the spouses's view of their partner was congruent with the partner's self-view. Surprisingly, intimacy was lowest when the spouse appraised the partner positively, but the partner appraised the self negatively. Similarly, a prospective study of college students showed that the participants were most satisfied with their roommates when the roommate's view of them was congruent with their own self view (McNulty & Swann, 1994). Although this finding is not surprising in general, it was surprising to find that low self-esteem participants preferred roommates who also viewed them negatively over roommates who viewed them positively.

Swann and his colleagues argue that this preference for self-verifying relationship partners is a product of an epistemological motive, or the need to view the world as stable and predictable (Giesler & Swann, 1999; Swann, 1990). People want to have stable self-concepts in order to understand the world as they experience it; it is their "point of reference" so to speak. Messages that contradict one's self-concept create confusion as to what one's point of reference should be, causing uncertainty about one's mastery over the most fundamental cognitive construct—the self. After all, if you don't know yourself, what *do* you know? This is the reason offered by Swann, Hixon, and de la Ronde (1992) as to why people desire to maintain their negative self-views. The best strategy for self-concept maintenance is to surround oneself with people who share one's self-view. For people with negative self-concepts, these cohorts are people who hold a less than desirable view of them. In their study of married couples, Swann, Hixon, and de la Ronde (1992) found that spouses with negative self-concepts

---

[1] Unfortunately, the judge's self-ratings on these items were not measured, so we could not control for actual similarity between roommates.

not only were viewed less favorably by their partners, but were also more committed to the relationship when their partner viewed them negatively than when their partner viewed them positively. Thus, it is to the advantage of people with highly relational self-construals to perceive their partners as their partners view themselves in the interest of maintaining the relationship, even if this perception is negatively biased. People with highly relational self-construals may still view their partners somewhat more positively than their partners view themselves, but the perception must be grounded in the partner's reality for the partner to feel validated and understood.

It seems rather strange that people with negative self-views would want to actively seek out negative feedback and appraisals from their spouses. It should be made clear, however, that people with negative self-concepts show initial signs of distress when they first receive negative feedback, but will later go on to seek unfavorable feedback from future interaction partners (Swann, Wenzlaff, Krull, & Pelham, 1992). It has been suggested that this striving toward receiving negative feedback is present because it fosters predictability and control (see Giesler & Swann, 1999). If negative feedback is judged to be irrelevant to the self, then the person with a negative self-view will dismiss the feedback in the same manner as people with positive self-views, especially if the feedback is extremely negative. Giesler and Swann (1999) argue that people with negative self-concepts have experienced past failures in their attempts to proactively control their interpersonal environment. Perhaps this is fostered by long-standing rejection or neglect from close others. As a result, people with negative self-views will control their environment by creating a negative social climate around them. So, they may purposefully neglect, reject, or derogate people who get close to them so that they can insure that the person knows the "real me". They may also engage in inappropriate social behaviors, such as self-disclosing too early in a relationship, or derogating themselves out of context for the purpose of creating an uncomfortable social atmosphere that will lead to a predicted rejection.

A challenge to the self-verification perspective on the role of accurate knowledge of one's relationship partner comes from research examining the role of positive illusions in relationships. Positive illusions are defined as people's idealistic views of their relationship partners in the sense that they "see their partners in a more positive light than the partners' self-perceptions justify" (Murray, Holmes, & Griffin, 1996a, p. 82). Positive illusions conflict with verification because illusions are rooted in inflated positivity regardless of whether they are accurate or not, whereas verification is rooted in accuracy regardless of whether it is flattering or not. Murray and her colleagues (1996a, 1996b) identified several benefits of idealization within close relationships. First, it resolves the tension between the commitment to one's partner and the doubts that arise when we recognize faults. For example, when a person is romantically involved with someone, that person tends to see the other person through a rosy filter. When in this stage, people use their image of the ideal partner to fill in the gaps of what they cannot see (Murray, Holmes, & Griffin, 1996a, 1996b). They give their partner the benefit of the doubt by applying ideal, positive characteristics to the other person even if there are no signs that they possess these characteristics. Idealization makes partners feel special and valued, and encourages them to live up to the idealized image, which strengthens the positive cycle. Idealization makes one's relationship seem more valuable than other people's relationships, thus diminishing the value of possible alternative partners and creating a stable, small ingroup. Idealization also increases *attributional charity*, which is defined as perceiving negative behaviors as external and uncontrollable, whereas positive behaviors are perceived as internal and controllable (Murray & Holmes, 1993). When people are motivated to view their partners in a positive light, they may find themselves explaining away negative behaviors they observe in their partners and bolstering positive behaviors. They may go so far as to see virtues in what may otherwise be perceived as a fault (Murray & Holmes,

1993). These behaviors may be especially evident in people with highly relational self-construals, who may give the benefit of the doubt to a close other as willingly as they do to themselves.

Idealization also is self-affirming as interdependence increases. The more people internalize their partners into their own self-concept (as suggested by research by Aron, Aron, and Smollen, 1992), the more their positive image reflects on one's own self-image. In addition, idealization undermines self-criticisms. When people begin to doubt themselves, idealizing partners who encourage the doubting person to see their better personal qualities quickly dispel these doubts and self-criticisms (Murray et al., 1996).

In short, idealization or positive illusions of one's relationship partners can have positive consequences for both the self and the relationships. If highly relational persons desire to develop and maintain close relationships, they may be more likely than others to view their relationships idealistically. To test this hypothesis, Cross and Morris (Study 2; 2003) asked students living with a new roommate to predict their roommate's responses to a measure of relationship depth of closeness. We also asked them to report their own feelings of depth in the relationship on this measure. Kenny and Acitelli (2001) point out that in dyadic data of this sort, the judge's predictions of the target's self-reports include two components: a bias effect (the extent to which the judge projects his or her own sense of closeness onto the target) and an accuracy effect, (the extent to which the judge's estimate reflects the target's actual feelings of closeness). These effects are best examined using muliple regression analysis, in which the predictor variables are the judge's ratings of themselves and the target's self-ratings, and the outcome variable is the judge's prediction of the target's ratings (Kenny & Acitelli, 2001). The path from the judges' ratings of their own depth of closeness to their prediction of their roommate's depth represents the bias effect, and the path from the roommate's self-rating of depth to the participant's prediction represents the accuracy effect. In our analysis, we first controlled for the bias and accuracy effects, then examined the association between the judges' self-construal scores and their estimates of the roommate's depth of closeness. As expected, the hierarchical regression analysis revealed that the judge's relational self-construal scores were significant predictors of their estimates of their roommate's depth, indicating that the highly relational judges held positive illusions of their roommate's depth of closeness in the relationship.

How can these highly relational judges be both accurate (as discussed earlier) and hold positive illusions? In part, these findings are due to different prediction tasks. In the study described earlier (Cross & Morris, 2003), participants with highly relational self-construals were better than lows at predicting their roommates' values and beliefs. This task is relatively objective, and is based primarily on the roommate's explicit disclosures. Estimation of one's roommate's depth of closeness in the relationship is more likely to be based on a variety of factors, including indirect or nonverbal communication, and the judge's own motivation and hopes for the relationship. We hypothesize that accurate knowledge of one's roommate's values and beliefs leads to specific strategies and behaviors that enhance the relationship (e.g., avoiding conflict and selecting activities appealing to the roommate), whereas positive illusions of the roommate's closeness motivates the person to make generous attributions for the other's behavior and to persist in the relationship (Murray et al., 1996). Similarly, Katz and colleagues (Katz, Anderson, & Beach, 1997; see also Katz, Beach, & Anderson, 1996) found that partner enhancement (positive illusions) and partner verification uniquely predict relationship satisfaction and intimacy in romantic relationships. They argue that the most satisfying and intimate relationships are those in which partners' views of each other are positive, yet bounded by reality. It is in the interest of people with highly relational self-construals to view their partners in a positive light, but it is also important for them to be accurate in their perceptions of close others (at least, accurate in the eyes of the partner). This way, the partner feels both understood and valued, which makes for a positive and long-lasting relationship.

THE RELATIONAL SELF-CONSTRUAL'S ROLE IN OTHER PROCESSES THAT CONTRIBUTE TO CLOSENESS AND INTIMACY

Extensive research has documented the role of the self in psychological processes that shape social behavior. For example, the self influences attention to and memory for others' behavior, the encoding and organization of information about others, and the interpretation of social information (see Baumeister, 1998; Brown, 1998; and Markus & Wurf, 1987, for reviews). Variation in the structure of the self may have pervasive and systematic consequences for these processes. Research is beginning to reveal that the relational self-construal importantly shapes the basic-level processes that form a foundation for the development of closeness and intimacy in relationships.

For example, information processing and aspects of social cognition depend upon the structure of the self. Individuals with a highly relational self-construal tend to have well-organized cognitive networks for relationship-oriented constructs, remember relationship-oriented information well, and organize information about others in terms of their relationships (Cross et al., 2002). Chronic or situational activation of the relational self-construal also promotes context sensitivity. Haberstroh, Oyserman, Schwarz, Kuhnen, and Ji (2002) experimentally primed either the relational self or the independent self of research participants. Compared with the independence-primed participants, relatedness-primed participants were more sensitive to the context in which questions were asked, and appeared to be more likely to take into account the questioner's prior knowledge in their responses. Other experimental research also primed either the independent or interdependent self and examined participants' performance on the embedded figures test, an oft-used measure of field dependence and independence (Kuhnen, Hannover, & Schubert, 2001). When the interdependent self was primed, participants were better able to detect the small figures that were embedded in the larger figures compared to when the independent self was primed. This sensitivity to the context may in part account for the association between the relational self-construal and empathy (see discussion by Cross & Madson, 1997) and the association between the relational self-construal and accurate predictions of the roommates values and beliefs (described above).

The relational self-construal is also associated with a mode of thinking that emphasizes similarity with close others and assimilation of the self to others. As Byrne (1971) articulated several decades ago, perceived similarity is one of the primary grounds for the development of a relationship. Perceived similarity can decrease the cognitive distance between oneself and the other and so create a sense of belonging in the relationship. In contrast, viewing oneself and another person as quite different can create a sense of differentiation, uniqueness, and individuality (Mikulincer, Orbach, & Iavnieli, 1998). In addition, perceptions of similarity may also contribute to the belief that one can predict the other's behavior and so promote relationship harmony. Research with romantic couples shows that viewing one's partner as similar to oneself, even if this perception is illusory, creates a sense that one has found a "kindred spirit" and promotes relationship satisfaction (Murray et al., 2002).

A variety of studies have shown that priming the relational self influences perceptions of similarity. For example, Stapel and Koomen (2001) found that priming the individual self promotes a mindset focused on differentiation of the self from others, whereas priming the relational self promotes a mindset focused on finding similarities between the self and others, or assimilation of the self and the other (see also

Brewer & Gardner, 1996). Other research suggests that the relational self is associated with behavioral assimilation in addition to cognitive assimilation. Many studies have shown that people tend to nonconsciously imitate the behaviors of others (Chartrand & Bargh, 1999). When people nonconsciously mimic the behaviors of their interaction partners (for example, they cross their arms or tap their feet like their partner), they demonstrate a form of assimilation of the self to the other, or an orientation towards similarity. Mimicry may also communicate to the partner one's interest in the relationship. Work by Sanchez-Burks (2002) suggests that individuals who are more likely to construct relational self-construals are also more likely to mimic the behavior of interaction partners, evidencing an orientation toward similarity and assimilation.

Likewise, research focused on chronic individual differences reveals that persons with a highly relational self-construal are more likely than others to view themselves and their relationship partners as similar on important dimensions. In two studies, Cross et al. (2002) examined students' descriptions of themselves and a close friend, using an indirect measure of similarity. Participants were asked to rate themselves and a friend on a variety of attributes, and an intraclass correlation between these ratings was used as the indicator of perceived similarity. In addition, the participants rated the typical college student at their university. As expected, participants with a highly relational self-construal were more likely than other participants to describe themselves and their close friend similarly. There was no relation between the self-construal scores and similarity for other students at one's university, however. In other words, the participants with highly relational self-construals do not regard all ingroup members as similar to themselves, but only close relationship partners.

These findings suggest that the relational self-construal promotes thinking about oneself and close others in ways that facilitate and support close relationships. These effects, however, are not predicted by many long-standing theories of the self. For example, the original version of self-evaluation maintenance theory (SEM; Tesser, 1988) predicted that when a close other performs better than oneself in a domain that is important to the self, one should feel threatened, and so seek to distance oneself from the other. But for the person with a relational self-construal, such distancing comes with a cost—the loss of a close relationship. In a study examining this process using pairs of close friends, Bacon (2001) found that highly relational participants were less likely to engage in the distancing behaviors that SEM theory predicts (but see also the extended version of SEM; Beach et al., 1996; Beach et al., 1998). Similarly other research shows that when the relational self is primed, people make fewer self-enhancing comparisons with close others compared to when the independent self is primed (Gardner, Gabriel, & Hochschild, 2002; see also Kemmelmeier & Oyserman, 2001).

In summary, these studies indicate that the relational self-construal importantly influences a variety of processes that contribute to closeness and intimacy. The possibilities for additional research seem almost limitless. For example, individuals with a highly relational self-construal may be more likely than others to accommodate to a relationship partner with the goal of maintaining a close relationship (Arriaga & Rusbult, 1998). Accomodation and assimilation processes promoted by the relational self-construal may result in high levels of self-concept change in the context of close relationships (Aron, Paris, & Aron, 1995). Individuals with a highly relational self-construal may be more likely than others to take the perspective of close others (Davis, 1994) resulting in higher levels of cognitive interdependence (Agnew, Van Lange, Rusbult, & Langston, 1998). They may use a different calculus than others when considering the costs and benefits of relationships (Rusbult & van Lange, 1996).

This conceptualization of the self overlaps with work by Aron and his colleagues (Aron, Aron, Tudor, & Nelson, 1991; Aron et al., 1992; Aron, Mashek, & Aron, chap. 3, this volume) on the notion of including others in the self. They suggest that almost everyone includes particular close relationships in the self (such as relationships with romantic partners), and they have examined how this representation of closeness influences cognitive processes. For example, Aron et al. (1991) found that when another person is included in the self, individuals tend to use the same kinds of thought processes with regard to that person that typically define information processing about the self. They argue that fundamentally, relationship closeness can be conceptualized as a cognitive closeness that can be explored using the tools of social cognition research. These two lines of research share a common interest in the cognitive processes that ensue when others are included in the self, but they have different aims. Whereas Aron et al.'s (1995) research focuses on the representation of closeness in specific relationships and the consequences of closeness for the self-concept, our research has focused on individual differences in the self and the role of the relational self-construal in a variety of cognitive, motivational, and relationship-oriented processes. Persons with a highly relational self-construal are more likely than those with low relational self-construals to include close others in the self (Cross et al., 2000), yet the consequences of the relational self-construal extend beyond effects for specific relationships, impacting other aspects of social cognition and motivation (Cross et al., 2002; Gore & Cross, 2003).

IS THERE A DOWNSIDE TO THE RELATIONAL SELF-CONSTRUAL?

The research on the influence of the relational self-construal is in its infancy, but this early work hints to its importance in understanding the development and maintenance of close and intimate relationships. We should note, however, that the relational self-construal may have potential negative consequences. Consider again the case of new roommates. If one of the roommates desires a close relationship, she may push for closeness more quickly than her roommate desires. This person may self-disclose inappropriately, insensitive to the gradual revelation of the self that characterizes the development of most close relationships. If the highly relational partner overestimates the similarity between herself and her roommate, she may have unrealistic expectations of the partner or the relationship. As a result, the partners of high relationals may feel that too much closeness is expected and feel smothered by the relationship (see Mashek & Sherman, chap. 19, this volume).

Persons with a highly relational self-construal may also experience difficulty in life transitions that require separation from close friends and family. Leaving home for college, studying abroad, or a work transfer to another state may challenge the self in ways that are not shared by individuals who have low relational self-construals. Certainly everyone uprooted from friends and family will miss social support and the activities they enjoyed with old friends, but the highly relational person may find it difficult to feel that they can be themselves until they have developed new close relationships. On the other hand, the person with a highly relational self-construal may be more likely to maintain long-distance relationships and to initiate new friendships in a new situation. In other situations, the highly relational person may find that their orientation toward supporting and maintaining relationships is not adaptive. For example, persons with a highly relational self-construal may be slow to leave an abusive relationship, making too generous attributions for the partner's harmful behavior.

Researchers have long been concerned about the potential relation between a relational or communal orientation and undesirable levels of self-denial or the loss of self (Helgeson, 1994; Jack, 1991; see also Mashek & Sherman, chap. 19, this volume). The person who defines the self relationally may sacrifice too much of the self for the sake of a close relationship. Meta-analytic studies, however, show no relation between a communal or relational orientation and depression (Bassoff & Glass, 1982; Whitley, 1984). Helgeson and her colleagues (Helgeson, 1994; Helgeson & Fritz, 1998) suggest that a relational orientation balanced by personal agency or independence promotes health and well-being. In contrast, individuals characterized by *unmitigated communion*, defined as a focus on others to the exclusion of the self, are more likely to experience depression than are others. Helgeson and Fritz (1998) suggest that individuals who are high in unmitigated communion pay more attention to the problems of close others and take those problems on as their own, which contributes to distress. The association between the relational self-construal and unmitigated communion has not yet been examined, but research conducted to date shows no association between scores on the relational-interdependent self-construal scale and measures of depression or distress (Cross et al., 2000). In research currently underway in our laboratory we are examining the ways that the relational self-construal is balanced by conceptions of an independent self to promote well-being and satisfying relationships.

A RETURN TO THE AMERICAN DILEMMA

Contemporary American ideology mandates that individuals should be their own person, do their own thing, seek what is best for themselves, and maintain their freedom at any cost. These ideals and goals are often challenged in close relationships, and people may find themselves making a choice between independence and connection. Research on the relational self-construal suggests that one solution to this dilemma is to question the razor-sharp separation of self and others that has characterized the American identity. When the self is defined in terms of close relationships, (or when others are included in the self, Aron et al., 1992), then the aims and goals of close relationships need not always conflict with or impinge upon one's own aims and goals.

How do these concepts and findings relate to persons from non-Western cultures? The relational-interdependent self-construal scale was explicitly developed to tap a Western conception of the self-in-relation (in contrast to the group-oriented interdependent self prevalent in many collectivist cultures). Before exporting this concept (and its measure) to a non-Western culture, it is important to thoroughly understand the basic beliefs, ideas, and values about both the self and close relationships that prevail in the new culture. The form that a relational self-view takes, and the understanding of closeness and intimacy in other cultures, may vary dramatically from that of Western cultures. Indigenous researchers in non-Western societies are best able to examine these processes using culture-relevant concepts and approaches.

Increasingly, Western psychologists are recognizing the negative consequences of individualism and independence that ignores basic needs for close social relationships (see Myers, 1999, for a review). Recognition of variation in the self-construal, examination of the ways that others are included in the self, and research on the consequences of relational conceptions of the self may lead to richer theories of relationship processes and new perspectives on identity that free people from the glorious but terrifying isolation of the American conception of the self.

REFERENCES

Agnew, C. R., Van Lange, P. A. M., Rusbult, C. E., & Langston, C. A. (1998). Cognitive interdependence: Commitment and the mental representation of close relationships. *Journal of Personality and Social Psychology, 74*, 939–954.

Allen, R. L., Dawson, M. C., & Brown, R. E. (1989). A schema based approach to modeling an African-American racial belief system. *American Political Science Review, 83*, 421–442.

Aron, A., Aron, E. N., & Smollen, D. (1992). Inclusion of other in the self scale and the structure of interpersonal closeness. *Journal of Personality and Social Psychology, 63*, 596–612.

Aron, A., Aron, E. N., Tudor, M., & Nelson, G. (1991). Close relationships as including other in the self. *Journal of Personality and Social Psychology, 60*, 241–253.

Aron, A., Melinat, E., Aron, E. N., Vallone, R. D., & Bator, R. J. (1997). The experimental generation of interpersonal closeness: A procedure and some preliminary findings. *Personality and Social Psychology Bulletin, 23*, 363–377.

Aron, A., Paris, M., & Aron, E. N. (1995). Falling in love: Prospective studies of self-concept change. *Journal of Personality and Social Psychology, 69*, 1102–1112.

Arriaga, X. B., & Rusbult, C. E. (1998). Standing in my partner's shoes: Partner perspective taking and reactions to accommodative dilemmas. *Personality and Social Psychology Bulletin, 24*, 927–948.

Bacon, P. L. (2001). Defending the self: The role of the relational-interdependent self-construal. Unpublished doctoral dissertation, Iowa State University, Ames, Iowa.

Bassoff, E. S., & Glass, G. V. (1982). The relationship between sex roles and mental health: A meta-analysis of twenty-six studies. *Counseling Psychologist, 10*, 105–112.

Baumeister, R. F. (1998). The self. In D. T. Gilbert, S. T. Fiske, & G. Lindzey (Eds.), *The handbook of social psychology:* (Vol. 1, 4th ed., pp. 680–740). New York: McGraw-Hill.

Baumeister, R. F., & Leary, M. R. (1995). The need to belong: Desire for interpersonal attachments as a fundamental human motivation. *Psychological Bulletin, 117*, 497–529.

Beach, S. R. H., Tesser, A., Mendolia, M., Anderson, P., Crelia, R., Whitaker, D. G., & Fincham, F. D. (1996). Self-evaluation maintenance in marriage: Toward a performance ecology of the marital relationship. *Journal of Family Psychology, 10*, 379–396.

Beach, S. R. H., Tesser, A., Fincham, F. D., Jones, D. J., Johnson, D., & Whitaker, D. J. (1998). Pleasure and pain in doing well, together: An investigation of performance-related affect in close relationships. *Journal of Personality and Social Psychology, 74*, 923–939.

Bellah, R. N., Madsen, R., Sullivan, W. M., Swidler, A., & Tipton, S. M. (1985). *Habits of the heart.* New York: Harper & Row.

Bernieri, F. J., Zuckerman, M., Koestner, R., & Rosenthal, R. (1994). Measuring person perception accuracy: Another look at self-other agreement. *Personality and Social Psychology Bulletin, 20*, 367–378.

Berscheid, E., & Reis, H. T. (1998). Attraction and close relationships. In D. T. Gilbert, S. T. Fiske (Eds.), *The handbook of social psychology*, (Vol. 2, 4th ed., pp. 193–281). New York: McGraw-Hill.

Berscheid, E., Snyder, M., & Omoto, A. M. (1989). The relationship closeness inventory: Assessing the closeness of interpersonal relationships. *Journal of Personality and Social Psychology, 57*, 792–807.

Brewer, M. B., & Gardner, W. (1996). Who is this "we"? Levels of collective identity and self-representations. *Journal of Personality and Social Psychology, 71*, 83–93.

Brown, J. D. (1998). *The self.* Boston: McGraw Hill.

Byrne, D. (1971). *The attraction paradigm.* New York: Academic Press.

Chartrand, T. L., & Bargh, J. A. (1999). The chameleon effect: The perception-behavior link and social interaction. *Journal of Personality and Social Psychology, 76*, 893–910.

Clark, M. S., Ouellette, R., Powell, M. C., & Milberg, S. (1987). Recipient's mood, relationship type, and helping. *Journal of Personality and Social Psychology, 53*, 94–103.

Cross, S. E., Bacon, P. L., & Morris, M. L. (2000). The relational-interdependent self-construal and relationships. *Journal of Personality and Social Psychology, 78*, 791–808.

Cross, S. E., & Gore, J. S. (2002). Cultural models of the self. In M. Leary & J. Tangney (Eds.), *Handbook of Self and Identity.* New York: Guilford.

Cross, S. E., & Madson, L. (1997). Models of the self: Self-construals and gender. *Psychological Bulletin, 122*, 5–37.

Cross, S. E., & Morris, M. L. (2003). Getting to know you: The relational self-construal, relational cognition, and well-being. *Personality and Social Psychology Bulletin, 29*, 512–523.

Cross, S. E., Morris, M. L., & Gore, J. S. (2002). Thinking about oneself and others: The relational-interdependent self-construal and social cognition. *Journal of Personality and Social Psychology, 82*, 399–418.

de la Ronde, C., & Swann, W. B. (1998). Partner verification: Restoring shattered images of our intimates. *Journal of Personality and Social Psychology, 75*, 374–382.

Gardner, W. L., Gabriel, S., & Hochschild, L. (2002). When you and I are "we," you are not threatening: The role of self-expansion in social comparison. *Journal of Personality and Social Psychology, 82*, 239–251.

Giesler, R. B., & Swann, W. B. (1999). Striving for confirmation: The role of self-verification in depression. In T. Joiner & J. C. Coyne (Eds.), *The interactional nature of depression: Advances in interpersonal approaches* (pp. 189–217). Washington, DC: American Psychological Association.

Gilligan, C. (1982). *In a different voice: Psychological theory and women's development.* Cambridge, MA: Harvard University Press.

Gore, J. S., & Cross, S. E. (2003). *There's more to me than just me: The relational self-construal and relational motivation.* Manuscript submitted for review.

Gore, J. S., Cross, S. E., & Morris, M. L. (2003). *Let's be friends: The relational self-construal and relationship maintenance among college roommates.* Manuscript in preparation.

Gottman, J. M. (1994). An agenda for marital therapy. In S. M. Johnson & L. S. Greenberg (Eds.), The heart of the matter: Perspectives on emotion in marital therapy (pp. 256–293). Philadelphia: Brunner/Mazel.

Haberstroh, S., Oyserman, D., Schwarz, N., Kuhnen, U., & Ji, L. J. (2002). Is the interdependent self more sensitive to question context than the independent self? Self-construal and the observation of conversational norms. Journal of Experimental Social Psychology, 38, 323–329.

Hays, R. B. (1985). A longitudinal study of friendship development. Journal of Personality and Social Psychology, 48, 909–924.

Helgeson, V. S. (1994). Relation of agency and communion to well-being: Evidence and potential explanations. Psychological Bulletin, 116, 412–428.

Helgeson, V. S., & Fritz, H. G. (1998). A theory of unmitigated communion. Personality and Social Psychology Review, 2, 173–183.

Hofstede, G. (1991). Cultures and organizations: Software of the mind. London: McGraw-Hill.

Jack, D. C. (1991). Silencing the self: Women and depression. Cambridge, MA: Harvard University Press.

Kashima, Y., Yamaguchi, S., Kim, U., Choi, S. C., Gelfand, M. J., & Yuki, M. (1995). Culture, gender, and self: A perspective from individualism-collectivism research. Journal of Personality and Social Psychology, 69, 925–937.

Katz, J., Anderson, P., & Beach, S. R. H. (1997). Dating relationship quality: Effects of global self-verification and self-enhancement. Journal of Social and Personal Relationships, 14, 829–842.

Katz, J., Beach, S. R. H., & Anderson, P. (1996). Self-enhancement versus self-verification: Does spousal support always help? Cognitive Therapy and Research, 20, 345–360.

Kemmelmeier, M., & Oyserman, D. (2001). The ups and downs of thinking about a successful other: Self-construals and the consequences of social comparisons. European Journal of Social Psychology, 31, 311–320.

Kenny, D. A., & Acitelli, L. K. (2001). Accuracy and bias in the perception of the partner in a close relationship. Journal of Personality and Social Psychology, 80, 439–448.

Kim, H., & Markus, H. R. (1999). Deviance or uniqueness, harmony or conformity? A cultural analysis. Journal of Personality and Social Psychology, 77, 785–800.

Kuhnen, U., Hannover, B., & Schubert, B. (2001). The semantic-procedural-interface model of the self: The role of self-knowledge for context-dependent versus context-independent modes of thinking. Journal of Personality and Social Psychology, 80, 397–409.

Laurenceau, J. P., Barrett, L. F., & Pietromonaco, P. R. (1998). Intimacy as an interpersonal process: The importance of self-disclosure, partner disclosure, and perceived partner responsiveness in interpersonal exchanges. Journal of Personality and Social Psychology, 74, 1238–1251.

Lepore, S. J. (1992). Social conflict, social support, and psychological distress: Evidence of cross-domain buffering effects. Journal of Personality and Social Psychology, 63, 857–867.

Lin, Y. C. (1992). The construction of the sense of intimacy from everyday social interaction. Unpublished doctoral dissertation, University of Rochester, Rochester, New York.

Lukes, S. (1973). Individualism. Oxford, England: Blackwell.

Maccoby, E. (1990). Gender and relationships: A developmental account. American Psychologist, 45, 513–520.

Marin, G., & Triandis, H. C. (1985). Allocentrism as an important characteristic of the behavior of Latin Americans and Hispanics. In R. Diaz-Guerrero (Ed.), Cross-cultural and national studies in social psychology (pp. 69–80). Amsterdam: North Holland.

Markus, H. R., & Kitayama, S. (1991). Culture and the self: Implications for cognition, emotion, and motivation. Psychological Review, 98, 224–253.

Markus, H., & Wurf, E. (1987). The dynamic self-concept: A social psychological perspective. Annual Review of Psychology, 38, 299–337.

McCombs, H. (1985). Black self-concept: An individual/collective analysis. International Journal of Intercultural Relations, 9, 1–18.

McNulty, S. E., & Swann, W. B. (1994). Identity negotiation in roommate relationships: The self as architect and consequence of social reality. Journal of Personality and Social Psychology, 67, 1012–1023.

Mikulincer, M., Orbach, I., & Iavnieli, D. (1998). Adult attachment style and affect regulation: Strategic variations in subjective self-other similarity. Journal of Personality and Social Psychology, 75, 436–448.

Murray, S. L., & Holmes, J. G. (1993). Seeing virtues in faults: Negativity and the transformation of interpersonal narratives in close relationships. Journal of Personality and Social Psychology, 65, 707–722.

Murray, S. L., Holmes, J. G., & Griffin, D. W. (1996a). The benefits of positive illusions: Idealization and the construction of satisfaction in close relationships. Journal of Personality and Social Psychology, 70, 79–98.

Murray, S. L., Holmes, J. G., & Griffin, D. W. (1996b). The self-fulfilling nature of positive illusions in romantic relationships: Love is not blind, but prescient. Journal of Personality and Social Psychology, 71, 1153–1180.

Murray, S. L., Holmes, J. G., Bellavia, G., Griffin, D. W., & Dolderman, D. (2002). Kindred spirits? The benefits of egocentrism in close relationships. Journal of Personality and Social Psychology, 82, 563–581.

Myers, D. G. (1999). Close relationships and quality of life. In D. Kahneman, E. Diener, & N. Schwartz (Eds.), Well-being: The foundations of hedonic psychology (pp. 374–391). New York: Sage.

Myers, D. G. (2000). The American Paradox. New Haven, CT: Yale University Press.

Pierce, G. R., Sarason, I. G., & Sarason, B. R. (1991). General and relationship-based perceptions of social support: Are two constructs better than one? Journal of Personality and Social Psychology, 61, 1028–1039.

Reis, H. T., & Patrick, B. C. (1996). Attachment and intimacy: Component processes. In E. T. Higgins & A. W. Kruglanski (Eds.), *Social Psychology: Handbook of basic principles* (pp. 523–563). New York: Guilford.

Reis, H. T., & Shaver, P. (1988). Intimacy as an interpersonal process. In S. Duck (Ed.), *Handbook of personal relationships: Theory, research and interventions* (pp. 367–389). Oxford, England: Wiley.

Rothbaum, F., Weisz, J., Pott, M., Miyake, K., & Morelli, G. (2000). Attachment and culture: Security in the United States and Japan. *American Psychologist, 55*, 1093–1104.

Rusbult, C. E. (1983). A longitudinal test of the investment model: The development (and deterioration) of satisfaction and commitment in heterosexual involvements. *Journal of Personality and Social Psychology, 45*, 101–117.

Rusbult, C. E., & van Lange, P. A. M. (1996). Interdependence processes. In E. T. Higgins & A. W. Kruglanski (Eds.), *Social psychology: Handbook of basic principles* (pp. 564–596). New York: Guilford Press.

Sanchez-Burks, J. (2002). Protestant relational ideology and (in)attention to relational cues in work settings. *Journal of Personality and Social Psychology, 83*, 919–929.

Sheldon, K. M., & Elliot, A. J. (1999). Goal striving, need satisfaction, and longitudinal well-being: The self-concordance model. *Journal of Personality and Social Psychology, 76*, 482–497.

Singelis, T. M. (1994). The measurement of independent and interdependent self-construals. *Personality and Social Psychology Bulletin, 20*, 580–591.

Stafford, L., & Canary, D. J. (1991). Maintenance strategies and romantic relationship type, gender, and relational characteristics. *Journal of Social and Personal Relationships, 8*, 217–242.

Stapel, D. A., & Koomen, W. (2001). I, we, and the effects of others on me: How self-construal level moderates social comparison effects. *Journal of Personality and Social Psychology, 80*, 766–781.

Swann, W. B. (1990). To be adored or to be known? The interplay of self-enhancement and self-verification. In E. T. Higgins & R. M. Sorrentino (Eds.), *Handbook of motivation and cognition: Foundations of social behavior, Vol. 2* (pp. 408–448). NY: Guilford Press.

Swann, W. B., Hixon, J. G., & de la Ronde, C. (1992). Embracing the bitter "truth": Negative self-concepts and marital attachment. *Psychological Science, 3*, 118–121.

Swann, W. B., Wenzlaff, R. M., Krull, D. S., & Pelham, B. W. (1992). Allure of negative feedback: Self-verification strivings among depressed persons. *Journal of Abnormal Psychology, 101*, 293–306.

Tesser, A. (1988). Toward a self-evaluation maintenance model of social behavior. *Advances in Experimental Social Psychology*. New York, Academic Press.

Triandis, H. C. (1995). *Individualism and collectivism*. Boulder, CO, Westview.

Whitley, B. E. (1983). Sex role orientation and self-esteem: A critical meta-analytic review. *Journal of Personality and Social Psychology, 44*, 765–778.

14

The Link Between the Pursuit of Intimacy Goals and Satisfaction in Close Relationships: An Examination of the Underlying Processes

Catherine A. Sanderson
Amherst College

Both theory and research on close relationships point to the connection between intimacy and relationship satisfaction (Berscheid, 1983; Kelley, 1979). Specifically, individuals who engage in self-disclosure, trust, and interdependence with their partners experience greater relationship satisfaction and longer relationship longevity (Altman & Taylor, 1973; Hendrick, 1981; Hendrick, Hendrick, & Adler, 1988; Hill, Rubin, & Peplau, 1976; Levinger & Senn, 1967; Reis & Shaver, 1988; Rubin, Hill, Peplau, & Dunkel-Schetter, 1980; Simpson, 1987). On the other hand, relationships with low levels of intimacy are more likely to end (Hendrick, 1981; Hendrick et al., 1988; Hill et al., 1976; Simpson, 1987). Thus, creating intimacy in a relationship plays an important role in predicting satisfaction in close relationships as well as in maintaining these relationships over time.

Although considerable research demonstrates that a strong focus on intimacy is associated with relationship satisfaction and longevity, relatively little is known about the specific processes underlying this association. Several prominent models of close relationships, however, describe various processes by which individuals' own distinct needs, traits, and goals influence patterns of relationship interaction, cognition, and behavior, which in turn predict satisfaction (Bradbury & Fincham, 1988, 1991; Reis & Shaver, 1988). For example, the contextual model of marriage proposed by Bradbury and Fincham (1988) describes how individual difference factors, including attachment styles, traits, and goals, influence the proximal context of a relationship, namely individuals' thoughts and feelings regarding their partner's behavior, and thereby lead to relationship satisfaction. Similarly, Reis and Shaver's (1988) model of the intimacy process describes how individuals' distinct needs, motives, and goals influence how they act toward their partner, which in turn is interpreted and responded to by their partner on the basis of his or her own distinct needs (see Laurenceau et al., 2004). Although both of these models describe the role of individual difference factors in influencing the creation of intimacy through various processes, and thereby leading to relationship satisfaction and longevity, it is certainly possible, and even likely, that the link between intimacy and satisfaction in a relationship is somewhat more complex and bidirectional than these models portray. For example, individuals who are, for whatever reason, in highly satisfying relationships may develop a strong focus on intimacy. Alternatively, a third variable, such as attachment style, neuroticism, or self-esteem, may predict both intimacy and satisfaction. Both of these possibilities are discussed in some detail at the end of this chapter.

This chapter first describes research showing that individuals vary in the extent to which they pursue intimacy goals in their close relationships, and that people who have a strong focus on the pursuit of such goals experience greater satisfaction. I will then review research examining five potential explanations for the goals-satisfaction link, namely whether individuals with a strong focus on intimacy goals in their romantic relationships (a) structure their relationships in particular ways (e.g., spend more time with their partners); (b) interact within these relationships in distinct ways (e.g., engage in more interdependence and self-disclosure); (c) resolve conflicts within these relationships in more constructive ways, (d) have similarly-focused partners, and (e) perceive their partners as intimacy focused. Although the vast majority of research on the link between intimacy and satisfaction has examined romantic relationships, friendships represent a distinct type of interpersonal relationships, and hence I also describe preliminary work that examines the link between intimacy goals and satisfaction in close same-sex friendships. Finally, I describe a number of lingering issues that should be examined in future research, including the processes underlying the goals-perception-satisfaction link, the causal direction of the link between goals and satisfaction, other potential mediators of the goals-satisfaction link, and the impact of culture on this link.

THE PURSUIT OF INTIMACY GOALS

Close relationships are typically viewed as forums for engaging in intimacy, including self-disclosure, interdependence, and trust (see, for example, Berscheid, 1983; Kelley et al., 1983; Rempel, Holmes, & Zanna, 1985). However, despite this general emphasis on the presence of intimacy in close relationships, individuals may differ in how interested they are in engaging in such behavior (Cantor & Malley, 1991). As described by the lifespan approach to personality (e.g., Cantor, 1994; Cantor & Kihlstrom, 1987), individuals within a given subculture may all "take on" a given task, but both situational and personal factors will influence exactly how they take on these tasks, including their distinct goals, strivings, and personal projects (Cantor & Zirkel, 1990; Emmons, 1989; Little, 1989; Little, Lecci, & Watkinson, 1992; Mischel & Shoda, 1995). For example, following the dissolution of a close relationship (e.g., through divorce or death of a spouse), an individual may be more interested in working on self-reliance than on interdependence (Cantor & Malley, 1991). Similarly, Zirkel's (1992; Zirkel & Cantor, 1990) research has shown that even though the task of independence is a salient one for college students, individuals themselves vary in the amount of anxiety they bring to this task. In turn, although one person may see a close relationship as an opportunity to engage in interdependence with a single other, another may see a relationship as an opportunity to explore a new identity or achieve independence from one's family of origin.

Individuals may differ not only in how interested they are in the pursuit of intimacy, but also in their ability to engage in such a pursuit. As described by the attachment styles model (Hazan & Shaver, 1987; Simpson, 1990), individuals who have developed insecure attachment models in early childhood may be reluctant to pursue intimacy in close relationships, because they lack a secure base on which to build such communion. Similarly, Erikson's (1950, 1968) theory of life stages proposes that those who have not yet successfully resolved their identities (Marcia, 1966; Orlofsky, 1978) may not be ready to focus on merging with another, and thus may engage in close relationships with a focus on self-exploration (but cf., Gilligan, 1982). In sum, both theory and research have shown that individuals vary in the extent to which they are focused on and adept at creating intimacy in a close relationship (e.g., Berscheid, Snyder, & Omoto, 1989; Cantor, Acker, & Cook-Flannagan, 1992; McAdams, 1984; Prager, 1995).

To examine individuals' general orientation toward the pursuit of intimacy goals in romantic relationships, Sanderson and Cantor (1995) created a 13-item self-report scale which is based on prior literature (Hazan & Shaver, 1987; Marcia, 1966). The goal of intimacy involves self-disclosure, mutual dependence, and emotional attachment, and hence items were created that assessed these general concerns within the specific context of romantic relationships (e.g., "in my dating relationships, I try to share my most intimate thoughts and feelings," and "in my dating relationships, I try to date those I can count on."). This scale meets the standard criteria for determining unidimensionality (Briggs & Cheek, 1993), including high internal consistency, a modest mean interitem correlation, and one factor accounting for a substantial portion of the variance. The intimacy goals scale is positively correlated with ego achievement and negatively correlated with interpersonal ego diffusion, indicating that those with a strong focus on intimacy goals have successfully resolved their identity issues (Sanderson & Cantor, 1995). Scores on the intimacy goals scale are also positively correlated with secure attachment and negatively correlated with anxious attachment (Sanderson & Cantor, 1995). There is no association between strength of intimacy goals and avoidant attachment, suggesting that people with a strong focus on intimacy in their relationships are not particularly fearful of or disinterested in such relationships. Similarly, there is no significant association between strength of intimacy goals and communal orientation (Sanderson, Rahm, & Beigbeder, in press), showing that people with a strong focus on intimacy goals in their close interpersonal relationships are not simply generally oriented toward helping others. The intimacy goals scale is negatively associated with the sociosexual orientation inventory, indicating that those with a strong focus on intimacy in their close relationships are less willing to engage in sexual activity in casual dating contexts (e.g., those lacking intimacy; Sanderson & Cantor, 1995).

Most importantly, scores on our intimacy goals scale are associated with satisfaction in and the longevity of romantic relationships. Specifically, individuals with a strong focus on the pursuit of intimacy goals in their close relationships experience greater satisfaction in both dating (Sanderson & Cantor, 1997; Sanderson & Evans, 2001; Sanderson & Karetsky, 2002) and marital relationships (Sanderson & Cantor, 2001). Individuals with intimacy goals are also more likely to maintain their dating relationships over time (Sanderson & Cantor, 1997). For example, individuals with stronger intimacy goals report a mean relationship length of 22 months as compared with 12 months for those with weaker intimacy goals (Sanderson & Cantor, 1995). They also report having fewer casual dating and sexual partners. This work therefore demonstrates that individuals do vary in the extent to which they are focused on the pursuit of intimacy goals in their close relationships, and that the pursuit of such goals is associated with related individual difference measures as well as the experience of romantic relationships.

FIVE POTENTIAL PATHWAYS LEADING TO THE
GOALS-SATISFACTION LINK

To examine the association between the pursuit of intimacy goals and satisfaction in close relationships, and in particular various factors that may mediate this link, I, in collaboration with various colleagues, conducted a series of correlational studies. In one sample, we collected measures from both members of 60 college student dating couples on time spent together, social support given, perception of one's partner's goals, and satisfaction (Sanderson & Cantor, 1997). We collected these measures as well as additional measures of self-disclosure (elicited and engaged in) in a sample of 100 undergraduate women in dating relationships (Sanderson & Evans, 2001). We also collected data on the pursuit of intimacy goals, relationship satisfaction, and conflict resolution strategies from a sample of 189 male and female undergraduates to examine whether individuals with a strong focus on intimacy goals are more likely to use constructive strategies to resolve interpersonal conflicts (Sanderson & Karetsky, 2002). Finally, to extend this research to marital relationships, we collected data on time spent together, social support provided, perceptions of spouses' goals, and satisfaction from 44 married couples (Sanderson & Cantor, 2001). As shown in Figure 14.1, in each of these samples, we first examined the association between intimacy goals and

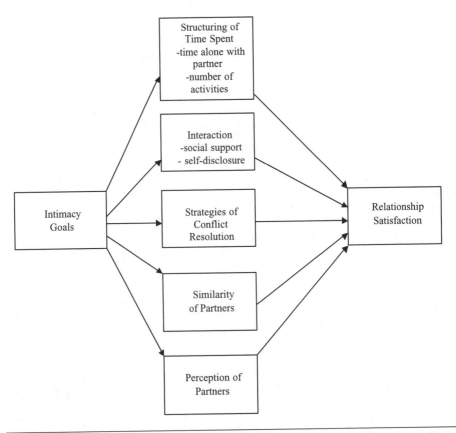

FIG. 14.1. A model portraying five distinct pathways through which the pursuit of intimacy goals may lead to relationship satisfaction. Sanderson, C. A., & Cantor, N. (2001). The association of intimacy goals and marital satisfaction: A test of four mediational hypotheses. *Personality and Social Psychology Bulletin, 27,* 1567–1577. Copyright © 2001 by Sage Publications, Inc. Reprinted by permission of Sage Publications.

satisfaction, and then examined whether various factors (e.g., structuring of time spent with partners, interaction with partners, strategies of conflict resolution, similarity of partners, perception of partners) mediated the goals-satisfaction link.

STRUCTURING OF TIME SPENT

A critical feature of achieving one's goals is planning where and when to engage in valued life tasks (Gollwitzer, 1993; Mischel, Cantor, & Feldman, 1996; Snyder & Ickes, 1985). Individuals choose to spend time in particular environments, namely those that facilitate goal-fulfillment, and hence the pursuit of a given goal is associated with characteristic methods of task pursuit and the structuring of daily life activity (Cantor & Fleeson, 1991; Cantor, Norem, Niedenthal, Langston, & Brower, 1987). For example, Emmons and colleagues (Emmons, Diener, & Larsen, 1986) found that extraverts and those high in need for affiliation gravitate towards social situations, whereas those high in endurance and need for achievement gravitate toward work situations. Similarly, in the domain of close relationships, women who see themselves as highly feminine (e.g., emotional, gentle, helpful to others) perform many household tasks (e.g., "woman-type" things), whereas men who see themselves as highly masculine (e.g., independent, self-confident, and competitive) perform few household tasks (Atkinson & Huston, 1984). Individuals therefore are quite adept at structuring their daily lives in order to spend time in goal-relevant situations.

Similarly, individuals with intimacy goals may spend more time alone with their partner and engage in more activities with their partner, which facilitate communication and companionship. For example, Silbereisen and colleagues (Silbereisen, Noack, & von Eye, 1992) found that adolescents in established relationships, who are presumably interested in engaging in self-disclosure and interdependence, select private settings over more public settings when spending time with their partners. Those with a strong focus on intimacy may also choose to engage in many activities with their partners as a way of fostering interdependence. For example, intimacy-focused individuals may prefer to work together with their spouse on various household tasks (e.g., balancing the checkbook, washing dishes, planning vacations) as opposed to dividing up such responsibilities, and may engage in more frequent and revealing conversations. Correspondingly, a beeper study by McAdams and Constantian (1983) demonstrated that individuals who are high in intimacy and affiliation motives engage in more interpersonal conversations and letter-writing than those without such motives. Individuals with a strong focus on intimacy goals in their close relationships are therefore expected to structure their relationships in distinct ways, namely those that facilitate the achievement of intimacy.

In turn, individuals with intimacy goals do report structuring their close relationships in particular ways (Sanderson & Cantor, 1997, 2001; Sanderson & Evans, 2001). For example, those with intimacy goals report spending more time alone with their dating partners. They do not, however, report spending more time with their partner and others or with their partner in school-related activities, suggesting that those with a strong focus on intimacy goals are spending more time only in those contexts that should facilitate the pursuit of intimacy goals. Similarly, research with married couples has shown that individuals with a strong focus on intimacy goals engage in more activities with their spouse, including watching television, eating meals, and even doing laundry.

However, our studies provide no evidence that this type of structuring of relationships, including spending time alone with one's partner and engaging in many activities with one's partner, mediates the link between intimacy and relationship satisfaction (Sanderson & Cantor, 1997, 2001; Sanderson & Evans, 2001). In fact, when we controlled for intimacy goals, there was no association between this type of structuring

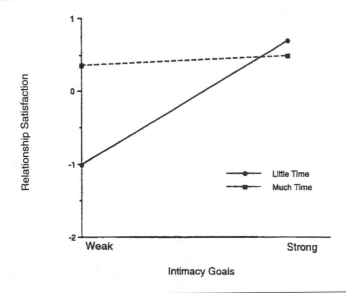

FIG. 14.2. The pursuit of intimacy goals moderates the association of time spent with one's partner on relationship satisfaction, such that individuals with a weak focus on intimacy goals need to spend considerable time with their dating partner to experience relationship satisfaction, whereas those with a strong focus on intimacy goals do not. From "Social dating goals in late adolescence: Implications for safer sexual activity," by C. A. Sanderson and N. Cantor, 1995, *Journal of Personality and Social Psychology, 68*, p. 1428. Copyright 1997 by the American Psychological Association. Reprinted with permisson.

of relationships and satisfaction in our dating samples. Moreover, and as shown in Figure 14.2, people with a strong focus on intimacy goals experienced high levels of satisfaction regardless of the amount of time they spent with their dating partner, whereas those with a less strong focus on intimacy goals needed to spend large amounts of time with their partner in order to experience satisfaction. These findings suggest that individuals with a strong focus on intimacy goals may be able to compensate for the absence of daily life situations that directly facilitate intimacy (e.g., spending time alone with their partner), perhaps through emphasizing the quality of their time alone together as opposed to its quantity. In contrast, although engaging in many activities with one's spouse was a significant predictor of satisfaction in our married sample (even after controlling for intimacy goals), intimacy goals also continued to predict satisfaction, indicating that the intimacy goals-marital satisfaction link is not explained simply by the amount of time spent engaging in activities with one's spouse. In sum, our findings indicate that those with a strong focus on intimacy goals can experience considerable relationship satisfaction even without spending large amounts of time and engage in many activities with their partners.

The difference in findings between our dating and married samples is likely to reflect the distinct nature of these different types of relationships. Specifically, dating couples, who at least in our samples were not living together, are likely to have considerable flexibility in terms of how much time they spend together and exactly what they do during such time. In turn, those who are highly focused on intimacy goals are likely to choose to spend considerable time with their partner (and considerable time alone with their partner), whereas those without such a focus are likely to make different choices. Married couples, on the other hand, have much less flexibility in their choice about how much time to spend together as well as in the activities they do together. The couples in our study, for example, all lived together and had children, and hence are likely to be "required" to spend a fair amount of time together and engage in various activities together (e.g., childrearing, household management), regardless of the intensity of their focus on intimacy goals in their marriage.

INTERACTION IN DATING RELATIONSHIPS

Individuals with a strong focus on a particular goal may not only spend more time in goal-relevant situations, but also may interact within these broadly goal-relevant situations in particular ways. Specifically, they may engage in specific goal-relevant behaviors and may even evoke particular actions, strategies and responses from others (Buss, 1987). For example, McAdams, Healy, and Krause (1984) found that people with a strong focus on intimacy-motivation were more likely to take on a listening role in one's interactions with friends, whereas those with high-power motivation were more likely to take on an agentic or striving orientation. This type of role, in turn, is likely to elicit particular types of responses and behaviors from one's friend.

Similarly, individuals with a strong focus on intimacy in their close relationships are expected to interact in and experience such relationships in distinct ways. First, individuals with intimacy goals may give substantial social support to their partners as a way of strengthening their bond. They may also be more dependent on their partner, and expect their partner to be dependent on them, for support, understanding, and resources. Moreover, given their greater focus on creating interdependence, their partners' feelings and needs may have more impact on their own thoughts, feelings, behaviors, and plans. Research by Clark and colleagues, for example, indicates that people who are oriented towards interdependence are more attentive to the needs of their partner (Clark, 1984; Clark, Mills, & Corcoran, 1989; Clark, Mills, & Powell, 1986). Second, one of the predominant goals of an intimate relationship is obtaining support and confirmation of self-worth, both of which are fostered through self-disclosure (Hendrick, 1981). In turn, individuals with intimacy goals may both share more personal information with their partners, and be particularly focused on and adept at eliciting self-disclosure from their partner. Finally, individuals with intimacy goals may engage in relationship-enhancing thoughts, such as their feelings about their partner and the positive experiences they have shared. These thoughts may enhance positive feelings about and commitment to both their partner and the relationship (e.g., Cate, Koval, Lloyd, & Wilson, 1995; Franzoi, Davis, & Young, 1985). In sum, individuals with intimacy goals may create opportunities within their romantic relationships to engage in particular types of intimacy-enhancing interactions, which in turn may be associated with greater satisfaction.

As predicted, individuals with a strong focus on intimacy goals in their romantic relationships do interact in and experience these relationships in distinct ways. First, individuals with a strong focus on intimacy goals provide more social support to their partners in both dating and marital relationships (Sanderson & Cantor, 1997, 2001; Sanderson & Evans, 2001). They also have greater influence on their partner's thoughts and feelings as well as on their future plans (Sanderson & Cantor, 2001). Finally, Sanderson and Evans (2001) found that individuals with intimacy goals both engage in and elicit more self-disclosure, and focus more on positive thoughts about the relationship. They do not, however, focus more on their partner's thoughts or on thoughts about others in their broader social network.

Moreover, our research provides some evidence that patterns of relationship interaction partially explain the intimacy goals-relationship satisfaction link. Specifically, data from one of our dating couples samples indicates that both social support given to one's partner and self-disclosure elicited from one's partner partially, although not entirely, mediates the goals-satisfaction link (Sanderson & Evans, 2001). Similarly, data from our married couple sample demonstrates that the link between intimacy goals and satisfaction is reduced, although not eliminated, when social support given is included in the analysis. Individuals with strong intimacy goals seem to benefit in terms of satisfaction from providing social support and a "listening ear" to their partner, suggesting that they may get more out of caring for others than they do out of being cared for (e.g., receiving social support and engaging in self-disclosure themselves; Brickman & Coates, 1987).

STRATEGIES OF CONFLICT RESOLUTION

Although close relationships involve some conflict, the specific strategies that people use to resolve these conflicts reveal much about the nature and quality of the relationship (Canary, Cupach, & Messman, 1995). Specifically, individuals who are invested in and satisfied with their relationships use more constructive strategies of conflict resolution, such as open discussion and compromise, and are less likely to engage in destructive strategies (e.g., emotional withdrawal, defensiveness, contempt, and criticism; Christensen & Heavey, 1990; Rusbult, Zembrodt, & Dunn, 1982). In line with this view, recent research indicates that people who are highly committed to their relationship are more likely to forgive their partner's misbehavior (Finkel, Rusbult, Kumashiro, & Hannon, 2002). Specifically, people who are highly committed to their dating relationships are more likely to choose relationship-maintaining responses to betrayal, such as voice (e.g., discussing the situation directly) and loyalty (e.g., remaining with the partner), than those who are less committed. Moreover, individuals who use constructive and relationship-enhancing strategies for managing the inevitable conflicts that emerge are likely to experience more positive and satisfying relationships (Canary et al., 1995). This research therefore suggests that the use of such constructive strategies is another possible explanation for the intimacy goals-relationship satisfaction link.

Given prior research demonstrating that the strength of an individual's focus on the pursuit of intimacy goals in their dating relationships is associated with the distinct patterning and experience of such relationships, it is certainly conceivable that individuals with a stronger focus on intimacy goals may respond more constructively to dating conflicts and hence achieve more beneficial resolutions to conflict. First, the more time partners spend together, the more time they have to get to know one another (Brehm, 1992; Rusbult et al., 1982). In turn, this knowledge should help couples both avoid conflicts and cope with any difficulties that do occur. Second, exchanging substantial social support with one's partner strengthens the bond of trust and loyalty and enhances feelings of responsibility for and commitment to the relationship (e.g., Brickman & Coates, 1987; Fincham & Bradbury, 1990; Pasch & Bradbury, 1998; Sarason, Shearlin, Pierce, & Sarason, 1987). Mutual social support may also lead partners to feel comfortable collaborating with one another or seeking one another's advice or guidance for particular problems, including problems that exist in the relationship. Third, open communication and self-disclosure should enhance individuals' ability to manage conflict more positively by increasing mutual awareness and empathy in the relationship, thereby leading to mutual decision making and compromise (Pasch & Bradbury, 1998). For example, self-disclosure could lead individuals to reveal information about their backgrounds and values to their partner, which provides insight into their actions and can help their partner make correct or beneficial attributions for their behavior (Hendrick, 1981). Individuals with a strong focus on intimacy goals may be particularly adept at avoiding potential areas of conflict that could disrupt relationship functioning. According to Ickes and Simpson's (1997) empathic accuracy model, most close relationships have *danger zones*, namely areas in which having an awareness of one's partner's thoughts and feelings could be detrimental to one's relationship (e.g., knowing that one's partner has romantic thoughts about an old dating partner or finds a person particularly attractive). Individuals with a strong focus on intimacy goals may be particularly likely to engage in *motivated inaccuracy* about their partners' thoughts and feelings during times of potential relationship threat.

As predicted, individuals with a strong focus on intimacy goals in their romantic relationships are more likely to use constructive strategies of conflict resolution (Sanderson & Karetsky, 2002). Specifically, individuals with intimacy goals are more likely to choose constructive methods of coping, such as relying on others for social support, using open discussion and compromise, and showing concern for partner's feelings, whereas they were less likely to avoid or deny the conflict. Our finding that individuals with a strong focus on intimacy goals use more constructive strategies for resolving conflicts is particularly impressive because individuals with a strong focus on intimacy goals, who have greater interdependence, are likely to have greater potential for conflict (see, for example, Braiker & Kelly, 1979). They are also more likely to successfully work through conflicts with their partners and thereby maintain the relationship, and less likely to break up as a result of the conflict.

Most importantly, this research demonstrated that the strategies individuals use for coping with conflict in their dating relationships serve as a partial mediator between intimacy goals and relationship satisfaction. Specifically, individuals with stronger intimacy goals were not only more likely to use open discussion and show concern for their partner's feelings in response to conflict, but also mediation analyses demonstrated that the use of these strategies was associated with increased relationship satisfaction. Thus, individuals with a stronger focus on intimacy goals apparently experience greater relationship satisfaction at least in part because they handle conflict within these relationships in beneficial ways.

PARTNER SIMILARITY

As described previously, individuals go to considerable lengths to structure their lives in ways that allow for goal fulfillment (Buss, 1987; Diener, Larsen, & Emmons, 1984; Emmons et al., 1986; Snyder, 1983). Because an important component of one's close relationship is obviously one's partner, individuals select particular interaction partners, namely those who will assist them in fulfilling their own needs and goals (Buss, 1987; Cantor, 1994; Mischel et al., 1996; Snyder & Ickes, 1985; Snyder & Simpson, 1984). Although some researchers have found little evidence that people select relationship partners who share their specific personality traits (e.g., Lykken & Tellegen, 1993), other researchers suggest that people do choose partners with similar physical characteristics, cognitive abilities, and personality traits (Caspi & Herbener, 1990; Epstein & Guttman, 1984; Mascie-Taylor & Vandenberg, 1988; Phillips, Fulker, Carey, & Nagoshi, 1988). However, much of this later work has examined specific dispositional traits, such as neuroticism and extraversion, that are unlikely to directly impact each individual's ability to fulfill their own goals. It is hard to imagine, for example, how having an introverted partner would impair one's own ability to engage in extraverted behavior, and in some cases, having such a contrasting partner could even be beneficial (e.g., a pairing of dominance and submission). However, some research does suggest that individuals are more likely to select relationship partners with specific traits that may directly impact one's own ability to accomplish desired goals (Miller, Cody, & McLaughlin, 1985; Miller & Read, 1991). For example, Snyder and Simpson's (1984) work on self-monitoring indicates that individuals with a relatively public orientation prefer to date "high-status individuals" who should facilitate their desire to enhance their social standing. This preference for a particular type of relationship partner makes sense in this case because fulfilling the goals and plans of one partner depends on such a selection.

In turn, because creating an intimacy-focused relationship necessarily requires the cooperation of both partners, individuals with strong intimacy goals may choose or create similarly-oriented partners. As Miller (1990) describes, engaging in open self-disclosure and mutual dependence requires the cooperation of both people. An intimacy-focused partner is also likely to act in ways to facilitate intimacy (e.g., by providing social support, eliciting self-disclosure, engaging in interdependent activities). Moreover, an individual with a strong desire to create intimacy is likely to feel frustrated when their partner is primarily focused on independence and self-reliance and lacks the ability or comfort to engage in such self-disclosure (Miller, 1990; Miller & Read, 1991). Because individuals with intimacy goals should find it easiest to fulfill their goals with a partner who is receptive to and even facilitates such behavior, they should be motivated to have intimacy-focused partners. On the other hand, individuals who have little desire for intimacy in a relationship might prefer a similarly-oriented partner, who should be less likely to demand this type of excessive self-disclosure and interdependence.

Although we predicted that individuals with a strong focus on intimacy goals in their close relationships might experience greater satisfaction as a result of choosing similarly-oriented partners, our findings generally do not support this hypothesis. Two of our three dating couple samples included data on the intimacy goals of both partners (Sanderson & Cantor, 1997; Sanderson & Evans, 2001), and in each of these cases, there was no significant association between each partners' goals. Similarly, although there was a significant correlation between partners' goals in our married couple sample (Sanderson & Cantor, 2001), the link between one's own focus on intimacy and satisfaction was significant even when the model included spouse's goals. In sum, individuals with a strong focus on intimacy goals experience high levels of relationship satisfaction regardless of whether they have similarly-oriented partners.

PARTNER PERCEPTION

Considerable research in close relationships has shown that individuals develop detailed models of their partner's goals and beliefs (Miller & Read, 1991), and these beliefs (regardless of their accuracy) may in turn influence relationship satisfaction (Murray, Holmes, & Griffin, 1996a, 1996b; Ptacek & Dodge, 1998). Murray and colleagues (Murray et al., 1996a, 1996b), for example, have found that both dating and married couples experience more satisfying and longer-lasting relationships when individuals hold idealized views about their partners. Similarly, the social support literature indicates that individuals' perceptions of the amount of social support they receive can be a stronger predictor of well-being than the actual amount of support received (Dunkel-Schetter & Bennett, 1990), and a study by Ptacek and Dodge (1995) found that the perceived similarity of coping styles between partners is a stronger predictor of satisfaction in both dating and married relationships than the actual similarity of coping styles. Thus, close relationships research across a variety of domains demonstrates that the mere perception of one's partner's traits and styles plays an important role in creating relationship satisfaction.

Given the considerable prior research demonstrating that individuals project their own traits onto their partners (Murray et al., 1996a), those with a strong focus on intimacy goals in their close relationships may see their partners as sharing such a focus. In fact, individuals with intimacy goals are likely to see a focus on intimacy as a highly relevant and important feature of their self-concepts, and hence may be particularly inclined to project this image onto their partners (Schaefer & Olson, 1981).

In line with this view, research by Ruvolo and Fabin (1999) indicates that such projection increases as intimacy increases in a relationship. Moreover, individuals with a strong focus on the pursuit of intimacy goals should be highly motivated to see their partners as sharing their desire for intimacy because such a perception would enable them to feel more comfortable engaging in the highly vulnerable act of open self-disclosure. As described by Murray and Holmes' (2000) dependency-regulation model, people have great difficulty engaging in dependency and vulnerability in a relationship when they believe these efforts will result in rejection and disappointment. We therefore predicted that individuals with intimacy goals may be so focused on creating intimacy that they see their worlds, and specifically their partners' goals, through *intimacy-colored glasses,* which in turn leads to satisfaction.

In line with our predictions, our analyses from all three samples provide some evidence for the power of projection. As predicted, women with intimacy goals in their dating relationships did believe their partners share their focus on intimacy, and this perception was an important predictor of relationship satisfaction (Sanderson & Evans, 2001). In fact, the relationship between own goals and satisfaction was reduced, although not eliminated, when perceptions of one's partner's intimacy goals were included in the analysis. Moreover, findings from our married couple sample revealed that individuals with a strong focus on intimacy goals in their marital relationships do see their spouses as sharing this focus, and that this perception entirely accounts for the link between intimacy goals and marital satisfaction (see Figure 14.3; Sanderson & Cantor, 2001).

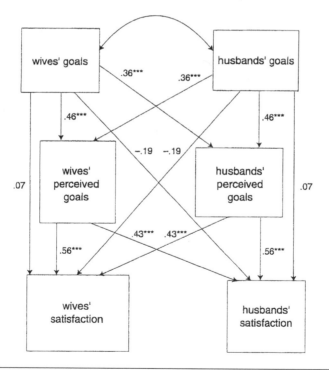

FIG. 14.3. The pursuit of intimacy goals is associated with relationship satisfaction because the pursuit of such goals leads one to perceive one's spouse as having a strong focus on intimacy. Sanderson, C. A., & Cantor, N. (2001). The association of intimacy goals and marital satisfaction: A test of four mediational hypotheses. *Personality and Social Psychology Bulletin, 27,* 1567–1577, Copyright © 2001 by Sage. Reprinted by permisson of Sage.

INTIMACY GOALS AND FRIENDSHIP SATISFACTION

Although the vast majority of research on the link between intimacy and satisfaction has focused on romantic relationships, friendships are another very important type of relationship. Friendships are experienced in one form or another by virtually everyone over the course of their lives. In the early stages of a friendship, friendship formation is motivated by a desire for companionship, a need for "belongingness," and to counter feelings of loneliness (Hays, 1988). Over time, friends become important sources of emotional support, physical aid, and intellectual stimulation, and provide individuals with a social context in which to interact. In these ways, a friend may contribute to one's individual happiness and satisfaction with life, personal identity development, and maintenance of self-esteem and overall health (Sullivan, 1953; Weiss & Lowenthal, 1975). In light of the numerous possibilities that abound for friendship formation and the positive features that friendships provide, it is not surprising that friendships are one of the most significant types of relationships engaged in by individuals across the lifespan.

Although the friendship task is a highly valued one for late adolescents, different people will approach this task with distinct goals and needs in mind (Hays, 1988). Hays, for example, notes that personal characteristics, such as friendship motivation and loneliness, influence individuals' focus on seeking friendships in general, and that individuals themselves vary in their friendship goals. Similarly, although Bakan (1966) describes *communion*, a particular orientation toward relationships character-ized by mutual disclosure and harmony, as a central need, individuals may differ in the extent to which they approach close friendships with a focus on intimate self-disclosure and listening. Moreover, individual differences in the pursuit of intimacy goals in friendships are particularly likely in late adolescence because those who have not yet resolved their identity issues (Marcia, 1966; Orlofsky, 1978) should be less likely to approach friendships with a focus on communion (Erikson, 1950; but cf., Gilligan, 1982). In sum, both theory and research suggest that individuals vary in the extent to which they are focused on and adept at creating intimacy in a close relationship.

To examine the link between the pursuit of intimacy goals in friendships and the experience of such relationships, we conducted two studies with undergraduate stu-dents (Sanderson et al., in press). In both of these samples we collected lengthy data from one person, and then brief data from their closest same-sex on-campus friend (e.g., intimacy goals, friendship satisfaction). These studies were based, in large part, on our prior research with dating and married couples, and hence included many of the same measures including time spent with friend, social support and self-disclosure (given and received), strategies of conflict resolution, perceptions of one's friend's intimacy goals, and friendship satisfaction.

These findings indicated people with a strong focus on the pursuit of intimacy goals in their close friendships structure and experience these relationships in distinct ways (Sanderson et al., in press). First, and in contrast to research on romantic relation-ships, there was no association between the pursuit of intimacy goals in friendships and the patterning of time spent in these relationships. These findings may indicate that college students in general (regardless of the intensity of their focus on inti-macy in friendships) spend considerable time with their friends (e.g., in dormitories, classes, dining halls, athletic teams, etc.). Second, and in line with our findings on the influence of intimacy goals in romantic relationships, those with a strong focus on intimacy in their friendships report eliciting and giving more self-disclosure, as well as receiving and giving more social support. People with a strong focus on the pursuit of intimacy goals in their close same-sex friendships do interact in these relationships in distinct, namely intimacy-inducing, ways. Third, these findings demonstrate that individuals with a strong focus on intimacy goals in their friendships were significantly more likely to respond to conflicts using constructive, communication-based strategies, including open communication and voice, whereas they were less likely to use destructive conflict resolution strategies, such as selfish responses, reciprocal blame and criticism, exit, and neglect. Finally, although there was no significant association between one's focus on intimacy and one's friend's focus on intimacy, those with a strong focus on intimacy in friendships saw their friends as sharing this focus. These findings once again are in line with those from our research on the influence of intimacy goals on interaction in romantic relationships showing that individuals with a strong focus on intimacy goals in their close friendships see their friends as sharing this focus.

We also conducted mediational analyses in both studies to examine which, if any, of the patterns of interaction and perception influenced the goals-satisfaction link (Sanderson et al., in press). These analyses indicated some aspects of individuals' interaction in their close friendships led to greater satisfaction. Specifically, individuals with a strong focus on intimacy goals in their close same-sex friends experience greater satisfaction at least in part because they report eliciting more social support and self-disclosure from their friend, and because they use more constructive strategies to resolve conflicts. Individuals with a strong focus on intimacy goals in their close same-sex friendship therefore experience greater friendship satisfaction at least in part because they use more constructive strategies to resolve conflict and dissatisfaction in such relationships. Interestingly, and in contrast to our research with couples in romantic relationships, individuals' perceptions of their friends' focus on intimacy did not mediate the goals-satisfaction link.

SUMMARY

This chapter describes the results from six distinct research studies (four focusing on interactions in romantic relationships, two focusing on interactions in close same-sex friendships) that examine various processes that may underlie the intimacy–satisfaction link. As shown in Table 14.1, this research provides quite consistent findings. First, this research provides no evidence that the goals–satisfaction link is caused

TABLE 14.1
Summary of Evidence for the Role of Each Process in Mediating the Intimacy Goals–Relationship Satisfaction Link

Sample	Structuring	Interaction	Conflict–Resolution	Partner Similarity	Perception
Dating relationships					
Couples[a]	–	–		–	+
Women[b]	–	+		–	+
Women and men[c]			+		
Married couples[d]	–	–		–	+
Close friends[e]	–	+	+	–	–

Note. Blank cells indicate unmeasured processes. – = no evidence for mediation; + = evidence for full or partial mediation.

[a]Sanderson & Cantor, 1997. [b]Sanderson & Evans, 2001. [c]Sanderson & Karetsky, 2001. [d]Sanderson & Cantor, 2001. [e]Sanderson, Rahm, Beigbeder, in press.

by individuals with strong intimacy goals structuring their relationships in distinct ways; although those with a strong focus on intimacy goals did spend more time alone with their partner and engage in more activities with their partner, this structuring was not associated with relationship satisfaction. Second, limited evidence suggests that both social support given and self-disclosure elicited partially mediate the link between intimacy goals and satisfaction in both dating relationships and close friendships. We also found evidence that individuals with a strong focus on intimacy goals use more constructive strategies of conflict resolution, which in turn was associated with greater satisfaction in both dating relationships and close friendships. Finally, although there was no association between similarity of individuals' intimacy goals and satisfaction, individuals' perceptions of their partner's focus on intimacy goals was a strong predictor of satisfaction in dating and marital relationships (but not close friendships). In sum, this program of research suggests that individuals with a strong focus on intimacy goals experience greater satisfaction in romantic relationships as well as friendships because they give more social support to their partner, elicit more self-disclosure from their partner, and use more constructive strategies of conflict resolution. Interestingly, and in line with prior research on the power of perception in romantic relationships (Acitelli, Douvan, & Veroff, 1993; Murray et al., 1996a, 1996b; Ptacek & Dodge, 1995), the intimacy goal-relationship satisfaction was partially mediated by individuals' perceptions of their partners' intimacy goals, even controlling for their partners' actual goals. The power of perception did not, however, mediate the goals-satisfaction link in our studies of close same-sex friendships, indicating that seeing one's partner through *intimacy-colored glasses* predicts satisfaction only in romantic relationships.

LINGERING ISSUES

These findings extend those of prior research on the association of intimacy goals and relationship satisfaction by exploring five distinct processes that may mediate the goals-satisfaction link, and hence have important implications for research on intimacy and closeness in interpersonal relationships. Although this chapter has reviewed prior research on several potential mediators of the intimacy goals-relationship satisfaction link, additional work is clearly needed to more definitively define the distinct associations between goals and relationship satisfaction. This section suggests several topics that should be examined in future research.

What Is the Process Underlying the Goals-Perception-Satisfaction Link?   Although our findings indicate that individuals' own intimacy goals predict their perceptions of their partners' goals (e.g., they see their partners through so-called intimacy-colored glasses), and that these perceptions in turn are associated with satisfaction, they do not answer the question of how exactly such perceptions mediate the goals-satisfaction link. First, individuals who perceive that their partner has intimacy-focused goals may act in particular ways in order to assist their partner in fulfilling these goals, and these efforts to directly facilitate intimacy in the relationship (e.g., they may themselves engage in more self-disclosure, provide more social support, etc.) may lead to satisfaction. According to this hypothesis, individuals' own behavior (which occurs as a result of their perceptions of their partner's goals) leads them to create opportunities for intimacy in the relationship, which thereby leads to satisfaction via self-fulfilling prophecy (e.g., Jussim, 1989; Snyder, Tanke, & Berscheid, 1977). Recent longitudinal research by Downey and colleagues (Downey, Freitas, Michaelis, & Khouri, 1998) has shown the negative implications of such a process, namely by demonstrating that individuals who are especially sensitive to rejection in their dating relationships actually behave in ways that elicit rejection from their dating partners.

On the other hand, it is also possible that simply having such a perception (regardless of its accuracy) may lead those with intimacy goals to perceive their spouse's behavior accordingly (e.g., one could interpret the behavior of a hard-working spouse who is rarely home as intensely focused on providing for his or her family and thereby quite concerned with communion). In other words, individuals with intimacy goals may feel content with their relationship merely through their belief that their partner is also interested in engaging in interdependence and communion (e.g., the power of seeing one's partner through intimacy-colored glasses). For example, individuals who believe (even erroneously) that their partner shares their intense focus on intimacy may feel comfortable engaging in various personally-relevant (e.g., intimacy-focused) behaviors (e.g., sharing thoughts and feelings, eliciting self-disclosure, spending time alone with one's partner), and as a result may experience satisfaction.

What Is the Causal Direction of the Goals–Satisfaction Link?   Although our findings provide some evidence for the role of various processes in mediating the goals-satisfaction link, with the exception of one of our samples (Sanderson & Cantor, 1997), these analyses assessed variables at a single time period, and therefore cannot demonstrate causality. It is certainly possible, for example, that greater relationship satisfaction leads one to form stronger intimacy goals, structure one's dating relationship in particular ways, and perceive one's partner as having intimacy-focused goals (e.g., Snyder, 1983). In fact, the perception that one's partner has intimacy goals may even lead people to act in particular ways that elicit intimacy-focused behavior, and even create intimacy-focused goals, from their partner (Snyder et al., 1977). Murray and colleagues (1996b), for example, have found that individuals' perceptions of their partners may actually have the power to become self-fulfilling prophecies (e.g., an individual actually creates the partner he or she envisions by modifying the partner's self-concept). Similarly, the *Michaelangelo effect* refers to the finding that people actually become more like their partner's images of them over time, which in turn is associated with greater relationship satisfaction and longevity (Drigotas, Rusbult, Wiselquist, & Whitton, 1999). Similarly, intimacy-focused individuals may assume their partners are intimacy-focused and work to elicit self-disclosure, and over time, as their partners became more and more comfortable with engaging in such behavior, their perceptions of their partners' goals would essentially be realized. Future longitudinal research would contribute to an understanding of the development of intimacy goals by assessing individuals' intimacy goals and their partners' goals at different points in time in order to gain a better understanding of how each individual's goals influence the other's goals, behavior, and satisfaction.

Although given the use of cross-sectional data we cannot determine the direction of the effects in this data, it is likely that the link between goals and satisfaction is complex and bidirectional. On the one hand, recent longitudinal work on the effects of personality on interpersonal relationships suggests that personality affects relationships whereas relationships have little impact on personality (Asendorpf & Wilpers, 1998). Similarly, research on close relationships has shown that spouses' behavior and interpretations seem to contribute to marital satisfaction as opposed to the reverse (e.g., marital satisfaction influencing such perceptions; Karney & Bradbury, 2000). However, research also suggests that experience in relationships has an impact on personality. Research in developmental psychology, for example, provides strong evidence that individuals' early relationship experiences color their interpersonal interactions later on (Hartup & van Lieshout, 1995). Similarly, Caspi and Herbener (1990) have shown that interaction between spouses influences personality development across the lifespan. Finally, research by Cook (1990) suggests that attachment security is reciprocally determined in relationships, with secure people providing support to their relationship partners, who in turn extend more support back to their partner, resulting in, in essence, a positive feedback loop. In sum, although intimacy goals may indeed lead to particular patterns of interaction and perception in close relation-ships, which thereby contributes to satisfaction, the association between goals and satisfaction is clearly complex and bi-directional.

Are There Other Mediators of the Goals-Satisfaction Link?   Although this re-search examined several possible mediators of the intimacy goals-relationship satis-faction link (e.g., time spent with partner, patterns of interaction, strategies of conflict resolution, partner's actual goals, partner's perceived goals), there are clearly other variables that may serve to mediate this association. Intimacy-focused individuals may structure their close relationships and interact with their partners in a variety of ways not addressed in this study, including making beneficial attributions, showing empathy, and engaging in "relationship talk" (e.g., Acitelli, 1992), which in turn may be associated with relationship satisfaction. For example, those who are pursuing in-timacy goals may be more aware of and focused on their partner's feelings regarding the relationship. Relatedly, research by Franzoi and colleagues (Franzoi et al., 1985) has shown that perspective-taking scores are significantly related to relationship sat-isfaction in college student couples. Individuals with intimacy goals, who are more likely to both engage in and elicit self-disclosure, may also make more accurate and positive attributions for their partner's behavior, and hence experience greater re-lationship satisfaction (Fincham & Bradbury, 1989). Future research should examine these as well as other potential mediators of the intimacy goal-relationship satisfaction link to provide insight into whether factors other than mere perception of partners' goals are associated with relationship quality.

How Does Culture Matter?   The research described throughout this chapter on the link between intimacy goals and relationship satisfaction is based on primarily white, middle to upper-class samples in the United States, and therefore these findings may or may not apply to other cultures. Cultures vary significantly in the value they place on interdependence versus independence as an overarching goal (e.g. Markus & Kitayama, 1991; Singelis, 1994), and even subcultures within a given population may vary in the emphasis they place on these two goals (Veroff, 1983). For exam-ple, African-American college students in the United States show a greater focus on collectivism and interdependence than white students (Baldwin & Hopkins, 1990). Although we have not tested our hypotheses regarding the link between intimacy goals and relationship satisfaction in non-Western samples, we do have data indicat-ing that people from more interdependent subcultures within the United States and who themselves have a strong focus on interdependence are better able to regulate their behavior in their dating relationships in a functional way (Cantor & Sanderson, 1997). Specifically, we collected data from approximately 1,300 college students at six different colleges in Georgia, which provided a range of respondents from differ-ent subcultures (47% white, 41% African American). This data included measures of their orientation toward interpersonal discussion with their dating partner regarding condom use as well as measures of safer sexual behavior. Findings indicated that subculture moderated the impact of interpersonal discussion orientation on number of sexual partners: for African-American students, weaker interpersonal orientation was associated with more sexual partners, and stronger interpersonal orientation was associated with fewer sexual partners; whereas for Whites, interpersonal orientation had little impact on number of sexual partners. In sum, individuals whose subculture emphasizes interdependence are particularly influenced in terms of their relation-ship behavior by the intensity of their focus on interpersonal orientation. Similarly, the impact of intimacy goals on relationship satisfaction may be particularly strong in subcultures that place a strong emphasis on communion and interdependence. Future research should clearly examine this important question.

ACKNOWLEDGMENTS

I wish to acknowledge the extremely helpful suggestions of Art Aron, John Holmes, Debra Mashek, and Harry Reis on an earlier version of this chapter and the assistance of Darren Yopyk in preparing this chapter.

Correspondence concerning this chapter should be addressed to Catherine A. Sanderson, Department of Psychology, P.O. Box 2236, Amherst College, Amherst, Massachusetts 01002-5000. E-mail: casanderson@amherst.edu

REFERENCES

Acitelli, L. K. (1992). Gender differences in relationship awareness and marital satisfaction among young married couples. *Personality and Social Psychology Bulletin, 18*, 102–110.

Acitelli, L. K., Douvan, E., & Veroff, J. (1993). Perceptions of conflict in the first year of marriage: How important are similarity and understanding? *Journal of Social and Personal Relationships, 10*, 5–19.

Altman, I., & Taylor, D. A. (1973). *Social penetration: The development of interpersonal relationships.* New York: Holt, Rinehart, & Winston.

Asendorpf, J. B., & Wilpers, S. (1998). Personality effects on social relationships. *Journal of Personality and Social Psychology, 74*, 1531–1544.

Atkinson, J., & Huston, T. L. (1984). Sex role orientation and division of labor early in marriage. *Journal of Personality and Social Psychology, 46*, 330–345.

Bakan, D. (1966). *The duality of human existence.* Boston, MA: Beacon.

Berscheid, E. (1983). Emotion. In H. H. Kelley, E. Berscheid, A. Christensen, H. Harvey, T. L. Huston, G. Levinger, et al. (Eds.), *Close relationships* (pp. 110–168). San Francisco: Freeman.

Berscheid, E., Snyder, M., & Omoto, A. M. (1989). The relationship closeness inventory: Assessing the closeness of interpersonal relationships. *Journal of Personality and Social Psychology, 57*, 792–807.

Bradbury, T. N., & Fincham, F. D. (1988). Individual difference variables in close relationships: A contextual model of marriage as an integrative framework. *Journal of Personality and Social Psychology, 54*, 713–721.

Bradbury, T. N., & Fincham, F. D. (1991). A contextual model for advancing the study of marital interaction. In G. Fletcher & F. Fincham (Eds.), *Cognition in close relationships* (pp. 127–147). Hillsdale, NJ: Lawrence Erlbaum Associates.

Braiker, H. B., & Kelley, H. H. (1979). Conflict in the development of close relationships. In R. L. Burgess & T. L. Huston (Eds.), *Social exchange in developing relationships* (pp. 135–168). New York: Academic Press.

Brehm, S. S. (1992). *Intimate relationships.* New York: McGraw Hill.

Brickman, P., & Coates, D. (1987). Commitment and mental health. In P. Brickman (Ed.), *Commitment, conflict, and caring* (pp. 222–309). Englewood Cliffs, NJ: Prentice Hall.

Briggs, S. R., & Cheek, J. M. (1986). The role of factor analysis in the development and evaluation of personality scales. *Journal of Personality, 54*, 106–148.

Buss, D. M. (1987). Selection, evocation and manipulation. *Journal of Personality and Social Psychology, 53*, 1214–1221.

Canary, D. J., Cupach, W. R., & Messman, S. J. (1995). *Relationship conflict.* Thousand Oaks, CA: Sage.

Cantor, N. (1994). Life task problem-solving: Situational affordances and personal needs. *Personality and Social Psychology Bulletin, 20*, 235–243.

Cantor, N., Acker, M., & Cook-Flannagan, C. (1992). Conflict and preoccupation in the intimacy life task. *Journal of Personality and Social Psychology, 63*, 644–655.

Cantor, N., & Fleeson, W. (1991). Life tasks and self-regulatory processes. *Advances in Motivation and Achievement, 7*, 327–369.

Cantor, N., & Kilhstrom, J. F. (1987). Personality and social intelligence. Englewood Cliffs, NJ: Prentice-Hall.

Cantor, N., & Malley, J. (1991). Life tasks, personal needs, and close relationships. In G. J. O. Fletcher & F. D. Fincham (Eds.), *Cognition in close relationships* (pp. 101–125). Hillsdale, NJ: Lawrence Erlbaum Associates.

Cantor, N., Norem, J. K., Niedenthal, P. M., Langston, C. A., & Brower, A. M. (1987). Life tasks, self-concept ideals, and cognitive strategies in a life transition. *Journal of Personality and Social Psychology, 53*, 1178–1191.

Cantor, N., & Sanderson, C. A. (1998). The functional regulation of adolescent dating relationships and sexual behavior: An interaction of goals, strategies and situations. In J. Heckhausen & C. Dweck (Eds.), *A life-span perspective on motivation and control* (pp. 185 to 215). New York: Cambridge University Press.

Cantor, N., & Zirkel, S. (1990). Personality, cognition, and purposive behavior. In L. Pervin (Ed.), *Handbook of personality theory and research* (pp. 135–164). New York: Guilford.

Caspi, A., & Herbener, E. S. (1990). Continuity and change: Assortative marriage and the consistency of personality in adulthood. *Journal of Personality and Social Psychology, 58*, 250–258.

Cate, R. M., Koval, J., Lloyd, S. A., & Wilson, G. (1995). Assessment of relationship thinking in dating relationships. *Personal Relationships, 2* 77–95.

Christensen, A., & Heavey, C. L. (1990). Sex and social structure in the demand/withdrawal pattern of marital conflict. *Journal of Personality and Social Psychology, 59*, 73–81.

Clark, M. S. (1984). Record keeping in two types of relationships. *Journal of Personality and Social Psychology, 47*, 549–557.

Clark, M. S., Mills, J., & Corcoran, D. M. (1989). Keeping track of needs and inputs of friends and strangers. *Personality and Social Psychology Bulletin, 15*, 533–542.

Clark, M. S., Mills, J., & Powell, M. (1986). Keeping track of needs in exchange and communal relationships. *Journal of Social and Personal Relationships, 2*, 403–413.

Cook, W. L. (2000). Understanding attachment security in family context. *Journal of Personality and Social Psychology, 78*, 285–294.

Diener, E., Larsen, R. J., & Emmons, R. A. (1984). Person*Situation interactions: Choice of situations and congruence response models. *Journal of Personality and Social Psychology, 47*, 580–592.

Downey, G., Freitas, A. L., Michaelis, B., & Khouri, H. (1998). The self-fulfilling prophecy in close relationships: Rejection sensitivity and rejection by romantic partners. *Journal of Personality and Social Psychology, 75*, 545–560.

Drigotas, S. M., Rusbult, C. E., Wiselquist, J., & Whitton, S. W. (1999). Close partners as sculptor of the ideal self: Behavioral affirmation and the Michelangelo phenomenon. *Journal of Personality and Social Psychology, 77*, 293–323.

Dunkel-Schetter, C., & Bennett, T. L. (1990). Differentiating the cognitive and behavioral aspects of social support. In I. G. Sarason, B. R. Sarason, & G. R. Pierce (Eds.), *Social support: An interactional view* (pp. 267–296). New York: Wiley.

Emmons, R. A. (1989). The personal striving approach to personality. In L. A. Pervin (Ed.), *Goal concepts in personality psychology* (pp. 87–126). Hillsdale, NJ: Lawrence Erlbaum Associates.

Emmons, R. A., Diener, E., & Larsen, R. J. (1986). Choice and avoidance of everyday situations and affect congruence: Two models of reciprocal interactionism. *Journal of Personality and Social Psychology, 51*, 815–826.

Epstein, E., & Guttman, R. (1984). Mate selection in man: Evidence, theory, and outcome. *Social Biology, 31*, 243–278.

Erikson, E. H. (1950). *Childhood and society.* New York: Norton.

Erikson, E. H. (1968). *Identity: Youth and crisis.* New York: Norton.

Fincham, F. D., & Bradbury, T. N. (1990). Social support in marriage: The role of social cognition. *Journal of Social and Clinical Psychology, 9*, 31–42.

Finkel, E. J., Rusbult, C. E., Kumashiro, M., & Hannon, P. A. (2002). Dealing with betrayal in close relationships: Does commitment promote forgiveness? *Journal of Personality and Social Psychology, 82*, 956–974.

Franzoi, S. L., Davis, M. H., & Young, R. D. (1985). The effects of private self-consciousness and perspective taking on satisfaction in close relationships. *Journal of Personality and Social Psychology, 48*, 1585–1595.

Gilligan, C. (1982). In a different voice. Cambridge, MA: Harvard University Press.

Gollwitzer, P. (1993). Goal achievement: The role of intentions. In W. Stroebe & M. Hewstone (Eds.), *European review of social psychology. Vol. 4* (pp. 141–185). London: Wiley.

Hartup, W. W., & van Lieshout, C. F. M. (1995). Personality development in social context. *Annual Review of Psychology, 46*, 655–687.

Hays, R. B. (1988). Friendship. In S. Duck (Ed.), *Handbook of personal relationships* (pp. 391–408). New York: Wiley.

Hazan, C., & Shaver, P. R. (1987). Romantic love conceptualized as an attachment process. *Journal of Personality and Social Psychology, 52*, 511–524.

Hendrick, S. S. (1981). Self-disclosure and marital satisfaction. *Journal of Personality and Social Psychology, 40*, 1150–1159.

Hendrick, S. S., Hendrick, C., & Adler, N. L. (1988). Romantic relationships: Love, satisfaction, and staying together. *Journal of Personality and Social Psychology, 54*, 930–988.

Hill, C. T., Rubin, Z., & Peplau, L. A. (1976). Breakups before marriage: The end of 103 affairs. *Journal of Social Issues, 3*, 147–168.

Ickes, W., & Simpson, J. A. (1997). Managing empathic accuracy in close relationships. In W. Ickes (Ed.), *Empathic accuracy* (pp. 218–250). New York: Guilford Press.

Jussim, L. (1989). Teacher expectations: Self-fulfilling prophecies, perceptual biases, and accuracy. *Journal of Personality and Social Psychology, 57*, 469–480.

Karney, B. R., & Bradbury, T. N. (2000). Attributions in marriage: State or trait? A growth curve analysis. *Journal of Personality and Social Psychology, 78*, 295–309.

Kelley, H. H. (1979). *Personal relationships: Their structures and processes.* Hillsdale, NJ: Lawrence Erlbaum Associates.

Kelley, H. H., Berscheid, E., Christensen, A., Harvey, J. H., Huston, T. L., Levinger, G., et al. (1983). Close relationships. New York: Freeman.

Levinger, G., & Senn, D. J. (1967). Disclosure of feelings in marriage. *Merril-Palmer Quarterly, 13*, 237–249.

Little, B. (1989). Personal projects analysis: Trivial pursuits, magnificent obsessions, and the search for coherence. In D. M. Buss & N. Cantor (Eds.), *Personality Psychology: Recent Trends and Emerging Directions* (pp. 15–31). New York: Springer-Verlag.

Little, B. R., Lecci, L., & Watkinson, B. (1992). Personality and personal projects: Linking big five and PAC units of analysis. *Journal of Personality, 60*, 501–525.

Lykken, D. T., & Tellegen, A. (1993). Is human mating adventitious or the result of lawful choices? A twin study of mate selection. *Journal of Personality and Social Psychology, 65*, 56–68.

Marcia, J. E (1966). Development and validation of ego identity status. *Journal of Personality and Social Psychology, 3*, 551–558.

Markus, H. R., & Kitiyama, S. (1991). Culture and the self: Implications for cognition, emotion, and motivation. *Psychological Review, 98*, 224–253.

Mascie-Taylor, C. G. N., & Vandenberg, S. G. (1988). Assortative mating for IQ and personality due to propinquity and personal preference. *Behavior Genetics, 18*, 339–345.

McAdams, D. P. (1984). Human motives and personal relationships. In V. J. Derlega (Ed.), *Communication, intimacy, and close relationships* (pp. 41–70). Orlando, FL: Academic Press.

McAdams, D. P., & Constantian, C. A. (1983). Intimacy and affiliation motives in daily living: An experience sampling analysis. *Journal of Personality and Social Psychology, 45*, 851–861.

McAdams, D. P., Healy, S., & Krause, S. (1984). Social motives and patterns of friendship. *Journal of Personality and Social Psychology, 47*, 828–838.

Miller, L. C. (1990). Intimacy and liking: Mutual influence and the role of unique relationships. *Journal of Personality and Social Psychology, 59*, 50–60.

Miller, L. C., Cody, M. J., & McLaughlin, M. L. (1985). Situations and goals as fundamental constructs in interpersonal communication research. In M. L. Knapp & G. R. Miller (Eds.), *Handbook of interpersonal communication* (pp. 162–198). Beverly Hills, CA: Sage.

Miller, L. C., & Read, S. J. (1991). On the coherence of mental models of persons and relationships: A knowledge structure approach. In G. O. Fletcher & F. D. Fincham (Eds.) *Cognition in close relationships* (pp. 69–99). Hillsdale, NJ: Lawrence Erlbaum Associates.

Mischel, W., Cantor, N., & Feldman, S. (1996). Principles of self-regulation: The nature of willpower and self-control. In E.T.Higgins & A. W. Kruglanski (Eds.), *Social psychology: Handbook of basic principles* (pp. 329–360). New York: Guilford.

Mischel, W., & Shoda, Y. (1995). A cognitive-affective system theory of personality: Reconceptualizing situations, dispositions, dynamics, and invariance in personality structure. *Psychological Review, 102*, 246–268.

Murray, S. L., & Holmes, J. G. (2000). Seeing the self through a partner's eyes: Why self-doubts turn into relationship insecurities. In A. Tesser (Ed.), *Psychological perspectives on self and identity* (pp. 173–197). Washington, DC: American Psychological Association.

Murray, S. L., Holmes, J. G., & Griffin, D. W. (1996a). The benefits of positive illusions: Idealization and the construction of satisfaction in close relationships. *Journal of Personality and Social Psychology, 70*, 79–98.

Murray, S. L., Holmes, J. G., & Griffin, D. W. (1996b). The self-fulfilling nature of positive illusions in romantic relationships: Love is blind, but prescient. *Journal of Personality and Social Psychology, 71*, 1155–1180.

Orlofsky, J. L. (1978). The relationship between intimacy status and antecedent personality components. *Adolescence, 13*, 419–441.

Pasch, L. A., & Bradbury, T. N. (1998). Social support, conflict, and the development of marital dysfunction. *Journal of Personality and Social Psychology, 66*, 219–230.

Phillips, K., Fulker, D. W., Carey, G., & Nagoshi, C. T. (1988). Direct marital assortment for cognitive and personality variables. *Behavior Genetics, 18*, 347–356.

Prager, K. J. (1995). *The psychology of intimacy.* New York: Guilford.

Ptacek, J. T., & Dodge, K. L. (1995). Coping strategies and relationship satisfaction in couples. *Personality and Social Psychology Bulletin, 21*, 76–84.

Reis, H. T., & Shaver, P. (1988). Intimacy as an interpersonal process. In S. Duck (Ed.), *Handbook of personal relationships* (pp. 367–389). New York: Wiley.

Rempel, J. K., Holmes, J. G., & Zanna, M. P. (1985). Trust in close relationships. *Journal of Personality and Social Psychology, 49*, 95–112.

Rubin, Z., Hill, C. T., Peplau, L. A., & Dunkel-Schetter, C. (1980). Self-disclosure in dating couples: Sex roles and the ethic of openness. *Journal of Marriage and the Family, 42*, 305–317.

Rusbult, C. E., Zembrodt, I. M., & Dunn, L. K. (1982). Exit, voice, loyalty, and neglect: Responses to dissatisfaction in romantic involvements. *Journal of Personality and Social Psychology, 43*, 1230–1242.

Ruvolo, A. P., & Fabin, L. A. (1999). Two of a kind: Perceptions of own and partner's attachment characteristics. *Personal Relationships, 6*, 57–79.

Sanderson, C. A., & Cantor, N. (1995). Social dating goals in late adolescence: Implications for safer sexual activity. *Journal of Personality and Social Psychology, 68*, 1121–1134.

Sanderson, C. A., & Cantor, N. (1997). Creating satisfaction in steady dating relationships: The role of personal goals and situational affordances. *Journal of Personality and Social Psychology, 73*, 1424–1433.

Sanderson, C. A., & Cantor, N. (2001). The association of intimacy goals and marital satisfaction: A test of four mediational hypotheses. *Personality and Social Psychology Bulletin, 27*, 1567–1577.

Sanderson, C. A., & Evans, S. M. (2001). Seeing one's partner through intimacy-colored glasses: An examination of the processes underlying the intimacy goals-relationship satisfaction link. *Personality and Social Psychology Bulletin, 27*, 461–471.

Sanderson, C. A., & Karetsky, K. H. (2002). The influence of intimacy goals on coping with conflict in dating relationships. *Journal of Social and Personal Relationships, 19*, 323–343.

Sanderson, C. A., Rahm, K. B., & Beigbeder, S. A. (in press). The link between the pursuit of intimacy goals and satisfaction in close same-sex friendships: An examination of the underlying processes. *Journal of Social and Personal Relationships.*

Sarason, B. R., Shearlin, E. N., Pierce, G. R., & Sarason, I. G. (1987). Interrelationships between social support measures: Theoretical and practical implications. *Journal of Personality and Social Psychology, 52*, 813–832.

Schaefer, M. T., & Olson, D. H. (1981). Assessing intimacy: The PAIR inventory. *Journal of Marriage and Family Therapy, 7*, 47–60.

Silbereisen, R. K., Noack, P., & von Eye, A. (1992). Adolescents' development of romantic friendship and change in favorite leisure contexts. *Journal of Adolescent Research,7*, 80–93.

Simpson, J. A. (1987). The dissolution of romantic relationships: Factors involved in relationship stability and emotional distress. *Journal of Personality and Social Psychology, 53*, 683–692.

Simpson, J. A. (1990). The influence of attachment styles on romantic relationships. *Journal of Personality and Social Psychology, 59*, 971–980.

Singelis, T. M. (1994). The measurement of independent and interdependent self-construals. *Personality and Social Psychology Bulletin, 20*, 580–591.

Snyder, M. (1983). The influence of individuals on situations: Implications for understanding the links between personality and social behavior. *Journal of Personality, 51*, 497–516.

Snyder, M., & Ickes, W. (1985). Personality and social behavior. In G. Lindsey & E. Aronson (Eds.), *Handbook of social psychology* (pp. 883–947). New York: Random House.

Snyder, M., & Simpson, J. A. (1984). Self-monitoring and dating relationships. *Journal of Personality and Social Psychology, 47*, 1281–1291.

Snyder, M., Tanke, E. D., & Berscheid, E. (1977). Social perception and interpersonal behavior: On the self-fulfilling nature of social stereotypes. *Journal of Personality and Social Psychology, 35*, 656–666.

Sullivan, H. S. (1953). *The interpersonal theory of psychiatry.* New York: Norton.

Veroff, J. (1983). Contextual determinants of personality. *Personality and Social Psychology Bulletin, 9*, 331–344.

Weiss, L., & Lowenthal, M. F. (1975). Life course perspective on friendship. In M. F. Lowenthal (Ed.), *Four stages of life* (pp. 48–61). San Francisco, CA: Jossey-Bass.

Zirkel, S. (1992). Developing independence in a life transition: Investing the self in the concerns of the day. *Journal of Personality and Social Psychology, 62*, 506–521.

Zirkel, S., & Cantor, N. (1990). Personal construal of a life task: Those who struggle for independence. *Journal of Personality and Social Psychology, 58*, 172–185.

15

The Impact of Adult Temperament on Closeness and Intimacy

Elaine N. Aron
State University of New York, Stony Brook

This purpose of this chapter is to discuss intimacy and closeness in the light of some of the current research on *adult temperament*, which is defined as inborn biological differences affecting style of behavior in a wide variety of situations. In this chapter closeness is viewed as an emotional, cognitive, and behavioral phenomena, defined below, and intimacy is conceptualized as a subset of closeness—that is, the emotional experience of it. Thus I begin with a discussion of adult temperament, and then proceed to research and theory regarding its relationship to closeness by considering one such temperament trait, referred to as *sensory-processing sensitivity* (E. N. Aron & A. Aron, 1997) (although it might well be called something else), and three types of effects that the characteristics associated with this trait, or any trait, have on closeness. These three effects are actor, partner, and relationship effects. (This organization is loosely based on Kenny's, 1994, social relations analysis.) Although this chapter is predominately theory-based and research oriented, it also benefits from the author's clinical experience when it has seemed useful in predicting research hypotheses.

TEMPERAMENT AS TWO INNATE, POSSIBLY UNIVERSAL STRATEGIES

That people can display dramatic individual differences in inherited temperament traits is not news. And surely these would affect closeness. Still, "individual differences," innate or otherwise, have often been a topic set aside as only confusing the real task of understanding close relationships in general, even if we admit that certain broad categories, especially introversion–extraversion and secure–insecure, can be interesting sidelines for study.

However, imagine if there were (at least) two quite different breeds of humans—as different as, say, a pit bull and a Chihuahua. *Breed* would become an essential variable, even if a nuisance. Would we study the more numerous or culturally ideal breed (CroMagnon rather than Neanderthal)? Report results on both breeds in every study? The issues are much like those surrounding gender, of course, but a different breed, with its own genders, would indeed complicate our research.

Welcome to the dawning reality of innate individual differences—that two or more "hard-wired" behavioral styles are typically present within a species, including the human species. This idea requires a major rethinking, in that we are accustomed to the idea that evolutionary theory implies an ideal, fittest prototype individual, perfectly adapted to its ecological niche. Although such an individual may not exist, and this prototype evolves as the niche changes, there is still only one ideal way to meet the challenges of that niche. But more recently it has been recognized (for a brief review of this literature and one example, see Wilson, Coleman, Clark, & Biederman, 1993) that many or perhaps most species have "subspecies" with two (or perhaps more) different survival strategies such that when one does not work, the other does. The two groups behave differently in most situations, whether avoiding predators, foraging, or mating (they may even harbor different parasites).

Two strategies in particular are seen as very basic—they are roughly what we have termed in humans introversion and extraversion (e.g., Eysenck, 1991). One, hypothesized (Gray, 1991) to be controlled by the behavioral activation system (BAS), causes an individual to advance towards and explore novel stimuli, whatever the consequences. We might call it the strategy of "go for it," or betting on long shots. When it is strong, one has the trait of sensation seeking (Zuckerman, 1990, 1994), extraversion, positive affect, or whatever one wishes to call it depending on the context (social, emotional, etc.).

The other strategy, the focus of this chapter, is hypothesized to be under the control of the Behavioral Inhibition System (BIS; Gray, 1991), promotes stopping to observe a novel situation and processing the information thoroughly before acting (except when preliminary processing warns of the need for fast action). It is a strategy of "do it once and do it right," or betting on the sure thing. When an individual has an innately active BIS, this strategy becomes the predominant behavioral style or temperament. By processing sensory details before proceeding, fewer risks are taken, less energy is expended, and a better cognitive map of the situation is maintained; but such individuals miss the benefits of being first. A predator will not catch them unaware in a clearing, for example, but by the time they enter it, the most nutritious grazing sites may be taken. Interestingly, in most populations, including humans, the sensation seeking strategy usually stabilizes around 70% to 85%, the sensation processing strategy around 15% to 30%. In humans, measuring the latter trait as sensory-processing sensitivity in adults (E. N. Aron & A. Aron, 1997), or "inhibitedness" (Kagan, 1994) in children, the percentage with the trait is about 15% to 20%.

Note, again, that this trait does not create a style of indiscriminate fearfulness, as observing may involve developing a clever strategy to acquire something desirable rather than avoiding something threatening, and observing is also a way to save unnecessary effort by exploring mentally rather than physically. Finally, note that our data from two diverse samples found that the two traits are independent, as one would expect if they are governed by separate systems. That is, one could be high in one trait and low on the other, or low on both or high on both. That is, counterintuitive as it may be, being highly sensitive is not the opposite of being a high-sensation seeker.

These two strategies, again, appear to be found within every species, and this makes sense given that they are not automatic ways of reacting in a given situation, but ways of processing and responding to information about any situation. Perhaps they are the only two ways, in the sense of their being only two ways to "play the odds." Certainly, in humans, the two strategies are well-known in adults (under labels such as extraversion–introversion, e.g. Eysenck, 1991, or Stelmack & Geen, 1992; harm avoidance vs. novelty seeking, Cloninger, 1987; or approach–avoidance, Eliot & Thrash, 2002). In children the strategies have been described as uninhibitedness or inhibitedness (Kagan, 1994). In other species the high sensory-processing style is mainly what is described in the literature because the more common sensation-seeking style is considered "normal" (e.g., see Higley & Suomi, 1989; Stevenson-Hinde, Stillwell-Barnes, & Zung, 1980; Suomi, 1983, 1987, 1991, for primates; see Bekoff, 1977; Fox, 1972; Goddard & Beilharz, 1985; MacDonald, 1983; Scott & Fuller, 1965, for canids; see Blanchard, Flannelly, & Blanchard, 1986; Blizard, 1981; Cooper, Schmidt, & Barrett, 1983, for rats; see Lyons, Price, & Moberg, 1988, for goats; and see Wilson, Coleman, Clark, & Biederman, 1993, for pumpkinseed sunfish).

That a preference for observation and processing versus quick action are a basic biological difference has been most recently supported by the finding of the allele determining these two strategies in the well-studied *Drosophila*, or fruit fly (Osborne, et al, 1997; Renger, Yao, Sokolowski, & Wu, 1999). Flies that are "sitters" (30%) as opposed to "rovers" (70%) in the presence of food have a greater neuronal excitability and connectivity, suggesting that in the presence of food they have substituted increased sensory processing for exploratory movement. In bees the same gene, termed *for* for "forager," turns on during development, changing nurse bees into nectar gatherers (Ben-Shahar, Robichon, Sokolowski, & Robinson, 2002).

Gray (1991) appears to have had an important insight about the two strategies in humans when he differentiated them from social introversion and extraversion by suggesting two separate trait dimensions, anxiety and impulsivity, controlled by the BIS and BAS. The term *anxiety* was used because the BIS is sensitive to anxiety–reducing medications. But identifying the sensory-processing strategy as anxiety, or the BIS as functioning mainly to lower the threshold for negative stimuli or punishment, has turned out to be highly problematic. Gray himself stated that the "central task" [of the BIS is] "to compare, quite generally, actual with expected stimuli" (1985, p. 8), and given the general sensitivity to stimuli created by the BIS, any argument that it only increases an awareness of threats of punishment would be "tortuous, assuming it to be viable at all (Gray, 1981, p. 270)." This reasoning makes sense, given that there is far more evolutionary advantage to a trait creating a preference to pause and match present stimuli to past memories—including but not limited to past dangers—over one that causes an indiscriminately anxious, inhibited response. Still, seeing the trait as fearfulness, avoidance, or withdrawal continues (e.g., Eliot & Thrash, 2002).

Although genes clearly do exist that create temperament styles or strategies, they do not come with labels. These genes require some name, however, and the names reflect our past ideas and also our future theory, research, and eventual application of those labels. In humans, this genetic difference in strategies is frequently observed in social situations, and each strategy is most popularly called *introversion* or *extraversion*. When the observing strategy becomes problematic for mental health it is labeled as a genetic tendency to shyness, social phobia, negative emotionality, or dispositional depression or anxiety.

What has been ignored in these descriptions, and which caused Gray (1981) to rethink the dichotomy, is the wealth of data indicating that those called introverts, compared to those called extraverts, are biochemically and neurologically more sensitive under most conditions. They are more aware of subtle stimulation, responsive to stimulants, and reactive to medications (for a review, see Koelega's 1992 meta-analysis; Stelmack & Geen's 1992 review; Kohn's 1987 discussion of arousability; and E. N. Aron & A. Aron, 1997). "Introverts" evidence more lability in the Pavlovian sense (central nervous system capacity for rapid information processing; Mangan & Sturrock, 1988), greater electrodermal lability (Crider & Lunn, 1971), and a greater electrodermal orienting response at moderate levels of stimuli (Zahn, Kruesi, Leonard, & Rapoport, 1994). Overall, "introverts" are "geared to inspect," according to Brebner (1980, p. 313), and more reflective and stringent in their criteria for responses according to Patterson and Newman (1993), but not necessarily different in fearfulness or sociability. Further, although some of this sensitivity may be sensory, most of it appears to be attributable to a difference in how information is processed.

SENSORY-PROCESSING SENSITIVITY (AND SENSATION SEEKING): STUDYING TEMPERAMENT IN ADULTS

Like Gray (1981), I was aware that introverts evidence more sensitivity to stimuli and thus I began to study this basic human difference under the new name of *high sensory-processing sensitivity,* or simply *high sensitivity*. Besides adopting the strategy of "look before you leap," those with the trait evidence a greater sensitivity to subtleties and to the consequences of an action. Highly sensitive individuals also have a tendency to become overaroused and fatigued by stimulation that is highly intense, persisting, or complex, and an understandable inclination to avoid such highly stimulating situations, including unfamiliar social environments (E. N. Aron & A. Aron, 1997; E. N. Aron, 1999).

The study of temperament (e.g., Kohnstam, Bates, & Rothbart, 1989) has been primarily carried out with infants and young children in longitudinal and twin studies because supposedly children have been least affected by personal history. To study temperament in adults without waiting for the results of longitudinal studies, researchers have tried to recognize how certain fundamental differences that are recognized in infants and other species, and that are biologically plausible, might be expressed in adult humans. This type of approach has already yielded measures and research on the BAS-based temperament traits of novelty or sensation seeking (e.g., Cloninger, 1987; Zuckerman, 1990, 1994). It is worth noting that sensation seeking is an equally interesting variable for the study of closeness, in that, at least men with the trait have been found to (a) have more partners in a year and over a lifetime, (b) change partners more frequently, (c) know sexual partners less time before first intercourse, (d) desire more partners in the next year, (e) desire more variety in sexual experiences, and (f) have more short-term relationships (Seto, Lalumiere, & Quinsey, 1995). A consideration of the relation of sensation seeking to the way closeness is experienced would no doubt yield interesting hypotheses—for example, that sensation seekers probably experience closeness as rapid mutual self-disclosures of interesting, arousing details followed quickly by boredom.

As for sensory-processing sensitivity in adults, others have described something like it: Fine (1972, 1973) explained field independence as greater sensory discrimination; Petrie (1967) studied augmenters and reducers of stimulation; Mehrabian (1991) created a measure of low stimulus screening; and a number of Japanese researchers have pursued research on sensitivity as an individual difference (e.g. Nagane, 1990; Satow, 1987).

My own research on sensory-processing sensitivity (E. N. Aron & A. Aron, 1997) began with a qualitative investigation intended to extract core potential characteristics from in-depth interviews followed by a series of questionnaire studies, including a random digit dialing telephone survey. In the process we created a unidimensional 27-item scale (see the appendix) for identifying highly sensitive persons (HSPs) and cross-validated it using a variety of samples and methods. We also used these studies to examine convergent and discriminant validity using several measures of introversion, neuroticism, and low sensory screening, and found that high sensitivity was related to but not identical to social introversion, emotionality, or a combination of these.

The moderate positive correlation between sensitivity and both introversion and emotionality seemed due to the effect of a grouping found in this study through hierarchical cluster analysis: About two thirds of HSPs did not differ from the rest of the population except on the sensitivity scale, but about one third also scored high on measures of negative family conditions in childhood, introversion, and emotionality. In a later series of studies (E. N. Aron, 1999; E. N. Aron & A. Aron, 2002), we further explored this association and found that HSPs with self-reported unhappy childhoods (measured by reasonably objective questions such as the presence of alcoholism or mental illness in the family, the physical presence of the father, the mother, etc.) are far more likely to be depressed, anxious, or shy than HSPs with adequate childhoods or nonHSPs with or without adequate childhoods. That is, there was a clear interaction, replicated across two samples and with different measures, between sensitivity and childhood environment in predicting shyness, depression, and anxiety; those with high sensitivity were more impacted by a problematic childhood than those low in sensitivity, but those with high sensitivity were as well or better off than those low in sensitivity if their childhoods were normal. (Since retrospective reports of unhappy childhoods were being used to study an interaction of reported childhood with temperament, and not as a study of reported childhood as a main effect, we presumed that any bias in self-report of childhood events does not operate differently in HSPs and nonHSPs.)

In these last results we see the obvious importance of both nurture and nature and how the trait of *high sensitivity* (i.e., a strategy of studying a situation closely before proceeding) can lead to a heightened expectation of bad outcomes, chronic anxiety, depression, or shyness, if past experiences were negative. Without these negative experiences the strategy of pausing to observe leads to no more anxiety, depression, or shyness than does the impulsive strategy.

HIGH SENSITIVITY AND CLOSENESS

In this chapter, I define closeness and intimacy in terms of emotion, cognition, and behavior (an extension of the findings of A. Aron, E. N. Aron, & Smollan, 1992, that distinguished feeling close, or emotional closeness, from behaving close or, behavioral closeness, as described by Berscheid, Snyder, & Omoto, 1989).

I define *emotional closeness* as intimacy, which, following Reis and Shaver (1988), is the degree to which one feels validated, cared for, and understood—especially during self-disclosures. In addition, intimacy can be defined as the degree to which one believes that the other has the same emotional reactions to a situation as the self, or at least the other thoroughly understands and appreciates one's reactions (an idea suggested by Stern, 1985, when describing infant–mother attunement).

Emotional closeness, or intimacy, is probably the main contributor to or detractor from *cognitive closeness*, which I define as the degree to which selves overlap or are confused with one another (A. Aron & E. N. Aron, 1986; A. Aron, E. N. Aron, Tudor, & Nelson, 1991; A. Aron, Mashek, E. N. Aron, chap. 3, this volume).

Behavioral closeness, in turn, is probably largely controlled by cognitive closeness, which I define as the degree to which two people spend time together, influence each other's behavior (Berscheid et al., 1989), and continue to self-disclose. All of these activities are probably indicators of how much two people have included each other in the self, so that spending time together or not, being influenced by the other or not, and talking or not have become automatic behavior. (However, behavioral closeness probably affects cognitive and emotional closeness.)

Clearly, temperament impacts all three of these aspects of closeness; but the effects of temperament are complex because of the immense role that prior relationship experience plays in present relationships—as is evidenced by the ubiquitous effects of attachment style on adult relationships (Cassidy & Shaver, 1999). Thus it was not surprising when I added my measure of sensitivity to a number of relationship studies being done for other purposes, and found no direct, unmodified correlation with sensitivity on the standard variables—relationship success, satisfaction, closeness, and intimacy—once I had partialed out neuroticism. In other words, a strategy of pausing to check before proceeding is unrelated to the ability to develop a close, satisfying relationship.

TEMPERAMENT AND PERSONAL HISTORY—INTERACTION EFFECTS ON CLOSENESS

The impact of sensitivity on closeness is still present, however. It is reflected heavily in the aforementioned interaction of the trait with a troubled childhood leading to depression, anxiety, and shyness. These two variables (trait, troubled childhood) are closely related to neuroticism and attachment style, and these variables, in turn, greatly impact relationships in a direct manner (Cassidy & Shaver, 1999; Karney & Bradbury, 1997). Researchers studying children longitudinally have found a similar interaction (trait and troubled childhood together leading to neuroticism and/or an insecure attachment style), and perhaps have even spotlighted some conditions that give rise to the interaction. For example, Hagekill (1996) reported that the most variance in children's neuroticism was accounted for by an interaction of temperament and negative life events such that young children evidencing initial low sociability (presumably evidence of a strategy of pausing to check and avoiding overstimulation) and having more negative life events were more neurotic at later ages than initially low-sociable children having fewer negative life events. Boyce et al. (1995) and Gannon, Banks, and Shelton (1989) both found that highly reactive children were more prone to illnesses and injuries if family and school life was highly stressful, but under less stressful conditions these more reactive children were less prone to illness or injury (which Boyce et al. suggested might be due to their greater reactivity to signs of security and affection as well as signs of stress). And returning to adult samples, Gilmartin (1987), although not reporting interactions, also found that a negative family environment during childhood and other negative life experiences were important contributors to love-shyness, a trait which he also found related to inherited sensitivity.

Catching this interaction almost as its causes are enacted, Gunnar (1994) reports studies measuring the physiological responses of inhibited and uninhibited children in a novel, highly stimulating laboratory full of toys and, at times, an adult stranger. In this situation inhibited children tend to pause upon entering and evidence an adrenaline response, as one would expect whereas uninhibited children generally rush forward without pause and have no adrenaline response. Gunnar reasoned, however, that it is not the immediate surprise response, indicated by adrenaline, that places a child at risk later in life, rather it is an evaluation of the situation as threatening, indicated by elevated cortisol following the initial surprise.

One study (Gunnar, Larson, Hertsgaard, Harris, & Brodersen, 1992) compared the behavior of inhibited toddlers who waited one hr with a responsive caregiver before entering the laboratory setting with the behavior of inhibited toddlers, who waited with an unresponsive caregiver. In another study (Nachmias, Gunnar, Mangelsdorf, Parritz, & Buss, 1996), uninhibited and inhibited toddlers already rated on security during the Strange Situation (Ainsworth, Blehar, Waters, & Wall, 1978) were exposed to the novel, highly stimulating laboratory situation. In both studies, uninhibited children showed, as usual, neither an adrenaline nor a cortisol response in the novel, highly stimulating laboratory environment, and all inhibited children evidenced a rise in adrenaline. There was also a rise in cortisol in the inhibited children left with an unresponsive caretaker in the Gunnar et al. (1992) study as well as in the inhibited children who were insecurely attached in the Nachmias et al. (1996) study. (Cortisol was also measured before and after the strange situation, and cortisol was high only in insecure–inhibited children.)

It seems that part of what the sensitive or inhibited child appraises when pausing to check a new situation is the amount of social support likely to be available if danger arises—in these studies, either from the temporary caretaker or from the ongoing mother–child attachment relationship. When support is chronically unreliable, sensitive children are more likely to perceive novel environments, presumably including new or suddenly more intimate relationships, as threatening. Or, in other words, future neuroticism and closeness appear to be the result of an interaction between temperament and sense of security in childhood.

Because of that interaction, in the next three sections (on actor, partner, and relationship effects) I offer hypotheses about the impact of sensitivity on closeness in adults, both for those with secure and insecure attachment styles. But my main goal is to generate thinking about temperament and to make clear that when formulating hypotheses about temperament in close relationships, one must look for interactions of temperament and the contributions of personal history, especially attachment style, rather than main effects. Although it would be interesting in itself to find that taking temperament into account modifies predictions about the degree of closeness, a major readjustment of current theories would be required if temperament has a moderating effect on, or sometimes even reverses, established patterns of association among key variables in basic relationship-relevant processes. Thus, I make a point of making some predictions of that sort.

Finally, as I make these predictions, I will be referring to some general effects of high sensitivity, as suggested by my interviews and other data, that are likely to increase or decrease closeness:

1. Low risk taking (part of the overall strategy of HSPs).

2. A greater than average need for quiet time for processing information (a self-reported need, probably because of the deeper processing).

3. A greater need to avoid overstimulation (a self-reported need, no doubt the result of lower sensory thresholds).

4. A preference for deeply meaningful conversations (a self-reported preference, probably because of the general preference for deeper processing, suggested by, for example, Thorne's, 1987, finding that pairs of introverts engaged in "focused problem talk" whereas extroverts discussed shared experiences, and an item not used on the HSP measure but which HSPs agree to significantly more than nonHSPs: "Would you be willing to sit at the bedside of a dying stranger and comfort them?").

5. A greater awareness of subtleties in emotional and nonverbal communication (inherent in the definition of the trait).

6. A sense of being different, the result of being a minority and, in North American culture, not being the ideal (e.g., Chen, Rubin, & Sun, 1992, found that peer popularity and being a sensitive, quiet child were positively correlated in China and negatively in Canada).

Actor Effects—How One's Own Sensitivity Might Affect One's Own Closeness

The following sections use Kenny's (1994) method of analyzing the effect of a variable on social relations by separately considering actor, partner, and relationship effects. Although what follows is a bit confusing, because we are looking at two variables—sensitivity and closeness—the distinctions seem worthwhile. Remember, sensitivity is that which varies, and the social impact is the impact on closeness. Thus, actor effects are the effect of the variable on the self, so in this first section I consider the effect of one's own sensitivity on one's own closeness, regardless of the sensitivity of the other.

Partner effects are the effects of the variable on the partner, so in the second section I consider the effects of the other's sensitivity on one's own closeness, regardless of sensitivity. Relationship effects, the third section, are the effect of a particular pattern of a variable within a relationship—in this case, the impact of the degree of *similarity* of one's own and the other's sensitivity on one's own closeness. Of course, a truly exhaustive discussion (in both senses) would consider other relationships among the variables, but the following provides examples only of how sensitivity might impact closeness.

Turning to the effects on one's own closeness (actor effects), I begin with the situation in which the sensitive person has a secure adult attachment style. Although HSPs should in general be cautious about any commitment, I predict that secure HSPs would not be as hesitant to commit to a close relationship as insecure HSPs. Indeed, secure HSPs might be more eager to commit than secure nonHSPs because HSPs can always benefit from situations that help calm them and reduce their level of arousal and close relationships can be the ideal setting for such soothing. Perhaps, from a biological standpoint, it is the most ideal, if one feels secure in making such an attachment.

As for maintaining a close relationship (being close after becoming close), secure HSPs should be prone to attempt to improve relationships rather than to impulsively exit them, avoiding the risk of leaving a troubled close relationship that might still be salvageable. Secure HSPs may also foresee further untried possibilities ("things still might change if I can get him to go to counseling") as well as the painful consequences of a break up ("she's difficult, but if I left her I would also miss her so much, and what are the odds of finding someone any better?). The preference for meaningful conversations should be a strong motivator for closeness in secure HSPs, as would be a rewarding sense of competence as they effectively use their awareness of the other's moods, meanings, and needs to maintain an intimate relationship. Finally, I predict that again because of the awareness of subtle emotional and nonverbal cues, secure HSPs, compared with nonHSPs, will notice more indicators of intimacy—that is, experience heightened validation and a sense of being cared for and understood, when these indicators are actually present (emotional closeness) and, therefore, readily include intimate others into the self (cognitive closeness).

As for hypothesized effects on the closeness of the insecure HSP, I predict that the HSP's general risk-avoidance would lead to an insecure HSP taking an even longer "pause to check" before entering a potentially close relationship, allowing very slow increases in self-disclosure, and having a high fear of commitment (affecting emotional, cognitive, and behavioral closeness). In clinical settings I have observed that the HSP's strategy of perceiving every subtle aspect of a person and considering the long-term consequences of all of these have the effect of causing most HSPs to take into far greater account any character flaw or irritating habit in a potential partner than would a nonHSP. Focusing on another's limitations will inevitably interfere with feelings of attraction and love, and after failing to commit several times as a result of such considerations, even a secure HSP begins to wonder if he or she is "capable of real love." But for insecure HSPs, the processing of the potential consequences of the other's flaws make for fine defenses against closeness ("she's so cheerful and talkative—it's kind of endearing now, but I know it will drive me crazy in a few years," or "ten years difference in age is small now, but what about when we are 70 and 80?"). Of course insecure attachment can also involve feeling unworthy, and the sense of being different from others could easily lead for an insecure HSP, to a sense of having a horrible flaw that will presumably be discovered as closeness increases.

As for maintaining closeness, the insecure HSP's awareness of subtleties can lead to a particular awareness of and obsessing about a partner's irritating bodily noises, odors, or nervous habits. This appears to be a defense against closeness unique to the insecure HSP because secure HSPs report noticing the same stimuli but seem to avoid focusing on them. One could also predict that insecure HSPs would have a keen awareness of any signs, actual or misinterpreted, of abandonment or betrayal just as secure HSPs are, happily, aware of the smallest signs of love. And because closeness for insecure people in general leads to inner conflict between a need for attachment and a fear and defense against it—as is evidenced, for example, by the lack of coherence and metacognitive monitoring during the Adult Attachment Inventory, leading to the repressive or excessively animated rhetorical styles of insecure people on that measure (Hesse, 1999)—behavioral closeness for insecures has to lead to high and often excessive levels of stimulation and arousal. And, HSPs more than others dread over arousal, in general from long experience with it. Thus HSPs' general need for "down time" becomes an understandable excusing of one's self to return to a calmer state, and for the insecure HSP that means in solitude, with less behavioral closeness.

Are there processes that are not just slower or faster but entirely different in HSPs (making temperament a moderator of patterns of association among relevant variables)? I have already mentioned that secure HSPs might even be quicker to commit than nonHSPs, given their desire to be in a soothing relationship. In the context of mutual self-disclosure, one might also predict that HSPs would be quicker to exit a dialogue in which information was revealed that would suggest the relationship could become difficult or threatening (for example, comments suggesting narcissism, unreasonable anger, a "paranoid streak," delusional or very idiosyncratic thinking, or sexual "oddities"), whereas nonHSPs would remain longer in such a discussion, perhaps finding them interesting. Similarly, HSPs might remain longer in subtle or deep conversations than they would in ordinary conversations, whereas nonHSPs might exit such a dialogue out of boredom sooner than they would leave an ordinary conversation. (This interaction pattern is not merely a case of an attraction of similars, because in most cases these variations from normal conversation would not be determined by the other's temperament. For example, the kinds of subtle, interesting conversations an HSP might enjoy could probably arise as often or more often between an HSP and a reasonably educated, erudite, or philosophical nonHSP.) Finally, if the conversation were unusually boring, we might again see an interaction, because the HSP would not wish to risk hurting the other person's feelings and so would exit more slowly than he or she would from an ordinary conversation, but a nonHSP would be less aware of or concerned about this risk and might exit more quickly from an unusually boring conversation.

In sum, I have considered the effect of sensitivity on one's own closeness, usually taking into account whether one's attachment style is secure or insecure. The next section turns to the impact on one's self of having a highly sensitive partner.

Partner Effects—How a Partner's Sensitivity Affects the Self (HSP or Not)

Once again I consider the secure and insecure person separately (realizing that there are many other situations to explore created by combinations of secure and insecure with HSP and nonHSP). If the self is secure, one can hypothesize that having an HSP partner who needs extra quiet time, perhaps the greatest potential obstacle to closeness for the self, could even be experienced as a benefit—for example, that it results in both taking more "down time." As for the impact of other qualities of an HSP partner, the secure self with an HSP partner should enjoy being easily understood during intimate interactions, having meaningful conversations happen more often, and feeling more secure in knowing his or her partner is skilled in maintaining the relationship and would not exit it impulsively. Such a secure self might well feel he or she has found a partner who differs favorably from the majority.

In contrast, one can hypothesize that an insecure self with an HSP partner will be troubled by the HSP occasionally "abandoning" him or her to be alone or involved in HSP-typical activities such as listening to classical music, hiking in silence, or writing in a journal (this is an example of lowered behavioral closeness feeding back to lower emotional closeness). While the avoidant insecure might seem to appreciate this aspect of having an HSP as a partner, it is my experience that when the HSP withdraws, the avoidant harshly denigrates such behavior or reveals a more preoccupied style and "lures" the HSP out of his or her needed down time.

The HSP's desire for deeper conversation or ability to sense the other's thoughts and feelings may be experienced by an insecure partner as intrusive or controlling, especially to an avoidant partner, intensifying defenses against emotional and cognitive closeness. The HSP's preference to avoid highly stimulating environments such as shopping malls, parties, or sports events could also interfere with an insecure partner's probably preferred method of being together—that is, doing activities together rather than being emotionally close. An HSP's desire to avoid overstimulation provides the insecure partner with the opportunity to create highly stimulating situations by initiating conflicts, and the HSP's differentness creates the additional opportunity to make and justify harsh criticisms, all of which will cause the HSP to withdraw— what the avoidant type ostensibly desires and the preoccupied type is always testing for. Finally, an avoidant–insecure type might see the HSP's differences as a type of inferiority and reason for avoiding all forms of closeness. The preoccupied type, on the other hand, might see the partner's unusualness as a reason for feeling intimidated and unworthy, another reason to avoid closeness.

In sum, the effect of having an HSP partner on an individual is partly determined by the individual's attachment style, and there are ample ways for that effect to occur.

What about predictions that would be different in direction, not just different in degree (that is, a crossover or interaction effect)? Communication or behavioral change techniques that are especially direct, forceful, or confronting might be highly useful in communicating one's needs to a nonHSP partner, but would be especially unhelpful when speaking to an HSP partner, who benefits more from gentle, indirect observations of difficulties with only a subtle inference about where the fault lies or how behavior should change. (Besides processing negative feedback deeply, HSPs can be distressed by the kind of direct criticism that helps nonHSPs because HSPs are often shame-prone as a result of the trait not being ideal in this culture.) Thus temperament determines the type of feedback that is helpful in a close relationship, not just the amount or volume of it.

In sum, I have considered the effect of a partner's sensitivity on one's own closeness, particularly when one's attachment style is secure or insecure. The next section turns to the impact on one's own closeness of how much sensitivity is found in the relationship itself—that is, the effect on one's self of the degree to which the partners' are similar or dissimilar in sensitivity.

Relationship Effects: The Impact of the Degree of Similarity of Sensitivity

Although, again, I have found no consistent direct effects of individual differences in sensitivity on individuals' scores on relationship-relevant variables, my data indicate a small but consistent mean tendency for established couples with similar temperaments to be more satisfied, which is consistent with general findings of relationship satisfaction for couples with personality similarities of all kinds.

I begin by discussing the general effects of dissimilarity in sensitivity, most of which would apply to both secure and insecure partners in dissimilar relationships, but I will add the interaction with attachment style when speaking of those effects which might differently affect a person who is insecure.

On the basis of intensive interviews I have done with members of sensitivity-dissimilar couples, I suspect that the typical slight negative impact of this dissimilarity is usually due to the conflicts that can arise as a result of any temperament differences. Temperament traits are often viewed as differences that ought to be modifiable when in fact they are not. Thus requests that one change can be perceived as rejections of one's basic self, thereby reducing the sense of emotional closeness or intimacy. Even if one were to decide to change, the inability to do so would lead to frustration and a sense for the one trying that he or she must not love the other enough. Thus, through cognitive dissonance or self-perception processes, what had seemed to be love would seem to become not really caring enough to make this change (e.g., of learning to like loud music). Also, failures of the other to change are perceived as stubbornness or not caring, no doubt having a similar impact on intimacy.

Fundamentally, partners who chose dissimilars do not understand that the qualities they initially loved are often the result of the same biological substrate that also causes the disliked qualities. They do not know they are experiencing a temperament trait or understand that such traits are essentially neutral, having advantages in some situations, disadvantages in others. Temperament traits are a "package deal," as I counsel (E. N. Aron, 2000).

However, if dissimilar couples do accept what they find problematic in each other's temperament, this increase in acceptance should increase intimacy (emotional closeness), because a person with a dissimilar personality who appreciates his or her partner could be perceived as showing even greater caring than when a person with a similar personality cares. Plus, intimacy may increase simply from obstacles to closeness that the two have overcome together.

Regarding cognitive closeness, dissimilarity could provide a sense of gaining a far broader perspective and having more abilities available than one has alone or gains by having a partner who is similar to him or herself (A. Aron & E. N. Aron, 1986). Provided a relationship seems possible at all, each might well view the other as surprising, refreshing, and mysterious (what one can never do, the other can do so easily and well). For example, nonHSPs might be delighted with the prospect of closeness with someone who introduced them to the novelty and pleasure of being quiet in the out of doors, discussing dreams, or spending time alone. HSPs might be highly interested in someone who brings to their life adventure and freedom from worry, who urges often that they as a couple should forget the budget and have fun, who might take the two hitchhiking across Europe, or plan for them to see far more movies and plays than the HSP would otherwise venture to try.

The period when the two are first becoming acquainted and are experiencing rapid self-expansion, and therefore feeling most in love (A. Aron & E. N. Aron, 1986), should be prolonged for dissimilar personalities, which should prolong all forms of closeness. During this time, each may also seek to find areas of nontemperament similarity and promote these in a compensatory way. ("Thank goodness she at least likes golf—I'll brush up on my game.") And not being able to assume they understand each other's point of view, each may feel he or she needs to give particular attention to the other so that they actually spend more time listening than similar personalities might. Through these extra efforts at emotional and behavioral closeness, cognitive dissonance or self-perception may operate to cause them to see themselves as closer to someone they have tried so hard to understand and spend time with. That which similar personalities enjoy automatically is truly an effort to love for dissimilar personalities.

The need of one partner to withdraw for down time no doubt impacts closeness—at least behavioral closeness, as it reduces time spent together. But it could shift the emphasis to "quality over quantity," which may well be the very essence of intimacy in a long-term relationship, in which constant, more superficial interaction may lead to boredom.

In regard to insecure partners, however, one would expect that all of these effects of dissimilarity could become negative. First, insecure people would be less likely to believe a relationship with a dissimilar personality could happen, given the insecure person's overall pessimism about relationships. And if he or she entered a relationship with a dissimilar personality, the mismatch in the desired amount of time spent together and of preferred activities seems likely to lead to reduced intimacy. As mentioned previously, under these circumstances, preoccupied insecure partners feel abandoned and avoidant partners use this as an opportunity to create conflicts that have the effect of distancing.

Other differences, such as preferred amount of risk taking, could lead each individual to feel less intimate on the basis of the assumption that the other does not like him or her because of such differences. For example, insecure nonHSPs would see their impulsiveness as a reason for their HSP partner to judge and reject them. The HSP would expect to be judged for being too cautious. In general, when the inevitable conflicts arise between dissimilar personalities, insecure partners would be likely to globalize and feel victimized as if their basic self were being misunderstood and rejected by the other. When the HSP partner perceives subtle cues about the moods and emotions of the nonHSP partner and shares these, it probably would not improve communications and intimacy between them, but would highlight the many subtle and deep negative feelings likely to be predominating, which would lead to further decreases in intimacy for both.

Because of all of the above, insecure individuals in dissimilar relationships would probably resist cognitive closeness (i.e., including other in the self). With time, differences would no longer seem to offer special benefits to be gained through inclusion of the other. Avoidant people would see these differences as the risk of including inferior qualities into the self, and preoccupied people would view them as the risk of being excluded from the other's self.

As for the impact on an individual's closeness when there is a high degree of similarity, I will consider only the case of two HSPs. For them, all types of closeness should be easier to develop, except when one or both has a negative view of this temperament trait. This self-contempt is quite frequent in the relatively "raw," insensitive immigrant cultures of the United States, Canada, Latin America, and Australia (Chen et al., 1992) and is probably only partially related to insecure attachment style. In these cases, over time, including the other into the self can only mean that the other is viewed in the same negative way. Most notice is given to those times when the trait is inevitably a disadvantage, as when the couple must endure something highly stimulating or make a difficult decision quickly.

Comparisons with other couples, so important to couple well being (Van Lange & Rusbult, 1995), will often be negative, especially when one or both members of the other couple are not HSPs. Accepting the general norms of what is ideal, HSPs are likely to focus on external accomplishments, of which nonHSPs are likely have more: joint income, number of children, size of house, number of exciting vacations or nights on the town. Negative views of their shared trait are likely to reduce intimate feelings, cognitions, and behaviors in each of them.

Are there predictions about when the degree of temperament similarity would interact with other processes? Murray, Holmes, Bellavia, Griffin, and Dolderman (2002) found that relationship partners are most satisfied when they assume the other is like one's self, even after controlling for actual similarity. But HSPs, who know they are fundamentally different from most others, would be much less likely to assume their partner is like themselves. Indeed, the degree of behavioral dissimilarity that would be evident to both sides might well reverse the process found in most couples in which assumed similarity is a benefit over and above actual similarity.

In sum, I have considered the effect on one's own closeness of sensitivity as a pattern within the relationship—that is, the effect on one's self of the couple's degree of similarity in sensitivity.

The Effect of Sensitivity on Sexual Intimacy

Even if the effect of high sensitivity on relationship quality is not a simple one, it is clear that it will play a substantial role in preferences and practices that would seem to create an "intimacy style" in the individual and in the couple, one which might be summed up as preferring a high quality (of activities, conversations, etc.) over a high quantity, which is a strategy, again, of doing a few things and enjoying them thoroughly. One area in which I was able to see such a style was in a study of temperament and sexual intimacy (E. N. Aron, 2000). This research was based on a sample of 450 respondents who were subscribers to a newsletter for HSPs. Subscribers were also asked to give the anonymous questionnaire to their nonHSP friends, who were to mail it in separately. These questionnaires included items about sexual experiences, practices, problems, and preferences, as well as a short-form of the HSP scale. Four main results, found for both genders, were obtained after controlling for measures of negative affectivity and traumatic events in childhood.

First, like overall relationship satisfaction, there was a near-zero difference between HSPs and nonHSPs in overall satisfaction with their sex lives and reports of sexual problems. Second, HSPs were substantially more likely to report that sex for them had a "sense of mystery and power." This may result from HSPs' tendency to reflect on experiences more deeply. (It does seem that sexuality has considerable potential to be reflected upon deeply, or not at all, depending on the person.) Third, HSPs report being less sexually responsive to explicit sexual cues such as pornography. This may be due to such cues being in fact overarousing for an HSP. In addition, HSPs may reflect guiltily on the social or personal consequences of using such materials. Fourth, responses to several items point to HSPs being more sensitive to stimulation during sex. They report being less interested in variety of sexual practices, more disturbed by slight sounds or "off" smells, more easily distracted, and more likely to feel so highly stimulated physically that it is painful or they feel a need to stop for a while.

Overall, as with relationship closeness, instead of finding a straight-forward difference in satisfaction, I found a difference in sexual style, one that could be, again, called a preference for quality over quantity of sexual stimulation. In this case the preference is for less direct stimulation and contact, apparently to avoid over arousal, and an appreciation of subtleties that might create as much or more of a sense of intimacy, but in a different way—in particular, sharing a mysterious and powerful experience together. The impact of different styles of sexual intimacy has not been explored, and is no doubt impacted by the style of general intimacy, which for HSPs, again, probably involves preferring in-depth discussions and attention to nuances and details of interactions. Such a style seems important for also achieving a similar style of sexual intimacy, because of the need to discuss fully each other's responses and preferences, especially when the two are dissimilar.

CONCLUSION

This chapter explores the potential impact of temperament on relationship closeness, beginning with a review of the research on one specific trait (high sensory-processing sensitivity) as one of two "breeds" or strategies—a preference to process information about a novel situation thoroughly before acting, a kind of psychological exploring, as opposed to preferring to advance immediately and explore physically. Something approximating these two strategies appears to be found throughout the animal world, from fruit flies to primates (in humans it is probably determined by an especially active BIS; whereas the other trait, novelty seeking, is probably the result of an especially active BAS). On the basis of their likely relevance, six qualities of HSPs were considered: low risk taking; the need for quiet, usually alone; the high motivation to avoid overstimulation; a preference for deeply meaningful conversations; a greater awareness of subtleties in emotional and nonverbal communication; and a sense of being different and not the ideal.

The impact of sensitivity or any temperament trait on closeness is generally not straightforward, however, because past relationship experiences are equally or more important. But when interactions with a troubled childhood or adult attachment style are considered, differences as a result of temperament do occur. In particular, I have found that chronic depression, anxiety, and shyness—all of which affect closeness—are more likely to develop in HSPs than nonHSPs who have had troubled childhoods, whereas HSPs and nonHSPs with good childhoods show no differences on these problems. Thus, as I make predictions specifically about the impact of high sensitivity on closeness, I speculate that this impact should depend on a person's attachment history. Most important, I suggest examples of predictions in which sensitivity may affect not only the degree of closeness, but should actually create reversals of established close relationship findings.

The main goal of this hypothesizing, however, is to generate thinking about temperament's impact on closeness and to stress that when making predictions about temperament in close relationships, one must look for interactions of temperament and relationship history, rather than main effects, and that there is indeed a fundamental difference between these two "breeds" of humans. This chapter attempts to shift that difference from being an unnoticed or neglected source of noise to becoming an interesting variable in its own right.

REFERENCES

Ainsworth, M. D. S., Blehar, M. C., Waters, E., & Wall, S. (1978). *Patterns of attachment: A psychological study of the strange situation.* Hillsdale, NJ: Lawrence Erlbaum Associates.

Aron, A., & Aron, E. N. (1986). *Love as the expansion of self: Understanding attraction and satisfaction.* New York: Hemisphere.

Aron, A., Aron, E. N., & Smollan, D. (1992). Inclusion of other in the self scale and the structure of interpersonal closeness. *Journal of Personality and Social Psychology, 63,* 596–612.

Aron, A., Aron, E. N., Tudor, M., & Nelson, G. (1991). Close relationships as including other in the self. *Journal of Personality and Social Psychology, 60,* 241–253.

Aron, E. N. (1999). High sensitivity as one source of fearfulness and shyness: Preliminary research and clinical implications. In L. A. Schmidt & J. Schulkin (Eds.), *Extreme fear, shyness, and social phobia: Origins, biological mechanisms, and clinical outcomes* (pp. 251–272). New York: Oxford.

Aron, E. N. (2000). *The highly sensitive person in love,* New York: Broadway.

Aron, E. N., & Aron, A. (1997). Sensory-processing sensitivity and its relation to introversion and emotionality. *Journal of Personality and Social Psychology, 73,* 345–368.

Aron, E. N., & Aron, A. (2002). *Adult shyness: The interaction of temperamental sensitivity and a negative childhood environment.* Manuscript submitted for review.

Bekoff, M. (1977). Mammalian dispersal and the ontogeny of individual behavioral phenotypes. *American Naturalist, 111,* 715–732.

Ben-Shahar, Y., Robichon, A., Sokolowski, M. B., & Robinson, G. E. (April 26, 2002). Influence of gene action across different time scales on behavior. *Science, 296,* 741–744.

Berscheid, E., Snyder, M., & Omoto, A. M. (1989). The relationship closeness inventory: Assessing the closeness of interpersonal relationships. *Journal of Personality and Social Psychology, 57,* 792–807.

Blanchard, R. J., Flannelly, K. J., & Blanchard, D. C. (1986). Defensive behaviors of laboratory and wild *Rattus norvegicus. Journal of Comparative Psychology, 100,* 101–107.

Blizard, D. A. (1981). The Maudsley reactive and nonreactive strains: A North American perspective. *Behavior Genetics, 11,* 469–489.

Boyce, W. T., Chesney, M., Alkon, A., Tschann, J. M, Adams, S., Chesterman, B., et al. (1995). Psychobiologic reactivity to stress and childhood respiratory illnesses: Results of two prospective studies. *Psychosomatic Medicine, 57,* 411–422.

Brebner, J. M. T. (1980). Reaction time in personality theory. In A. T. Welford (Ed.), *Reaction times* (pp. 309–320). London: Academic Press.

Cassidy, J., & Shaver, P. R. (1999). *Handbook of attachment: Theory, research, and clinical applications.* New York: Guilford.

Chen, X., Rubin, K., & Sun, Y. (1992). Social reputation and peer relationships in Chinese and Canadian children: A cross-cultural study. *Child Development, 63,* 1336–1343.

Cloninger, C. R. (1987). A systematic method for clinical description and classification of personality variants: A proposal. *Archives of general psychiatry, 44,* 573–588.

Cooper, D. O., Schmidt, D. E., & Barrett, R. J. (1983). Strain specific cholinergic changes in response to stress: Analysis of a time-dependent avoidance variation. *Pharmacology, Biochemistry, and Behavior, 19,* 457–462.

Crider, A., & Lunn, R. (1971). Electrodermal lability as a personality dimension. *Journal of Experimental Research in Personality, 5,* 145–150.

Eliot, A. J., & Thrash, T. M. (2002). Approach-avoidance motivation in personality: Approach and avoidance temperaments and goals. *Journal of Personality and Social Psychology, 82,* 804–818.

Eysenck, H. J. (1991). Biological dimensions of personality. In L. A. Pervin (Ed.), *Handbook of personality* (pp. 244–276). New York: Guilford Press.

Fine, B. J. (1972). Field-dependent introvert and neuroticism: Eysenck and Witkin united. *Psychological Reports, 31,* 939–956.

Fine, B. J. (1973). Field-dependence-independence as "sensitivity" of the nervous system: Supportive evidence with color and weight discrimination. *Perceptual and Motor Skills, 37,* 287–295.

Fox, M. L. (1972). Socioecological implications of individual differences in wolf litters: A developmental and evolutionary perspective. *Behaviour, 41,* 298–313.

Gannon, L., Banks, J., & Shelton, D. (1989). The mediating effects of psychophysiological reactivity and recovery on the relationship between environmental stress and illness. *Journal of Psychosomatic Research, 33,* 165–175.

Gilmartin, B. G. (1987). *Shyness and love: Causes, consequences, and treatment.* Lanham, MD: University Press of America.

Goddard, M. E., & Beilharz, R. G. (1985). A multivariate analysis of the genetics of fearfulness in potential guide dogs. *Behavior Genetics, 15,* 69–89.

Gray, J. A. (1981). A critique of Eysenck's theory of personality. In H. J. Eysenck (Eds.), *A model for personality* (pp. 246–276). New York: Springer.

Gray, J. A. (1985). Issues in the neuropsychology of anxiety. In A. H. Ruma & J. D. Maser (Eds.), *Anxiety and disorder* (pp. 5–25). Hillsdale, NJ: Lawrence Erlbaum Associates.

Gray, J. A. (1991). The neurophysiology of temperament. In J. Strelau & A. Angleitner (Eds.), *Explorations in temperament: International perspectives on theory and measurement* (pp. 105–128). New York: Plenum.

Gunnar, M. R. (1994). Psychoendocrine studies of temperament and stress in early childhood: Expanding current models. In J. E. Bates & T. D Wachs (Eds.), *Temperament: Individual differences at the interface of biology and behavior* (pp. 175–198). Washington, DC: American Psychological Association.

Gunnar, M, Larson, M., Hertsgaard, L., Harris, M., & Brodersen, L. (1992). The stressfulness of separation among 9-month-old infants: Effects of social context variables and infant temperament. *Child Development, 63,* 290–303.

Hagekill, B. (1996, October). *Influences of temperament and environment in the development of personality.* Paper presented at the Occasional Temperament Conference XI, Eugene, Oregon.

Hesse, E. (1999). The adult attachment interview: Historical and cultural perspectives. In J. Cassidy & P. R. Shaver (Eds.), *Handbook of attachment* (pp. 395–433). New York: Guilford.

Higley, J. D., & Suomi, J. D. (1989). Temperamental reactivity in nonhuman primates. In G. A. Kohnstamm, J. E. Bates, & M. K. Rothbart (Eds), *Temperament in childhood* (pp. 152–167). Chichester, England: Wiley.

Kagan, J. (1994). *Galen's prophecy: Temperament in human nature.* New York: Basic Books.

Karney, B. R., & Bradbury, T. N. (1997). Neuroticism, marital interaction, and the trajectory of marital satisfaction. *Journal of Personality and Social Psychology, 72,* 1075–1092.

Kenny, D. A. (1994). Interpersonal perception: A social relations analysis. New York: Guilford.

Koelega, H. S. (1992) Extraversion and vigilance performance: 30 years of inconsistencies. *Psychological Bulletin, 112,* 239–258.

Kohn, P. M. (1987). Issues in the measurement of arousability. In J. Strelau & H. J. Eysenck, (Eds.), *Personality dimensions and arousal* (pp. 233–250). New York: Plenum.

Kohnstam, G. A., Bates, J. E., & Rothbart, M. K. (1989). *Temperament in childhood.* New York: Wiley.

Lyons, D. M., Price, E. O., & Moberg, G. P. (1988). Individual differences in temperament of domestic dairy goats: Constancy and change. *Animal Behavior, 36,* 1323–1333.

MacDonald, K. (1983). Stability of individual differences in behavior in a litter of wolf cubs (*Canis lupus*). *Journal of Comparative Psychology, 97,* 99–106.

Mangan, G. L., & Sturrock, R. (1988). Lability and recall. *Personality and Individual Differences, 9,* 519–523.

Mehrabian, A. (1991). Outline of a general emotion-based theory of temperament. In J. Strelau & A. Angleitner (Eds.), *Explorations in temperament: International perspectives on theory and measurement* (pp. 75–86). New York: Plenum.

Murray, S. L., Holmes, J. G., Bellavia, G., Griffin, D. S., & Dolderman, D. (2002). Kindred spirits? The benefits of egocentrism in close relationships. *Journal of Personality and Social Psychology, 82,* 563–581.

Nachmias, M., Gunnar, M., Mangelsdorf, S., Parritz, R. H., & Buss, K. (1996). Behavioral inhibition and stress reactivity: The moderating role of attachment security, *Child Development*, 67, 508–522.

Nagane, M. (1990). Development of psychological and physiological sensitivity indices to stress based on state anxiety and heart rate. *Perceptual and Motor Skills*, 70, 611–614.

Osborne, K. A., Robichon, A., Burgess, E., Butland, S., Shaw, R. A., Coulthard, A., et al. (August 8, 1992). Natural behavior polymorphism due to a cGMP-dependent protein kinase of *Drosophila*. *Science*, 277, 834–836.

Patterson, C. M., & Newman, J. P. (1993). Reflectivity and learning from aversive events: Toward a psychological mechanism for the syndromes of disinhibition. *Psychological Review*, 100, 716–736.

Petrie, A. (1967). *Individuality in pain and suffering*. Chicago: University of Chicago

Reis, H. T., & Shaver, P. (1988). Intimacy as an interpersonal process. In S. Duck (Ed.), *Handbook of personal relationships* (pp. 367–389). New York: Wiley.

Renger, J. J., Yao, W.-D., Sokolowski, M. B., & Wu, C.-F. (1999). Neuronal polymorphism among natural alleles of a cGMP-dependent kinase gene, *foraging*, in *Drosophila*. *Journal of Neuroscience*, 19, RC28, 1–8.

Satow, A. (1987). Four properties common among perceptions confirmed by a large sample of subjects: An ecological approach to mechanisms of individual differences in perception: II. *Perceptual and Motor Skills*, 64, 507–520.

Scott, J. P., & Fuller, J. (1965). *Genetics and the social behavior of the dog*. Chicago: University of Chicago Press.

Seto, M. C., Lalumiere, M. L., & Quinsey, V. L. (1995). Sensation seeking and males' sexual strategy, *Personality and individual differences*, 19, 669–675.

Stelmack, R. M., & Geen, R. G. (1992). The psychophysiology of extraversion. In A. Gale & M. W. Eysenck (Eds), *Handbook of individual differences: Biological perspectives*, 227–254. Chichester, England: Wiley.

Stern, D. N. (1985). *The interpersonal world of the infant*. New York: Basic Books.

Stevenson-Hinde, J., Stillwell-Barnes, R., & Zung, M. (1980). Individual differences in young rhesus monkeys: Continuity and change. *Primates*, 21, 61–62.

Suomi, S. J. (1983). Social development in rhesus monkeys: Consideration of individual differences. In A. Oliverio & M. Zappella (Eds.). *The behavior of human infants* (pp. 71–92). New York: Plenum.

Suomi, S. J. (1987). Genetic and maternal contributions to individual differences in rhesus monkey biobehavioral development. In N. A. Krasnegor, E. M. Blass, M. A. Hoffer, & W. P. Smotherman (Eds.), *Perinatal behavioral development: A psychobiological perspective* (pp. 397–419). San Diego, CA: Academic Press.

Suomi, S. J. (1991). Uptight and laid-back monkeys: Individual differences in the response to social challenges. In S. E. Brauth, W. S. Hall, & R. J. Dooling (Eds.), *Plasticity of development* (pp. 27–56). Cambridge, MA: MIT Press.

Thorne, A. (1987). The press of personality. *Journal of Personality and Social Psychology*, 53, 718–726.

Van Lange, P. A. M., & Rusbult, C. E. (1995). My relationship is better than—and not as bad as—yours is: The perception of superiority in close relationships. *Personality and Social Psychology Bulletin*, 21, 32–44.

Wilson, D. S., Coleman, K., Clark, A. B., & Biederman, L. (1993). Shy–bold continuum in pumpkinseed sunfish (*Lepomis gibbosus*): An ecological study of a psychological trait. *Journal of Comparative Psychology*, 107, 250–260.

Zahn, T. P., Kruesi, M. J. P., Leonard, H. L., & Rapoport, J. L. (1994). Autonomic activity and reaction time in relation to extraversion and behavioral impulsivity in children and adolescents. *Personality and Individual Differences*, 16, 751–758.

Zuckerman, M. (1994). Impulsive unsocialized sensation seeking: The biological foundations of a basic dimension of personality. In J. E. Bates & T. D. Wachs (Eds), *Temperament: Individual differences at the interface of biology and behavior* (pp. 219–255). Washington, DC: American Psychological Association.

Zuckerman, M. (1990). The psychophysiology of sensation seeking, *Journal of Personality*, 58, 313–343.

APPENDIX

The Highly Sensitive Person Scale

INSTRUCTIONS: This questionnaire is completely anonymous and confidential. Answer each question according to the way you personally feel, using the following scale:

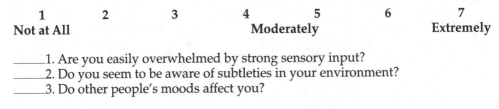

1	2	3	4	5	6	7
Not at All			Moderately			Extremely

_____1. Are you easily overwhelmed by strong sensory input?

_____2. Do you seem to be aware of subtleties in your environment?

_____3. Do other people's moods affect you?

____4. Do you tend to be more sensitive to pain?

____5. Do you find yourself needing to withdraw during busy days, into bed or into a darkened room or any place where you can have some privacy and relief from stimulation?

____6. Are you particularly sensitive to the effects of caffeine?

____7. Are you easily overwhelmed by things like bright lights, strong smells, coarse fabrics, or sirens close by?

____8. Do you have a rich, complex inner life?

____9. Are you made uncomfortable by loud noises?

____10. Are you deeply moved by the arts or music?

____11. Does your nervous system sometimes feel so frazzled that you just have to get off by yourself?

____12. Are you conscientious?

____13. Do you startle easily?

____14. Do you get rattled when you have a lot to do in a short amount of time?

____15. When people are uncomfortable in a physical environment do you tend to know what needs to be done to make it more comfortable (like changing the lighting or the seating)?

____16. Are you annoyed when people try to get you to do too many things at once?

____17. Do you try hard to avoid making mistakes or forgetting things?

____18. Do you make a point to avoid violent movies and TV shows?

____19. Do you become unpleasantly aroused when a lot is going on around you?

____20. Does being very hungry create a strong reaction in you, disrupting your concentration or mood?

____21. Do changes in your life shake you up?

____22. Do you notice and enjoy delicate or fine scents, tastes, sounds, works of art?

____23. Do you find it unpleasant to have a lot going on at once?

____24. Do you make it a high priority to arrange your life to avoid upsetting or overwhelming situations?

____25. Are you bothered by intense stimuli, like loud noises or chaotic scenes?

____26. When you must compete or be observed while performing a task, do you become so nervous or shaky that you do much worse than you would otherwise?

____27. When you were a child, did parents or teachers seem to see you as sensitive or shy?

V

What Situational Factors Play a Role in Closeness and Intimacy?

Beyond the Individual: Concomitants of Closeness in the Social and Physical Environment

Ximena B. Arriaga and Wind Goodfriend
Purdue University

Andrew Lohmann
Claremont Graduate University

The domain of couple closeness extends well beyond the individual couple members themselves. Although couple members' cognitions and feelings about each other are important indicators of closeness, there are other key indicators that reside in the couple's social environment (e.g., among family and friends) and even in their physical environment. This chapter describes research that examines whether couple members' closeness is reflected in (a) the level of support they receive from family and friends, and (b) the way that they arrange the objects in their home. Extant research on closeness has examined the facets (Aron, A. & Fraley, 1999), antecedents (Feeney, 1999), development (Montgomery, 1993), and outcomes of closeness (Aron, A., Aron, E. N., Tudor, & Nelson, 1991). Less is known about the social and physical environmental concomitants of closeness, which are the focus of this chapter.

Like others, we have adopted a broad conceptualization of closeness, suggesting that it involves an ongoing process of mutual influence between two members of a dyad (e.g., Berscheid, Snyder, & Omoto, Chap. 6, this volume; see also Kelley et al., 1983; Mashek & Sherman, chap. 19, this volume). Closeness is the culmination of getting along well with another person, wanting to continue an association with that person, assuming that such an association will continue into the long-term future, feeling psychologically connected to another person, and perceiving one's self as having incorporated aspects of the other. In this chapter, we examine three different indicators of closeness: (a) the extent to which individuals include aspects of their partner in their sense of self (cf. Aron, A., & Fraley, 1999); (b) levels of relationship commitment, defined as feeling psychologically attached to a partner, adopting a long-term orientation, and intending to continue in the relationship, and (c) levels of couple functioning.

We use the term social environment to refer to the network of important individuals with whom couple members feel close bonds. This conceptualization is similar to the way in which other researchers define social environments, largely focusing on the interrelations linking couples to their respective networks of kin relations, friends, and acquaintances (cf. Milardo, 1982). In short, the social environment is made up of individuals who influence and are influenced by the couple members. In contrast to our analysis of the social environment, our analysis of physical environments focuses on the objects and spaces that have special meaning for a couple. Specifically, we examined the arrangement of objects in a couple's home, which presumably influences and is influenced by the couple.

In discussing the social and physical environments in which close relationships exist, we underscore the importance of situational and physical constraints that channel relationship behavior. Social environments can be powerful in directing the course of a relationship. For example, the lack of parental support may channel a romantic relationship in predictable ways; the couple members may struggle with the lack of support from parents by questioning their levels of closeness (Felmlee, 2001), or, alternatively, by defying their parents and becoming even closer (Driscoll, Davis, & Lipetz, 1972). As will become clear below, we also suggest that elements of the physical environment can guide behaviors.

A central idea of this chapter is that social and physical environments have, to some degree, a functional purpose. For example, in the domain of arranging physical environments, one important function served by the careful placement of meaningful home objects is to communicate to others something about the inhabitants (Altman & Rogoff, 1987). Similarly, couple members may allow close others to figure prominently in their relationship if they are supportive, or they may try to avoid interactions with, or even conversations about, close others who are not supportive.

As such, our assumptions about environments fall into a Lewinian tradition (Lewin, 1951): Individuals must negotiate their immediate environments. They do so by perceiving and interpreting the environment in terms of their own goals and abilities—that is, they see the environment through the lens of their "life space." But they are, to some extent, limited by the forces that facilitate and constrain movement toward their goals. For example, couple members who rent an apartment that is already furnished may find it relatively effortful to display objects that say something about their couplehood. Similarly, couples who have been ostracized by family members are certainly influenced by them, but they probably are not influenced by them in desired ways.

SOCIAL ENVIRONMENT

An Interdependence Analysis

Our analysis of the links between social support and relationship closeness begins with the basic premise that situations shape behavior. This has been an assumption of many theories and interdependence theory is no exception (Kelley & Thibuat, 1978; Thibaut & Kelley, 1959). Interdependence theory posits that over time dyad members bring about situations that are aligned with their interpersonal goals—that is, this theory provides a functional analysis of interpersonal behavior (Kelley, 1983; 1991).

In every interaction, couple members are first confronted with the given situation. The given situation is the situation as it initially and objectively exists. Some situations may initially involve the couple members wanting the same things, whereas others may involve a conflict of interest at the outset. Each couple brings specific characteristics that shape a given situation, such as personal characteristics (e.g., personality traits, each person's past experiences with that situation) as well as situational characteristics (Kelley, 1991). One situational characteristic concerns whether close others support or undermine the relationship. Having unsupportive family members is likely to affect how relationship partners interact with one another. For example, if a woman's family members are completely unsupportive of her partner, she may have relatively more power over her partner than he has over her, because her family members may be encouraging her to leave him. If she becomes tempted to heed that advice, she will become less dependent on the relationship—that is, she will be less affected by what he does and by what unfolds than he will be. Thus, the extent of social support is one factor that may shape the given situation.

According to interdependence theory, not all couples will react to a given situation in the same way. In fact, a major impetus behind the development of interdependence theory was to account for the fact that different dyads react to the same situation in different ways; different reactions reflect a combination of each person taking in the given situation and exerting his or her unique interpersonal goals (e.g., wanting what is best for the partner vs. wanting to quash a partner, wanting to get relatively more out of interactions than the partner, wanting both self and partner to get a lot out of interactions; Kelley, 1991).

Over time, couple members will vary in the way that they manage social support situations. If couple members feel close to their partners, they will seek situations that feature strong support from close others. Similarly, couples will want to avoid situations in which they sense a lack of support from close others. When an interaction problem arises that involves social network members—such as having a social obligation with a person who happens to dislike one of the partners—couple members who are close may attempt to cognitively reconceptualize the situation as one that affords better outcomes (i.e., transformation of motivation; Kelley & Thibaut, 1978). For instance, partners might place relatively less emphasis on interactions with the unsupportive person (i.e., the outcomes in interacting with that person will have a lower value and involve less dependence). However, if the situation is too taxing to produce such reconceptualizations, the couple members will experience negative outcomes and avoid those situations in the future (Kelley, 1983). In this way, over repeated experiences, couple members who desire to be close to one another exhibit a process of adaptation that may include consideration of support from one's social network.

Social Support and Relationship Closeness

An important implication of interdependence theory as it pertains to a couple's social environment is that members of one's social network (i.e., close friends and family members) are not mere spectators of an unfolding relationship. Instead, they make up part of the (given) situations that couple members come across. Indeed, social network members often have opinions about a relationship (Agnew, Loving, & Drigotas, 2001), they often provide social support (Sprecher & Felmlee, 1992), and they may even exert efforts to direct a relationship (Felmlee, 2001). Thus, social-network members can channel a couple's interpersonal behavior.

A large body of research has focused on how a couple influences, and is influenced by, the important others in their social environment (Milardo & Allan, 1997). This research suggests that social-network members direct couple members' levels of closeness. Specifically, couple members with supportive social environments tend to have high levels of intimacy and commitment, and their relationships are more likely to endure over time (Cox, Wexler, Rusbult, & Gaines, 1997; Felmlee, Sprecher, & Bassin, 1990; Milardo, 1982; Sprecher, 1988). Perceiving support for one's relationship from friends has consistently been linked to positive relationship outcomes (e.g., Felmlee, 2001). Moreover, as couple members become closer to one another, the amount of overlap in their friend networks increases (Milardo & Helms-Erikson, 2000).

Whereas lack of friend support consistently has negative consequences, evidence on the effect of lacking family support is mixed. Some studies reveal that relationship benefits are associated with having supportive family members (e.g., Sprecher & Felmlee, 1992). However, one study suggested that high levels of commitment and closeness can also occur when parents disapprove of the relationship, referred to as the "Romeo and Juliet effect" (Discoll et al., 1972).

We examined several aspects of social support as it relates to couple closeness, with a sample of individuals in heterosexual dating relationships. First, we attempted to replicate previous research that reveals a positive correlation between relationship closeness and social support for the relationship.[1] We were primarily interested in the associations between relationship closeness and perceived support from others. Regardless of actual support from others, ultimately it is the perception of support from others that is likely to shape couple interactions (Felmlee, 2001).

Second, we were interested in exploring the causal direction among these variables. On the basis of our interdependence analysis, we have indicated that support from close others influences and partly defines the given situations that couple members come across and to which they must respond. Thus, social support from friends and family members influences closeness. However, this same analysis suggests that couple members' interaction goals (such as increasing closeness) will affect whether they seek out situations that involve supportive others. Thus, closeness may drive perceived support from others. In short, both causal directions are plausible. We examined these issues using a longitudinal design, which did not allow us to affirm causal claims but did potentially allow us to rule out plausible causal claims.

Third, we explored whether relationship closeness and perceived social support predicted whether a relationship was intact at a later point in time. In particular, we were interested in the unique effects of closeness and social support in predicting later breakup status.

Predicting Changes in Closeness and Social Support

We analyzed data derived from two studies, each using a multiwave longitudinal design involving 10 measurement occasions (or *times*) conducted one week apart, along with a follow-up session conducted approximately four months after Time 10. Because social support measures were obtained at the odd-numbered times, we examined data from Times 1, 3, 5, 7, and 9 in the current analyses. Participants were in relationships that were primarily exclusive in nature and eight weeks in duration, on average, at Time 1. Given that the two studies used almost identical procedures and to maximize statistical power, the two samples were combined in the analyses to yield a total sample size of 98 individuals who completed all Times (cf. Arriaga, 2001, for details regarding the sample). This sample excluded any individuals whose relationships ended before Time 10.

Data collection sessions were conducted on a weekly basis in a small classroom; 10–18 participants took part in each session. At Time 1, the experimenter described the study tasks and obtained written consent from the participants. At each time thereafter, the experimenter reviewed the activities for the day's session, assured the participants that their responses would remain confidential, and distributed questionnaires. Each session lasted approximately 15 min.

---

[1] Our measure of social support included separate questions for friend support and parental support, which allowed us to explore the *Romeo and Juliet* effect (i.e., a negative correlation between couple closeness and parental support for the relationship). However, as has been the case in other studies (Parks, 1997), we did not find support for this effect.

At each occasion, three items tapped social support (*Do your good friends approve of and support your relationship?; Does your family—your parents, brothers, sisters, etc.—approve of and support your relationships?; In general, do people you care about—your family and friends—approve of or support your relationship?*; Time 1 $\alpha = .93$), each followed by a 9-point response scale, ranging from 0 (*don't approve at all*), to 8 (*approve completely*).

We also measured general closeness, commitment level, and dyadic adjustment, which we used as approximate indicators of closeness. As a measure of general closeness, participants completed the inclusion of the other in the self (IOS) scale (Aron, A., Aron, E. N., & Smollan, 1992). Three items from Rusbult (1983) were used to measure commitment (*I intend to stay in this relationship; I feel very attached to our relationship—very strongly linked to my partner; I am oriented toward the long-term future of my relationship (for example, imagine being with my partner several years from now)*; $\alpha = .80$), along with a 9-point response scale. Couple functioning was measured using a shortened version of Spanier's (1976) dyadic adjustment scale (Time 1 $\alpha = .86$). Respondents indicated how often they disagreed with their partners with respect to a variety of issues (e.g., friends, amount of time spent together) on a scale ranging from 1 (*always disagree*) to 8 (*always agree*). Respondents also indicated the frequency with which they engaged in several types of interaction (e.g., *How often do you have a stimulating exchange of ideas?*), on a scale ranging from 1 (*never*), to 6 (*more often* [than once a day]). We derived measures of social support, commitment, and dyadic adjustment by averaging the items tapping each of these constructs.

Breakup status was assessed at follow-up (four months after the last time) by asking participants whether they were still dating their Time 1 partners. Participants whose relationships ended were also asked whether the participant or the partner was responsible for the breakup. On the basis of responses to these questions at the follow-up session, participants were categorized into three breakup groups: (a) those individuals whose relationships endured, or *stayers*; (b) those individuals who ended their relationships, or *leavers*; and (c) those individuals whose partner ended the relationship, or *abandoned individuals*. Across the two samples, there were 44 stayers, 35 leavers, and 19 abandoned individuals.[2]

To obtain measures of change over time in social support, general closeness, commitment level, and dyadic adjustment, we adopted a growth curve analytic approach (cf. Karney & Bradbury, 1995). First, we derived estimates of change by modeling a linear trajectory of change for each participant.[3] Specifically, each participant's ratings of a given variable at all five measurement occasions (e.g., social support at Times 1, 3, 5, 7, and 9) were regressed onto time, yielding a set of estimates unique to that person. For the current research aims, we were particularly interested in two parameters that were estimated: (a) the *intercept*, which provides an unbiased indicator of an individual's initial level of a given variable (i.e., just prior to Time 1), and (b) the *slope* of the linear regression line, which provides an unbiased estimate of that individual's rate of linear change over time in the levels of a given variable. Means and standard deviations of change estimates for each variable are presented in Table 16.1 (see first column, "Entire sample"). These parameters were then included in regression models.

---

[2] In the first sample, participants had the option of reporting that their relationship ended by mutual consent. The four participants who indicated this option could not be categorized into a breakup group, so they were excluded from the final sample. In the second sample, participants completed a measure that did not provide a mutual consent option.

[3] We used a linear model (i.e., we assumed that an individual's repeated social support or closeness ratings follow a linear pattern more closely than other patterns, such as a curvilinear trend), given that linear models sufficiently approximate change over short periods of time even if the true model of change follows another pattern (Rogosa et al., 1982). In the current data set, a linear model fit the data better than a curvilinear model.

TABLE 16.1

Means and Standard Deviations of Change Parameters, for Entire Sample and for Each Breakup Group

		Breakup Groups		
	Entire Sample	Stayers	Abandoned	Leavers
	(n = 98)	(n = 44)	(n = 19)	(n = 35)
Social support from friends and family				
Initial level	6.34 (1.71)	6.76 (1.13)	5.98 (2.00)	5.99 (2.05)
Linear trend	−.01 (.18)	.05$_a$ (.09)	.04$_a$ (.13)	−.10$_b$ (.23)
General relationship closeness				
Initial level	4.36 (1.60)	4.81$_a$ (1.53)	4.30$_{ab}$ (1.64)	3.83$_b$ (1.54)
Linear trend	.01 (.18)	.06$_a$ (.15)	−.02$_{ab}$ (.20)	−.05$_b$ (.18)
Level of relationship commitment				
Initial level	5.58 (1.82)	6.18$_a$ (1.69)	5.53$_{ab}$ (1.46)	4.87$_b$ (1.93)
Linear trend	−.00 (.20)	.06$_a$ (.14)	.00$_{ab}$ (.17)	−.09$_b$ (.25)
Level of dyadic adjustment				
Initial level	4.80 (0.55)	4.98$_a$ (0.47)	4.60$_b$ (0.64)	4.66$_b$ (.54)
Linear trend	.01 (.06)	.02$_a$ (.04)	.00$_{ab}$ (.07)	−.01$_b$ (.07)

Note. Table values are means (with standard deviations in parentheses) for the entire sample and for each breakup group. Means in the same row that do not share subscripts differ at $p < .05$ in the Tukey multiple range test. All table values are raw scores, not standardized; some of the measures have different scales and variances.

Does social support predict changes in closeness? To determine whether initial level of social support predicted changes in each indicator of closeness, we conducted three regression analyses, predicting the slope of each closeness indicator from initial level of social support, controlling for initial level of closeness.[4] Initial level of social support was not uniquely associated with changes in general closeness, $\beta = .10$, $p < .276$, changes in commitment level, $\beta = .17$, $p < .114$, or changes in dyadic adjustment, $\beta = .05$, $p < .637$, when controlling for initial closeness. Thus, these results failed to show that individuals who initially felt strong support grew closer over time or that those who initially felt a lack of support grew less close.

To increase our confidence in these findings, we examined our data using a second analysis strategy in which we regressed each closeness indicator at Time 9 onto social support at Time 1, controlling for the Time 1 level of the closeness indicator. The unique association of Time 1 social support was marginal with Time 9 general closeness, $\beta = .15$, $p < .082$, and with Time 9 commitment level $\beta = .17$, $p < .063$; the unique association with Time 9 dyadic adjustment was not significant, $\beta = .09$, $p < .314$. Thus, at best, the data provide unreliable support for social support as a plausible causal mechanism in shaping relationship closeness over time. A more conservative interpretation is that they fail to support this causal direction.

---

[4] Social support and each indicator of closeness were highly correlated. Thus, in predicting changes in closeness, we controlled for initial levels of closeness. That is, we assessed whether there was an effect of initial social support above and beyond the effect of initial closeness. In predicting changes in social support, we controlled for initial social support, which indicates whether the was an effect of initial closeness above and beyond initial social support.

Does Closeness Predict Changes in Social Support? We conducted parallel analyses to determine whether initial level of closeness predicted changes in social support. We conducted three regression analyses, regressing changes in social support onto initial level of each closeness indicator, controlling for initial level of social support (cf. footnote 4). Initial level of general closeness exhibited a marginal unique association with change in social support, $\beta = .18$, $p < .059$, and initial level of commitment exhibited a significant unique association, $\beta = .23$, $p < .027$, when controlling for initial level of social support; initial level of dyadic adjustment, $\beta = .01$, $p < .886$, was not uniquely associated with change in social support. We obtained similar findings using our second data analysis approach, in which we conducted three regression analyses (one for each Time 1 closeness indicator, controlling for Time 1 social support): Time 9 social support was significantly predicted from Time 1 general closeness, $\beta = .21$, $p < .010$, and Time 1 commitment level, $\beta = .24$, $p < .007$, but not from Time 1 dyadic adjustment, $\beta = .02$, $p < .790$. Thus, we could not rule out high levels of general closeness and commitment as plausible causal mechanisms for bringing about perceptions of strong social support.

Causal Implications. Although social support did not predict changes in closeness in our study, other studies have suggested that social support brings about more committed and loving relationships. For example, in a two-year longitudinal study with three time periods, Sprecher and Felmlee (1992) found that earlier levels of perceived social network support predicted later levels of relationship satisfaction, commitment, and love. Moreover, the reverse was only partly true: Only earlier level of commitment predicted later perceived social support, whereas the association of earlier satisfaction and love with later social support was not significant. Why do Sprecher and Felmlee's data suggest that social support leads to more closeness, and our data suggest that closeness leads to more support?

The Sprecher and Felmlee (1992) study differed from ours in several ways. First, there was more time between measurement occasions in their study than in ours. Thus, it is difficult to draw direct comparisons. Second, they examined slightly different relationship variables than we examined, although all of these variables tend to exhibit high positive correlations. Third, and importantly, their study involved relationships that had been intact longer than the relationships of participants in our study; our participants were in recently initiated relationships.

We speculate that the two sets of results—ours versus Sprecher and Felmlee's (1992)—in fact complement each other and reflect more general changes over the developmental course of a relationship. Early on, when couple members are in the stage of establishing their relationship (as was the case in our study), the dominant process may be to create a social environment that reflects and bolsters subjective feelings of closeness. Those who feel close to their partner may seek others who are supportive of the relationship; if they fail to find support, they may even adopt positively biased beliefs about their network, *perceiving* support despite evidence to the contrary. Indeed, their aim is to create more reasons for being with the partner. Those who do not feel particularly close to their partners and foresee a breakup in the future may look for reasons to end the relationship and, consequently, they may undermine actual support or perceive less support than actually exists. However, over time as the relationship unfolds (as was the case in the study by Sprecher and Felmlee), it becomes increasingly difficult to sustain perceptions of social support that have no basis in reality. At that point, the dominant process may be to alter perceptions to reflect reality. Couples who truly lack support may become at risk and those who truly have support may thrive. In sum, whereas closeness may influence perceptions of social support in recently initiated relationships, in ongoing relationships (i.e., those

TABLE 16.2

Logistic Regression Analyses Predicting Breakup Status From Changes
in Relationship Closeness and Changes in Social Support
From Friends and Family

| | | Simultaneous Regression Analysis | |
| | Simple Association | Individual Parameter | Overall Model |
Models Predicting Breakup Status	χ^2	χ^2	χ^2
Associations of changes in general closeness and social support			
Changes in general closeness	6.84***	1.90	18.65***
Changes in social support	12.38***	8.33***	
Associations of changes in commitment level and social support Changes in commitment	10.84***	3.33*	20.02***
Changes in social support	12.38***	6.08**	
Associations of changes in dyadic adjustment and social support			
Changes in dyadic adjustment	6.79***	0.68	17.33***
Changes in social support	12.38***	7.61***	

Note. *$p < .10$. **$p < .05$. ***$p < .01$.

that lasted beyond Time 9), the real presence or absence of support may influence
closeness and the ensuing course of those relationships.

Relationship Processes in Social Context. Although none of the studies that we
described above provide definitive support for a causal sequence, they all suggest that
examining only an individual's reports of his or her feelings of closeness will provide
an incomplete picture of what the future holds for that relationship. One must look
beyond the individual's thoughts and feelings about his or her relationship, and take
into account others' actual or perceived opinions of the relationship.

In our own research, we compared changes in closeness and changes in perceived
social support as predictors of whether relationships lasted until the follow-up occasion, eight months after the start of the study. Specifically, in a series of logistic
regression analyses, we examined whether changes in social support and changes in
each indicator of closeness each predicted later breakup status (stayer, abandoned, or
leaver, measured approximately four months after Time 9). The simple associations
are displayed in the first column of Table 16.2.

As can be seen in Table 16.1, stayers and leavers differed in almost every linear
trend variable, whereas abandoned individuals exhibited levels between the other
two groups. Thus, compared to stayers, leavers exhibited significant decreases in
general closeness, commitment, and dyadic adjustment. The exception was in social
support: Stayers and abandoned individuals did not differ, whereas leavers exhibited
significantly greater decreases in social support. Although abandoned individuals
were in relationships that ended, they perceived as much support for their relationships as did individuals whose relationships persisted.

In three additional analyses—one for each indicator of closeness—we examined
whether changes in social support and changes in closeness simultaneously predicted breakup. This allowed us to determine whether changes in social support add

something above and beyond the effect of changes in closeness in the prediction of whether a relationship lasts. As can be seen in Table 2, the results were surprising: Changes in social support predicted breakup above and beyond the effect of changes in each indicator of closeness, whereas only changes in commitment continued to provide marginal prediction of breakup status above and beyond the effect of changes in social support; changes in general closeness and in dyadic adjustment were not significant predictors. One interpretation of these results is that changes in social support mediate the effects of changes in closeness on breakup; in Table 16.2, the simple effects for changes in closeness were significant, but these effects dropped to marginal or nonsignificance when controlling for changes in social support.

Summary

Two sets of results regarding social support are pertinent. In the first set, perceived social support at the outset of recently initiated dating relationships did not predict changes in closeness, but closeness at the outset predicted changes in perceived social support. Thus, at a very early point in a relationship, closeness appears to have a more prominent role in predicting relationship changes than does social support. However, in a second set of findings, changes in social support over the course of the ensuing 10 weeks had a unique effect on breakup (measured four months after the tenth week) whereas changes in closeness did not. Moreover, other research on established relationships (Sprecher & Felmlee, 1992) suggests that the effect of social support on relationship qualities is more robust than the effect of relationship qualities on social support.

We speculated about a model that would integrate these findings, in which we suggest that the effects of social support vary over the course of a relationship. Early on, it is possible that individuals who do not feel close attribute the lack of closeness to members of their social network; thus, their Time 1 levels of closeness predict changes in social support. Moreover, for these individuals who do not feel close, changes in their perceptions of social support may continue to reflect a lack of closeness. Thus, changes in social support predict which relationships will end. However, in relationships that endure over time (i.e., beyond the follow up), it becomes difficult to maintain perceptions of support that reflect projected feelings of closeness and have no basis in reality. At that point, social support predicts changes in relationship qualities, as was shown by Sprecher and Felmlee (1992).

These results suggest that perceived social support provides additional information beyond subjective closeness—arguably even better information than closeness—in predicting the course of a relationship. Regardless of whether the effects of perceived social support are real or instead reflect masked feelings of closeness, examining factors beyond the individual—even if one must rely on the individual's reports of these factors—can be critically important in understanding what unfolds in intimate relationships. In the next section, we extend our analysis of examining factors beyond the individual by focusing on meaningful aspects of couple members' physical environments.

PHYSICAL ENVIRONMENT

Research in the area of environmental psychology describes the symbolic nature of objects, noting that objects in the home represent to others (such as guests) one's values and characteristics (Gosling, Ko, Mannarelli, & Morris, 2002; Werner, 1987). Moreover, recent theorizing on the situated nature of cognition suggests that the arrangement of spatial environment is a fundamental medium for bringing about behavioral goals (Kirsh, 1995). We applied these ideas to an interpersonal context (cf. Lohmann, Arriaga, & Goodfriend, 2003). In particular, we examined a process that Altman has referred to as *placemaking*—the physical and symbolic creation of a home as represented operationally in the acquisition and placement of shared objects (Altman, Brown, Staples, & Werner, 1992). We focused specifically on the arrangement of objects in a couple's home and suggest that jointly acquired objects may reflect various aspects of a couple's relationship, namely closeness, relationship commitment, and dyadic adjustment.

Objects in the physical environment serve many purposes. For instance, in public areas, objects may indicate that a particular area is claimed (Brown, 1987), such as leaving a jacket on a chair to mark temporary "ownership." In private spaces, such as one's home, objects take on symbolic value by reflecting aspects of one's personal identity (Altman, 1975; Altman & Ginat, 1996; Brown, 1987; Gosling et al., 2002).

In the specific context of intimate relationships, objects can serve at least two primary functions. First, couple members may use objects to communicate things about their couple identity to others. For example, newlyweds may prominently place photos from their honeymoon, which subsequently become the topic of conversation with those who visit their home. Second, home objects may cue certain relationship qualities to the couple members themselves—that is, objects may inwardly direct couple members' behaviors. For instance, an object may seem unimportant to others but may have special meaning to the couple, reminding them of a special moment in their lives together. These two functions have distinct, but mutually relevant, theoretical roots. We briefly review these theoretical roots below.

Outward Function: Objects as Symbols to Others

One important function served by the careful placement of meaningful home objects is to communicate to others something about the inhabitants (Altman, 1987; Altman & Ginat, 1996; Brown, 1987; Gosling et al., 2002). The idea that objects reflect aspects of the self to others was described by Heider (1958), who wrote that an individual "reveals [what] belongs to him in order to produce a positive reaction" (p. 78). For example, family heirlooms may be located in a central location of a home for the express purpose of evoking particular cognitions or emotions that reflect pride in one's lineage to those who visit one's home. Prominently placed religious icons serve to identify membership with a specific religious community (McMillan & Chavis, 1986); objects such as expensive art can reflect how one wishes to represent his or her status to others (Amaturo, Costagliola, & Ragone, 1987); objects may even act as symbols of social integration, as exemplified by the number of homes that display the U.S. flag on Independence Day (Csikszentmihalyi, & Rochberg-Halton, 1981).

Similarly, home objects can communicate something about one's intimate relationship. For instance, couple members may exhibit wedding pictures or other relationship-symbolizing objects to communicate to others that they are a unit. We were particularly interested in objects that couple members acquire together, given that they reflect their couple identity more than do objects that they acquire individually. One primary variable in our analysis of placemaking was *couple displays*: objects that couple members acquire together and are placed in prominent locations in their home for visitors to notice. We expected that, compared with less close couple members, relatively close couple members would have a high number of couple displays to communicate their "couplehood." On the other hand, couple members who are not necessarily as eager to communicate their joint identity might make other choices for the objects they put in prominent places; they may opt to display objects that are not relationship-centric, such as objects that they acquire individually.

Inward Function: Objects as Behavioral Cues for Couple Members

We also examined a second function that home objects may serve in the context of intimate relationships: They cue relationship qualities to the couple members themselves. Others have touched on the idea that home objects and spatial arrangements can direct thoughts and behavior. The Russian psychologist L. S. Vygotsky was fascinated by the psychological function of objects (Holland & Valsiner, 1988). As Holland and Valsiner note (1988, p. 248), for Vygotsky these symbolic objects function in the mental world as tools do in the physical world. For example, one may tie a string around one's finger to remember to do something; the string alone has no meaning, but when placed around one's finger, it takes on special meaning.

Cognitive scientists interested in situated cognition have expressed similar ideas. A major theme of situated cognition is that individuals manipulate their physical environment for the sake of facilitating their personal goals. For example, dieters keep certain foods out of view (out of a pantry or refrigerator) to prevent snacking (Kirsch, 1995, p. 404). Cognitive representations that are most adaptive are those that are specific to the immediate environment (Smith & Semin, in press). For example, a general script on how to complement a partner may not bring about the desired consequence (e.g., when a person plops down on the couch after a long day at work, a partner who says "You look wonderful!" is not likely to be taken seriously). On the other hand, specific cognitions that take into account the immediate moment are more likely to advance one's goal (e.g., when a person plops down on the couch, a partner might say "It's amazing how you can manage a long day at work and still look wonderful"). Moreover, the environment may cue personal goals—in this case, couple-relevant cognitions—in ways that become automatic after repeated activation (Bargh, 1990). Whereas Vygotsky might describe the string around one's finger as a symbol that directs mental events in a conscious and deliberate way, those interested in situated cognition would suggest that the string is a way of managing and manipulating the environment so as to be automatically directed toward certain behaviors over others, thereby simplifying the behavioral choices one must make (Kirsh, 1995). Thus, the physical environment constrains thoughts and behaviors, and thoughts and behaviors, in turn, reflect contingencies in the environment.

Following this reasoning, we suggest that prominently placed home objects provide enviornment-specific ways of directing a couple member's thoughts, feelings, and actions. Just as there are ways of arranging items to informationally cue behaviors (i.e., "jigging" the environment; Kirsh, 1995), there are ways that couple members may arrange the physical environment of their home to cue their couple identity. For most American couples, this process begins when the couple members first move into a shared physical environment. Typically they integrate their individually owned objects into a mixture of things that furnish the home (Altman et al., 1992). However, over time, couple members replace these things with objects that they acquire together. Thus, it comes as no surprise that studies describe homes as more than mere dwellings: Insofar as "home" reflects one's identity and prompts feelings of "belonging" (Altman et al., 1992; Cooper, 1974; Csikszentmihalyi & Rochberg-Halton, 1981), "home" may also prompt thoughts of one's couplehood. As such, over time the tangible objects that make up a couple's physical dwelling (e.g., brick walls, rooms, possessions) transform into a space commemorating the couple members' joint identities.

However, not all couple members infuse special meaning into the objects that they have acquired together. Some couple members may reside in homes that are filled with jointly acquired prominent objects, yet their favorite objects may be ones that were not acquired together. Although they are surrounded by objects that reflect their couplehood, they prefer their individually acquired objects that serve as cues of individuality-oriented cognitions over relationship-oriented cognitions. Either they are not motivated to see their environment in ways that promote the relationship (Rusbult & Buunk, 1993), or, more simply, they may find less closeness to be more optimal (cf. Brewer, 1993).

On the other hand, other couple members may take a strong liking to objects that they have acquired together. These objects cue more relationship-oriented cognitions, suggesting greater cognitive interdependence between partners (cf. Agnew, Van Lange, Rusbult, & Langston, 1998). Thus, a second primary variable in our analysis of placemaking was *couple markers*: jointly acquired objects that have become the favorite objects of a couple member. We expected that, compared with less close couple members, relatively close couple members would have a high number of couple markers to cue their "couplehood." On the other hand, couple members whose favorite objects are individually acquired will not be directed toward favorable relationship thoughts, feelings, and actions.

Physical Environment as a Concomitant of Closeness

We conducted a study in which we examined how objects that are prominently placed in one's home communicate information to visitors as well as to the couple members themselves (Lohmann et al., 2003). Both couple displays and couple markers were presumed to communicate closeness, commitment, and general relationship functioning. We anticipated that a higher prevalence of couple displays and couple markers each would be positively associated with general closeness, commitment, and dyadic adjustment.

We did not seek to identify the exact causal direction between home objects and relationship qualities. Instead, we adopted a correlational approach, even though such an approach would not allow us to rule out causal processes stemming from an unaccounted, third variable. Instead, we aimed to provide an initial test of the possibility that key relationship features may direct the placement of and preference for objects, but also to allow for the more intriguing possibility that the arrangement of objects in a couple's home environment may shape key relationship features. Together, both processes functionally serve to maintain a relationship.

We recruited participants from university campuses, office areas, local businesses, and shopping centers in a small-sized Midwestern city and in the Southern California area. To qualify for the study, participants had to be at least 18 years of age and they had to be in a romantic relationship with someone with whom they had been living for at least one year. Participants completed a questionnaire in the privacy of their home and then mailed their completed questionnaire to us. The response rates were 80% and 50% for the Midwest and Southern California subsamples, respectively, for a total response rate of 64%. The final sample consisted of 110 individuals (49 men; 61 women).

Three percent of participants were age 55 or older, 25% were age 40 to 54, 55% were age 25 to 39, and 16% were age 24 or younger. The mean relationship duration was 10 years and 4 months; 79% were married whereas the other 21% were in nonmarital cohabitating relationships. Participants had lived together an average of 9 years and 4 months.

We included measures of closeness, relationship commitment, and dyadic adjustment that were almost identical to those described in the section on social environments (see Lohmann et al., 2003, for details). The sample consisted of individuals who were relatively close on a scale ranging from 1 to 7 ($M = 4.98$, $SD = 1.67$), moderately to highly committed on a scale ranging from 1 to 7 ($M = 5.89$, $SD = 0.91$), and in relatively well-functioning relationships as indicated by their dyadic adjustment scores on a scale ranging from 9 to 57 ($M = 44.65$, $SD = 6.75$). As might be expected, level of commitment varied by relationship type with married individuals being more committed ($M = 6.02$, $SD = 0.83$) than cohabitating individuals ($M = 5.41$, $SD = 1.06$), F (1, 109) $= 8.88$, $p < .004$.

The measures of couple markers and couple displays involved having participants list objects in their home, complete additional measures (that were beyond the scope of this research), and then indicate who acquired the object (self, partner, or both self and partner together). Importantly, we included several instructions to ensure that, when asked how the object was acquired, participants would not change the objects that were listed. Specifically, participants were instructed to make themselves comfortable in the room of their home where they were most likely to entertain guests. They were asked to indicate which room they were in (e.g., living room). They then read instructions in which we defined objects and asked them to indicate the five objects or things that they like most in that room. On the following page, participants were asked to list the five objects that they most wanted a visitor to notice, which could be the same or different objects that they most like in the room.

After completing several measures that were for purposes beyond the current research, participants were instructed to once again list their five most favorite objects that they had previously listed, without changing any of the objects that they had listed; no participants listed new objects that had not appeared earlier. After relisting the relevant objects, participants were asked to label each object as being acquired by them (e.g., purchased by them, heirloom of their family), by the partner, or by both of them. The measure of couple markers was based on the percentage of favorite objects that were jointly acquired (e.g., a person who indicated that four of the five favorite objects listed were jointly acquired would obtain a score of .80).

On the next page, participants were instructed to once again list the five objects that they had previously listed as those they most wanted a visitor to notice, without making any changes to this list. Then, participants were asked to label each object as being acquired by them, by the partner, or by both of them. The measure of couple displays was based on the percentage of objects they wanted a visitor to notice that were jointly acquired. On average, approximately half of visitor-relevant and favorite objects were jointly acquired (54% of couple displays, 49% of couple markers); the proportions of couple displays and markers were positively correlated ($r(105) = .76$, $p < .001$).

Levels of the relationship variables varied in the two sub-samples,[5] so we combined the two subsamples but retained subsample as a covariate in all additional analyses. Moreover, the proportion of couple displays varied by relationship duration, so we included relationship duration as a second covariate in analyses.[6] (There were no significant statistical interactions involving subsample or duration; thus, these variables did not moderate any of the expected associations.)

---

[5] Compared to individuals from the Southern California sample, those from the Midwest sample felt marginally closer to their partners ($M = 5.22$, $SD = 1.47$ vs. $M = 4.64$, $SD = 1.87$), $F(1, 108) = 3.20$, $p < .076$, had significantly better functioning relationships ($M = 45.81$, $SD = 5.84$ vs. $M = 43.04$, $SD = 7.61$), $F(1, 109) = 4.66$, $p < .033$, and were significantly more committed ($M = 6.09$, $SD = 0.79$ vs. $M = 5.62$, $SD = 1.00$), $F(1, 109) = 7.76$, $p < .006$. The two subsamples also differed in the relationship type: A significantly larger proportion of the Midwest sample was comprised of married individuals (88%; 12% cohabitating individuals) than in the Southern California sample (67%; 33% cohabitating, $\chi^2(1, 110) = 6.54$, $p < .011$). However, these two groups did not differ in relationship duration ($F(1, 101) = 1.27$, $p < .263$).

[6] Compared to individuals in relationships that were relatively shorter in duration, those in longer relationships reported a significantly greater proportion of jointly acquired objects among those they wanted others to notice, $r(101) = .29$, $p < .004$. The correlation of relationship duration with proportion of jointly acquired "favorite" objects was not significant, $r(100) = .16$, $p < .103$.

We calculated correlations between couple displays and each indicator of closeness, partialling out the effects of relationship duration and subsample. Couple displays were significantly correlated with closeness ($pr[107] = .21$, $p < .042$), marginally correlated with commitment level ($pr[107] = .19$, $p < .057$); the simple correlation between couple displays and commitment was significant, ($r[107] = .20$, $p < .043$), and significantly correlated with dyadic adjustment ($pr[107] = .34$, $p < .001$). Thus, compared with individuals who indicated a relatively lower proportion of jointly acquired objects as the objects they most wanted others to notice, those who indicated a higher proportion of visitor-relevant jointly acquired objects felt closer to their partner and had better functioning relationships. They also were relatively more committed, although this association was marginal. These results suggest a strategic and functional placement of home objects to convey the characteristics of the relationship to others outside the family.

To examine couple markers, we calculated partial correlations between couple markers and each indicator of closeness, controlling for relationship duration and subsample. Couple markers were significantly correlated with general closeness ($pr[108] = .24$, $p < .017$), marginally correlated with commitment ($pr[108] = .19$, $p < .067$); the simple correlation with commitment was significant, ($r[108] = .26$, $p < .007$), and significantly correlated with dyadic adjustment ($pr[108] = .27$, $p < .008$). Thus, compared with individuals who indicated a relatively lower proportion of jointly acquired objects as their favorite objects, those who indicated a higher proportion of jointly acquired favorite objects felt closer to their partner and had better functioning relationships. They also were relatively more committed, although this association was marginal. These results suggest that home furnishings may cue relationship characteristics to the couple members themselves.

Causal Implications.   We have suggested that couple members affect and are affected by their environment, although we did not directly examine this bidirectional association. We adopted a correlational approach, which can only provide evidence of an association but cannot clarify the nature of this association. Is it only the case that couple members arrange their home to reflect current levels of closeness? Or, could it also (or only) be the case that couple displays and markers cue certain levels of closeness to the couple members? Of course, it is also possible that a third factor brings about changes in home arrangement and closeness.

The possibility that markers cause closeness is intriguing. This would involve a process whereby objects bring about relationship-oriented behaviors, and these behaviors bring about closeness. Thus, relationship-specific behaviors would mediate the association between markers and closeness. Such a process would have important practical implications, namely that changing a couple's home environment could improve their levels of closeness, commitment, and functioning.

Summary.   Individuals who indicated a relatively higher proportion of visitor-relevant and favorite jointly acquired objects felt closer to their partner and had better functioning relationships. They were also more likely to be committed, although this effect was marginal in our study. We suggested that partners arrange the objects in their homes in ways that reflect levels of closeness—that is, high closeness may cause jointly acquired objects to be placed prominently whereas relatively lower closeness may cause the prominent placement of individually acquired objects. However, we also suggested that the opposite causal sequence may occur, that prominently-placed jointly acquired objects elicit greater closeness and prominently placed individual object elicit less closeness. We speculated about the causal mechanisms that might account for this link as well as the practical implications.

CAVEATS

Some caveats should be noted. First, we do not wish to suggest that social and physical environments are the only, or even the most important, types of environmental influences. Conceivably, there are other types of environments that influence couple members, such as work environments, neighborhoods, and religious institutions.

Second, the research described in this chapter pertains to a specific population: American dating, cohabitating, and marital couples. It remains to be determined whether the current findings apply to other cultures and types of relationships. For instance, given that home may be thought of differently in other cultures (Csikszentmihalyi & Rochberg-Halton, 1981), there may be variations in the extent to which a home reflects the inhabitants' joint identities. Moreover, the dynamics of couplehood may vary, as is the case in polygamous cultures (Altman & Ginat, 1996). Similarly, the influence of family and friends may be more pronounced in some cultures than in others, and such variations may even occur within American subcultures—for instance, extended family members tend to have a greater presence among Latinos and African American families (Mindel, 1980). It is conceivable that the current findings may generalize to other types of close relationships. For example, parents may decorate their office spaces to reflect their parental status and college roommates who are friends may cover their dorm room walls with photos of things that they have done together (cf. Gosling et al., 2002).

THE POWER OF THE ENVIRONMENT

Regardless of the type of relationship or culture being examined, the idea that environments shape our behavior is universal. We have suggested that individuals organize their immediate social and physical environments to facilitate their relationship goals. Our findings revealed that relationship partners who are relatively close perceive that friends and family members support their relationship. They also organize objects in their home so as to reflect and sustain closeness. In the language of interdependence theory, social network members and physical objects constitute factors that partly define a given situation. Couple members size up the given situation and respond in ways that reflect their relationship goals. Subsequently, they recreate situations and environments that promote these goals. In the language of situated cognition, couple members actively arrange their social engagements and physical spaces in ways that will bring to mind and direct their relationship goals. Both theoretical orientations suggest that relationship goals influence how couple members manage their immediate environment, and, in turn, the immediate environment brings about thoughts, feelings, and behaviors that reflect closeness.

Understanding relationships involves examining the social and physical environment in which couple members' lives unfold. In short, Lewin's (1951) adage that behavior is a function of the person and environment could be expanded to also state that the environment is a function of the person and interpersonal behavior.

REFERENCES

Agnew, C. R., Loving, T. J., & Drigotas, S. M. (2001). Substituting the forest for the trees: Social networks and the prediction of romantic relationship state and fate. *Journal of Personality and Social Psychology, 81,* 1042–1057.

Agnew, C. R., Van Lange, P. A. M., Rusbult, C. E., & Langston, C. A. (1998). Cognitive interdependence: Commitment and the mental representation of close relationships. *Journal of Personality and Social Psychology, 74,* 939–954.

Altman, I. (1975). *The environment and social behavior.* Monterey, California: Brooks/Cole.

Altman, I., Brown, B. B., Staples, B., & Werner, C. M. (1992). A transactional approach to close relationships: Courtship, weddings, and placemaking. In B. Walsh, K. Craik, & R. Price (Eds.), *Person-environment psychology* (pp. 193–241). Hillsdale, NJ: Lawrence Erlbaum Associates.

Altman, I., & Ginat, J. (1996). *Polygamous families in contemporary society*. Cambridge, MA: Cambridge University Press.

Altman, I., & Rogoff, B. (1987). World views in psychology: Trait, interactional, organismic, and transactional perspectives. In D. Stokols, & I. Altman (Eds.), *Handbook of environmental psychology* (vol. 1, pp. 7–40). New York: Wiley.

Amaturo, E., Costagliola, S., & Ragone, G. (1987). Furnishing and status attributes: A sociological study of the living room. *Environment and Behavior, 19*, 228–49.

Aron, A., Aron, E. N., & Smollan, D. (1992). Inclusion of other in the self scale and the structure of interpersonal closeness. *Journal of Personality and Social Psychology, 63*, 596–612.

Aron, A., Aron, E. N., Tudor, M., & Nelson, G. (1991). Close relationships as including other in the self. *Journal of Personality and Social Psychology, 60*, 241–253.

Aron, A., & Fraley, B. (1999). Relationship closeness as including the other in the self: Cognitive underpinnings and measures. *Social Cognition, 17*, 140–160.

Arriaga, X. B. (2001). The ups and downs of dating: Fluctuations in satisfaction in newly formed romantic relationships. *Journal of Personality and Social Psychology, 80*, 754–765.

Brewer, M. B. (1993). The role of distinctiveness in social identity and group behavior. N. M. A. Hogg & D. Abrams (Eds.), *Group motivation: Social psychological perspectives* (pp. 1–16). Hertfordshire, England: Harvester Wheatsheaf.

Brewer, M. B. (1993). The role of distinctiveness in social identity and group behavior. N. M. A. Hogg & D. Abrams (Eds.), *Group motivation: Social psychological perspectives* (pp. 1–16). Hertfordshire, England: Harvester Wheatsheaf.

Brown, B. B. (1987). Territoriality. In D. Stokols & I. Altman (Eds.), *Handbook of environmental psychology* (Vol. 1, pp. 505–531). New York: Wiley.

Cooper, C. (1974). The house as a symbol of self. In J. Lang, C. Burnette, W. Moleski, & D. Vachon (Eds.), *Designing for human behavior: Architecture and the behavioral sciences* (pp. 130–146). Stroudsberg, PA: Dowden, Hutchinson, & Ross.

Cox, C. L., Wexler, M. O., Rusbult, C. E., & Gaines, S. O., Jr. (1997). Prescriptive support and commitment processes in close relationships. *Social Psychology Quarterly, 60*, 79–90.

Csikszentmihalyi, M., & Rochberg-Halton, E. (1981). *The meaning of things: Domestic symbols and the self*. Cambridge, MA: Cambridge University Press.

Driscoll, R., Davis, K. F., & Lipetz, M. E. (1972). Parental interference and romantic love: The Romeo and Juliet effect. *Journal of Personality and Social Structure, 24*, 1–10.

Feeney, J. A. (1999). Issues of closeness and distance in dating relationships: Effects of sex and attachment style. *Journal of Social and Personal Relationships, 16*, 571–590.

Felmlee, D. H. (2001). No couple is an island: A social network perspective on dyadic stability. *Social Forces, 79*, 1259–1287.

Felmlee, D., Sprecher, S., & Bassin, E. (1990). The dissolution of intimate relationships: A hazard model. *Social Psychology Quarterly, 53*, 13–30.

Gosling, S. D., Ko, S. J., Mannarelli, T., & Morris, M. E. (2002). A room with a cue: Personality Judgments Based on Offices and bedrooms. *Journal of Personality and Social Psychology, 82*, 379–398.

Heider, F. (1958). *The psychology of interpersonal relations*. New York: Wiley.

Holland, D. C., & Valsiner, J. (1988). Cognition, symbols, and Vygotsky's developmental psychology. *Ethos, 16*, 247–272.

Karney, B. R., & Bradbury, T. N. (1995). Assessing longitudinal change in marriage: An introduction to the analysis of growth curves. *Journal of Marriage and the Family, 57*, 1091–1108.

Kelley, H. H. (1983). The situational origins of human tendencies: A further reason for the formal analysis of structures. *Personality and Social Psychology Bulletin, 9*, 8–36.

Kelley, H. H. (1991). Lewin, situations, and interdependence. *Journal of Social Issues, 47*, 211–233.

Kelley, H. H., Berscheid, E., Christensen, A., Harvey, J. H., Huston, T. L., Levinger, G., et al. (Eds.) (1983). *Close relationships*. New York: W. H. Freeman.

Kelley, H. H., & Thibaut, J. W. (1978). *Interpersonal relations: A theory of interdependence*. New York: Wiley.

Kirsh, D. (1995). The intelligent use of space. *Artificial Intelligence, 73*, 31–68.

Lewin, K. (1951). *Field theory in social science*. New York: Harper.

Lohmann, A., Arriaga, X. B., & Goodfriend, W. (2003). Close relationships and placemaking: Do objects in a couple's home reflect couplehood? *Personal Relationships, 10*, 437–449.

McMillan, D. W. & Chavis, D. M. (1986). Sense of community: A definition and theory. *Journal of Community Psychology, 14*, 6–23.

Milardo, R. M. (1982). Friendship networks in developing relationships: Converging and diverging social environments. *Social Psychology Quarterly, 45*, 162–172.

Milardo, R. M., & Allan, G. (1997). Social networks and marital relationships. In S. Duck (Ed.), *Handbook of personal relationships: Theory, research, and interventions* (2nd ed., pp. 506–522). New York: Wiley.

Milardo, R. M., Helms-Erikson, H. (2000). Network overlap and third-party influence in close relationships. In C. Hendrick & S. Hendrick (Eds.), *Close relationships: A sourcebook* (pp. 33–45). Thousand Oaks, CA: Sage.

Mindel, C. H. (1980). Extended familism among urban Mexcian Americans, Anglos, and Blacks. *Hispanic Journal of Behavioral Sciences, 2*, 21–34.

Parks, M. R. (1997). Communication networks and relationship life cycles. In S. Duck (Ed.), *Handbook of personal relationships: Theory, research, and interventions* (2nd ed., pp. 351–372). New York: Wiley.

Rogosa, D., Brant, D., & Zimowski, M. (1982). A slow growth curve approach to the measurement of change. *Psychological Bulletin, 92*, 726–748.

Rusbult, C. E., & Buunk, B. P. (1993). Commitment processes in close relationships: An interdependence analysis. *Journal of Social and Personal Relationships, 10*, 175–204.

Smith, E. R., & Semin, G. R. (in press). The foundations of socially situated action: Socially situated cognition. *Advances in Experimental Social Psychology*.

Spanier, G. B. (1976). Measuring dyadic adjustment: New scales for assessing the quality of marriage and similar dyads. *Journal of Marriage and the Family, 38*, 15–28.

Sprecher, S. (1988). Investment model, equity, and social support determinants of relationship commitment. *Social Psychology Quarterly, 51*, 318–328.

Sprecher, S., & Felmlee, D. (1992). The influence of parents and friends on the quality and stability of romantic relationships: A three-wave longitudinal investigation. *Journal of Marriage and the Family, 54*, 888–900.

Thibaut, J. W., & Kelley, H. H. (1959). *The social psychology of groups*. New York: Wiley.

Werner, C. M. (1987). Home interiors: A time and place for interpersonal relationships. *Environment and Behavior, 19*, 169–179.

17

Loss of an Intimate Partner Through Death

Camille B. Wortman
State University of New York at Stony Brook

Karin Wolff
University of Trier

George A. Bonanno
Teachers College, Columbia University

Megan P. and her husband were making plans to celebrate their 25th anniversary when he died of a heart attack. Although it has been over six years since his death, Megan continues to struggle with powerful feelings of depression and loneliness. She feels that she must hide these feelings from her friends, who expect her to have "moved on" by now. How should her intense and prolonged distress following her husband's death be interpreted? Perhaps she and her husband shared such a close bond that she finds it unbearable to go on without him. Alternatively, her continuing grief may reflect preexisting psychological problems or an absence of coping resources.

John T. lost his wife of 18 years after a lengthy battle with cancer. Although only three months have passed since her death, John is showing few outward signs of distress. In fact, he has expressed interest in dating. What is the best way to understand John's reaction? Is he denying his grief and running away from his pain? Does his apparent lack of grief signify that he is a shallow, superficial person who was not really attached to his wife? Perhaps he is showing little distress because her death brought about feelings of relief—either because the marriage was an unhappy one, or because he was burdened by caregiving responsibilities. Alternatively, his reaction may signify a healthy resilience in coping with the death of his spouse.

To date, most of the work on closeness and intimacy has focused on how intimacy is established and maintained. Some research has examined how people react to the loss of an intimate relationship following a breakup or divorce. However, close relationships researchers have focused almost no attention on how people deal with the loss of an intimate partner through death. This issue is important in its own right because death of a partner is a universal experience among couples in a long-term relationship.

Indeed, the only way that a person can avoid losing one's partner through death is to die first. Moreover, by learning more about how people react to a close partner's death, what factors shape their reactions, and what issues they struggle with as they attempt to continue on their own, we can learn a great deal about the nature of intimacy itself. By intimacy we are referring to relationships characterized by deep affection, strong dependency, or both. In examining research on partner loss, we focus almost exclusively on long-term relationships among heterosexual partners. Although it is important to understand how those in gay and lesbian relationships react to partner loss, the empirical research base is limited at present.

In this chapter, we draw from our own research and that of others to explore how people are affected by the death of an intimate partner. We focus on four interlocking sets of issues. First, how do people react when they lose an intimate partner through death? In Western culture there are strong expectations that following the death of a spouse, the surviving spouse will exhibit intense distress. Over the next year or so survivors are expected to "work through" their feelings and return to their earlier level of functioning. Because there is little scientific evidence to support these expectations (Bonanno & Kaltman, 1999; 2001), we have come to label them "myths of coping with loss" (Wortman & Silver, 1987; 1989; 2001). In the first section of this chapter, we highlight the implications of this work for understanding closeness and intimacy.

In the second section of the chapter, we attempt to understand the extraordinary variability that characterizes peoples' reactions to the death of a spouse or partner. Why do some people respond with intense and prolonged distress whereas others seem to be relatively unscathed, and perhaps even strengthened, by the loss? To address these questions, we focus on current research as well as a new prospective study that assesses people on average 3 years before the death of their spouse and at 6 and 18 months following the death (Bonanno et al., 2002). In the third section of the chapter, we focus on the following question: When a person loses an intimate partner, what role, if any, is played by other close relationships in facilitating recovery from the loss? Although social support has been shown to play an important role in adjustment to bereavement (see, e.g., Sanders, 1993; Stylianos & Vachon, 1993), there is considerable evidence that bereaved people often have difficulty obtaining the support they need (Wortman, Battle, & Lemkau, 1997). We explore the bereaved person's relationships with others in some detail to elucidate the nature of these problems. The final issue we address in this chapter concerns the possible reestablishment of intimacy in new relationships following the death of one's spouse or partner. Once a spouse has died, what factors predict whether the surviving spouse will show interest in establishing a new romantic or sexual relationship? Given the greater preponderance of men to women, are both genders equally likely to express interest in forming new attachments?

REACTIONS TO THE DEATH OF A SPOUSE

In all cultures, there are strong and powerful assumptions about how people should react to the death of a loved one. Assumptions in the industrialized West are derived in part from the theories of loss offered by prominent writers in the area, including Freud's (1917/1957) grief work perspective and Bowlby's (1980) attachment model of loss. They are based in part on books and articles written by clinicians that describe the grieving process (see, e.g., Jacobs, 1993; Rando, 1993; Worden, 1991). Finally, they are drawn from books and articles written for and by the bereaved themselves (e.g., Sanders, 1999). These assumptions are likely to have a pervasive impact on how a person's reactions to loss are evaluated by others, as well as people's judgments about the appropriateness of their own responses. For this reason, it is important to subject them to careful empirical scrutiny. Below, we identify four assumptions that we believe to be very prevalent in the grief literature, and examine the empirical evidence for each.

The Expectation of Intense Distress

When a person experiences the death of a spouse or partner, it is assumed that the normal way to react is with intense distress or depression. The most prevalent theories in the area (e.g., Freud, 1917/1957; Bowlby, 1980) are based on the assumption that at some point, people will confront the reality of their loss and go through a period of depression. Books written by grief researchers, as well as those written by and for the bereaved, convey the same view. As Shuchter (1986) has indicated, "virtually everyone whose spouse dies exhibits some signs and symptoms of depression" (see also Sanders, 1999).

What percentage of people actually experience depression in the first few months after the death of a spouse? Available evidence suggests that around 20% of the bereaved manifest clinically significant levels of depression, depending on the sample and the assessment procedure used (see Bonanno & Kaltman, 1999, 2001; Wortman & Silver, 2001, for reviews). Of course, it is possible to become depressed following the loss without manifesting major depression. To determine the prevalence of depression, it is important to include a measure of mild as well as clinically diagnosable depression. In fact, three studies on conjugal loss have included such measures (Bruce, Kim, Leaf, & Jacobs, 1990; Cleiren, 1993; Zisook, Paulus, Shuchter, & Judd, 1997). Each has found that after the death of a spouse, a substantial minority of respondents experience little distress or depression. For example, Zisook et al. (1997) used elderly widowers' and widows' ratings on symptom inventories to classify them into DSM-IV categories of major depression, minor depression, subsyndromal depression (endorsing any two symptoms from the symptom list) and no depression (endorsing one or no items reflecting depression). Two months after the partner's death, 20% were classified as showing major depression, 20% evidenced minor depression, 11% were classified as showing subsyndromal depression, and 49% were classified as evidencing no depression.

Failure to Experience Distress Is Viewed as Problematic

Historically, the failure to exhibit grief or distress following the loss of a spouse has been viewed as an indication that the grieving process has gone awry (e.g., Deutsch, 1937; Marris, 1958). As Marris (1958) has argued, "grieving is a process which 'must work itself out'... if the process is aborted from too hasty a readjustment... the bereaved may never recover" (p. 33). Indeed, most practicing clinicians continue to maintain, either explicitly or implicitly, that there is something wrong with bereaved individuals who do not exhibit grief or depression. In a survey of expert clinicians and researchers in the field of loss (Middleton, Moylan, Raphael, Burnett, & Martinek, 1993), a majority (65%) endorsed the belief that "absent grief" exists, that it typically stems from denial or inhibition, and that it is maladaptive in the long run. It is also believed that if they are not expressed, feelings of grief or depression will emerge at a later point, either in the form of a delayed grief reaction or physical health problems (see, e.g., Bowlby, 1980; Rando, 1993). Consistent with the notion that "absent grief" signals unhealthy denial and repression of feelings, it is believed that bereaved people who have not begun grieving will benefit from clinical intervention designed to help them work through their unresolved feelings (see, e.g., Bowlby, 1980; Deutsch, 1937; Jacobs, 1993; Rando, 1993; Worden, 1991). As Jacobs (1993) has suggested, such individuals "ought to be offered brief psychotherapy by a skilled therapist" (p. 246).

The failure to exhibit distress following the loss of a loved one has also been viewed as evidence for character weakness. Horowitz (1990) has maintained that those who show little overt grief following a loss are "narcissistic personalities" who are "immature" (p. 301; see also Raphael, 1983). It has also been suggested that those who fail to exhibit distress were only superficially attached to their spouses (Fraley & Shaver, 1999; Rando, 1993).

Although these ideas are firmly entrenched among theorists and practitioners working in the field of grief and loss, there is virtually no empirical evidence to support them (Bonanno et al., 2002; Wortman & Silver, 2001). In the previous section of this paper, we reviewed evidence indicating that a large percentage of bereaved individuals exhibit little or no distress in the early months following their spouse's death. The prevalence of this response alone raises questions about the appropriateness of viewing it as pathological. Moreover, if distress is not experienced during the first several months following the loss, it is unlikely to emerge later (see Bonanno et al., 2002, for a review). In most studies that have assessed delayed grief, it has emerged in a very small percentage of cases (typically around 2%). This is the case even in studies that have followed the bereaved for as long as five years (Bonanno & Field, 2001). Nonetheless, a substantial majority (76.6%) of researchers and clinicians endorsed the belief that delayed grief does occur (Middleton et al., 1993).

The Importance of "Working Through" the Loss

Among researchers as well as practitioners, it is commonly assumed that to adjust successfully to the death of a loved one, a person must "work through" what has happened. Although there is some debate about exactly what it means to "work through" a loss (Wortman & Silver, 2001), most grief theorists would agree that people need to reflect on, process, and express the thoughts, feelings, and memories associated with their loss. Attempts to deny the implications of the loss, or block feelings or thoughts about it, are ultimately regarded as unproductive. This view of the grieving process has constituted the dominant perspective on bereavement for the past 50 years. However, evidence fails to support this assumption. "Working through" has been operationalized in many ways, including thinking about the loss, confronting versus avoiding reminders, expression of feelings verbally or through facial expressions, and expression of feelings through writing. Although some studies provide support for the notion that "working through" is important for adjustment to the death of a loved one, most do not. In fact, results of most studies run directly counter to what the "working through" hypothesis would predict (see Bonanno & Kaltman, 1999; 2001, or Wortman & Silver, 2001, for reviews). For example, in a study of gay men who lost a partner to AIDS, Nolen-Hoeksema, McBride, and Larson (1997) found that those who thought about the loss and how they had changed as a result of it, had higher depression scores 12 months later even when initial depression was controlled. Similarly, Bonanno and Keltner (1997) found that those who expressed negative feelings or showed facial expressions reflecting negative emotions (e.g., anger) during an interview 6 months after the death showed higher interviewer-rated grief 14 months following their spouse's death, even when initial levels of grief were controlled (see also Bonanno, Keltner, Holen, & Horowitz, 1995; Bonanno & Field, 2001).

Therapeutic treatments developed for the bereaved focus heavily on helping them work through their feelings (Rando, 1993; Worden, 1991). If working through is indeed beneficial, we would expect treatment studies of bereavement interventions to show positive results. Over the past few years, three reviews of treatment studies have appeared in the literature (Allumbaugh & Hoyt, 1999; Kato & Mann, 1999; Neimeyer, 2000). Each of these reviews reached the same disturbing conclusion: that in most cases, bereavement treatments are ineffective and in a significant minority of cases, they are actually harmful.

The Expectation of Recovery

Once a person has completed the process of working through the loss, it is generally believed that he or she will achieve a state of recovery. Individuals who are recovered can encounter reminders of the loss without pain, and are able to return to normal functioning (Parkes & Weiss, 1983). Those who fail to recover after an "appropriate" amount of time are considered to be displaying *chronic grief* (Jacobs, 1993; Middleton et al., 1993). Grief theorists have rarely discussed how much time is appropriate. However, bereaved people typically comment that within a year or so after the loss, they are expected to be finished with the morning process and be "back to normal" (Wortman & Silver, 1987).

Several studies have suggested that following the loss of a spouse, it often takes longer than one or two years to return to a state of equilibrium (see Wortman & Silver, 2001, for a review). In one study of over 800 people who lost a spouse between 1 and 60 years ago (Wortman & Silver, 2001), it took widowed respondents more than 30 years to reach the level of depression of married respondents, and over 15 years to reach the level of life satisfaction of married respondents. Although painful feelings about the deceased spouse declined over time, it took bereaved respondents nearly 40 years to reach a point at which they experienced such painful feelings "rarely" (see also Lehman, Wortman, & Williams, 1987). These studies suggest that although symptoms often lessen over time, many people who have lost a spouse continue to experience distressing symptoms, painful memories, and impaired quality of life for several years.

ACCOUNTING FOR VARIABILITY IN RESPONSE TO LOSS

The previous review has illustrated that the so-called normal or common pattern of grief, which involves experiencing intense distress that declines over time, is by no means universal. Some people, like the man who was mentioned at the beginning of the chapter (John T.), appear to experience relatively little distress following the death of a spouse or partner, while others, like Megan P., appear to experience prolonged or chronic grief following the loss. In order to enhance our understanding of the grieving process, it is critically important to learn more about these different patterns of grieving. One important issue concerns the prevalence of these different patterns—normal grieving, "absent grief" or resilience, and chronic grief. Do the majority of people show the so-called normal pattern, with a smaller percentage showing little distress or prolonged distress following the loss? With few exceptions (e.g., Levy, Martinkowski, & Derby, 1994), most bereavement studies have examined grief or depression by aggregating data across respondents, making it impossible to determine what percentage of respondents follow different trajectories over time. A second important issue concerns the antecedents of these patterns. Past studies provide little information about antecedents because in most cases respondents are assessed only after the loss has occurred. By using a prospective, longitudinal design in which the bereaved are assessed prior to and following the loss, it becomes possible to examine the validity of many of the hypotheses advanced to account for these patterns. For example, we can determine whether absent grief is indicative of denial or inhibition, lack of attachment, or resilience in the face of loss. Similarly, we can assess whether those exhibiting chronic grief had very close, or very conflictual relationships with the deceased, as well as whether they had pre-existing mental health problems or vulnerabilities.

Another advantage of assessing bereaved people prior to, as well as following the loss of their spouse is that it makes it possible to identify patterns that cannot otherwise be assessed. One such pattern is preloss depression followed by improvement after the loss. This pattern has received little discussion in the bereavement literature. However, life event researchers have noted that when the marital relationship is stressful, the death may provide fortuitous relief and result in an improvement in mental health (Wheaton, 1990). Another pattern that may emerge if people are assessed prior to the loss is chronic depression. Some people who show a chronic grief reaction, scoring high in depression following the loss and remaining depressed, may have been depressed before the loss. These chronically depressed people may differ in important ways from people who were not previously depressed, but who display intense and prolonged depression in reaction to the loss.

To learn more about these patterns of grief and their antecedents, we conducted a study in which we examined patterns of change in depression among a sample of adults prior to and following the death of their spouses (Bonanno, Wortman, et al., 2002). Data for this investigation were obtained as part of the changing lives of older couples (CLOC) study, a prospective study that involved conducting baseline interviews with 1,532 individuals from the Detroit area. All respondents were married, and all were at risk to become bereaved because the husband was age 65 or older. Participants who subsequently lost a spouse were identified through monthly death record tapes provided by the state of Michigan. Bereaved individuals were invited to participate in follow-up interviews at 6 and 18 months after their spouse's death.

At each wave, depression was measured using the Center for Epidemiological Studies depression scale (CES-D; Radloff, 1977). To identify patterns of response and the prevalence of each, we first categorized participants into low and high pre-loss depression. Next, we assessed changes in depression by comparing each participant's CES-D score at pre-loss with his or her scores at the 6-month and 18-month follow-ups. As expected, most of the sample (90.2%) were captured by the five conceptually relevant patterns defined above: normal or common grief (an increase in depression shortly after the death, followed by a decrease in depression over time, (10.7%), "absent grief" or resilient pattern (45.9%), depressed-improved (10.2%), chronic grief (15.6%), and chronic depression (7.8%). For an illustration of each pattern, see Figure 17.1. Only a few participants, less than 5%, showed delayed grief.

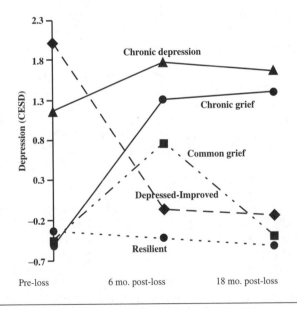

FIG. 17.1. Patterns of grief response.

It is interesting to note that the so-called common grief pattern is actually far less common than the stable low depression or resilient pattern, which categorized nearly half of the sample. Given the prevalence of this pattern, it becomes all the more important to clarify its antecedents. The prebereavement data indicated that those in the resilient group were indeed attached to their spouse, rating their marriage positively. There was no evidence to support the hypothesis that prior to the loss, they were cold and unfeeling, as interviewers rated them highly on interpersonal comfort, skill, and warmth. They also appeared to be well-adjusted prior to the loss. Finally, they held certain world views prior to the loss, such as acceptance of death, that may have made it easier to deal with the loss. In contrast to the resilient respondents, those in the depressed-improved group rated their marriage negatively and expressed ambivalence toward their spouse. They were also likely to have an ill spouse. Hence, the death may have brought an end to the stress they experienced in their marriage. They also showed other indications of being maladjusted and self-absorbed prior to the loss. In the absence of pre-loss data, these qualities may be inadvertently attributed to resilient individuals, because bereaved people who do not show distress are often described as maladjusted and self-absorbed.

In examining the antecedents of chronic grief, we found no evidence to suggest that those with conflictual or problematic marriages, or those who were ambivalent toward their spouse, were most likely to exhibit chronic grief. In fact, chronic grievers had the most positive and the least ambivalent relationships with their spouses of any of the groups. Ratings of the chronic grief respondents contrasted sharply with those of the chronically depressed respondents, who rated their marriages as significantly more negative and more ambivalent than those in the chronic grief condition. Those who were more dependent on their spouse, and who had more dependent personalities, were more likely to manifest chronic grief. However, chronic depression respondents also scored very high on both of these kinds of dependency. Surprisingly, chronic grievers showed no signs of enhanced vulnerability, or poor coping ability, prior to the loss. Hence, very few of the variables hypothesized in the literature as antecedents of chronic grief (conflictual or ambivalent relationship with one's spouse, poor coping efficacy, or a history of mental health problems) reached statistical significance. In contrast, several pre-loss variables assumed in the literature to underlie chronic grief were instead strongly associated with chronic depression. These findings suggest that much of clinical theory regarding the nature of chronic grief may be misinformed by the failure to distinguish between these two groups.

To learn more about these trajectories, we also asked questions designed to determine how these groups react to and process the loss (Bonanno, Wortman, & Nesse, 2003). These results provided strong corroboration for our argument that respondents in the resilient group are in fact showing genuine resilience in the face of loss. They showed relatively little grief. In addition, they scored low on items designed to assess processing the loss, such as thinking or talking about the loss. They also scored low on avoidance/distraction, suggesting that their lack of distress is indicative of good adjustment rather than defensive denial.

This study provides clear evidence that there are many distinct ways that a person may react to the loss of a spouse. Results suggest that some people become depressed following the loss, whereas others were already depressed before the loss. Many people continue to do well after the loss, and this seems indicative of resilience rather than pathology or lack of attachment. And some actually do better after their spouse dies, most likely because the death is associated with relief from a stressful marital situation.

As it has become increasingly clear that peoples' reactions to the death of a spouse are quite variable, researchers have become interested in identifying those who are at greatest risk to develop subsequent problems. One factor that typically emerges as predictive of difficulties during conjugal bereavement is the mode of death. Although the literature is not entirely consistent, deaths that are sudden, untimely, occur in a violent manner, or are brought about by the actions of another person appear to cause the greatest difficulty. Other factors that are typically associated with poor outcome include reduced financial resources; the presence of other stressors such as unemployment or physical health problems; the perceived absence of social support; and gender, with men showing substantially greater morbidity and mortality following the death of their spouse than do women. (see, Sanders, 1993; Stroebe & Schut, 2001, for reviews).

Regarding gender differences, there are several reasons why women might be expected to be more vulnerable to partner loss than men (see Miller & Wortman, 2002, for a more detailed discussion). First, women are more dependent on men for economic resources. The income of women decreases by nearly a third following widowhood, whereas the income of men stays the same. Second, men are more likely to define themselves in terms of their jobs, whereas the identity of women is much more closely tied to their relationships. Third, as we discuss in more detail below, widowed men are far more likely than women to become involved in subsequent romantic relationships and to remarry. It is typical for women who lose a spouse to remain widowed for the rest of their lives. Despite these reasons, however, it is now well-established that men do worse following bereavement. There are several studies showing that men become more depressed following the death and evidence greater mortality than widowed women (Stroebe, Stroebe, & Schut, 2001; Miller & Wortman, 2002).

One explanation for these gender differences is that for several reasons, the marital role may be more beneficial to men. If so, the loss of this role may be more stressful for men than for women. Consistent with this view, there is evidence that women typically have many more close social relationships than men, who rely heavily on their wives for support. Women also perform more housework and childcare than men do. Because men rely on their wives in these domains, they may experience stress when they have to handle these matters on their own (Miller & Wortman, 2002). A second mechanism has been suggested by Umberson (1987, 1992), who has found that women typically take greater responsibility for their spouse's health care, diet, nutrition, and exercise than do men. They are also more likely to place constraints on negative health behaviors, such as drinking and driving. Umberson's (1987, 1992) findings indicate that the poorer health of men following the death of their spouse stems from the loss of this positive influence on their health behavior. A final explanation that has been advanced is that these differences in depression and in mortality may stem from gender differences in coping with the death. It has been suggested, for example, that widowed men may do worse than widowed women because they rely almost exclusively on distraction to deal with the loss, and sometimes distract themselves in ways that are deleterious to their health (e.g., heavy drinking). To date, however, few studies have focused on gender differences in coping with conjugal loss (Stroebe et al., 2001).

We have included this information on gender differences in response to spousal loss because it sets the stage for our subsequent discussion about the formation of new relationships following the spouse's death. As we will see, the tendency to become involved in new relationships is also strongly influenced by gender. The hypotheses regarding why men may have more difficulty in coping with widowhood can help us understand why they pursue new relationships.

SOCIAL SUPPORT FROM FAMILY AND FRIENDS: DOES IT HELP?

Following the loss of an intimate partner, what role, if any, do family members and friends play in the process of recovery and healing? There is abundant evidence that supportive relationships with others can protect people from the deleterious effects of stress (House, Umberson, & Landis, 1988; Schwarzer & Leppin, 1989; Stroebe & Stroebe, 1996). Moreover, several studies have shown a positive relationship between perceived social support and adjustment among the bereaved (see Sanders, 1993, and Stylianos & Vachon, 1993, for reviews). Initially, it was generally assumed that social networks were supportive and that those with social ties should do better, when exposed to stress, than those without them. However, studies began to emerge which suggested that having a social network is not always helpful and that we must pay more attention to the negative aspects of relationships (Ingram, Betz, Mindes, Schmitt, & Smith, 2001; Laireiter, Baumann, Perkonigg, & Himmelbauer, 1997; Rook, 1984; Rook, 1992). The problematic aspects of support have also begun to surface in studies on bereavement. There is evidence to suggest that when left to their own devices, others often make support attempts that are judged to be unhelpful by the recipient (Davidowitz & Myrick, 1984; Lehman, Ellard, & Wortman, 1986).

These findings take on increasing significance in light of evidence that nonsupportive interactions may have important implications for mental health. In fact, there is accumulating evidence to suggest that the negative elements of social interactions are more strongly related to mental health than positive elements (see, e.g., Manne, Taylor, Dougherty, & Kemeny, 1997; Rook, 1992; Morgan, Neal, & Carder, 1997; Schuster, Kessler, & Aseltine, 1990). For this reason, it is important to understand how those in the bereaved person's social environment approach social interactions with the bereaved, what their underlying assumptions and motivations are, and why they so frequently make support attempts that fail.

One reason why outsiders may make inappropriate support attempts is because they lack information about what a person goes through after losing an intimate partner. For example, outsiders may be unaware of all the things that are lost when a person's spouse or partner dies. They may not recognize that in addition to the loss of their partner, the surviving spouse may also be grieving such things as the loss of their identity as a helpmate, their financial security, and their hopes and dreams for the future (Rando, 1993).

A second factor that may influence others' reactions to the bereaved has to do with the kinds of feelings that are elicited by major losses. Interacting with someone whose spouse has died often evokes powerful feelings of helplessness and vulnerability (Wortman, Battle, & Lemkau, 1997). Feelings of helplessness may be evoked because there is little one can do to effect any improvement in the survivor's situation. As Caine (1974) has expressed it, "no one knows what to do with a tumultuous, angry, sobbing woman who is railing at the fates" (p. 30). Consequently, encounters with the bereaved may be awkward and uncomfortable because the support provider is uncertain about what to say or do. The more distressed the survivor, the more helpless others are likely to feel, and the more social support is likely to be eroded (Bolger, Foster, Vinokur, & Ng, 1996).

Several theories in social psychology have relevance for understanding how feelings of vulnerability can affect reactions to survivors of a major loss. These theories suggest that peoples' feelings about others who are less fortunate are determined in large part by their own needs for security (e.g., Lerner's just world theory; see Wortman, Carnelley, Lehman, Davis, & Juola Exline, 1995). Feelings of vulnerability can lead others to avoid, derogate, and blame the bereaved for their fate. By so doing, people can maintain the belief that they don't deserve to suffer and that nothing bad will happen to them. Indeed, widows often report that married friends are uncomfortable in their presence, perhaps because they serve as a reminder that death and widowhood are a real possibility (Morgan, Carder, & Neal, 1997).

We believe that people's misconceptions about the process of coming to terms with the death of a spouse, and their feelings of vulnerability and helplessness, can lead them to respond to the bereaved in ways that are unintentionally damaging. There is evidence to suggest that people engage in three types of behaviors that are often detrimental: (a) they discourage open expression or discussion of feelings about the loss; (b) they encourage recovery; and (c) they fall back on automatic or scripted support attempts which may seem to dismiss or trivialize the survivor's problems (Ingram, Jones, & Smith, 2001; Ingram, Betz, et al., 2001; Marwit & Carusa, 1998; Wortman & Lehman, 1985; Lehman, Ellard, & Wortman, 1986).

Bereaved individuals commonly report that when they attempt to discuss or display feelings about what has happened, they are blocked from doing so and experience this as upsetting (Lehman et al., 1986; Ingram, Betz, et al., 2001). For example, one person who had lost her husband in an accident said, "I needed to talk about the accident, but when I started talking to my closest friend about it for the second time, she became visibly annoyed. 'You told me that already,' she said." (Wortman et al., 1995; p. 92). Attempts to prevent or discourage open communication about negative feelings may take many specific forms, such as minimizing the loss (e.g., "You had many good years together"), or encouraging the bereaved person to look on the bright side (e.g., "You have so much going for you and so much to live for"). There is evidence to suggest that if people want to talk about the loss and perceive their social milieu as blocking them from doing so, they become increasingly depressed over time (Lepore, Silver, Wortman, & Wayment, 1996).

Others also attempt to encourage recovery from the loss, and the bereaved do not find this to be helpful (Ingram, Betz, et al., 2001; Lehman et al., 1986). They often try to arouse the surviving spouse's interest in new activities or in the resumption of old hobbies or interests. One way others may encourage recovery is to bring up the topic of remarriage. There is evidence that discussions of this topic are often initiated within a few days or weeks of the spouse's death (Wortman & Lehman, 1985). Glick, Wess, and Parkes (1974) reported that "widows invariably found early suggestions that they consider remarriage unpleasant and even jarring" (p. 22).

As a result of the anxiety and uncertainty inherent in interactions with the bereaved, people may have difficulty focusing on the bereaved person's needs. Instead, support providers may respond to the pressure inherent in the situation by relying on scripted or automatic support behaviors. In the United States and Western Europe, these behaviors are part of our cultural understanding of how to help others; therefore, they can be invoked automatically and with little thought. Such behaviors may include giving advice (e.g., "You should consider getting a dog; they're wonderful companions"), providing a philosophical or religious perspective on what happened (e.g., "It was his time to go"; "It was God's will"), offering platitudes (e.g., "Time heals all wounds"; "It's time you moved on"), or attempting to identify with the survivor's feelings (e.g., "I know how you feel—I lost my great uncle"). As one widower expressed it, "On the same day that my wife died, I had to listen to her cousin go on and on about how her dog had recently died after a long illness." Each of these types of support is typically regarded as unhelpful by the bereaved (Ingram et al., 2001; Ingram, Betz, et al., 2001; Lehman et al., 1986; Marwit & Carusa, 1998). Another thing people may do to fill awkward moments is to ask inappropriate questions. If their loved one died in an accident, the bereaved person may be asked whether there was a lot of blood, or whether the deceased was wearing a seat belt. People may also ask questions about such matters as money (e.g., "How are you going to spend all that insurance money?"), or about the loved one's possessions (e.g., "What are you going to do with his tools?").

Studies have shown that unsupportive social interactions account for a significant amount of the variance in depression among the bereaved, beyond the variance explained by the level of present grief (Ingram et al., 2001). Despite having a negative impact on the bereaved, however, support providers may rarely receive feedback on the adequacy of their support attempts. When a bereaved person finds another's comment to be annoying, he or she may be reluctant to point this out. Consequently, providers may frequently conclude that their support attempt was appreciated.

One might expect unhelpful remarks to be more prevalent among strangers or casual acquaintances than among the survivors' relatives or close friends. However, this does not appear to be the case. In one study, slightly more than half of all unhelpful comments were made by relatives or friends (Lehman et al., 1986). In another study, family members were consistently rated by the bereaved as less helpful than friends (Marwit & Carusa, 1998). Because those closest to the survivor may have the greatest stake in his or her recovery, it is perhaps not surprising that they have little tolerance for displays of distress. Unlike casual acquaintances, family members and close friends may also invest considerable energy in attempting to alleviate the bereaved person's distress and may be frustrated if the person shows little improvement (Lehman et al., 1986; Morgan et al., 1997). In addition, bereavement is usually a crisis of the entire social network. The surviving spouse's children and other close relatives may have difficulty providing support because they are grieving themselves (Marwit & Carusa, 1998; Stylianos & Vachon, 1993).

What do survivors find to be beneficial? Evidence indicates that they value the opportunity to talk with others about their feelings when they choose to do so (Lehman et al., 1986; Marwit & Carusa, 1998). They also find it helpful when others express concern (e.g., "I care what happens to you" or reaffirm a supportive presence (e.g., "I am here for you.") (Laireiter et al., 1997; Marwit & Carusa, 1998). Contact with a similar other is also regarded as very helpful (Lehman et al., 1986). Others who have experienced the death of a spouse may be in a unique position to offer effective support. Unlike outsiders, they typically have a more accurate understanding of what the bereaved person is going through. Similar others may also feel more comfortable with a bereaved person than those who have not lost a loved one, and may therefore be less prone to making automatic or scripted comments. Moreover, contact with similar others can reassure the bereaved that their own feelings and behaviors are normal.

Considered together, the available evidence suggests that support from family members and friends is unlikely to fill the void left by a partner's death (Stroebe, Stroebe, Abakoumkin, & Schut, 1996), and in many cases may not promote healing and recovery. Interestingly, there is evidence that people know what behaviors are regarded as supportive by the bereaved, but are unable to implement these behaviors in encounters with the bereaved, perhaps because of the anxiety inherent in such interactions (Lehman et al., 1986; Marwit & Carusa, 1998). Hence, instead of teaching people specific support strategies that have been found to be helpful, it may be more worthwhile to teach them to control and manage the negative feelings that are evoked in encounters with the bereaved.

THE REESTABLISHMENT OF INTIMACY FOLLOWING PARTNER LOSS

Following partner loss, how common is it for people to become involved in new intimate relationships? Should the formation of new attachments be viewed as adaptive or maladaptive? Should John T.'s interest in dating be regarded as an indication of recovery and healing, or a sign that he is running away from his pain? Under what conditions are such relationships most likely to occur? As it turns out, one of the most important factors in determining whether a bereaved person will become involved in a new relationship is gender. Several studies have shown that men are far more likely than women to seek out subsequent relationships. For example, in a study involving a middle aged sample of bereaved people, Hustins (2001) found that 54% of the men, but only 7% of the women had developed some form of sexual relationship by the end of the first year of bereavement. Similarly, in a study of widows and widowers over the age of 65, Davidson (2001) found that 31% of the widowers developed a new relationship within two years, whereas only 4% of widows did so. Schneider, Sledge, Shuchter, and Zisook (1996) have reported that in a sample of bereaved individuals with a mean age of 61, 61% of the men became involved in new romantic relationships and 25% remarried by 25 months after the loss, whereas only 19% of the women became involved in new relationships and 5% remarried during the same time period. The women who remarried took twice as long to do so as the men did.

What is the best way to understand these gender differences? One factor that must be taken into account is the greater opportunity that men have to pursue new relationships. According to Schneider et al. (1996), the ratio of widows to widowers is at least 5 to 1, and this ratio becomes increasingly skewed with age (the ratio in people over 85 is 15 to 1). Moreover, men typically become involved with women younger than themselves, providing them an even bigger pool of women to choose from.

Another reason why men may be more likely to pursue new relationships following widowhood is because they are more devastated by the loss. Earlier, we summarized evidence indicating that men suffer more following the death of their spouse than women do. Some investigators have suggested that men may seek a new relationship in order to "replace" household services previously provided by the wife (cf. Davidson, 2001). However, recent evidence has suggested that the major reason why men form new relationships is to reestablish emotional closeness. Carr (2002) has found that men who were most emotionally reliant on their wives reported the greatest desire to date and remarry. In contrast, the more emotionally reliant women were on their husbands, the less interested they were in pursuing subsequent relationships. Whereas widowed men showed lower self-esteem than married controls, women showed higher self-esteem following their partner's death than married controls. For women, these results were most pronounced among those who were involved in an emotionally dependent marriage, suggesting that such marriages rob women of their self-esteem. For many women, the end of the marriage provides an opportunity for them to regain their self-esteem.

Why do women show little interest in forming new relationships following conjugal loss? In studies in which widows were asked to provide reasons why they had not become involved with someone new, they almost never mention the shortage of available men. Instead, they frequently commented that they had come to value the independence associated with widowhood. In a qualitative study of elderly widowed people, Davidson (2001) found that 92% of the widows, but none of the widowers, mentioned that they had not remarried because they did not want to look after another person. Fifty-six percent of the widows mentioned that they were enjoying their freedom; none of the widowers mentioned this factor. Interestingly, widows regarded their newfound freedom with some guilt, and described it as "selfish." Many women expressed interest in going out socially, but felt that there would be too many "strings attached" if they became involved in a new relationship. As one widow expressed it, "First it's the 'home cooked meal,' then it's the shirt that needs ironing. No . . . Not any more. . . I've done my bit." (Davidson, 2001, p. 311). The theme that women had "paid their dues" in their first marriage was expressed frequently. As one woman indicated, "you know, if you get 'life' [in prison] you only do 25 years. I did 50!" (Davidson, 2001, p. 311).

An important component of not wanting to "take on another man" was women's awareness that because of prevailing norms, they would most likely end up with a man older than they were. They found this unappealing for two reasons. First, they recognized that older men are more likely to require caregiving. Second, they had reservations about becoming sexually involved with an older man. One woman said,

"I'm 70. Who wants to marry a man about 75? Oh, I couldn't go to bed with an old man like that. I couldn't bear the thought of it." (Davidson, 2001, p. 312).

Despite these gender differences, available evidence suggests that involvement in a new relationship is adaptive and healthy. In one study, both men and women who were involved in a new romance 25 months after their spouse's death were significantly less depressed, and were more likely to rate their adjustment to widowhood as good or excellent (Schneider et al., 1996).

CONCLUSIONS AND IMPLICATIONS

In this chapter, we examine prevailing norms about how those in Western cultures react to the loss of a spouse or partner. We attempt to account for the striking variability in responses that has been found to occur. We have explored difficulties that survivors may encounter in obtaining support from family members and friends. And we have attempted to explain why some people seek to establish new relationships following partner loss whereas others do not. Because most studies have been conducted on heterosexual couples in this culture, it is not clear whether the conclusions we have drawn will generalize to other kinds of close relationships (gay, lesbian, friendship) or to other cultural contexts.

The findings reviewed in this chapter suggest that it is important to remain open minded about what is the "normal" or appropriate way to react to the death of a partner. Reactions like that shown by John T, who evidenced little distress following his partner's death, are actually surprisingly common. Moreover, such reactions are likely to signify resilience in the face of loss, not callousness or narcissism. There are also many ways of understanding a reaction like that of Mary P., who may have suffered the traumatic loss of a great love, and may be dealing with other stressors, such as chronic health problems as well. Continuing distress does not necessarily mean that she is a weak person who is "wallowing in her grief."

Following the loss of a spouse, there is every indication that people may have problems obtaining adequate support from others. We have attempted to explain how their own needs and concerns often lead potential support providers to respond to the bereaved in ways that are unhelpful. In future research, it will be important to determine how positive exchanges between the bereaved and their family and friends can be facilitated. One possibility is to provide information to support providers about why interactions with the bereaved can be threatening and upsetting, and how these negative feelings can result in support attempts that fail.

We believe that the bereaved face a dilemma in obtaining adequate support. There is evidence that following the loss of a spouse, people desire and benefit from opportunities to talk openly about their feelings and concerns. However, if the bereaved maximize their chances for personal adjustment by conveying their distress, they may risk driving their social network away. Given the interpersonal costs of expressing one's distress, are there alternative means of expression that might be beneficial, such as artistic expression or keeping a diary? Are some negative emotions, such as bitterness or rage, more difficult to tolerate than others, such as sorrow? Are support providers more capable of tolerating another's distress if it is conveyed in a controlled manner? Is the equation affected by gender, with others' having more difficulty with males' displays of distress than females'?

There is evidence to indicate that if the bereaved are able to genuinely laugh while talking about their loved one, they evoke more favorable responses from untrained observers who watch them on videotape (Keltner & Bonanno, 1997). Conversely, those who convey that they are coping poorly with a life crisis elicit powerful negative feelings from others (Silver, Wortman, & Crofton, 1990). The implications of these findings are distressing, as they suggest that those in greatest need of social support may be least likely to get it. Should the bereaved be cautioned about the potentially negative impact of displays of distress on potential supports?

Available research suggests that how much people suffer following the loss of their spouse, as well as how soon they become involved in other relationships and remarry, is strongly influenced by gender. Although the reasons for these gender differences are still being debated, it appears that men's greater dependence on their wives for emotional support, for assistance in maintaining their health, and for help with household tasks all play a role. As marital relationships continue to change, with men and women becoming more equal partners, it will be interesting to see whether gender differences in reaction to partner loss will continue to occur.

REFERENCES

Allumbaugh, D. L., & Hoyt, W. J. (1999). Effectiveness of grief therapy: A meta-analysis. *Journal of Counseling Psychology, 46*, 370–380.

Bolger, N., Foster, M., Vinokur, A. D., & Ng, R. (1996). Close relationships and adjustment to a life crisis: The case of breast cancer. *Journal of Personality and Social Psychology, 70*, 283–294.

Bonanno, G. A., & Field, N. P. (2001). Evaluating the delayed grief hypothesis across 5 years of bereavement. *American Behavioral Scientist, 44*, 798–816.

Bonanno, G. A., & Kaltman, S. (1999). Toward an integrative perspective on bereavement. *Psychological Bulletin, 125*, 760–786.

Bonanno, G. A., & Kaltman, S. (2001). The varieties of grief experience. *Clinical Psychology Review, 21*, 705–734.

Bonanno, G. A., & Keltner, D. (1997). Facial expressions of emotion and the course of conjugal bereavement. *Journal of Abnormal Psychology, 106*, 126–137.

Bonanno, G. A., Keltner, D., Holen, A., & Horowitz, M. J. (1995). When avoiding unpleasant emotion might not be such a bad thing: Verbal-autonomic response dissociation and midlife conjugal bereavement. *Journal of Personality and Social Psychology, 46*, 975–985.

Bonanno, G. A., Wortman, C. B., Lehman, D., Tweed, R., Sonnega, J., Carr, D., & Nesse, R. (2002). Resilience to loss, chronic grief, and their pre-bereavement predictors. *Journal of Personality and Social Psychology, 83*, 1150–1164.

Bonanno, G. A., Wortman, C. B., & Nesse, R. M. (2003). Prospective patterns of resilience and maladjustment during widowhood. Manuscript under review.

Bowlby, J. (1980). *Loss: Sadness and depression. Attachment and loss; Vol 3*. New York: Basic Books.

Bruce, M. L., Kim, K, Leaf, P. J., & Jacobs, S. (1990). Depressive episodes and dysphoria resulting from conjugal bereavement in a prospective community sample. *American Journal of Psychiatry, 147*, 608–611.

Caine, L. (1974). *Widow*. New York: Basic Books.

Carr, D. (2002, November 23). *Life after death: Gender differences in resilience among the elderly widowed*. Paper presented at the 55th Annual Scientific Meeting, Gerontological Society of America, Boston, MA.

Cleiren, M. P. H. D. (1993). *Bereavement and adaptation: A comparative study of the aftermath of death*. Philadelphia, PA: Hemisphere.

Davidowitz, M., & Myrick, R. D. (1984). Responding to the bereaved: An analysis of "helping" statements. *Death Education, 8*, 1–10.

Davidson, K. (2001). Late life widowhood, selfishness and new partnership choices: A gendered perspective. *Aging and Society 21*, 297–317.

Deutsch, H. (1937). Absence of grief. *Psychoanalytic Quarterly, 6*, 12–22.

Fraley, R. C., & Shaver, P. R. (1999). Loss and bereavement: Bowlby's theory and recent controversies concerning "grief work" and the nature of detachment. In J. Cassidy & P. R. Shaver (Eds.), *Handbook of attachment theory and research: Theory, research, and clinical applications* (pp. 735–759). New York: Guilford.

Freud, S. (1957). Mourning and melancholia. In J. Strachey (Ed.), *The standard edition of the complete works of Sigmund Freud* (Vol. 14, pp. 152–170). London: Hogarth Press. (Original work published 1917)

Glick, I. O., Wess, R. S., & Parkes, C. M. (1974). *The first year of bereavement*. New York: Wiley.

Horowitz, M. J. (1990). A model of mourning: Change in schemas of self and other. *Journal of American Psychoanalytic Association, 38*, 297–324.

House, J. S., Umberson, D., & Landis, K. R. (1988). Structures and processes of social support. *Review of Sociology, 14*, 293–318.

Hustins, K. (2001). Gender differences related to sexuality in widowhood: Is it a problem for the male bereaved? In D. A. Lund (Ed.) *Men coping with grief: Death, value, and meaning series* (pp. 207–213). Amityville, NY: Baywood Publication Company.

Ingram, K. M., Betz, N. E., Mindes, E. J., Schmitt, M. M., & Smith, N. G. (2001). Unsupportive responses from others concerning a stressful life event: Development of the unsupportive social interactions inventory. *Journal of Social and Clinical Psychology, 20,* 173–207.

Ingram, K. M., Jones, D. A., & Smith, N. G. (2001). Adjustment among people who have experienced AIDS-related multiple loss: The role of unsupportive social interactions, social support and coping. *Omega: Journal of Death & Dying, 43,* 287–309.

Jacobs, S. (1993). *Pathological grief: Maladaptation to loss.* Washington, DC: American Psychiatric Press, Inc.

Kato, P. M., & Mann, J. (1999). A synthesis psychological intervention for the bereaved. *Clinical Psychology Review, 19,* 275–296.

Keltner, D., & Bonanno, G. A. (1997). A study of laughter and dissociation: Distinct correlates of laughter and smiling during bereavement. *Journal of Personality and Social Psychology, 73,* 687–702.

Laireiter, A.-R., Baumann, U., Perkonigg, A., & Himmelbauer, S. (1997). Social support resources in inter-personal relationships (social networks) during stressful life conditions: Results from two pilot studies. *European Review of Applied Psychology, 47,* 123–129.

Lehman, D. R., Ellard, J. H., & Wortman, C. B. (1986). Social support for the bereaved: Recipients' and provider's perspectives on what is helpful. *Journal of Consulting and Clinical Psychology, 54,* 438–446.

Lehman, D. R., Wortman, C. B., & Williams, A. F. (1987). Long-term effects of losing a spouse or child in a motor vehicle crash. *Journal of Personality and Social Psychology, 52,* 218–231.

Lepore, S. J., Silver, R. C., Wortman, C. B., & Wayment, H. A. (1996). Social constraints, intrusive thoughts, and depressive symptoms among bereaved mothers. *Journal of Personality and Social Psychology, 70,* 271–282.

Levy, L. H., Martinkowski, K. S., & Derby, J. F. (1994). Differences in patterns of adaptation in conjugal bereavement: Their sources and potential significance. *Omega: Journal of Death & Dying, 29,* 71–87.

Manne, S. L., Taylor, K. L., Dougherty, J., & Kemeny, N. (1997). Supportive and negative responses in the partner relationship: Their association with psychological adjustment among individuals with cancer. *Journal of Behavioral Medicine, 20,* 101–125.

Marris, P. (1958). *Widows and their families.* London: Routledge and Kegan Paul.

Marwit, S. J., & Carusa, S. S. (1998). Communicated support following loss: Examining the experiences of parental death and parental divorce in adolescence. *Death Studies, 22,* 237–255.

Middleton, W., Moylan, A., Raphael, B., Burnett, P., & Martinek, N. (1993). An international perspective on bereavement related concepts. *Australian & New Zealand Journal of Psychiatry, 27,* 457–463.

Miller, E., & Wortman, C. B. (2002). Gender differences in mortality and morbidity following a major stressor: The case of conjugal bereavement. In G. Weidner, S. M. Kopp, & M. Kristenson (Eds.), *Heart Disease: Environment, Stress and Gender* (NATO Science Series, Series I: Life and Behavioural Sciences, Vol. 327). Amsterdam: IOS Press.

Morgan, D., Carder, P., & Neal, M. (1997). Are some relationships more useful than others? The value of similar others in the networks of recent widows. *Journal of Social and Personal Relationships, 14,* 745–759.

Morgan, D. L., Neal, M., & Carder, P. C. (1997). Both what and when: The effects of positive and negative aspects of relationships on depression during the first 3 years of widowhood. *Journal of Clinical Geropsychology, 3,* 73–91.

Neimeyer, R. A. (2000). Searching for the meaning of meaning: Grief therapy and the process of reconstruction. *Death Studies, 24,* 541–558.

Nolen-Hoeksema, S., McBride, A, & Larson, J. (1997). Rumination and psychological distress among be-reaved partners. *Journal of Personality and Social Psychology, 72,* 855–862.

Parkes, C. M., & Weiss, R. S. (1983). *Recovery from bereavement.* New York: Basic Books.

Radloff, L. S. (1977). The CES-D Scale: A self-report depression scale for research in the general population. *Applied Psychological Measurement, 1,* 385–401.

Rando, T. A. (1993). *Treatment of complicated mourning.* Champaign, IL: Research Press.

Raphael, B. (1983). *The anatomy of bereavement.* New York: Basic Books.

Rook, K. S. (1984). The negative side of social interaction: Impact on psychological well-being. *Journal of Personality and Social Psychology, 45,* 1097–1108.

Rook, K. S. (1992). The detrimental aspects of social relationships: Taking stock of an emerging literature. In H. O. F. Veiel & U. Baumann (Eds.), *The meaning and measurement of social support* (pp. 157–170). New York: Hemisphere.

Sanders, C. M. (1993). Risk factors in bereavement outcome. In M. Stroebe, W. Stroebe, & R. O. Hansson (Eds.), *Handbook of bereavement: Theory, research and intervention* (pp. 255–267). New York: Cambridge University Press.

Sanders, C. M. (1999). *Grief: The mourning after* (2nd ed.). New York: Wiley.

Schneider, D. S., Sledge, P. A., Shuchter, S. R., & Zisook, S. (1996). Dating and remarriage over the first two years of widowhood. *Annals of Clinical Psychiatry, 8,* 51–57.

Shuchter, S. R. (1986). *Dimensions of grief: Adjusting to the death of a spouse.* San Francisco/London: Jossey-Bass.

Schuster, T., Kessler, R. C., & Aseltine, R. H. (1990). Supportive interactions, negative interactions, and depressed mood. *American Journal of Community Psychology, 18,* 423–438.

Schwarzer, R., & Leppin, A. (1989). Social support and health: A meta-analysis. *Psychology & Health, 3,* 1–15.

Silver, R. C., Wortman, C. B., & Crofton, C. (1990). The role of coping in support provision: The self-presentational dilemma of victims of life crises. In B. R. Sarason, I. G. Sarason, & G. R. Pierce (Eds.), *Social support: An interactional view* (pp. 397–426). New York: Wiley.

Stroebe, M. S., & Schut, H. (2001). Models of coping with bereavement: A review. In M. S. Stroebe, R. O. Hansson, & W. Stroebe, *Handbook of bereavement research: Consequences, coping, and care* (pp. 375–403). Washington, DC: American Psychological Association.

Stroebe, W., & Stroebe, M. (1996). The social psychology of social support. In E. T. Higgins, & A. W. Kruglanski (Eds.), *Social psychology: Handbook of basic principles* (pp. 597–621). New York: Guilford Press.

Stroebe, W., Stroebe, M., Abakoumkin, G., & Schut, H. (1996). The role of loneliness and social support in adjustment to loss: A test of attachment versus stress theory. *Journal of Personality and Social Psychology, 70*, 1241–1249.

Stroebe, M., Stroebe, W., & Schut, H. (2001). Gender differences in adjustment to bereavment: An empirical and theoretical review. *Review of General Psychology, 5*, 62–83.

Stylianos, S. K., & Vachon, M. L. (1993). The role of social support in bereavement. In M. S. Stroebe, R. O. Hansson, & W. Stroebe (Eds.), *Handbook of bereavement:Theory, research, and intervention* (pp. 397–410). New York: Cambridge University Press.

Umberson, D. (1987). Family status and health behaviors: Social control as a dimension of social integration. *Journal of Health & Social Behavior, 28*, 306–319.

Umberson, D. (1992). Gender, marital status, and the social control of health behavior. *Social Science & Medicine, 34*, 907–917.

Wheaton, B. (1990). Life transitions, role histories, and mental health. *American Sociological Review, 55*, 209–223.

Worden, J. W. (1991). *Grief counseling and grief therapy: A handbook for the mental health practitioner* (2nd ed.). New York: Springer.

Wortman, C. B., Battle, E. S., & Lemkau, J. P. (1997). Coming to terms with sudden, traumatic death of a spouse or child. In R. C. Davis & A. J. Lurigio (Eds.), *Victims of crime* (pp. 108–133). Thousand Oaks, CA.: Sage.

Wortman, C. B., Carnelley, K. B., Lehman, D. R., Davis, C. G., & Juola Exline, J. (1995). Coping with the loss of a family member: Implications for community-level research and intervention. In S. E. Hobfoll & M. W. deVries (Eds.), *Extreme stress and communities: Impact and intervention*. Dordrecht, the Netherlands: Kluwer.

Wortman, C. B., & Lehman, D. R. (1985). Reactions to victims of life crises: Support attempts that fail. In I. G. Sarason & B. R. Sarason (Eds.), *Social support: Theory, research, and applications*. Dordrecht, The Netherlands: Martinus Nijoff.

Wortman, C. B., & Silver, R. C. (1987). Coping with irrevocable loss. In G. R. VandenBos & B. K. Bryant (Eds.), *Cataclysms, crises, and catastrophes: Psychology in action (Master lecture series), 6*, 189–235. Washington, DC: American Psychological Association.

Wortman, C. B., & Silver, R. C. (1989). The myths of coping with loss. *Journal of Consulting and Clinical Psychology, 57*, 349–357.

Wortman, C. B., & Silver, R. C. (2001). The myths of coping with loss revisited. In M. S. Stroebe, R. O. Hansson, W. Stroebe, & H. Schut (Eds.), *Handbook of bereavement research: Consequences, coping, and care*. Washington, DC: American Psychological Association.

Zisook, S., Paulus, M., Shuchter, S. R., & Judd, L. L. (1997). The many faces of depression following spousal bereavement. *Journal of Affective Disorders, 45*, 85–94.

18

The Cultural Grounding of Closeness and Intimacy

Glenn Adams and Stephanie L. Anderson
University of Kansas

Joseph K. Adonu
Brunel University

THE CULTURAL GROUNDING OF CLOSENESS AND INTIMACY

The purpose of this chapter is to consider closeness and intimacy from a cultural perspective. Although popular understandings equate a cultural perspective with exploration of diversity, the goal of the chapter is not to describe how closeness and intimacy vary across cultures.[1] Instead, the goal is to illuminate a more general process that is typically invisible in mainstream accounts: the extent to which observed patterns of closeness and intimacy are not "just natural", but are instead grounded in particular cultural worlds.

The cultural grounding of closeness and intimacy is typically invisible in mainstream accounts because of the common practice of conducting research in a small set of possible worlds. To help illuminate this process, we describe examples from research in diverse West African worlds—settings in which everyday realities differ from those that prevail in both psychological science and the North American worlds that tend to inform social-psychological imagination.[2] The purpose of these examples is not to provide a descriptive account of love (or closeness and intimacy), West African style. Instead, these examples help to illuminate how the experience of closeness and intimacy in North American worlds—and the study of these phenomena in psychological science—reflect particular constructions of self and social reality.

---

[1] For a review of personal relationship from a cross-cultural perspective, see Goodwin (1999).

[2] We acknowledge in advance an emphasis on North American settings at the apparent expense of research in Europe and other settings. Mostly this emphasis reflects the location of our research. However, this emphasis also reflects the extent to which—with a few important exceptions (e.g., Moscovici, 1984)— the shape of modern social psychology, even as it flourishes in Europe and other settings, may have its historical and conceptual roots mainly in North American realities. For an elaboration of this statement, see Farr (1996).

Culture: What Is It?

Corresponding to the sense that a cultural perspective means exploration of diversity across groups, social psychologists are likely to define culture in ways that imply group membership. Sometimes the association of culture with group is explicit, as when writers define culture as "customary beliefs, social forms, and material traits of a racial, religious, or social group" (p. 352) (Lau, Chiu, & Lee, 2001). More often, the association of culture with group membership is implicit, as when writers refer to *members of culture X* or use *culture* synonymously with *society*, *nation*, or *ethnicity*.

Rather than membership in monolithic groups, we instead define culture as explicit and implicit patterns of historically derived and selected ideas and their embodiment in institutions, practices, and artifacts (based on Kroeber & Kluckhohn, 1952, p. 357). This definition deemphasizes "groupness" and instead locates culture in more diffuse models or social representations (see Morris, Menon, & Ames, 2001; Moscovici, 1984). The important implication is that we do not use *North American* and *West African* to refer to monolithic entities, but instead to refer to the multiple, diffuse patterns that form the common ground for experience in diverse North American and West African worlds.[3]

Implicit Constructions of Self and Social Reality

The patterns that are the focus of this chapter are implicit constructions of self and social reality (or *constructions of self* for easier reference). Theory and research in a variety of disciplines have emphasized the extent to which psychological experience in contemporary North American worlds is rooted in individualist, atomistic, or independent constructions of self (Baumeister, 1987; Bellah, Madsen, Sullivan, Swindler, & Tipton, 1985; Dumont, 1970; Fiske, Kitayama, Markus, & Nisbett, 1998; Markus, Kitayama, & Heiman, 1996). As illustrated at the top of Figure 18.1, these constructions locate self and identity in the internal properties of inherently separate particles. They frame connection as a secondary product, not necessarily in the sense of less valued, but in the sense of derived or manufactured. Rather than a default fact of existence, these constructions regard connection as a voluntary, often tenuous arrangement of more basic, unconnected selves.

In contrast, Africanist writers have used phrases like *relational self* (Piot, 1999) or *relational individualism* (Shaw, 2000) to describe the constructions of self that are prominent in social discourse and material reality of diverse West African worlds. These labels are meant to contrast first with the constructions of self that prevail in North American settings and in mainstream social science.[4] Rather than internal properties of bounded entities, these constructions locate self-experience in preexisting fields

---

[3] The key features to note about cultural patterns are that (a) they can be both explicit and implicit; (b) they include both mental and material components; and (c) these components represent the conceptual and material legacy of previous human activity. Although cultural patterns can be explicitly recognized in traditions and ideology, they more often exist as the implicit common ground that underlies experience in various communities. This perspective clarifies that the nature of cultural engagement is not *membership* in groups (e.g., "Protestants"), but *engagement* with cultural patterns (e.g., Protestantism) that need not be associated with clearly defined groups. An important advantage of this conception is to accommodate the fact of multiplicity. People are not "monocultural", but instead engage overlapping sets of cultural patterns in their everyday existence (e.g., a Catholic woman who encounters the cultural legacy of Protestantism in the policies of her corporate workplace). For a discussion of this and other conceptions of culture, see Adams and Markus (2001).

[4] This characterization is not equally applicable to all social science perspectives. For example, the symbolic interactionist perspective explicitly recognizes the relational grounding of self (Stryker, 1997). However, these perspectives are relatively marginalized in contemporary psychology.

Independent Constructions of Self and Social Reality

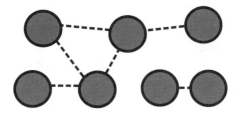

Interdependent Constructions of Self and Social Reality

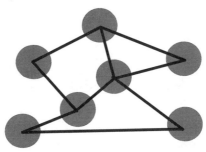

FIG. 18.1. Implicit constructions of self and social reality. The top half of the diagram represents independent constructions of self and social reality. These constructions locate psychological experience in internal properties of inherently separate individuals (represented by solid circles). They promote an experience of relational connection (represented by dashed lines) as the relatively tenuous, secondary product of ontologically prior selves. Rather than a barrier to closeness and intimacy, independent constructions of self may both (a) foster the prominence of closeness and intimacy in many North American settings and (b) shape the study of these phenomena in mainstream social science.

The bottom half of the diagram represents interdependent constructions of self and social reality. These constructions locate psychological experience in fields of relational connection (represented by solid lines) that are ontologically prior to individual experience (represented by shaded circles). Relationship is not a tenuous creation, but instead is an inescapable fact of human existence. Rather than facilitate the experience of closeness and intimacy, the interdependent constructions of self that are prominent in many West African settings promote cautious ambivalence regarding closeness and intimacy.

of relational force (Gyekye, 1992; Jackson, 1982; see the bottom half of Figure 18.1). Rather than a derivative product, these constructions frame relationship as a default fact of social existence. They promote an experience of inescapable connection, not only to other people (living and dead), but also to place, spiritual forces, and a sense of built-in order (Ferme, 2001; Fiske, 1991; Kirby, 1986; Riesman, 1986; Tengan, 1991).

In addition, these labels are meant to contrast with notions like collectivist or communal self. Africanist writers object to such labels to the extent that they imply mindless assimilation to an anonymous collective or diffusion of individuated, personal identity into deindividuated, group identity (Appiah, 1992; Mudimbe, 1988). Rather than a loss of individual self, Africanist writers emphasize that the individual self of Western intellectual traditions takes a more relational form in many West African worlds (Piot, 1999; Shaw, 2000).

Translating into a common framework in the field of social psychology, one might use the label *interdependent* to refer to the constructions of self that are prominent in West African settings and *independent* to refer to the constructions of self that are prominent in contemporary North American settings (Dion, K. L., & Dion, K. K., 1988; Cross & Gore, chap. 13, this volume; Markus & Kitayama, 1991). Given popular understandings of these labels (e.g., Li, 2002), one might then predict that closeness and intimacy would carry greater psychological weight in West African worlds (where interdependent constructions are prominent) than in North American worlds (where independent constructions are prominent). Instead, research suggests an opposite pattern. Closeness and intimacy tend to carry greater psychological weight in North American worlds but are regarded with cautious ambivalence in social discourse of many West African worlds (Adams, G., 2000; Adams, G., & Plaut, 2003; Shaw, 2000).

How is one to resolve this apparent paradox? As we explain in the following sections, the key is to understand independence and interdependence as implicit constructions of self and social reality. This key represents an elaboration of the independence-interdependence framework in two ways.

The first elaboration is an explicit shift in emphasis away from value dimensions to ontological beliefs. From this perspective, interdependence is not a synonym for collectivist values or a desire for interpersonal connection; instead, it refers to an ontological experience of self in terms of inherent connection. The essence of interdependence is not that relational connection is valued but that it is constructed and experienced as an inescapable fact. Likewise, independence is not a synonym for individualist values or the desire for personal autonomy; instead, it refers to an ontological experience of a bounded self that is inherently unconnected. The essence of independence is not that relational connection is devalued, but that it is constructed and experienced as the secondary creation of inherently separate selves.

The second elaboration is a shift in emphasis from construal to construction. Although *construal* highlights ontological aspects of cultural representations, it also has a connotation of mere belief. In contrast, *construction* refers not only to beliefs about self, but also to realities of self—psychological experience built into the structure of everyday worlds (see Arriaga, Goodfriend, & Lohmann, chap. 17, this volume; Brown, Werner, & Altman, 1994). The independent constructions of self that are prominent in many North American worlds are not just ideas about separation. Instead, these ideas are linked to realities of separation like residence in self-contained apartment units, eating from individual place settings, and the practice of "leaving home" in young adulthood. Likewise, the interdependent constructions of self that are prominent in many West African worlds are not just ideas about connection. Instead, these ideas are linked to realities of connection like lifelong residence in family compounds, eating from communal bowls, and the practice of arranged marriage. In the sections that follow, we consider the implications of these different constructions for the experience of closeness and intimacy.

Definitions of Closeness and Intimacy

First, however, we pause to consider definitions of closeness and intimacy. Although definition is an important step in any theoretical analysis, it assumes special importance from a cultural perspective. To consider closeness and intimacy across cultural and historical settings implies that there is a context-general or *etic* (Pike, 1954) definition of these phenomena that applies equally well across settings. However, closeness and intimacy may also have context-specific or *emic* (Pike, 1954) definitions that resonate with particular constructions of self. For example, in contrast to definitions that emphasize positive feeling, phenomena in West African settings suggest definitions of *closeness* that include the possibility of hatred and ill will. In contrast to definitions that emphasize self-disclosure, phenomena in West African settings suggest definitions of *intimacy* that emphasize interpersonal responsiveness. We elaborate on these statements in later sections. The point for now is to define closeness and intimacy broadly—perhaps as intense, interpersonal involvement and experience of intersubjectivity—to avoid an *imposed etic* definition (Berry, 1969) that is more precise but distorts local experience in the process.

THE CULTURAL GROUNDING OF CLOSENESS AND INTIMACY IN WEST AFRICAN WORLDS

Despite the prevailing association of interdependence with the pursuit of closeness and intimacy, ideologies of relationship in many West African settings—where relatively interdependent constructions of self are prominent—advocate cautious ambivalence about closeness and intimacy (Adams, G., 2000; Adams, G., & Plaut, 2003; Ferme, 2001; Shaw, 2000). This cautious ambivalence is evident across multiple relationship forms.

Love and Marriage

Because most discussions of closeness and intimacy refer to marriage or love relationships, we begin our discussion of closeness and intimacy in West African worlds with these relationship forms. As in many regions of the postcolonial world, there is some evidence that relationship ideologies in many West African settings increasingly advocate the emotional intimacy, exclusive intensity, and open disclosure associated with the North American ideal (Bleek, 1976; cf. Dion, K. K., & Dion, K. L., 1993; Hatfield & Rapson, 1996). However, this trend exists against a background reality in which marriage and love relationships are neither constructed nor experienced as intensely intimate connections (Bohannan, 1971). Instead of intimate companionship, partners in many West African settings cite mutual fulfillment of complementary obligations as their goal for the relationship (Franklin, Odongo, & Binka, 1998; Robertson, 1984). Rather than open disclosure, relationship ideology in many West African settings advocates that partners should exercise caution in their revelations to each other (Kilson, 1974; Mikell, 1995). Rather than the idea that "two shall become one flesh", constructions of marriage in many West African settings advocate that spouses resist potentially self-indulgent intimacy and instead focus on a broader range of obligations (Mikell, 1995; Oppong, 1981).

In part, this ambivalence about intimacy in marriage and love relationships is a reflection of everyday realities that diverge from assumed realities of psychological science. Perhaps most salient in this respect is the practice of polygamy. Although the assumption in psychological science is official monogamy, contemporary estimates suggest that as many as 25% of married adults across diverse, West African settings are in openly polygamous unions (Dodoo, 1998; Klomegah, 1997; see Hatfield & Rapson, 1996). Even in those settings where polygamy has declined, scholars claim that its historical legacy persists in formalized interactions and a decrease in psychological intimacy between love partners (Karanja, 1987).

Another feature of everyday realities that contributes to ambivalence about closeness and intimacy is the practice of arranged marriage. Rather than an agreement between individuals based primarily on the experience of love, relationship ideology in many West African worlds holds that marriage is an arrangement between family groups (Kilson, 1974; Nukunya, 1969; Sow, 1985). Although local ideologies allow that closeness and intimacy may develop over time, the prevailing sense is that closeness and intimacy are not essential to a healthy marriage or love relationship and may even lead to undesirable outcomes (Mikell, 1995).

Social psychologists tend to associate the practice of arranged marriage with collectivist forms of interdependence and a corresponding submersion of personal identity into collective, family identity (e.g., Hatfield & Rapson, 1996). However, one can also frame this practice in terms of relational emphases. Resonating with interdependent constructions of self, the prototypical forms of relationship in many West African settings tend to be those, like kinship relations, that entail the experience of inherent connection. From this perspective, kinship connections are more real or consequential (but not necessarily more desired) than manufactured connections like marriage. The implicit contrast is the experience of family relationship in many North American worlds. Resonating with independent constructions of self, it tends to be ascribed connections like kinship that seem like artificial impositions. The more real or consequential connections are those, like love and marriage, that reflect the creative efforts of autonomous selves (Bohannan, 1971).

Here again, different relational prototypes are linked to differences in everyday realities. Perhaps the most salient example is residence patterns. Although the typical pattern in contemporary North American settings is *neolocal* residence—that is, the creation of a separate home apart from that of either partner's family of birth—there is less expectation in many West African settings that conjugal partners will establish a joint, neolocal residence. In contrast to North American settings where nightly cosleeping and conjugal intimacy are something like a moral imperative (Shweder, Jensen, & Goldstein, 1995), it is often the case in many West African settings that happily married partners neither reside in the same house nor expect to sleep together as a nightly routine (cf. Franklin et al., 1998; Mikell, 1995; Oppong, 1981).

Kinship

This idea of relational prototypes suggests a possible explanation for ambivalence about closeness and intimacy in West African constructions of love relationship: Perhaps closeness and intimacy are as valued in West African experience as in North American experience, but they occur in the context of kinship connections rather than love connections.[5] However, evidence suggests that cautious ambivalence about closeness and intimacy characterize kinship connections, too. Intimate contact between family members can foster a sense of social equality in what, given many West African constructions of self, are inherently unequal connections. Accordingly, relationship ideology in many West African settings emphasizes authority ranking within family relationships (see Fiske, 1991) and includes practices—like parent–child avoidance (Riesman, 1992), sending children to be raised by relatives (Goody, 1982), and proscriptions against addressing one's older siblings by name—all of which are designed to prevent intimate contact.

---

[5] For a general statement of this idea, see Dion, K. L., & Dion, K. K., 1993. More specific to West African settings, Fortes (1950) claimed of the Asante in the colonial Gold Coast (now Ghana) that "next to the bond between mother and child none is so strong as that between siblings by the same mother" (p. 273). He explicitly contrasted intimacy in marriage and sibling relationships:

> Quoting their own experiences, men say that it is to his sister that a man entrusts weighty matters, never to his wife. He will discuss confidential matters . . . with his sister, secure in the knowledge that she will tell nobody else. He will give his valuables into her care, not into his wife's. . . . Women, again, agree that in a crisis they will side with their brothers against their husbands (Fortes, 1950, p. 275).

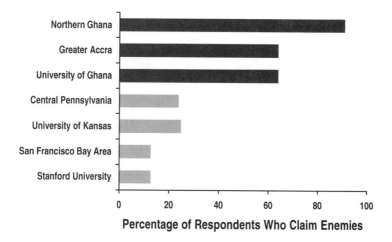

FIG. 18.2. Cultural variation in the experience of personal enemies. The percentage of people who claim enemies is greater in diverse Ghanaian settings (dark bars) than in diverse American settings (light bars). There are also cultural differences within national settings, such that the percentage of people who claim enemies is greater in rural or less educated settings (like Northern Ghana and Central Pennsylvania) than people in urban or more educated settings (like Greater Accra, the San Francisco Bay Area, Stanford University, and the Universities of Ghana and Kansas).

Enemyship

Additional evidence that cautious ambivalence toward closeness and intimacy extends to relationship in general comes from research on *enemyship*: a personal relationship of hatred and malice in which one person seeks another's downfall or tries to sabotage another's progress (Adams, G., 2000). Although nearly absent as a topic of study in psychological science (Felmlee & Sprecher, 2000; Wiseman & Duck, 1995), a concern with enemyship tends to be prominent in many West African worlds. Across diverse demographic categories, the percentage of respondents who claim enemies— defined as *people who hate you, personally, to the extent of wishing for your downfall or trying to sabotage your progress*—is several times greater across settings in the West African country of Ghana than across comparison settings in the USA (Adams, G., 2000) (see Figure 18.2).

At first, the prominence of enemyship may seem to contradict the claim that interdependent constructions of self are prominent in West African worlds.[6] The key to this apparent contradiction is to understand *interdependence* as a reference, not to value orientations or desire for intimacy, but instead to ontological beliefs; that is, the extent to which people experience themselves to be embedded in fields of relational force. From this perspective, interdependent constructions of self do not attenuate the experience of enemyship by causing people to behave more harmoniously; instead they promote an experience of relationship, including enemyship, as a built-in feature of the natural order.

Likewise, the prominent experience of enemyship in West African settings is not antithetical to the experience of closeness and intimacy; instead it reflects the anticipation

---

[6] Indeed, when students in North American universities predict who is more likely to claim enemies— people in "independent, North American settings or interdependent, West African settings"—the vast majority in sample after sample incorrectly guess the former.

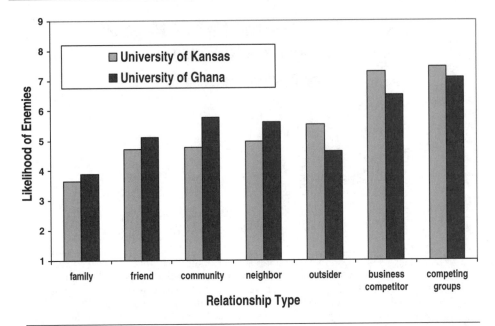

FIG. 18.3. Where do enemies lurk? Students at the University of Ghana (dark bars) rate the likelihood of enemies from relatively close sources (like *family, friends, people in the community,* and *neighbors*) to be greater than do students at the University of Kansas (light bars).

of deliberate harm from close, intimate spaces. The association of enemyship with intimate spaces is evident in numerous public representations, including vehicle slogans and proverbs like "[h]atred comes from the house" or "[a]n insect that bites you will surely be hiding inside your cloth" (Dolphyne, 1996, p. 128; see Kyei & Schreckenbach, 1975, and Rowlands, 1996, for more examples). This association is also evident in studies that ask participants to rate a series of relationship forms according to the likelihood that they will produce an enemy. Results portrayed in Figure 18.3 come from a single study (Adams, G., Anderson, Mensah, & Adonu, 2003) but are representative of a more general pattern (Adams, G., 2000). People in West African settings rate the likelihood of enemies in close relationship sources (e.g., family, friends, neighbors, and people in the community) to be significantly greater than do people in North American settings. In contrast, people in North American settings rate the likelihood of enemyship in relatively distant sources (e.g., outsiders and members of competing groups) to be significantly greater than do people in West African settings.[7]

In general, research on the prominence of enemyship in West African worlds highlights the fact that intimate connections are not just a source of benefits; in addition, they can be a source of harm. To the extent that one recognizes the potential for harm

---

[7] Similarly, when North American audiences learn about the prominence of enemyship in West African settings, they often propose explanations that emphasize tribalism, intergroup conflict, or other collectivist varieties of interdependence (Brewer & Gardner, 1996; Cross, Bacon, & Morris, 2000). This inclination to construct enemies as an intergroup phenomenon—like the disinclination to experience enemyship in close spaces—may have its source in independent constructions of self that frame sociality in terms of a distinction between personal self and collective self, rather than a personal self that is inherently more relational (Piot, 1999; Shaw, 2000).

in close relationships, it is likely that one will regard closeness and intimacy with caution and ambivalence. Thus, research on enemyship helps to explain why closeness and intimacy are regarded with more cautious ambivalence in West African worlds than in North American worlds. Moreover, this research suggests that differences in experience of enemyship are not a coincidence, but instead reflect parallel differences in constructions of self and social reality.

Summary

Contrary to popular misunderstandings of a cultural perspective, the point of this section has not been to declare cautious ambivalence about closeness and intimacy to be a defining characteristic of some monolithic entity called *West African culture*. Instead, the point has been to link cautious ambivalence about closeness and intimacy to the interdependent constructions of self and social reality that underlie psychological experience across diverse, West African worlds.

THE CULTURAL GROUNDING OF CLOSENESS AND INTIMACY IN NORTH AMERICAN WORLDS

On the basis of research described in the previous section, it may be premature to conclude that interdependent constructions of self are everywhere associated with cautious ambivalence about closeness and intimacy. After all, there are likely to be peculiar features of West African worlds—for example, a legacy of slavery and violent upheaval (Ferme, 2001; Piot, 1999; Shaw, 2000), belief in sorcery (Assimeng, 1989; Geschiere, 1997; Meyer, 1998), or the pervasive experience of extreme poverty (Foster, 1965; Mullings, 1984)—that promote unique varieties of interdependence.

For this reason it is important to consider research that compares the experience of closeness and intimacy in contemporary North American worlds with more varied cultural settings beyond the West African case. This research yields similar conclusions. People who inhabit contemporary North American worlds tend to rate relationships to be closer and appear more prone to engage in intimate self-disclosure than do people who inhabit comparison settings where more interdependent constructions of self are prominent (e.g., Chinese and Korean settings; see Chen, 1995; You & Malley-Morrison, 2000).

A Cross-Cultural Perspective on Intimate Self-Disclosure

If North American settings are so independent, then why are people in these settings especially likely to engage in intimate disclosure? Again, the key to this apparent paradox is to understand independence in terms of ontological beliefs rather than value orientations. On the basis of popular understandings that frame independence as a tendency to value autonomy and devalue connection, one might expect that independent constructions of self—whether considered as patterns that vary between cultural worlds (Li, 2002) or as psychological tendencies that vary between individuals within contemporary North American worlds (cf. Cross & Gore, this volume; Dion, K. K., & Dion, K. L., 1993)—would constitute a barrier to the experience of closeness and intimacy. In contrast, cross-cultural evidence suggests that the independent constructions of self that are prominent in contemporary North American worlds may facilitate both an emphasis on intimate disclosure and its consequences for production of closeness.

Why should this be the case? First, consider motivations *for* intimate disclosure and closeness. If a goal of self-disclosure is the creation of intimate connection, then this goal may be more critical in worlds that do not readily afford connection. To the extent that independent constructions of self promote the experience of inherent solitude, a key to relational well-being may be the creation of intimate connection with large numbers of people as a safeguard against the experience of loneliness (Adams, G., & Plaut, 2003). As a result, people who inhabit worlds that promote independence may be particularly motivated to engage in processes, like self-disclosure, that help build intimate connections. In contrast, people who inhabit worlds that promote interdependence may have a greater experience of inherent connection and may feel less motivated to engage in intimate disclosure to create additional connections.

Second, consider motivations against intimate disclosure and closeness. Revealing sensitive information can leave a person vulnerable to malicious gossip, emotional blackmail, and other betrayals of trust. These dangers may carry less psychological weight in worlds that promote independence, especially to the extent that relationship networks are less dense, less overlapping, and less embedded (Feld & Carter, 1998) than in worlds that promote interdependence (Triandis et al., 1988; Wheeler, Reis, & Bond, 1989). Because individual dyads share fewer structural links, a person is better able to control the damage that results from any given betrayal. Moreover, the relative isolation of individual connections from the larger social context affords the possibility of avoidance or escape from problem cases. From this perspective, the independent constructions of self that are prominent in contemporary North American worlds promote the pursuit of closeness and intimacy by affording the sense that one is sufficiently unconnected to avoid the potential problems of intimate connection.

Finally, consider the means by which intimate self-disclosure is said to generate closeness. Theorists have proposed that self-disclosure produces its effects through the mutual discovery, expression, and validation of personal attributes and emotionally sensitive information (Laurenceau, Rivera, Schaffer, & Pietromonaco, chap. 5, this volume). It follows that disclosure should then assume a more prominent place in settings where, consistent with independent constructions, the key to self and social perception lies in internal attributes of bounded objects. If, consistent with the interdependent constructions, the key to self and social perception lies in fields of relational force, then the exploration and expression of personal attributes should be less relevant or rewarding.

A related reason why self-disclosure should be associated with independent constructions of self is the influence of these constructions on emotional experience. Disclosure of emotionally sensitive information may be more rewarding in settings where emotions are constructed and experienced as private phenomena that signal internal states of bounded selves (Mesquita, 2001). In that case, sharing emotion information not only brings direct benefits of self-validation, but also contributes to production of common ground and the process of self-expansion (Aron, A., Mashek, & Aron, E. N., chap. 3, this volume). In contrast, disclosure of emotionally sensitive information may be less appropriate, permissible, or rewarding in settings in which—consistent with interdependent constructions of self—emotions are constructed and experienced as interpersonal events with objectively obvious meaning (Mesquita, 2001). In that case, disclosure of emotionally sensitive information (like expression of emotion in general) may be constructed and experienced as a self-indulgent act—one that contributes little to the production of common ground or the process of self-expansion.

A Historical Perspective on Intimate Self-Disclosure

Additional support for a link between intimate self-disclosure and independent constructions of self comes from research that considers closeness and intimacy from a historical perspective. From this perspective, the emphasis on closeness and intimacy in contemporary North American settings is not natural or inevitable, but instead is a relatively recent development associated with the rise of affective individualism; that is, constructions of self characterized not only by an ontological sense of separate and autonomous individuals, but also a value emphasis on exploration and expression of unique, individual feelings (Baumeister, 1987; Bellah et al., 1985; Stone, 1977).

According to these accounts, the rise of affective individualism was a product of social changes in Europe and North America around 1800. One change was a philosophical emphasis on individual independence from ascribed social position and an associated "self-evident truth" of interpersonal equality. This sense of inherent equality fostered not only declarations of political independence, but also a shift toward less hierarchical constructions of relationship. Another force was a religious emphasis on personal reflection and self-knowledge. This change helped trigger a shift in attitudes about introspection and self-exploration, from a pastime of elites to an activity increasingly required of ordinary individuals. A third force was increasing affluence and mobility (both physical and social) that fostered increased opportunities for privacy and greater resources to devote to leisurely self-expression (Bellah et al., 1985; Stone, 1977).

Associated with these changes was a shift in the construction and experience of personal relationship. Prior to this time, marriage and family relations were typically characterized by "distance, deference, and patriarchy" (Stone, 1977, p. 18). Satisfaction in these relationships was less about emotional closeness or intimate disclosure and more about (ideally) cheerful performance of relational obligations. With the rise of affective individualism, close relationships became an important arena in which to explore and express personal feelings. This was particularly true of women, who shared the growing imperative of exploration and self-expression but had a smaller range of opportunities to do so outside of personal relationships (Oliker, 1998). Thus, a historical perspective suggests not only how cultural practices of intimacy developed in tandem with larger forces of individualism, but also how the pursuit of closeness and intimacy became a gendered activity.

Summary

On the basis of research about individual differences in tendencies toward independence within contemporary North American worlds, one might conclude that independent constructions of self constitute a barrier to the pursuit of closeness and intimacy (Cross & Gore, chap. 13, this volume; Dion, K. K., & Dion, K. L., 1993; Dion, K. L., & Dion, K. K., 1988). A cultural perspective on closeness and intimacy, based on both cross-cultural and historical research, suggests a different conclusion. Although independent constructions of self may indeed render the pursuit of closeness and intimacy problematic (see Baumeister, 1997; Bellah et al., 1985), a cultural perspective suggests that the prominent concern with closeness and intimacy is ultimately grounded in (rather than at odds with) independent constructions of self.

IMPLICATIONS FOR THE EXPERIENCE OF CLOSENESS AND INTIMACY

The preceding sections focus on the possibility that closeness and intimacy are more prominent or carry greater psychological weight in some settings than in others. An alternative possibility is that cultural differences are not about different amounts, but instead reflect different conceptions of closeness and intimacy. Rather than context-general, etic concepts that one can easily transport across settings, closeness, intimacy, and related concepts may have context-specific, emic expressions that resonate with local constructions of self.

Emic Constructions of Relational Interdependence

For example, local constructions of relational may vary depending on local constructions of self. The independent constructions of self that are prominent in North American worlds may promote conceptions of relational that resonate with the experience of relationship as voluntary creation. Given these constructions, a *relational* person may be one who desires intimate connection and behaves in a friendly, sociable manner conducive to creating it. In contrast, the interdependent constructions of self that are prominent in many West African settings may promote conceptions of relational that resonate with the experience of relationship as inherent connection. Given these constructions, a relational person may be one who, for better or worse, is immersed in fields of relational force.

Evidence for this difference comes from a study in which students at Stanford University and the University of Ghana considered a set of complementary target pairs (e.g., *men and women*; Adams, G., 2000, Study 1). For each pair, participants were to indicate which member had (a) more friends and (b) more enemies. To the extent that students identify one member (e.g., women) as having more friends but the *other* member (e.g., men) as having more enemies, it suggests a conception of being relational that resonates with an independent construction of self and associated experience of relationship as an optional agreement. It is as if people consider which member of each pair is more "relational" in this sense and then indicate this member as having more friends, but fewer enemies, than the other, less relational member. In contrast, to the extent that respondents select one member as having more friends and the same member as having more enemies, it suggests a conception of being relational that resonates with an interdependent construction of self and associated experience of relationship as immersion in fields of inherent connection. It is as if people consider which member of each pair is more "relational" in this sense and then indicate this member as having both more friends and more enemies than the other, less relational member. Consistent with hypothesized differences in constructions of self, Ghanaian students were significantly more likely than Stanford students to respond according to the latter pattern.

Closeness and Intimacy

For much of this chapter, we have implicitly adopted a context-general, etic definition of closeness and intimacy that heavily emphasizes disclosure of personal feelings. Adopting this etic definition and evaluating diverse settings accordingly, one might be tempted to conclude—given ideologies that warn against intimate disclosure (Shaw, 2000)—that relationship life in West African settings is characterized by a deficit of closeness and intimacy. An alternative possibility is that closeness and intimacy are just as relevant in West African settings, but that the disclosure-centric definition adopted in psychological research functions as an imposed etic (Berry, 1969) that obscures the experience of closeness and intimacy in these settings.

How might closeness and intimacy be experienced differently in West African settings? Research on the association between self-disclosure and relationship satisfaction suggests a speculative possibility. This research indicates that mutual self-disclosure does not serve as a powerful determinant of satisfaction in settings, like many West African worlds, where people experience relationship in terms of complementarity rather than companionship (Hendrick, 1981; Franzoi, Davis, & Young, 1985; Yelsma & Athappilly, 1988). But if not disclosure and validation of emotionally sensitive information, then what else could be the basis of closeness and intimacy in West African settings? Research described elsewhere in this handbook suggests an alternative possibility: perceptions of responsiveness to relational obligations (Laurenceau et al., chap. 5, this volume; Reis, Clark, & Holmes, chap. 12, this volume; cf. Clark & Reis, 1988; Fiske, 1991).

Theoretical support for this possibility comes from research on the cultural grounding of emotional experience (Mesquita, 2001). This research proposes different understandings of sharing emotion that suggest parallel differences in understandings of closeness and intimacy. According to this research, independent constructions of self promote an experience of emotion as a private event, and they direct efforts at appraisal inward to understanding the subjective meaning of this event. Resonating with the association between disclosure and closeness, sharing emotion has the sense of disclosing information about one's private, subjective experience. In contrast, interdependent constructions of self promote an experience of emotion as an interpersonal event, and they direct efforts at appraisal outward to understanding the objective meaning of this event. Resonating with the proposed association between responsiveness and closeness, sharing emotion has the sense of sharing concern. It is not limited to validation of disclosed information (Laurenceau et al., this volume; Reis et al., this volume), but includes readiness to respond with appropriate action (Mesquita, 2001).

Empirical support for this possibility comes from a study that compared interview participants' definitions of *friend* (Adams, G., & Plaut, 2003). Consistent with a hypothesized link between disclosure of personal feelings and the experience of closeness, the percentage of respondents who spontaneously mentioned emotional support as a defining feature of *friend* was greater among participants in North American settings (specifically, the San Francisco Bay area; 52%) than West African settings (specifically, the Greater Accra and Upper East regions of Ghana; 32%). In contrast, but consistent with the hypothesized link between responsiveness to obligation and the experience of closeness, the percentage of respondents who spontaneously mentioned instrumental support (e.g., material help, financial assistance, and advice) as a defining feature of *friend* was greater among participants in West African settings (56%) than North American settings (12%). These results support the idea that interdependent constructions of self promote an experience of close relationship that is based more on perceived responsiveness to obligations than on intimate disclosure of personal feelings.

Summary

Research discussed in this section suggests that the cultural grounding of closeness and intimacy is not simply a matter of quantitative differences: the extent to which closeness and intimacy are more prominent in some settings than others. More important, this research suggests a qualitative difference. Closeness and intimacy may mean different things, have different bases, and take different forms depending on the constructions of self and social reality that inform relationship experience in different cultural worlds.

IMPLICATIONS FOR THE STUDY OF CLOSENESS AND INTIMACY

The possibility that psychological science imposes an etic definition of closeness and intimacy—one in which disclosure of emotionally sensitive information plays a disproportionate role—is one example of a larger phenomenon that is also the focus of a cultural perspective; that is, the extent to which psychological science is itself grounded in particular constructions of self and social reality. From this perspective, the independent constructions of self that are prominent in North American settings do not just influence the experience of closeness and intimacy. They also influence the

TABLE 18.1

Profile of the Empirical Studies Cited in This Handbook
as a Function of Relationship Type

Relationship Type	Frequency	Percentage
Marriage and Love	68	62
Friendship	11	10
Intergroup	6	6
Relatives	2	2
Other	11	10
Multiple categories	11	10

Note. $N = 109$. Other = acquaintance, mentor, roommate, stranger, and volunteer relationships.

study of closeness and intimacy (cf. Gergen, Gulerce, Locke, & Misra, 1996; Markus & Kitayama, 1994; Markus et al., 1996; Stryker, 1997).

An important way in which implicit constructions of self influence the study of closeness and intimacy concerns the topics chosen for research. The phenomena that have received the most attention in psychological research are topics—like disclosure, satisfaction, and intimacy within love relationships—that resonate with independent constructions of self and the associated experience of relationship as voluntary creation. There has been less attention to topics—like obligation, harmony, and intimacy within kin relationships—that resonate with an interdependent construction of self and the associated experience of relationship in terms of inherent, inescapable connection. To conclude this chapter, we consider two examples of the emphasis on voluntary connection as indications of the extent to which the study of closeness and intimacy is based on independent constructions of self.

Relational Types

Is it really true that the study of closeness and intimacy is based on relatively voluntary connections? To evaluate this claim, we categorized the empirical studies referred to in this handbook according to the relationship type that they investigated. Studies that were cited multiple times in the same chapter or by authors in multiple chapters counted only once in the resulting totals. Results of this analysis (Table 18.1) suggest that the study of closeness and intimacy, as represented by research in this handbook, is based largely on studies that focus exclusively on marriage and love relationships (62%).

A cultural perspective suggests two points about this state of affairs. The first is to note again that the emphasis on love relationship in the study of closeness and intimacy is not a coincidence. Instead, it reflects the independent constructions of self that disproportionately inform social—psychological imagination. If social—psychological imagination were grounded in West African worlds or other settings where interdependent constructions of self were prominent, one can speculate that less voluntary forms of connection (like kinship) would dominate the study of relationship (Mogghadam, Taylor, & Wright, 1993).

Related to this is the second point: Conventional scientific wisdom about closeness and intimacy may be what it is not only because research is based in settings where independent constructions are prominent, but also because the study of personal relationship is often based on voluntary connections like love and marriage. Conventional scientific wisdom might be different if the study of closeness and intimacy were based in relationship forms, like kinship, that resonate more closely with interdependent constructions of self. For example, responsiveness to obligation might feature as prominently as self-disclosure in scientific discourse about closeness and intimacy. One can observe confirmation of this idea in the relative emphasis on responsiveness versus disclosure in attachment theory perspectives, which have a stronger basis than most other theories in kin connections (Collins & Feeney, chap. 10, this volume; Reis et al., chap. 12, this volume).

University Student Worlds

The preceding section suggests that scientific knowledge about closeness and intimacy is disproportionately based in worlds where independent constructions of self are prominent. This statement refers not only to worlds associated with European heritage, but also to the common-ground realities—like high mobility, universal literacy, and narrow age distribution—that characterize university student worlds.

Is it really true that the study of closeness and intimacy is based in university student worlds? To evaluate this claim, we again categorized the empirical studies referred to in this handbook, this time according to the source of participants. We first categorized the 44 out of 109 cases for which handbook chapters reported sample information. This preliminary analysis revealed that university student worlds were the setting for 24 (or 55%) of these 44 cases. We then consulted original reports to obtain information about the source of participants for the remaining 68 studies for which handbook chapters did not report sample information. This follow-up analysis revealed that university student worlds were the setting for 51 (or 75%) of these 68 cases.

How is the cultural grounding of the study of closeness and intimacy evident in these results? First, the combined analyses indicate that university student worlds were the setting for at least 75 (or 69%) of the 109 studies cited in the handbook. This pattern suggests the extent to which university student worlds are the actual norm or modal setting for studies of closeness and intimacy. Second, results of the follow-up analysis indicate that university student worlds were the setting for 75% of the studies for which handbook chapters did not report sample characteristics. This pattern suggests the extent to which university student worlds are the implicit norm or default standard for studies of closeness and intimacy—the background against which only deviations (i.e., studies conducted in off-campus worlds) are considered noteworthy or require special mention.

A cultural perspective on the study of closeness and intimacy again suggests two points about this state of affairs. The first is simply to note that the common-ground realities of university worlds are especially likely to promote both (a) independent constructions of self and (b) the study of closeness and intimacy in the context of relationships (e.g., friendship and romantic love) that resonate with independent constructions of self. Although this does not invalidate research based in university worlds, it does suggest that scientists should devote greater consideration to the role of these worlds in shaping observed patterns. Observed patterns are not just so, but instead reflect particular constructions of self. Associated with this point is the possibility that conclusions about closeness and intimacy from research conducted in university student worlds may not apply as well to settings where less independent constructions of self are prominent. These include not only "other cultures" and kin relationships, but also older adult, working-class, high-school educated, or off-campus worlds (Adams, R. G., Blieszner, & de Vries, 2000; Allan, 1977; Argyle, 1994; Markus, Curhan, Ryff, & Palmersheim, 2003).

The second point concerns interpretation of cross-cultural research. The typical practice of cross-cultural psychology is to develop a measure in settings associated with European heritage and then compare responses to this measure among university students from two or more nations. If one finds a difference between these groups of students, the implication is that this difference has something to do with the larger national populations from which the samples of students are drawn. The problem for interpretation arises when one does not observe a between-groups difference. The implication in this case, often made explicit, is that the pattern of results indicates lack of a cultural difference.

In contrast, the idea of university culture suggests that just because one includes cross-national samples of students, it does not mean that one's study is necessarily cross-cultural. Instead, one may be tapping shared meanings, institutions, and practices associated with cultural patterns of university life. So if one observes that intimate disclosure or "close" dating relationships are increasing in psychological weight among university students in diverse nations, it is not necessarily evidence that accounts claiming cultural variation in relationship are invalid. Rather than evidence against the cultural grounding of closeness and intimacy, these results can be evidence for the cultural grounding of closeness and intimacy—in particular, evidence that experience of relationship is shaped by shared cultural realities of university student worlds.[8]

CONCLUSION

A cultural perspective on closeness and intimacy is still in its infancy. As a result, discussion in this chapter has necessarily consisted of relatively speculative observations on the basis of a few studies rather than the definitive conclusions of systematic research. Given the preliminary state of research on these questions, it would be premature to claim strong conclusions. Instead, the goal of this chapter has been to illuminate a process—the cultural grounding of closeness and intimacy—that is typically invisible in psychological science.

The importance in illuminating this process is to better understand closeness and intimacy, not just in other cultures, but especially in the apparently acultural studies that make up the bulk of psychological science. From the present perspective, patterns observed in typical studies of closeness and intimacy are not natural or inevitable, but instead reflect independent constructions of self that resonate with North American worlds, university settings, and an emphasis on voluntary connections like love and marriage.

ACKNOWLEDGMENTS

Glenn Adams and Stephanie L. Anderson, Department of Psychology, University of Kansas; and Joseph K. Adonu, Department of Psychology, Brunel University.

The research reported in this chapter is partly based on field research in Ghana conducted by Glenn Adams from August, 1996 to August, 1997; October, 1998 to August, 1999; and June, 2002 to August, 2002. This field research was supported by the Social Science Research Council International Predissertation Fellowship Program, the J. William Fulbright Fellowship Board, and the New Faculty General Research

---

[8] A similar point applies to the concept of change. Suppose it were true that intimate disclosure is increasingly assuming a larger place in marriage and love relationships across all regions of the contemporary world. If so, it would not necessarily constitute evidence *against* the cultural grounding of closeness and intimacy. Instead, it might constitute evidence *for* the cultural grounding of closeness and intimacy—in particular, evidence that experience of relationship is increasingly shaped by constructions of self associated with an emergent, global culture (see Arnett, 2002).

Fund of the University of Kansas Center for Research. The Department of Psychology at the University of Ghana in Legon, the Tamale Institute of Cross-Cultural Studies, and the University for Development Studies in Navrongo also supported this field research in Ghana by granting affiliation to Glenn Adams.

We thank Kwarteng Ofosuhene Mensah for his assistance with the research reported in this chapter. We also thank Arthur Aron, Debra Mashek, and the Culture and Psychology Research group at the University of Kansas for their comments on earlier versions of the chapter.

Correspondence concerning this chapter should be addressed to Glenn Adams, Department of Psychology, University of Kansas, 1415 Jayhawk Blvd., Lawrence, Kansas 66045-7556. Email: adamsg@ku.edu

REFERENCES

Adams, G. (2000). *The collective construction of enemyship in Ghana and the USA: Implications for the study of psychology and culture.* Unpublished doctoral dissertation, Stanford University, Palo Alto, CA.

Adams, G., Anderson, S. A., Mensah, K. O., & Adonu, J. A. (2003). Cultural variation in perceived sources of enemies. Unpublished data. University of Kansas, Lawrence, Kansas.

Adams, G., & Markus, H. R. (2001). Culture as patterns: An alternative approach to the problem of reification. *Culture and Psychology, 7,* 283–296.

Adams, G., & Plaut, V. C. (2003). The cultural grounding of personal relationship: Friendship in North American and West African worlds. *Personal Relationships, 10,* 335–349.

Adams, R. G., Blieszner, R., & de Vries, B. (2000). Definitions of friendship in the third age: Age, gender, and study location effects. *Journal of Aging Studies, 14,* 117–133.

Allan, G. (1977). Class variation in friendship patterns. *British Journal of Sociology, 28,* 389–393.

Appiah, K. A. (1992). *In my father's house: Africa and the philosophy of culture.* New York: Oxford University Press.

Argyle, M. (1994). *The psychology of social class.* London: Routledge.

Arnett, J. J. (2002). The psychology of globalization. *American Psychologist, 57,* 774–783.

Assimeng, J. M. (1989). *Religion and social change in West Africa: An introduction to the sociology of religion.* Accra, Ghana: Ghana University Press.

Baumeister, R. F. (1987). How the self became a problem: A psychological review of historical research. *Journal of Personality and Social Psychology, 52,* 163–176.

Baumeister, R. F. (1997). The self and society: Changes, problems and opportunities. In R. D. Ashmore & L. J. Jussim (Eds.), *Self and identity: Fundamental issues. Rutgers series on self and social identity, Vol. 1.* (pp. 191–217). New Brunswick, NJ: Rutgers University Press.

Bellah, R., Madsen, R., Sullivan, W., Swindler, A., & Tipton, S. (1985). *Habits of the heart: Individualism and commitment in American life.* New York: Harper & Row.

Berry, J. W. (1969). On cross-cultural comparability. *International Journal of Psychology 4,* 119–128.

Bleek, W. (1976). *Sexual relationships and birth control in Ghana: A case study of a rural town.* Amsterdam: University of Amsterdam Press.

Bohannan, P. J. (1971). Dyad dominance and household maintenance. In F. L. K. Hsu (Ed.), *Kinship and culture* (pp. 42–66). Chicago: Aldone.

Brewer, M. B., & Gardner, W. (1996). Who is this "we"? Levels of collective identity and self-representations. *Journal of Personality and Social Psychology, 71,* 83–93.

Brown, B. B., Werner, C. M., & Altman, I. (1994). Close relationships in environmental context. In A. L. Weber & J. H. Harvey (Eds.), *Perspectives on close relationships* (pp. 340–358). Needham Heights, MA: Allyn & Bacon.

Chen, G. M. (1995). Differences in self-disclosure among Americans versus Chinese: A comparative study. *Journal of Cross-Cultural Psychology, 26,* 84–91.

Clark, M. S., & Reis, H. T. (1988). Interpersonal processes in close relationships. *Annual Review of Psychology, 39,* 609–672.

Cross, S. E., Bacon, P. L., & Morris, M. L. (2000). The relational-interdependent self-construal and relationships. *Journal of Personality and Social Psychology, 78,* 791–808.

Dion, K. K., & Dion, K. L. (1993). Individualistic and collectivistic perspectives on gender and the cultural context of love and intimacy. *Journal of Social Issues, 49,* 53–69.

Dion, K. L., & Dion, K. K. (1988). Romantic love: Individual and cultural perspectives. In R. J. Sternberg & M. L. Barnes (Eds.), *The psychology of love.* (pp. 264–289). New Haven, CT: Yale University Press.

Dodoo, F. N.-A. (1998). Marriage type and reproductive decisions: A comparative study in sub-Saharan Africa. *Journal of Marriage and the Family, 60,* 232–242.

Dolphyne, F. A. (1996). *A comprehensive course in Twi (Asante) for the non-Twi learner.* Accra, Ghana: Ghana Universities Press.

Dumont, L. (1970). *Homo Hierarchicus.* Chicago: University of Chicago Press.

Farr, R. M. (1996). *The roots of modern social psychology, 1872–1954.* Cambridge, MA: Blackwell.

Feld, S., & Carter, W. C. (1998). Foci of activity as changing contexts for friendship. In R. G. Adams & G. Allan (Eds.), *Placing friendship in context* (pp. 136–152). Cambridge, England: Cambridge University Press.

Felmlee, D., & Sprecher, S. (2000). Close relationships and social psychology: Intersections and future paths. *Social Psychology Quarterly, 63,* 365–376.

Ferme, M. C. (2001). *The underneath of things: Violence, history, and the everyday in Sierra Leone.* Berkeley, CA: University of California Press.

Fiske, A. P. (1991). *Structures of social life: The four elementary forms of social relations: communal sharing, authority ranking, equality matching and market pricing.* New York: Free Press.

Fiske, A. P., Kitayama, S., Markus, H. R., & Nisbett, R. E. (1998). The cultural matrix of social psychology. In D. T. Gilbert & S. T. Fiske (Eds.), *The handbook of social psychology, Vol. 2* (4th ed.) (pp. 915–981). Boston: McGraw-Hill.

Fortes, M. (1950). Kinship and marriage among the Ashanti. In A. R. Radcliffe-Brown & D. Forde (Eds.), *African systems of kinship and marriage* (pp. 252–284). London: Kegan Paul.

Foster, G. M. (1965). Peasant society and the image of the limited good. *American Anthropologist, 67,* 293–315.

Franklin, N., Odongo, P., & Binka , F. (1998). *Life narratives from Navrongo, Ghana: A cultural census of the Kassena-Nankana.* (Available from the Navrongo Health Research Centre, Ministry of Health, P. O. Box 114, Navrongo, Upper East Region, Ghana)

Franzoi, S. L., Davis, M. H., & Young, R. D. (1985). The effects of private self-consciousness and perspective taking on satisfaction in close relationships. *Journal of Personality and Social Psychology, 48,* 1584–1594.

Gergen, K. J., Gulerce, A., Lock, A., & Misra, G. (1996). Psychological science in cultural context. *American Psychologist, 51,* 496–503.

Geschiere, P. (1997). *The modernity of witchcraft: Politics and the occult in postcolonial Africa.* Charlottesville, VA: University of Virgina Press.

Goodwin, R. (1999). *Personal relationships across cultures.* London: Routledge.

Goody, E. N. (1982). *Parenthood and social reproduction: Fostering and occupational roles in West Africa.* Cambridge, England: Cambridge University Press.

Gyekye, K. (1992). Person and community in Akan thought. In K. Wiredu & K. Gyekye (Eds.), *Person and community: Ghanaian philosophical studies* (pp. 101–121). Washington, DC: Council for Research in Values and Philosophy.

Hatfield, E., & Rapson, R. L. (1996). *Love and sex: Cross-cultural perspectives.* Boston: Allyn & Bacon.

Hendrick, S. S. (1981). Self-disclosure and marital satisfaction. *Journal of Personality and Social Psychology, 40,* 1150–1159.

Jackson, M. S. (1982). *Allegories of the wilderness: Ethics and ambiguity in Kuranko narratives.* Bloomington, IN: Indiana University Press.

Karanja, W. W. (1987). "Outside wives" and "inside wives" in Nigeria: A study of changing perceptions in marriage. In D. Parkin & D. Nyamwaya (Eds.), *Transformations of African Marriage* (pp. 247–262). Manchester, England: Manchester University Press.

Kilson, M. (1974). *African urban kinsmen: The Ga of central Accra.* New York: St. Martin's Press.

Kirby, J. P. (1986). *God, shrines and problem solving among the Anufo of Northern Ghana.* Berlin, Germany: Dietrich-Reimer-Verlag.

Klomegah, R. (1997). Socio-economic characteristics of Ghanaian women in polygynous marriages. *Journal of Comparative Family Studies, 28,* 73–88.

Kroeber, A. L., & Kluckhohn, C. (1952). *Culture: A critical review of concepts and definitions.* New York: Random House.

Kyei, K. G., & Schreckenbach, H. (1975). *No time to die.* Accra, Ghana: Catholic Press.

Lau, I. Y. M., Chiu, C. Y., & Lee, S. I. (2001). Communication and shared reality: Implications for the psychological foundations of culture. *Social Cognition, 19,* 350–371.

Li, H. Z. (2002). Culture, gender, and self-close-other connectedness in Canadian and Chinese samples. *European Journal of Social Psychology, 32,* 93–104.

Markus, H. R., Curhan, K. B., Ryff, C. D., & Palmersheim, K. (2003). Social class and well-being in America: A sociocultural approach. Manuscript submitted for publication.

Markus, H. R., & Kitayama, S. (1991). Culture and self: Implications for cognition, emotion, and motivation. *Psychological Review, 98,* 224–253.

Markus, H. R., & Kitayama, S. (1994). Collective fear of the collective: Implications for selves and theories of selves. *Personality and Social Psychology Bulletin, 20,* 568–579.

Markus, H. R., Kitayama, S., & Heiman, R. (1996). Culture and "basic" psychological principles. In E. T. Higgins & A. W. Kruglanski (Eds.), *Social psychology: Handbook of basic principles* (pp. 857–913). New York, NY: Guilford Press.

Mesquita, B. (2001). Emotions in collectivist and individualist contexts. *Journal of Personality and Social Psychology, 80,* 68–74.

Meyer, B. (1998). 'Make a complete break with the past': Memory and post-colonial modernity in Ghanaian Pentecostalist discourse. *Journal of Religion in Africa, 28*, 316–349.

Mikell, G. (1995). The state, the courts, and "value": Caught between matrilineages in Ghana. In J. Guyer (Ed.), *Money matters: Instability, values and social payments in the modern history of West African communities* (pp. 225–244). Portsmouth, NH: Heinemann.

Moghaddam, F. M., Taylor, D. M., & Wright, S. C. (1993). *Social psychology in cross-cultural perspective.* New York: W. H. Freeman.

Morris, M. W., Menon, T., & Ames, D. (2001). Culturally conferred conceptions of agency: A key to social perception of persons, groups, and other actors. *Personality and Social Psychology Review, 5*, 169–182.

Moscovici, S. (1984). The phenomena of social representations. In R. M. Farr & S. Moscovici (Eds.), *Social representations* (pp. 3–69). Cambridge, England: Cambridge University Press.

Mudimbe, V. Y. (1988). *The invention of Africa: Gnosis, philosophy, and the order of knowledge.* Bloomington, IN: Indiana University Press.

Mullings, L. (1984). *Therapy, ideology, and social change: Mental healing in urban Ghana.* Berkeley, CA: University of California Press.

Nukunya, G. K. (1969). *Kinship and marriage among the Anlo Ewe.* London: Athlone Press.

Oliker, S. J. (1998). The modernization of friendship: Individualism, intimacy, and gender in the nineteenth century. In R. G. Adams & G. Allan (Eds.), *Placing friendship in context* (pp. 18–42). Cambridge, England: Cambridge University Press.

Oppong, C. (1981). *Middle class African marriage: A family study of Ghanaian senior civil servants.* London: George Allen & Unwin. (Original work published in 1974, *Marriage among a matrilineal elite: A family study of Ghanaian senior civil servants.* London: Cambridge University Press).

Pike, K. L. (1954). *Language in relation to a unified theory of the structure of human behavior.* Dallas, TX: Summer Institute of Linguistics.

Piot, C. (1999). *Remotely global: Village modernity in West Africa.* Chicago: University of Chicago Press.

Riesman, P. (1986) The person and the life cycle in African social life and thought. *African Studies Review, 29*, 71–138.

Riesman, P. (1992). *First find your child a good mother: The construction of self in two African communities.* D. L. Szanton, L. Abu-Lughod, S. Hutchinson, P. Stoller, & C. Trosset (Eds.). New Brunswick, NJ: Rutgers University Press.

Robertson, C. C. (1984). *Sharing the same bowl: A socioeconomic history of women and class in Accra, Ghana.* Ann Arbor, MI: University of Michigan Press.

Rowlands, M. (1996). Consumption of an African modernity. In M. J. Arnoldi, C. M. Geary, & K. L. Hardin (Eds.), *African material culture* (pp. 188–213). Bloomington, IN: Indiana University Press.

Shaw, R. (2000). "Tok af, lef af": A political economy of Temne techniques of secrecy and self. In I. Karp & D. A. Masolo (Eds.), *African philosophy as cultural inquiry* (pp. 25–49). Bloomington, IN: Indiana University Press.

Shweder R. A., Jensen, L. A., & Goldstein, W. M. (1995). Who sleeps by whom revisited: A method for extracting the moral goods implicit in practice. In J. J. Goodnow & P. J. Miller (Eds.), *Cultural practices as contexts for development* (pp. 21–39). San Francisco: Jossey-Bass.

Sow, F. (1985). Muslim families in contemporary Black Africa. *Current Anthropology, 26*, 563–573.

Stone, L. (1977). *The family, sex, and marriage: In England, 1500–1800.* New York: Harper & Row.

Stryker, S. (1997). "In the beginning there is society": Lessons from a sociological social psychology. In C. McGarty & S. A. Haslam (Eds.), *The message of social psychology: Perspectives on mind in society* (pp. 315–327). Malden, MA: Blackwell.

Tengan, E. (1991). *The land as being and cosmos: The institution of the Earth Cult among the Sisaala of northern Ghana.* Frankfurt, Germany: Peter Lang.

Triandis, H. C., Bontempo, R., Villareal, M. J., Asai, M., et al. (1988). Individualism and collectivism: Cross-cultural perspectives of self-ingroup relationships. *Journal of Personality and Social Psychology, 54*, 323–338.

Wheeler, L., Reis, H. T., & Bond, M. H. (1989). Collectivism and individualism in everyday life: The middle kingdom and the melting pot. *Journal of Personality and Social Psychology, 57*, 79–86.

Wiseman, J. P., & Duck, S. (1995). Having and managing enemies: A very challenging relationship. In S. Duck & J. T. Wood (Eds.), *Confronting relationship challenges: Understanding relationship processes series, 5* (pp. 43–72). Thousand Oaks, CA: Sage.

Yelsma, P., & Athappilly, K. (1988). Marital satisfaction and communication practices: Comparison among Indian and American couples. *Journal of Comparative Family Studies, 19*, 37–54.

You, H. S., & Malley-Morrison, K. (2000). Young adult attachment styles and intimate relationships with close friends: A cross-cultural study of Koreans and Caucasian Americans. *Journal of Cross-Cultural Psychology, 31*, 528–534.

VI

Is There a Dark Side to Closeness and Intimacy?

19

Desiring Less Closeness
With Intimate Others

Debra J. Mashek
George Mason University
Michelle D. Sherman
Oklahoma City VA Medical Center and University of Oklahoma Medical Center

Most people acknowledge the desire for closeness with romantic partners. However, a more complex picture of closeness emerges when one moves beyond the range of closeness often examined by much of the research on romantic relationships, and instead explores the situation where closeness becomes suffocating. This chapter explores a facet of this complex picture—the desire for less closeness—by integrating data from Mashek's (2002) laboratory research and Sherman's clinical experience.

The present chapter (a) builds on A. Aron, Mashek, and E. N. Aron's (chap. 3, this volume) definition of closeness to operationalize what it means to desire less closeness; (b) explores possible causes of desiring less closeness, highlighting the hypothesized causal role of interpersonal control; and (c) offers a preliminary framework and supporting data for delineating the desire for less closeness from related constructs such as avoidant attachment and fear of intimacy.

WHAT IS CLOSENESS AND WHAT DOES IT MEAN TO DESIRE LESS CLOSENESS?

We adopt A. Aron, Mashek, and E. N. Aron's view (chap. 3, this volume) that closeness is the state of including others in the self. When a close other is part of myself, that person influences who I am by influencing my identities, resources, and perspectives (Aron, A., & Aron, E. N., 1986). Additionally, close others shape us by influencing how we think (Agnew, Van Lange, Rusbult, & Langston, 1998) and how we behave (Bersheid, Snyder, & Omoto, 1989).

So what does it mean to desire less closeness with someone? We propose that desiring less closeness with someone, or feeling "too close," means feeling that another person's influence (or even demands) on the self is too strong or intense, overpowering, unwelcome, or misguided. People who report a desire for less closeness describe the experience using powerful words such as caged up, controlled, imbalanced, locked down, merged, not being able to get out, oppressed, overwhelmed, possessed, imprisoned, restricted, smothered, suffocated, and trapped.[1] These descriptions certainly capture the theme of other influencing self; indeed, these descriptions evoke a sense of extreme influence or control. The qualitative connection between these control-themed words and the desire for less closeness is not surprising. In fact, we propose that this connection is a causal one: that perceived threat to personal control is one *cause* of feeling too close.

This chapter focuses on those individuals who report more current closeness than desired closeness, assessed by Mashek (2002) using a modified version of A. Aron, E. N. Aron, and Smollan's (1992) Inclusion of other in self (IOS) scale (for a detailed description of the IOS see Agnew, Loving, Le, & Goodfriend, chap. 7, this volume). Mashek modified the IOS slightly by asking respondents to answer two questions. First, using the seven pairs of circles originally used by Aron and colleagues, respondents indicate the picture that best describes their *current* relationship with their partners. Second, Mashek presents respondents with another set of overlapping circles. Respondents circle the picture that best describes their *desired* relationship with the partner. A more extreme score for actual closeness (e.g., 6) than for desired closeness (e.g., 5) is interpreted as indicating a desire for less closeness.

Examples of Feeling Too Close

Social lore and clinical writings describe the experience of feeling too close to romantic partners. For example, a passage from Kahlil Gibran's popular *The Prophet* prescribes distance between the self and other as optimal: "And stand together yet not too near together: For the pillars of the temple stand apart, And the oak tree and the cypress grow not in each other's shadow." Given the ability of popular magazines to both influence and reflect social lore, it is telling to note article titles such as *Fighting the Urge to Merge* (Harper's Bazaar, November 1985) and *Privacy vs. Intimacy: How close can you get and still breathe* (Glamour, March 1983). Perhaps the most illustrative examples of feeling too close come from first-person accounts. One female student from the U.S. who felt too close stated, "For seven years every decision, from what to eat for dinner to where to live, has been made by the two of us together. I want to make some decisions on my own, I don't want my life to be tied to my partner." A male college student who desired less closeness said, "I stopped pursuing many of the activities and interests that were previously a part of who I was. I gave them up because my partner wasn't interested and I wanted to spend time with her."

Clinical description offers yet another source of examples of feeling too close. A hypothetical case presentation (derived from a composite of Sherman's clientele) may illustrate the complex interplay involved in discrepant desires for closeness. Mary and Bob have been married for 6 years. They sought out couples therapy due to difficulties with "getting their needs met" in the relationship. Mary was widowed eight years before marrying Bob, and she had greatly enjoyed the independence of her single lifestyle. Mary reported significant enjoyment of Bob and the marriage, yet an equally strong distaste for his "clinginess" and his frequent pulls for closeness (e.g., Bob would

---

[1] These descriptions were provided by participants in Mashek's research.

follow her around the house and resented her doing activities with her girlfriends). Typical of the closeness–distance dance (cf. Lerner, 1985), the more Bob pursued, the more Mary distanced. Mary felt that Bob was never satisfied—it was simply "never enough" for him. Bob was frustrated and jealous of the time, energy, and emotion Mary gave to others (e.g., her church, extended family) instead of to him. Mary struggled to maintain her sense of separateness from Bob, who was trying to emotionally consume her. Bob didn't understand why she was so selfish and repeatedly ignored his needs; he often felt rejected, hurt and lonely.

Prevalence of Feeling Too Close

Taken together, the examples above suggest that it is *possible* to desire less closeness, or to feel "too close." But how *prevalent* is this experience?

A few research papers explicitly report both actual and desired levels of closeness in romantic relationships (e.g., Davis & Bibace, 1999; Eshel, Sharabany, & Friedman, 1998; Larrieu & Leibsohn, 1988; Schaefer & Olson,1981). Unfortunately, none of these studies report the prevalence of discrepancies between actual and desired closeness. However, it is possible to get a rough estimate of the prevalence of differences between actual and desired closeness. When looking at data from studies that used college student samples, we estimate (based on the descriptive information provided in these reports) that 12% to 30% of respondents report more actual closeness than desired closeness. The prevalence among married individuals (estimated in the same way) seems much less, ranging from 3% to 9%. Although the percentage is low for wedded individuals overall, the closeness/distance issue is certainly a common one addressed in marital therapy (e.g., Christensen, 1988a, 1988b; Christensen & Jacobson, 2000; Jacobson, 1989; Napier, 1978). The fact that college students are still experimenting with intimate relationships and navigating the challenges of Erikson's (1963) "intimacy versus isolation" stage of psychosocial development (marked by trying to create trusting, love relationships or becoming quite isolated and self-absorbed), may partially explain the differences across generations.

When using the modified IOS scales to measure actual and desired closeness, Mashek (2002) finds that approximately 13–19% of the dating undergraduate students surveyed feel too close (38–46% appear to desire more closeness, whereas approximately 35–49% are satisfied with current levels of closeness). When using an alternate measure of closeness (a numerical Likert scale as opposed to a pictorial measure) she finds that approximately 7–9% of respondents report more current closeness than desired closeness. (We suspect that these lower estimates may be a function of the visual metaphor offered by the IOS scale, which really seems to tap participants' intuitive understanding of closeness.) Thus, after collecting data from nearly 1,200 dating undergraduates from Long Island (but who are likely typical of North American students in general), Mashek estimates that 7% to 19% of North American undergraduate students feel too close at any given time. (Approximately 11% of the females desired less closeness compared to 15% of the males, a difference that is not statistically significant.) Consistent with estimates based on previous research with adults, only 5% of respondents in a community sample ($N = 100$) reported greater actual than desired closeness (using the IOS scale).

As another indicator of prevalence, Mashek asked 611 undergraduate participants to indicate, *How often do you feel too close to your romantic partner? Everyday, Once per week, Once per month, Once per semester, Never.* Surprisingly, 57% of respondents reported feeling too close to the current partner at least once per semester. That is, over half of the sample reported feeling too close in the context of their current relationship at least once in the preceding three months. That so many people report desiring less closeness at least once in the recent past, yet comparatively fewer people report desiring less closeness at any given point in time, suggests that the desire for closeness waxes and wanes over time (Christensen & Jacobson, 2000), possibly in response to the partner's behavior, fluctuations in the relationship, changes in the environment, extra-relationship events, or some combination of factors. (Of course, the different measurement methods—difference scores based on present feelings versus qualitative descriptors of past feelings—might also account for some or all of this difference.)

Taken together, the data suggest that feeling too close is a real and pervasive phenomenon. A next logical line of inquiry involves studying the relationship quality correlates of wanting less closeness. Across samples, the general pattern of results is quite clear. People who are satisfied with the level of closeness in their relationship (that is, people whose actual closeness equals their desired closeness) report exceptionally high relationship quality. However, the reported relationship quality of people who desire less closeness is just as low as people who desire more closeness. Mashek finds this curvilinear pattern across measures of relationship satisfaction, commitment, and passionate love. Beyond general measures of relationship quality, people who desire less closeness differ in important ways from both people who desire more closeness and people who are satisfied with their current levels of closeness. We discuss these differences in-depth later in the chapter.

Another interesting correlate is the correspondence between the closeness discrepancies of members of a couple. In a given relationship, is one person's desire for less closeness related to the partner's closeness wishes? The answer to this question is uncertain. Christensen (1988a, 1988b) and Jacobson (1989) discuss a pattern often seen in clinical settings where one person seeks increased affiliation and the other seeks increased distance; as each partner makes her or his move, the couple becomes increasingly polarized. In a similar vein, Lerner (1985) describes emotional pursuers and emotional distancers. Pursuers deal with angst by seeking closeness, whereas distancers deal with angst by withdrawing. Lerner points out that if a couple is made up of one pursuer and one distancer, a "dance" of closeness is likely to ensue in times of stress. These clinical accounts, then, suggest that if one person withdraws emotionally because of a need for space or feeling suffocated, the partner's insecurity may be sparked, resulting in attempts to achieve more closeness. Data collected by Mashek and her colleagues lends empirical support to this idea. Preliminary analysis of data collected from 43 dating couples using the modified IOS scales suggest that when one person desires less closeness, the partner desires more closeness $(r = -.27)$.

To summarize, clinical accounts and research findings provide a descriptive account of desiring less closeness. Formal conceptualizations of closeness unite the construct of closeness with the idea of influence of other on self, or control. In the following section, we propose that the reason desiring less closeness co-occurs with feeling controlled is because threat to personal control causes the desire for less closeness.

WHAT CAUSES THE DESIRE FOR LESS CLOSENESS?

Threat to Personal Control

People are fundamentally motivated to expand the self by acquiring resources, perspectives, and identities (Aron, A., & Aron, E. N., 1986; see also Aron, Mashek, & Aron, chap. 3, this volume). Furthermore, people have a need for autonomy (e.g., self-direction and personal volition; Ryan & Deci, 2000). When a close other exerts control over us, that person threatens our autonomy, thus restricting our ability to seek out new perspectives, identities, and social and material resources. This threat to control, we propose, may create a sense of too much closeness.

Why might threat to control catalyze the desire for less closeness? To answer this question, it is useful to return for a moment to the nature of closeness. Closeness entails influence across many domains. In a very real sense, to control someone is to influence that person. Close others are in a position to not only influence us, but to control us on some level (although this is an oversimplification of actual relationship dynamics, this logic introduces the connection between closeness and control). If a partner controls us such that our access to, or freedom to seek out, resources, perspectives, and identities is limited, then we should desire less closeness with this person because she or he is limiting our ability to achieve the fundamental goal of self-expansion. A desire for less closeness may reflect a desire to reestablish our own control. (Of course, in extreme cases of control, closeness may not even exist in the relationship. For example, if a husband beats his wife and won't let her talk to her friends, she is highly controlled, but likely to feel afraid and not at all close.)

If someone were to respond to the desire for less closeness by actually becoming less close to a controlling partner, autonomy would be effectively reestablished, thus decreasing the ability of the other person to exert control over the self. The vulnerability inherent in sharing the self with others may contribute to feeling out of control (an idea reflected in the language used to describe the early phase of romantic relationships—"falling" in love, "falling" head over heals, being on an "emotional roller coaster"); in an effort to regain personal control, we may seek distance.

Different literatures offer insights into how and why control might develop in the context of close relationships. For example, the power literature (e.g., French & Raven, 1959; Lips, 1991; Pence & Shepard, 1988) suggests that certain types of power, such as affectionate rewards and referent power, do seem to require closeness. Attachment theory (Bowlby 1982, 1988) details the consequences of intrusiveness—another form of control—in the context of closeness (e.g., Ainsworth, 1969): Inappropriate or insensitive "support" may be viewed as intrusive. Finally, using a compensatory model of control, Stets (1995) describes why control might develop in relationships. She argues that when one person feels a general lack of control (not simply in the relationship domain), that person may attempt to compensate for this lack of control by exerting control over a romantic partner. Thus, a theoretical base exists across clinical, social, and developmental psychology literatures for the hypothesis that threat to control causes the desire for less closeness.

Mashek and Aron (2003) provide preliminary evidence linking threat to control to the desire for less closeness. In two college samples and in one community sample of people involved in romantic relationships, the desire for less closeness correlated strongly and positively with threat to control. That is, as levels of threat to control increased in the relationships, so too did the desire for less closeness. Further, this effect was robust across different quetionnaire methods and for both females and males, even after controlling for relationship quality. Althogh these data are correlational in nature, they are nevertheless important because they highlight the existence of a relationship between these two constructs. Additional experimental research, of course, is needed to explore a possible causal mechanism.

Threat to Personal Identity

Although we highlighted the role of threat to control in precipitating the desire for less closeness, any number of factors might play equally important roles. This phenomenon, after all, is exceptionally complex and multidimensional. Literatures such as optimal distinctiveness theory and object relations theory point to personal identity threat as another likely cause of desiring less closeness.

One's identity may be threatened if distinctions between self and other become unclear, as suggested by optimal distinctiveness theory (Brewer & Pickett, 1999). If the differences between self and other are excessively blurred, then the dyad becomes a highly inclusive category. Being a member of a highly inclusive group may motivate an active search for differentiation (Brewer, 1993). Put another way, over inclusion in the dyad may lead to an active search for the self through a desire for less closeness with the other. Additionally, object relations theory argues that the self should be able to differentiate its own perceptions, ideas, and feelings from those of the other (Stierlin, 1976) and that this self–other differentiation is a fundamental goal of development. Stierlin (1976) suggests that the ability to differentiate between self and other is most likely to break down when trying to establish closeness or empathy. It seems possible that individuals may be able to tolerate only a certain degree of this inability to differentiate between self and others. When this threshold is crossed, the self may feel too close to the other.

Considering the Person, the People, and the Situation

A complete understanding of what causes the desire for less closeness will likely involve delineating factors originating in Person A (the person who desires less closeness), factors originating in Person B (A's partner); factors originating in the unique relationship between A and B (AXB); and factors external to the relationship (C) (cf. Kenny, 1994).

For example, it could be that Person A is hypersensitive to control threat, possibly interpreting perfectly "normal" behaviors by Person B as threatening when in fact most other people would not interpret B's behavior similarly. Or it could be that Person B is indeed controlling and that Person A accurately interprets B's behavior as threatening. Or it could be that an attribute of Person A only triggers a desire for less closeness when paired with a particular attribute of Person B (for example, A may have an avoidant attachment orientation and B may be preoccupied with closeness). Finally, it could be that a contextual factor (such as a period of intense stress at work) may create an arena in which A might be temporarily sensitive to control. Then again, any combination of these factors might interact to set the stage for desiring less closeness.

As researchers and clinicians more clearly articulate the psychological and environmental conditions that lead Person A to shift from feeling "okay with closeness" to "feeling too close," it may be helpful to articulate whether each condition is an A, B, AXB, or C factor. By doing so, the pattern of effects might gel into a coherent, even clearer picture. Additionally, in order to understand the implications of desiring less closeness on the larger dyadic system, it will be necessary to keep in mind that both members of the dyad could potentially feel too close at either the same time or at different times. And, the closeness desires of dyad members likely wax and wane over time, probably in response to any of the A, B, AXB, and C factors. As such, a prospective study mapping A, B, AXB, and C factors from both dyad members' perspective may be a useful tool in illuminating the intricacies of this phenomenon.

Although the desire for less closeness is complex, a systematic consideration of the many factors (and the interactions between factors) that might contribute to the desire for less closeness will likely yield meaningful information with real implications for relationship satisfaction, longevity, and well-being.

To summarize, little is known about what causes one to desire less closeness. Mashek's (2002) experimental study provides empirical support for the hypothesis that threat to personal control catalyzes the desire for less closeness. Other factors likely contribute to the desire for less closeness, including threat to personal identity. Finally, given the complexity of the desire for less closeness, researchers and clinicians may find it useful to delineate which potential causal factors originate in the person who desires less closeness, which factors originate in that person's partner, which factors originate as a function of the unique relationship between these two people, and which factors originate in circumstances external to the dyad.

HOW IS THE DESIRE FOR LESS CLOSENESS SIMILAR TO AND DIFFERENT FROM RELATED CONSTRUCTS?

As we noted earlier, the desire for less closeness is commonly experienced. More than 50% of undergraduate students reported desiring less closeness with their romantic partners in the preceding months. Given this prevalence, one might question whether certain people are more likely than others to desire less closeness in romantic relationships. For example, is the desire for less closeness experienced only by people with an avoidant attachment style? Or maybe the desire for less closeness co-occurs with a fear of intimacy?

This section of the chapter is devoted to trying to map the desire for less closeness onto individual difference variables highlighted by various theoretical approaches. Importantly, unlike individual difference variables (e.g., attachment orientation), the desire for less closeness seems to be a reaction to a specific relationship (vs. an attribute characterizing a person's perception of all of her or his relationships) and seems to be bounded by time (that is, I might desire less closeness with my partner today, but desire more closeness with her two weeks from now).

Attachment Anxiety and Avoidance

As part of a questionnaire study, Mashek (2002) asked 323 undergraduates to complete the experiences in close relationships (ECR) measure of adult attachment (Brennan, Clark, & Shaver, 1998). As part of this same study, participants completed verbal analogues of the IOS scales (i.e., "[h]ow would you characterize your ACTUAL relationship with your partner?" "[h]ow would you characterize your DESIRED relationship with your partner?" Responses ranged from 1 (*not at all close*) to 7 (*extremely close*).

We mentioned earlier that many relationship quality measures show a curvilinear relationship with the difference between desired and current closeness. Might the avoidance and anxiety dimensions of attachment map similarly onto these difference scores? The squared difference between desired and current closeness significantly predicts avoidance ($\beta = .17$, R^2 change $= .02$, $p = .006$; see Figure 19.1), above what is predicted by the unsquared difference scores and attachment anxiety. A plot of the resulting equation shows a near-perfect U-shape: people who want less closeness and people who want more closeness tend to be quite avoidant, but people who are satisfied with the closeness in their relationship report very little avoidance. However, the squared difference does not significantly predict anxiety ($\beta = .09$, R^2 change $= .006$, $p = .15$), above what is predicted by the unsquared difference scores and avoidance. Thus, avoidance, but not anxiety, shows a curvilinear relationship with wanting more, wanting the same, and wanting less closeness.

Interestingly, anxiety, but not avoidance, shows a significant linear relationship with the difference between desired and actual closeness. Controlling for avoidance, the unsquared difference between desired and actual closeness significantly predicts anxiety ($\beta = .15$, $p = .008$; see Figure 19.1). However, controlling for anxiety, the unsquared difference fails to significantly predict avoidance ($\beta = .08$, $p = .17$). The least anxious people are those who want less closeness and the most anxious people are

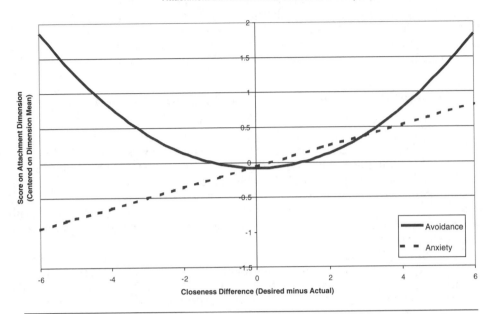

FIG. 19.1. Desire for less closeness as a function of attachment anxiety and attachment avoidance.

those who want more closeness. It's important to note that the anxiety measured by the ECR focuses on anxiety about relationships, as opposed to anxiety more generally. This distinction is important because, as Sherman finds in her clinical experience, oftentimes those who want less closeness are anxious in a more general sense—torn between feeling they "should" give more yet not wanting to.

Clearly, the above analyses each report on only one of the attachment dimensions at a time. (The results are the same when the analyses for each dimension are run without controlling for the other dimension.) To understand the relationship between desiring less closeness and the two dimensions of attachment, we predicted the Anxiety × Avoidance interaction term from avoidance, anxiety, and the unsquared difference between desired and current closeness. When controlling for both anxiety and avoidance, the unsquared difference score was not a significant predictor of the interaction term ($\beta = .009$, $p = .51$). Similarly, the squared difference score was not a significant predictor of the interaction term ($\beta = -.003$, R^2 change $= .000$, $p = .84$), above what is predicted by anxiety, avoidance, and the unsquared difference.

To summarize, avoidance shows a clear curvilinear relationship with the difference between desired and actual closeness such that the least avoidant individuals are those whose desired closeness matches their current closeness; people who want more closeness and people who want less closeness are highly avoidant. Anxiety, on the other hand, shows a clear linear relationship with the closeness difference such that the least anxious individuals are those who want less closeness. Finally, no significant relationship (linear or curvilinear) exists between the closeness difference and the interaction between anxiety and avoidance.

People who want more closeness tend to be both highly avoidant and highly anxious, whereas those who want less closeness are highly avoidant but minimally anxious. These results suggest that anxiety is the dimension that best differentiates between those people who want less closeness from those who want more closeness.

The anxiety and avoidance scores of people who want less closeness fit the pattern described as "dismissing" (dismissive of relationships) by Bartholomew and Horowitz (1991; see also Brennan et al., 1998). However, it seems unlikely that all people who desire less closeness are also dismissive.

In a study of over 1,000 people, Brennan et al. (1998) administered the ECR to assess anxiety and avoidance. On the basis of this measure, approximately 21% of people fell into the dismissing cluster. Yet, across studies (as we reported earlier) we find that as many as 57% of undergraduate students report desiring less closeness over the preceding months. Given the discrepancy between estimated prevalence of dismissing attachment orientations (21%) and estimated prevalence of feeling too close (57%), it seems that individuals with dismissive attachment orientations have not cornered the market on feeling too close. Thus, it seems that feeling too close does not perfectly parallel attachment orientations. Nevertheless, as indicated by our regression results, the attachment dimensions of avoidance and anxiety certainly offer useful frameworks for understanding the desire for less closeness.

Fear of Intimacy

A construct conceptually related to feeling too close is "fear of intimacy" (see Firestone & Firestone, chap. 21, this volume, for a discussion of intimacy fears). Descutner and Thelen (1991) define fear of intimacy as "the inhibited capacity of an individual, because of anxiety, to exchange thoughts and feelings of personal significance with another individual who is highly valued" (p. 219). It seems intuitive that fear of intimacy should be related to a desire for less closeness—fear of the emotional risks and vulnerability involved in closeness could certainly cause one to desire less closeness.

Competing hypotheses come to mind regarding the association between fear of intimacy and the desire for less closeness. It could be that people who are more fearful of intimacy are the same people who desire less closeness. After all, anxiety about relationships seems to play a key role in Descunter and Thelen's (1993) conceptualization of fear of intimacy, and, as we saw earlier, attachment anxiety is predictive of the unsquared difference between desired and current closeness. Thus, we might expect a similar relationship between fear of intimacy and the desire for less closeness as exists between attachment anxiety and the desire for less closeness. Then again, it may be that people who are fearful of intimacy may actually desire more closeness. They may lack of social skills, confidence or experience required for developing and maintaining intimate relationships, but want closeness very badly. Much like the trepidation experienced by a hydrophobic individual at a pool's edge on a sweltering summer day, someone who is fearful of intimacy might like to "take the plunge" (i.e., get close) but be unable to do so out of fear.

Data from a small sample of 47 dating individuals who completed the modified IOS scales and the fear of intimacy scale (Descutner & Thelen, 1993) show that neither the unsquared ($\beta = .05$, $p = .7$) nor the squared difference ($\beta = .24$, R^2 change $= .056$, $p = .13$) between desired and current closeness significantly predicts fear of intimacy. However, the size of the beta for the squared difference, over and above the effect of the unsquared difference, is relatively large ($\beta = .24$; the non-significance apparently a function of the small sample size). A plot of the resulting equation shows a U-shape: People who want less closeness and people who want more closeness are more fearful of intimacy than people who are satisfied with their current closeness. This finding offers preliminary support for both of the competing hypotheses. It appears that people who are fearful of intimacy might actually represent at least two distinct groups.

Although people who desire less closeness may be more likely to fear intimacy, it seems reasonable to expect that not everyone who feels too close is fearful of intimacy.

It could be that characteristics of the partner or the relationship might serve as a catalyst for the desire for less closeness. For example, the partner might be especially needy or the relationship might be especially demanding time wise. Thus, even if a person is not fearful of intimacy, it is still possible to have too much of it (as a metaphor, even if a person is not fearful of water, he or she would nevertheless desire less water if his or her house were flooded).

Dimensions of Social Relating

Social absorption (the tendency to "merge" with others) and social individuation (the tendency to keep the self distinct from others) represent two surprisingly orthogonal dimensions of social relating (see Ickes, Hutchinson, & Mashek, chap. 20, this volume). People who are highly socially absorbed have a behavioral propensity to become interdependent with others. People who are highly socially individuated, on the other hand, have a propensity to maintain clear cognitive distinctions between self versus others. And, as with any two-dimensional space, individuals can be low on one dimension but high on the other.

It seems that people low on the social absorption scale might be the people who tend to desire less closeness with others. The people who are low in social absorption, as a general rule, do not behave in an interdependent fashion with those around them. Thus, closeness behaviors might be uncomfortable for low social absorption individuals because of the interdependence typical of close relationships (see Berscheid, Snyder, & Omoto, 1989). In the previous section, we argue that people who are fearful of intimacy might actually want more closeness. However, this same argument is not appropriate with respect to social relating. Unlike someone who is fearful of—but interested in—closeness, people who are lowly socially absorbed may have zero interest in closeness. Rather than "standing at the pool's edge," people who are low in social absorption are nowhere near the water.

In terms of social individuation, the second and more cognitively oriented dimension of social relating, we predict the opposite pattern as predicted for social absorption. In particular, higher social individuation should be associated with the desire for less closeness.

Participants who completed the aforementioned measure of attachment also completed the dating relationship specific version of the social orientation scale (see Ickes, Hutchinson, & Mashek, chap. 20, this volume).

The unsquared difference between desired and actual closeness significantly predicts social absorption ($\beta = -.11, p = .04$), above what is predicted by social individuation. Contrary to our expectations, people who desire less closeness actually have higher social absorption scores. This result may suggest that people who are highly socially absorbed get in over their heads in terms of behavioral interdependence. They may become so intensely socially absorbed that they desire less closeness as a means of "coming up for air."

The squared difference does not add anything to the predictive model over and above what's predicted by the unsquared difference and social individuation ($\beta = -.04, R^2$ change $= .001, p = .50$).

Neither the unsquared nor the squared difference significantly predicts social individuation (for the unsquared difference $\beta = .09, p = .11$; for the squared difference $\beta = -.01, R^2$ change $= .000, p = .844$).

To examine the interaction between social absorption and social individuation, we conducted a regression analysis to parallel the analysis conducted in the attachment section of this chapter. In particular, we predicted the Absorption × Individuation interaction term from absorption, individuation, and the unsquared difference between desired and current closeness. When controlling for both absorption and individuation, the unsquared difference score was not a significant predictor of the interaction term ($\beta = .005$, $p = .48$). Similarly, the squared difference score was not a significant predictor of the interaction term ($\beta = -.004$, R^2 change $= .000$, $p = .63$), above what is predicted by absorption, individuation, and the unsquared difference.

To summarize, absorption (but not individuation) shows a significant linear relationship with the difference between desired and actual closeness such that the most absorbed individuals are those who desire less closeness. Neither absorption nor individuation show a significant curvilinear relationship with the closeness difference. Finally, no significant relationship (linear or curvilinear) exists between the closeness difference and the interaction between absorption and individuation.

When looking at the four groups created by crossing the two dimensions of social absorption and social individuation, one group consistently stands out as unique (see Ickes et al., chap. 20, this volume). This group consists of those people who score low on the social absorption scale and high on the social individuated scale (Ickes and colleagues note that this group demonstrate an "individuated aloofness"). Compared with an average of all the other groups, these individuals are two times as likely to report feeling too close (30% compared to 15%). Given their high level of need for separateness, their threshold for intimacy may be comparatively low. Thus, they could be primed to experience relationships as too close.

Much like the other constructs discussed thus far, it seems that although the dimensions of social relating are useful in understanding the complexities of desiring less closeness, these dimensions cannot account for the totality of the phenomenon.

Risk in Intimacy

Risk in intimacy is another construct related to the desire for less closeness. Pilkington and Richardson (1988) believe that people vary in their sensitivity to the perils associated with closeness and intimacy. If this is the case (and their data suggest it is), then it's possible that people come to desire less closeness when their schemas for intimacy risk are primed. Although we are not aware of any data speaking directly to this question, Pilkington's 1989 study (as cited in Pilkington & Woods, 1999) showed a significant relationship between perceived risks in intimacy and attachment orientation. Specifically, secure individuals perceived the least risk associated with intimacy and closeness, and dismissing individuals perceived the greatest risk (preoccupied people perceived an intermediary level of risk; their data did not include the fearful category). This result, in conjunction with the idea that people who want less closeness seem to include those who are fearful of closeness and those that are dismissive of closeness, suggests that people who desire less closeness might also be the same people who perceive more risks associated with intimacy.

To summarize, existing data mapping the desire for less closeness onto other constructs suggests that our understanding this phenomenon can be enriched by considering the full constellation of psychological correlates. Similarly, exploring the differences between desired and current closeness can further enhance our understanding of these other constructs. Importantly, these data also suggest that the desire for less closeness (a time bound, relationship specific experience), although certainly related to other neighboring constructs (namely individual differences), is a unique enough an experience to justify additional empirical and theoretical exploration.

CONCLUSIONS

This chapter built on established conceptualizations of closeness to offer an operationalization of what it means to desire less closeness. The connection between closeness and interpersonal influence, or control, played a central role in this operationalization. We then extended the idea of influence into the realm of interpersonal control, presenting empirical data to support a hypothesized causal role between threat to control in close relationships and the subsequent desire for less closeness. Finally, we turned to neighboring theories and constructs to begin delineating what "too much closeness" is and is not.

Four conclusions can be drawn from this synthesis. First, not surprisingly given what clinicians and commentators on the human condition have known for decades, it is possible to desire less closeness with intimate others. Second, the desire for less closeness is a relatively common experience, occurring in as many as 57% of undergraduate dating relationships. Third, the desire for less closeness seems to be precipitated, at least in part, by threat to personal control. And, fourth, the desire for less closeness maps onto individual differences in theoretically and practically meaningful ways.

Without a doubt, many questions remain unanswered, indeed unexplored. The current discussion offers a springboard from which researchers and clinicians can pursue interest in this theoretically and practically important area. As the inquiry into the desire for less closeness continues, a more complete picture of closeness, and relationship processes more generally, will come into focus. An important next step in this area of research should be to develop models for understanding the waxing and waning of the desire for less closeness at the dyadic level. And, in doing so, special attention might be paid to identifying other causes and consequences of feeling too close.

The desire for less closeness might stem from fearing the consequences of self exposure, including anxiety regarding how the other person might experience the "real me." Previous relationship experiences with rejection and hurt might sensitize people to the risks associated with closeness. Life events, such as death in the family, health concerns, or work demands might decrease the emotional and physical resources necessary for negotiating the closeness continuum with a partner. Additionally, what role does threat to identity play in making people feel too close? Further, does the desire for less closeness precipitate for different reasons, or through different mechanisms, or with different consequences for people who are becoming close (e.g., newly established relationships) versus people who are already close (e.g., long-term relationships).

Of course, the social, cultural, and historical environments influence our expectations and experiences of closeness in relationships. The experience of feeling too close to others is likely a heterogeneous phenomenon that varies across relationships and cultures. As researchers further investigate the experience of feeling too close to others, it will be important to describe and account for similarities and differences in the experience across different personal, relationship, and cultural contexts. Similarly, do people at different levels of identity status development (Erikson, 1963) differ in their sensitivity to, recognition of, or response to feeling too close? The process of negotiating and solidifying boundaries (e.g., Katherine, 1991) may be central to the phenomenon. Additionally, future thinking and research on this topic might seek greater specificity in the various aspects of closeness (e.g., emotional sharing, physical intimacy, spiritual closeness, shared activities).

In terms of practical applications, therapists may help couples more fully explore each person's desire for closeness. Although the observable behavior of each partner may be different, oftentimes both partners are fearful of losing the relationship. Therefore, assisting couples to explore and express their own unique wishes for intimacy can be quite healing. Gaining respect and tolerance for the partner's needs and feelings is essential. The "closeness seeker" may feel quite alone and desperate, and his or her previous attempts at seeking connection may have resulted in further polarization. Important treatment goals for the intimacy seeker include finding effective means to a) solicit closeness from the partner in a nondemanding manner and b) engage in self-soothing when the bid for intimacy is rejected. The "distance seeker" may feel depleted and frustrated with the never-ending demands of his or her partner, yet feel committed to maintaining the relationship. Treatment goals for the distance seeker include learning effective means of a) challenging him or herself to give of the self even when it may be difficult, and b) learning to reject the partner's solicitations in a nonhurtful nor attacking manner.

As research into the desire for less closeness continues, we propose that a major goal should be to clearly map out the constellation of behaviors, affect, and cognitions associated with too much closeness. And, importantly, collaborative efforts between researchers and clinicians are needed to fully think through how these insights might contribute to therapy and how therapeutic insights might shape theoretical understanding.

REFERENCES

Ainsworth, M. D. S. (1969). *Maternal sensitivity scales*. From mimeograph. Johns Hopkins University. Revised 3/10/69. Accessed September 22, 2003 at http://www.psychology.sunysb.edu/attachment/pdf/mda_sens_coop.pdf

Agnew, C. R., Van Lange, P. A. M., Rusbult, C. E., & Langston, C. A.(1998). Cognitive interdependence: Commitment and the mental representation of close relationships. *Journal of Personality and Social Psychology, 74*, 939–954.

Aron, A., & Aron, E. N. (1986). *Love as the expansion of self: Understanding attraction and satisfaction*. New York: Hemisphere.

Aron, A., Aron, E. N., & Smollan, D. (1992). Inclusion of other in the self scale and the structure of interpersonal closeness. *Journal of Personality and Social Psychology, 63*, 596–612.

Bartholomew, K., & Horowitz, L. M. (1991). Attachment styles among young adults: A test of a four-category model. *Journal of Personality and Social Psychology, 61*, 226–244.

Berscheid, E., Snyder, M., & Omoto, A. M. (1989). The relationship closeness inventory: Assessing the closeness of interpersonal relationships. *Journal of Personality and Social Psychology, 75*, 792–807.

Bowlby, J. (1982). *Attachment and loss, Vol. I. Attachment* (2nd ed.). New York: Basic Books.

Bowlby, J. (1988). *A secure base: Parent–child attachment and healthy human development*. New York: Basic Books.

Brennan, K. A., Clark, C. L., & Shaver, P. R. (1998). Self-report measurement of adult attachment: An integrative overview. In J. A. Simpson & W. S. Rholes (Eds.), *Attachment theory and close relationships* (pp. 46–76). New York: Guilford.

Brewer, M. B. (1993). The role of distinctiveness in social identity and group behavior. In J. A. Hogg & D. Abrams (Eds.) *Group motivation: Social psychological perspectives*. London: Harvester Wheatsheaf.

Brewer, M. B., & Pickett, C. L. (1999). Distinctiveness motives as a source of the social self. In T. R. Tyler & R. M. Kramer (Eds.), *The psychology of the social self*. Mahwah, NJ: Lawrence Erlbaum Associates.

Cameron, J. (November, 1985). Fighting the urge to merge. *Harper's Bazaar*, p. 106+.

Christensen, A. (1988a). Detection of conflict patterns in couples. In K. Hahlweg & M. J. Goldstein (Eds.), *Understanding major mental disorders: The construction of family interaction research*. (pp. 250–265). New York: Family Process Press.

Christensen, A. (1988b). Dysfunctional interaction patterns in couples. In P. Noller & M. A. Fitzpatrick (Eds.), *Perspectives on Marital Interaction*. (pp. 31–52). Clevedon, England: Multilingual Matters.

Christensen, A., & Jacobson, N. S. (2000). *Reconcilable differences*. New York: Guilford.

Davis, M. J., & Bibace, R. (1999). Dating couples and their relationships: Intimacy and contraceptive use. *Adolescence, 34*, 1–7.

Descutner, C. J., & Thelen, M. H. (1991). Development and validation of a fear-of-intimacy scale. *Psychological assessment: A journal of consulting and clinical psychology, 3*, 218–225.

Erikson, E. (1963). *Childhood and society*. (2nd ed.). New York: Norton.

Eshel, Y., Sharabany, R., & Friedman, U. (1998). Friends, lovers and spouses: Intimacy in young adults. *British Journal of Social Psychology, 37*, 41–57.

French, J. R. P., & Raven, B. H. (1959). The bases of social power. In D. Cartwright (Ed.), *Studies in social power*. Ann Arbor, MI: University of Michigan Press.

Gibran, K. (1923). *The Prophet*. New York: Random House.

Jacobson, N. S., (1989). The politics of intimacy. *The behavior therapist, 12*, 29–32.

Katherine, A. (1991). *Boundaries: Where you end and I begin*. New York: Hazelden.

Kenny, D. A. (1994). *Interpersonal perception: A social relations analysis*. New York: Guilford.

Laiken, D. (March 1983). Privacy vs. intimacy: How close can you get and still breathe? *Glamour*, p. 238+.

Larrieu, J. A., & Leibsohn, M. (1988, April). Actual and expected intimacy in dating couples. Paper presented at the 68th Annual Meeting of the Western Psychological Association, Burlingame, California.

Lerner, H. G. (1985). *The dance of anger*. New York: Harper & Row.

Lips, H. M. (1991). *Women, men, and power*. Mountain View, CA: Mayfield Publishing.

Mashek, D. & Aron, A. (under review). Threat to control and the desire for less closeness.

Napier, A. Y. (1978). The rejection-intrusion pattern: A central family dynamic. *Journal of Marriage and Family Counseling, 4*, 5–12.

Pence, E., & Shepard, M. (1988). Integrating feminist theory and practice: The challenge of the battered women's movement. In K. Ylloe, & M. Bograd (Eds.), *Feminist perspectives on wife abuse* (pp. 282–298). Newbury Part, CA: Sage.

Pilkington, C. J., & Richardson, D. R. (1988). Perceptions of risk in intimacy. *Journal of Social and Personal Relationships, 5*, 503–508.

Pilkington, C. J., & Woods, S. P. (1999). Risk in intimacy as a chronically accessible schema. *Journal of Social and Personal Relationships, 16*, 259–263.

Ryan, R. M., & Deci, E. L. (2000). Self-determination theory and the facilitation of intrinsic motivation, social development, and well-being. *American Psychologist, 55*, 68–78.

Schaefer, M. T., & Olson, D. H. (1981). Assessing intimacy: The PAIR inventory. *Journal of Marital and Family Therapy, 7*, 47–60.

Stets, J. E. (1995). Modeling control in relationships. *Journal of Marriage and the Family, 57*, 489–501.

Stierlin, H. (1976). The dynamics of owning and disowning: Psychoanalytic and family perspectives. *Family Process, 15*, 277–289.

20

Closeness as Intersubjectivity: Social Absorption and Social Individuation

William Ickes and Joanna Hutchison
University of Texas at Arlington
Debra Mashek
George Mason University

A personal relationship, in order to qualify as such, must be more than merely subjective. It must be intersubjective. At the very least, the participants in the relationship must be aware of each other. They must also acknowledge that some kind of relationship exists between them. If these minimal intersubjective criteria are not met, one person might believe that he or she has a personal relationship with the other, whereas from the other's standpoint this belief is the stuff of fantasy or delusion, rather than reality.

To be sure, the illusion of intersubjectivity can foster the corollary illusion that a personal relationship exists when in fact one does not. If Hector spends all of his free time surfing the Internet for any news, images, or music featuring Jennifer Lopez, his increasing knowledge of and "involvement" with her might eventually be viewed as a "personal relationship" within Hector's fantasy-steeped mind. But if Jennifer has never heard of Hector and doesn't acknowledge any relationship with him, then Hector is a nonentity as far as she is concerned.[1] Similarly, although Lucinda may have read every word that Nicholas Evans (*The Horse Whisperer*) has ever published, her sense that she has developed a personal relationship with an author who knows nothing of her existence is also based on an illusion. Indeed, the only possible exception

---

[1] Lest the reader think that such examples are not found in everyday life, a friend of D. Mashek's told her about a listserv devoted to discussing Playboy Playmates. He said that it is not uncommon for one or more of the men on the listserv to proclaim that Miss October (choose your own month) is his "best friend" and that he "knows all about her." Apparently, such men can get very defensive if anyone is critical of their "best friend." We presume that most of the monthly Misses have never heard of these guys.

to such cases requires the supernatural assumption that the absent Other can actually read one's mind, as when a religious convert professes to have developed "a personal relationship with Jesus Christ."

To put it simply, true relationships demand intersubjectivity. Individual subjectivity is never enough. For example, Duard may fervently believe that Trixie was destined to be his soulmate, and that it was her image that has haunted his dreams since his early adolescence. However, unless he attempts with some success to convince Trixie of these "facts," they will remain little more than a subjective reality for Duard himself. Much to his chagrin, they will fail to define an agreed-upon, intersubjective reality that Duard and Trixie can share as a couple. Moreover, to the extent that perceptions of closeness within a relationship depend upon the degree of intersubjectivity that each partner perceives, Duard may eventually be forced to conclude that Trixie will never share his vision of the two of them as soulmates, and that she will never feel as close to him as he does to her.[2] Intersubjectivity, then, is more than two people's mutual awareness of each other's existence; it is the extent to which they share—and agree that they share—a common interpretation of events that lie within their joint experience.

Intersubjectivity is an important basis for the development of intimacy within a relationship. It is important because intimacy—the extent to which the partners share knowledge regarding each other's personally meaningful and emotionally charged experiences—will typically not develop until both partners feel assured that they have already established a "common ground" understanding that is not likely to break down or betray them when such idiosyncratic insights, confidences, and vulnerabilities are revealed. And intimacy, in turn, begets feelings of closeness, which—according to our definition—are the affectively tinged judgments that partners make about the current level of intimacy in their relationship. Implicit in these judgments, we would argue, are corresponding assessments of the levels of intersubjectivity and mutual trust that underlie and sustain that level of intimacy.

Although most people attain a sense of closeness through the development of genuine intersubjectivity in their personal relationships, there are at least some people who, like Hector and Lucinda, will settle for a sense of closeness that is based on the illusion, rather than the fact, of intersubjectivity. Even sadder than those people, however, are the ones who seem to be averse to intersubjectivity and the sense of closeness it entails. These individuals, who hold themselves apart from others and resist becoming cognitively and behaviorally interdependent with them, offer what is perhaps the most poignant illustration of the central thesis of this chapter: that genuine closeness depends upon intersubjectivity and can rarely be sustained in its absence.

In the present chapter, we explore the links between intersubjectivity and perceptions of closeness in personal relationships. We begin by noting the similarities in various philosophical and psychological conceptions of intersubjectivity. We then consider the two major dimensions—social absorption and social individuation—that appear to underlie the different modes of relating to others, and that enable us to achieve a broader theoretical integration. Next, using an individual difference approach, we examine some preliminary research findings that are relevant to the different modes of social relating, and we then go on to consider the implications of these

---

[2] These asymmetries in the subjective relationships of self and other can have strange effects on the dynamics of the objective relationship. For example, people entering a new relationship often spend a great deal of time playing out in their fantasies possible interaction scenarios with the other person. These directed ruminations can contribute to a weirdness in the objective relationship when the "dreamer" subsequently interacts with the other as if the fantasized events (e.g., tender words and looks) have actually occurred. Such asymmetries in the partners' respective "subjective relationships" can offer quite a challenge to establishing a true intersubjectivity.

findings for relationship closeness. In particular, we identify a category of individuals who seem to be so averse to closeness that they actively shun it, and we conclude by sketching a tentative psychological profile of these individuals.

PHILOSOPHICAL AND PSYCHOLOGICAL CONCEPTIONS OF INTERSUBJECTIVITY

Philosophical Conceptions

Certain philosophers were the first to propose that there are at least two fundamentally different modes of relating to other people. Perhaps the most widely acknowledged of these philosophers is Buber (1970), who, in his book *I and Thou*, contrasted an "I–It" mode of relating with an "I–Thou" mode of relating. According to Buber, the first mode is one in which I maintain my separateness from other people and relate to them more as objects of my own consciousness than as individuals whose subjectivity is as real and important as my own. In contrast, the second mode is one in which I am so fully engaged and interdependent with others that we are able to transcend our individual subjectivities and have a genuinely intersubjective experience instead.

As the philosopher Crossley has noted, Buber was only one of a number of philosophers who have made a conceptually similar distinction. These philosophers, who also include Husserl (1960, 1970), Merleau-Ponty (1962, 1964), Sartre (1956), and Schutz (1967, 1970), have all observed that genuine intersubjectivity is different from other modes of social relating. In his book *Intersubjectivity: The Fabric of Social Becoming*, Crossley (1996) attempted to synthesize the thinking of these philosophical predecessors by proposing what he regards as a fundamental contrast between the mode of "egological intersubjectivity" and the mode of "radical intersubjectivity."

According to Crossley (1996), in the mode of *egological intersubjectivity* the ego (i.e., one's subjective point of view) is always interposed between the self and the other person. I try to understand the other by empathically "putting myself in the other's place," but in doing so I aspire merely to create a model of the other's subjective experience that is based on my own subjective experience; I do not attempt to apprehend the other's experience more directly. When I relate to others within this "egological" mode, I tend to regard them as constructed "social objects" whose inner lives are defined by their objective attributes and their social-category memberships. In other words, I tend to relate to the other as a mental representation—as a personality type, a social-category member, or a role-occupant—instead of experiencing the other's subjectivity through an intersubjective exchange. It is, perhaps, not too much of an oversimplification to say that I relate to my image or mental construction of the other person rather than to the other person's subjectivity (i.e., as it is "glimpsed" or apprehended throughout our intersubjective exchange).

In contrast, in the mode of *radical intersubjectivity* I am highly engaged and interdependent with the other person. During the time we interact together in this mode, we effectively transcend the self-other distinction and experience ourselves as constituting what Merleau-Ponty (1962) has called "an intersubjective system." In doing so, we no longer relate merely to our image or mental construction of each other, but instead experience each other's subjectivity more directly through our intersubjective exchange. Citing Merleau-Ponty, Crossley has described this intersubjective experience as one in which "a 'common ground' is constituted between self and other; they are 'woven into a single fabric' [in which] . . . 'perspectives blend' into a shared 'common world'. We grasp the other's thoughts 'the moment they come into being'" (Crossley, 1996, p. 33).

Of these two modes of relating to others, egological intersubjectivity might appear to be the more unnatural—treating other people, for example, as specific exemplars of a personality type, a social category, or a social role. However, Crossley (1996) has argued that we do this in our everyday life whenever we treat a waiter or a cashier as just a role-occupant—someone whose function is merely to take an order and bring food or to accept our payment and give us a receipt. A more extreme example is the bigot who sees another person as an abstraction—i.e., as a "deviant" individual whose subjective experience is not seriously considered—rather than seeing a unique human being whose subjective experience must be respected and taken into account. Perhaps the most extreme example is the solipsist, the person who acts as if other people have no subjective experience and are merely constructions or projections of the solipsist's own mind.

By contrast, radical intersubjectivity does not seem so radical at all. Indeed, it seems to be the more natural way to relate to others—accepting that their subjectivity is as real and valid as one's own and cooperating with them to create an "intersubjective system" that encompasses and transcends the subjective experience of the individual participants. We should keep in mind, however, that egological intersubjectivity and radical intersubjectivity might be theoretical end points on a continuum that could include more mixed and intermediate forms of social relating. These mixed and intermediate forms might be evident, for example, when we at one moment treat the bus driver as a mere role occupant who takes our change and drives us to our destination, but in the next moment ask him about his family and sympathize with him about his financial problems.

Psychological Conceptions

Not surprisingly, social psychologists have also theorized about the different modes of social relating. In particular, Zimbardo (1969) has contrasted the mode of *individuation* with the mode of *deindividuation*; A. Aron and his colleagues (1992, 1997) have contrasted a mode of *low self-expansion* with a mode of *high self-expansion* in which the other is "included in the self"; and Ickes (2002) has contrasted a mode of *subjective social cognition* with one of *intersubjective social cognition*. Interestingly, these psychological conceptions not only appear to have much in common with each other but also reveal some intriguing points of convergence with the philosophical conceptions reviewed above.

Zimbardo (1969) has characterized individuation as a psychological state in which the social identities and distinguishing characteristics of the participants are clearly evident. In this state, it is easy to construct cognitive representations that differentiate self and other as individuals who have their own separate identities, roles, and unique responsibilities. It is also relatively easy to resist becoming cognitively and behaviorally interdependent with the other in a way that blurs this perception of separate identities, roles, and responsibilities. The state of individuation contrasts strongly with the state of deindividuation, which Zimbardo characterizes in polar-opposite terms. In this state, individual identities and distinguishing characteristics are *not* clearly evident. The participants feel anonymous and lose sight of their separate identities, roles, and responsibilities. They experience a kind of intersubjective "merging" with each other in which the boundary between self and other tends to dissolve as the level of cognitive and behavioral interdependence increases.

The idea of an intersubjective merging has actually been validated empirically in the self-expansion research of A. Aron and his colleagues (Aron & Aron, 1997; Aron, A. Aron, E. N., & Smollan, 1992). In their studies of the changes that take place when heterosexual partners first fall in love, they have found that a "cognitive confounding" of self and other begins to occur, such that characteristics of the self and characteristics of the partner tend to become so closely associated in both partners' memories that they are demonstrably confused during memory retrieval tasks. The self-concepts of the partners appear to expand to include each other in a way that suggests the development of Merleau-Ponty's (1962) intersubjective system—a system that both encompasses and transcends the partners' individual identities. Similar to Zimbardo's (1969) theory, the self-expansion model contrasts a subjective mode of social relating, in which individual identities are separate and distinct, with an intersubjective mode of social relating, in which the self/other distinction tends to dissolve as the level of cognitive and behavioral interdependence increases.

A similar contrast is evident in the distinction that Ickes (2002) has made between subjective social cognition and intersubjective social cognition. According to Ickes, subjective social cognition is the product of remembered, imagined, or anticipated social interaction rather than real, ongoing social interaction. It occurs in only one person's head and is therefore entirely subjective. As a form of social cognition, it is relatively detached and egocentric, making it more susceptible to fantasy and projective bias. And because it relies heavily on stereotypes and abstractions, it leads us to view others as being compelled by their social identities, roles, and personal attributes to think and act the way that they do. It also leads us to attempt to construe or construct other people's subjectivity rather than enabling us to experience it more directly through an intersubjective exchange.

In contrast, intersubjective social cognition is the product of real, ongoing social interaction. It is intersubjective as well as subjective. It is less susceptible to fantasy and projective bias. And because it occurs when we are engaged with others in an intersubjective system of interdependent cognition and behavior, it enables us to apprehend the other's subjectivity as it aligns with and "blends into" our own. It also enables us to appreciate others as being capable of greater self-determination, of being able to transcend their ascribed identities, roles, and attributes to think and act in novel and unexpected ways. And in contrast to subjective social cognition, which requires us to construe or construct the other's subjectivity, intersubjective social cognition enables us to apprehend the other's subjectivity more directly through its contribution to the intersubjective exchange.

In general, we experience subjective social cognition when we are not interacting with others, and we experience intersubjective social cognition when we are interacting with them. As Ickes (2002) has suggested, however, dispositional influences may moderate, or even override, the situational influence of being alone or in interaction with others. For example, a person who is self-absorbed and solipsistic could experience egological intersubjectivity and subjective social cognition even during face-to-face interactions with others. In contrast, a person who is needy and interdependence-seeking could—like Hector and Lucinda—experience a fantasized version of radical intersubjectivity and intersubjective social cognition even while alone.

Similarities in the Various Conceptions of Intersubjectivity

Although the differences in these various conceptions of intersubjectivity are certainly of interest, in the present chapter we are primarily concerned with their points of conceptual overlap and similarity. In all of these conceptions, at least two modes of social relating are posited. One of these modes is characterized by (a) a relatively strong distinction between self and other (i.e., one that entails the perception of self and other as separate individuals who each have their own unique identities, roles, and attributes); (b) a relatively low level of behavioral interdependence; and (c) a lack of the experiential sense of having "merged" with the other. In contrast, the other mode is characterized by (a) a relatively weak distinction between self and other,

(b) a relatively high level of behavioral interdependence, and (c) the experiential sense of having "merged" with the other.

DIMENSIONS OF SOCIAL RELATING: SOCIAL ABSORPTION AND SOCIAL INDIVIDUATION

Given the commonality of these distinctions across the various philosophical and psychological conceptions, the first author decided to try to capture them in a set of self-report items. The goal of this effort was to determine whether such items might be used to assess individual differences in the propensity to relate to others through either the first or the second of the two contrasting modes.

To this end, some items were written to assess the strength of the respondent's self—other distinction ("In my interactions with others, I have a clear and definite sense of the difference between my perspective and theirs," "I like to have a clear sense of who I am dealing with, and of how that person is different from me."). Other items were written to assess the respondent's overall level of behavioral interdependence ("In conversations, the things I say are so interconnected with the things my partner says that I don't even try to separate them," "It's easy for me to get so caught up in a conversation with someone that I lose all track of time."). And still other items were written to assess the respondent's predisposition to "merge" with others ("It's easy for me to get 'in synch' with other people and to 'merge' with them during the time we're together," "I like the experience of merging with others and becoming part of something larger than myself.")

Social Absorption and Social Individuation as Independent Factors

Surprisingly, when Hutchison and Ickes (1999) conducted an exploratory factor analysis of these items in data collected from an initial sample of 437 respondents, they found evidence for two, rather than three, underlying factors (see Table 20.1). The first factor, labeled *social absorption* (SA), concerns the degree to which the respondent tends to "merge" with others, becoming absorbed into the intersubjective system ("I tend to get completely absorbed in my interactions with other people," "I can get so absorbed in a conversation or shared activity with someone that I forget about everything else."). The second factor, labeled *social individuation* (SI), concerns the degree to which the respondent tends to distinguish self from others ("I like I like to have a clear sense of who I am dealing with, and of how that person is different from me," "I like to maintain a clear distinction between myself and others when I interact with them.")

When Hutchison and Ickes collected data on their 18-item social orientation scale (SOS) from four new samples, their confirmatory factor analyses repeatedly confirmed that this two-factor solution best accounted for the total factor variance, and that the factors of social absorption and social individuation were almost perfectly orthogonal. The correlations between SA and SI ranged from $-.08$ to $.05$ across the five samples, with an average correlation of $.00$. In addition, the internal consistencies of both factors were acceptable in all five samples, with an average alpha for the 9-item SA subscale of $.77$ and an average alpha for the 9-item SI subscale of $.72$.

Taken together, the results from the first five samples (combined $N = 1,711$ respondents) revealed that SA and SI are two independent dimensions of social relating. This outcome was neither expected nor guaranteed. As noted above, a plausible alternative possibility was that three modestly correlated factors might emerge: one measuring the strength of the self–other distinction, one measuring the degree of behavioral interdependence, and one measuring the degree to which the experience of "merging" is reported. A second plausible alternative possibility was that only a single common factor might emerge, one that contrasted an egological intersubjective mode

TABLE 20.1

Items Loading on the Social Absorption (SA) and Social Individuation (SI) Factors (Sample 1 Data)

Factor 1: Social Absorption (Items 1, 3, 5, 7, 9, 10, 12, 14, 17)

.68 I tend to get completely absorbed in my interactions with other people. (I3)
.68 I can get so absorbed in a conversation or a shared activity with someone that I forget everything else. (I9)
.66 It's easy for me to get so caught up in a conversation with someone that I lose all track of time. (I1)
.65 I like the experience of merging with others and becoming part of something larger than myself. (I17)
.64 In my social relationships, I experience such a strong sense of connection and sharing that I think in terms of "we" rather than in terms of "me" and "you." (I5)
.61 It's easy for me to get "in synch" with other people and to "merge" with them during the time we're together. (I7)
.61 I feel comfortable opening up to other people and sharing experiences with them. (I14)
.57 I have such a strong sense of rapport with others that I can assume without question that we understand each other. (I10)
.46 In conversations, the things I say are so interconnected with the things my partner says that I don't even try to separate them. (I12)

Factor 2: Social Individuation (Items 2, 4, 6, 8, 11, 13, 15, 16, 18)

.68 I like to have a clear sense of who I am dealing with, and of how that person is different from me. (I11)
.65 I like to maintain a clear distinction between myself and others when I interact with them. (I8)
.64 It's important to me to have a distinct sense of my own identity and to know how it differs from that of other people. (I4)
.61 As a person, I have clearcut boundaries and I expect other people to respect them. (I18)
.57 In my interactions with others, I have a clear and definite sense of the difference between my perspective and theirs. (I2)
.57 When I interact with other people, I am aware of the "invisible barrier" that separates us. (I13)
.54 In conversations with others, I am very aware of the thoughts and feelings I should keep to myself. (I15)
.52 It's easy for me to keep track of what I contribute and what the other person contributes to a discussion. (I6)
.51 I tend to stay absorbed in my own thoughts and feelings, even in social situations. (I16)

of relating to others (strong self–other distinction, low interdependence, weak sense of "merging") with a radical intersubjective mode (weak self/other distinction, high interdependence, strong sense of "merging").

Hutchison and Ickes's data were clear and unequivocal, however, in identifying SA and SI as two orthogonal dimensions of social relating. It is useful to note that the first dimension, SA, appears to reflect the respondent's *behavioral* propensity to merge and become interdependent with others, whereas the second dimension, SI, appears to reflect the respondent's *cognitive* propensity to maintain a strong distinction between the identities, perspectives, and attributes of self versus others.

A Revised Theoretical Framework: Four Modes of Social Relating

Given the conceptual independence of SA and SI in the self-report data, Ickes and Hutchison (2000) wondered if these two orthogonal dimensions could provide the

Social Absorption

		Low	High
Social Individuation	**Low**	**Anonymous Independence** Anomie	**Deindividuated Merging** Radical intersubjectivity Deindividuation Including the other in the self
	High	**Individuated Aloofness** I-It relationship Egological intersubjectivity Objectifying self and other	**Individuated Interdependence** Working relationship Respectful cooperation

FIG. 20.1. Four modes of social relating.

basis for a revised theoretical framework in which the earlier philosophical and psychological conceptions might be integrated. The interesting complication, of course, is that a theoretical framework based on two orthogonal dimensions would result in four modes of social relating instead of just two. What are these four modes of social relating? And what implications do they have for our understanding of closeness and intimacy?

Our current interpretation of these four modes is depicted in Figure 20.1. *Anonymous independence* is the label we have given to the upper-left mode, in which social individuation and social absorption are both low. Although this mode was not identified by the various theorists noted above, it does seem to correspond to what the sociologists have termed *anomie*. Anomie is the experience of living anonymously and in relative independence from others. In this mode, individuals do not become absorbed in their interactions with others, and self and others remain relatively anonymous and deindividuated. According to sociologists, this anomic mode of relating to others is characterized by impersonal interactions of the sort that strangers typically have.

Individuated aloofness is the label we have assigned to the lower-left mode, in which social individuation is high but social absorption is low. In terms of the theoretical distinctions we have discussed, this mode best exemplifies Buber's (1970) "I-It" relationship and Crossley's (1996) egological intersubjectivity. In this mode, people individuate self and others in terms of their cognitive representations. At the same time, however, they resist any involvement with each other that could result in a high level of behavioral interdependence and the intersubjective experience of "merging." According to Buber, individuals in this mode tend to objectify others as a means of maintaining distance and separation from them. According to Sartre (1956), the need to objectify others derives from a fear that others might do the same to you, thereby turning you into a social object that they can analyze and attempt to manipulate and control.

Deindividuated merging is our label for the upper-right mode, in which social individuation is low but social absorption is high. This is the mode that Crossley (1996) calls *radical intersubjectivity*, Zimbardo (1969) calls *deindividuation*, and Aron and colleagues

(1992) call *including the other in the self.* In this mode, self and other participate in what Merleau-Ponty (1962) has described as an intersubjective system. The distinction between self and other blurs and dissolves as intersubjectivity supersedes individual subjectivity. According to Aron and Aron (1997), this mode of relating often gives rise to the exhilarating perception that one's self has expanded to include the other (and vice versa). It is as if the separate pronouns *you* and *I* have ceased to be as relevant as the single pronoun *we.*

Finally, *individuated interdependence* is the label we have assigned to the lower-right mode, in which social individuation and social absorption are both high. In this mode, self and other retain a clear sense of their differences as individuals, but they are still able to become absorbed in their interaction with each other. Their behavior is therefore highly interdependent. However, their sense of merging must be incomplete because the distinction between self and other does not blur and dissolve, but remains intact. We suggest, somewhat speculatively, that this mode of social relating is the one used most often with nonintimates. That is, it represents the typical mode in which we relate to our neighbors in the community and our colleagues at work—a mode in which we engage in cooperative, interdependent interaction with them but never fail to respect the self–other boundaries imposed by our different identities, roles, commitments, and obligations.

Clearly, our revised theoretical framework incorporates the two modes of social relating that have been emphasized by previous theorists: egological intersubjectivity and radical intersubjectivity. However, it complements them with two additional modes: the mode of deindividuated isolation that sociologists have called *anomie,* and the mode of individuated interdependence that appears to be our typical way of relating to our fellow citizens, neighbors, and coworkers.

But if two modes of social relating aren't sufficient, are four modes really enough? Probably not. We suspect that our four-mode typology is a transitional one, and that it will eventually be superseded by a more inclusive typology that delineates even more of these modes. For the present, however, the four-mode typology seems to be heuristic and worthy of further exploration, particularly given the apparent orthogonality of its two underlying dimensions. So, in the research described below, we examine both the correlates of these two underlying dimensions and the four modes of social relating that these dimensions imply.

PRELIMINARY RESEARCH FINDINGS

Correlates of Social Absorption and Social Individuation

To gain a better understanding of SA and SI as personality constructs, Hutchison and Ickes (1999) correlated respondents' SA and SI scores with their scores on several other personality measures. The resulting correlations are presented in Table 20.2, where they are organized in terms of the samples from which they were drawn.

In Sample 1, we found that the respondents' scores on our measure of social individuation (SI) were completely uncorrelated (.00) with their scores on Maslach, Stapp, and Santee's (1985) individuation scale. This is an important finding from the standpoint of discriminant validity, because Maslach et al.'s individuation scale assesses people's need to stand out behaviorally and become the center of attention in social situations, whereas our SI measure assesses their need to cognitively differentiate self from other. Despite the fact that the word "individuation" appears in the name of both scales, the two scales clearly measure very different types of individuation (i.e., the need to attract other people's attention versus the need to differentiate between self and other).

TABLE 20.2

Personality Correlates of Social Absorption (SA) and Social
Individuation (SI) for the Individual Respondents in Hutchison
and Ickes' (1999) Samples

Sample	SA	SI
1 (N = 437)		
Individuation Scale (Maslach et al., 1985)	−.28***	.00
2 (N = 253)		
Extraversion	.40***	−.13*
Agreeableness	.36***	−.14*
Conscientiousness	−.11	.16*
Neuroticism	.20**	.00
Openness	.26***	.04
Impulsivity	.33***	−.12
Anxious attachment style	.26***	−.08
Avoidant attachment style	−.41***	.27***
6 (N = 32)		
Extraversion	.53**	.11
Agreeableness	.38*	.09
Conscientiousness	.21	.31†
Neuroticism	.29†	−.09
Openness	.56***	.34*

†$p < .10$, *$p < .05$, **$p < .01$, ***$p < .001$

On the other hand, we found that the same respondents' scores on Maslach et al.'s individuation scale were negatively correlated (−.28) with their scores on our measure of social absorption (SA). This correlation is also important, but from the standpoint of offering convergent validity evidence for our measure of SA. Why? Because high SA people should desire to blend in and merge with others, and this desire should be antithetical to the need to set themselves apart from others and become the center of attention.

In Samples 2 and 6, we found that social absorption was positively correlated with *extraversion, agreeableness, openness to experience, impulsivity, neuroticism,* and *anxious attachment,* but was negatively correlated with *avoidant attachment.* Viewed as a whole, this pattern of correlations suggests that high SA individuals are people who are exceptionally open to social experience—people who actively (and perhaps impulsively) seek to affiliate and "merge" with others in an agreeable way. The data further hint that their desire to blend in and merge with others may in part be attributable to a somewhat neurotic and anxious attachment style.

In contrast, the only replicable personality correlate of social individuation in both samples was its positive correlation with conscientiousness. This finding suggests that high SI individuals—people who strongly distinguish self from others—may have a general tendency to "sort, order, and categorize" the various people and things with whom they come in contact. Indeed, the apparent need of high SI individuals to keep things separate and in their proper place might help to account for the evidence of their avoidant attachment style in the Sample 2 data. Quite simply, high SI individuals might prefer to keep other people separate, and to avoid "getting mixed up" with them.

The Four Modes of Social Relating: A Dyadic Interaction Study

Having examined the personality correlates of SA and SI as independent dimensions, we next examined the four modes of social relating that these dimensions imply. Extending our individual difference approach, Hutchison (1999) used her participants' pretest data to create four different dyad types to study during their initial, unstructured interactions. Extreme scorers, rather than those who merely scored above or below the medians on the SA and SI dimensions, were recruited by telephone to participate as the members of these four dyad types.

The first dyad type was composed of same-sex (male–male or female–female) strangers who were both low in SA and low in SI (low SA–low SI dyads). The second dyad type was composed of same-sex strangers who were both low in SA but high in SI (low SA–high SI dyads). The third dyad type was composed of same-sex strangers who were both high in SA but low in SI (high SA–low SI dyads). And the fourth dyad type was composed of same-sex strangers who were both high in SA and high in SI (high SA–high SI dyads). There were twelve pairs of strangers in each of the four dyad types, with male-male and female-female pairs represented about equally.

When the members of each dyad reported for the study, the experimenter seated them together on a couch in a large lab room and asked them to wait there for a few minutes until she returned. A hidden video camera unobtrusively recorded their initial interaction during the six-minute period while she was away. When she returned to the lab, she probed for suspicion, explained the necessity of doing the videotaping without the dyad members' prior knowledge, and then asked for their signed consent to allow us to use the videotape as a source of data in her study.

It was at this point that something unusual happened—something we had not previously observed in over twenty years of conducting dyadic interaction research using the same procedure. As usual, the majority of the participants had no problem with the covert videotaping once the experimenter had explained that it was necessary in order to avoid biasing their spontaneous interaction behavior. However, several of the dyad members in the low SA–high SI condition reacted in a highly unexpected way, by strongly (and in some cases, emotionally) protesting our videotaping procedure. Despite the fact that all participants had been warned earlier that certain information might be withheld from them in order to avoid biasing their responses during the study, these low SA–high SI participants were visibly upset that we had captured their behavior on videotape without their prior knowledge.

Even in these cases, the experimenter was ultimately successful in calming the participants down and obtaining their signed consent to allow us to use their tape (given her repeated assurances that no one but the members of our research team would ever see it). Still, the reactions displayed by these low SA–high SI participants were dramatically indicative of what Sartre has described as the fear of becoming an object for others. Indeed, the protesting participants expressed this fear quite directly, assaulting the experimenter with one anxious question after another about the possible uses to which the videotape of their interaction might be put. In these people, as in almost no others previously, our covert videotaping procedure had obviously touched a nerve. It seemed clear to us that the low SA–high SI people were expressing what Crossley (1996) has described as "a paranoid sense of being objectified from the outside and of losing the ability to determine the meaning of their own actions" (p. 61).

It was, in retrospect, quite fortunate that Hutchison recognized the importance of the fact that this paranoid-like behavior was limited primarily to low SA–high SI participants. Because her data revealed few behavioral differences among the four dyad types on measures such as the amount of talking, gazing, gesturing, and smiling, she decided to ask our undergraduate research assistants to view each videotape and make subjective ratings of the degree to which each of the dyad members seemed wary and suspicious during their interaction. Her goal was to see whether the paranoid-like reactions she had observed in the low SA–high SI participants during the post-interaction debriefing would also be evident in the videotaped interaction itself.

And the answer was: they were. Observer-rated suspiciousness was found to be uniquely high in the low SA–high SI dyads, compared to the other three dyad types. Our own strong impression upon viewing the videotapes of their interactions was consistent with that of our undergraduate raters: the low SA–high SI participants seemed to display a kind of "social paranoia" that led them to regard each other, as strangers, with evident wariness and suspicion. "Who *is* this person?" they each seemed to be asking themselves. "And do I really want to get involved with him/her?"

This finding raises a number of questions. Just how generalizable is this kind of reaction in low SA–high SI individuals? Is it only strangers whom they hold "at arm's length," or do they treat their so-called intimates in a similar way? How, for example, would low SA–high SI individuals characterize their perceptions and feelings about their relationship with their own current dating partners? Would they tend to hold these people "at arm's length" as well?[3]

The Four Modes of Social Relating: Two Studies of Dating Respondents

These questions were addressed in studies conducted by Debra Mashek and her colleagues at the State University of New York at Stony Brook. Mashek administered a relationship-specific version of Ickes and Hutchison's (1998) social orientation scale (SOS) to two independent samples of students who were involved in close relationships at the time of testing. The items for the relationship-specific version of the SOS emphasized interactions with the partner, rather than interactions with people more generally. For example, the first item from the original scale reads, "It's easy for me to get so caught up in a conversation with someone that I lose all track of time." The revised item reads, "It's easy for me to get so caught up in a conservation with my partner that I lose all track of time."

Findings From the First Study. Mashek's (2002) first study sought to determine whether the constellation of behaviors and cognitions displayed by low SA–high SI individuals in the context of stranger relationships is also present in intimate relationships. In particular, she wanted to see whether the low SA–high SI individuals would exhibit the wariness and suspicion in their dating relationships that Hutchison had observed in her laboratory study of initial same-sex interactions. To explore this possibility, 128 respondents (79 women and 49 men) were asked to complete the dating-partners version of the SA and SI subscales. They were also asked to complete relationship-relevant measures of commitment (Rusbult, 1983), satisfaction (Hendrick, 1988), passionate love (Hatfield & Sprecher, 1986), and attachment style (Bartholomew & Horowitz, 1991).

Interestingly, the SA and SI subscales were slightly negatively correlated with each other in this sample, $r = -.21$ ($p < .05$). That this relationship exists when focusing

---

[3] Another question left unanswered by Hutchison's (1999) study concerns the extent to which the reactions observed in the low SA–high SI dyads reflected an "actor effect" as opposed to a "partner effect" (cf. Campbell and Kashy, 2002). The answer to this important question must await the results of a study in which the SA/SI typology of one dyad member is varied independently of that of his or her interaction partner. The most we can say about the findings from Hutchison's study is that dyads in which both partners have low SA–high SI status are distinctive in the high degree of "social paranoia" that their members display.

explicitly on dating relationships, but does not exist when looking at stranger relationships, may suggest a difference between intersubjectivity in close relationships and in relationships with strangers. This difference warrants exploration in future research.

Of primary interest to us were the relationships between SA and SI and closeness. To assess closeness, Mashek administered the inclusion of other in self scale (IOS; Aron, Aron, & Smollan, 1992). The IOS is a single-item pictorial measure consisting of seven pairs of circles, each pair overlapping slightly more than the preceding pair. One of the circles is labeled *self* and the other circle is labeled *other*. The amount of overlap between the two circles ranges from barely touching to almost completely overlapped (see Aron & Mashek, chap. 4, this volume). Each respondent completed the IOS two times—once for current closeness ("Which pair of circles best describes your current relationship with your partner?") and once for desired closeness ("Which pair of circles best describes your desired relationship with your partner?").

Not surprisingly, the respondents' social absorption scores correlated moderately and positively with their perceptions of both current and desired closeness (.36 and .35, respectively). The relationship between social absorption and closeness (whether actual or desired) makes sense, given that both constructs emphasize a sense of merging and "becoming one." In fact, Aron and his colleagues (1992) devised the IOS scale as a means of tapping into the idea of "including other in self," and it was intended to serve as a visual metaphor for "becoming one" with the other.

It is also not surprising that the respondents' social individuation scores correlated negatively with their perceptions of both current and desired closeness (−.26 and −.22 respectively). The more that an individual makes a strong distinction between self and partner (as measured by the SI subscale), the less does that same individual report feeling close to the partner. Importantly, the pattern and strength of the correlations between the closeness measures and each dimension of the SOS hold up even when controlling for the other dimension. Thus, even though the dating-relationship versions of the SI and SA subscales were slightly negatively correlated with each other, this slight departure from orthogonality does not account for the pattern of correlations between each of the subscales and the two closeness measures.

As mentioned earlier, we can identify four general types of social relating within the two-dimensional space defined by SA and SI. Of particular interest are the type of people who fall into the low SA–high SI category. As we noted in the previous section, these individuals displayed a uniquely high level of social paranoia and anxiety in dyadic interactions with strangers. Do these individuals also display uniquely "alienated" perceptions of the dating relationships in which they are currently involved? The data from Debra's first study revealed that they do.

Compared to all of the other respondents in the sample, the low SA–high SI respondents reported feeling significantly less close to their current romantic partners, (see Table 20.3 for the means and other relevant statistics). In addition, the low SA–high SI group reported that they desired less closeness than did the other groups combined. Interestingly, 30% of the respondents in the low SA–high SI group indicated that they desired less closeness than was currently present in the relationship, compared to only 15% of the other respondents.

This latter finding suggests that low SA–high SI individuals are more likely than other people to feel "too close" in the context of a romantic relationship. That is, they may have a greater tendency to feel suffocated, smothered, and enmeshed in their intimate relationships. (For a detailed discussion of how the perception of "too much closeness" can create problems in close relationships, see the chapter by Mashek in this volume.)

Clearly, low SA–high SI individuals feel less close to their partners than do individuals in the remaining three groups. But do low SA–high SI individuals also diverge from others on relationship-relevant dimensions such as commitment, satisfaction, or

TABLE 20.3

Correlates of Social Absorption (SA) and Social Individuation (SI)
for the Dating Respondents in Mashek's Two Samples

	SA	SI
Study 1 (N = 128)		
Current closeness (Aron et al., 1992)	.36**	−.26**
Desired closeness	.35**	−.22*
Commitment (Rusbult, 1983)	.42**	−.20*
Satisfaction (Hendrick, 1988)	.47**	−.31**
Passionate love (Hatfield & Sprecher, 1986)	.60**	−.17
Fearful attachment	−.16	.10
(Bartholomew & Horowitz, 1991)		
Secure attachment	.34**	−.11
Preoccupied attachment	.00	.16
Dismissive attachment	−.04	.05
Study 2 (N = 321)		
Current closeness (Aron et al., 1992)	.40**	−.04
Desired closeness	.34**	−.12*
Avoidance (Brennan et al., 1998)	−.56**	.25**
Anxiety	.07	.08
Fearful attachment	−.27**	.20**
Secure attachment	−.19**	.17**
Preoccupied attachment	−.11*	.15**
Dismissive attachment	−.38**	.23**

* $p < .05$, ** $p < .01$, *** $p < .001$

passionate love? The answer, not surprisingly and consistent with Ickes and Hutchi-son's findings, is yes. Compared to individuals representing the other three types, the low SA–high SI individuals reported feeling less committed to their current partner and less satisfied with their relationship ($ps < .001$). Moreover, the low SA–high SI individuals were less likely than those in other groups to report "symptoms" of pas-sionate love, as measured by Hatfield and Sprecher's (1986) passionate love scale ($p < .01$). Finally, this group more strongly endorsed a statement reflecting a fearful attachment orientation and less strongly endorsed a statement reflecting a secure at-tachment orientation ($ps < .01$). Table 20.3 displays the correlations between various relationship relevant scales and the SA and SI subscales.

To get a more vivid impression of just how "closeness averse" the low SA–high SI respondents appear to be, it is useful to consider their responses to some of the individual items on the survey questionnaire. Compared to the individuals in the other groups, the low SA–high SI individuals reported that they were less likely to desire affection from their partner; more likely to wish they hadn't gotten into the relationship; more likely to want the relationship to end; less likely to want to know all about the partner; less likely to want the partner to know all about them; more likely to feel humiliated or embarrassed; and more likely to hate themselves (see Table 20.4 for a complete list). In summary, these individuals shun closeness and prefer to actively distance themselves from even their most "intimate" others.

Findings From the Second Study.   Mashek's second study of dating respondents gave us additional insights into the relationships between SA and SI and various measures of closeness. The sample included 321 respondents (175 women and 146

TABLE 20.4

Items on Which the Low SA/High SI Group Differed From the Other Groups in Mashek's (2002) First Sample

Compared to the individuals in other groups, low SA/high SI individuals:

(Relevant to Closeness Aversion)
1. are more likely to want to end the relationship in the near future. ($p < .001$)
2. are less committed to the relationship. ($p < .002$)
3. are less likely to want to be with their partner more than anyone else. ($p < .02$)
4. are less likely to believe that they will love their partner for ever. ($p < .02$)
5. are less likely to desire affection from their partner. ($p < .01$)
6. are less likely to feel that life without their partner would be dark and dismal. ($p < .04$)
7. are less satisfied with the relationship. ($p < .001$)
8. are more likely to wish that they hadn't gotten into the relationship. ($p < .005$)
9. are less likely to report that they love their partner. ($p < .03$)
10. are more likely to report that they see problems in the relationship. ($p < .03$)

(Relevant to Self-Disclosure)
1. are more likely to hide their true self. ($p < .05$)
2. are less likely to want to know all about their partner. ($p < .005$)
3. are less likely to want their partner to know all about them. ($p < .02$)
4. are more likely to be unhappy with the way their family of origin communicated when they were growing up. ($p < .02$)

(Relevant to Resistance to Partner's Influence)
1. are less likely to get excited at the sight of their partner. ($p < .002$)
2. are less likely to feel their body responding to their partner's touch ($p < .01$)
3. are less likely to report that their partner can make them feel bubbly ($p < .02$)
4. are more likely to try to control events and people. ($p < .06$)
5. are more afraid to let things happen naturally. ($p < .10$)

(Relevant to Self-Criticism and Health Concerns)
1. are more likely to pick on themselves for everything, including the way they think, feel, look, act, behave. ($p < .10$)
2. are more likely to feel humiliated or embarrassed. ($p < .002$)
3. are more likely to hate themselves. ($p < .003$)
4. are more worried about medical problems, namely bladder, bowel, and stomach problems. ($p < .01$)
5. are more likely to feel ill and run down ($p < .001$)
6. are more preoccupied with the idea of their body failing. ($p < .002$)
7. are more likely to feel that their general health is poor. ($p < .02$)

men). They each completed the relationship-specific version of the social orientation scale (our measure of SA and SI), two items to assess current and desired closeness, and Brennan, Clark, and Shaver's (1998) measure of the anxious and avoidant attachment dimensions. As in the previous study, the dating-relationship versions of the SA and SI measures correlated slightly negatively with each other ($r = -.13$, $p < .05$).

The results replicated Mashek's previous finding of a positive relationship between SA and both current and desired closeness ($rs = .40$ and $.34$, respectively), even though closeness was assessed in this study using a non-pictorial measure. On the other hand, her previous finding that social individuation correlated negatively with both current and desired closeness was only partially replicated. In the Study 2 sample, SI had a zero (.00) correlation with current closeness and only a slight negative ($-.12$) correlation with desired closeness.

As we have already seen, however, the negative effect of high social individuation might be evident only in combination with a low level of social absorption. And, in Mashek's second study, this was definitely the case. First, the low SA–high SI individuals reported significantly less current closeness than the other individuals in the sample, $p < .001$. In addition, the low SA–high SI individuals reported that they *desired* significantly less closeness than the other individuals did ($p < .001$). These results clearly replicate the closeness data from the first study of dating respondents.

The attachment orientation data added further detail to this picture. As expected, the low SA–high SI individuals differed significantly from the remaining individuals in their scores on the avoidance attachment dimension ($p < .001$). Specifically, the low SA–high SI group was markedly more avoidant than any other group. Furthermore, and paradoxically, this group was also significantly more fearful, more secure, and more dismissive than any other group. Once again, the data suggest that there is something unique and rather odd about low SA–high SI individuals, who appear to shun closeness while simultaneously describing themselves as more fearful, more secure, and more dismissive than other individuals do. These individuals appear to have "social self-concepts" that are highly conflicted and perhaps even pathological.

Taken together, the data from Mashek's studies of dating respondents consistently indicate that, compared to other people, low SA–high SI individuals report a host of behaviors and cognitions that are typically considered negative in close relationships. Most important for the present chapter is the finding that these individuals seem to be resistant to closeness, and in fact seem to shun it. In the following section, we consider the implications of our data for the study of closeness and for our understanding of the "socially paranoid," closeness-averse individual.

CONCLUSIONS

In the present chapter, we have argued that genuine closeness depends upon intersubjectivity and can rarely be sustained in its absence. Using this premise as our point of departure, we identified a common core of distinctions made by various philosophical and psychological conceptions of intersubjectivity (the strength of the self–other distinction, the level of behavioral interdependence, and the presence or absence of the sense of "merging" with others). We then factor-analyzed a set of self-report items that were written to capture these core distinctions and found that they reflected two orthogonal dimensions—social absorption and social individuation.

By examining the quadrants created by these two orthogonal dimensions, we identified four different modes of relating to others: *anonymous independence, individuated aloofness, individuated interdependence,* and *deindividuated merging.* We proposed that the first mode is the one that sociologists have termed anomie; that the second mode is the one that Sartre (1956) has characterized as objectifying self and others; that the third mode is the conventional one in which we relate to neighbors and coworkers; and that the fourth mode is the one that Crossley (1996) has called radical intersubjectivity.

In our individual difference research comparing these four modes, we found that individuals who endorsed the second mode (individuated aloofness) as self-descriptive were strikingly different from all other respondents. These individuals are unusually wary and suspicious. They resist becoming involved and interdependent with others, and they are so averse to closeness and intimacy that they take little pleasure in their current dating relationships and look forward to seeing them end. They strongly objectify both self and others, and they display an aversion to self that parallels a similar aversion to others. In essence, they appear to embody the existential alienation from self and others that Sartre has delineated so precisely in his novels, plays, and philosophical essays.

These existentially alienated, closeness-averse individuals clearly warrant further study. Their behaviors and perceptions appear to cohere into the kind of psychological syndrome that is analogous to a psychological and/or personality disorder. It remains to be seen, however, if there are any standard psychological or personality disorders to which our syndrome of individuated aloofness might prove to correspond. Testing for such correspondence should be an important goal of future research, as it promises to tell us much about the nature of "closeness aversion" as a psychological and social-psychological phenomenon.

REFERENCES

Aron, A., & Aron, E. N. (1997). Self-expansion motivation and including other in the self. In S. Duck, K. Dindia, W. Ickes, R. Milardo, R. Mills, & B. Sarason (Eds.), *Handbook of personal relationships: Theory, research and interventions* (2nd ed. pp. 251–270). Chichester, England: Wiley.

Aron, A., Aron, E. N., & Smollan, D. (1992). Inclusion of other in the self scale and the structure of interpersonal closeness. *Journal of Personality and Social Psychology, 63*, 596–612.

Bartholomew, K., & Horowitz, L. M. (1991). Attachment styles among young adults: A test of a four-category model. *Journal of Personality and Social Psychology, 61*, 226–244.

Brennan, K. A., Clark, C. L., & Shaver, P. (1998). Self-report measurement of adult attachment: An integrative overview. In J. A. Simpson & W. S. Rholes (Eds.), *Attachment theory and close relationships* (pp. 46–76). New York: Guilford Press.

Buber, M. (1970). *I and Thou* (W. Kaufman, Trans.) New York: Scribner.

Campbell, L., & Kashy, D. A. (2002). Estimating actor, partner, and interaction effects for dyadic dates using proc mixed and HLM: A user-friendly guide. *Personal Relationships, 9*, 327–342.

Crossley, N. (1996). *Intersubjectivity: The fabric of social becoming.* London: Sage.

Hatfield, E., & Sprecher, S. (1986). Measuring passionate love in intimate relationships. *Journal of Adolescence, 9*, 383–410.

Hendrick, S. S. (1988). A generic measure of relationship satisfaction. *Journal of Marriage and the Family, 50*, 93–98.

Husserl, E. (1960). *Cartesian meditations: An introduction to phenomenology.* The Hague: M. Nijhoff.

Husserl, E. (1970). *The crisis of European sciences and transcendental phenomenology: An introduction to phenomenological philosophy.* Evanston, Ill: Northwestern University Press.

Hutchison, J. (1999). *Correlates of social absorption and social individuation in the unstructured interactions of opposite-sex strangers.* Unpublished master's thesis, University of Texas at Arlington.

Hutchison, J., & Ickes, W. (1999). *Personality correlates of social absorption and social individuation.* Unpublished data, University of Texas at Arlington.

Ickes, W. (2002). The social self in subjective and intersubjective research paradigms. In J. P. Forgas & K. D. Williams (Eds.), *The social self: Cognitive, interpersonal and intergroup perspectives* (pp. 205–218). Philadelphia: Psychology Press.

Ickes, W., & Hutchison, J. (1998). *The Social Orientations Scale (SOS): A measure for assessing the independent dimensions of social absorption and social individuation.* Unpublished personality scale, University of Texas at Arlington.

Ickes, W., & Hutchison, J. (2000, February). *Social absorption and social individuation: Independent dimensions of social relating.* Invited talk given at the preconference on relationships, first annual meeting of the Society for Personality and Social Psychology, Nashville, Tennessee.

Maslach, C., Stapp, J., & Santee, R. T. (1985). Individuation: Conceptual analysis and assessment. *Journal of Personality and Social Psychology, 49*, 729–738.

Merleau-Ponty, M. (1962). *The phenomenology of perception.* London: Routledge.

Merleau-Ponty, M. (1964). *Signs.* Evanston, Ill: Northwestern University Press.

Rusbult, C. E. (1983). A longitudinal test of the investment model: The development (and deterioration) of satisfaction and commitment in heterosexual involvements. *Journal of Personality and Social Psychology, 45*, 101–117.

Sartre, J.-P. (1956). *Being and nothingness: An essay on phenomenological ontology.* New York: Philosophical Library.

Schutz, A. (1967). *The phenomenology of the social world.* Evanston: Northwestern University Press.

Schutz, A. (1970). *On phenomenology and social relations: Selected writings.* Chicago: The University of Chicago Press.

Zimbardo, P.G. (1969). The human choice: Individuation, reason, and order versus deindividuation, impulse, and chaos. *Nebraska Symposium on Motivation, 17*, 237–307.

21

Methods for Overcoming
the Fear of Intimacy

Robert W. Firestone and Lisa Firestone
The Glendon Association

An intimate relationship is one in which neither party silences, sacrifices, or betrays the self.

—Lerner (1989, p. 3)

People's basic sense of self is formed originally in a relationship constellation that predisposes their attitudes toward themselves, others, and the world at large. Studies have demonstrated that people often replicate early patterns of attachment with care givers in their adult romantic relationships (Ainsworth & Eichberg, 1991; Bartholomew, 1993; Bretherton, Ridgeway, & Cassidy 1990; Feeney, Noller, & Hanrahan, 1994; George & Solomon, 1996, 1999; Main, Kaplan, & Cassidy, 1985; Shaver & Hazan, 1993). Research has also shown that early attachments with parents or other significant figures create feelings of wholeness and security or states of anxiety and insecurity that can persist for a lifetime (Ainsworth, 1989; Bartholomew, 1993; Bowlby, 1988; DeWolff & van IJzendoorn, 1997; Fonagy, 1998; Main, et al., 1985; Scharfe & Bartholomew, 1994; Shaver & Hazan, 1993).

Intimate relationships can be the ultimate source of happiness and fulfillment; at the same time, they have the potential to generate considerable pain and suffering. Although other issues in life cause us concern—crime, poverty, war, existential issues of aloneness and death—we seem to experience the most distress in relation to the problems we face in our closest associations. This chapter focuses on understanding the difficulties that people encounter as they strive to develop and sustain intimacy in their personal relationships, and describes methods for helping individuals overcome these barriers.

A DEFINITION OF INTIMACY

According to Sexton and Sexton (1982), "the word intimacy is derived from the Latin *intimus*, meaning inner or inmost. To be intimate with another is to have access to, and to comprehend, his or her inmost character" (p. 1). The authors believe that intimacy also involves "seeing" and being "seen," that is, having an empathic perception and a depth of understanding of the other. Intimate relating is made up of positive behavioral components that are not merely ideational but have an outward manifestation, a style of communication where both partners experience a sense of shared meaning. We view intimacy as characterized by affectionate companionship, nondefensiveness, and honest communication, an essential component in a close, loving relationship. Intimacy is usually experienced through a wide range of emotions, including kindness, tenderness, sexual attraction, pleasure in satisfying the wants and needs of the other, and joy in sharing meaningful moments, activities, and projects.

Maintaining intimacy presupposes an ongoing capacity for giving and receiving love. Fundamental to maintaining intimacy is the willingness to experience the poignant feelings of sadness that inevitably arise at times when one feels especially close, both sexually and emotionally (Firestone, 1985; Schnarch, 1991). Schnarch asserted that

> when couples far exceed their wildest imaginations of increased intimacy and sexual pleasure, the resulting increased desire for the partner triggers physical pain and sorrow. Some patients experience it as 'bittersweet' melancholy, while others report it as chest-bursting heartache. (p. 192)

Firestone and Catlett (1999) explained the psychodynamics involved in this type of poignant sadness: "People who have suffered painful childhoods are often deeply saddened by love and tenderness in their sexual lives" (p. 27). Viewing this phenomenon from an existential perspective, loving sexuality and emotional closeness remind us that

> we are truly alive and really do exist, and in embracing life and love we are forced to be cognizant of our personal death as well. Giving value to our existence makes us poignantly aware of our mortality. (Firestone, Firestone, & Catlett, 2003, p. 384)

BARRIERS TO INTIMACY

From our experience with individuals representing both clinical and nonclinical populations, we found that the key issues in distressed couples and the corresponding breakdown in relationships are not those commonly thought to be responsible: economic hardship, religious differences, problems with inlaws, breakdown of church and family, sexual incompatibility, etc. It seems that relationships fail primarily because the defensive processes that each person brings to the relationship limit his or her ability to develop and maintain closeness and intimacy. This intolerance of intimacy is based on negative attitudes toward self and others as well as an essential fear of vulnerability, abandonment, rejection, and potential loss.

Individuals who become involved in a romantic relationship sooner or later find themselves faced with a basic dilemma. Most have a fear of intimacy and at the same time they are terrified of being alone. Their solution is to form a fantasy bond—an illusion of connection and closeness—that allows them to stay together while maintaining a nonthreatening emotional distance (Firestone & Catlett, 1999).

In *Intrusiveness and Intimacy in the Couple*, Ruszczynski and Fisher (1995) emphasized the importance of distinguishing between "apparent" and genuine intimacy. Their approach is in line with our own thinking in relation to a vital function served by the fantasy bond, that of maintaining the form of the relationship after the substance (the behavioral operations of love, companionship and, sexuality) has deteriorated.

> Sometimes the wish to be close, to be intimate, is associated with a concern for the other.... Sometimes, however, the apparent intimacy is an expression of an intrusive

determination to control the other. At heart, such an intrusiveness consists in treating the other as an extension of the self. . . . In other words, it is an "intimacy," . . . we suggest, that is delusional insofar as it denies separateness. (Ruszczynski & Fisher, 1995 p. 1)

In the following pages, the authors define the fantasy bond and describe a conceptual model integrating psychoanalytic and existential frameworks that helps clarify why people retreat from closeness and intimacy. It explains why so many marriages end in divorce and why so often those that remain intact do so at great expense to the individuality of the participants, why sexual relationships often deteriorate or become routinized, and why so many couples distance themselves from one another and become, in effect, intimate enemies (Firestone, 1997).

The second part of the chapter focuses on the application of the techniques of voice therapy in the context of a couples' group. Voice therapy, a cognitive–affective–behavioral methodology, can be used to help individuals identify and counter negative thoughts or internalized "voices" about themselves and their partners that interfere with intimacy. Preliminary results from a small pilot study of four couples in the couples' group are reported. A case study of one of these couples is presented, along with data from a three-year follow-up using an initial version of the Firestone voice scale for couples (FVSC) and the experiences in close relationships inventory (Brennan, Clark, & Shaver, 1998). Findings are discussed in terms of their implications for theory development and empirical research.

SEPARATION THEORY

A Developmental Perspective

The theoretical approach described here, Separation Theory, elucidates how painful experiences early in childhood lead to defense formation and how these original defenses are reinforced as the developing child gradually becomes aware of his or her own mortality (Firestone, 1997). There are two primary sources of psychological pain, *interpersonal* and *existential*, that impinge on children and lead to the development of self-protective defenses. Interpersonal pain is caused by frustration and separation experiences in addition to the intentional and unintentional aggression and mistreatment that children experience to varying degrees in their earliest relationships with parents or caretakers. Existential pain refers to the pain of aloneness, potential loss of love objects, and the inevitability of aging and death. Both factors continue to have an impact on an individual's personality development and personal relationships throughout the life span.

Formation of the Fantasy Bond

The fantasy bond is the primary defense against interpersonal pain, separation anxiety, and later, the fear of death. It is formed originally in early childhood as a substitute for love and care that may be missing in the infant's environment (Firestone, 1984). The fantasy bond is highly effective as a defense because a human being's capacity for imagination provides partial gratification of needs and reduces tension. The illusion of being connected to the mother (or primary caregiver), together with self-gratifying, self-soothing patterns such as thumb sucking, nail biting, and excessive masturbation, are an attempt to heal the fracture in separation experiences and compensate for emotional deprivation. They lead to a posture of pseudoindependence in the developing child, an attitude that "I don't need anyone, I can take care of myself." The irony is that the more individuals come to rely on this fantasy process, the more they strive to keep other people in the background and the more helpless and ineffective they become in coping with the real world.

Once children form a fantasy bond, they feel this false sense of self-sufficiency because they have taken into themselves the image of the "good and powerful" parent. At the same time, they take on their parent's rejecting attitudes toward them as well as the negative beliefs and attitudes their parents held toward themselves. These internalized parental attitudes form the basis of their negative self-image. Children tend to idealize their parents and see themselves as bad, unlovable, or undeserving of love. It is important that the image of the parent is positive because it would be impossible for the child to feel safe or secure with an internalized parent perceived as inadequate or destructive.

In effect, children simultaneously develop a feeling of being the strong, good parent and the weak, bad child. In denying their needs and wants in relation to other people, they become a system unto themselves. The more seriously deprived children are, the more they depend on the fantasy bond as a compensation and reject genuine closeness and affection from others. As adults, they continue to parent or treat themselves the way they were treated as children, and often the way their parents treated themselves. Bollas (1987) described the *self as object* in similar terms when delineating the defensive functions of this form of self-parenting. According to Bollas,

> [e]ach person transfers elements of the parents' child care to his own handling of himself as an object.... If we look closely at our patients we would probably all agree that each has his or her own sense of existence but that, by virtue of the persistent pathology of their defences, they live by disowning the self. (pp. 59–63)

A number of theorists, beginning with Kaiser, have dealt with the modes of relating based on fantasy processes or a delusion of fusion (Karpel, 1976, 1994; Wexler & Steidl, 1978). Kaiser (Fierman, 1965) asserted that the universal psychopathology was "the attempt to create in real life by behavior and communication the illusion of fusion" (pp. 208–209). Kaiser's germinal idea that this illusion represents the universal symptom of neurotic disturbance is analogous to the conceptualization of the *fantasy bond* or self-parenting process as the primary defense mechanism in neurosis (Firestone, 1984).

It is important to differentiate the specific use of the word *bond* from its other uses in the literature. It is not a bond as in *bonding* (a secure maternal–infant attachment) in a positive sense, nor does it refer to a relationship characterized by real loyalty, devotion, and genuine love. The authors' concept of the fantasy bond uses *bond* rather in the sense of bondage or limitation of freedom. It describes an imaginary connection to a parent or significant figure in one's adult life rather than a real attachment (Firestone, 1985).

Children develop their original defenses to protect themselves against interpersonal pain in the family. Later, these defenses are strongly reinforced or crystallized when they learn about death. Sometime between the ages of three and seven, children come to realize that the life they thought and experienced as permanent is in fact impermanent (Anthony, 1971/1973; Kastenbaum, 1974, 1995; Lester, 1970; Nagy, 1948/1959; Rochlin 1967). Their world is turned upside down by the dawning awareness of first their parent's death, and eventually their own death. The defenses that they developed in relation to interpersonal distress are now used in an attempt to relieve this existential pain. From this point on, both kinds of pain, interpersonal and existential, trigger the defensive process and contribute to people's tendencies to lead inward, self-protective lives and to retreat from closeness and intimacy in interpersonal relationships (Firestone, 1994, 1997; Greenberg, et al., 1990; Solomon, Greenberg, & Pyszczynski, 1991).

Understanding the functions of the fantasy bond in protecting the child (and later the adult) against death anxiety helps explain why people tend to make self-limiting choices in life and in their relationships that condemn them to repeat the unfortunate circumstances of their early lives. In order to protect the fantasy connection, which they erroneously consider to be a matter of life and death, people can only tolerate gratification in fantasy. Real gratification and genuine loving relationships actually threaten an individual's psychological equilibrium and pseudoindependent posture. Therefore, in a seeming paradox, many people avoid personal gratification and prefer not to be loved or valued by others because it makes them more vulnerable and aware of their own death. They choose to merge with others and lose their distinctive characteristics rather than invest in a life they must certainly lose.

DESTRUCTIVE EFFECTS OF THE FANTASY BOND ON INTIMATE RELATING

By the time individuals reach adulthood, they have crystallized their defenses and exist in a psychological equilibrium that they do not wish to disturb. Conflict develops as partners strive to preserve their defenses while trying to hold on to their initial feelings of closeness and affection. As noted, the two conditions tend to be mutually exclusive. Eventually one or both partners unconsciously choose to preserve long-standing psychological defenses to maintain an illusion of security, thus threatening the intimacy they once shared. To mask this painful fact, both partners develop a fantasy of enduring love, substituting form for the substance of the relationship. Everyday routines, customs, and role-determined behaviors provide the structure and form of the relationship, often replacing the original warmth, affection, trust, and respect for one another.

Once an illusion of connection with the partner has been formed, experiences of genuine love and intimacy interfere with its defensive function, whereas symbols of togetherness and images of love strengthen the illusion. Any event that arouses an awareness of separateness threatens the fantasy of fusion, precipitating anxiety states that predispose anger and hostility. To protect the fantasy bond against these intrusions, most people recreate the destructive aspects of their family of origin in their current relationship using three methods: selection, distortion, and provocation. People tend to select partners who are similar to significant figures in their early lives because these are the people who fit in with their defenses and who they feel comfortable with. They distort their mates and see them more like the people in their past than they really are. If all else fails, they try to provoke responses in their partner that will duplicate their past. In effect, they relive rather than live their lives.

MANIFESTATIONS OF THE FANTASY BOND IN COUPLE RELATIONSHIPS

One early symptom of deterioration in a relationship can be observed in the couple's style of communication, which tends to become less honest and direct. Exchanges are characterized by small talk, bickering, speaking for the other, interrupting, or talking as a unit. Both partners tend to forsake their independence and begin to manipulate by playing on the other's guilt, becoming childlike and dependent, or by giving angry and parental responses.

As these methods of relating take a toll on the relationship, other symptoms of the fantasy bond become more apparent. Individuals who in the early phases of their relationship spent hours in conversation begin to lose interest in both talking and listening, and spontaneity and playfulness gradually disappear. They become less personal in their exchanges and stop taking the time to make contact or to really notice how the other person is feeling. Often the partners develop a routinized, mechanical style of lovemaking and experience a reduction in the level of sexual attraction. As one or both participants sacrifice their individuality to become one half of a couple, their basic attraction to each other is jeopardized. In fact, people in a fantasy bond often experience the other as an appendage, a condition that causes their feelings of sexual attraction to wane.

In some cases, one partner may attempt to control various aspects of the relationship due to underlying feelings of insecurity and fears of potential rejection or loss. If the other partner submits to this form of control, he or she tends to become less attractive or appealing, and the couple's sexual relating often deteriorates accordingly. It is important to stress that this decline is generally not the inevitable result of familiarity, as many people assume. It is due to deadening habit patterns, exaggerated dependency, negative projections, loss of independence, and a sense of obligation.

In addition, one or both partners may begin to hold back the positive qualities that originally attracted the other in order to maintain a comfortable distance, and this withholding leads to a sense of guilt and remorse. Consequently, both may begin to act out of a sense of obligation and responsibility rather than out of a genuine desire to be together.

THE VOICE PROCESS

Within each person there exists an essential dualism, a primary split between forces that represent the self and those that oppose the self. These elements can be conceptualized as the "self system" and the "antiself system." The two systems develop independently; both are dynamic and continually evolve over time. In other words, people possess conflicting points of view and beliefs about themselves, others, relationships, and events in the world, depending upon which aspect of the personality, self or antiself, is dominant. One point of view is rational, objective, and life-affirming, while the other is made up of a destructive thought process or voice, an overlay on the personality, that is opposed to the ongoing development of the self.

The authors propose that the voice represents the introjection of destructive thought patterns and attitudes based on an identification with negative attitudes and defenses of one's parents. We have hypothesized that the voice is the intrapsychic mechanism primarily responsible for the transmission of negative traits, behaviors, and defense patterns from one generation to the next.

The voice represents the language of the defensive process. It functions as a secondary defense that supports the fantasy bond (or primary defense) and self-parenting, inward behavior patterns. For example, to protect one's illusion of complete self-sufficiency or posture of pseudoindependence, one may tell oneself, in the form of the voice: *Even if you do find someone to love, relationships don't last forever. Watch out, don't get too involved so you won't get disappointed later on.* These are a few, among the many, deep-seated beliefs, expectations, or critical voices that people have reported using as rationalizations to push away another person who genuinely loved and valued them.

The voice is a form of intrapsychic communication that ranges from minor self-criticisms to major self-attacks and fosters self-soothing habit patterns, isolation, and self-destructive lifestyles. Voice attacks are directed toward others as well as toward oneself. People generally anticipate rejection from a relationship partner based on both aspects of the voice. For example, they may have self-depreciating thoughts such as: "You're so uninteresting. What do you have to offer this relationship?" Or they may have cynical or hostile thoughts toward their partner, such as: "He/She doesn't care about you any more. When was the last time the two of you went out together?" Both types of voices, belittling and attacking self and others, predispose alienation and provide each partner with rationalizations for retreating to a more defended, pseudoindependent posture.

In terms of attachment theory, the voice process can be conceptualized as a fundamental aspect of what have been described as *internal working models*. These intervening variables help explain the psychodynamics involved in interpersonal relationships and the intergenerational transmission of negative attitudes, behaviors, and defenses. Attachment researchers (Batgos & Leadbeater, 1994; Bowlby, 1973, 1980, 1982; Bretherton & Munholland, 1999; Bretherton, et al., 1990) have proposed that these internal working models represent children's beliefs about self and relationships and mediate their attachment behavior. Their formulations agree in substance with the authors' findings, both those regarding the voice process that influences different styles of relating in adult relationships, and those related to children's reactions during those moments when their parents manifested abusive, neglectful, or intrusive behavior. Attachment theorist Bretherton (1996) argued that "insecure individuals develop working models of self and attachment figure in which some schema or schema networks [cognitive processes] may be dissociated from others" (p. 14). In examining adult romantic attachments, Shaver and Clark (1996) asserted that "a child with a negative model of both self and attachment figures can become an adolescent or adult who implicitly distrusts relationship partners, expects them to be cruel, neglectful, or unpredictable, and feels unworthy of anyone's love" (p. 34).

The concept of the voice is similar in many respects to certain constructs in attribution and appraisal theory (see Higgins, 1987). Experimental studies conducted to assess the role of causal attributions in psychopathology beginning with those of Peterson, et al. (1982) and more recent research reported by Kinderman and Bentall (1996) have shown that many people make attribution errors on the basis of experiences from the past. For example, Roseman and Kaiser (2001) noted that "*Pathogenic experiences and maladaptive learning* [in childhood] may be the most common sources of appraisal inaccuracy" (p. 255).

Researchers Kinderman and Bentall (2000), investigating the effects of causal attribution errors and self-discrepancies in relationships, found that some individuals attribute the causes of events to self, while others attribute the "causes of events to the actions or omissions of identifiable others" (p. 262). Fincham and Bradbury (1992) stated that

> [d]istressed spouses are hypothesized to make attributions for negative events that accentuate their impact (e.g., they locate the cause in their partner, see it as stable or unchanging, and see it as global or influencing many areas of the relationship. (p. 457)

We contend that both types of attribution errors (about self and others) represent distortions mediated by the voice process, and that thought patterns contributing to relationship distress need to be further explicated through empirical studies. The resultant findings could then be used to broaden our understanding of several intervening variables currently under investigation by attribution theorists, including factors influencing "rejection sensitivity" as described by Downey, Feldman, and Ayduk (2000).

DESTRUCTIVE EFFECTS OF THE VOICE ON INTIMATE RELATING

The nature of the fantasy bond and related defensive processes as they are manifested in intimate relationships is that both individuals, more often than not, are "listening" to the dictates of their respective voices. Their communications are filtered, in a sense, through a biased or alien point of view that distorts their partner's real image. Both parties ward off loving responses from the other, using rationalizations promoted by the voice to justify their anger and distancing behavior. They tend to project their own self-attacks on one another and often respond as though they were being victimized or depreciated by their mates. In terms of appraisal theory, partners who inaccurately interpret each other's behavior often have maladaptive emotional responses in their interactions with each other. According to appraisal theorists Roseman and Smith (2001), "[c]onflicting, involuntary, or inappropriate appraisal may account for irrational aspects of emotions" (p. 8). Regarding "rejection sensitive" individuals, Ayduk, et al. (2000) argued that "people who expect rejection act in more hostile, aggressive ways in relationships" (p. 776), while Downey, et al. (2000) contended that such a person "will readily perceive intentional rejection in the ambiguous behavior of a significant other," that will in turn "elicit cognitive-affective overreactions including hurt and anger" (p. 46).

Until these projections are understood and essentially taken back within the couple (or these inaccurate appraisals and expectations corrected) and other manifestations of the fantasy bond identified and consistently challenged, there will be no sustained therapeutic progress or improving in the relationship. From this perspective, for a psychotherapy to be effective, symptoms of the fantasy bond as well as internalized voices about oneself and one's partner need to be exposed and understood in the context of each partner's fears and anxieties. Voice therapy achieves these goals and also facilitates partners relating to each other with more compassion and frees them to experience genuine loving feelings (Firestone & Catlett, 1999).

VOICE THERAPY: APPLICATION IN COUPLES THERAPY

Voice therapy was so named because it represents a process of giving spoken words to negative thought processes or internalized voices. This cognitive–affective–behavioral methodology helps uncover destructive thoughts, attitudes, and beliefs that interfere with intimacy. Developing insight into the sources of these negative thoughts facilitates the development of compassion for oneself and others. Through modifying behaviors that are regulated by these thoughts, individuals become more self-assertive and less self-destructive. The overall purpose of voice therapy, in both individual and couples psychotherapy, is to separate and bring out into the open those elements of the personality that are antagonistic toward self and hostile toward others, together with the associated negative affect (Firestone, 1988, 1997).

The primary goal with couples is to help each individual identify the voice attacks that are influencing distancing behaviors and creating conflict in the relationship. Couples learn to distinguish between projections and distortions that are a result of the voice process, and realistic perceptions of their partner's traits, both negative and positive. Each partner also learns to realistically assess his or her own assets and liabilities. This process leads to acceptance of ambivalent feelings toward oneself and one's partner and therefore offers a more stable and honest perspective. Moreover, by identifying specific self-criticisms as well as judgmental, hostile thoughts about one another, partners are able to communicate more honestly and to achieve more closeness and intimacy in the relationship.

The goals of voice therapy are similar in several respects to the aims of object relations approaches in couple therapy. Interventions informed by object relations theory are focused on the reinternalization of disowned and projected views of the self as described in Scharff and Scharff's (1991) book, *Object Relations Couple Therapy*. According to object relations theorist Zinner (1976), who delineated the psychodynamics underlying projection, "the contents of the projected material contain highly conflicted elements of the spouse's object relationships with his or her own family of origin" (p. 297).

THE STEPS IN THE THERAPEUTIC PROCESS

In individual as well as conjoint and couple's group sessions, clients generally progress through the following steps over the course of treatment:

1. Each partner formulates the problem he or she perceives is limiting his or her satisfaction within the relationship, while learning not to attribute blame to the other.

2. The principal technique of voice therapy involves each partner verbalizing his or her self-critical thoughts in the second person format, that is, in the form of statements toward themselves, for example, *"You're unattractive, you're unlovable,"* rather than **I'm** unattractive, **I'm** unlovable." When clients express themselves in this format, they often reveal feelings of intense anger toward themselves as well as feelings of painful sadness. By articulating self-attacks in the second person, each partner facilitates the process of separating his or her own point of view from the hostile thought patterns that make up this alien point of view.

Hostile, cynical thoughts toward one's partner are verbalized in the third-person format, as though someone else were imparting negative information to the individual about his or her partner, for example, *"He doesn't want to commit to the relationship,"* or *"She's so childish and melodramatic,"* *"He/She doesn't give as much to the relationship as you do."*

The process of identifying the voice can be approached intellectually as a primarily cognitive technique or more emotionally as a cathartic technique. In both procedures, the client learns to verbalize negative thoughts in the second person as though someone else were addressing him or her. In the latter technique, there is an emphasis on the release of the affect accompanying the voice attacks. For example, the client is encouraged to "say it louder," "really feel that," or "let go and say anything that comes to mind." Clients often adopt this style of expression of their own volition. When asked to verbalize their negative thoughts in the second person, they often spontaneously begin to speak louder and with more intensity of feeling, as described earlier. With this release of emotions, valuable material is revealed. Clients often verbalize thoughts and beliefs that they were previously unaware of. A number of clinicians and researchers have emphasized the importance of accessing and experiencing emotions associated with cognitive distortions and painful events in one's past to achieve significant positive shifts in core schemas or concepts of oneself, which in turn facilitates change in psychotherapy (Diamond & Liddle, 1996; Fraiberg, Adelson, & Shapiro, 1980; Greenberg, 2002; Johnson & Greenberg, 1995; Kennedy-Moore & Watson, 1999; Lieberman & Pawl, 1993; Lieberman & Zeanah, 1999).

In sessions where both partners are present, each individual reveals negative thoughts and attitudes toward him or herself as well as toward the other. In a real sense, they are sharing each other's individual psychotherapy. When verbalizing hostile attitudes toward the other, partners express what their voices are telling them regarding negative behaviors they perceive in the other person. During this process, they often become aware that their tone of voice has taken on a sarcastic, derisive quality and that these attacks are exaggerating their partner's undesirable characteristics. Disclosing harsh, judgmental views of their partner in the form of the voice helps people separate these views from a more realistic or congenial view of their mate. Clients are encouraged to relinquish residual cynical thoughts and grudges even though their critical views may have some basis in reality.

3. Partners discuss their spontaneous insights and their reactions to verbalizing the voice. They then attempt to understand the relationship between their voice attacks and behavior patterns that are interfering with intimacy in the relationship. In tracing the source of their self-attacks and hostile attitudes to early family interactions, partners gain perspective into each other's problems and feel more compassion for their mates as well as for themselves. Recognizing their voice attacks as the primary source of dissatisfaction in their relating takes pressure off the relationship and has a powerful effect on improving attitudes toward their mates as well as on enhancing each individual's personal growth.

4. The therapist and the individual partners identify the specific behaviors that are influenced or controlled by each partner's negative cognitive process and that are causing distress in the relationship, and then work together to formulate ideas about altering routine responses and habitual patterns of behavior. The corrective suggestions they arrive at are in accord with each partner's personal goals and are specific to those problem areas he or she wishes to correct or improve. These goals invariably represent personal risk and increased vulnerability in the sense of breaking with defenses that protect each partner from experiencing painful emotions. For example, a woman reveals voice attacks that she is boring and that her husband is not interested in anything she has to say. The corrective suggestions she and her therapist arrived at are to reveal her self-attacks to her husband and arrange to spend time with him discussing her thoughts, feelings, and point of view. Each partner learns to accommodate to the anxiety associated with breaking inward, self-protective defenses and is gradually able to tolerate more intimacy in his or her life.

A SMALL PILOT STUDY APPLYING VOICE THERAPY WITH FOUR COUPLES

In this section, the authors provide a case example of the application of voice therapy techniques in the context of a couples group made up of eight individuals (four couples). All of the participants in the group were highly successful in other areas of their lives, but had been unable to maintain a long-lasting and meaningful intimate relationship. The series of meetings was videotaped and transcribed.

Participants

Participants included four men and four women. All were Caucasian and ranged in age from 27 to 52 years of age, with an average age of 38. Three participants, two women and one man, had been previously married (the male participant had divorced twice), and five had never been married. The duration of the participants' current relationships (at the time of the original study) ranged from three months to three years, with a mean of 18 months. This case example focuses on a single couple, Sheryl and Mark, who were 38 and 41 years old respectively.

In the group discussions, the participants essentially followed the steps outlined above. Each partner revealed his or her self-attacks and critical attitudes toward the other and discussed the resulting insights while the other listened. Partners were sensitive and empathic toward each other during this process. They became increasingly aware that the hostile and judgmental attitudes expressed in their voice dialogues were more harsh or cynical than were warranted by the real situation. The participants formulated a number of goals for altering behaviors that were causing distress or creating distance in the relationship. The group was generally compassionate and supportive, and there was a good deal of cross identification between individuals and couples.

CASE EXAMPLE: SHERYL AND MARK

Background

Some years ago, Sheryl and Mark became romantically involved; however, they were unable to sustain their initial feelings of attraction, friendship, and affection. Eventually they separated, but remained friends. In a discussion that took place shortly after the breakup, Mark and Sheryl revealed the inner voices they had experienced during the early phases of their relationship:

> Mark: Immediately after the first date, I had voices that I should do things. *"You should call her, you should treat her nicely. She likes you, so you should be calling her right away. You should give her what she wants."*

As Mark spoke, his voice took on a derisive tone and became progressively louder and more angry:

> *"Don't be like most of these men. Men are nasty, men are really mean. Don't be like one of them. Be a nice man. Be different from how they are. Don't be one of these lousy bastards like most of these other men. Don't be a bastard like your father was. Just be nice. And you'd better hold on to her! You're lucky to have her. But she's going to see you're not a very attractive man. She's going to see everything when she really gets to know you."*

In the same discussion, Sheryl articulated destructive attitudes toward herself:

> Sheryl: *"Don't disappoint him. Say yes. If you say no, you won't get what you want. Say yes.* (angry) *You'd better give him whatever he wants. If you don't give him what he wants he's going to leave you, and you're going to be alone. You won't meet a nice guy ever again. He's nice, he's successful, he'll take care of you, you better not screw this up."* (loud, agitated) *"You'd better hold on to him. You know how long it takes you to meet people. Men don't like you, you're lucky to have this one. You're lucky to have anybody!"*

Mark had voices that he should take care of a woman, and Sheryl had reciprocal voices that she needed to be taken care of. Their self-attacks created a desperation to stay in the relationship and to hold on to each other, in effect, to form a fantasy bond, which in turn contributed to a deterioration in their original feelings for each other.

Four years following their breakup, Mark and Sheryl became reinvolved. During the intervening years, both individuals had developed personally and had altered many of their defensive behaviors. For example, Mark challenged his distorted perceptions of men and women and found that these views were based on his observations of his parents' relationships as well as their negative attitudes toward themselves, each other, and the opposite sex. He recognized that he identified not only with his father's animosity toward women and negative views of himself as a man, but also with his mother's negative view of men—and thus of himself—as being harsh and aggressive. He came to understand why he attempted to compensate by pleasing women or by deferring to them.

During the same period, Sheryl explored her fears of being vulnerable in an intimate relationship and traced these fears to early childhood experiences. She uncovered voices depreciating her as a woman and recognized how they contributed to the difficulties she and Mark had encountered when they were originally involved.

THE SERIES OF COUPLES GROUPS[1]

Mark and Sheryl's renewed relationship started off well, but as time went on, they began to experience problems reminiscent of their past relationship. Mark noticed, for example, that he had begun to pursue Sheryl in a desperate manner at times. Sheryl became aware of struggling to control strong impulses to push Mark away whenever he was simply being loving and affectionate. Both individuals asked if they could participate in the group mentioned previously. In the couples group, first Sheryl and then Mark worked on the steps in voice therapy.

1. *Formulating the problem.* In this discussion, Sheryl describes her negative reaction to the affection and intimate feelings that have been developing in the relationship:

Sheryl: The feeling that I have is that I've always just simply liked you, but partly I feel like I can't stand it that you're nice to me or that you like me. I feel like I have a mean streak.
Facilitator: In response to his liking you.
Sheryl: Yes.

2. *Verbalizing negative thoughts and releasing affect.*

Facilitator: What do you tell yourself about the relationship?
Sheryl: It's like, "*Don't show him anything, don't show him you like him.*" That's what I tell myself—"*Just don't show it. You'll be such a sucker, you're such a sucker if you show it.*" At times when he's really nice, I'll just want to squash him. When he's vulnerable I just want to smash him, and it's for no reason except that he's vulnerable and he's being sweet. (sad)

3. *Discussing insights.*

Sheryl: I've had so many thoughts of ways I've seen myself like my mother, and in previous relationships I've acted so much like her and didn't even know it. Every relationship ended basically the same way, for no reason really, just getting rid of it. But I know that's like my mother's point of view. She was very critical of my father and she would be mean to him. She was humiliated to be seen with him when he was sick. Actually, he had a brain tumor and when I went home for the holidays, we were all playing Monopoly, and he was watching us. He couldn't really speak because he was losing his physical abilities. He started drooling, and she said: "Stan, ugh!" She was humiliated by him, and so he went to his room. I felt so bad for him because there was no kindness in her at all. But I feel like sometimes I act like that myself.
Facilitator: So it's almost like a compulsion to reenact those patterns. Like it's barely under your control.
Sheryl: Yes, it's like that. It's like in the movie, *Alien*, where this thing comes out of my stomach and I'm surprised by it and by the things that I say. It's for no reason except to take the pleasure away, the happiness that he might have just from being nice to me. I want to smash that. (sad, tearful)

4. *Formulating plans for behavioral change.*

Facilitator: So the hope is for you to hang in there and to tolerate the anxiety in giving up these defenses, actually breaking with the imaginary connection that you have with your mother in that sense, and learn to really control that destructive acting out and allow yourself to get a perspective or an empathic view of the person you're with. Basically if

---

[1] Portions of this case example are adapted from *Fear of Intimacy* (Firestone & Catlett, 1999). Copyright © 1999 by The American Psychological Association. Adapted with permission.

you do sweat it out, you'll be able to have more in your life. It takes a lot of courage to go through that process but it's really worth it.

Sheryl: I feel like it would make me sad, too, because I would feel a lot. When I'm in that other point of view I feel big and mean. And when I just let things be I feel like a soft, sweet person.

1. *Formulating the problem.*

Mark: In all of my close relationships, I've had a pattern of pushing the woman away because on some level, I don't want to accept the love, I don't want to accept the friendship. (To Sheryl) When we were involved years ago, I remember how quickly our relationship became routine, habitual, but even more than that, I was pursuing you in a desperate way and at the same time losing myself. I gave up interest in other friends, and if you wanted to see me, I would drop anyone else in my life to see you. In fact, I would anticipate your desire to see me and drop them before you would even ask. And I lost my old friends and I lost you at the same time.

Facilitator: When partners give up their independence, they lose their attractiveness.

Mark: Absolutely. I pushed you away so quickly by doing that. I don't want that to happen this time. But sometimes I feel myself starting to do the same thing, trying to pursue you in that same desperate way.

2. *Verbalizing negative thoughts and releasing affect.*

Facilitator: What are you telling yourself at those times?

Mark: I think it's a voice that I've incorporated in myself about not being a real man. That was my mother's voice. If I were to say the voices about myself and about men, they would be: *"You're a weak piece of shit! Just like your father. You're nothing. You can't compete in a man's world. You're just not a man. You'd better grovel. You'd better take care of women. You'd better give us what we want. You're not a strong man. You just don't have it in you. And you're stupid. You think you're smart? You think you fit into the rest of the world, but women run it all. You men are just some drones that are out there!"* (loud voice, enraged) *"We control it all! So just play the role. Play the role like a big man. But you're not a big man, we both know it, don't we?"* (sarcastic)

   I feel those voices from both sides. I feel them from my mother and I feel them from my father. He felt that same way about himself and about men.

3. *Discussing insights.*

Mark: Today when I heard other people standing up for themselves in relation to their voice attacks, I felt like standing up for myself and saying: "That's not me. I'm not really a weak piece of shit and I don't have to be that way. I don't have to play that role, just to try to cover up that feeling of being weak." Saying that made me very sad. I really don't have to be that way. Not only can I be different, I can actually have different actions and sweat out the anxiety as it comes up.

   I realize that when I'm into that other point of view, I don't want to feel like a man. So if I pursue you [Sheryl] in a desperate way, I'm so much weaker, I'm so much more the type of man that my mother saw men as.

   Last week, Sheryl and I talked about this and I expressed my feeling that being sensitive and expressing tenderness is not the same as being weak. I told her, "I don't want you to interpret my sensitivity or kindness toward you or my affection as weakness." And saying that gave me a real sense of myself in a way that I was shocked. I felt so centered after that conversation.

4. *Formulating plans for behavioral change.*

Mark: I realize that it's important to stick to the plans I made not to give up other friendships and activities, like I did in the past, just because we're involved. I think it's also a good idea to let you initiate some of the activities we share instead of my always being the one to suggest that we get together, go to a movie or go out to eat, or make love, even.

I know that I'll probably be anxious if I stop pursuing you in that way, but right now I feel like I can go through whatever feelings come up.

Follow-Up Interview

In an interview two months after the discussion described above, Mark and Sheryl reported progress both in terms of an increased sense of independence, self-confidence, and personal growth and experiencing more gratification in their relationship. Here they describe some of these important changes.

> Sheryl: I feel like we've grown closer since we had that last talk. I still get scared sometimes. Even this week, I recognized a shift in my feelings, to really caring a lot about you (Mark). Instead of just learning how to accept you caring about me, I started feeling a deep sense of caring for you, too.
> Mark: Since we've been talking, I've felt really close to you. I noticed I felt more grounded in myself, especially revealing some of the ways I might push you away. That seemed to give me some insight, and I learned more about how I would feel desperate toward you and how that worked into the whole situation.
> A couple of other things I noticed, when we were together, and you started feeling sad when we were making love, I felt so close to you. I felt in love with you. I couldn't feel any closer than how I felt at that moment.
> Sheryl: For some reason, what's happening is bringing up a lot of sadness in me lately, and I think I'm really resistant to that.
> Facilitator: Yes, it's the fear of the sadness. It's ironic that people are afraid of sadness and to feel sadness, when in fact, if they do feel it and let it out, they actually feel better.
> Mark: It's followed by closeness and happiness.
> Facilitator: Yes, the sadness seems to center people in themselves.

In the course of the group discussions, the participants came to realize that they had been living their lives and conducting their relationships based on destructive thought processes and parental prescriptions rather than on fulfilling their own desires and goals. Once they recognized the profound influence of these early parental introjects (internal working models), they could begin to identify and challenge the thought processes that were limiting them. For example, as Mark and Sheryl effectively countered their self-attacks and cynical views of themselves and one another through modifying behavior patterns that had been creating distance in their relationship, they gained in self-confidence and strengthened their own point of view, which was more congenial toward self and other. Several months later, they married and the following year had a baby boy.

Preliminary Results[2]

Seven participants completed the initial version of the Firestone voice scale for couples (FVSC) prior to the discussions that took place over a 3-month period. The FVSC assesses the frequency of destructive thoughts the subject is currently experiencing toward self, toward his or her partner, and about relationships in general. Following these meetings, participants again completed an initial version of the FVSC, which

---

[2]Material from the series of meetings were compiled into two video documentaries entitled *Voices About Relationships* (Parr, 1997) and *Coping with the Fear of Intimacy* (Parr, 1999). A more detailed description of the pilot study and pre and posttest results on the FVSC can be found in *Fear of Intimacy* (Firestone & Catlett, 1999).

FVSC

Instructions

All people experience thoughts that are critical towards themselves and others. For example, when a person is worried about his (her) relationship, he (she) might think:
"You'd better hang onto him (her). This may be your last chance. You may never get anybody again."

Or a person might have critical thoughts about a potential partner:
"Don't get involved. You might get hurt because he (she) is so unreliable."

These thoughts are a part of everyone's thinking process. Please indicate the frequency with which you experience the following thoughts by circling the corresponding number.

1 – NEVER 2 – RARELY 3 – ONCE IN A WHILE 4 – FREQUENTLY 5 – MOST OF THE TIME

Fore example, you think or say to yourself:

1 2 ③ 4 5   "You're unattractive. Why should she (he) want to go out with you?"

1.	You'd better put on a good front. Put your best foot forward or he (she) won't be interested.	1	2	3	4	5
2.	You'd be better off on your own.	1	2	3	4	5
3.	He (she) doesn't give a damn about you. If he (she) did he (she) would remember to do what he (she) promised.	1	2	3	4	5
4.	He (she) never spends time with you. He (she) is always with his (her) friends.	1	2	3	4	5
5.	He (she) doesn't want to hear your opinions, so keep them to yourself.	1	2	3	4	5
6.	You've got to be careful of what you say to a man (woman).	1	2	3	4	5
7.	What you feel and think isn't important to him (her)	1	2	3	4	5
8.	Even if your marriage isn't romantic anymore, it's better than most couples have.	1	2	3	4	5
9.	You've got to keep him (her) interested.	1	2	3	4	5
10.	He (she) can be such a jerk (bitch)!	1	2	3	4	5

FIG. 21.1. Firestone Voice Scale Couples. © 1999, The Glendon Association.

consisted of 171 items derived from clinical material, discussion groups with couples, and from graduate students studying psychology. (See Figure 21.1.)

Three years later, the participants again completed the FVSC and the *experiences in close relationships inventory* (ECR-R; Fraley, Waller, & Brennan, 2000). The ECR-R is a 36-item self-report attachment measure and is derived from four categories or regions (secure, preoccupied, dismissing, and fearful) represented in a two-dimensional (low anxiety to high anxiety and low avoidance to high avoidance) space. See Figures 21.2 and 21.3 for a graphic representation of Mark and Sheryl's scores on the FVSC prior to

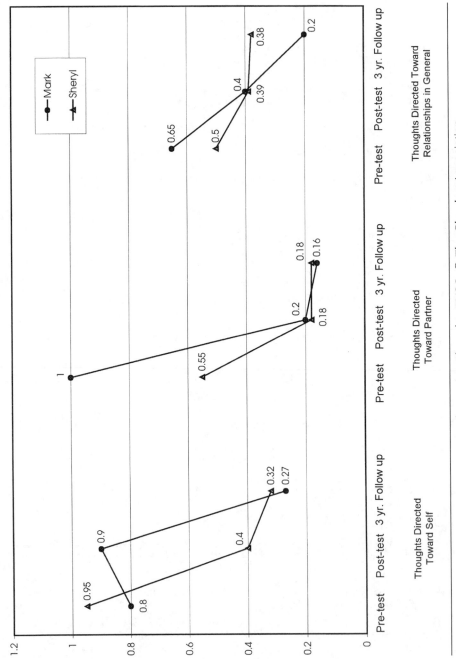

FIG. 21.2. Frequency of Negative Thoughts-FVSC. © The Glendon Association.

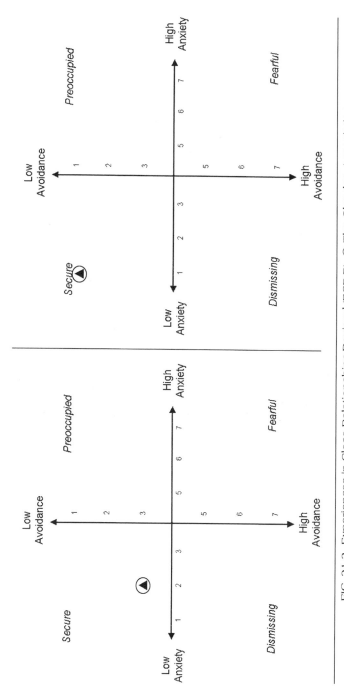

FIG. 21.3. Experiences in Close Relationships-Revised (ECR-R). © The Glendon Association.

the series of discussions, at 2-month follow-up, and at 3-year follow-up testings, and their scores on the ECR-R at follow-up. Results from pre and posttests and from the follow-up assessment using the FVSC indicated that Mark and Sheryl had progressed significantly in terms of a decrease in their negative views of self, each other, and the relationship.

DISCUSSION

Both Sheryl and Mark reported positive changes in terms of a happier, more optimistic outlook, more loving responses toward the other, and greater satisfaction in their relationship. This was a consistent pattern among the other couples in the group. The participants all commented on the value of learning to be nondefensive and open in listening as their partner verbalized his or her self-attacks. They found that they could reveal their feelings of anger and withholding patterns of behavior, admit critical, hostile voices toward themselves and their partner, and face up to the emotional pain and sad feelings they experienced as they attempted to restore intimacy, or as in the case of Mark and Sheryl, they once again tried to develop and sustain a close relationship. The participants reported that the group setting afforded a safe place in which to expose their fears of being alone and their anxieties about potential rejection, abandonment, and existential issues of life and death.

Findings from the preliminary study with this small sample could ideally serve as an impetus for further investigations into how negative thought processes predispose distancing behaviors in couples. Perhaps future investigations assessing the frequency with which destructive thoughts are experienced by individual partners will add to our knowledge of the relationship between maladaptive attributions and the deterioration of intimacy and closeness in many long-term relationships. According to Johnson, Karney, Rogge, and Bradbury (2001).

> [c]orrelational data on the relationship between attributions and marital satisfaction make it clear that unhappy spouses, as compared with happy spouses, tend to make more negative attributions. Yet, the measurement of thought is a difficult matter, and attributions are not an exception. (p. 176)

In addition, empirical studies or random clinical trials (comparing voice therapy with empirically validated treatments) potentially could establish the efficacy of voice therapy as a treatment for distressed couples.

CONCLUSION

Our approach, based on separation theory, suggests that by giving up illusions of connection and destructive modes of thinking, people can develop the capacity to both offer and accept love, closeness, and intimacy in their relationships. In breaking with defensive programming from the past, they can maintain feeling for self and others.

It was interesting to note that although the participants came to the couples group originally to improve their relationships, the significant outcome of this series of meetings was that each individual became more aware of his or her negative thinking and developed a step-by-step strategy for relating more closely to the other. In contrast with many couple therapies, where the emphasis is on preserving the relationship, we view the dyad as an abstraction and are concerned with helping individuals challenge their own defenses rather than maintaining the couple or marriage. We believe that each partner's individual defenses are the primary issue that interferes with intimacy; in essence, with our approach, individuals are receiving help in a couples' setting.

The men and women who took part in the series of discussions have continued to involve themselves in the process of learning how to love. They struggle to remain open and vulnerable in situations where previously they had tried to protect themselves from the possibility of being hurt again in the new relationship. They discovered that the most effective way to counter destructive thought patterns is to take risks and change defensive behaviors that were influenced by the voice.

Lastly, to break a fantasy bond and sustain genuine intimacy in one's relationship, one must go through the anxiety of giving up core defenses and attempt to remain close to one's partner, despite the increased sense of vulnerability. In our work with couples, we encourage individual partners to tolerate the anxiety of change rather than act out behaviors that alter the situation. As they overcome their resistance to change and avoid destructive patterns, they become more aware of the voice or destructive thought process and its detrimental effects and achieve better control of their behavior. They discover that the anticipatory anxiety involved in following through on a corrective suggestion is worse than the actual anxiety experienced when they engage in the action itself.

Intimacy and mutual regard can only be achieved when couples struggle through the anxiety aroused in movement toward closeness and individuation. Indeed, the hope for the couple as well as for the future of the family, is for the individuals to break out of the imprisonment of their defensive self-parenting posture. Freeing themselves from destructive ties (fantasy bonds) and moving toward independence and autonomy offers the possibility for a genuinely loving relationship.

REFERENCES

Ainsworth, M. D. S. (1989). Attachments beyond infancy. *American Psychologist, 44*, 709–716.

Ainsworth, M. D. S., & Eichberg, C. G. (1991). Effects on infant–mother attachment of mother's unresolved loss of an attachment figure, or other traumatic experience. In C. M. Parkes, J. Stevenson-Hinde, & P. Marris (Eds.),. *Attachment across the life cycle* (pp. 160–183). New York: Tavistock/Routledge.

Anthony, S. (1973). *The discovery of death in childhood and after*. Harmondsworth, England: Penguin Education. (Original work published in 1971).

Ayduk, O., Mendoza-Denton, R., Mischel, W., Downey, G., Peake, P. K., & Rodriguez, M. (2000). Regulating the interpersonal self: Strategic self-regulation for coping with rejection sensitivity. *Journal of Personality and Social Psychology, 79*, 776–792.

Bartholomew, K. (1993). From childhood to adult relationships: Attachment theory and research. In S. Duck (Ed.), *Learning about relationships* (pp. 30–62). Newbury Park, CA: Sage.

Batgos, J., & Leadbeater, B. J. (1994). Parental attachment, peer relations, and dysphoria in adolescence. In M. B. Sperling & W. H. Berman (Eds.), *Attachment in adults: Clinical and developmental perspectives* (pp. 155–178). New York: Guilford Press.

Bollas, C. (1987). *The shadow of the object: Psychoanalysis of the unthought known*. New York: Columbia University Press.

Bowlby, J. (1973). *Attachment and loss: Vol. II. Separation: Anxiety and anger*. New York: Basic Books.

Bowlby, J. (1980). *Attachment and loss: Vol. III. Loss: Sadness and depression*. New York: Basic Books.

Bowlby, J. (1982). *Attachment and loss, Vol. I: Attachment* (2nd ed.). New York: Basic Books.

Bowlby, J. (1988). *A secure base: Parent-child attachment and healthy human development*. New York: Basic Books.

Brennan, K. A., Clark, C. L., & Shaver, P. R. (1998). Self-report measurement of adult attachment: An overview. In J. A. Simpson & W. S. Rholes (Eds.), *Attachment theory and close relationships* (pp. 46–76). New York: Guilford Press.

Bretherton, I. (1996). Internal working models of attachment relationships as related to resilient coping. In G. G. Noam & K. W. Fischer (Eds.), *Development and vulnerability in close relationships* (pp. 3–27). Mahwah, NJ: Lawrence Erlbaum Associates.

Bretherton, I., & Munholland, K. A. (1999). Internal working models in attachment relationships. In J. Cassidy & P. R. Shaver (Eds.), *Handbook of attachment: Theory, research, and clinical applications* (pp. 89–111). New York: Guilford Press.

Bretherton, I., Ridgeway, D., & Cassidy, J. (1990). Assessing internal working models of the attachment relationship. In M. T. Greenberg, D. Cicchetti, & E. M. Cummings (Eds.), *Attachment in the preschool years: Theory, research, and intervention* (pp. 273–308). Chicago: University of Chicago Press.

DeWolff, M., & van IJzendoorn, M. H. (1997). Sensitivity and attachment: A meta-analysis on parental antecedents of infant attachment. *Child Development, 68*, 571–591.

Diamond, G., & Liddle, H. A. (1996). Resolving a therapeutic impasse between parents and adolescents in multidimensional family therapy. *Journal of Consulting and Clinical Psychology, 64*, 481–488.

Downey, G., Feldman, S., & Ayduk, O. (2000). Rejection sensitivity and male violence in romantic relationships. *Personal Relationships, 7*, 45–61.

Feeney, J. A., Noller, P., & Hanrahan, M. (1994). Assessing adult attachment. In M. B. Sperling & W. H. Berman (Eds.), *Attachment in adults: Clinical and developmental perspectives* (pp. 128–152). New York: Guilford Press.

Fierman, L. B. (1965). Afterword. In L. B. Fierman (Ed.), *Effective psychotherapy: The contribution of Hellmuth Kaiser* (pp. 203–212). New York: Free Press.

Fincham, F. D., & Bradbury, T. N. (1992). Assessing attributions in marriage: The Relationship Attribution Measure. *Journal of Personality and Social Psychology, 62*, 457–468.

Firestone, R. W. (1984). A concept of the primary fantasy bond: A developmental perspective. *Psychotherapy, 21*, 218–225.

Firestone, R. W. (1985). *The fantasy bond: Structure of psychological defenses.* Santa Barbara, CA: Glendon Association.

Firestone, R. W. (1988). *Voice therapy: A psychotherapeutic approach to self-destructive behavior.* Santa Barbara, CA: Glendon Association.

Firestone, R. W. (1994). Psychological defenses against death anxiety. In R. A. Neimeyer (Ed.), *Death anxiety handbook: Research, instrumentation, and application* (pp. 217–241). Washington, DC: Taylor & Francis.

Firestone, R. W. (1997). *Combating destructive thought processes: Voice therapy and separation theory.* Thousand Oaks, CA: Sage.

Firestone, R. W., & Catlett, J. (1999). *Fear of intimacy.* Washington, DC: American Psychological Association.

Firestone, R. W., Firestone, L., & Catlett, J. (2003). Creating a life of meaning and compassion: The wisdom of psychotherapy. Washington, DC: American Psychological Association.

Fonagy, P. (1998). An attachment theory approach to treatment of the difficult patient. *Bulletin of the Menninger Clinic, 62*, 147–169.

Fraiberg, S., Adelson, E., & Shapiro, V. (1980). Ghosts in the nursery: A psychoanalytic approach to the problems of impaired infant–mother relationships. In S. Fraiberg (Ed.), *Clinical studies in infant mental health: The first year of life* (pp. 164–196). New York: Basic Books.

Fraley, R. C., Waller, N. G., & Brennan, K. A. (2000) An item-response theory analysis of self-report measures of adult attachment. *Journal of Personality and Social Psychology, 78*, 350–365.

George, C., & Solomon, J. (1996). Representational models of relationships: Links between caregiving and attachment. *Infant Mental Health Journal, 17*, 198–216.

George, C., & Solomon, J. (1999). Attachment and caregiving: The caregiving behavioral system. In J. Cassidy, & P. R. Shaver (Eds.), *Handbook of attachment: Theory, research, and clinical applications* (pp. 649–670). New York: Guilford Press.

Greenberg, J., Pyszczynski, T., Solomon, S., Rosenblatt, A., Veeder, M., Kirkland, S., & Lyon, D. (1990). Evidence for terror management theory II: The effects of mortality salience on reactions to those who threaten or bolster the cultural worldview. *Journal of Personality and Social Psychology, 58*, 308–318.

Greenberg, L. S. (2002). *Emotion-focused therapy: Coaching clients to work through their feelings.* Washington, DC: American Psychological Association.

Higgins, E. T. (1987). Self-discrepancy: A theory relating self and affect. *Psychological Review, 94*, 319–340.

Johnson, M. D., Karney, B. R., Rogge, R., & Bradbury, T. N. (2001). The role of marital behavior in the longitudinal association between attributions and marital quality. In V. Manusov & J. H. Harvey (Eds.), *Attribution, communication behavior, and close relationships* (pp. 173–194). Cambridge, England: Cambridge University Press.

Johnson, S. M., & Greenberg, L. S. (1995). The emotionally focused approach to problems in adult attachment. In N. S. Jacobson & A. S. Gurman (Eds.), *Clinical handbook of couple therapy* (pp. 121–141). New York: Guilford Press.

Karpel, M. (1976). Individuation: From fusion to dialogue. *Family Process, 15*, 65–82.

Karpel, M. A. (1994). *Evaluating couples: A handbook for practitioners.* New York: W. W. Norton.

Kastenbaum, R. (1974, Summer). Childhood: The kingdom where creatures die. *Journal of Clinical Child Psychology*, 11–14.

Kastenbaum, R. (1995). *Death, society, and human experience* (5th ed.). Boston: Allyn & Bacon.

Kennedy-Moore, E., & Watson, J. C. (1999). *Expressing emotion: Myths, realities, and therapeutic strategies.* New York: Guilford Press.

Kinderman, P., & Bentall, R. P. (1996). A new measure of causal locus: the Internal, Personal and Situational Attributions Questionnaire. *Personality and Individual Differences, 20*, 261–264.

Kinderman, P., & Bentall, R. P. (2000). Self-discrepancies and causal attributions: Studies of hypothesized relationships. *British Journal of Clinical Psychology, 39*, 255–273.

Lerner, H. (1989). *The dance of intimacy: A woman's guide to courageous acts of change in key relationships.* New York: Harper Perennial.

Lester, D. (1970). Relation of fear of death in subjects to fear of death in their parents. *Psychological Record, 20*, 541–543.

Lieberman, A. F., & Pawl, J. H. (1993). Infant-parent psychotherapy. In C. H. Zeanah, Jr. (Ed.), *Handbook of infant mental health* (pp. 427–442). New York: Guilford Press.

Lieberman, A. F., & Zeanah, C. H. (1999). Contributions of attachment theory to infant–parent psychother-apy and other interventions with infants and young children. In J. Cassidy & P. R. Shaver (Eds.), *Handbook of attachment: Theory, research, and clinical applications* (pp. 555–574). New York: Guilford Press.

Main, M., Kaplan, N., & Cassidy, J. (1985). Security in infancy, childhood, and adulthood: A move to the level of representation. *Monographs of the Society for Research in Child Development, 50(1–2)*, 66–104.

Nagy, M. H. (1959). The child's view of death. In H. Feifel (Ed.), *The meaning of death* (pp. 79–98). New York: McGraw-Hill. (Original work published 1948).

Parr, G. (Producer and Director). (1997). *Voices about relationships* [Videotape]. Santa Barbara, CA: Glendon Association.

Parr, G. (Producer/Director). (1999). *Coping with the fear of intimacy* [Videotape]. Santa Barbara, CA: Glendon Association.

Peterson, C., Semmel, A., Von Baeyer, C., Abramson, L., Metalsky, G.I., & Seligman, M. E. P. (1982). The attributional style questionnaire. *Cognitive Therapy and Research, 6,* 287–300.

Rochlin, G. (1967). How younger children view death and themselves. In E. A. Grollman (Ed.), *Explaining death to children* (pp. 51–85). Boston: Beacon Press.

Roseman, I. J., & Kaiser, S. (2001). Applications of appraisal theory to understanding, diagnosing, and treating emotional pathology. In K. R. Scherer, A. Schorr, & T. Johnstone (Eds.), *Appraisal processes in emotion: Theory, methods, research* (pp. 249–267). New York: Oxford University Press.

Roseman, I. J., & Smith, C. A. (2001). Appraisal theory: Overview, assumptions, varieties, controversies. In K. R. Scherer, A. Schorr, & T. Johnstone (Eds.), *Appraisal processes in emotion: Theory, methods, research* (pp. 3–19). New York: Oxford University Press.

Ruszczynski, S., & Fisher, J. (1995). Introduction. In S. Ruszczynski & J. Fisher (Eds.), *Intrusiveness and intimacy in the couple* (pp. 1–9). London: Karnac Books.

Scharfe, E., & Bartholomew, K. (1994). Reliability and stability of adult attachment patterns. *Personal Relationships, 1,* 23–43.

Scharff, D. E., & Scharff, J. S. (1991). *Object relations couple therapy.* Northvale, NJ: Jason Aronson.

Schnarch, D. M. (1991). *Constructing the sexual crucible: An integration of sexual and marital therapy.* New York: W. W. Norton.

Sexton, R. E., & Sexton, V. S. (1982). Intimacy: A historical perspective. In M. Fisher & G. Stricker (Eds.), *Intimacy* (pp. 1–20). New York: Plenum.

Shaver, P. R., & Clark, C. L. (1996). Forms of adult romantic attachment and their cognitive and emotional underpinnings. In G. G. Noam & K. W. Fischer (Eds.), *Development and vulnerability in close relationships* (pp. 29–58). Mahwah, NJ: Lawrence Erlbaum Associates.

Shaver, P. R., & Hazan, C. (1993). Adult romantic attachment: Theory and evidence. In D. Perlman & W. Jones (Eds.), *Advances in personal relationships, Vol. 4* (pp. 29–70). London: Jessica Kingsley.

Solomon, S., Greenberg, J., & Pyszczynski, T. (1991). A terror management theory of social behavior: The psychological functions of self-esteem and cultural worldviews. *Advances in Experimental Social Psychology, 24,* 93–159.

Wexler, J., & Steidl, J. (1978). Marriage and the capacity to be alone. *Psychiatry, 41,* 72–82.

Zinner, J. (1976) The implications of projective identification for marital interaction. In H. Grunebaum & J. Christ (Eds.), *Contemporary marriage: Structure, dynamics, and therapy.* (pp. 293–308). Boston, MA: Little, Brown.

22

Avoidant Attachment: Exploration of an Oxymoron

Robin S. Edelstein and Phillip R. Shaver
University of California, Davis

To say of a child that he is attached to, or has an attachment to, someone means that he is strongly disposed to seek proximity to and contact with a specific figure and to do so in certain situations, notably when he is frightened, tired, or ill.

—Bowlby (1982, p. 371)

The metaphor of attachment, which Bowlby (1969/1982) used to characterize the emotional bond between an infant and his or her primary caregiver, implies proximity, affection, and being "fastened on" (*Oxford American Dictionary*, 1980). How then could an attachment be "avoidant"? How could a magnet attracted to iron be, at the same time, repelled by it? Although the imagery seems improbable, one of Ainsworth's major categories of infant attachment to mother was *avoidant* (Ainsworth, Blehar, Waters & Wall, 1978). This designation was based on the infant's behavior in a laboratory assessment procedure called the *strange situation* (Ainsworth et al., 1978).

The strange situation was based on the assumption that even a brief separation from a caregiver in an unfamiliar setting would activate an infant's attachment system (the innate behavioral system assumed by Bowlby, 1982, to regulate closeness to a caregiver or attachment figure) and heighten attachment behaviors (e.g., crying, following, clinging). And in fact a majority of infants in the strange situation become preoccupied and upset when their caregiver quietly leaves the room, and then seek proximity to the caregiver when he or she returns. Avoidant infants, however, do not appear distressed by their caregiver's departure and do not display attachment behaviors when he or she returns. These infants actively create distance from caregivers by turning away or ignoring their greetings.

Ainsworth's home observations revealed that mothers of avoidant infants were emotionally unexpressive, discouraged close physical contact, and were likely to reject or ignore their infants' bids for comfort when the infants were distressed (Ainsworth et al., 1978). Over time, these infants were hypothesized to develop an adaptive strategy of minimizing attachment behavior and displays of distress to avoid punishment, distancing, or rejection on the part of primary attachment figures who were uncomfortable with closeness. In other words, avoidant infants have learned to "deactivate" their attachment systems as a defensive strategy to prevent further distress. The defensive nature of this behavior is confirmed by evidence that avoidant infants do maintain proximity to caregivers in non-threatening situations (Grossmann, Grossmann, & Schwan, 1986) and, despite the outward appearance of indifference, show heightened physiological arousal during separations (Spangler & Grossmann, 1993; Sroufe & Waters, 1977).

In adulthood, attachment is generally assessed not through observation, as in the strange situation, but rather with self-report or interview measures (see Crowell, Fraley, & Shaver, 1999, for a review). Nevertheless, there are striking parallels between the behavior of avoidant infants and that of adults classified as avoidant. Both avoidant infants and adults appear to defensively regulate proximity to close others when they themselves or their partners are threatened or stressed (e.g., Edelstein et al., in press; Fraley & Shaver, 1998; Mikulincer, Florian, & Weller, 1993; Simpson, Rholes, & Nelligan, 1992). Like avoidant infants, avoidant adults inhibit expressions of distress (Fraley & Shaver, 1997) and minimize displays of attachment behavior toward romantic partners (Fraley, Davis, & Shaver, 1998). Adults with an avoidant attachment style seem to be less emotionally close to romantic partners, to self-disclose less (Anders & Tucker, 2000; Mikulincer & Nachshon, 1991), to dislike physical and emotional intimacy (Fraley et al., 1998), and to grieve less following a breakup compared to nonavoidant adults (Fraley & Shaver, 1999). These findings suggest that avoidant individuals may maintain physical and psychological distance from romantic partners as a way to prevent attachment system activation, thereby preventing the rejection, punishment, or distress they have learned to associate with close relationships.

Recent research provides further evidence for the defensive nature of avoidant adults' responses to threat: Whereas nonavoidant individuals show increased accessibility of mental representations of attachment figures when primed subliminally with attachment-related threat words (e.g., *separation*) as well as more general threat words (e.g., *failure*), avoidant individuals show heightened accessibility of mental representations of attachment figures only in response to general threats. When they are primed with attachment-related threats (e.g., *separation*), avoidant individuals actually inhibit mental representations of their attachment figures (Mikulincer, Gillath, & Shaver, 2002). In other words, discomfort with closeness and reliance on close relationship partners may occur primarily under certain specifiable conditions of attachment-related threat (e.g., loss, separation, rejection), which may remind an avoidant person, perhaps unconsciously, of situations in which he or she was punished for expressing attachment needs and seeking closeness.

In this chapter, we are particularly interested in the interpersonal and intrapsychic dynamics of avoidance in adulthood, and how these dynamics play out in the context of close relationships. Although the topic of adult attachment has received considerable attention in recent years (e.g., Cassidy & Shaver, 1999; Simpson & Rholes, 1998), relatively few comprehensive reviews of avoidance per se exist (but see Cassidy & Kobak, 1988; Fraley et al., 1998; Main, 1981). Thus, we will provide a systematic review of the theoretical and empirical literature on avoidant attachment and attempt to answer the following questions:

1. How does avoidant attachment work, both intrapsychically and interpersonally (i.e., behaviorally)?
2. How does avoidant attachment differ from secure attachment?
3. Are avoidant individuals really "attached" in a measurable sense? (If not, given their wariness concerning closeness and intimacy, what are they doing in long-term relationships?)

4. Are avoidant adults truly "insecure," or can avoidance 'work' smoothly as a style of relating to others?
5. Can avoidance be transformed into security?

By addressing these questions in the context of a book about closeness and intimacy, we hope to shed light on the distinction between secure and insecure approaches to intimacy and dependency, or interdependence, in close relationships. We will begin by describing the normative function of the attachment behavioral system in adulthood, followed by a discussion of individual differences in the way this system is organized and regulated. Next, we will consider the unique features of avoidant attachment as they relate to interpersonal closeness and intimacy, including the ways in which avoidant individuals regulate psychological and physical closeness to others.

By *close* and *intimate* we mean both physical closeness and intimacy—spending a lot of time with a relationship partner, having an extensively interdependent relationship, and being physically intimate (e.g., touching, hugging, kissing, caressing, having sexual relations)—and psychological intimacy: being very familiar with each other and being able to talk with each other about personal feelings, wishes, and needs. When closeness and intimacy are considered within the purview of attachment theory, one thinks naturally of the kinds of closeness and intimacy experienced in an infant-mother relationship, where the infant is held by the mother, often nurses from her breasts, is kissed, hugged, and tickled by her, and is bathed and has diapers changed by her. The infant falls asleep in the mother's lap or on her shoulder and may sleep next to her or on top of her in bed. The mother, for her part, experiences intense feelings of caring and affection for the infant while having the infant literally and figuratively attached to her presence and her body. As the infant matures, he or she will have an increasingly complex mind and imagination, which can be shared with close relationship partners. By adolescence and adulthood, perhaps the primary form of intimacy is psychological, but the physical aspects should not be underestimated. Anyone who has carried on a long-term relationship both by e-mail and in person knows that both modes of communication have their intimate aspects, but if one had to be abandoned in favor of the other, e-mail would usually be the loser.

THE ATTACHMENT BEHAVIORAL SYSTEM

According to Bowlby (1982), the mechanism driving attachment behavior across the lifespan is the attachment behavioral system, one of several behavioral systems (e.g., caregiving, exploration, affiliation, sexual mating), evolved to promote survival and reproductive fitness. The attachment system is automatically activated by experiences of danger or threat; in response, proximity-seeking and other attachment behaviors (e.g., clinging, crying, following) are intensified. These behaviors are adaptive in that they promote proximity to attachment figures, which in turn facilitates the threatened individual's immediate protection and ultimate survival. A central function of the attachment behavioral system is therefore the regulation of proximity (which is one form of closeness) to attachment figures in relation to perceived threat: When threat or stress is high, closeness and protection are necessary for survival and are particularly desired. When threat or stress is low, the attachment system is not normally activated, thus closeness may be less essential.

The regulation of proximity is central to attachment relationships in adulthood as well. Although more directly concerned with the infant-caregiver bond, Bowlby (1982) proposed that the attachment behavioral system remains influential throughout the lifespan. The normative motivation to establish affectional bonds with others, combined with the caregiving and sexual behavioral systems, contributes to the formation and maintenance of adult romantic relationships (Fraley & Shaver, 2000;

Shaver, Hazan, & Bradshaw, 1988). In part on the basis of this hypothesis, an extensive research effort has been devoted to the nature, function, and dynamics of attachment relationships in adulthood, including adult romantic relationships. Results from these studies reveal a number of similarities between certain aspects of infant-caregiver relationships and adult romantic relationships. For example, both infants and adults tend to seek support, comfort, and proximity to attachment figures when threatened and are likely to protest separations from attachment figures (Ainsworth et al., 1978; Fraley & Shaver, 1998; Simpson et al., 1992). These findings are consistent with the idea that the attachment system is a human behavioral system motivating individuals across the lifespan to establish bonds with caregivers and other attachment figures (Bowlby, 1982).

Researchers have provided further empirical support for the normative functioning of the attachment system in adults (e.g., Mikulincer, Birnbaum, Woddis, & Nachmias, 2000; Mikulincer & Arad, 1999; Mikulincer & Shaver, 2001). For instance, Mikulincer et al. (2000) subliminally exposed individuals to threatening words such as *failure, illness, death,* and *separation,* presumed to activate attachment-related thoughts and emotions, and measured their lexical decision times to attachment-related words reflecting both proximity and distance, such as *closeness* and *abandonment.* The closeness-related words became more accessible for all subjects, regardless of differences in security, suggesting that threats to the attachment system automatically activate thoughts related to proximity seeking.

Similarly, Mikulincer et al. (2002) found that attachment-related threats increased the cognitive accessibility of mental representations of attachment figures compared to nonattachment figures: Subliminal priming of *failure* facilitated reaction times to the names of attachment figures in lexical decision tasks for all subjects, regardless of differences in security. In a Stroop color-naming task, the threatening primes resulted in increased interference with naming the ink colors in which names of attachment figures were printed, reflecting the increased mental accessibility of attachment figures' names. In contrast, threatening primes did not increase the accessibility of nonattachment figures' names, nor did neutral primes influence reaction times for the names of attachment figures or nonattachment figures.

Results from these studies suggest that there are at least two normative reactions to attachment-related threats: heightened activation of the attachment system (as evidenced by increased accessibility of mental representations of attachment figures) and a heightened desire to establish proximity to close others (as evidenced by increased accessibility of words related to closeness and security). That neither of these responses appears to be moderated by individual differences in attachment security suggests that they are universal, at least in the populations studied thus far. However, as we discuss in the following section, individual differences do play a role in the way these reactions get played out in mentation and behavior.

INDIVIDUAL DIFFERENCES IN ADULT ATTACHMENT

Despite the normative motivation to maintain proximity to protective caregivers and form close emotional bonds with them, experiences with attachment figures influence the way this motivation is experienced and expressed, including an individual's comfort with, desire for, and striving for closeness. For instance, repeated experiences with an attachment figure who rebuffs or punishes displays of distress and attachment behavior may eventually lead an individual to inhibit such behavior, thereby decreasing opportunities for closeness. In contrast, an inconsistently responsive attachment figure may inadvertently elicit a heightened desire and striving for closeness on the part of a person who is trying to assure reliable attention to attachment needs.

Recent research suggests that individual differences in adult attachment, which are related to these kinds of interpersonal experiences, are best characterized by a person's placement on two relatively independent continuous dimensions, attachment-related *anxiety* and *avoidance*, rather than by the person's placement into a discrete category (Fraley & Waller, 1998). These dimensions are conceptually similar to those underlying Ainsworth's infant attachment patterns (Ainsworth et al., 1978, Figure 10, p. 102; Brennan, Clark, & Shaver, 1998): The anxiety dimension concerns the extent to which the attachment system is activated by environmental and interpersonal stressors. Anxious infants and adults are overly concerned with fears of abandonment and rejection, and as a result tend to be especially vigilant regarding the whereabouts of attachment figures (Ainsworth et al., 1978; J. A. Feeney, 1998). Adults high on the anxiety dimension are more easily distressed by brief separations from attachment figures (J. A. Feeney & Noller, 1992; Fraley & Shaver, 1998) and often do not feel that their needs for closeness are satisfied by relationship partners (Hazan & Shaver, 1987).

The avoidance dimension concerns the regulation of attachment behavior in anxiety-producing situations. Avoidance in infancy as well as in adulthood appears to reflect deactivation or inhibition of the attachment system (Cassidy & Kobak, 1988), resulting in infrequent displays of proximity seeking and other attachment behaviors. Adults high on the avoidance dimension report discomfort with close relationships and find it difficult to depend on close others. Their relationships with others are characterized by low levels of interdependence, trust, and commitment (Levy & Davis, 1988; Simpson, 1990).

Individuals who score low on both dimensions (i.e., who are classified as secure) are comfortable with closeness but not preoccupied with relationship partners. In threatening situations, secure infants and adults actively seek support and comfort from relationship partners (e.g., Grossmann et al., 1986; Mikulincer et al., 1993; Simpson et al., 1992.) and find that this support readily terminates activation of the attachment system. Adults with a secure attachment style tend to be in satisfying relationships characterized by trust, commitment, and interdependence (Collins & Read, 1990; Hazan & Shaver, 1987; Levy & Davis, 1988; Simpson, 1990; Stackert & Bursik, 2003).

Individual differences in attachment are therefore closely tied to variations in the need for and comfort with closeness: Attachment security involves a healthy balance between closeness and independence. Secure individuals have an internal sense of security and do not generally worry about losing relationship partners, but they can seek support from attachment figures when threatened. Anxious individuals desire more closeness than do their relationship partners, resulting in dissatisfaction when these needs are not met. Avoidant individuals are uncomfortable with closeness and overly concerned with self-reliance and independence.

UNIQUE FEATURES OF AVOIDANT ATTACHMENT

Distancing Strategies

Like avoidant infants, avoidant adults may (either consciously or unconsciously) fear that seeking proximity to others is not a feasible way to regulate and protect against distress because it sometimes leads to punishment or rejection. Instead, particularly under conditions of attachment-related stress or threat, avoidant adults tend to increase physical, emotional, and psychological distance from others.

Several different lines of research suggest that avoidant individuals use distancing as a coping strategy in response to certain kinds of threats. First, observational studies of romantic couples suggest that emotional support and caregiving provided to a partner are predicted by an interaction between the caregiver's self-reported attachment avoidance and the partner's visible level of distress (B. C. Feeney & Collins, 2001; Fraley & Shaver, 1998; Rholes, Simpson, & Orina, 1999; Simpson et al., 1992). When threat or stress is low, avoidance is unrelated (and sometimes even slightly positively related) to the provision of emotional support; however, when threat or stress is high, avoidance and the provision of emotional support are negatively related. For instance, Simpson et al. (1992) led the female members of heterosexual romantic couples to believe that they were about to participate in a painful, anxiety-provoking activity. When women were less distressed, men high on avoidance were slightly more supportive than men low on avoidance, but highly avoidant men were less supportive than low-avoidant men when their partners were distressed (see also B. C. Feeney & Collins, 2001). Fraley and Shaver (1998) also reported that, among couple members separating at an airport, self-reported attachment avoidance was negatively related to caregiving behavior, whereas this pattern was slightly reversed among nonseparating couples.

Similarly, Mikulincer et al. (1993) examined Israeli individuals' coping strategies in response to Scud missile attacks during the Gulf war. Whereas nonavoidant individuals tended to seek support from others, avoidant individuals were more likely to distance themselves from others and attempt to cope in a self-reliant manner. This difference was evident, however, only among individuals living in a dangerous, vulnerable area; secure and avoidant individuals living in less threatened areas did not differ in their use of coping strategies.

Taken as a whole, these findings suggest that avoidant individuals may be unsupportive, distant, or overly self-reliant primarily in certain kinds of situations, specifically those that are threatening because they activate attachment-related thoughts and emotions. These behavioral findings are paralleled by recent research suggesting that avoidant individuals may also distance themselves psychologically from others and/or sources of distress, and that this tendency is intensified in response to threat. For instance, in an examination of subjective self–other similarity, Mikulincer, Orbach, and Iavnieli (1998) found that, compared to secure and anxious individuals, avoidant individuals perceived the least similarity between themselves and members of an in-group with respect to shared traits and opinions. This finding was particularly evident following a negative mood induction, suggesting that avoidant individuals may create psychological distance from others as a mood repair strategy.

Creating psychological distance from others may also serve as a way for avoidant individuals to enhance their self-views. By projecting their own undesired traits onto others, avoidant individuals can increase self–other discrepancies, thereby inflating their self-view (Mikulincer & Horesh, 1999). Mikulincer and Horesh (1999) found that, compared to nonavoidant individuals, avoidant individuals could more easily retrieve an example of a person possessing their own unwanted self-traits, were more likely to attribute their unwanted self-traits to unknown others, and showed memory biases in favor of these unwanted self-traits. This process of "defensive projection" may be a mechanism used by avoidant individuals to enhance or maintain a positive self-view and maintain interpersonal distance by excluding unwanted information about the self and projecting that information onto others (Mikulincer & Horesh, 1999). This process may be magnified in threatening situations: After receiving failure feedback, avoidant individuals' self-appraisals became more positive, whereas the self-appraisals of nonavoidant individuals either remained unchanged or became slightly more negative (Mikulincer, 1998).

Dismantling Avoidant Defensive Strategies

The findings discussed thus far suggest that avoidant individuals employ a variety of defensive strategies, especially in stressful or threatening situations, to distance themselves from others, maintain positive self-views, and regulate negative emotions. Such strategies are also likely to prevent the establishment of closeness and intimacy with others. Further research, however, suggests that the effectiveness of these strategies may be undermined by situational constraints or additional sources of information. Moreover, at times, these strategies may even involve costs to those who employ them. For instance, avoidant individuals' self-views become less inflated when they are threatened but then prevented from using regulatory strategies (Mikulincer, 1998).

Mikulincer (1998) manipulated distress by providing failure feedback (vs. no feedback) to participants on a problem-solving task. He then used a bogus pipeline manipulation, in which participants were told that the veracity of their responses would be closely monitored through physiological instruments, to inhibit the use of regulatory mechanisms. Participants in the no-bogus-pipeline condition were connected to the instruments but were not told that their responses would be monitored. Consistent with previous findings, failure feedback (vs. no feedback) led avoidant individuals to inflate their self-views compared to nonavoidant individuals, but this result was evident only in the no-bogus-pipeline condition. When the bogus pipeline was used, there were no differences across attachment groups in self-inflation following failure feedback. Moreover, the bogus pipeline manipulation had no effect on avoidant individuals' self-evaluations when no feedback was given. These findings are consistent with the idea that the positive self-views of avoidant individuals are defensive in nature and may result from an effortful strategy in response to threat.

The defensively positive self-views of avoidant individuals are further called into question by other sources of information, such as peer ratings, projective measures, and physiological indexes. Although avoidant individuals do not report high levels of psychological distress, their peers rate them as more anxious and hostile and less ego-resilient than nonavoidant individuals (Kobak & Sceery, 1988). Similar discrepancies are evident in avoidant individuals' responses to the Adult Attachment Interview (AAI; George, Kaplan, & Main, 1984). When asked to describe their childhood attachment figures and their relationships with them, avoidant individuals appear unable to substantiate their own claims (Hesse, 1999). They may, for instance, describe a caregiver as loving and supportive, but then seem unable to provide congruent examples of caregiver behavior to support that description.

Mikulincer, Florian, and Tolmacz (1990) also reported inconsistencies in avoidant individuals' responses to conscious and unconscious measures of death anxiety: Although avoidant individuals reported low levels of conscious death anxiety, their responses to a TAT story measure revealed high levels of unconscious death anxiety. Avoidant individuals have also been shown to display heightened physiological responses indicative of anxiety to AAI questions concerning attachment-related childhood events, despite their tendency to claim lack of memory for those events (Dozier & Kobak, 1992). Dozier and Kobak suggest that these physiological responses reflect avoidant individuals' use of deactivating strategies when faced with probing questions about attachment-related experiences. Moreover, these findings, coupled with those of Kobak and Sceery (1988) and Mikulincer (Mikulincer, 1998; Mikulincer et al., 1990), provide substantial support for the defensive nature of avoidant individuals' self-views: When the use of regulatory strategies is inhibited or when nonself-report measures are used, the self-evaluations of avoidant individuals lose their positive glow.

Similarly, Mikulincer et al. (2000) found that, when primed with attachment-related threat words (e.g., *separation*), avoidant individuals showed increased accessibility of closeness-related words (e.g., *love, closeness*) but not distance-related words (e.g., *rejection, abandonment*). This pattern of results was similar to that found for secure individuals and different from what was found for anxious individuals, whose minds immediately turned to both closeness and distance-related words. With the addition of a cognitive load, however, avoidant individuals responded like anxious ones, exhibiting activation of distance- as well as closeness-related words. These findings suggest that avoidant individuals are normally suppressing or inhibiting worries about rejection and abandonment, and that this defensive process requires measurable cognitive effort or resources.

Moreover, these results allude to conditions under which avoidant coping strategies might break down and indicate that there may be potential costs associated with the use of such strategies. Although avoidant individuals may often succeed in preventing attachment-related distress (or at least the expression of that distress) and the establishment of closeness and intimacy with others, their efforts to do so may take a toll on their physical and psychological well-being. This may be particularly evident in highly stressful situations, or in situations in which avoidant individuals are prevented from using their characteristic regulatory strategies. For instance, avoidance was related to increased distress during the process of divorce (Birnbaum, Orr, Mikulincer, & Florian, 1997), a finding that may seem somewhat surprising given that avoidance is generally unrelated to reported distress, even among couples temporarily separating at an airport (Fraley & Shaver, 1998). Moreover, among dating couples, avoidance was negatively related to distress in response to a break-up (Fraley et al., 1998). Yet, according to Birnbaum et al., the experience of permanently separating from a spouse may overwhelm avoidant individuals and render their defensive strategies, which are generally successful in preventing attachment-related distress, less effective. Along these same lines, avoidance was positively related to distress among new mothers adjusting to the transition to parenthood (Mikulincer & Florian, 1998).

In Mikulincer et al.'s (1993) study of reactions to Scud missile attacks on Israel, avoidant individuals coped by attempting to ignore the problem, distancing themselves from it, and not seeking social support. This strategy was related to later psychosomatic symptoms attributable to stress. Even more dramatic evidence for the limitations of avoidant coping strategies comes from a one-year longitudinal study of mothers' adjustment to a highly stressful event—their infants' being born with congenital heart disease (Berant, Mikulincer, & Florian, 2001). At a first assessment, shortly after learning of the diagnosis, mothers scoring high on attachment avoidance evidenced poorer mental health and were less likely to seek social support than less avoidant mothers. Further, mothers' avoidance at the first assessment predicted a negative change in their mental health status one year later. That is, the mental health of avoidant mothers, bad from the start, deteriorated over this one-year period. The deterioration was mediated by avoidant women's increased reliance on emotion-focused coping strategies and by their increasingly pessimistic appraisals of their ability to cope with the situation.

That avoidance was associated with the use of emotion-focused coping strategies in this study may provide further evidence for the breakdown of avoidant defenses. These kinds of strategies are generally found to be more characteristic of anxious, rather than avoidant, individuals. Unlike avoidant individuals, those who are highly anxious easily become overwhelmed by negative events and are often preoccupied with their own emotional reactions to those events. It is possible that, in highly stressful situations, avoidant individuals have greater difficulty relying on their typical defensive strategies (or find them less effective) and instead are forced to rely on alternative strategies. The findings of Berant et al. (2001) suggest that reliance on these secondary strategies is partially responsible for the deterioration of avoidant mothers' mental health. Highly stressful situations may therefore leave avoidant individuals unusually defenseless, in that they cannot rely on their typical (and normally effective) coping strategies.

Another possibility is that the limitations of avoidant individuals' defensive strategies are simply more evident in high-stress situations. That is, there may be hidden costs to those using these defenses that become perceptible only when indirect measures are used, or when levels of stress reach a certain threshold. This possibility would be consistent with observations of avoidant infants, whose apparent indifference to separation is betrayed by a physiological reaction indicative of anxiety (Spangler & Grossmann, 1993; Sroufe & Waters, 1977).

Thus, the defensive strategies relied upon by avoidant individuals, although often successful in regulating attachment-related distress and maintaining distance from others, may at times prove costly to these individuals' own physical and psychological well-being. As will be discussed next, by preventing the establishment of closeness and intimacy with others, such strategies are also likely to disrupt close relationships and damage romantic partners.

Relationship Dynamics

Although there may be negative effects of avoidant individuals' chronic reliance on deactivating and distancing strategies, these effects may not always be apparent, especially in the short-term. More readily apparent are the negative effects of these strategies on the avoidant person's close relationships and relationship partners. Avoidant individuals' tendencies to distance themselves from others, affirm their independence, and suppress negative emotion may lead relationship partners to become dissatisfied and relationship quality to deteriorate. For instance, as discussed earlier, a growing body of research suggests that avoidance is negatively related to caregiving behavior, particularly when relationship partners are distressed or upset (B. C. Feeney & Collins, 2001; Fraley & Shaver, 1998; Simpson et al., 1992). Perhaps as a way to distance themselves from expressions of negative emotion and others' distress, avoidant individuals seem to be unresponsive precisely when their partners most need their support. Those on the receiving end of this unsupportive behavior, although dissatisfied with their partners' response, may learn to avoid seeking support or expressing distress for fear of further rejection.

Avoidance has similarly been related to poor communication during couple members' discussions of conflictual issues in their relationship (Collins & B. C. Feeney, 2000; Simpson, Rholes, & Phillips, 1996). For couples including avoidant individuals, the quality of discussion appears to decrease as the level of conflict being discussed increases. Along these same lines, Guerrero (1998) found that avoidant individuals were less likely to talk to their romantic partners when they were suspicious about their partner's fidelity. Instead, they tended to distance themselves from their partners, to deny the problem, or to use other indirect coping strategies (e.g., giving their partner the "silent treatment"). Rather than easing suspicions or resolving conflicts, this kind of behavior may further alienate romantic partners. Moreover, insofar as open discussions of conflict can increase feelings of intimacy, evading such discussions may be another way for avoidant individuals to maintain interpersonal distance from relationship partners.

By preventing the establishment of intimacy in their close relationships, avoidant individuals may seek to prevent the attachment-related distress they have learned to associate with closeness. Compared to nonavoidant individuals, they are more likely to date more than one person at a time (Kirkpatrick & Hazan, 1994) and to become attracted to or involved with someone else while in a relationship (Guerrero, 1998; Schachner & Shaver, 2002). Perhaps as a way to justify their reluctance to invest fully in and commit to relationship partners, avoidant individuals are more likely to perceive their partners unfavorably. For instance, they perceive their partners as less trustworthy (B. C. Feeney & Collins, 2001) and are more likely to suspect them of infidelity

(Guerrero, 1998). If partners are devalued, threats of rejection or abandonment by them may be less distressing.

Moreover, avoidant behavior may preclude even the initial formation of close relationships. Avoidant individuals prefer to work alone (Hazan & Shaver, 1990), use work or other solitary activities to avoid social interactions (Hazan & Shaver, 1990; Mikulincer, 1997), and find themselves attracted to potential relationship partners who do not reciprocate their feelings (A. Aron, E. N. Aron, & Allen, 1998). After completing tasks (e.g., self-disclosure exercises) designed to foster closeness in previously unacquainted dyads, avoidant individuals report feeling less close to their partners than do nonavoidant individuals (A. Aron, Melinat, E. N. Aron, Vallone, & Bator, 1997).

In addition, avoidance is associated with the regulation of *physical* intimacy in the context of romantic relationships. Avoidant individuals are less likely than nonavoidant individuals to use physical touch to communicate affection and comfort to relationship partners, and are more likely to find touch aversive (Brennan et al., 1998). Nevertheless, avoidant adults are more likely than nonavoidant adults to engage in promiscuous sexual behavior (Brennan et al., 1998; Brennan & Shaver, 1995; Schachner & Shaver, 2002), suggesting that it is not sexual touch per se that they find aversive, but rather more affectionate or intimate aspects of touch (see also Hazan, Zeifman, & Middleton, 1994). Avoidance of physical intimacy, particularly when coupled with efforts to maintain psychological distance, may serve to prevent the establishment of genuine attachment bonds. Consistent with this suggestion, Fraley and Davis (1997) found that avoidant adults were less likely to be in relationships characterized as "full-blown" attachments (i.e., in which relationship partners satisfied all requisite attachment functions).

In consideration of these findings, it is not surprising that avoidant individuals tend to be in romantic relationships characterized by lower levels of satisfaction, intimacy, interdependence, and longevity (Brennan & Shaver, 1995; B. C. Feeney & Collins, 2001, J. A. Feeney, 1998, 1999; Kirkpatrick & Davis, 1994; Kirkpatrick & Hazan, 1994; Lussier, Sabourin, & Turgeon, 1997). Nevertheless, most avoidant individuals do find themselves in close relationships, despite their apparent dissatisfaction with them. Moreover, they are much more likely to become involved in relationships with securely attached or even anxious partners than with other avoidant individuals (Collins & Read, 1990; Kirkpatrick & Davis, 1994; Simpson, 1990), which may serve a relationship-maintaining function (Kirkpatrick & Davis, 1994). Given their apparent discomfort with closeness and intimacy, what then motivates avoidant individuals to pursue close relationships?

We propose that avoidant adults are in roughly the same situation as avoidant infants: Like every other human being, they have a need for care and security, and do not feel fully sufficient on their own, but they have learned to maintain a certain degree of self-protective distance to avoid vulnerability and rejection. Under low-stress conditions, avoidant and nonavoidant individuals are often indistinguishable, and when a *general* (not specifically attachment-related) threat is encountered, the minds of avoidant individuals turn automatically to thoughts of attachment security and mental representations of attachment figures. Only when issues like separation and rejection (i.e., attachment-related injuries; Johnson, Makinen, & Millikin, 2001) arise, or when the level of distress goes beyond the ability of avoidant defenses to contain, do avoidant individuals' defensive strategies become evident.

Yet these strategies are not without costs. Avoidance is negatively related to relationship satisfaction (J. A. Feeney, 1999), including satisfaction with sexual experiences (Hazan, Ziefman, & Middleton, 1994), and to relationship longevity (Kirkpatrick & Hazan, 1994). Avoidant individuals are less likely to discuss their sexual histories with relationship partners, which may lead to unsafe sex (Schachner & Shaver, 2002). Other relationships may also suffer: Avoidant individuals have poor parenting skills

(Rholes, Simpson, & Blakely, 1995; Rholes, Simpson, Blakely, Lanigan, & Allen, 1997) and have difficulty getting along with their colleagues at work (Hazan & Shaver, 1990). They are cut off from their own emotional memories (Mikulincer & Orbach, 1995), out of touch with some of their own deep fears (e.g., of death, Mikulincer et al., 1990), and unaffected by infusions of positive affect (Mikulincer & Sheffi, 2000). Avoidant individuals use alcohol to blot out negative concerns and feelings (Brennan & Shaver, 1995; Tracy, Shaver, Albino, & Cooper, 2003) and seem to crumble when put under strain (Berant et al., 2001; Mikulincer et al., 1993). They systematically distort their social perceptions, including their own self-perceptions, and have to struggle to maintain a false sense of self-esteem and self-reliance (Mikulincer, 1998).

Prospects for Change

Can avoidant individuals' destructive approach to close relationships be changed? Unfortunately, given their tendency to deny problems and needs, and their stated dislike of self-disclosure and of people who encourage disclosure, avoidant individuals may be particularly difficult to treat in therapy. Nevertheless, we are encouraged by several promising therapeutic techniques currently being developed and used to treat symptoms associated with avoidance, such as fear of intimacy and defensive reactions to conflict.

Clinicians at the Glendon Association propose that fears of intimacy are rooted in destructive thoughts, attitudes, and beliefs about the self and relationship partners (Firestone & Catlett, 1999). These internalized "voices" lead people to distance themselves from others and to perceive them in a negative light, both being characteristic of avoidant individuals. Through a therapeutic intervention called "voice therapy," individuals can learn to acknowledge, understand, and change their critical internal voices. Recent evidence suggests that voice therapy is successful in decreasing the frequency of negative thoughts about the self, relationship partners, and relationships in general (Firestone, Firestone, & Catlett, this volume). In addition, participants report greater optimism about the future and greater relationship satisfaction following the voice therapy intervention. Voice therapy may thus be an effective way to modify avoidant approaches to closeness and intimacy.

Another approach used to treat relational difficulties is emotionally focused therapy (EFT; Johnson, 1996), an attachment-based therapeutic intervention for couples. According to this approach, relationship partners' inability to manage their own attachment insecurities results in defensive responses to conflict, such as unresponsiveness and inaccessibility, which in turn result in further conflict and dissatisfaction. Defensive responses may also prevent relationship partners from providing support to and seeking support from one another during times of stress. The goal of EFT is to transform a distressed relationship into a secure attachment bond by minimizing defensive reactions to conflict and teaching partners to use one another as sources of comfort. Given avoidant individuals' tendency to rely on defensive strategies, especially in the face of conflict, and their apparent difficulties in both seeking and providing support, interventions such as EFT may be particularly useful (see also, McCullough, 2001, for a discussion of emotionally focused techniques). Although research on the effectiveness of this kind of therapy for treating avoidance per se has not yet been conducted, EFT has been shown to increase participants' relationship satisfaction (Johnson & Sims, 2000).

Avoidant defenses, particularly the defensive enhancement of self-views and the desire to be self-sufficient and independent of others, have also been treated with some success by therapists in the object-relations and self-psychology traditions. According to these perspectives, defensive responses result from early relations with caregivers, in which dependence and vulnerability are discouraged or punished, and the child does not feel that his or her true self is accepted (Kohut, 1966). Treatment generally involves dismantling defensive strategies by encouraging clients to give up the false self they have constructed to protect themselves from rejection and vulnerability, and by fostering recognition of needs for closeness with others (e.g., Johnson, 1987).

In addition, experimental research indicates that avoidant individuals respond positively to security-inducing primes: Like secure individuals, they become less hostile toward out-groups (Mikulincer & Shaver, 2001), more open to new ideas (Mikulincer, 1998), more empathic (Mikulincer et al., 2001), and more attracted to secure relationship partners (Baldwin, Keelan, Fehr, Enns, & Koh-Rangarajoo, 1996). Although tasks designed to foster closeness in dyads may be less effective for avoidant compared to nonavoidant participants, they have nevertheless been shown to increase attachment security (at least temporarily) for both groups (A. Aron et al., 1997). These findings suggest that therapeutic interventions that serve similar security-enhancing functions could be used successfully with avoidant individuals. Along these same lines, secure relationship partners, by serving as repeated, chronic security primes, may temper avoidant defenses and increase avoidant individuals' desire for and comfort with closeness.

CONCLUSIONS

We began by asking five questions to which we can now offer preliminary answers.

1. How does avoidant attachment work, both intrapsychically and interpersonally (i.e., behaviorally)? For some people, avoidance is a necessary compromise between an innate need for reliable protection, safety, and support from a few select people—attachment figures—and fear of punishment, rejection, or abandonment by those figures. Theoretically, this compromise is accomplished through a network of inhibitory neural circuits (Shaver & Mikulincer, 2002). That is, the attachment behavioral system itself remains intact; however, under conditions that remind a person of potential vulnerability to punishment, loss of control, or rejection, he or she automatically inhibits needs for closeness and protection and instead opts for self-reliance and avoidant coping strategies. Outwardly, as observed by relationship partners and researchers, this inhibitory process may suggest the absence of distress, and even a failure to become emotionally attached to others. Inwardly, it is a costly process that can lower a person's quality of life and poison his or her close relationships.

2. How does avoidant attachment differ from secure attachment? Secure individuals can generally be self-reliant because they have found that safety, support, and encouragement are reliably provided by relationship partners when needed. Their autonomy is not propped up by defensive, inhibitory circuitry that keeps them from experiencing the full range of emotion, distorts perceptions of self and relationship partners, and (in the long run) damages health and close relationships. Both secure and avoidant individuals view themselves as having high self-esteem, but avoidant self-views are maintained through a combination of defensive projection of their own unwanted traits onto others and suppression or repression of threats and fears. Secure individuals generally make good relationship partners by virtue, in part, of being competent, empathic caregivers. Avoidant individuals generally do not respond well to partners who are in need, and have trouble providing empathic care.

3. Are avoidant individuals really "attached" in a measurable sense? Yes. When asked to complete the WHOTO questionnaire (Trinke & Bartholomew, 1997), which asks who participants would turn to in times of need, avoidant

individuals list the same kinds of people that nonavoidant individuals do—parents, romantic partners, siblings, and friends (Mikulincer et al., 2002). Moreover, when avoidant research participants are primed with threatening words such as "failure," the lexical decision times for their named attachment figures decrease just like those of nonavoidant participants. Moreover, when avoidant individuals are asked to vividly imagine breaking up with their long-term relationship partner, their level of concern and autonomic arousal are similar to those of nonavoidant individuals (Fraley & Shaver, 1997). What makes them different is that they can shut off thinking about this painful topic at will, which less avoidant people (especially those who are high in attachment anxiety) have difficulty doing. Although avoidant individuals may look less attached in many situations (e.g., being more interested in extra-relationship sex, grieving less intensely following breakups), they are likely to be attached to their primary relationship partners in very real ways. Their reasons for being involved in long-term relationships are probably more or less the same as the reasons of nonavoidant individuals.

4. Are avoidant adults truly "insecure," or can avoidance 'work' smoothly as a style of relating to others? Avoidant individuals are truly insecure, even if they do not say so on common measures of psychological distress. Their insecurity is often detected by indirect measures, such as assessments of peer reports and physiological indices of distress, and is reflected in their relationships with others. Although avoidant individuals may be relatively successful at regulating attachment-related distress much of the time, their ability to relate to others is severely hindered by their repertoire of defensive strategies. Their close relationships are less intimate, interdependent, satisfying, and long-lasting than those of secure individuals.

5. Can avoidance be transformed into security? Because avoidant research participants respond to security primes in the same ways, and to the same extent, as anxious and secure participants (Mikulincer & Shaver, 2001), we are optimistic that their attachment systems are capable of being transformed in the direction of security. Therapeutic interventions that serve a security-enhancing function have the potential to help avoidant individuals overcome their fear of intimacy.

ACKNOWLEDGMENTS

We thank Arthur Aron, Elaine Aron, Joyce Catlett, Lisa Firestone, and Debra Mashek for their helpful comments and suggestions on previous versions of this chapter. Correspondence concerning this chapter should be addressed to Robin S. Edelstein or Phillip R. Shaver at Department of Psychology, University of California, Davis, One Shields Avenue, Davis, CA 95616-8686. E-mail: redelstein@ucdavis.edu or prshaver@ucdavis.edu.

REFERENCES

Ainsworth, M. D. S., Blehar, M. C., Waters, E., & Wall, S. (1978). *Patterns of attachment: A psychological study of the strange situation*. Hillsdale, NJ: Lawrence Erlbaum Associates.

Anders, S. L., & Tucker, J. S. (2000). Adult attachment style, interpersonal communication competence, and social support. *Personal Relationships, 7*, 379–389.

Aron, A., Aron, E. N., & Allen, J. (1998). Motivations for unreciprocated love. *Personality and Social Psychology Bulletin, 24*, 787–796.

Aron, A., Melinat, E., Aron, E. N., Vallone, R., & Bator, R. (1997). The experimental generation of interpersonal closeness: A procedure and some preliminary findings. *Personality and Social Psychology Bulletin, 23*, 363–377.

Baldwin, M. W., Keelan, J. P. R., Fehr, B., Enns, V., & Koh-Rangarajoo, E. (1996). Social cognitive conceptualization of attachment working models: Availability and accessibility effects. *Journal of Personality and Social Psychology, 71*, 94–104.

Berant, E., Mikulincer, M., & Florian, V. (2001). Attachment style and mental health: A 1-year follow-up study of mothers of infants with congenital heart disease. *Personality and Social Psychology Bulletin, 27*, 956–968.

Bowlby, J. (1969/1982). *Attachment and loss, Vol. I. Attachment.* New York: Basic Books.

Birnbaum, G. E., Orr, I., Mikulincer, M., & Florian, V. (1997). When marriage breaks up: Does attachment style contribute to coping and mental health? *Journal of Social and Personal Relationships, 14*, 643–654.

Brennan, K. A., & Shaver, P. R. (1995). Dimensions of adult attachment, affect regulation, and romantic relationship functioning. *Personality and Social Psychology Bulletin, 21*, 267–283.

Brennan, K. A., Clark, C. L., & Shaver, P. R. (1998). Self-report measurement of adult attachment: An integrative overview. In J. A. Simpson & W. S. Rholes (Eds.), *Attachment theory and close relationships* (pp. 46–76). New York: Guilford Press.

Cassidy, J., & Kobak, R. R. (1988). Avoidance and its relationship with other defensive processes. In J. Belsky & T. Nezworski (Eds.), *Clinical implications of attachment* (pp. 300–323). Hillsdale, NJ: Lawrence Erlbaum Associates.

Cassidy, J., & Shaver, P. R. (Eds.). (1999). *Handbook of attachment: Theory, research, and clinical applications.* New York: Guilford Press.

Collins, N. L., & Feeney, B. C. (2000). A safe haven: An attachment theory perspective on support seeking and caregiving in intimate relationships. *Journal of Personality and Social Psychology, 78*, 1053–1073.

Collins, N. L., & Read, S. J. (1990). Adult attachment, working models, and relationship quality in dating couples. *Journal of Personality and Social Psychology, 58*, 644–663.

Crowell, J. A., Fraley, R. C., & Shaver, P. R. (1999). Measurement of individual differences in adolescent and adult attachment. In J. Cassidy & P. R. Shaver (Eds.), *Handbook of attachment: Theory, research, and clinical applications* (pp. 434–465). New York: Guilford Press.

Dozier, M., & Kobak, R. R. (1992). Psychophysiology in attachment interviews: Converging evidence for deactivating strategies. *Child Development, 63*, 1473–1480.

Edelstein, R. S., Alexander, K. W., Shaver, P. R., Schaaf, J. M., Quas, J. A., Lovas, G. S., & Goodman, G. S. (in press). Adult attachment style and parental responsiveness during a stressful event. *Attachment and Human Development.*

Feeney, B. C., & Collins, N. L. (2001). Predictors of caregiving in adult intimate relationships: An attachment theoretical perspective. *Journal of Personality and Social Psychology, 80*, 972–994.

Feeney, J. A. (1999). Adult attachment, emotional control, and marital satisfaction. *Personal Relationships, 6*, 169–185.

Feeney, J. A. (1998). Adult attachment and relationship-centered anxiety: Responses to physical and emotional distancing. In J. A. Simpson & W. S. Rholes (Eds.), *Attachment theory and close relationships* (pp. 189–218). New York: Guilford Press.

Feeney, J. A., & Noller, P. (1992). Attachment style and romantic love: Relationship dissolution. *Australian Journal of Psychology, 44*, 69–74.

Firestone, R. W., & Catlett, J. (1999). *Fear of intimacy.* Washington, DC: American Psychological Association.

Fraley, R. C., & Davis, K. E. (1997). Attachment formation and transfer in young adults' close friendships and romantic relationships. *Personal Relationships, 4*, 131–144.

Fraley, R. C., Davis, K. E., & Shaver, P. R. (1998). Dismissing avoidance and the defensive organization of emotion, cognition, and behavior. In J. A. Simpson & W. S. Rholes (Eds.), *Attachment theory and close relationships* (pp. 249–279). New York: Guilford Press.

Fraley, R. C., & Shaver, P. R. (1997). Adult attachment and the suppression of unwanted thoughts. *Journal of Personality and Social Psychology, 73*, 1080–1091.

Fraley, R. C., & Shaver, P. R. (1998). Airport separations: A naturalistic study of adult attachment dynamics in separating couples. *Journal of Personality and Social Psychology, 75*, 1198–1212.

Fraley, R. C., & Shaver, P. R. (1999). Loss and bereavement: Attachment theory and recent controversies concerning "grief work" and the nature of detachment. In J. Cassidy & P. R. Shaver (Eds.) *Handbook of attachment: Theory, research and clinical applications* (pp. 735–759). New York: Guilford Press.

Fraley, R. C., & Shaver, P. R. (2000). Adult romantic attachment: Theoretical developments, emerging controversies, and unanswered questions. *Review of General Psychology, 4*, 132–154.

Fraley, R. C., & Waller, N. G. (1998). Adult attachment patterns: A test of the typological model. In J. A. Simpson & W. S. Rholes (Eds.), *Attachment theory and close relationships* (pp. 77–114). New York: Guilford Press.

George, C., Kaplan, N., & Main, M. (1984). *Adult Attachment Interview.* Unpublished manuscript. University of California, Berkeley.

Grossmann, K. E., Grossmann, K., & Schwan, A. (1986). Capturing the wider view of attachment: A reanalysis of Ainsworth's strange situation. In C. E. Izard & P. B. Read (Eds.), *Measuring emotions in infants and children* (Vol. 2, pp. 124–171). New York: Cambridge University Press.

Guerrero, L. K. (1998). Attachment-style differences in the experience and expression of romantic jealousy. *Personal Relationships, 5*, 273–291.

Hazan, C., & Shaver, P. R. (1987). Romantic love conceptualized as an attachment process. *Journal of Personality and Social Psychology, 52*, 511–524.

Hazan, C., & Shaver, P. R. (1990). Love and work: An attachment-theoretical perspective. *Journal of Personality and Social Psychology, 59*, 270–280.

Hazan, C., Zeifman, D., & Middleton, K. (1994, July). *Adult romantic attachment, affection, and sex.* Paper presented at the 7th International Conference on Personal Relationships, Groningen, the Netherlands.

Hesse, E. (1999). The Adult Attachment Interview: Historical and current perspectives. In J. Cassidy & P. R. Shaver (Eds.), *Handbook of attachment: Theory, research, and clinical applications* (pp. 395–433). New York: Guilford Press.

Johnson, S. M. (1987). *Humanizing the narcissistic style.* New York: W. W. Norton & Company.

Johnson, S. M. (1996). *The practice of emotionally-focused marital therapy: Creating connection.* New York: Brunner/Mazel.

Johnson, S. M., Makinen, J. A., & Millikin, J. W. (2001). Attachment injuries in couple relationships: A new perspective on impasses in couples therapy. *Journal of Marital and Family Therapy, 27*, 145–156.

Johnson, S. M., & Sims, A. (2000). Attachment theory: A map for couples therapy. In T. M. Levy (Ed.), *Handbook of attachment interventions* (pp. 169–191). San Diego CA: Academic Press.

Kirkpatrick, L. A., & Davis, K. E. (1994). Attachment style, gender, and relationship stability: A longitudinal analysis. *Journal of Personality and Social Psychology, 66*, 502–512.

Kirkpatrick, L. A., & Hazan, C. (1994). Attachment styles and close relationships: A four-year prospective study. *Personal Relationships, 1*, 123–142.

Kobak, R., & Sceery, A. (1988). Attachment in late adolescence: Working models, affect regulation, and representations of self and others. *Child Development, 59*, 135–146.

Kohut, H. (1966). Forms and transformations of narcissism. *Journal of the American Psychoanalytic Association, 14*, 243–272.

Levy, M. B., & Davis, K. E. (1998). Lovestyles and attachment styles compared: Their relations to each other and to various relationship characteristics. *Journal of Social and Personal Relationships, 5*, 439–471.

Lussier, Y., Sabourin, S., & Turgeon, C. (1997). Coping strategies as moderators of the relationship between attachment and marital adjustment. *Journal of Social and Personal Relationships, 14*, 777–791.

Main, M. (1981). Avoidance in the service of attachment: A working paper. In K. Immelmann, G. Barlow, L. Petrinovich, & M. Main (Eds.), *Behavioral development: The Bielefeld interdisciplinary project* (pp. 651–693). New York: Cambridge University Press.

McCullough, L. (2001). Desensitization of affect phobias in short-term dynamic psychotherapy. In M. Solomon, R. J. Nebarsky, L. McCullough, M. Alpert, F. Shapiro, & D. Malan (Eds.), *Short-term therapy for long-term change* (pp. 54–82). New York: Norton.

Mikulincer, M. (1997). Adult attachment style and information processing: Individual differences in curiosity and cognitive closure. *Journal of Personality and Social Psychology, 72*, 1217–1230.

Mikulincer, M. (1998). Adult attachment style and affect regulation: Strategic variations in self-appraisals. *Journal of Personality and Social Psychology, 75*, 420–435.

Mikulincer, M., & Arad, D. (1999). Attachment, working models, and cognitive openness in close relationships: A test of chronic and temporary accessibility effects. *Journal of Personality and Social Psychology, 77*, 710–725.

Mikulincer, M., Birnbaum, G., Woddis, D., & Nachmias, O. (2000). Stress and accessibility of proximity-related thoughts: Exploring the normative and intraindividual components of attachment theory. *Journal of Personality and Social Psychology, 78*, 509–523.

Mikulincer, M., & Florian, V. (1998). The relationship between adult attachment styles and emotional and cognitive reactions to stressful events. In J. A. Simpson & W. S. Rholes (Eds.), *Attachment theory and close relationships* (pp. 143–165). New York: Guilford Press.

Mikulincer, M., Florian, V., & Tolmacz, R. (1990). Attachment styles and fear of death: A case of affect regulation. *Journal of Personality and Social Psychology, 58*, 273–280.

Mikulincer, M., Florian, V., & Weller, A. (1993). Attachment styles, coping strategies, and posttraumatic psychological distress: The impact of the Gulf War in Israel. *Journal of Personality and Social Psychology, 68*, 817–826.

Mikulincer, M., Gillath, O., Halevy, V., Avihou, N., Avidan, S., & Eshkoli, N. (2001). Attachment theory and reactions to others' needs: Evidence that activation of the sense of attachment security promotes empathic responses. *Journal of Personality and Social Psychology, 81*, 1205–1224.

Mikulincer, M., Gillath, O., & Shaver, P. R. (2002). Activation of the attachment system in adulthood: Threat-related primes increase the accessibility of mental representations of attachment figures. *Journal of Personality and Social Psychology, 83*, 881–895.

Mikulincer, M., & Horesh, N. (1999). Adult attachment style and the perception of others: The role of projective mechanisms. *Journal of Personality and Social Psychology, 76*, 1022–1034.

Mikulincer, M., & Nachshon, O. (1991). Attachment styles and patterns of self-disclosure. *Journal of Personality and Social Psychology, 61*, 321–331.

Mikulincer, M., & Orbach, I. (1995). Attachment styles and repressive defensiveness: The accessibility and architecture of affective memories. *Journal of Personality and Social Psychology, 68*, 917–925.

Mikulincer, M, Orbach, I., & Iavnieli, D. (1998). Adult attachment style and affect regulation: Strategic variations in subjective self-other similarity. *Journal of Personality and Social Psychology, 75*, 436–448.

Mikulincer, M., & Shaver, P. R. (2001). Attachment theory and intergroup bias: Evidence that priming the secure base schema attenuates negative reactions to out-groups. *Journal of Personality and Social Psychology, 81,* 97–115.

Mikulincer, M., & Sheffi, E. (2000). Adult attachment style and cognitive reactions to positive affect: A test of mental categorization and creative problem solving. *Motivation and Emotion, 24,* 149–174.

Oxford University Press. *Oxford American dictionary.* (1980). New York: Author.

Rholes, W. S., Simpson, J. A., & Blakely, B. S. (1995). Adult attachment styles and mothers' relationships with their young children. *Personal Relationships, 2,* 35–54.

Rholes, W. S., Simpson, J. A., Blakely, B. S., Lanigan, L., & Allen, E. A. (1997). Adult attachment styles, the desire to have children, and working models of parenthood. *Journal of Personality, 65,* 357–385.

Rholes, W. S., Simpson, J. A., & Orina, M. M. (1999). Attachment and anger in an anxiety-provoking situation. *Journal of Personality and Social Psychology, 76,* 940–957.

Schachner, D. A., & Shaver, P. R. (2002). Attachment style and human mate poaching. *New Review of Social Psychology, 1,* 122–129.

Shaver, P. R., Hazan, C., & Bradshaw, D. (1988). Love as attachment: The integration of three behavioral systems. In R. J. Sternberg & M. Barnes (Eds.), *The psychology of love* (pp. 68–99). New Haven, CT: Yale University Press.

Shaver, P. R., & Mikulincer, M. (2002). Attachment-related psychodynamics. *Attachment and Human Development, 4,* 133–161.

Simpson, J. A. (1990). Influence of attachment styles on romantic relationships. *Journal of Personality and Social Psychology, 59,* 971–980.

Simpson, J. A., & Rholes, W. S. (Eds.) (1998). *Attachment theory and close relationships.* New York: Guilford Press.

Simpson, J. A., Rholes, W. S., & Nelligan, J. S. (1992). Support seeking and support giving within couples in an anxiety-provoking situation: The role of attachment styles. *Journal of Personality and Social Psychology, 62,* 434–446.

Simpson, J. A., Rholes, W. S., & Phillips, D. (1996). Conflict in close relationships: An attachment perspective. *Journal of Personality and Social Psychology, 71,* 899–914.

Spangler, G., & Grossmann, K. E. (1993). Biobehavioral organization in securely and insecurely attached infants. *Child Development, 64,* 1439–1450.

Sroufe, L. A., & Waters, E. (1977). Heart-rate as a convergent measure in clinical and developmental research. *Merrill–Palmer Quarterly, 23,* 3–27.

Stackert, R. A., & Bursik, K. (2003). Why am I unsatisfied? Adult attachment style, gendered irrational relationship beliefs, and young adult romantic relationship satisfaction. *Personality and Individual Differences, 34,* 1419–1429.

Tracy, J. L., Shaver, P. R., Albino, A. W., & Cooper, M. L. (2003). Attachment styles and adolescent sexuality. In P. Florsheim (Ed.), *Adolescent romance and sexual behavior: Theory, research, and practical implications* (pp. 137–159). Mahwah, NJ: Lawrence Erlbaum Associates.

Trinke, S. J., & Bartholomew, K. (1997). Hierarchies of attachment relationships in young adulthood. *Journal of Social and Personal Relationships, 14,* 603–625.

Conclusion

23

Conclusion

Arthur P. Aron
State University of New York at Stony Brook
Debra J. Mashek
George Mason University

As we noted at the outset, the chapters in this *Handbook* focus specifically on closeness and intimacy, bringing together the latest thinking from a group of the most active and widely recognized researchers who have addressed these topics in social psychology, clinical psychology, communication studies, and related disciplines. In general, the authors of each chapter spelled out what they mean by closeness or intimacy; summarized an ongoing program of theory-based research focusing on its relevance to closeness or intimacy as they have defined it; and offered a variety of new ideas, new applications, and previously unstated theoretical connections.

Our intention from the beginning was that this *Handbook* would be more than a collection of isolated contributions. We did expect some degree of spontaneous integration and cross-reference to arise automatically by virtue of the common disciplinary heritage of many authors and the connections with relationship science that nearly all authors shared. However, the study of closeness and intimacy has been very diverse and not previously brought together in one place. Thus, we also made systematic efforts as editors to promote lines of connection. Our initial guidelines to authors focused contributors on a common structure and approach. We also arranged for most of the authors to serve as peer reviewers for other papers in the volume (thus, exposing them as reviewers in a deep way to each other's contributions as well as providing them as reviewees with input from other perspectives). In addition, our own two reviews of each chapter consistently urged authors to consider in their revisions specific linkages we recognized between their work and others'—something authors generally took to with enthusiasm and creativity. Finally, we have organized the chapters into sections that we hope provide some overarching structure and pattern.

In this concluding chapter we want to add one more layer of integration. Our goal for this chapter is to attempt to articulate, both from our perspective as editors and contributors, whatever common themes can be gleaned from this developing and variegated field. We also attempt to identify seemingly untapped opportunities for bringing different lines of thinking and research to bear on each approach. In addition, we point out issues that have been considered minimally or not at all. To keep the discussion manageable, we will mainly consider these issues section by section, and then conclude briefly with an even more general integration.

SECTION 1: WHAT ARE CLOSENESS AND INTIMACY?

The first section focused on just what it is we are trying to understand: What are closeness and intimacy? Each of the four chapters in this section answers this question slightly differently. However, there seems to be at least two points of commonality. As viewed by the authors of these chapters, closeness and intimacy (a) involve the self, and (b) are fundamentally interactional in nature.

Fehr's (chap. 2) chapter provides a scientific discussion of nonscientific conceptualizations of intimacy. Rather than defining intimacy, Fehr draws on people's intuitive understanding to identify commonly held beliefs about the events that precipitate intimacy. She concludes that "intimacy is inherently interactional" and that "intimacy expectations are based on knowledge of specific patterns of relating between self and others." That is, lay people understand intimacy to be fundamentally based on interactions between selves. This is a key conclusion, given it sets the stage for subsequent theoretical articulations. After all, if the theoretical descriptions fail to map onto lay understandings, one could question whether the theories are actually describing the human experience.

In Chapter 3, A. Aron, Mashek, and E. N. Aron define closeness as the inclusion of others in the self. Selves are central to this articulation. In particular, who I am is fundamentally altered because of my interactions with you; and who you are is fundamentally altered because of your interactions with me. Dovetailing nicely with the ideas discussed by Fehr, the notion of "overlapping selves" seems to capture the intuitive understanding some lay people have of closeness. Importantly, A. Aron and his coauthors wed this intuitive allure with a theoretical framework (and associated empirical evidence) that clearly emphasizes the importance of interaction between and among selves.

At the outset of their chapter, Prager and Roberts (chap. 4) caution that intimacy is not exclusively interactional. Not all interactions are intimate and not all interactions contribute to an intimate relationship. Rather, true intimacy both requires the engagement of the self and touches the self. Importantly, Prager and Roberts emphasize the role "authentic selves" play in connecting with others in ways that facilitate openness, positivity, and shared understanding.

Finally, Laurenceau, Rivera, Shaffer, and Pietromonaco (chap. 5) review the vast body of empirical support for Reis and Shaver's (1988) interpersonal process model of intimacy. The model itself, and the evidence supporting the accuracy of the model, make transparent that interaction between selves is paramount to establishing intimacy in a relationship. Issues at the core of selfhood (e.g., motivations, needs, fears) color what gets disclosed to a relationship partner, how that partner interprets and responds to those disclosures, and how the self responds to the partner's response. In sum, this interpersonal process model is fundamentally one of selves interacting to create a sense of shared intimacy.

As we noted, the chapters in this section convey strongly the message that closeness and intimacy engage the self—perhaps the deepest most authentic self—and may even create the self. As we also noted, closeness and intimacy seem to be process driven phenomena, as opposed to mere states (at the same time, authors such as Prager and Roberts highlight that specific moments or experiences can also be intimate, but this is different than what they call true intimacy). Closeness and intimacy build over time as a function of selves interacting, which creates prototypical knowledge of specific patterns of relating to others, the inclusion of others in the self, opportunities to engage with others in a positive, self-revealing way that creates shared understanding, and the possibility of feeling cared for, validated, and understood. More generally, common themes emerge in the processes and experiences that the authors of these chapters (as well as the authors of subsequent chapters) characterize as close or intimate. Generally, these themes include such features as a sense of connectedness, shared understandings, mutual responsiveness, mutual dependence, self-disclosure, or intersubjectivity.

At the same time, even just focusing on the chapters in this section, there is considerable opportunity for connecting and contrasting ideas from different approaches in theoretically compelling ways. For example, does the interpersonal process model of intimacy work differently depending on the authenticity of the selves involved? Is someone who is unwilling or unable to reveal her or his genuine self capable of feeling cared for, validated, and understood? Do the prototypes of how intimacy is created differ for people who do and don't make available their authentic selves in their own interactions? In what ways does the process of including the other in the self contribute to feeling cared for, validated and understood? Or are being cared for, validated, and understood in and of themselves expanding to the self? And, given the explicit role selves play in closeness and intimacy processes, how do these processes unfold in cultural contexts that do not assume an independent self (see Adams, Anderson, & Adonu, chap. 18, for a discussion of this topic).

There is not a single common approach for conceptualizing closeness and intimacy, as evidenced by the fact that opportunities exist for integration across different approaches. That is, ordinary people (at least in Western cultures) do seem to hold a common prototype of what creates intimacy and we can recognize common themes in researchers' definitions that are not unlike layperson's understandings. Yet, we do not by any means have a common definition. First, it is not at all clear that closeness and intimacy are the same thing. On the one hand, looking at the book as a whole, those authors who especially emphasize closeness (Agnew et al.; Arriaga et al.; A. Aron et al., Berscheid et al.; Ickes et al.; Mashek & Sherman; Rusbult et al.) generally stress patterns of interaction, interdependence, mutual influence, and the ongoing cognitive connectedness of selves or intersubjectivity. That is, the focus tends to be on patterns and structures and on behavioral and cognitive aspects. Much (though not all) of these ideas emerge from interdependence and self-expansion models. On the other hand, those authors who especially emphasize intimacy (e.g., Fehr; R. W. Firestone, & L. Firestone; Kouneski & Olson; Prager & Roberts; Laurenceau et al., Reis et al.; Sanderson; Vohs & Baumeister) generally stress themes such as self-disclosure, responsiveness, vulnerabilities, mutual understanding, touching, social support, and caring. That is, the focus tends to be on communication and affect. Much (but not all) of these ideas emerge from work on self-disclosure and in many cases are specifically informed by the Reis–Shaver intimacy model. (Several authors in this volume took positions somewhere in the middle, typically explicitly attempting to discuss both intimacy and closeness as considered in the various ways noted above. These included the Collins and Miller and Edelstein and Shaver chapters on attachment and the Cross and Gore chapter on interdependent self construal, all of which directly addressed both intimacy and closeness as considered in the ways we defined above; plus Adam's chapter on culture, Wortman et al.'s chapter on grief and loss, and E. N. Aron's chapter on temperament, all of which applied to intimacy/closeness issues that have not usually been considered by relationship scientists.)

Even within each of the broad areas of closeness and intimacy, the chapters in this *Handbook* suggest that there is considerable diversity of details. Within closeness, there seemed to be at least three general emphases: closeness as density of interaction (amount of time spent together, diversity of activities, and perhaps shared social network), closeness as mutual influence (strength of influence and mutual dependence for outcomes), and closeness as cognitive connectedness (inclusion of other in the self and intersubjectivity). Similarly, there appeared to be some relatively distinct themes within the general intimacy emphasis: intimacy as moments of felt connection and mutuality, intimacy as self-disclosure and vulnerability, intimacy as mutual responsiveness and felt concern for the other's welfare, and intimacy as physical touch and sexuality.

Given the large number of research papers on the topics of closeness and intimacy (we had nearly 4,200 PsycINFO database hits on *intimacy* or *closeness* just considering the past 10 years), we think a major challenge facing relationship scientists is sorting out the differences and commonalities among different understandings of these core phenomena (or this core phenomenon). That is, an important area for future research will be to identify the commonalities and differences among these different approaches. We realize that this kind of work when it has been done with regard to other core concepts in relationship science (e.g., commitment, love, satisfaction, power) has not, in any case of which we are aware, led to universally accepted definitions, distinctions, or understandings. Thus, it would seem unrealistic to expect such a conclusion for closeness and intimacy. At the same time, precisely this kind of work on other core concepts has been quite fruitful in clarifying major theoretical questions and furthering research by making clear conceptualizations available and facilitating comparisons among different studies and models. We think this kind of advance can be facilitated by such work on closeness and intimacy. We are hopeful that this process will be advanced by the appearance of this *Handbook*, which spells out and puts next to each other various major current conceptualizations of closeness and intimacy.

SECTION 2: HOW CAN CLOSENESS AND INTIMACY BE MEASURED?

Having considered (thought not settled) what is meant by closeness and intimacy, the next section turned to operationalizations. At least two themes were apparent in the chapters in this section. The first theme is multidimensionality and complexity. Specifically, each chapter offered strong arguments that we need multi-faceted measurement tools to capture adequately the complexity of closeness and intimacy. The second theme might be labeled *flexibility*. Each of the chapters in this section championed measurement strategies that are inherently flexible, thus allowing researchers and clinicians to collect rich and well-defined data across diverse contexts.

In Chapter 6, Berscheid, Snyder, and Omoto based their operationalization on an interdependence framework that led them to assess closeness with a partner in terms of amount of time spent with the partner, diversity of activities shared with the partner, and the strength of influence the partner has over the self. Importantly, assessment of this triad of factors (frequency, diversity, and strength), though by self-report, focuses on observable behaviors that occur within a tightly limited window of time. Berscheid et al. note that the three aspects are reasonably highly intercorrelated, as would be expected from the well-defined theoretical perspective on which the measure is based. At the same time they also emphasize that closeness is multidimensional in two senses. First, the three dimensions are far from perfectly correlated so that the pattern among them can be significantly informative. And second, a full picture of relational life depends on measuring other closeness-like (though conceptually distinct) constructs such as sentiment, longevity of the relationship, and cognitive interconnectedness.

It is also clear that part of the reason for the widespread and successful use of Berscheid et al's (1989) relationship closeness inventory (RCI) lies in its flexibility. Consider, for example, the adaptability of the Diversity subscale. The authors point out that the list of shared activities used in this subscale can—indeed, should—be altered as a function of the population of interest, an approach employed successfully in research they review. By utilizing population-specific activities, researchers who use the RCI enhance the sensitivity of the measure by making it more content valid. The importance of flexibility is again echoed in Berscheid et al's review of the different kinds of relationships that have been studied with the RCI (i.e., peer friendships, parental-adolescent relationships, adult romantic dyads), the populations with which the RCI has been used (i.e., adolescents, adult, cross-cultural), and the setting in which the RCI has been employed (i.e., cognitive processes, sexual satisfaction).

Agnew, Loving, Le, and Goodfriend (chap. 7) continue the discussion of multidimensional measurement and flexibility, focusing their chapter on A. Aron, E. N. Aron, and Smollan's (1992) inclusion of other in the self (IOS) Scale. The IOS scale consists of seven pairs of overlapping circles, labeled self and other, that vary in their degree of overlap. The respondent's task is to select the pair of circles that best describes his or her relationship with a particular other. The IOS Scale has historically been used as a global assessment of "oneness." However, the authors of this chapter consider whether new types of questions might be asked by looking at the multiple, diverse facets of closeness that feed into these global assessments. In the process of considering this multiplicity, they also illustrate the flexibility of the IOS Scale by demonstrating how this measure can be adapted to study any number of facets of closeness, such as "physical closeness" and "social closeness."

Kouneski and Olson (chap. 8) make apparent the benefits of assessing intimacy through the use of typologies, based on a multidimensional mapping of peaks and valleys across intimacy domains. By considering a full constellation of relationship strengths, clinicians become able to evaluate the relationship in its totality, thus avoiding the pitfall of reducing a complex social relationship to a single number. This broad-picture perspective gives way to clinical flexibility in terms of how the therapist makes use of the empirical data to help a couple recognize their particular strengths and make progress toward addressing their particular weaknesses.

All told, the chapters in this section suggest two clear take-home messages. First, it is important to use multidimensional measurement tools to capture the complex nature of closeness and intimacy. And second, relationship research and clinical practice can be made richer by using available measurement tools in creative ways, as allowed by the inherent adaptability of the measures.

At the same time, it is clear that the focus of the approaches in these different chapters, both substantively and methodologically are quite distinct. In this vein, what opportunities might there be for creative connections among these diverse approaches? As discussed in the Berscheid et al. chapter, there have been studies examining the relations of the RCI and the IOS scale, and studies contrasting the RCI with measures of "sentiment"—which may in part be what is assessed by the Enriching Relationship, Issues, Communication, and Happiness ENRICH. Still, both as represented by the chapters in this section and more generally, there has been little systematic examination of the links between measures in the closeness tradition (which are generally interdependence and social cognition rooted, such as the RCI and IOS scale) and those in the intimacy tradition (such as the ENRICH and measures that seem to tap related constructs described in other chapters in the *Handbook*).

As noted in our discussion of definitions, closeness and intimacy may be quite different constructs, in which case one would expect different measures. But as also noted in that section, they should be related in significant ways and identifying both the similarities and differences is important for advancing knowledge in this area. Such work will depend centrally of course on measures and in identifying the latent structure of relations among the different operationalizations of closeness. Thus, for example, one might ask whether couples with particular ENRICH profiles predictably indicate particular patterns of IOS scale and RCI subscale scores? When the IOS scale is used to asked about specific aspects of closeness, do responses map onto particular ENRICH domains in meaningful ways?

To add yet another dimension to the measurement of closeness and intimacy, might we learn even more by asking about both current and desired relationships (as Mashek & Sherman describe in their chapter in their use of the IOS scale and as has been done using the personal assessment of intimacy in relationships; Shaefer & Olson, 1981)? Even within the closeness domain, one might ask for example, whether actual strength of influence differs from desired strength of influence? What might such differences mean in terms of relationship quality and relationship trajectory? Additional insights might be gleaned by asking about ideal and/or socially prescribed levels of closeness and intimacy and perceptions of a partner's closeness and intimacy expectations.

In terms of what is largely missing in the domain of assessment, it is notable that, as in relationship research generally, all three of the measures of closeness and intimacy described in this section (the RCI, the IOS scale, and the ENRICH inventory) rely on self-report. Of course, the RCI minimizes this limitation by focusing on observable behaviors (if an unbiased observer were to trail the couple for a few weeks, her or his assessment of the couple's closeness should correspond with the assessments of the couple members); the IOS scale minimizes this limitation by being non-obvious in its wording and having demonstrated correlations with various relevant nonobvious measures (e.g., reaction times); and the ENRICH minimizes this limitation by drawing on the perspectives of both people in a particular dyad. Might adding implicit measures to our arsenal of tools advance the scientific understanding of closeness and intimacy even further? Certainly, Agnew, Van Lange, Rusbult, and Langston's (1988) thought-listing paradigm (described in the Agnew et al. chapter here), which focuses on spontaneous plural pronoun use, seems to be a step in this direction. The response-time and other cognitive measures described in A. Aron et al.'s chapter in this volume are another possible approach. Yet another, is the interaction diary study method (developed by Reis & Wheeler, 1991, and described in this volume in the Laurenceau et al. chapter) that enlists self-reports, but does so very close to when they occur, minimizing memory distortions. However, these examples are all considerably more demanding than is practical in many studies, particularly where closeness or intimacy is not the major focus or where participant time is limited. Thus, one direction for future research may well be the development of psychometrically sound nonobvious measures that are easy to apply in a wide variety of relationship research contexts.

Aside from the issue of possible limitations of self-report assessment, the measures described in this section (and even expanding them to include all those described throughout the volume) only cover a small part of the conceptual domain of closeness and intimacy. Just as a few examples, there seem to be no easily adaptable measures of momentary feelings of intimacy or closeness, of ideals of intimacy or closeness, of an individual's unique prototype of intimacy or closeness, of perceived dependence or influence of self on other, or of situational intersubjectivity. Thus a measurement challenge facing closeness and intimacy researchers and practitioners is to continue thinking creatively about theoretically and practically meaningful methods of assessing the complexities of closeness and intimacy across time and contexts.

SECTION 3: WHAT ARE THE GENERAL PROCESSES OF CLOSENESS AND INTIMACY?

As we noted in the introduction, all of the chapters in this volume discuss closeness and intimacy processes to some degree, but what stands out about the chapters in this section is their relatively direct focus on these issues. They also stand out from many of the other chapters in that they consider closeness and intimacy in the context of larger relationship-based models. Thus, each sees closeness and intimacy as part of the ongoing context of the relationship. Closeness and intimacy, in the view of these chapters, can not be isolated from more general issues such as the relationship's interdependence structure, the combination of attachment histories the individuals bring to the relationship, the attachment models the relationship evokes, the links with other relationship processes such as passion and sexuality, and how each partner perceives the other's responsiveness to their needs.

Rusbult, Kumashiro, Coolsen, and Kirchner (chap. 9) summarize in some detail the intricacies of the interpersonal structures of mutual outcome dependence, including their evolution over time, which shape motivation and experience in a relationship. In this context, one is close to one's partner to the extent one depends on the partner for meeting one's needs. Thus, the processes that drive closeness are those that drive dependence, including the satisfaction the relationship provides, the investments one has put into the relationship that would be lost without the relationship, and the alternatives to the relationship that are foregone by maintaining the relationship. What is central to this analysis is that closeness is more than a subjective state or even an emergent property of specific interactions. Rather, understanding closeness requires taking into account the ongoing context of how a person's well-being is linked to what the relationship affords and can be expected to afford in the future.

Collins and Feeney (chap. 10) link their contribution to understanding closeness and intimacy to attachment theory, another major conceptual framework in the relationship area and one that takes a quite different perspective than interdependence theory. Attachment theory focuses on a normative process of a relational partner providing security in the face of threats. It also, and most centrally, focuses on individual differences, based mainly on the working models people hold of what kind of support they can expect from a relational partner when faced with threat. Because intimate interactions involve people making themselves vulnerable, such interactions engage the attachment system. The opportunity and experience of such interactions are thus heavily constrained by individual differences in attachment styles.

Vohs and Baumeister (chap. 11) delineate a model in which rapid increases in intimacy are what generate the experience of passion. In this context, they suggest that there might be gender differences in the formula by which intimacy leads to passion, so that identical increases in intimacy will cause more passion in the man than in the woman. Drawing from varied sources of evidence, they contend that men in general have stronger sex drives than women and, interestingly, that the female sex drive shows more plasticity than the male sex drive, responding to social, cultural, and situational factors.

Finally, Reis, Clark, and Holmes (chap. 12) integrate for the first time broadly diverse strands of relationship research and theory to make the argument that the fundamental ingredient promoting experienced intimacy is perceiving the partner as responsive to ones own needs—"a process by which individuals come to believe that relationship partners both attend to and react supportively to the self." This conclusion is supported by a variety of evidence and theoretical reasoning, notably including work on interpersonal processes guided by the Reis-Shaver intimacy model (detailed in chap. 5 of this volume) in which intimacy depends on a partner's response to an emotional self-disclosure showing understanding, validation, and caring; Clark and Mills' (1993) work on normative relationship processes in "communal relationships" in which the key ingredient is attending to the other's needs; and work on social support processes showing that both the perception and reality of the partner's positive regard and sympathetic caring are important predictors of felt intimacy.

As noted, the four chapters in this section share the clear theme that an understanding of the processes of intimacy and closeness is greatly enriched by considering the larger relationship context. Thus, Rusbult et al. show how closeness is not an isolated cognitive phenomenon, but a result of an interpersonal process in which what matters are the circumstances of mutual dependence with the other; Collins and Feeney show how the experience and expression of intimacy can be conceptualized in the context of normative attachment processes that arise under threat (including the vulnerabilities engendered by intimacy-related based interactions) and how they are constrained by individual differences in the expectations of partner response developed in attachment interactions with early caregivers; Vohs and Baumeister show how intimacy operates in an interactive system with passion, with the core process being rate of change in intimacy over time; and Reis et al. show how a wide variety of relationship research converges on a core process in which intimacy is dependent on perceived partner responsiveness.

However, in spite of this broad common theme, as we have seen in the previous sections, the various approaches appear as relatively isolated lines of thinking and research. Thus, a central opportunity for future research that emerges from this section is the systematic exploration of similarities and differences in the implications for closeness and intimacy of different general relationship models. Here are just a few examples of seemingly important questions in relation to the four chapters in this section: Is the extent to which a given interdependence situation creates subjective dependence moderated by individual differences in attachment? How does the central importance of responsiveness to other's needs apply in the context of sexual intimacy? Does a rapid increase in dependence (and thus closeness) create passion? How is responsiveness to the other's needs shaped by the interdependence situation?

Aside from what might be integrated, what is missing entirely in this picture of the role of larger relationship theories in understanding closeness and intimacy processes? First, there are other major relationship models that would seem to be potentially important in understanding closeness and intimacy processes. These include evolutionary approaches (e.g., Buss & Kenrick, 1998), social cognitive models (e.g., Baldwin, 1995; Andersen, Glassman, & Gold, 1998), theories of relational ideals (e.g., Fletcher & Simpson, 2001), social learning approaches to marital interaction (e.g., Bradbury, Cohan, & Karney, 1998); empathic processes (e.g., Ickes, 1993); and many others that are not represented here. We did not invite contributions in these areas because we felt that too little had been done to date based on these approaches that explicitly focused on closeness or intimacy, though we may well have missed such work. There are also important potential contributions from relationship models that are associated with authors in this volume but who chose to focus on other sides of their work (e.g., Ickes' work on empathic processes, Aron & Aron's work on self-expansion motivation, Clark's work on communal versus exchange orientation). In all these cases, we are hopeful that the present volume will inspire consideration of possible links of these models with closeness and intimacy processes.

SECTION 4: WHAT INDIVIDUAL DIFFERENCES PLAY A ROLE IN CLOSENESS AND INTIMACY?

The chapters in this section focus on how individual differences constrain and promote closeness and intimacy. Over and above general relationship processes, the characteristics people bring to a relationship shape how close and intimate that relationship will be. Cross and Gore's and Sanderson's chapters focus on individual differences directly linked to relationships, while E. N. Aron's chapter focuses on more general individual differences. But in all three cases, the emphasis is centrally on the general role of these individual differences in shaping closeness and intimacy. Several other chapters in this Volume also stress individual differences, notably Collins and

Feeney's and Edelstein and Shaver's chapters that stress individual differences in attachment style, the Firestones' chapter on individual differences in fear of intimacy, and Ickes et al.'s chapter on individual differences in social absorption and individuation. However, in the case of each of these individual-difference related chapters we have put in other sections, individual differences are part of a larger model of relational or clinical thinking that also has a fairly substantial normative element. In contrast, the chapters in this section focus very directly and largely exclusively on the individual difference aspect. For the most part they limit more general consideration to, at most, the corresponding individual difference of the partner. Thus, in terms of Lewin's famous equation for describing behavior as a function of the person and the environment, these chapters focus in on the person.

Cross and Gore (chap. 13) describe an individual difference variable they label relationship-interdependent self-construal, the propensity to view the self as fundamentally connected with others. Relationship-interdependent self-construal implies a lower level of self-other distinctiveness. Thus, it facilitates a variety of relational processes that permit those in a highly individualistic Western culture to nevertheless experience closeness and intimacy with others.

Sanderson (chap. 14) focuses on individual differences in the importance of intimacy as a goal. She shows that those who pursue intimacy goals report greater relationship satisfaction in their romantic and friendship relationships. She further provides evidence that this link is due at least in part to those who have a strong focus on intimacy goals giving more social support to their partner, eliciting more self-disclosure from their partner, and using more constructive strategies of conflict resolution.

Finally, E. N. Aron (chap. 15) focuses on individual differences in temperament, characteristics that appear early in life and seem to be innate. She takes as her main example sensory processing sensitivity, a tendency to process information deeply so that highly sensitive individuals are more easily overwhelmed by high levels of stimulation but also are more attuned to subtleties in their environment. She describes findings showing how this variable has a variety of influences on the generation, experience, and effects of closeness on the individual whether viewed from the perspective of the sensitivity of the individual, the sensitivity of the individual's partner, or the degree of similarity of the individual and partner.

Overall, these three chapters illustrate that what people bring to a relationship dramatically impacts the closeness and intimacy in those relationships. Thus, people whose self-other boundaries are less rigid or for whom relational intimacy is a central goal clearly enjoy more closeness and intimacy in their relationships, and they do so because they function in relationships in a variety of discernable ways that promote closeness and intimacy. Also, the closeness and intimacy people enjoy depends, in ways that can be well delineated, on broader individual differences such as innate temperament, both their own and their partners'.

The role of individual differences in closeness and intimacy seems yet one more area in which there are striking opportunities for comparing and contrasting different views that have developed relatively independently. Just considering these three chapters, several questions immediately jump to mind. Conceptually and empirically, what is the link between interdependent self-construal and intimacy goals? How is each of these shaped by innate temperament? Yet another area for potential integration would be to apply E. N. Aron's approach of using Kenny's (1994) social relations model analysis into actor effects, partner effects, and relationship effects in exploring the role of interdependent self-construal and intimacy goals in closeness and intimacy. Indeed, these same kinds of integrative opportunities apply with regard to the individual difference variables covered in other chapters in this *Handbook*: attachment styles, fear of intimacy, and social orientation.

In terms of what is missing entirely here, one area that would seem important for future exploration is the relation of closeness and intimacy to other individual differences that have proven important in social behavior more generally, but have not been much or at all investigated in terms of closeness and intimacy. Some notable examples would be general personality characteristics such as those in the "Big Five"; self-esteem and differences in various self-related motives such as self-verification and self-assessment; intelligence, creativity, and other cognitive abilities; general and specific social skills; constellations of social attitudes such as authoritarianism, social dominance, conservatism; lay theories and world views; and demographic variables such as age, social class, and relationship experience. Another entire approach that is largely missing in work on the relation of individual differences to closeness and intimacy is the implications of closeness and intimacy for changing people. That is, individual differences (or at least their expression) are modified by experience. The most important such experiences would seem to be those that occur in the context of closeness and intimacy.

SECTION 5: WHAT SITUATIONAL FACTORS PLAY A ROLE IN CLOSENESS AND INTIMACY?

A key component of any relationship is the social nature of the environment in which that relationship unfolds. Thus, it may not be surprising that a common theme apparent in this section is that social environments play an especially palpable role in our closeness and intimacy experiences. Obviously, relationships neither develop nor dissolve in a social vacuum. What the chapters in this section make clear is exactly how profoundly our social worlds shape and reflect our closeness and intimacy experiences. That is, in the Lewinvan tradition of considering behavior as a function of the person and the environment, these chapters focus in on the environment.

Actually, most of the chapters in this *Handbook* consider the situation to some degree (though the chapters in the previous section the least). Indeed, most of the chapters in this book emphasize the exquisite dependence of closeness and intimacy processes on the situational context of the partner and the relationship. What led us to separate out the chapters in this section is their strong focus on situational factors over and above the immediate relationship context, notably including the qualities of the social network and the culture in which a relationship is embedded.

In the first chapter in this section, Arriaga, Goodfriend, and Lohmann (chap. 16), based on an interdependence framework, argue that couples arrange both their physical and social environments in ways that facilitate the couple's relationship goals. Importantly, their analyses suggest that high levels of closeness and commitment possibly bring about perceptions of strong social support. Another striking finding they present is that people who leave relationships had significantly lower levels of social support from their social network than people who do not leave relationships. In terms of the physical environment, the data suggest that people might actually arrange the objects in their homes in ways that reflect levels of closeness.

Wortman, Wolff, and Bonanno (chap. 17) explore the bereavement experiences of people who have recently suffered the loss of an intimate partner. The death of a partner creates a context wherein issues of intimacy must be negotiated. As such, a great deal can be learned about the very nature of intimacy by considering how people react to and recover from the loss of an intimate partner. Much of the focus of the chapter is on the survivor's interactions with people in their immediate social environment, who often approach the bereaved with a host of inaccurate assumptions about bereavement and varying motivations that can contribute to less than helpful—possibly even hurtful—attempts at social support. The authors suggest that the social situation created by interactions with members of social networks can alter how the bereaved deal with the loss of an intimate partner, and possibly even their willingness to enter into new relationships.

Adams, Anderson, and Adonu (chap. 18) investigate culture as an omnipresent situational factor that clearly colors how people view, study, and experience closeness and intimacy. This chapter points out that the study of closeness and intimacy has been grounded historically in a cultural context that is essentially invisible to those likewise embedded in this context. Importantly, Adams and his colleagues point out that empirical findings on closeness and intimacy from studies conducted in a Western cultural context must not be assumed to be "natural" or "inevitable." Rather they should be interpreted as falling from a Western cultural reality that emphasizes the voluntary connections of independent selves.

The message that most clearly resonates through the three chapters in this section is that layers of social context blanket our closeness and intimacy experiences. Perceptions that our friends and family endorse our relationships contribute to our willingness to remain in these relationships. Inappropriate or insensitive comments from those in our social circles can pile additional psychological strain onto the experience of coping with intimate loss. And, without being aware of it—indeed, without the ability to be aware of it—our closeness and intimacy experiences float about in a medium of culturally determined assumptions.

Some seemingly fascinating potentials for future research lie at the intersections of the chapters in this section. For example, how do bereaved individuals structure their social and physical environments as they relate to the partner who died? Do attempts at making the deceased partner more salient (e.g., hanging additional photos in the living room) depend on relationship goals (e.g., "to always remember")? What assumptions about death and dying exist in non-Western cultures and are these assumptions reflective of cultural conceptualizations of self and selfhood? What might a social network analysis or physical environment analysis (such as those conducted by Arriaga et al.) reflect in a culture where voluntary connections of inherently separate selves are not the norm? Further, all of these larger-than-the couple situational influences certainly bear on the findings and approaches to intimacy and closeness described in other chapters of this *Handbook* (and beyond). Cross and Gore's chapter on interdependent self-construal is one interesting example of a relevant integration of cultural variables with individual differences within a culture. Other possibilities include the impact of the physical environment and social network and cultural context on the relation to closeness and intimacy of variables such as attachment style or fear of intimacy, or the effect of these larger situational influences on issues ranging from lay understandings of intimacy, intimacy processes, and moments of intimacy, to behavioral and cognitive closeness.

Some issues that seem largely missing from the consideration of the larger-than-the-couple situation, include variables such as social class and ethnicity, wealth and physical security, historical era and cohort effects, and technological developments.

Finally, as we focus on the larger situational factors in and beyond these chapters, should we also ask about the limits of larger situational influences when it comes to closeness and intimacy? Is it possible that there are core closeness and intimacy processes, or sufficiently general ways to describe such processes without losing all meaning, that hold up regardless of the larger situational context? Even if the larger social context varies, are there any constants in the closeness and intimacy equation?

SECTION 6: IS THERE A DARK SIDE TO THE PROCESS OF CLOSENESS AND INTIMACY?

The chapters in the first five sections of this volume tend to paint a bright, rosy picture of closeness and intimacy. However, as the chapters in this final section emphasize, closeness and intimacy also have a shadowed, grey side. They show how there can be too much of a good thing, so that closeness can be smothering or threatening, and many people are actively averse to closeness, fear intimacy, or have a working model of others that is distrustful of closeness and intimacy. The chapters in this section spell out these processes and individual differences, emphasizing in each case that this dark side of intimacy is a natural, understandable response. It is one that at least in the short run, from the perspective of the experience of the individual, serves important self-protective or other social and personal functions.

Mashek and Sherman (chap. 19) operationalize being too close to a relational partner as describing the interconnectness with their partner as higher than their desired interconnectedness with their partner. They show that this experience is actually quite common in romantic relationships. They argue that it arises when a person feels that the partner or the relationship threatens their control over their own outcomes or the sense of having a unique identity. Thus, while closeness is generally desirable, when it threatens other important personal goals, it becomes aversive.

Ickes, Hutchinson, and Mashek (chap. 20) focus on the central role of intersubjectivity in closeness. They integrate various conceptualizations of intersubjectivity, mainly from the philosophical literature, along with empirical exploration of the latent structure of individual difference items based on these notions. This analysis yields a two dimensional scheme of social absorption and social individuation. The focus of their chapter is then on findings regarding the interesting group of individuals who are low on social absorption and high on social individuation, a group who are "unusually wary and suspicious" with regard to closeness and intimacy. Ickes and his colleagues do not explore why some people fall into this category, but they do emphasize that it is a way of experiencing the world that is consistent with a coherent philosophical position described by philosophers as objectifying others.

R. W. Firestone and L. Firestone (chap. 21) bring a clinical perspective to the table, focusing on how to understand people with a strong fear of intimacy, though also emphasizing that everyone who enters a significant personal relationship has to face the dilemma of deciding between the costs of intimacy and the costs of being alone. Those who clinicians often see, however, have both an especially deep dread of intimacy and an especially deep dread of being alone. According to the Firestones, the solution of such individuals (and sometimes of all of us) is to form a fantasy bond. A *fantasy bond* is an illusion of connection and closeness, it serves to allow the couple "to stay together while maintaining a nonthreatening emotional distance." This fantasy bond not only substitutes for genuine intimacy, but is actively threatened by it. Yet it is also a clearly self-protective response to what is perceived as an impossible situation.

Finally, Edelstein and Shaver (chap. 22) examine how people can have an "attachment" style that is "avoidant" of attachment. They argue that such individuals have made a trade off between a basic need for security with a primary attachment figure and their expectation that such attachment figures cannot be counted on to provide that security. Avoidant individuals still need an attachment figure and do indeed form relationships in which they are dependent on others; yet avoidant individuals put up various defensive barriers against experiencing much intimacy or closeness in those relationships. Again, from the perspective of their experience, avoidant attachment is the best compromise available.

Overall, it is clear from these chapters that people in general often, and some people more often than others, experience closeness or intimacy as aversive. Once in a relationship, people may frequently feel they are losing control over themselves and that the partner or the relationship is submerging their identity. And some people are highly prone to avoid intimacy or closeness, fearing intimacy, objectifying others, and avoiding the vulnerability of connections. Rather than an idiosyncracy, feeling too close seems to be a normal reaction to threats to ones control or identity. Among those who are especially prone to fear closeness or intimacy, this seems to be a coherent position rooted in early experience—one that at least from the perspective of the individual is self-protective, even if in the long run it interferes with achieving the benefits of closeness and intimacy.

As we have seen in each of the preceding sections, in this section too there would seem to be considerable opportunities for future work exploring the potential points of convergence and divergence of the themes expressed in these chapters. For example, is the being "too close" that is normatively undesirable the same thing as what is aversive or irrelevant to those who objectify others, who fear intimacy, or who are avoidantly attached? And just considering the individual differences presented in these chapters, how much overlap is there? Are these the same phenomena under different names or do they represent distinct experiences with different causes and effects? And considered more broadly (that is in terms of the themes expressed in other chapters in this *Handbook*), under what circumstances can there be too much of the usually more positive expressions of intimacy (such as the experiences of deep interactional intimacy described by Prager & Roberts, the sexual intimacy described by Vohs & Baumeister, the mutual dependence described by Rusbult et al., or the responsiveness emphasized by Reis et al.). How do the larger circumstances of social network and culture play out in undermining or promoting true closeness and intimacy?

Finally, what is missing from the picture of the dark side presented in the chapters in this section? First, there are probably other dark sides to closeness and intimacy besides those covered here. Indeed, the Wortman et al. chapter suggests that one such dark side is that high levels of closeness and intimacy in a relationship can lead to greater distress when the partner is lost. Other possible dark sides of closeness and intimacy might relate to overly focusing on these issues at the expense of other life goals (e.g., too much attention to closeness between marital partners at the expense of attending to children or too much attention to intimacy with relational partners in adolescence at the expense of attending to educational achievement), too much closeness or intimacy with partners who are detrimental to the self (e.g., women who are close to abusing partners, adolescent friendships with aggressive peers), or just so much closeness or intimacy with a person that one is overly trusting, making the self more vulnerable than might be beneficial.

IN CLOSING: FINAL THOUGHTS ON CLOSENESS AND INTIMACY

The chapters in this *Handbook* provide an abundance of findings and ideas that enrich our understanding of closeness and intimacy. We clearly know a great deal about what these terms mean, how to measure them, how their processes relate to larger themes in relationships, how they are impacted by individual differences and larger-than-relationships situational factors, and their dark side. We also believe that these chapters represent an impressive illustration of the kind of masterful methodological and conceptual work that can be done to further the understanding of central phenomena in the important domain of human relational life.

Indeed, we hope that bringing these chapters together in one place, with their great diversity of approaches, will inspire new work in terms of both research and practice. Even staying completely within the frameworks of each chapter, most of the research and findings are explicitly preliminary and ripe for further refinement and expansion. Second, as we have suggested throughout this concluding chapter, there are opportunities not to be missed for creative integrations, exploring linkages and distinctions of the elements of each of the different approaches. And finally, by presenting much of what is known, we have stressed what remains nearly untouched. Indeed, there are additional overarching holes in what is known above and beyond what we have considered in our section by section analysis. These include the almost exclusive emphasis on intimacy in adult-adult heterosexual relationships (to say nothing of the limitations largely to North American romantic relationships, mostly among college students, already noted); the almost complete lack of consideration of biological or neural factors at play; and the primary focus on the causes and concomitants of closeness and intimacy as opposed to their effects.

In sum, we hope that this *Handbook* will make available to students, scientists, scholars, and clinicians a single comprehensive and accessible source that encompasses much of what is known about closeness and intimacy. We also hope that having such a comprehensive and accessible source will help establish closeness and intimacy as a focus of relationship science important in its own right, comparable to the focus on other major relationship phenomena such as commitment or satisfaction. Most important, we hope that this *Handbook of Closeness and Intimacy* will serve as a foundation for an innovative new wave of research and practice on these very central features of the human life.

REFERENCES

Agnew, C. R., Van Lange, P. A. M., Rusbult, C. E., & Langston, C. A. (1988). Cognitive interdependence: Commitment and the mental representation of close relationships. *Journal of Personality and Social Psychology, 74*, 939–954.

Andersen, S. M., Glassman, N. S., & Gold, D. (1998). Mental representations of the self, significant others, and nonsignificant others: Structure and process of private and public aspects. *Journal of Personality and Social Psychology, 75*, 845–861.

Aron, A., Aron, E. N., & Smollan, D. (1992). Inclusion of other in the self scale and the structure of interpersonal closeness. *Journal of Personality and Social Psychology, 63*, 596–612.

Baldwin, M. W. (1995). Relational schemas and cognition in close relationships. *Journal of Social and Personal Relationships, 12*, 547–552.

Bradbury, T. N., Cohan, C. L., & Karney, B. R. (1998). Optimizing longitudinal research for understanding and preventing marital dysfunction. In T. N. Bradbury (Ed.), *The developmental course of marital dysfunction* (pp. 279–311). New York: Cambridge University Press.

Buss, D. M., & Kenrick, D. T. (1998). Evolutionary social psychology. In D. T. Gilbert, S. T. Fiske, & G. Lindzey (Eds.), *The handbook of social psychology: Vol. 2* (4th ed., pp. 982–1026). Oxford, England: Oxford University Press.

Clark, M. S., & Mills, J. (1993). The difference between communal and exchange relationships: What it is and is not. *Personality and Social Psychology Bulletin, 19*, 684–691.

Fletcher, G. J. O. & Simpson, J. A. (2001). Ideal standards in close relationships. In J. P. Forgas, K. D. Williams, & L. Wheeler (Eds.), *The social mind: Cognitive and motivational aspects of interpersonal behavior* (pp. 257–273). New York: Cambridge University Press.

Kenny, D. A. (1994). *Interpersonal perception: A social relations analysis.* New York: Guilford.

Ickes, W. (1993). Empathic accuracy. *Journal of Personality, 61*, 587–610.

Reis, H. T. &, Shaver, P. (1988). Intimacy as an interpersonal process. In S. Duck (Ed.), *Handbook of personal relationships* (pp. 367–389). Chichester, England: Wiley.

Reis, H. T., & Wheeler, L. (1991). Studying social interaction with the Rochester interaction record. In M. P. Zanna (Ed.), *Advances in experimental social psychology: Vol. 24* (pp. 269–318). San Diego, CA: Academic Press.

Shaefer, M. T. & Olson, D. H. (1981). Assessing intimacy: The PAIR Inventory. *Journal of Marital and Family Therapy, 7*, 47–60.

Author Index

Note: Numbers in italics indicate pages with complete bibliographic information; n indicates footnote.

I

Iavnieli, D., 239, *244*, 402, *411*
Ickes, W., 69, 70, *76*, *78*, 89, 93, 94, *97*, 145, *160*, 204, 210, 213, 223, 251, 254, 255, *264*, *266*, 360, 361, 362, 363, 365, 368, *373*, 422, *428*
Impett, E. A., 174, 176, *185*
Ingram, K. M., 313, 314, *319*
Inman, C. C., 12, *26*

J

Jack, D. C., 241, *244*
Jackson, M. S., 323, *338*
Jacobs, S., 306, 307, 309, *318*, *319*
Jacobson, N. S., 61, 66, 67, *76*, 204, *223*, 345, 346, *355*
Jacogson, N. S., 145, *158*
Jaffe, K., 171, 181, *184*
James, P., 67, *76*
James, W. H., 191, *199*
Jensen, L. A., 326, *339*
Ji, L. J., 239, *244*
Johnson, B. T., 31, 34, *41*
Johnson, D., 30, *40*, 240, *243*
Johnson, D. J., 143, 151, *160*
Johnson, F. L., 12, *24*
Johnson, M. D., 392, *394*
Johnson, M. P., 83, *97*, 141, *160*
Johnson, S. M., 45, 47, *58*, 63, 66, 75, *76*, 205, *223*, 383, *394*, 406, 407, 408, *411*
Joiner, T. E., 210, *223*
Jones, D. A., 314, *319*
Jones, D. J., 30, *40*, 240, *243*
Jones, E. E., 31, *40*, 106, *115*
Jourard, S., 44, *58*, 63, *76*
Judd, L. L., 307, *320*
Jung, C. G., 36, *40*
Juola Exline, J., 313, 314, *320*
Jussim, L., 260, *264*

K

Kagan, J., 268, 269, *281*
Kaiser, S., *394*
Kaltman, S., 306, 307, 308, *318*
Kanin, E. J., 193, *199*
Kaplan, H. S., 51, *58*
Kaplan, N., 166, *186*, 375, *394*, 403, *410*
Karanja, W. W., 325, *338*
Karetsky, K. H., 249, 250, 255, *266*
Karney, B. R., 261, *264*, 272, *281*, 291, *302*, 392, *394*, 422, *428*
Karpel, M., 378, *394*

Kashima, Y., 231, *244*
Kashy, D. A., 368n.3, *373*
Kasser, T., 61, *78*
Kastenbaum, R., 378, *394*
Katherine, A., 354, *355*
Kato, P. M., 308, *319*
Katz, I., 210, *223*
Katz, J., 238, *244*
Katz, L. F., 205, *223*
Keelan, J. P. R., 156, *158*, 174, *185*, 408, *410*
Keeley, M. P., 62, *76*
Kelley, H. H., 2, *6*, 10, 13, *25*, 30, *40*, 82, 83, 84, 85, 86, 87, 88, 92, 96, *96*, *97*, *98*, 137, 138, 138n.1, 139, 139n.2, 140, 143, 144, 146, 147, 148, 148n.4, 149, 150, 151, 152, *160*, *161*, 206, 218, *223*, 247, 248, 255, *263*, *264*, 287, 288, 289, *302*, *303*
Kelly, G. A., 43, *58*
Keltner, D., 308, 317, *318*, *319*
Kemeny, N., 313, *319*
Kemmelmeier, M., 240, *244*
Kennedy-Moore, E., 383, *394*
Kenny, D. A., 71, *76*, 212, *223*, 238, *244*, 273, *281*, *355*, 423, *428*
Kenrick, D. T., 139, *160*, 422, *428*
Kerns, K. A., 72, *76*, 174, 175, 177, 181, *185*
Kerr, N. L., 137, 138n.1, 139, 140, 143, 144, 148n.4, *160*
Kessler, R., 211, 212–213, *222*, 313, *319*
Khouri, H., 156, *159*, 209, 211–212, *223*, 260, *264*
Kiecolt-Glaser, J. K., 163, 169, *187*
Kihlstrom, J. F., 34, *40*, 47, *58*, *59*, 248, *263*
Kilson, M., 325, *338*
Kim, H., 230, *244*
Kim, K., 307, *318*
Kim, U., 231, *244*
Kim, Y., 61, *78*
Kinderman, P., 381, *394*
Kinsey, A. C., 193, *199*
Kirby, J. P., 323, *338*
Kirkland, S., 378, *394*
Kirkpatrick, L., 179, *185*, 405, 406, *411*
Kirsh, D., 296, 297, *302*
Kirson, D., 11, *25*
Kitayama, S., 45n.1, 49, *59*, 74, *77*, 230, *244*, 262, *265*, 322, 324, 334, *338*
Klein, M., 44, *59*
Klein, S. B., 34, *40*, 47, *58*
Klomegah, R., 325, *338*
Kluckhohn, C., 322, *338*
Knee, C. R., 71, *76*, 104, *115*
Ko, S. J., 295, 296, 301, *302*

Subject Index

8524